Old
Testament Law
for
Christians

Old Testament Law

for

Christians

ORIGINAL CONTEXT
AND ENDURING APPLICATION

Roy E. Gane

B

Baker Academic

a division of Baker Publishing Group
Grand Rapids, Michigan

© 2017 by Roy E. Gane

Published by Baker Academic
a division of Baker Publishing Group
P.O. Box 6287, Grand Rapids, MI 49516-6287
www.bakeracademic.com

Printed in the United States of America

Library of Congress Cataloging-in-Publication Data
Names: Gane, Roy, 1955– author.
Title: Old Testament law for Christians : original context and enduring application / Roy E. Gane.
Description: Grand Rapids : Baker Academic, 2017. | Includes bibliographical references and index.
Identifiers: LCCN 2017010891 | ISBN 9780801049040 (pbk.)
Subjects: LCSH: Law (Theology) | Christianity and law.
Classification: LCC BS1199.L3 G36 2017 | DDC 241/.2—dc23
LC record available at https://lccn.loc.gov/2017010891

17 18 19 20 21 22 23   7 6 5 4 3 2 1

Contents

Abbreviations

General and Bibliographic

AB	Anchor Bible
ABD	*Anchor Bible Dictionary*, ed. David Noel Freedman, 6 vols. (New York: Doubleday, 1992)
acc.	accommodation
AD	anno Domini
ANE	ancient Near East(ern)
AUSS	*Andrews University Seminary Studies*
b.	Babylonian Talmud
BBR	*Bulletin for Biblical Research*
BC	before Christ
BCE	before the Common Era
BDAG	W. Bauer, F. W. Danker, W. F. Arndt, and F. W. Gingrich, *A Greek-English Lexicon of the New Testament and Other Early Christian Literature*, 3rd ed. (Chicago: University of Chicago Press, 2000)
BibSem	The Biblical Seminar
BRev	*Bible Review*
BSac	*Bibliotheca Sacra*
BZABR	Beihefte zur Zeitschrift für altorientalische und biblische Rechtsgeschichte
BZAW	Beihefte zur Zeitschrift für die alttestamentliche Wissenschaft
CahRB	Cahiers de la Revue biblique
CBC	Cambridge Bible Commentary
CBQ	*Catholic Biblical Quarterly*
CE	Common Era
CEB	Common English Bible
cf.	*confer*, compare
CHANE	Culture and History of the Ancient Near East
chap(s).	chapter(s)

COS	*The Context of Scripture*, ed. W. W. Hallo, 3 vols. (Leiden: Brill, 1997– 2002), vol. 4 forthcoming
D	Deuteronomic source of the Pentateuch
DCH	*Dictionary of Classical Hebrew*, ed. David J. A. Clines, 9 vols. (Sheffield: Sheffield Phoenix, 1993–2014)
ECC	Eerdmans Critical Commentary
ed(s).	editor(s), edited by, edition
e.g.	*exempli gratia*, for example
EncJud	*Encyclopedia Judaica*, ed. Fred Skolnik and Michael Berenbaum, 2nd ed., 22 vols. (Detroit: Macmillan Reference USA, 2007)
esp.	especially
ESV	English Standard Version
etc.	*et cetera*, and so forth, and the rest
FAT	Forschungen zum Alten Testament
Gk.	Greek
GR	Greco-Roman
H	Holiness Code/source of the Pentateuch
Heb.	Hebrew
HUCA	*Hebrew Union College Annual*
i.e.	*id est*, that is
ISBE	*International Standard Bible Encyclopedia*, ed. Geoffrey W. Bromiley, re- vised ed., 4 vols. (Grand Rapids: Eerdmans, 1979–88)
ITC	International Theological Commentary
JAOS	*Journal of the American Oriental Society*
JATS	*Journal of the Adventist Theological Society*
JBL	*Journal of Biblical Literature*
JETS	*Journal of the Evangelical Theological Society*
JJS	*Journal of Jewish Studies*
JPS	Jewish Publication Society
JRE	*Journal of Religious Ethics*
JSOT	*Journal for the Study of the Old Testament*
JSOTSup	Journal for the Study of the Old Testament Supplement Series
JSS	*Journal of Semitic Studies*
KJV	King James Version
LAI	Library of Ancient Israel
LBI	Library of Biblical Interpretation
LH	Laws of Hammurabi
LHBOTS	The Library of Hebrew Bible/Old Testament Studies
lit.	literally
LXX	Septuagint (the Greek Old Testament)
m.	Mishnah
MAL	Middle Assyrian Laws
masc.	masculine
MT	Masoretic Text
NASB	New American Standard Bible (1995)
NICNT	New International Commentary on the New Testament
NICOT	New International Commentary on the Old Testament

NIGTC	New International Greek Testament Commentary
NIV	New International Version (2011)
NJPS	*The Tanakh: The Holy Scriptures: The New JPS Translation according to the Traditional Hebrew Text* (1985)
NKJV	New King James Version
no(s).	number(s)
NT	New Testament
OBO	Orbis Biblicus et Orientalis
OT	Old Testament
OTS	Old Testament Studies
P	Priestly source of the Pentateuch
pl.	plural
PMW	Progressive Moral Wisdom
RBS	Resources for Biblical Study
repr.	reprint, reprinted
SBL	Society of Biblical Literature
SBLDS	Society of Biblical Literature Dissertation Series
SBLSP	Society of Biblical Literature Seminar Papers
ScrHier	Scripta Hierosolymitana
sing.	singular
SSN	Studia Semitica Neerlandica
STI	Studies in Theological Interpretation
STRev	*Sewanee Theological Review*
TDOT	*Theological Dictionary of the Old Testament*, ed. G. J. Botterweck and H. Ringgren, trans. J. T. Willis et al., 15 vols. (Grand Rapids: Eerdmans, 1974–2006)
TOTC	Tyndale Old Testament Commentaries
trans.	translator, translated by, translation
UDHR	Universal Declaration of Human Rights
VT	*Vetus Testamentum*
VTSup	Supplements to Vetus Testamentum
v(v).	verse(s)
WBC	Word Biblical Commentary
ZA	*Zeitschrift für Assyriologie*

Old Testament

Gen.	Genesis	2 Sam.	2 Samuel
Exod.	Exodus	1 Kings	1 Kings
Lev.	Leviticus	2 Kings	2 Kings
Num.	Numbers	1 Chron.	1 Chronicles
Deut.	Deuteronomy	2 Chron.	2 Chronicles
Josh.	Joshua	Ezra	Ezra
Judg.	Judges	Neh.	Nehemiah
Ruth	Ruth	Esther	Esther
1 Sam.	1 Samuel	Job	Job

Ps(s).	Psalm(s)	Amos	Amos
Prov.	Proverbs	Obad.	Obadiah
Eccles.	Ecclesiastes	Jon.	Jonah
Song	Song of Songs	Mic.	Micah
Isa.	Isaiah	Nah.	Nahum
Jer.	Jeremiah	Hab.	Habakkuk
Lam.	Lamentations	Zeph.	Zephaniah
Ezek.	Ezekiel	Hag.	Haggai
Dan.	Daniel	Zech.	Zechariah
Hosea	Hosea	Mal.	Malachi
Joel	Joel		

New Testament

Matt.	Matthew	1 Tim.	1 Timothy
Mark	Mark	2 Tim.	2 Timothy
Luke	Luke	Titus	Titus
John	John	Philem.	Philemon
Acts	Acts	Heb.	Hebrews
Rom.	Romans	James	James
1 Cor.	1 Corinthians	1 Pet.	1 Peter
2 Cor.	2 Corinthians	2 Pet.	2 Peter
Gal.	Galatians	1 John	1 John
Eph.	Ephesians	2 John	2 John
Phil.	Philippians	3 John	3 John
Col.	Colossians	Jude	Jude
1 Thess.	1 Thessalonians	Rev.	Revelation
2 Thess.	2 Thessalonians		

Introduction

"Wisdom" has been defined as "the capacity to realize what is of value in life for oneself and others."[1] Anyone in touch with current developments in our world can recognize that Christians need informed discussion and effective inculcation of such wisdom more than ever before. Seismic shifts in social morality, controversial Supreme Court rulings, political debates and ethics, business practices, behaviors of church members, and clashes between adherents of Christian and non-Christian religious civilizations revolve around differences in values. How can we intentionally and proactively stabilize our own value system and gain a sense of perspective regarding our negotiable and nonnegotiable principles so that we can navigate the complexity of modern life in appropriate relation to others who hold values that diverge from our own?

A Neglected Source of Wisdom regarding Values

A rich source of wisdom regarding values is contained in OT laws. However, Christians have generally neglected these laws, to our loss, because we have not regarded them as relevant to our lives. There are at least three reasons for this.

First, post-NT Christian tradition has tended to isolate the Ten Commandments as the only "moral law" that remains applicable and have not adequately taken into account the web of relationships between these commandments and other laws that also exemplify moral/ethical principles.

---

1. Nicholas Maxwell, *The Human World in the Physical Universe: Consciousness, Free Will, and Evolution* (Lanham, MD: Rowman & Littlefield, 2001), 38.

Second, there are many OT laws that Christians simply cannot keep because the earthly sanctuary/temple, with its rituals and regulations, no longer exists and has been superseded by Christ's heavenly temple ministry. Furthermore, we lack other institutions and cultural practices governed by OT laws, such as theocratic administration of justice, cities of refuge, the Jubilee, bonded servitude, polygamy, and levirate marriage. Additionally, modern society has moved away from an agricultural subsistence economy, so for most of us, at least in the developed world, OT laws for farmers are unrelated to our lives.

Third, a significant number of OT laws are somewhat obscure or disturbing to Christians because they illustrate values within the context of ancient Israelite culture, which is quite foreign to us. For instance, why did God prescribe a special ritual to judge the case of a suspected adulteress (Num. 5:11–31) and provide no corresponding procedure to judge a husband whose wife suspects him of adultery? Why could a father or husband annul a vow made by his daughter or wife, respectively (30:3–16 [30:4–17 MT])?

Goal of This Book

This book shows Christians how OT laws are relevant, interesting, accessible, and useful; how to navigate around them; how to uncover their wise values (cf. 2 Tim. 3:15, "to make you wise for salvation"); and how to arrive at answers to questions regarding their interpretation and application to modern life. The aim is to aid Christians, especially those who teach others, in understanding how OT laws reveal wise and enduring values and principles, even when certain laws do not directly apply to us today. The values and principles reflect the divine character of love (Matt. 22:36–40; 1 John 4:8), in continuity with the rest of biblical instruction (including that of the NT), in ways that are meaningful and helpful to Christians saved by grace through faith (Eph. 2:8–9) who are serious about following the God who transforms their lives (e.g., Rom. 8:1–17; Titus 3:3–7).

A key task of the present work is to evaluate and draw from existing methods for applying values and principles of OT laws to modern Christian life in order to develop a fresh and balanced approach that is faithful to both Testaments and is also clear and useable. In utilizing this approach, the author strives to consistently follow biblical evidence to its logical conclusions, without constraints from postbiblical traditions regarding interpretation or implementation of OT laws. The results are likely to generate discussion because they are not 100 percent in harmony with the prescribed practice of any existing Christian denomination, to my knowledge.

The book introduces OT law. It does not try to comprehensively elucidate all biblical laws, which would be impossible because the issues involved with them are complex and the relevant secondary literature is vast. Some historical issues are addressed here, but this is basically a synchronic study that lacks space for engaging the ongoing scholarly debates concerning the historical development (including sources) of OT law texts from their prehistory to their final canonical form.

Parts of This Book

This volume is divided into four parts. Part 1, "Getting into Old Testament Law" (chaps. 1–3), introduces the relevance, nature, and purpose of OT law. Part 2, "Literature and Background of Old Testament Law" (chaps. 4–6), identifies locations of laws in the OT and law concepts in other genres, explains how OT law communicates values through its literary genre, and describes ancient historical contexts that shed light on OT laws. Part 3, "Applying Old Testament Laws" (chaps. 7–10), exposes issues involved in direct and indirect application of OT laws to modern Christian life, reviews and critiques methods for applying OT laws, synthesizes a Progressive Moral Wisdom approach, and illustrates this approach through a case study. Part 4, "Values in Old Testament Law" (chaps. 11–16), explicates moral values in the Ten Commandments and in social-justice laws, grapples with serious theodicy problems raised by some OT laws, and addresses questions regarding ongoing observance of several OT laws. The book concludes with a reflection on the value of obedience to God's will, followed by a select bibliography that guides the reader to further resources, some with additional helpful bibliographies.[2]

Biblical Citations

The present book develops concepts and reaches conclusions on the basis of interaction with biblical texts. This sometimes requires reference to the

2. E.g., Raymond Westbrook and Bruce Wells, *Everyday Law in Biblical Israel: An Introduction* (Louisville: Westminster John Knox, 2009); Raymond Westbrook, *Law from the Tigris to the Tiber: The Writings of Raymond Westbrook*, ed. Bruce Wells and Rachel Magdalene, 2 vols. (Winona Lake, IN: Eisenbrauns, 2009); Richard M. Davidson, *Flame of Yahweh: Sexuality in the Old Testament* (Peabody, MA: Hendrickson, 2007); Joe M. Sprinkle, *Biblical Law and Its Relevance: A Christian Understanding and Ethical Application for Today of the Mosaic Regulations* (Lanham, MD: University Press of America, 2006); and esp. John W. Welch, *Biblical Law Cumulative Bibliography*, CD-ROM (Provo, UT: Brigham Young University Press; Winona Lake, IN: Eisenbrauns, 2005).

original Hebrew and Greek, although in as untechnical a manner as possible for the benefit of readers without training in these languages. Biblical citations adhere to the following patterns:

Quotations of the Bible in English translation are from ESV unless otherwise indicated.

Explanatory words in brackets within a biblical quotation are supplied and not part of the quoted English version.

Verse references follow English Bible numbering. When Hebrew Bible versification differs, it appears after the English reference and is labeled MT.

Transliterations of Hebrew and Greek words are according to the general-purpose style in the second edition of *The SBL Handbook of Style*.[3] Of the options for the letters *bet*, *kaf*, and *pe* when they lack the *dagesh lene*, this book uses the following: *bet* = *v*, *kaf* = *k*, and *pe* = *f*. Also, *vav* = *v* and *khet* = *kh*.

Names of basic Hebrew stems (*qal*, *niphal*, etc.) are according to *The SBL Handbook of Style*.[4]

Acknowledgments

I am grateful to Jim Kinney of Baker Academic for inviting me to undertake this project and for his initiative, wise insights, and supportive collaboration along the way. Hearty thanks go to my Andrews University colleagues Richard M. Davidson and Robert M. Johnston for carefully reading an entire preliminary manuscript and offering excellent ideas and suggestions for improvement. I am also grateful to my colleagues P. Richard Choi, Jo Ann Davidson, and John C. Peckham for expert advice regarding parts of the book. Trisha Broy, my research assistant, gathered some of the secondary sources utilized here.

3. *The SBL Handbook of Style: For Biblical Studies and Related Disciplines*, 2nd ed. (Atlanta: SBL Press, 2014), 58–60.
4. Ibid., 57.

PART 1

Getting into Old Testament Law

1

Is Old Testament Law Relevant for New-Covenant Christians?

We live in a world of competing value systems, which are at the center of much debate. What does the system of values in ancient OT law have to offer modern new-covenant Christians? If we are saved by divine grace through faith in Christ's once-for-all atoning sacrifice, not by our works of keeping God's law (Eph. 2:8–9; cf. Heb. 9:25–28), why should we invite outmoded values to play a role in directing our lives? Now that we enjoy the more glorious revelation of God in Jesus Christ, why do we still need the eclipsed revelation delivered through Moses (2 Cor. 3)? To put it in contemporary terms, why bother with an obsolete operating system when we are already enjoying a satisfying upgrade?

The NT is not an operating system that replaces the earlier OT one. Rather, the NT is the continuation of the OT story of redemption, in which earlier episodes provide crucial background for climactic later ones, which bring plotlines together toward the conclusion.[1] It is possible to read only the final portions of a story, but this approach misses a lot of the meaning. In the case of the Bible, the meaning is crucial wisdom, not mere entertainment or information.

This chapter addresses the relevance of OT law by considering the NT evaluation and use of it and its worth for providing background and context to the NT. Topics developed here include Jesus's approach to OT law, OT laws as background to his life and ministry, Paul's approach to OT law, and how

---

1. See, e.g., how genealogies in Matt. 1:1–17 and Luke 3:23–38 link the OT and NT periods, and how OT prophecies are fulfilled in the NT (Matt. 1:23; 2:6, 15, 18; etc.).

OT contexts (including law) illuminate values for Christians. It will begin to become clear that modern Christians can gain much practical wisdom from the rich and fascinating world of OT laws and the values encapsulated in them.[2] The remainder of the present volume will reinforce this impression.

Jesus's Approach to Old Testament Law

Continuing Authority

In the Gospels we read that Jesus regarded the OT laws given through Moses as coming from God and carrying continuing authority. For example, he responds to some opponents: "You have a fine way of rejecting the commandment of God in order to establish your tradition! For Moses said, 'Honor your father and your mother'; and, 'Whoever reviles father or mother must surely die.' But you say . . ." (Mark 7:9–11). Here "the commandment of God" (cf. v. 13, "the word of God") is what Moses said. The laws that Jesus cites on this occasion are not only from the Decalogue (Exod. 20:12; Deut. 5:16) but also from Exod. 21:17 (cf. Lev. 20:9).

In his Sermon on the Mount, Jesus strongly upholds the permanence of "the Law" (i.e., Torah, "Instruction" = the Pentateuch) along with the rest of the OT ("the Prophets"):

> Do not think that I have come to abolish the Law or the Prophets; I have not come to abolish them but to fulfill them. For truly, I say to you, until heaven and earth pass away, not an iota, not a dot, will pass from the Law until all is accomplished. Therefore whoever relaxes one of the least of these commandments and teaches others to do the same will be called least in the kingdom of heaven, but whoever does them and teaches them will be called great in the kingdom of heaven. (Matt. 5:17–19)

Bearing Witness to Christ

Jesus also viewed the (OT) Scriptures, which include the "Law of Moses" (Torah = Pentateuch) as bearing witness to himself (John 5:39), and thus he concludes a discourse to his critics: "For if you believed Moses, you would

---

2. Joe M. Sprinkle summarizes some important ways in which the Mosaic law continues to carry value for modern Christians: The law "*serves to restrain sinners, . . . is a prelude to the gospel, . . . is a guide for Christian living, . . . shows the holy yet merciful character of God, . . . [and] points to Christ who is the fulfillment of the law.*" Furthermore, "*Biblical civil laws are suggestive for modern jurisprudence.*" *Biblical Law and Its Relevance: A Christian Understanding and Ethical Application for Today of the Mosaic Regulations* (Lanham, MD: University Press of America, 2006), 26–27, emphasis original.

believe me; for he wrote of me. But if you do not believe his writings, how will you believe my words?" (vv. 46–47). When Jesus appeared to two disciples on the road to Emmaus after his resurrection, "beginning with Moses and all the Prophets, he interpreted to them in all the Scriptures the things concerning himself" (Luke 24:27). That night, he declared to more disciples,

> "These are my words that I spoke to you while I was still with you, that every-thing written about me in the Law of Moses and the Prophets and the Psalms must be fulfilled." Then he opened their minds to understand the Scriptures, and said to them, "Thus it is written, that the Christ should suffer and on the third day rise from the dead." (Luke 24:44–46)

The typological ritual laws prescribing the Passover sacrifice (Exod. 12:3–13, 21–27; cf. Lev. 23:5) and the "elevated sheaf" (so-called wave sheaf) firstfruits offering of barley on "the day after the Sabbath" (Lev. 23:10–11) could have been among the OT Scriptures in the Law of Moses to which Jesus referred to show that he had to suffer and then rise from the dead on the third day. Indeed, Jesus died on Friday ("the day of Preparation"; Mark 15:42; John 19:31) at the time of Passover (John 18:28, 39; 19:14; cf. Matt. 26:2) and rose on the third day, which was the first day of the week after the Sabbath (Matt. 28:1), when the elevated sheaf would have been offered. Paul explicitly referred to the crucified Christ as "our Passover lamb" (1 Cor. 5:7) and to the risen Christ as "the firstfruits of those who have fallen asleep" (1 Cor. 15:20).

Such correlations between the enacted redemptive typology of the OT ritu-als and what happened to Jesus of Nazareth contributed to confirmation—for his disciples and also for us—of John the Baptist's identification of him as "the Lamb of God, who takes away the sin of the world" (John 1:29), mean-ing the Messiah/Christ whom the ritual system prefigured and in this sense prophesied.[3] Today our only access to this ritual system is through pentateuchal texts, mostly in the form of laws/instructions.

The OT laws testify to Christ in another important way. When he was asked which is the greatest commandment in the law (Matt. 22:36), he replied: "You shall love the Lord your God with all your heart and with all your soul and with all your mind. This is the great and first commandment. And a second is like it: You shall love your neighbor as yourself. On these two command-ments depend all the Law and the Prophets" (vv. 37–40).

---

3. The OT sacrificial system also provides crucial background to Christ's heavenly priesthood, as presented in the books of Hebrews (esp. chaps. 7–10) and Revelation (esp. in introductory temple scenes; 1:12–20; chaps. 4–5; 8:2–5; etc.).

Here Jesus cites two laws (Deut. 6:5 and Lev. 19:18) outside the Ten Commandments to summarize all of OT law and also the messages of the prophets. That which unifies this divine revelation is the value of love, which is nothing less than the character of God: "God is love" (1 John 4:8). Because God loved the world, he gave Christ, "his only Son," to save those who believe in him (John 3:16). Christ is God (e.g., John 8:58; 10:30; Col. 1:19), so he is love (cf. John 15:9). Therefore all of OT law testifies to Christ's love, which he asks his followers to emulate (John 15:12).

Old Testament Laws as Background to Jesus's Life and Ministry

Some OT laws provide illuminating background to more specific aspects of Jesus's life and ministry. Following are three examples from Luke, all of which concern women.

Offering by a Poor Mother

Luke 2 tells us what Jesus's parents did soon after he was circumcised (eight days after he was born): "When the time came for their purification according to the Law of Moses, they brought him up to Jerusalem to present him to the Lord . . . and to offer a sacrifice according to what is said in the Law of the Lord, 'a pair of turtledoves, or two young pigeons'" (vv. 22, 24).

This refers to Lev. 12, according to which a woman who gave birth would undergo a period of purification, at the end of which she would offer "a one-year-old lamb as an entirely burned offering and a pigeon or turtledove as a purification offering" (v. 6 CEB); if she could not afford a sheep, she could sacrifice "two turtledoves or two pigeons—one for the entirely burned offering and the other for the purification offering" (v. 8 CEB). Thus Luke 2:24 implies that Jesus's parents offered two birds because they were poor. They could not even afford a lamb for Mary's purification after the birth of "the Lamb of God"!

Female Impure Discharge

Another purity law sheds light on an incident recounted in Luke 8. As a crowd of people pressed around Jesus, a woman with a chronic discharge of blood

came up behind him and touched the fringe of his garment, and immediately her discharge of blood ceased. And Jesus said, "Who was it that touched me?"

. . . But Jesus said, "Someone touched me, for I perceive that power has gone out from me." And when the woman saw that she was not hidden, she came trembling, and falling down before him declared in the presence of all the people why she had touched him, and how she had been immediately healed. And he said to her, "Daughter, your faith has made you well; go in peace." (Luke 8:44–48; cf. Matt. 9:20–22; Mark 5:25–34)

Why did she come trembling? She must have known that according to Lev. 15, her chronic genital discharge of blood made her physically and ritually impure, as during her menstrual period (vv. 25–27). Therefore, anyone who touched her would be impure until evening (cf. v. 19). No doubt hoping not to make Jesus impure, she only touched the fringe (Gk. *kraspedon*, "edge, border, hem") of his garment (Luke 8:44). But when he asked, "Who was it that touched me?" and insisted that someone had done so (8:45–46), she felt caught and likely thought he was angry because she had defiled him. In response to her confession, however, he affirmed her faith and reassured her that there was no problem.

Two other OT laws illuminate this story. First, the "fringe" or "tassel" (Heb. *tsitsit*; LXX *kraspedon*) that Jesus had on his garment was required by a law in Num. 15:37–40 (cf. Deut. 22:12) as a sign of remembering and following all of God's commandments and being holy to him. The tassel on each corner of a garment was to have a violet (or blue) cord attached to it (Num. 15:38). This color appeared in the holy priestly garments (Exod. 28:5, 6, 8, 15, 31, 33), and violet cords belonged to the high priest's vestments (28:28, 36–37; 39:21, 30–31). Given this connection, it appears that the violet cords on tassels belonging to Israelites who were not Levitical priests, such as Jesus, evoked the idea that these persons were members of God's "kingdom of priests and a holy nation" (Exod. 19:6).[4] Therefore the woman with the discharge of blood, who was ritually impure, touched a sign of Jesus's holiness.

Second, there is no indication that the woman's touch rendered Jesus impure. Rather, he perceived that power had gone out from him (Luke 8:46) to cure her impure discharge. There was a one-way flow of healing, with no backwash of impurity, just as when Jesus touched lepers to heal them (Matt. 8:2–3; Mark 1:40–42; Luke 5:12–13). As in the law of Lev. 11, Jesus was like "a spring or a cistern holding water," which could not be made impure (v. 36; contrast vv. 29–35) because it was a source of purity.[5]

---

4. Violet color also evoked royalty because this kind of dye was very expensive. Cf. Jacob Milgrom, *Numbers*, JPS Torah Commentary (Philadelphia: Jewish Publication Society, 1990), 127.

5. Roy Gane, *Leviticus, Numbers*, NIV Application Commentary (Grand Rapids: Zondervan, 2004), 216–17.

A Woman Considered Immoral

On another occasion, Jesus was invited to eat at the home of a Pharisee.

> And behold, a woman of the city, who was a sinner, when she learned that he was reclining at table in the Pharisee's house, brought an alabaster flask of ointment, and standing behind him at his feet, weeping, she began to wet his feet with her tears and wiped them with the hair of her head and kissed his feet and anointed them with the ointment. Now when the Pharisee who had invited him saw this, he said to himself, "If this man were a prophet, he would have known who and what sort of woman this is who is touching him, for she is a sinner." And Jesus answering said to him, "Simon, I have something to say to you." (Luke 7:37–40)

In this situation there are several striking points of comparison and contrast with the suspected adulteress ritual in Num. 5:11–31. As in the Num. 5 scenario, the woman's reputation is under scrutiny, with a man inquiring of the Lord whether she is guilty; she has a gift for the Lord but is in an attitude of mourning; her hair is let down, and she contacts holiness. "However, in Luke 7 (cf. Matt. 26:6–13; Mark 14:3–9; John 12:1–8) the focus of the woman's sorrow is on Christ, her gift consists of sweet-smelling perfume, the man who questions regarding her (Simon, the host; Luke 7:40, 43–44) is not her husband, he has no doubt that she has been guilty of indiscretion, and his accusation is only to himself rather than out in the open."[6]

In Num. 5 the Lord only renders a verdict of guilty or innocent (vv. 27–28), but Christ's verdict on the woman in Luke 7 is different: She is guilty as charged, but forgiven (vv. 47–50)! "Christ's forgiveness did not mean that he was lowering the moral standard. In his Sermon on the Mount he raised it by condemning even lust of the eyes (Matt. 5:27–28). It is not that his standard is weaker, but that his 'new covenant' forgiveness is stronger."[7] In fact, Christ's forgiveness is so powerful that the new covenant is based on it (Jer. 31:34, "For I will forgive their iniquity"; cf. 31:31–33).

Paul's Approach to Old Testament Law

Like Jesus, Paul upheld the ongoing worth of the (OT) Scriptures, which include OT law. He encouraged Timothy to continue learning from "the sacred writings, which are able to make you wise for salvation through faith in

6. Ibid., 527.
7. Ibid.

Christ Jesus. All Scripture is breathed out by God and profitable for teaching, for reproof, for correction, and for training in righteousness, that the man of God may be complete, equipped for every good work" (2 Tim. 3:15–17).

Paul was an expert in OT teachings, educated by the Pharisee Gamaliel (Acts 22:3), who was "a teacher of the law held in honor by all the people" (5:34). Paul said a lot about various aspects of law (Gk. *nomos*), but for our purpose here we will focus on his approach to the continuing relevance of pentateuchal law as divine instruction for Christian life.[8]

Good Works Resulting from Salvation

The book of Ephesians can serve as an example, starting with Paul's clear and concise summary of the way we are saved in 2:8–10 and then moving into his counsel regarding the Christian "walk," the manner of life, in later chapters.[9]

> For by grace you have been saved through faith. And this is not your own doing; it is the gift of God, not a result of works, so that no one may boast. For we are his workmanship, created in Christ Jesus for good works, which God prepared beforehand, that we should walk in them. (Eph. 2:8–10)

We are not saved by our own works in any sense. Rather, we are the workmanship, God's work! We are incapable of performing our salvation because that is a work of creating (i.e., re-creating) us in Christ (cf. Eph. 2:4–7), and we cannot create ourselves. God creates us anew so that we can fulfill his ideal plan by doing good works as he designed (v. 10). While these works of ours do not produce salvation, they result from it and demonstrate that our faith is ongoing and genuine (cf. James 2:26).

Salvation by grace through faith is not the end of the Christian life; it is for the whole life. In Eph. 3 Paul prays for the believers in Ephesus, who have already received Christ (cf. 1:1, 15),

> that according to the riches of his glory he may grant you to be strengthened with power through his Spirit in your inner being, so that Christ may dwell in your hearts through faith—that you, being rooted and grounded in love, may have strength to comprehend with all the saints what is the breadth and length

---

8. Cf., e.g., Richard B. Hays, *Echoes of Scripture in the Letters of Paul* (New Haven: Yale University Press, 1989), 97, 165–67, pointing out that Paul interpreted OT laws as directly speaking to Christians in his day.

9. Cf. use of the Hebrew term *halakah*, literally referring to walking or going, for traditional Jewish law.

and height and depth, and to know the love of Christ that surpasses knowledge, that you may be filled with all the fullness of God. (3:16–19)

The experience of faith and love that Paul wishes for the Ephesians, which he expresses in general terms, is progressive and growing (e.g., "being rooted and grounded in love"; cf. 4:11–16; cf. 1 Thess. 3:12–4:1).

Paul is more specific in Eph. 4: "I therefore, a prisoner for the Lord, urge you to walk in a manner worthy of the calling to which you have been called, with all humility and gentleness, with patience, bearing with one another in love, eager to maintain the unity of the Spirit in the bond of peace" (vv. 1–3). Walking in a worthy manner is equivalent to walking in good works (cf. 2:10). Here in chapter 4 the Christian "walk," or manner of conducting one's journey through life, is characterized by several virtues, positive attitudes that govern corresponding actions (including speech). These radically depart from the traits of the unconverted, futile-minded Gentile "walk," in which negative attitudes manifest themselves in impure practices (vv. 17–19).

Ephesians 4–6 Drawing on Old Testament Laws

As Paul continues in Eph. 4, he becomes even more specific. Christians who have "put on the new self, created after the likeness of God in true righteousness and holiness" (4:24) will live differently in many ways, and he provides some examples in a series of exhortations:

Therefore, having put away falsehood, let each one of you speak the truth with his neighbor, for we are members one of another. Be angry and do not sin; do not let the sun go down on your anger, and give no opportunity to the devil. Let the thief no longer steal, but rather let him labor, doing honest work with his own hands, so that he may have something to share with anyone in need. Let no corrupting talk come out of your mouths, but only such as is good for building up, as fits the occasion, that it may give grace to those who hear. And do not grieve the Holy Spirit of God, by whom you were sealed for the day of redemption. Let all bitterness and wrath and anger and clamor and slander be put away from you, along with all malice. Be kind to one another, tenderhearted, forgiving one another, as God in Christ forgave you. (Eph. 4:25–32)

The idea that behaviors such as telling the truth, controlling anger, and doing honest work represent good and beneficial values and that behaviors such as speaking falsehood, sinning as a result of anger, and stealing are bad and destructive did not originate with Paul. He is drawing on OT teaching, including OT law, and treating it as normative for Christians. Some of his exhortations—such as not to speak falsehood or to steal—relate quite directly to the Ten Commandments (Exod. 20:15–16; Deut. 5:19–20).[10] However, the backgrounds to most of his instructions here are clustered in Lev. 19, which belongs to the so-called Holiness Code (Lev. 17–27): not stealing, deceiving, or lying to one another (19:11); not nursing a grudge or prolonged anger (v. 18a); not slandering (v. 16); and not hating (v. 17), but loving your neighbor as yourself (v. 18b).

Reinforcing the idea that Paul has Lev. 19 in mind, he begins Eph. 5: "Therefore be imitators of God, as beloved children. And walk in love, as Christ loved us and gave himself up for us, a fragrant offering and sacrifice to God" (vv. 1–2). The first command in Lev. 19 is to imitate God: "You shall be holy, for I the LORD your God am holy" (v. 2). And a command to love is at the heart of that chapter: "You shall love your neighbor as yourself" (v. 18).

Verse 34 combines love with implicit imitation of God: "You shall treat the stranger who sojourns with you as the native among you, and you shall love him as yourself, for you were strangers in the land of Egypt: I am the LORD your God." Here the motive clause, "for you were strangers in the land of Egypt," reminds the Israelites that they are to empathize with others and treat them with the same kindness that they have received from the Lord, who delivered them from slavery in Egypt (cf. v. 36).

Christians are to emulate divine love manifested in a greater deliverance: "And walk in love, as Christ loved us and gave himself up for us, a fragrant offering and sacrifice to God" (Eph. 5:2). Christ's sacrifice delivers us from condemnation resulting from sin (cf. Rom. 8:1–2; Col. 2:13–14), as foreshadowed by animal sacrifices prescribed in Leviticus.

Paul's instructions in Eph. 5–6 contain additional allusions to OT laws. He speaks against sexual immorality and covetousness/greed (5:3, 5; cf. Lev. 18, 20; Exod. 20:17; Deut. 5:21) as well as drunkenness (Eph. 5:18; cf. Lev. 10:8–11). He also explicitly reiterates the Decalogue command to honor one's parents (Eph. 6:1–3; cf. Exod. 20:12; Deut. 5:16), and he urges masters not to treat their servants harshly (Eph. 6:9; cf. Exod. 21:26–27; Lev. 25:39–43).

In this brief exploration of Ephesians we have found that Paul's unpacking of the concept that we are God's workmanship, re-created in Christ to walk

---

10. The ninth commandment of the Decalogue prohibits a particular kind of falsehood: bearing false witness in a judicial setting (cf. Exod. 23:1–2, 7; Deut. 19:16–19). The law against lying in general is in Lev. 19:11.

in good works (2:10), is saturated with values already revealed in OT law. The apostle doesn't need to reinvent these values; instead, he selects, adapts, applies, and connects them together in the context of the gospel.

Other NT books contain plenty of other reflections of OT values (e.g., James 1:27–2:17), and exploring these would be interesting and profitable. However, the examples from Ephesians suffice to establish the point that the NT builds on OT law as useful and authoritative teaching.

Old Testament Contexts Illuminating Values for Christians

Need for Old Testament Contextualization

Granted that the OT provides background to the NT, why should we take time to directly examine OT law itself, rather than limiting our study to the digested-for-Christians transmission of values in the NT? If the NT teaches values that apply to the Christian life, why should we go back to the earlier expressions of these values in the OT, which are outside the new-covenant context, sometimes involve ancient Israelite cultural elements that are foreign and obscure to us, and in some cases may be obsolete?

Paul could have saved busy Timothy a lot of time by advising him to confine his study to the newly developing body of Christian writings, which more directly applied to Christians within the Greco-Roman culture. However, Paul viewed the "sacred writings," the OT Scriptures themselves—not predigested, abridged, or censored—as a rich resource to provide wisdom in various ways (teaching, reproof, correction, training) "for salvation through faith in Christ Jesus" (2 Tim. 3:15–17). Even the entire NT is far from complete in this way. Concepts and values that are barely or not at all mentioned in the NT are thoroughly exposed in the OT in contexts that illuminate them and their effects and implications.[11] The NT needs the OT contextual background, which the NT supplements and culminates.

Just as contextual usage determines meanings of words in a given language, it is the operation of values in particular life situations that reveals their dynamic nuances. Lists of virtues and vices (as in Eph. 4:25–32 discussed above) provide some important knowledge, but wisdom, which Paul desired Timothy to possess, involves the ability to choose, balance, and apply values in varied and often complex circumstances. The NT contains some significant contextualizations of values, but the OT offers much more in several genres,

11. Cf. Walter C. Kaiser Jr., *Toward Old Testament Ethics* (Grand Rapids: Zondervan, 1983), 33–34.

including law, narrative, wisdom literature, and prophetic writings. The following sections provide a few examples.

Immorality Excluded from God's Community

In Eph. 5:3 Paul identifies categories of sins that are totally inappropriate among Christians: "But sexual immorality and all impurity or covetousness must not even be named among you, as is proper among saints." As a young church leader, Timothy would be responsible for dealing with such problems if they arose, but he would need more guidance than this. So he could draw on Paul's counsel to the church at Corinth, illuminated by OT background.

In the particular context of 1 Cor. 5, Paul illustrates the proper treatment of a kind of sexual immorality that should not exist in a Christian community: "It is actually reported that there is sexual immorality among you, and of a kind that is not tolerated even among pagans, for a man has his father's wife. . . . Let him who has done this be removed from among you" (vv. 1–2). On what basis did Paul demand that the man be removed from fellowship enjoyed by members of the Christian community (cf. vv. 4–5, 9–13)? According to the law in Lev. 20:11, individuals who commit such incest incur capital punishment under the theocratic governance of ancient Israel, which removed the perpetrators from the community of God's people.

Paul did not condemn the Corinthian culprit to death at the hands of the church members, but he called for them "to deliver this man to Satan for the destruction of the flesh, so that his spirit may be saved in the day of the Lord" (1 Cor. 5:5). In the Christian setting, the equivalent of the OT death penalty is disfellowshipping (not dismembering!) to purge the church community,[12] which can serve a redemptive purpose so that the sinner ultimately may be saved, no doubt by impressing on the person the sense of being lost and desperately needing divine forgiveness and moral cleansing.

Further investigation of OT law, especially Lev. 18 and 20, would show Timothy that the case in Corinth exemplified only one among several kinds of sexual immorality that must be excluded from God's community. Although the NT speaks of adultery (Matt. 5:27–28; John 8:3–4; Rom. 2:22; 13:9; etc.; cf. Lev. 18:20; 20:10) and homosexual practice (Rom. 1:26–27; 1 Cor. 6:9; 1 Tim. 1:10; cf. Lev. 18:22; 20:13), it never even mentions bestiality (Lev. 18:23; 20:15–16) or varieties of incest aside from the one identified in 1 Cor. 5 (Lev. 18:6–7, 9–18; 20:12, 14, 17, 19–21).

---

12. Cf. Deut. 13:5 (13:6 MT); 17:7, 12; 19:19; 21:21; etc. of purging evil from the Israelite community.

Covetousness Leading to Immorality

In Eph. 5:3–8, why does Paul juxtapose sexual immorality, (moral) impurity, and covetousness, which he calls idolatry (cf. Col. 3:5)? He does not explain dynamic relationships between these violations of the Decalogue (Exod. 20:4–6, 14, 17). However, some OT narratives illustrate how covetousness can lead to sexual immorality. For example, David coveted Bathsheba (2 Sam. 11:2–3), (idolatrously) putting his desire for her above his relationship to God, and consequently he took her sexually. Balaam (idolatrously) coveted a reward for cursing Israel and ultimately sought to achieve his goal by plotting to entice the Israelites into sexual immorality and idolatry at Baal Peor (Num. 22–25; 31:8, 15–16; cf. 2 Pet. 2:15).

Paul's warning to Christians—"Let no one deceive you with empty words, for because of these things the wrath of God comes upon the sons of disobedience. Therefore do not become partners with them" (Eph. 5:6–7)—is vividly illustrated by Num. 25, which recounts the Israelites' disastrous Baal Peor experience:

> While Israel lived in Shittim, the people began to whore with the daughters of Moab. These invited the people to the sacrifices of their gods, and the people ate and bowed down to their gods. So Israel yoked himself to Baal of Peor. And the anger of the Lord was kindled against Israel. . . . Nevertheless, those who died by the plague were twenty-four thousand. (Num. 25:1–9)

Setting YHWH aside to covet Moabite women (a form of idolatry) and become their partners soon led the Israelites into idolatrous worship of their god Baal. No wonder OT law forbade covenants and marriages with idolaters (Exod. 23:31–33; Deut. 7:1–6)![13] Revelation 2:14 (in the message to the church at Pergamum) points out that the danger continues for Christians: "But I have a few things against you: you have some there who hold the teaching of Balaam, who taught Balak to put a stumbling block before the sons of Israel, so that they might eat food sacrificed to idols and practice sexual immorality."

Mercy for the Fallen

The OT laws delineate the scope of sexual immorality and emphasize its seriousness, but what about the possibility of mercy for those who have fallen into such sins? Paul emphasizes mercy for sinners in Eph. 2:4–5: "But God, being rich in mercy, because of the great love with which he loved us, even

---

13. Cf. Solomon's flagrant violation of this prohibition and its initial results (1 Kings 11). The idolatry that Solomon's wives introduced had a devastating long-term effect on the nation.

when we were dead in our trespasses, made us alive together with Christ—by grace you have been saved." The NT illustrates this magnificent gospel message in the lives of people (e.g., Luke 7:36–50 [see above]; John 8:11), and the OT provides additional contextualization of divine mercy.

For example, the narrative about David and Bathsheba (2 Sam. 11–12) and David's prayer of repentance in Ps. 51 hold out hope that one whose heart is broken by regret for deep sin can receive forgiveness and cleansing (2 Sam. 12:13; contrast the death penalty in Lev. 20:10).[14] Divine mercy is found here in narrative and a hymn, rather than in laws regarding sexual offenses, because mercy is usually not prescribed in laws. Mercy is over and above law, which is the standard against which obedience or violation and the need for mercy are measured.

Mercy does appear in pentateuchal laws prescribing animal sacrifices, through which the Israelites received the benefit of Christ's future sacrifice (Heb. 9–10): expiation prerequisite to forgiveness (e.g., Lev. 4:1–6:7 [4:1–5:26 MT]). However, David recognized that his capital offenses of taking Bathsheba by "power rape"[15] and murdering her husband by abuse of royal power (2 Sam. 11) were beyond the scope of remedies by animal sacrifices (Ps. 51:16 [51:18 MT]. He could only cling to a higher level of divine mercy, which was directly available through the coming sacrifice of Christ, by whom, according to Paul, "everyone who believes is freed from everything from which you could not be freed by the law of Moses" (Acts 13:39).[16]

The above discussion has shown that both Testaments of the Bible work together to inculcate wisdom for salvation by demonstrating the operation of values in a variety of contexts and through several genres complementing each other. This wisdom is comprehensive in that it equips a person of God "for every good work" (2 Tim. 3:17). However, it is not so exhaustive that those who are thoroughly equipped by studying Scripture can always safely and confidently rely on their own wisdom. A key piece of biblical wisdom is recognizing that humans are not adequately wise (e.g., Prov. 14:12; 16:25), so we need to depend on God for wisdom, which he "gives generously to all" (James 1:5).

---

14. The NT account of the woman caught in adultery magnificently demonstrates Christ's mercy (John 8:3–11), but the exquisitely detailed report in 2 Sam. 11–12 concerning David and Bathsheba shows how sin works in a complex stream of events from temptation to fall and then cover-up until God rips off the covers but accepts honest confession and unconditional surrender.

15. Richard M. Davidson, *Flame of Yahweh: Sexuality in the Old Testament* (Peabody, MA: Hendrickson, 2007), 535.

16. Cf. God's mercy on King Manasseh, whose appalling sins were not expiable through animal sacrifices (2 Chron. 33). Davidson points out that in 2 Samuel, even though the Lord forgave David, "his son born out of the illegitimate sexual encounter died as judgment for David's sin (12:14)," perhaps as "an intimation of the ultimate Son of David, the Messiah, who died to take the penalty of all repentant sinners" (ibid., including note 119).

2

What Is Old Testament Law?

Moses defined the authority, nature, and purpose of OT law in a stirring appeal to the Israelite nation:

> See, I have set before you today life and good, death and evil, in that I command you today to love the LORD your God, to walk in His ways, and to keep His commandments, His statutes, and His judgments, that you may live and multiply; and the LORD your God will bless you in the land which you go to possess. But if your heart turns away so that you do not hear, and are drawn away, and worship other gods and serve them, I announce to you today that you shall surely perish; you shall not prolong your days in the land which you cross over the Jordan to go in and possess. I call heaven and earth as witnesses today against you, that I have set before you life and death, blessing and cursing; therefore choose life, that both you and your descendants may live; that you may love the LORD your God, that you may obey His voice, and that you may cling to Him, for He is your life and the length of your days; and that you may dwell in the land which the LORD swore to your fathers, to Abraham, Isaac, and Jacob, to give them. (Deut. 30:15–20 NKJV)

The authority who has given laws to the Israelites and holds them accountable for obeying is "the LORD your God." He is "your God," the Deity whom the Israelites are to love because they enjoy a special relationship with him, and he has graciously given them the covenant promise of land that they are about to possess. The Lord is powerful and beneficent, providing "your life and the length of your days." Following his instructions involves accepting his authority, but disregarding his laws amounts to rejecting him, which goes with worshiping other gods. Unlike law in Greek thought, OT law "is not the expression of an impersonal natural reason, the rational order of the cosmos; rather, it is the expression of a personal divine being's *will*, which can take the form of detailed written instruction and legislation."[1]

The words "I call heaven and earth as witnesses today against you" (cf. Deut. 4:26; 31:28; 32:1) identify this passage as part of a treaty/covenant formulation. YHWH's laws function as stipulations of his covenant with Israel, also accompanied by blessings for obedience and curses for disobedience (esp. Deut. 28).[2] God's law is good in that those who choose to obey will receive life, good (i.e., prosperity), and blessing from God, "for He is your life" (Deut. 30:20 NKJV). Those who disobey forfeit the good life that God offers and incur the consequences of death, evil (i.e., adversity), and cursing.[3] Therefore the divine laws are normative and prescriptive, not merely descriptive.

The nature of OT law is expressed as "His ways, . . . His commandments, His statutes, and His judgments" (Deut. 30:16 NKJV). The Lord's law consists of his personal directives, which are based on his own character and behavior and cannot be separated from the relationship with him. Obedience includes loving *the Lord*, walking in *his* ways, obeying *his* voice, and clinging to *him*. Therefore, *the Lord* is the comprehensive Law as the standard of justice because "all his ways are justice" (32:4). While his commandments/laws do not constitute an exhaustive code, they provide valuable examples of his comprehensive justice.

The purpose of OT law is not merely to control humans by listing required and prohibited behaviors with penalties for violations. Rather, the purpose is to teach God's covenant people how they can enjoy the life, the good, and the blessing that he promises to those who love him and "walk in His ways" (Deut. 30:16 NKJV). A vital aspect of this instruction is to set out before them the contrast between God's ways and the alternatives so that they can understand the difference and be persuaded to make their own wise choices.[4]

In Deut. 30 the law is not simply "Mosaic." Moses does not promulgate his own law; instead, he stands outside the divine law to present the overall choice between following its instructions and disregarding them. Within themselves the OT laws lay out components of the contrasting options by

1. Christine Hayes, *What's Divine about Divine Law? Early Perspectives* (Princeton: Princeton University Press, 2015), 2, emphasis original.

2. On ANE and OT treaty/covenant formulations and their components, see John H. Walton, *Ancient Israelite Literature in Its Cultural Context: A Survey of Parallels between Biblical and Ancient Near Eastern Texts*, LBI (Grand Rapids: Zondervan, 1989), 101–5.

3. Cf. NJPS of Deut. 30:15, "life and prosperity, death and adversity."

4. On persuasive rhetorics in the Pentateuch, see James W. Watts, *Reading Law: The Rhetorical Shaping of the Pentateuch*, BibSem 59 (Sheffield: Sheffield Academic, 1999).

teaching particular distinctions between right and wrong and in many cases by indicating consequences of decisions regarding them. The Decalogue commandment concerning idolatry is an especially powerful case in point because its formulation is a microcosm of Moses's appeal in Deut. 30. Not only does it define right and wrong by forbidding idolatry (Exod. 20:4–5a), but it also supplies motivation by contrasting the results of disobedience with those of obedience: "for I the LORD your God am a jealous God, visiting the iniquity of the fathers on the children to the third and the fourth generation of those who hate me, but showing steadfast love to thousands of those who love me and keep my commandments" (vv. 5b–6).[5]

Thus far we have found that OT law is normative, exemplary, covenantal divine instruction.[6] The rest of the present chapter further addresses the question "What is Old Testament law?" through exploration of the authority of OT law, its absolute moral standards and the people's accountability to it, and its nature. The next chapter will explore the purpose of OT law.

Authority of Old Testament Law

Divine Source and Authority

Old Testament law is distinguished from other bodies of law by the source and authority that the Bible claims for it: the Deity YHWH, the Lord. Human societies can develop customary norms; rulers, legislatures, and courts can issue and enforce decrees and laws within their limited spheres of influence.[7] But YHWH as the Creator (Gen. 1–2; Exod. 20:11; 31:17) possesses vastly greater authority because he has established and controls even the "laws"/ norms of the cosmic natural order,[8] so he can encourage obedience and discourage disobedience to the laws that he gives human beings by means of blessings and curses that affect people through physical conditions within their natural environment (Lev. 26:4–5, 9–10, 16, 19–20, 22, 25; Deut. 28:4–5, 8, 11–12, 17–18, 21–24, 27–28; etc.).

5. Cf. Deut. 7:9, "The faithful God who keeps covenant and steadfast love with those who love him and keep his commandments, *to a thousand generations*" (emphasis added).

6. I am indebted to Kenneth Bergland, who characterizes OT law as "normative covenantal instruction." See "Torah and Prophets: Case-Studies of Inner-Biblical Reuse and Appropriation between the Ethical Laws of the Torah and the Classical Prophets" (PhD diss., Andrews University, forthcoming).

7. For human decrees, see *khoq*, "statute," in Gen. 47:26; Exod. 5:14; Isa. 10:1. For social norms in Egypt and Canaan, see Lev. 18 and 20.

8. See *khoq* in Job 28:26; Prov. 8:29; Jer. 31:36; *khuqqah*, "statute," in Job 38:33; Jer. 5:24; 31:35; 33:25.

It is impossible for humans to escape the domain of the all-knowing control of YHWH (Pss. 89:11 [89:12 MT]; 139; Jon. 1:9–10), who "judges the world" (Ps. 9:8 [9:9 MT]; cf. 98:9). His international reach is shown by his ability to expel powerful immoral nations from Canaan so that the Israelites can live there (Exod. 34:24; Lev. 18:24–25; Deut. 4:38; 7:1), and he can similarly expel the Israelites if they disregard his laws (Lev. 18:28; 20:22).

Transmission through Human Representatives

According to biblical narratives, laws for Israel originated with YHWH, who conveyed them to his people through his special representatives, especially Moses. The book of Exodus reports that the Israelites heard YHWH's voice when he delivered the Decalogue (20:19, 22; Deut. 5:4, 22–23). This terrified them, so they begged Moses to receive the divine messages and then tell them, and they would receive his words as the words of God (Exod. 20:18–21; Deut. 5:5, 24–27). Thus YHWH himself is the source and authority of the laws and holds his people accountable for obeying his voice (Num. 14:22).

YHWH's authority did not change when his presence and place of revelation moved from Mount Sinai to the tabernacle (Exod. 40:34–35), and he gave Moses many more laws there (Lev. 1:1ff.; cf. Exod. 25:22; Num. 7:89–8:1ff.). Nor was God's authority diminished when he answered legal questions that Moses asked him on behalf of the people as the need arose, generating authoritative precedents (e.g., Num. 15:32–36) and new divine case laws (cf. Lev. 24:10–23, etc.; see below).

Divine laws came to Israel through an especially transparent and therefore reliable medium because Moses is described as being supremely humble and having a relationship to the Lord transcending that of other prophets, as demonstrated by his unique face-to-face communication with YHWH (Num. 12:3, 6–8; Deut. 34:10–12). When biblical authors attribute pentateuchal instruction to Moses (e.g., 1 Kings 2:3; Ezra 3:2; Luke 24:44; John 7:19, 23), the point is not that the laws originated from him but that they were transmitted from God through Moses, who recorded them (Exod. 24:4; 34:27; Deut. 31:9, 22, 24).

Basic writing and compilation of pentateuchal laws by Moses would not rule out the possibility that some later individuals arranged and edited them to form the canonical corpus that has been handed down to us today.[9] We

---

9. Some of the most likely later additions include Gen. 12:6 ("At that time the Canaanites were in the land"), Num. 12:3 ("Now the man Moses was very meek, more than all people who were on the face of the earth"), and the account of the death of Moses in Deut. 34.

do not possess adequately solid data to determine the extent of such literary work, which would not undermine divine authority because "all Scripture is breathed out by God" (2 Tim. 3:16).

Our attitude toward the relevance of pentateuchal law for our lives depends on whether we accept or reject its divine origin and authority. Without divine authority, the laws may be good and helpful in many ways, like some other human laws, yet would lack YHWH's wisdom, and YHWH would not hold people accountable to them or bless their obedience. Such a toothless Torah can neither bite nor smile.

Absolute Moral Standards and Accountability

Absolute versus Subjective Morality

The Pentateuch presents many of its laws, such as the Ten Commandments (Exod. 20; Deut. 5) and laws derived from them (e.g., Exod. 21:12–17), as expressing or applying standards of morality that are absolute because their source is YHWH, who transcends human subjectivity and faultiness. Much of our contemporary society, especially in the Western world, tends to be hostile toward unbending absolute authority or at least uncomfortable with it. Collective and changing human wisdom has been replacing the Bible as the ethical standard.

What happens when members of a society set themselves adrift from the anchor of absolute morality, choosing to rely on their own subjective rationales rather than submit to divine authority, which sometimes is countercultural? Even a superficial review of history in so-called Christian countries shows that supplanting biblical values can yield gruesome results. There is no guarantee that subjective morality will counter human rights abuses in the future for the simple reason that it is no better than the society it reflects. Without real absolutes, anything can happen, as Rabbi Stewart Vogel points out:

> If each of us creates his own meaning, we also create our own morality. I cannot believe this. For if so, what the Nazis did was not immoral because German society had accepted it. Likewise, the subjective morality of every majority culture throughout the world could validate their heinous behavior. It comes down to a very simple matter: Without God there is no *objective meaning* to life, nor is there an *objective morality*. I do not want to live in a world where right and wrong are subjective.[10]

10. Laura Schlessinger and Stewart Vogel, *The Ten Commandments: The Significance of God's Laws in Everyday Life* (New York: Cliff Street Books, 1998), xxix.

Absolute Accountability

Along with absolute moral standards, divine authority provides absolute accountability, which humans also need in any era. People who think they are only accountable to other humans, who may or may not catch the wrongs they commit, tend to suppose that they can get away with some ethical violations. Consequently, others cannot fully trust them. Such lack of trust is detrimental to family relationships, business, society, and government.

As Jesus taught, crimes such as murder and adultery begin with inner attitudes, such as hatred and lust (Matt. 5:21–22, 27–28). Human authorities would not attempt to make laws that regulate attitudes before they reach outward expression, because humans cannot read thoughts and such statutes could not be enforced. Biblical laws show no such constraint: The Decalogue concludes with a commandment against coveting (Exod. 20:17; Deut. 5:21), and the Holiness Code prohibits bearing a grudge but commands Israelites to love others as they love themselves (Lev. 19:18; cf. v. 34). YHWH can require such laws because he can read thoughts (Ps. 139:2, 23). He can hold people accountable for secret violations that are undetected by other humans or exonerate innocent individuals who are suspected of committing such offenses (Num. 5:11–31).

Those for whom the "fear of the LORD is the beginning of wisdom" (Ps. 111:10; cf. Prov. 9:10) do not try to escape YHWH's omniscient perception, which awes, comforts, protects, and challenges them (Ps. 139; 2 Chron. 16:9). Such people accept full accountability to divine principles that reach into all areas of their lives, whether or not any humans are watching.

Divine Principles and Values

Morality involves "principles" and "values." A moral "principle" is an objective, absolute, changeless truth that governs human nature and relationships. Society corporately agrees on principles (e.g., that it is wrong to murder, steal, and commit adultery), and individuals can also accept them. A moral "value," on the other hand, is a subjective, changeable perspective of an individual or group that has developed from past experiences and interactions within culture and places a relatively high degree of importance on a course of action regarded as right (not intrinsically right) and results in a good life.[11] Examples

11. Bernard S. Jackson refers to values as "messages transmitted within society, often qualifications of other messages: that such behaviour is good, pleasant, revolting, etc." See *Studies in the Semiotics of Biblical Law*, JSOTSup 314 (Sheffield: Sheffield Academic, 2000), 171. He explores the nature of values and some ways in which they are expressed in OT laws (171–207).

of social values are justice, freedom, peace, and equality. All humans, including criminals, have values of some kind, whether good or evil. But people can bring their values into harmony with principles that they choose to guide them.

Much of OT law expresses or exemplifies absolute principles to guide human life.[12] By seeking to persuade people to make its moral principles their own, OT law encourages them to bring their personally held values into alignment with divine principles, which are based on objective, permanent, and inherently good divine values united by the overarching value of unselfish love (Lev. 19:18; Deut. 6:5; cf. Matt. 22:37–40; 1 John 4:8, 16).

Human values are subjective, changeable, and affected by culture; divine values remain constant, although OT law can temporarily constrain expressions of divine values and principles to varying degrees in order to accommodate human weakness as God seeks to meet people where they are. For example, God allowed divorce (Deut. 24:1–4), which compromises the ideal permanence of marriage (Matt. 19:3–9, referring to Gen. 1:27; 2:24), and OT law sanctioned levirate (brother-in-law) marriage (Deut. 25:5–10) as an exception to the incest law against union of a man and his sister-in-law (Lev. 18:16; 20:21).[13] The OT laws also regulated rather than abolished the cultural institutions of polygamy and servitude, which God permitted as less-than-ideal accommodations to human weakness (cf. chaps. 13–14).

If divine values are like principles in that they are objective and changeless, what is the difference between divine values and divine principles? In a sense they can be viewed as interchangeable, but the term "values" also conveys the idea of things assessed as carrying high priority on a scale of relative worth or importance, as contrasted with things that are less valuable or rejected. Moral values are preferences for what is regarded as right, appropriate, and beneficial. As such, they tend to shape attitudes and behaviors and to serve as benchmarks for measuring outcomes.

Divine values are God's priorities, which God shares with human beings in order to guide their lives in accordance with his reliable, good, and beautiful will and character. For example, a basic divine value is "You have loved righteousness and hated wickedness" (Ps. 45:7 [45:8 MT]; quoted in Heb. 1:9), as opposed to the values of a wicked man: "You love evil more than good, lying rather than speaking righteousness" (Ps. 52:3 [52:5 MT]). Galatians 5:19–23 lists several divine values as virtues in contrast to named vices:

12. E.g., the Ten Commandments, Exod. 20 (Deut. 5), and laws based on their principles.
13. This prohibition continues after the brother's death because it lacks a limitation such as that which appears in Lev. 18:18: "while her sister is still alive." Cf. Jacob Milgrom, *Leviticus 17–22: A New Translation with Introduction and Commentary*, AB 3A (New York: Doubleday, 2000), 1545, 1549.

Now the works of the flesh are evident: sexual immorality, impurity, sensuality, idolatry, sorcery, enmity, strife, jealousy, fits of anger, rivalries, dissensions, divisions, envy, drunkenness, orgies, and things like these. I warn you, as I warned you before, that those who do such things will not inherit the kingdom of God. But the fruit of the Spirit is love, joy, peace, patience, kindness, goodness, faithfulness, gentleness, self-control; against such things there is no law.[14]

The Bible generally conveys divine values/priorities by exemplifying them in various ways (including through different genres) rather than by directly stating them as prioritizations. In OT law, divine values underlie and are expressed by "principles," which encapsulate the values and make them normative by predicating or exemplifying ways in which they are to govern life and conduct, whether positively by carrying out what is worthwhile or negatively by avoiding that which is not. The following table shows some values and corresponding principles:

Values/Priorities	Principles
Rather than selfishness, God values love (Matt. 22:37–40; contrast 2 Tim. 3:2–5, "lovers of self," etc.).	*positive:* "You shall love the LORD your God" (Deut. 6:5); "You shall love your neighbor as yourself" (Lev. 19:18).
Rather than harming or taking life, God values its preservation (Gen. 45:5; Pss. 97:10; 138:7).	*negative example:* "You shall not murder" (Exod. 20:13).
Rather than unbridled sexuality, God values sexual fidelity within permanent marriage (Gen. 2:24; Lev. 18; Matt. 19:3–6).	*negative example:* "You shall not commit adultery" (Exod. 20:14).

Values do not merely prioritize what is good over what is evil; they also prioritize the relative importance of good principles. Thus a lawyer tested Jesus by asking him: "Teacher, which is the great commandment in the Law?" (Matt. 22:36). Jesus replied by citing love for God (Deut. 6:5) as "the great and first commandment" (Matt. 22:37–8) and adding a second that is like it: love for one's neighbor (Lev. 19:18; Matt. 22:39). Then he stated: "On these two commandments depend all the Law and the Prophets" (Matt. 22:40). Jesus issued a rebuke on another occasion: "Woe to you, scribes and Pharisees, hypocrites! For you tithe mint and dill and cumin, and have neglected the weightier matters of the law: justice and mercy and faithfulness. These you ought to have done, without neglecting the others" (Matt. 23:23).

14. Cf. Phil. 4:8, "Whatever is true, whatever is honorable, whatever is just, whatever is pure, whatever is lovely, whatever is commendable, if there is any excellence, if there is anything worthy of praise, think about these things."

Divine values provide the framework for divine principles by forming the conceptual, philosophical basis for the latter and by structuring their prioritized relationships to one another within a coherent system.[15] The ability to weigh values and principles and implement them in life is one of the hallmarks of wisdom.

Nature of Old Testament Law

Categorization of Old Testament Law

The meaning of the word "law" depends on the context in which it is used. In the context of law (in general, not limited to OT law) that governs human beings, a system of law consists of value-based norms that mediate relations between people and regulate their behavior within the social system to which they belong. While law is concerned with behavior, it is more than an external regulator:

> Law is the order of justice and right to which individuals and groups should conform and which judicial authority should enforce. Rules will necessarily play some role in this order, but there also will be principles and values which form a consistent system, cover all possible situations, and belong to the collective conscience of the community. By this definition, explicit rules—laws—are only the tip of the iceberg of the phenomenon of Law.[16]

There are several kinds of law governing human beings, and scholars are investigating how OT law relates to them in order to better understand the nature of OT law. Following are some relevant categories of law to which OT law can be compared or contrasted, plus some concepts involved with them. These are categories that modern people use to study law, but most of them are not stated in the Bible, so the biblical authors may not have thought about law in these ways. Nevertheless, relating OT law to our categories assists us as part of a process of cultural translation.

"Positive law," formulated and enforced by a human authority, posits regulation of actions and establishment of rights. By contrast, "natural law" is not human-made: it consists of standards of conduct and inherent rights based on traditional and widely accepted moral principles or nature and reason. Divine law is "religious law" taught by religious traditions.

Positive law includes prescriptive "statutory law," which is written law established by an officially governing legislature or legislator (as distinguished

---

15. On the hierarchy of value-based principles in OT law, see chap. 7 below.
16. Dale Patrick, *Old Testament Law* (Atlanta: John Knox, 1985), 4.

from unwritten/oral law or "common law"). Positive law also includes "common law" or "case law," which is developed by judges and courts, whose rulings in individual cases serve as descriptive precedents that affect decisions in subsequent cases. Statutory law is subordinate to "constitutional law," which is the fundamental written or unwritten law that defines the principles by which a government exercises its authority, thereby determining its nature and relationships between its branches. A "law code" is a collection of written laws, usually covering a certain subject area or organized by subjects.

"Moral law" refers to a system of guidelines for right (versus wrong) conduct that people may follow out of personal conscience, especially when such criteria are viewed as universal, permanent, ordained by a deity, or constituting a truth of human reason. Such moral guidelines may not be codified, and they may go beyond what is legislated and enforced or enforceable in positive law. Conversely, positive law includes regulation of situations in which morality is not in question. So moral law and positive law are distinct but overlap.[17]

After we have recognized moral law, it is helpful for us to ascertain the relationship between "morality" and "ethics." Both of these have to do with distinctions between right and wrong conduct, motives, and attitudes. Scott B. Rae distinguishes between "morality" and "ethics" as follows:

> Most people use the terms *morality* and *ethics* interchangeably. Technically, morality refers to the actual content of right and wrong, and ethics refers to the process of determining right and wrong. In other words, morality deals with moral *knowledge* and ethics with moral *reasoning*. . . . Morality is the end result of ethical deliberation, the substance of right and wrong.[18]

Common Hebrew terms for OT law clearly identify it as law in the sense of regulation to which people are held accountable. Aside from *torah* and *mitsvah*, which respectively emphasize the didactic role of OT law and its origin as divine command, some OT law is called *mishpat*, "judgment," a word that can refer to legal decisions (e.g., Deut. 1:17; 17:9, 11; 25:1) as well as to a divine law/rule (Exod. 21:1; Lev. 24:22). The term *khoq*, "statute, rule,"

17. Cf. ibid., 5.
18. Scott B. Rae, *Moral Choices: An Introduction to Ethics*, 3rd ed. (Grand Rapids: Zondervan, 2009), 15, emphasis original; cf. Scott B. Rae, *Introducing Christian Ethics: A Short Guide to Making Moral Choices* (Grand Rapids: Zondervan, 2016), 13: "Ethics refers to the discipline of discovering morality. Ethics is more the 'how we get there,' and morality is the 'what the standards are.'" Robert M. Johnston (Andrews University) suggests: "Ethics is the science of which morals are the application" (personal communication).

can be used of a legal regulation instituted by a human ruler (Gen. 47:26) or by God (Exod. 18:16; Deut. 4:5), and *khuqqah*, "statute," can refer to a human custom (e.g., Lev. 18:3, 30; 1 Kings 3:3) or a divine ordinance (e.g., Exod. 12:14; Lev. 23:41). Some usages of the Hebrew terms for law tend to be specific to certain kinds of contexts, such as *torah* for a rule of ritual procedure (e.g., Lev. 6:9, 14, 25 [6:2, 7, 18 MT]; 7:1) and *khoq* for an allocation/due (e.g., Exod. 29:28; Lev. 7:34; 10:15).

The relationship between OT law and modern categories of law is complex.[19] If the law originated with God, who gave it to his people through prophets such as Moses, this divine law is "religious law." It resembles the prescriptive "statutory law" category of human-made "positive law" in that it is written law originating from the divine legislator, who officially governed Israel under the theocracy (but see further below). Such OT law can also be classed as "moral law," which serves as a system of guidelines for right living as ordained by the Deity YHWH and includes elements that positive law cannot enforce, such as regulation of internal attitudes (e.g., Exod. 20:17; Lev. 19:17–18).[20]

Some parts of OT law are similar to common/case law in that decisions of the divine judge in particular cases served as precedents for similar and related future situations (Lev. 24:10–23; Num. 9:6–14; 27:1–11). In these instances, YHWH explicitly expanded the precedents into prescriptive statutes. Moreover, many of the OT laws are formulated as "case"/"casuistic" law (as contrasted with "apodictic law"): such a law consists of a "protasis" ("If/When . . .") that describes a given situation, followed by an "apodosis" ("then . . ." expressed or implied) that prescribes the legal consequence, the way in which the situation should be addressed (see chap. 5).[21] For example:

19. Christine Hayes elucidates the character of the biblical view of divine law as an expression of divine will, an expression of divine reason, and grounded in historical narrative, a multidimensional conception that is difficult to categorize in terms of modern theories of law (*What's Divine about Divine Law?*, 3, 12, 14–53). Hayes integrates the three dimensions of OT law: "Insofar as biblical law is grounded in the nation's story about itself, its addressees and ideal human type are members of a covenant community whose *historical encounter* with a divine sovereign underwrites its continuing fidelity to his *will* for the formation and preservation of a holy, just, and *wise* community" (52–53, emphasis original).

20. David VanDrunen also finds some resemblance and functional equivalence between Mosaic law, which regulated Israel, and natural law, which regulated Israel's pagan neighbors. See *Divine Covenants and Moral Order: A Biblical Theology of Natural Law* (Grand Rapids: Eerdmans, 2014), 282–366.

21. This does not require the conclusion that the OT case laws originated as common/case law that was formed descriptively through collection of precedents from human judges. In any case, their formulation reflects that of casuistic ANE collections such as the Laws of Hammurabi; cf. David P. Wright, *Inventing God's Law: How the Covenant Code of the Bible Used and Revised the Laws of Hammurabi* (Oxford: Oxford University Press, 2009).

protasis:	"If a man steals an ox or a sheep, and kills it or sells it,
apodosis:	he shall repay five oxen for an ox, and four sheep for a sheep."
	(Exod. 22:1 [21:37 MT])

The OT laws constituted "covenantal law" in that they explicitly served as stipulations of the unique (in the ANE) covenant that YHWH gave to Israel (e.g., Exod. 19–24; Lev. 26; Deut. 27–31; see chap. 3). Then OT law also contributed to "constitutional law," which defined basic principles of theocratic governance under the terms of the covenant. For example, civil leaders are responsible to the Lord's priestly representatives (e.g., Deut. 17:8–20).

Laws can be classified according to the kinds of wrongs that they address. Modern law is divided into two branches, criminal law and civil law. A "crime" is viewed as harming the entire community, so that public authority is responsible for apprehending the culprit, and punishment of that person is for the sake of the public. On the other hand, a "civil delict (tort)" is considered to wrong only the victim, who may seek financial reparation through legal action against the wrongdoer.[22] However, Raymond Westbrook and Bruce Wells propose that three categories can be roughly identified in OT law:

1. Offenses against a hierarchical superior, especially a king or God, that call for disciplinary action.
2. Morally grave offenses against another individual that call for revenge.
3. Offenses against the interests of an individual involving less moral culpability, for which the remedy is compensation.[23]

Function of Old Testament Law in Ancient Israel

Scholars have become aware that the OT laws were not like modern legislation in the sense of directly guiding judicial practice in lawcourts.[24] Westbrook defines "legislation" in his essay "Cuneiform Law Codes and the Origins of Legislation":[25]

22. Ibid., 69.
23. *Everyday Law in Biblical Israel: An Introduction* (Louisville: Westminster John Knox, 2009), 69–70; cf. 71–87). Ze'ev W. Falk points out that defining "crimes" in OT law is problematic because wrongs that we would call crimes were often dealt with by private action that the wronged party or his relatives carried out. See *Hebrew Law in Biblical Times: An Introduction*, 2nd ed. (Provo, UT: Brigham Young University Press; Winona Lake, IN: Eisenbrauns, 2001), 71.
24. Michael LeFebvre, "Written Law in Ancient Israel," in *Collections, Codes, and Torah: The Re-characterization of Israel's Written Law*, LHBOTS 451 (New York: T&T Clark, 2006), 31–54.
25. Originally published in *ZA* 79 (1989): 201–22.

Legislation is an authoritative source of law; the courts are bound to obey its precepts. That binding quality begins at a certain point in time, when the legislation is promulgated. And once promulgated, the text of the legislation takes on a life of its own—the text is the exclusive source of the law. For this reason, the courts must pay great attention to the wording of the text, interpret its meaning, and cite it in their decisions. Even if the legislation does not change the existing law but merely codifies it, the effect is to exclude reliance on the earlier sources.[26]

The pentateuchal narrative presents laws as authoritative because they were promulgated by YHWH at certain points in time. So they could be viewed as legislation to this limited extent. However, the source of law was not simply the written laws themselves, but the justice of YHWH that they exemplified. While some aspects of the formulation and arrangement of the laws could lend themselves to lawcourt usage, others would not. Furthermore, biblical narratives concerning lawcourt situations do not indicate that judges consulted lawbooks to arrive at their decisions. We will discuss these factors of formulation and court practice in order.

Regarding formulation, many of the OT laws articulate principles, cases, and penalties for violation that could be administered by human beings, as in modern legislation. However, a significant number of the OT laws do not specify penalties, or the penalties that they mandate are administered by God, and in some instances enforcement by humans is impossible (e.g., "You shall not covet," Exod. 20:17). Unlike modern legislation, many of the OT laws contain motivational elements clearly designed to persuade hearers/readers to comply.

Like modern legislation, many OT laws are placed in major collections, including what scholars have called the "Covenant Code" (or "Book of the Covenant"; Exod. 21–23), the "Holiness Code" (Lev. 17–26 [or 17–27]),[27] and the "Deuteronomic Code" (Deut. 12–26). Arrangement of laws in these portions of the Pentateuch involves literary sophistication and some grouping by topics.[28] However, these law collections differ from modern codified law in that they provide examples of principles and ways in which they can be

26. Raymond Westbrook, *Law from the Tigris to the Tiber: The Writings of Raymond Westbrook*, ed. Bruce Wells and Rachel Magdalene, 2 vols. (Winona Lake, IN: Eisenbrauns, 2009), 1:74.

27. Many scholars view Lev. 27 as an appendix to the Holiness Code.

28. For grouping by topics, see, e.g., Exod. 22:1–15 [21:37–22:14 MT] on problems involving property and its restitution and Lev. 18 on sexual behavior. For an important proposal regarding sophisticated literary structure in the Deuteronomic law collection, see Stephen A. Kaufman, "The Structure of the Deuteronomic Law," *Maarav* 1, no. 2 (1978–79): 105–58.

applied but do not try to cover comprehensively every kind of case that would need to be considered by the ancient Israelite legal system.

Moreover, the ways in which OT laws are organized differ from what we would expect in a modern law code. Rather than sequential and unified treatment of topics in discrete sections, the OT "codes" often present diverse topics together (esp. in Lev. 19) and reiterate certain laws in various places.[29] Also, whereas different modern codes regulating society would be dedicated to distinct topic areas (e.g., civil code, penal code, labor code), there is significant overlap between the contents of the OT collections.[30]

Regarding court practice, biblical narratives do not support the idea that judges were to rely on written laws, equating them with the Law in the sense of the ultimate source of justice. Shortly before the Israelites reached Mount Sinai, Moses described to his father-in-law how he judged the people who came to him to inquire of God: "When they have a dispute, they come to me and I decide between one person and another, and I make them know the statutes of God and his laws" (Exod. 18:16). As a prophet, Moses brought cases to God (cf. v. 19) and taught divine law (cf. v. 20). His judicial rulings were based on his knowledge of justice as informed by YHWH through oracles.[31] In Deuteronomy, after the Lord has given many laws at Sinai, judges are to judge justly because the judgment belongs to God as the source of justice, and they should refer to Moses any case that is too hard for them, but Moses does not instruct them to make their decisions according to a written law collection (Deut. 1:16–17; 16:18–20).

After the death of Moses, local judges are to take difficult cases to the Levitical priests and the national judge at YHWH's sanctuary in order to receive their ruling and follow their instruction (Deut. 17:8–13). The word for "instruction" here is *torah* (v. 11), but it comes from the priests and judge; it is not a written law that they consult in order to reach their decision. The fact that the Israelite high court is at the sanctuary and involves priests who can inquire of the Lord implies that the ultimate source of Israel's law is YHWH himself, whose decisions are accessed through oracles.[32]

No biblical narrative includes consultation of a lawbook in a description of a judicial deliberation.[33] Some narratives recount verdicts that correlate to varying degrees with specific OT laws and their penalties, which implies possible acquaintance with them but no attempt to follow them to the letter.

---

29. E.g., reiteration in Lev. 20 of earlier laws, esp. those in chap. 18.
30. E.g., Exod. 21:2–6 and Deut. 15:12–18 on slavery.
31. Cf. Deborah, a prophetess who served as a judge (Judg. 4:4–5).
32. LeFebvre, "Written Law," 44–46.
33. Patrick, *Old Testament Law*, 193–98.

For example, when Nathan told David a juridical parable about a rich man who took a poor man's ewe lamb (2 Sam. 12:1–4), the king angrily reacted with his opinion regarding a verdict: "As the Lord lives, the man who has done this deserves to die, and he shall restore the lamb fourfold, because he did this thing, and because he had no pity" (vv. 5–6). Fourfold reparation for a sheep accords with Exod. 22:1 (21:37 MT), where a person who steals a sheep "shall repay . . . four sheep for a sheep." The OT law never mandates capital punishment for theft of property, but David added this because of the aggravating circumstance that the rich man (representing himself!) was utterly pitiless.[34]

David was reluctant to publicly forgive the son of the woman of Tekoa, a (fictitious, although David did not know that) murderer (2 Sam. 14:8), perhaps because he did not want to violate the categorical prohibition in Num. 35:31, 33 against any penalty but death for a murderer. Nevertheless, the royal judge did grant amnesty in this difficult case (2 Sam. 14:11), no doubt because of the circumstance that the young man's mother and her dead husband would be left without an heir if their remaining son were executed (cf. vv. 5, 7).[35] David was able to grant such mercy only because he possessed the social power of a monarch to restrain clan justice (cf. vv. 7, 11). Even then, he knew that he was culpable for violating a norm through his judicial clemency, but he accepted the legal fiction offered by the "widow": "On me be the guilt, my lord the king, and on my father's house; let the king and his throne be guiltless" (v. 9).

It can be argued that such narratives show deviation from God's intent for judicial use of his law, which does not approve of capital punishment for theft of property or allow a murderer to escape the death penalty, although the Lord himself has the right to slay someone who steals from him (cf. Acts 5:1–10) or to let a murderer walk free (Gen. 4:8–16; 2 Sam. 12:9, 13; 2 Chron. 33:6, 13). But although the narratives demonstrate extreme cases, they seem to illustrate the flexible approach used and advocated by Moses in Exodus and Deuteronomy (see above).

---

34. Another instance of pitiless royal behavior was Jezebel's destruction of Naboth by manipulating the judicial system (1 Kings 21). She called for false witnesses to accuse him of cursing God and the king (vv. 10, 13), which would have violated the law of Exod. 22:28 (22:27 MT)—"You shall not revile God, nor curse a ruler of your people" (cf. Lev. 24:15–16)—whether or not she was actually citing this OT law. Punishment of Naboth went beyond OT law: His ancestral property (1 Kings 21:15–16), which should have belonged to his heirs, was confiscated by the crown, and his sons, the heirs, were also killed (2 Kings 9:26). On the possible relationship between this egregious abuse of Israelite jurisprudence and OT law, cf. Patrick, *Old Testament Law*, 195–96; and LeFebvre, "Written Law," 35–36.

35. Cf. Patrick, *Old Testament Law*, 195.

If the OT laws are not fully "legislation" as defined by Westbrook, could they constitute academic treatises? Westbrook describes this category as follows:

> An academic treatise on the law may be good evidence of what the law is, but it is not an authoritative source. The treatise in describing the law in effect refers the court to the real authoritative sources thereof, whether they be statute, precedent, or custom. The date of the treatise is therefore of less significance; there is no particular point in time at which it comes into effect. And its text has no independent value. Courts need not cite it or pay attention to its wording, since they are essentially looking beyond it to the source that it reflects.[36]

It appears that the early ANE law collections, such as that of Hammurabi, were academic treatises that gathered, edited, organized, and supplemented existing legal customs and precedents.[37] That they did not function as normative legislation is shown by the fact that extant Mesopotamian court records and contracts, of which there are thousands, do not explicitly refer to the Laws of Hammurabi or any other written law collection, so these collections were not used to directly govern day-to-day legal practice.[38]

The Israelites did not feel obligated to use the OT law collections to directly dictate their judicial verdicts, at least not in every case, and these laws pointed beyond themselves to an authoritative source (the character of YHWH; see above). There is a close relationship between the philosophy and contents of OT law and those of biblical Wisdom literature (see chap. 4), both of which teach application of values and principles and can be called *torah* "instruction, teaching, rule," and *mitsvah*, "commandment" (Exod. 24:12; Deut. 30:10; Prov. 3:1; 6:20, 23; 7:2).[39] However, the OT law collections are not academic wisdom treatises. Rather, they are presented as covenant stipulations that come into effect at particular points in time (see chap. 3), they are public rather than academic, and they are normative.[40]

---

36. Westbrook, *Law from the Tigris to the Tiber*, 1:74. On the contrast between legislative law codes and nonlegislative law collections/treatises, see LeFebvre, "Written Law," 23–28.

37. Westbrook, *Law from the Tigris to the Tiber*, esp. 1:91–92, 95; cf. John H. Walton, *Ancient Near Eastern Thought and the Old Testament: Introducing the Conceptual World of the Hebrew Bible* (Grand Rapids: Baker Academic, 2006), 287–91.

38. Martha T. Roth, *Law Collections from Mesopotamia and Asia Minor*, SBL Writings from the Ancient World 6 (Atlanta: Scholars Press, 1995), 5–7.

39. Anne Fitzpatrick-McKinley characterizes the Book of the Covenant (or Covenant Code) in Exodus as "a list of wisdom-moral rules." *The Transformation of Torah from Scribal Advice to Law*, JSOTSup 287 (Sheffield: Sheffield Academic, 1999), 144.

40. Cf. Walton, *Ancient Near Eastern Thought*, 293, 297. Anthony Phillips observes that the collection of laws in Exod. 21:12–22:17 (21:12–22:16 MT) seems to be "intended as a statement of actual statutes and precedents to be put into effect by Israel's judges. All the laws specify

The priests were responsible for teaching "the people of Israel all the statutes that the LORD has spoken to them by Moses" (Lev. 10:11; cf. Deut. 33:10), and Moses commanded the priests and elders to read "this law" (*torah*; possibly Deuteronomy) to the assembled Israelites every seven years at the Festival of Booths (Deut. 31:9–13).[41] All Israelites, including the judges, were to be informed by the law as a whole, and they were to act in accordance with its principles and ethos of justice. Therefore, OT law was to have public prescriptive influence,[42] even if its impact on individual court cases was less direct than that of modern statutory law.[43] Because the laws were available to everyone, primary parties could settle matters between them in many cases,[44] but third-party arbitrators or judges could become involved if necessary (cf. Matt. 5:23–25).

The OT law stipulates obligatory norms, which carry penalties for violation to be carried out by the human community under the theocracy and/or by YHWH himself (see chaps. 5, 14). Lest the Lord's commandments and penalties are thought to be merely theoretical, the Pentateuch explicitly records compliance with some of his cultic laws (e.g., Exod. 12:28, 50; 40:23, 25, 27, 29, 32; Lev. 16:34; Num. 8:3) and reports divinely mandated execution of individuals who violated other kinds of laws (Lev. 24:23; Num. 15:36). Even where no penalties are specified with individual laws, accumulated violations lead to divinely administered curses for breach of the covenant (esp. Lev. 26; Deut. 28). In light of biblical narratives that record fulfillment of these curses (e.g., 2 Kings 17; 2 Chron. 36), such divine punishments should not be taken lightly.

So how could OT laws be normative if they were not comprehensive and if they could be flexibly applied to individual cases? First, the laws are paradigmatic examples that guide positive behaviors, and when problems arise, the laws are to serve as starting points for deliberation of cases that are related but present variables. For example, Exod. 21:35 ("When one man's ox butts another's, so that it dies, then they shall sell the live ox and share its price, and

---

sanctions which can be enforced, whether it is execution or damages." *Essays on Biblical Law*, JSOTSup 344 (London: Sheffield Academic, 2002), 51–52.

41. Cf. Deut. 17:18–20, where the future king is to have his own copy of the law and read it throughout his life in order to learn and follow it.

42. Cf. Shalom M. Paul, *Studies in the Book of the Covenant in the Light of Cuneiform and Biblical Law*, VTSup 18 (Leiden: Brill, 1970; repr., Eugene, OR: Wipf & Stock, 2006), 38–39.

43. On the basis of Exod. 18, LeFebvre ("Written Law," 47) observes, "Laws are published for national exhortation, but are not assigned to the court as legislation."

44. Bernard S. Jackson refers to "'self-executing laws': laws designed for implementation by the parties themselves, without the need for recourse to third-party adjudication." *Wisdom-Laws: A Study of the Mishpatim of Exodus 21:1–22:16* (Oxford: Oxford University Press, 2006), 29 (referring to examples in Exod. 25–28, including Exod. 21:35).

the dead beast also they shall share") refers to a typical situation in which the values of the two oxen are equal or roughly equivalent.[45] Presumably, adjustments could be made for cases in which the values of oxen are significantly different. Persons deciding the cases would need to be able to justify their decisions by referring to relevant factors that influenced them. Notice the clarity with which such factors are indicated in the narratives that include pronouncements of judgment by King David on the rich man in Nathan's parable and on behalf of the "son" of the "widow" of Tekoa (see above). No doubt customary concepts and practices of justice were to inform the way in which details were worked out within the framework provided by OT law.

Second, the source of justice that guided any Israelite, and especially a judge (Deut. 1:16–17; 16:18–20), was not only the particular law that most closely addressed the situation before him. Normative justice was revealed by YHWH's own character of justice (e.g., Exod. 34:6–7), as revealed by the entire corpus of available divine law, including motive clauses and accompanying exhortations. In other words, while the letter of the law was important, it was to be sensitively and contextually applied in light of the spirit of the law as a whole, recognizing that no law code can explicitly account for all the complexities of human life.

Therefore, our interpretation of a given law should take into account the "underlying postulates" of the law system to which it belongs. We must "go beyond the individual rules; for it is not possible to comprehend the law of any culture without an awareness of its key concepts, its value judgments."[46]

Discrepancies between Laws

Understanding the nature of OT law assists assessment of discrepancies (or apparent discrepancies) within it. Given that the Lord himself is the ultimate source of the Law, according to the Pentateuch,[47] he can maintain justice

45. Ibid., 27. Here Jackson uses Exod. 21:35 to illustrate a narrative, rather than literal semantic, approach to the biblical text: "It applied to the typical cases whose images are evoked by the words of the rule" (cf. 24–26, 28–29).

46. Moshe Greenberg, "Some Postulates of Biblical Criminal Law," in *Yehezkel Kaufmann Jubilee Volume*, ed. Menahem Haran (Jerusalem: Magnes, 1960), 8.

47. Jacob Milgrom has suggested that when the Pentateuch introduces laws with the words "YHWH spoke to Moses, saying," this merely means that the anonymous authors "were certain that the laws they proposed were not of their invention, but were derivable from Mosaic principles (i.e., traceable to Moses himself)" (*Leviticus 17–22*, 1369). As biblical support for this idea, Milgrom cites two postexilic passages that refer to compliance with Mosaic law in some ways that have no precise antecedent in pentateuchal law (1368–69): Neh. 10:29 [10:30 MT] speaks of "a curse and an oath to walk in God's Law that was given by Moses the servant of God" (cf. 9:38–10:39 [10:1–40 MT]), and in 2 Chron. 30:16 priests and Levites "took their accustomed

through variable circumstances by giving somewhat different laws to different people for different situations. Thus OT law is dynamic and adaptable rather than static and rigid. Following are brief discussions of three examples.

First, Lev. 17 requires Israelites who wish to eat meat of domestic sacrificable animals to offer them as well-being offerings at the central sanctuary (vv. 3–9). By contrast, Deut. 12 allows them to slaughter and eat such animals at any of their settlements, without sacrificing them, provided that they drain out the blood (vv. 15–16, 20–25). The difference is not a legal contradiction or polemic between two schools of authorship, because the law in Lev. 17 regulates the wilderness setting during the journey from Sinai to Canaan, where all the Israelites camped around the sanctuary (v. 3, "the camp"; cf. Num. 2–3), but the law in Deut. 12 is to apply once they have spread out in the land of Canaan, where they may dwell too far from the sanctuary to go there every time they want to eat meat of a sacrificable animal (vv. 20–21; cf. chap. 6).[48]

Second, Moses's sermonic recounting of the Ten Commandments to the younger generation in Deut. 5 somewhat differs from the Exod. 20 version, which is presented as words directly spoken by God. The most significant

posts according to the Law of Moses the man of God." However, these are instances of later application of Mosaic law, which should be distinguished from the pentateuchal formula of initial law-giving ("YHWH spoke to Moses, saying") that is an integral part of the pentateuchal narrative, as shown, for example, by the way Lev. 1:1 ("[And] YHWH called [*vayiqra*'; with the *vav* consecutive] to Moses and spoke to him from the tent of meeting, saying," my trans.) continues the narrative from the end of Exodus. If there was a tabernacle that Moses set up and on which YHWH's cloud settled (Exod. 40), YHWH spoke to him from there (Lev. 1:1) as he had earlier spoken the Decalogue from Mount Sinai (Exod. 20). So this calls into question the logic of Milgrom's suggestion that the Mosaic principles behind the traditions in the Pentateuch derive from the Decalogue (1369). Many other laws are clearly based on principles exemplified in the Decalogue, but if we discount the transmission of these laws from YHWH through Moses, there is no reason to accept the divine origin of the Decalogue either, and if we reject that, there were no principles of divine-Mosaic origin from which to derive additional laws. Note that as support for the derivative nature of pentateuchal laws, Milgrom cites theological pluralism reflected by discrepancies between some of them (1370–71). Examination of these discrepancies is beyond the scope of the present volume, but it appears that factors such as legal supplementation and revision due to developments within the narrative framework of the Pentateuch, including problems of unfaithfulness by the Israelites, can account for at least some of them better than pluralism from schools of tradents that contributed to the composition of the Pentateuch.

48. Roy Gane, *Leviticus, Numbers*, NIV Application Commentary (Grand Rapids: Zondervan, 2004), 301–2. Critical scholars have long blown way out of proportion this difference between sacrificial slaughter in Leviticus and "profane" (i.e., nonsacred) slaughter in Deuteronomy. They do not adequately take the *Sitz im Leben* (situation in life) into account because they do not accept the historicity of the wilderness setting, and therefore they claim that the difference represents a polemic between two schools of thought: H (i.e., the Holiness source, which is part of P, the Priestly source) versus D (i.e., the Deuteronomic source). See, e.g., Julius Wellhausen, *Prolegomena to the History of Ancient Israel* (1885; repr., Atlanta: Scholars Press, 1994), 50–51.

change in Deut. 5 is the motivation that Moses provides for the Sabbath command, which refers to the national experience of the Israelites' redemption from slavery in Egypt (v. 15) rather than creation (Exod. 20:11). This does not mean that creation is irrelevant in Deuteronomy (see 4:32; 32:6). However, viewing the Sabbath as redemption from slavery to work, which also benefited slaves of the Israelites, would enhance the relevance of the Sabbath for the new generation of Israelites, who needed reminders of God's deliverance (5:14–15).

Third, Jacob Milgrom singles out a classic case of inconsistency between OT laws:

> For example, the tithe laws are revealed to Moses three times. In Leviticus the farmer gives his tithes to God (27:30); in Numbers, to the Levites (18:21); and in Deuteronomy, to himself (14:23). Moreover, Numbers and Deuteronomy limit the tithe to grain (barley and wheat), must (fresh wine), and oil (olive), whereas Leviticus imposes the tithe on all produce and animals. How can these flatly contradictory tithe laws be ascribed to one author, Moses?[49]

The tithe laws all relate to life in the land of Canaan. So discrepancies between them cannot be explained on the basis of changes from one setting to another, as in the relationship between Lev. 17 and Deut. 12 (see above). However, the differences are not as serious as Milgrom makes them appear.

It is true that in Leviticus the agricultural tithes belong to the Lord (27:30, 32). Numbers 18:21 does not contradict this and reports YHWH saying: "To the Levites I have given every tithe in Israel for an inheritance, in return for their service that they do, their service in the tent of meeting." Thus the tithes belong to God, who then assigns them to his servants, the Levites, and a tithe of the Levites' share then goes to the priests (vv. 26–28).[50] Leviticus and Numbers refer to the same 10 percent of an Israelite's income. Deuteronomy, however, calls for an additional tithe (another 10 percent) that the Israelites are to use two out of every three years for a special celebration before the Lord at the sanctuary with their families and guests (14:22–27), and every third year they are to give this tithe to the poor (vv. 28–29; 26:12–13).

Regarding differences in the kinds of items from which tithes are to be given, Num. 18:21 assigns "every tithe," on which Milgrom comments that

---

49. *Leviticus: A Book of Ritual and Ethics*, Continental Commentary (Minneapolis: Fortress, 2004), 1–2.

50. Jacob Milgrom recognizes this in his comment on Num. 18:24: "The tithe properly belongs to the Lord, which He, in turn, assigns to the Levites" (*Numbers: The Traditional Hebrew Text with the New JPS Translation*, JPS Torah Commentary [Philadelphia: Jewish Publication Society, 1990], 155). Cf. Lev. 7:6–10, 31–36 regarding portions of YHWH's sacrifices that he assigned to his priests.

this expression "may be a reference to the same phrase in Lev. 27:30, in which case this passage also holds that the tithe falls due on all crops."[51] We can add that "every tithe" in Num. 18:21 could also include tithes on herd and flock animals (Lev. 27:32). Deuteronomy 14:23 does specify only "the tithe of your grain, of your wine, and of your oil," but this is the separate, second tithe, so there is no contradiction with Leviticus or Numbers.

Closer examination has revealed two tithing systems, one in Leviticus-Numbers and the other in Deuteronomy, but with no real contradictions. For further information on tithing, see chapter 15.

Divine Endorsement of Human Ideas

Divine promulgation of OT law by YHWH bestows authority to ideas that may be new, already existing, or adapted combinations of new and existing elements; it does not require originality of all ideas. Even if some or many of the OT laws as such were preceded by decisions of human judges, which could include an oracular judge, such as Moses, operating under divine inspiration (e.g., Exod. 18:15–16, 19–20),[52] the Pentateuch presents its laws as coming from, and therefore endorsed by, YHWH.

The same is true of some components of OT law that definitely have precedents in Mesopotamian laws. For example, the law of the goring ox in Exod. 21:35 is identical in content to law §53 of the Laws of Eshnunna,[53] and the lex talionis ("law of retaliation; e.g., "an eye for an eye") element, which first appears in the Laws of Hammurabi §§196–97, 200, is later included in Exod. 21:23–25; Lev. 24:19–20; and Deut. 19:19, 21.[54] Even if this is direct borrowing, it does not negate divine authority of OT law any more than when the daughters of Zelophehad came up with the idea that they should inherit

51. Ibid. On Num. 18:27 ("As with the new grain from the threshing floor or the flow from the vat," NJPS), Milgrom queries but does not answer whether this verse implies that here the tithe comes only from grain, wine, and oil or from all produce (156). However, the point of the similes (with preposition *k*) in this verse is not to specify the kinds of products from which the tithe is collected, but that they are treated as though the Levites were farmers who had processed them.

52. LeFebvre ("Written Law," 46) points out that in Exod. 18, "the teaching of 'God's decrees and laws' (v. 16) *follows* inquiry and arbitration. Law publication arises out of—and procedurally follows—inquiry and adjudication" (emphasis original).

53. "If an ox gores another ox and thus causes its death, the two ox-owners shall divide the value of the living ox and the carcass of the dead ox" (trans. Martha Roth, "The Laws of Eshnunna," COS 2.130:335; cf. Roth, *Law Collections*, 67). Exodus 21:32 is somewhat similar to law §55: "If it gores a slave and thus causes his death, he shall weigh and deliver 15 shekels of silver" (trans. Roth, "Laws of Eshnunna," COS 2.130:335).

54. D. Wright (*Inventing God's Law*) has shown in detail that the Covenant Code (which he delimits as Exod. 20:23–23:19) is closely modeled on the Laws of Hammurabi.

their father's ancestral property (Num. 27:1–4), and YHWH affirmed that they were right (v. 7) and turned this precedent into a law (v. 8).

Since God's values are based on his character of love (1 John 4:8, 16), since he created human beings in his image (Gen. 1:26–27), and since his Word enlightens everyone (John 1:4–5, 9),[55] it is not surprising that humans are capable of formulating some principles in harmony with his values. However, due to our moral brokenness resulting from the fall into sin (Gen. 3), we need divine guidance in filtering our ideas to retain the truly love-based elements while discarding the aspects that creep in from selfish ulterior motives. It is the purpose of OT law to provide such guidance, as discussed in the next chapter of the present book.

55. In John 1:14 the Word is incarnated and so identified as Christ.

3

The Purpose
of Old Testament Law

In order to protect against behaviors viewed as harmful, a system of law generally has the purpose of guiding individuals and groups within a society according to its value-based principles. As divine teaching, however, the OT laws are not simply designed to control a list of behaviors according to fixed rules. Unlike modern positive law, they instruct and motivate people in a wise system of values that beneficially guides their choices and corrects their mistakes within the context of a redemptive covenant with the Deity. Therefore they contribute to the human moral journey from fallen attitudes and practices (beginning with Gen. 3) toward restoration of creation ideals in the new earth (Rev. 21–22).

Because the OT laws were initially given to ancient Israelites to assist their stage of the journey, with some accommodation to human weakness (cf. Deut. 24:1–4; Matt. 19:8), they are not always the last word on ethics for the people of God. However, they are foundational for understanding his ways and the direction in which they are leading (see chaps. 7–9).

This chapter identifies several interconnected aspects of the purpose of OT law: revealing God's character, specifying terms for accepting his covenant grace, teaching wisdom in response to fallen life, and guiding a model society that serves as a light to the nations.

Revealing God's Character

God's Love as Model for His People

Just as biblical narratives and other genres show YHWH's justice and mercy,[1] his laws also reflect and reveal his character. For example, Lev. 19 begins,

> And the LORD [YHWH] spoke to Moses, saying, "Speak to all the congregation of the people of Israel and say to them, You shall be holy, for I the LORD your God am holy. Every one of you shall revere his mother and his father, and you shall keep my Sabbaths: I am the LORD your God." (vv. 1–3)

YHWH is the God of the Israelites, so they are to live in harmony with his holy character, imitating him. In the divine speech that constitutes the rest of Lev. 19, the following laws teach God's people how to apply his value of holiness to their lives, beginning with respect for parents and observance of the Lord's Sabbaths (v. 3).[2] In this part of Leviticus (chaps. 17–26), holiness "is a relational category that comes into being in, by, and through enacted relationships based on justice, integrity, honesty, and faithfulness."[3]

At the center of Lev. 19, verse 18 formulates a fundamental principle that underlies more specific laws governing relations and interactions between human beings: "You shall love [verb from root '-h-b] your neighbor as yourself" (cf. v. 34). The context of this law within a chapter concerning human emulation of divine holiness indicates that unselfish love is a basic principle of YHWH's holy character. Thus the moral/ethical model and standard for God's people is nothing less than his loving character (cf. 1 John 4:8, 16, "God is love"; Matt. 22:37–40).

The concepts of God's love for his people and his requirement that they love him in return are explicit in several pentateuchal passages, such as these:

> [YHWH is] showing steadfast love [khesed] to thousands of those who love [participle of '-h-b] me and keep my commandments. (Exod. 20:6; paralleled in Deut. 5:10)

---

1. E.g., Exod. 3–15 (deliverance of Israel from Egypt); Pss. 9, 33, 103; Isa. 42, 61.
2. Referring to the fifth and fourth of the Ten Commandments, reversing the order of Exod. 20:8–11 (fourth commandment) and v. 12 (fifth commandment), and with "his mother and his father" (Lev. 19:3) reversing the order of the parents in Exod. 20:12. On such reversals indicating citations in the Bible, see Pancratius C. Beentjes, "Discovering a New Path of Intertextuality: Inverted Quotations and Their Dynamics," in *Literary Structure and Rhetorical Strategies in the Hebrew Bible,* ed. L. J. de Regt, J. de Waard, and J. P. Fokkelman (Assen, Netherlands: Van Gorcum, 1996), 31–50.
3. Frank H. Gorman Jr., *Divine Presence and Community: A Commentary on the Book of Leviticus,* ITC (Grand Rapids: Eerdmans, 1997), 100.

The LORD, the LORD, a God merciful and gracious, slow to anger, and abounding in steadfast love [*khesed*] and faithfulness, keeping steadfast love [*khesed*] for thousands. (Exod. 34:6–7)

You shall love [verb from *'-h-b*] the LORD your God with all your heart and with all your soul and with all your might. (Deut. 6:5)

Variety of Laws Reflecting God's Character

The large number of laws that the Israelites received at Sinai and later in the wilderness represents a massive demonstration of the divine character. In fact, according to the Pentateuch, they were receiving laws from YHWH through Moses before they reached Sinai (Exod. 16:4–5, 16, 23, 28–29; 18:16).

The Israelites already inherited a rich pre-Mosaic legal heritage from their ancestors and shared a number of legal principles with other ANE peoples.[4] Did these law materials also reflect God's character? The following paragraphs address this question.

Pentateuchal narratives regarding earlier periods record awareness of values such as respect for life (Gen. 9:4) as well as the wrongfulness of and punishability of murder (4:8–16; 9:5–6), various kinds of sexual immorality (homosexual rape, 19:4–13; adultery, 20:3; heterosexual rape, 34:1–2, 7; incest, 35:22; 49:4; promiscuity, 38:24), and theft (31:30, 32; 44:1–10).

Early family law had customary legal procedures for inheritance (Gen. 25:31–34; 27:1–40; 48:13–20), including by a servant adopted as heir (15:2–3), contracting marriage with a bride-gift (34:4, 8, 11–12), levirate (brother-in-law) marriage in the event that a dead man's widow was childless (38:6–8), and surrogate motherhood by servant women as secondary wives (16:1–4; 30:3–5, 9–10).

Early religious practices included sacrificial rituals (Gen. 4:3–4; 8:20; 22:13; 31:54; 46:1), prayer (20:17; 25:21), circumcision (17:10–14, 23–27), personal physical purification (35:2), tithing (14:20; 28:22), and setting up monuments to the Lord (28:18). YHWH's chosen people knew that it was wrong to worship deities other than YHWH, including through idolatry (35:2, 4; cf. Exod. 12:12).

The biblical text explicitly indicates that at least some of the Israelites' values and norms came from YHWH (e.g., permanent marriage, Gen. 2:18, 20–24; against murder, 4:8–16; respect for life, 9:4–6; circumcision, 17:10–14), but the origin of some others is unspecified. From comparison with other

---

4. For relationships between OT and ANE (as well as early rabbinic) law collections, see Samuel Greengus, *Laws in the Bible and in Early Rabbinic Collections: The Legal Legacy of the Ancient Near East* (Eugene, OR: Cascade, 2011).

ANE texts, we know that a number of principles and practices belonged to the shared cultural heritage of the ANE.

For example, early Mesopotamian law collections prohibit murder, sexual immorality, and theft.[5] Customs and laws regarding aspects of life such as family status (including marriage and adoption), property and inheritance, and legal transactions (including contracts) are well attested outside Israel from early times.[6] So are religious practices such as sacrifice, prayer, circumcision, personal purification, tithing, and setting up monuments to deities.[7]

If the Israelites already possessed legal principles and customs that apparently kept their society going quite well,[8] why did YHWH need to promulgate so many laws when the nation of Israel was established? It is easily understandable that new laws particularly applicable to them, especially concerning their unique religious system, would be needed, but why would YHWH repeat legal principles that already existed in ANE culture? John H. Walton explains:

> Israel had laws before to insure the smooth functioning of society, and it is logical to believe that they would have been heavily dependent on other cultures of their day for those guidelines. The revelation, though, had to do with providing a foundation for those norms (the covenant) and establishing YHWH as the source of those norms. One does not refrain from adultery merely because adultery disrupts society. Rather, adultery is prohibited because it goes against an absolute standard of morality by which YHWH himself is characterized.[9]

So whether laws that Israel inherited or received through Moses were original, borrowed, or shared within a common ANE cultural heritage is beside the point. YHWH's covenant law-giving provided the framework within which all of Israel's moral and religious values were to operate in harmony with his character.

5. On these law collections, see further in chap. 6.
6. See, e.g., ANE background materials provided in Raymond Westbrook and Bruce Wells, *Everyday Law in Biblical Israel: An Introduction* (Louisville: Westminster John Knox, 2009); Raymond Westbrook, *Property and the Family in Biblical Law*, JSOTSup 113 (Sheffield: JSOT Press, 1991). For a major resource, see Raymond Westbrook, ed., *A History of Ancient Near Eastern Law*, 2 vols., Handbook of Oriental Studies, Section 1, The Near and Middle East 72 (Leiden: Brill, 2003).
7. See, e.g., ANE backgrounds on biblical texts referring to these practices in John H. Walton, ed., *Zondervan Illustrated Bible Backgrounds Commentary*, vol. 1, *Genesis, Exodus, Leviticus, Numbers, Deuteronomy* (Grand Rapids: Zondervan, 2009).
8. Presumably including norms in addition to those mentioned above.
9. John H. Walton, *Ancient Israelite Literature in Its Cultural Context: A Survey of Parallels between Biblical and Ancient Near Eastern Texts*, LBI (Grand Rapids: Zondervan, 1989), 90.

The role of the OT laws in demonstrating the character of the divine lawgiver[10] parallels the purpose of the Laws of Hammurabi, according to the prologue and epilogue that frame them: This legal collection was to exemplify the just character of the king and his worthiness to rule.[11]

Selection and Adaptation in Harmony with God's Character

The OT laws for which there are ANE antecedents do not simply copy laws but select materials and adapt them to produce a special synthesis.[12] For example, it seems clear that the divine law regarding assault in Lev. 24 ("As he has done it shall be done to him, fracture for fracture, eye for eye, tooth for tooth," vv. 19–20) incorporated the lex talionis (law of retaliation) penalty of pure justice from the ANE legal environment, as shown by the fact that this kind of penalty appears in the earlier Laws of Hammurabi §§196–97, 200 in cases of assault. However, whereas the Laws of Hammurabi apply variable penalties for assault, depending on the relative social statuses of assailants and victims, and specify monetary compensation in a number of cases (e.g., §§196–214),[13] in Lev. 24:19–20 there are no monetary compensations or class distinctions. Shalom M. Paul points out benefits of the way in which the lex talionis is applied in OT law: It confines retaliation to the offender himself, limits it to the precise degree of the injury, and, unlike other ANE laws, treats people (except slaves) equally, so that the poor are protected to the same degree as the rich by the deterrent factor provided by talionic punishment.[14]

10. Cf. John H. Walton, *Covenant: God's Purpose, God's Plan* (Grand Rapids: Zondervan, 1994), 65.

11. Trans. Martha Roth, "The Laws of Hammurabi," COS 2.131:335–37, 351–53; Martha T. Roth, *Law Collections from Mesopotamia and Asia Minor*, SBL Writings from the Ancient World 6 (Atlanta: Scholars Press, 1995), 71–72, 76–81, 133–40.

12. See, e.g., David P. Wright, *Inventing God's Law: How the Covenant Code of the Bible Used and Revised the Laws of Hammurabi* (Oxford: Oxford University Press, 2009).

13. Trans. Roth, "The Laws of Hammurabi," 2.131:348; Roth, *Law Collections*, 121–23.

14. *Studies in the Book of the Covenant in the Light of Cuneiform and Biblical Law*, VTSup 18 (Leiden: Brill, 1970; repr., Eugene, OR: Wipf & Stock, 2006), 40, 76–77. On the difference between use of the lex talionis in OT and other ANE laws, Pamela Barmash observes (esp. relating to Lev. 24:17–21):

> Lex talionis is a flexible concept. In biblical law, it is used as a principle expressing equivalence. The penalty must be equivalent to the harm inflicted. In the case of a human death, the offender must be killed, and in the case of an animal death, the animal victim must be replaced. The penalty for homicide in cuneiform law is death, but it is not an expression of lex talionis. The death penalty is the penalty for serious offenses. The concern manifest in cuneiform law is on the fixing of the status of the victim in certain categories and how that status affects the punishment. (*Homicide in the Biblical World* [Cambridge: Cambridge University Press, 2005], 175)

Use of the term *mum* (defect/disfigurement) in Lev. 24:19 implies a strong connection between assault and murder. In 21:16–23 a descendant of Aaron who has a *mum* is disqualified from officiating as a priest, lest he profane (verb from root *kh-l-l*) YHWH's sacred precincts (v. 23). In 22:17–25 an animal victim acceptable for holy sacrifice must be *tamim* (cf. 1:3, 10; 3:1; etc.), which means that it does not have a *mum*, "defect" (22:19–21). Therefore having a *mum* diminishes the holiness of a living being, which means that inflicting a *mum* on another human being made in the image of God (cf. Gen. 1:26–27) is an act of sacrilege. Murder destroys a life made in God's image and thus incurs the destruction of the murderer's life (cf. Gen. 9:6). Assault resulting in a permanent defect is partial murder, destroying part of a life made in God's image, and thus incurs equivalent (according to the lex talionis) partial destruction of the assailant's body.[15]

Specifying Terms for Accepting God's Covenant Grace

Covenant Framework of God's Law

At the time of the exodus from Egypt, YHWH had a preexisting relationship with the Israelites because of his covenant with their ancestors, Abraham, Isaac, and Jacob (Exod. 2:23–24; 3:15–17; 6:2–8). YHWH regarded them as his "firstborn son" (4:22) and redeemed them from slavery in Egypt (6:6; 15:13). Because YHWH was their deliverer, they owed him allegiance as their Lord (*'adon*; Exod. 23:17; 34:23) if they wanted to continue enjoying the benefits of their relationship with him.[16] In fact, the existence of their nation depended on their ongoing acceptance of the covenant that YHWH offered them.[17]

The land of Canaan belonged to YHWH (Lev. 25:23) because all the earth is his (Exod. 19:5), and he took Canaan from the inhabitants of the land (Lev. 18:24–25; Josh. 23:9) and gave it to the Israelites (Josh. 21:43). Therefore YHWH had the right to establish the laws of the land, which the Israelites would be required to observe if they were to live there (Lev. 18:26, 28; 20:22).

See chaps. 13 and 14 on laws concerning injury to slaves due to excessive discipline by their masters (Exod. 21:20–21, 26–27), for which there is no mere monetary compensation but also no talionic punishment of the masters.

15. Cf. Roy Gane, *Leviticus, Numbers*, NIV Application Commentary (Grand Rapids: Zondervan, 2004), 426.

16. Cf. Exod. 15:18, where the song celebrating deliverance at the Red Sea ends "The Lord will reign forever and ever."

17. Cf. Bernard M. Levinson, *"The Right Chorale": Studies in Biblical Law and Interpretation*, FAT 54 (Tübingen: Mohr Siebeck, 2008), 49–50. "Assent must continue for each generation within ancient Israel and must finally include the assent of the reader" (50).

The Israelites who entered Canaan were not born there, so they did not become citizens of it automatically. Therefore they needed to undergo formalization of their relationship with the Lord of the land by consenting to a binding agreement, a covenant (*berit*), by which they promised to accept his sovereignty and obey his laws (Exod. 24:3–8). In this way they accepted God's gracious gift of the land, which he had promised as an important part of his covenant with their forefather, Abraham (Gen. 12:7; 13:14–17). So in this sense, the covenant between YHWH and Israel could be regarded as a kind of "naturalization."

A closer analogy is a covenant between a monarch and his subjects when they choose him to reign over them because he has already demonstrated his ability to successfully lead them against their enemies (as David in 2 Sam. 5:2–3).[18] Thus YHWH's first words to Israel through Moses at Mount Sinai proposed to the nation:

> You yourselves have seen what I did to the Egyptians, and how I bore you on eagles' wings and brought you to myself. Now therefore, if you will indeed obey my voice and keep my covenant, you shall be my treasured possession among all peoples, for all the earth is mine; and you shall be to me a kingdom of priests and a holy nation. These are the words that you shall speak to the people of Israel. (Exod. 19:4–6)

Here YHWH as the superior party reminds the Israelites of what he has done for them and offers them an ongoing beneficial relationship with himself on condition that they obey him and keep his covenant (i.e., his covenant stipulations = laws).

These relational dynamics parallel ANE suzerainty treaties between greater rulers (suzerains) and lesser rulers (vassals) under their spheres of influence and protection. Such a treaty formulation logically explicates the basis of the relationship and ongoing expectations, and it seeks to persuade the lesser party to comply with the stipulations. Typically ANE treaties included the following elements: introduction of the speaker, historical prologue reviewing the past relationship between the two parties, stipulations, statement concerning public reading and possibly also storing of the document, divine witnesses to enforce the treaty terms if necessary, and curses and blessings

---

18. Cf. 2 Kings 11:17, where Jehoida the priest "made a covenant between the LORD and the king and people, that they should be the LORD's people, and also between the king and the people." Here there is a close connection between the divine-human covenant and the monarch-subject covenant. Elsewhere the divine-human covenant is analogous to a marriage (e.g., Jer. 3:1–10; Ezek. 16, esp. v. 8; Hosea).

specifying divine actions against or for the vassal, depending on whether the vassal complies with the stipulations or not.[19]

Scholars have shown that enactments of the covenant between YHWH and the Israelites expressed in Exodus-Leviticus and the renewed covenant for the next generation in Deuteronomy are structured like ANE suzerainty treaties, with law collections constituting the stipulations.[20] However, whereas a suzerainty treaty was an international agreement contracted between human rulers, the YHWH-Israel covenant was between the nation (then lacking a human ruler) and its divine ruler, who claimed a kinship bond with them as the father of Israel, his "firstborn son" (Exod. 4:22). Compare 2 Sam. 5:1, where the Israelite tribes said to David, "Behold, we are your bone and flesh," before they made a covenant with him and anointed him as king over them (v. 3).

Additional evidence for the suzerain-vassal relationship between YHWH and Israel is found in the requirement for all Israelite males to appear before the Lord, at his sanctuary, to celebrate three pilgrim festivals (Exod. 23:14–17; 34:18, 22–24; Deut. 16:16–17), and none were to appear before him "empty-handed" (Exod. 23:15; Deut. 16:16). This indicates that to show their loyalty to YHWH, the Israelites were to come as vassals before their covenant suzerain, bringing sacrificial offerings as tribute. This tribute not only acknowledged YHWH's superiority, but it also expressed gratitude for his grace, because the value of a man's gift was to be "as he is able, according to the blessing of the LORD your God that he has given you" (Deut. 16:17).

Notice that the Israelites were individual vassals of YHWH within their corporate vassal nation. "Israel's vassalage made any individual trespass against the Law an act of rebellion, for the person concerned might in this way cause the annulment of the divine promises and the basis of Israel's existence. It was therefore the responsibility of the whole community to prevent such an act or to exclude the offenders from its midst."[21]

19. For an introduction to ANE treaties in relation to the OT covenants, see Walton, *Ancient Israelite Literature*, 95–109. For detailed presentation of the ANE treaties as well as laws, see Kenneth A. Kitchen and Paul J. N. Lawrence, *Treaty, Law and Covenant in the Ancient Near East*, 3 vols. (Wiesbaden: Harrassowitz, 2012).
20. See, e.g., Walton, *Ancient Israelite Literature*, 101–5; Kenneth A. Kitchen, *On the Reliability of the Old Testament* (Grand Rapids: Eerdmans, 2003), 283–94, esp. table on 284, including comparisons with ANE treaty formulations of various periods and implications for dating the biblical covenant texts (like Hittite treaties, within ca. 1400–1200 BC). Notice that early first millennium BC (ca. 900–650 BC) Assyrian treaties lack several elements, including historical prologues that express what the suzerain has graciously done for the vassal (287–91).
21. Ze'ev W. Falk, *Hebrew Law in Biblical Times: An Introduction*, 2nd ed. (Provo, UT: Brigham Young University Press; Winona Lake, IN: Eisenbrauns, 2001), 7–8.

Thus far it is clear that YHWH gave laws to the Israelites within the framework of his covenant with them,[22] just as emperors issued stipulations to their vassals within treaties. The covenant framework is crucial for understanding the function of OT law. The law is not a self-standing phenomenon: it contributes to preservation of an ongoing divine-human relationship that provides important benefits for God's people.

In the historical prologue of a treaty, a human suzerain could cite some things that he had done for the lesser party, which demonstrated his goodwill and ability to help in the future. For example, the prologue of the treaty between the Hittite king Suppiluliuma I (the suzerain) and Huqqanas and the Hayasa people reads as follows: "See now, Huqqanas, you (as) a mere dog(?) I have elevated, and have done you good. In the midst of Hattusa, and amongst the Hayasans (there), I have advantageously presented you, and have given you my sister in marriage. Now the whole Hatti-land, the land of [Hay]asa, and all the lands both far and near have heard of you."[23]

No human suzerain could compete with the unique divine YHWH, who accomplished unprecedented wonders for Israel (e.g., Deut. 4:34–39). He had already delivered them from slavery in Egypt before he gave them his covenant stipulations at Mount Sinai, as he reminded them in Exod. 20:2 and Deut. 5:6 in his historical prologue to the Ten Commandments: "I am the LORD your God, who brought you out of the land of Egypt, out of the house of slavery."[24] This prologue placed YHWH's covenant within the framework of grace, shown in the form of deliverance that his people could not earn by keeping covenant stipulations because he had already accomplished their salvation from slavery before they received the laws.[25] Their only appropriate response to his love for them would be to gratefully accept it and love him with loyal obedience;[26] as 1 John 4:19 puts it, "We love because he first loved us."

---

22. Cf. O. Palmer Robertson, *The Christ of the Covenants* (Phillipsburg, NJ: Presbyterian and Reformed, 1980), 170–71; Dale Patrick, *Old Testament Law* (Atlanta: John Knox, 1985), 26.

23. Trans. Kitchen and Lawrence, *Treaty, Law and Covenant*, 1:441.

24. Similarly, he had fulfilled his promise to Noah and his family by rescuing them from the great flood (Gen. 6–8) before he gave them an ongoing covenant (chap. 9), which included some stipulations (vv. 4–6).

25. Cf. Joe M. Sprinkle, *Biblical Law and Its Relevance: A Christian Understanding and Ethical Application for Today of the Mosaic Regulations* (Lanham, MD: University Press of America, 2006), 7: "Laws were not the means of salvation, but were guidelines for those already saved; . . . before the Mosaic law (Abraham), after the Mosaic law, and during the Mosaic law, salvation was and is a matter of God's grace rather than human merit."

26. On covenantal love, see Jon D. Levenson, *The Love of God: Divine Gift, Human Gratitude, and Mutual Faithfulness in Judaism*, Library of Jewish Ideas (Princeton: Princeton University Press, 2016), 1–58.

Law as Guide, Not Remedy for Violation

God's laws can benefit people only when they are kept. Thus YHWH commands: "You shall therefore keep my statutes and my rules; if a person does them, he shall live by them: I am the LORD" (Lev. 18:5). This is not about legalistic salvation from sin to eternal life by good works but about cause and effect in the present life.[27] In the context of Lev. 18, the opposite of "shall live" (v. 5) includes exile from the land (vv. 25, 28), so the life in view here must include life in that current era.[28] Elsewhere, harmony with sound principles yields the good result of life in the promised land, as in Deut. 5:33: "You shall walk in all the way that the LORD your God has commanded you, that you may live, and that it may go well with you, and that you may live long in the land that you shall possess."[29]

Law-keeping is not, cannot be, and never was intended to be a means of salvation or a basis of salvation from consequences of failure to keep it (Gal. 3:10–14, quoting Lev. 18:5; cf. Rom. 10:5–13). This is true even of limited salvation in the present era. When the Israelites departed from YHWH and suffered at the hands of their enemies (e.g., Judg. 2:11–15), their return to loyal obedience was essential for reaccepting the covenant connection with him and its benefits (10:15–16), but it could not pay for past sins or buy deliverance; they were totally at God's mercy (2:16, 18; 3:9, 15; 10:10–16; etc.).[30] Laws generally do not offer mercy to those who are accountable for keeping them, because mercy is over and above the law.[31]

Present and future rightdoing cannot redeem anyone from the ultimate result of wrongdoing because all humans have already incurred the terminal penalty of eternal death by committing sin (Rom. 3:23; 6:23). The reason for such death is that sin violates God's law (1 John 3:4), which is love (Matt. 22:37–40; Rom. 13:10), "the only basis on which intelligent beings with free

27. Cf. Walter Kaiser, "Leviticus 18:5 and Paul: Do This and You Shall Live (Eternally?)," *JETS* 14 (1971): 28.

28. Violation of the laws in Lev. 18 also results in the terminal divine punishment of being "cut off" (v. 29), which involves forfeiture of an afterlife, such as through loss of one's line of descendants (see chap. 5). While obedience can prevent this, it cannot provide forgiveness for sins that is necessary for ultimate salvation because "all have sinned" (Rom. 3:23) and "the wages of sin is death" (Rom. 6:23).

29. See also the motive clause of the Decalogue commandment to honor parents (Exod. 20:12; Deut. 5:16) and Deut. 30:16.

30. For the idea that violation of a divine law carries consequences that subsequent law-keeping cannot undo and divine mercy offers the only way out, see also Lev. 4:1–6:7 (4:1–5:26 MT); Ps. 51; Gal. 3:10–14.

31. However, laws regarding expiatory sacrifices (e.g., Lev. 4:1–6:7 [4:1–5:26 MT]) provide for merciful divine forgiveness, and in Num. 30 a woman whose father or husband annuls her vow is forgiven by statute (vv. 5, 8, 12).

choice can coexist harmoniously."[32] So a being who is not in full harmony with love is dangerous and therefore cannot live forever in God's universe. The Lord would be unjust and irresponsible, thereby violating his character of love, if he allowed such danger to continue.

God's law is holy, just, good, and spiritual (Rom. 7:12, 14 NKJV). The fact that it cannot save anyone who has broken it does not mean that it is defective, just as nobody would expect that the Surgeon General's warning against smoking would provide anyone who ignores it with a cure for lung cancer. Law is the beneficial guide regarding cause and effect, not a remedy for violation of it. According to the NT, there is only one way that a person who has violated divine law can be saved from the curse of capital condemnation: "Christ redeemed us from the curse of the law by becoming a curse for us" (Gal. 3:13).

Teaching Wisdom in Response to Fallen Life

Wisdom regarding Consequences

Paul treats OT law as divinely authoritative teaching that is designed to instruct and motivate God's people to wisely follow his values. Thus in Eph. 5 he warns: "For you may be sure of this, that everyone who is sexually immoral or impure, or who is covetous (that is, an idolater), has no inheritance in the kingdom of Christ and God" (v. 5). Here a major reason for not violating God's commandments (e.g., Exod. 20:14, 17; Lev. 18, 20) is to avoid forfeiting a place in the divine kingdom. The law makes people "wise for salvation" (2 Tim. 3:15) by giving them perspective, including about potential consequences, so that they can make informed choices before deciding what to do.

God's law already provides wisdom regarding consequences in OT passages such as Lev. 18, which urges his people to live according to his values of sexual purity, abstaining from the practices listed earlier in the chapter "lest the land vomit you out when you make it unclean, as it vomited out the nation that was before you. For everyone who does any of these abominations, the persons who do them shall be cut off from among their people" (vv. 28–29).[33] The laws of Lev. 18 were intended to make the Israelites "wise for salvation" in the sense of helping them choose to keep their continued enjoyment of God's gift of deliverance to a life of freedom in their own land. Choosing otherwise would lead to catastrophic consequences.

32. Roy Gane, *Altar Call* (Berrien Springs, MI: Diadem, 1999), 269–70.
33. On being "cut off," see chap. 5.

YHWH's laws are for the benefit and protection of human beings. They are not simply arbitrary to assert his control but are helpful (Ps. 119:175) and conducive to life (Lev. 18:5) and well-being (Deut. 10:13) because they reveal principles of cause and effect in the world that he, the wise Creator (e.g., Isa. 40:28), initially set up and continues to sustain (cf. Dan. 5:23, "the God in whose hand is your breath"). Humans need his insight to guard them from harmful effects of wrong actions and attitudes and to optimize their happiness and prosperity (e.g., Deut. 4:6).[34] In this light, it is astonishing that modern people eagerly spend money and time on how-to books and on tips through various media so that they can be happy and successful, yet they fail to recognize the value of the Bible as a source of wisdom to attune them to the Creator and his creation.

Stated and Unstated Cause and Effect

A few biblical laws quite directly express the relationship between cause and effect. For example, "And you shall take no bribe, for a bribe blinds the clear-sighted and subverts the cause of those who are in the right" (Exod. 23:8).

However, the stated outcome of a divine law is often a penalty or negative consequence for violation that does not appear to naturally and obviously flow as an effect from the causative action, as in the summary statement of Lev. 20:9: "For anyone who curses his father or his mother shall surely be put to death; he has cursed his father or his mother; his blood is upon him." Although it is clear that cursing one's parents incurs capital punishment, the text does not explain why.

Even in the first biblical prohibition, YHWH did not explain why Adam would incur death if he ate fruit from the tree of knowledge of good and evil (Gen. 2:17, also applicable to Eve in 3:3). The negative outcome of violation served only as the motivation for obedience.

Many OT laws, including most commandments of the Decalogue (Exod. 20:2–3, 8–11, 13–17), do not even express any consequences. However, summary statements (Exod. 15:26; Deut. 4:40; 6:1–3; 26:16–19) and especially the covenant blessings and curses in Lev. 26 and Deut. 28 emphasize that the

---

34. Thus James 1:25 speaks of "the perfect law, the law of liberty." John R. Donahue observes regarding the Ten Commandments, "Far from limiting human freedom, these commands make life in community possible, and protect vulnerable individuals" (*Seek Justice That You May Live: Reflections and Resources on the Bible and Social Justice* [New York: Paulist Press, 2014], 50). Martin Luther emphasized the positive protective function of the Ten Commandments. For example, on "You shall not bear false witness" (Exod. 20:16), he commented, "Thus a wall has been built around our good reputation and integrity to protect it against malicious gossip and deceitful tongues." *A Simple Way to Pray* (Louisville: Westminster John Knox, 2000), 54.

Israelites are responsible for keeping all of God's laws, with positive outcomes if they obey and negative results if they disobey. Therefore, every law carries a consequence, whether or not it is stated.

The fact that most of the pentateuchal laws do not specify their relationships between cause and effect means that the hearer/reader must figure them out or simply trust that the Lord knows what is best for his people, even if they must obey without knowing the reasons (cf. Deut. 29:29 [29:28 MT]).[35] Thus, what appears to be a lack in the laws is actually an invitation to ponder Scripture and to exercise faith.

Diagnostic Role of Law

The law warns people so that they can avoid danger that they would incur by breaking principles, and if they do violate them, the law shows them where they have gone wrong. By illuminating differences between right and wrong and their consequences, God's law plays an important initial role in the redemptive process by identifying problems to be addressed (Rom. 3:20; 7:7–13) so that sinners realize their need of a remedy (redemption through Christ, received by faith; 3:21–26).

For Israelites who committed inadvertent sins to realize their need to sacrifice purification offerings in order to receive expiation, they first had to be made aware of their violations of God's laws (Rom. 3:22–23, 27–28; cf. vv. 13–14).[36] Before David could receive divine forgiveness for his crime against Bathsheba and her husband, Uriah, he had to be confronted with and acknowledge the fact that he had broken the law and was condemned by it (2 Sam. 12). On the national level, it was when Josiah heard the "Book of the Law" read to him that he comprehended the depth of Judah's apostasy, humbled himself before God, and initiated a sweeping reform (2 Kings 22–23; 2 Chron. 34–35).

Knowledge of sin through awareness of God's law is unpleasant and can cause intense emotional pain (e.g., Ps. 51), but this pricking of our conscience is a necessary feedback mechanism, like physical pain, without which we could unknowingly damage ourselves.[37] Thus the law plays an important diagnostic role in moral healing and maintaining moral health, although it cannot heal (including justify/forgive) by itself (Rom. 3:20).

Christians often fail to grasp the benefit of biblical law in identifying sin because we take it for granted and are eager to move on to divine grace

---

35. On such "radical obedience," see Gane, *Leviticus, Numbers*, 208–9.

36. Cf. James 4:17, "So whoever knows the right thing to do and fails to do it, for him it is sin."

37. People with modern leprosy (Hansen's disease) can lose parts of their extremities because nerve damage removes their ability to feel pain.

and mercy through Christ, which is the basis of our salvation (Rom. 5; Eph. 2:8–9). But what if we didn't have God's law to reveal his character and will, showing the height of his mercy in view of the depth of our fallenness? How could we cope with the level of uncertainty and consequent anxiety that we would experience if the omniscient Deity would hold us accountable for actions that we do not perceive to be faulty because he has not identified them as such?

Outside Israel, the ANE people who lacked divine law often lived in fear that they may have committed unwitting sin because they attributed bad experiences to the fickle will of various gods whom they may have offended because they did not understand the divine will and wishes.[38] Against this background, YHWH's law is a wonderful gift to his people, in which he reveals himself as the only God, who is predictable, rational, just, concerned for their well-being, and willing to guide them. The Lord's ritual laws even prescribe sacrificial remedies for nondefiant violations of his commands (e.g., Lev. 4:1–6:7 [5:26 MT]).[39] No wonder the psalmist treasures the law of the Lord (e.g., Pss. 19:7–8 [19:8–9 MT]; 119:18, 72, 97)!

Laws Addressing Situations in Fallen Life

The OT laws provide divine guidance for life situations in various ways. Some specify rights, such as this: "If a man sells a dwelling house in a walled city, he may redeem it within a year of its sale" (Lev. 25:29). Others require or forbid certain attitudes, like these: "You shall not . . . bear a grudge, . . . but you shall love your neighbor as yourself" (Lev. 19:18) and "You shall not covet" (Exod. 20:17). Many laws command or prohibit behaviors, as in "Honor your father and your mother" (Exod. 20:12) and "You shall not steal" (v. 15). Instructions for expiatory sacrifices provide remedies for nondefiant violations of commandments, prerequisite to divine forgiveness (e.g., Lev. 4:26, 31, 35; 5:10).

To fully grasp the purpose of an OT law, we must understand the situation in fallen life that it addresses. Many laws have to do with scenarios that we

---

38. See Roy E. Gane, "Leviticus," in *Zondervan Illustrated Bible Backgrounds Commentary*, ed. Walton, 1:294; cf. Karel van der Toorn, *Sin and Sanction in Israel and Mesopotamia*, SSN 22 (Assen: Van Gorcum, 1985), 94–97; Jacob Milgrom, *Leviticus 1–16: A New Translation with Introduction and Commentary*, AB 3 (New York: Doubleday, 1991, 361–63). "Since the Hittites believed that divine displeasure was the ultimate source of most evils, they developed a science of divination in order to communicate with their gods, ascertain the reasons for their anger, and bargain about required restitution" (Gary Beckman's introduction to his translation of "Excerpt from an Oracle Report," *COS* 1.78:204).

39. Cf. Gane, "Leviticus," 294.

can readily understand, but some are obscure to us unless we can discover the long-lost situations to which they relate.

For example, Lev. 26:1 includes the prohibition "You must not place any carved stone ['*even maskit*] in your land, bowing down upon it."[40] Why would anyone bow down upon a "carved stone"? Such an object appears only here in the Bible, so we lack another biblical context to elucidate it. Nevertheless, in light of comparison with an ancient Assyrian text, Victor Hurowitz describes the carved stone and its function as "a stone slab placed in the ground, possibly in a doorway, decorated with engraved divine symbols and bowed down upon, enabling the supplicant to kiss the ground with the purpose of having his or her wish granted. We may translate it as 'decorated wishing stone.'"[41] Therefore, the law against doing this has the purpose of preventing a kind of idolatry (cf. Exod. 20:4–5). Even if the engraved divine symbols represent YHWH, such material portrayals would diminish the sense of his incomparable transcendence (cf. Deut. 4:15–18; 12:3–4). A request for divine aid in fulfilling a wish should be expressed by prayer to the Lord (cf. 1 Sam. 1:10–11; Matt. 7:7–11), without idolatry or magic.

A Model Society as a Guiding Light to the Nations

International Purpose of Covenant Stipulations

We have found that God's laws operate within the covenant framework of divine love and grace[42] for people who have experienced his salvation and choose to continue enjoying more and more of the benefits of their relationship with him. They do this not simply for themselves but also for the purpose of drawing others into a saving relationship with him (see, e.g., Ps. 72:17). Thus YHWH's covenant with Abraham and his descendants, the nation of Israel, commissioned them to serve as a channel of blessing to all peoples on earth (Gen. 12:2–3; 18:18; 22:18) because he has a whole world to save (cf. John 3:16; 2 Cor. 5:19). The Israelites could fulfill this purpose because the Lord revealed himself to them (cf. Exod. 6:6–7; Deut. 4:35; Ps. 106:8; cf. Rom. 3:1–2, "entrusted with the oracles of God").[43]

40. CEB, except that I render "upon it" instead of "to it."
41. V. Hurowitz, "Wish upon a Stone: Discovering the Idolatry of the *Even Maskit*," *BRev* (October 1999): 51.
42. Cf. Blu Greenberg, "Hear, O Israel: Law and Love in Deuteronomy (Deuteronomy 1–34)," in *Preaching Biblical Texts: Expositions by Jewish and Christian Scholars*, ed. F. C. Holmgren and H. E. Schaalman (Grand Rapids: Eerdmans, 1995), 150–53.
43. On the revelatory purpose of the divine covenants, see Walton, *Covenant*, 24.

The ultimate international purpose of God's covenant with Israel accounts for the fact that his laws (= covenant stipulations) were to contribute to the well-being of his chosen people, who would be blessed through his enhancement of good results (Lev. 26:3–13; Deut. 28:1–14) when they followed his sound principles of cause and effect (e.g., Deut. 10:13, "commandments . . . for your good"). Their well-being would draw others to the divine source of wisdom and blessing.

The first verses of Deut. 28 highlight the international significance of the covenant blessings, and Deut. 26 fleshes out the meaning of "set you high above":

> And if you faithfully obey the voice of the LORD your God, being careful to do all his commandments that I command you today, the LORD your God will set you high above all the nations of the earth. And all these blessings shall come upon you and overtake you, if you obey the voice of the LORD your God. (28:1–2)[44]

> And the LORD has declared today that you are a people for his treasured possession, as he has promised you, and that you are to keep all his commandments, and that he will set you in praise and in fame and in honor high above all nations that he has made, and that you shall be a people holy to the LORD your God, as he promised. (26:18–19)

These passages indicate the connection between YHWH's favor on the Israelites (cf. 7:6–8, unmerited by their previous numbers) and their enjoyment of lavish covenant blessings, with preeminence over all other nations. There can be no doubt that YHWH intended for others to notice his people! He wanted other nations to see his principles in action in their lives so that they would be attracted to his values and thereby to his character as the lawgiver (cf. Isa. 2:2–4; Mic. 4:1–3).[45] Israel's prosperity was not an end in itself; it was a tool of divine self-revelation.

YHWH's laws were to guide his people in maintaining harmony with him and his principles so that they would properly represent him to others. If they failed to do this, thereby in a larger sense taking his name (= reputation) in vain (cf. Exod. 20:7),[46] he could not bless them (Lev. 26:14–39; Deut. 28:15–68) lest he reinforce a wrong view of himself and thereby defeat his

---

44. Cf. 28:13, "And the LORD will make you the head and not the tail."
45. See the language of height ("highest of the mountains") in Isa. 2:2 and Mic. 4:1 as in the Deuteronomy passages above. Note that human perception of God's character as lawgiver has been a central issue since the first temptation (Gen. 3:1–6).
46. Cf. Patrick, *Old Testament Law*, 49.

purpose of revealing his true character and nature to all peoples on earth so that they could have the opportunity to choose him and his beneficial ways.[47]

Israel was to be God's model nation, showing to all other peoples how well a society could function if it followed YHWH's unique value system.[48] The society would reveal the values, which in turn would reveal the Lord. While other kinds of well-being enjoyed by the Israelites would be noticeable, the harmonious dynamics of their social interactions would be most significant in revealing the paramount divine value of love and the wisdom of principles flowing from it.[49] Their obedience to God's instructions would show their "wisdom and . . . understanding in the sight of the peoples, who, when they hear all these statutes, will say, 'Surely this great nation is a wise and understanding people'" (Deut. 4:6).

Foreigners who turned to gaze on the physical, material, and social prosperity of the Israelites and who encountered their distinctive ethics would try to reason back from effect to cause: What is the secret of the Israelites' success? Investigation will reveal that the key is the wise system of values that guides their lives and society. From where do they get these values? They have received them from their Deity, YHWH, whose character the values reflect. He loves them (Exod. 15:13; 19:5–6; Deut. 4:37–38), has demonstrated justice and mercy to them, and has delivered and cared for them in many ways (Exod. 19:4; Deut. 10:17–18, 21–22). Therefore he expects them to treat each other with corresponding justice and mercy (Deut. 10:19–20; cf. Mic. 6:8). What other deity is so good and reasonable?

Some Fulfillment of God's Purpose

The logical trajectory from curious admiration of God's covenant people to appreciation for God himself and his values was not meant to be merely theoretical. After a long period of national failure during the period of the judges, the Lord's plan finally achieved some fulfillment during the early reign of Solomon.

First Kings 3 reports that soon after Solomon became king, YHWH appeared to him in a dream and said, "Ask what I shall give you" (v. 5). Solomon requested: "Give your servant therefore an understanding mind to govern your

---

47. Some pentateuchal narratives show the seriousness of misrepresenting God, in these cases by Israelite leaders before their own people (Lev. 10:1–3; Num. 20:7–12).

48. On the distinctiveness of Israel's society, esp. in terms of ethics, and its function as the Lord's "paradigm," see Christopher J. H. Wright, *Old Testament Ethics for the People of God* (Downers Grove, IL: InterVarsity, 2004), 48–74. Israel was intended to be "a showcase of the way God longs for human society as a whole to operate" (74).

49. See further in chap. 10 regarding the witness of peace and unity among God's people.

people, that I may discern between good and evil, for who is able to govern this your great people?" (v. 9). His response pleased the Lord, who granted him not only unparalleled wisdom "to discern what is right" but also unmatched riches, honor, and long life on condition that Solomon "walk in my ways, keeping my statutes and my commandments" (vv. 10–14).

Soon afterward, Solomon's divine gift of wisdom was demonstrated to the nation when he solved a seemingly impossible legal dispute between two prostitutes (vv. 16–28). The people "stood in awe of the king, because they perceived that the wisdom of God was in him to do justice" (v. 28). Solomon's God-given wisdom in many areas became so great (4:29–33) that the fame of it went internationally viral: "And people of all nations came to hear the wisdom of Solomon, and from all the kings of the earth, who had heard of his wisdom" (v. 34).

One prominent visitor was the Queen of Sheba.

> And she said to the king, "The report was true that I heard in my own land of your words and of your wisdom, but I did not believe the reports until I came and my own eyes had seen it. And behold, the half was not told me. Your wisdom and prosperity surpass the report that I heard. Happy are your men! Happy are your servants, who continually stand before you and hear your wisdom! Blessed be the LORD your God, who has delighted in you and set you on the throne of Israel! Because the LORD loved Israel forever, he has made you king, that you may execute justice and righteousness." (1 Kings 10:6–9)

Thus her initial curiosity about Solomon's God-given wisdom led her to inquire and then to give glory to God.[50]

Mission of the New-Covenant Model Community

In every age, the obedience, allegiance, and praise of God's people are missiological instruments. When they are loyal and celebrate him among the nations for what he has done for them (Pss. 18:49 [18:50 MT]; 57:9 [57:10 MT]), "All the ends of the earth shall remember and turn to the LORD, and all the families of the nations shall worship before you" (22:27 [22:28 MT]; cf. vv. 25–26 [vv. 26–27 MT]).[51]

Jesus encapsulated the global role of his new-covenant followers and their actions: "You are the light of the world. . . . Let your light shine before others,

---

50. Contrast Hezekiah's failure to glorify God when Babylonian envoys came, resulting in disaster (2 Kings 20:12–19; Isa. 39).

51. Cf. Jesus's instruction to a man whom he had delivered from demons: "Go home to your friends and tell them how much the Lord has done for you, and how he has had mercy on you" (Mark 5:19).

so that they may see your good works and give glory to your Father who is in heaven" (Matt. 5:14–16). Through coming to know God in this way, precious people have the opportunity to enjoy eternal life (John 17:3). Like ancient Israel, the new-covenant community is to be God's model of goodness in a broken world. Above all, loving unity among Christians testifies to the fact that Jesus has come to be one with them (John 17:20–23).[52]

52. William J. Webb identifies several Pauline texts that depict a new-creation community in Christ: 1 Cor. 12:13; Gal. 3:28; Eph. 2:15; 4:22–24; Col. 3:11. *Slaves, Women & Homosexuals: Exploring the Hermeneutics of Cultural Analysis* (Downers Grove, IL: IVP Academic, 2001), 146–47.

PART 2

Literature and Background of Old Testament Law

4

Navigating Old Testament Laws and Related Literature

Ongoing divine laws in the OT are heavily concentrated in the Pentateuch, which has come to be called the *Torah*, meaning "Instruction." The Torah includes not only law instruction[1] but also instruction in the form of narratives. The pentateuchal narrative framework recounts the establishment (Exod. 19–31), restoration (Exod. 34, after the golden calf episode), and renewal (Deuteronomy) of the divine-human covenant with its stipulations = laws, as well as YHWH's theocratic governance of his people during their wilderness journeyings, which generated needs for some more laws (Leviticus, Numbers).

The rest of the OT (including Former and Latter Prophets and Writings) is based on and applies the Torah/Pentateuch, illustrating the results of loyal obedience to YHWH or rejection of him and violation of his principles, as laid out in the covenant blessings and curses (Lev. 26; Deut. 28). Thus there are many reflections of pentateuchal legal principles in other biblical genres, including narrative, prophecy, and Psalms and Wisdom literature (see below).[2]

1. See "Book of the Law [*torah*] of Moses" (Josh. 8:31; 23:6; 2 Kings 14:6; Neh. 8:1; cf. 2 Chron. 25:4; 34:14), which refers to at least a portion of the Pentateuch. According to a widely accepted rabbinic tradition, the Pentateuch contains 613 commandments (*b. Makkot* 23b).

2. In this sense, the three parts of the Hebrew canon (Torah, Prophets, and Writings) are Torah, Torah, Torah (Isaac Kikawada, presidential address, Pacific Coast meeting of the Society of Biblical Literature, Santa Clara, CA, 1986). For an introduction to guidance in moral formation from books throughout the OT, see Joel B. Green and Jacqueline E. Lapsley, eds., *The Old Testament and Ethics: A Book-by-Book Survey* (Grand Rapids: Baker Academic, 2013).

The present chapter helps readers find laws and related passages in various parts of the Bible and grasp some overall relationships between them.

Locations of Law Materials in the Old Testament

Groups of Pentateuchal Laws

Important pentateuchal law collections include the Decalogue (Ten Commandments) in Exod. 20:1–17, paralleled by Deut. 5:6–21; the so-called Covenant Code or Book of the Covenant in Exod. 21–23;[3] the cultic (so-called Priestly) laws in Lev. 1–7, 11–16;[4] the so-called Holiness Code, generally regarded as consisting of Lev. 17–26, followed by an appendix in Lev. 27;[5] and the Deuteronomic laws in Deut. 12–26. There are lesser clusters or series of laws in Gen. 9:3–6; 17:9–14; Exod. 12:1–27, 43–49; 13:1–16; 34:11–26;[6] Lev. 24:13–22; and Num. 5–6; 15; 18–19; 28–30; 35. Some isolated laws appear in Gen. 2:16–17; 17:1, 9–14; Exod. 29:38–42; 31:12–17; Lev. 10:8–11; Num. 8:1–2, 23–26; 9:9–14; 27:8–11; 36:6–9.

Narrative Contexts of Law-Giving

According to the narrative framework of the Pentateuch, YHWH gave laws at various times. First, he allowed Adam and Eve to eat from any tree but one (Gen. 2:16–17). Later he instructed Noah and his sons concerning respect for life (9:3–6). Then he commanded Abraham to walk before him and be blameless (17:1) and to perform the covenant sign of circumcision (vv. 9–14). According to Gen. 26:5, the Lord told Isaac that "Abraham obeyed my

---

3. Some scholars (e.g., Shalom M. Paul, *Studies in the Book of the Covenant in the Light of Cuneiform and Biblical Law*, VTSup 18 [Leiden: Brill, 1970; repr., Eugene, OR: Wipf & Stock, 2006], 28–29, 34) have included Exod. 20:22–26 in the Book of the Covenant (see 24:7 for this term), but 21:1, "Now these are the rules that you shall set before them," seems to introduce at least the main body of this law collection (cf. ibid., 43).

4. Leviticus 8–10 is narrative, describing the establishment of the Israelite sanctuary system. The first part of Lev. 11 presents noncultic dietary distinctions between meats that are permitted for eating and those that are "impure," thus unfit for food (vv. 1–23). Most of the rest of the chapter deals with transferable impurity from some kinds of dead animals (vv. 24–44), which has cultic significance in that such impurity must not be brought into contact with holy things (e.g., 7:20–21).

5. The blessings and curses in Lev. 26 bring the book to a logical conclusion, with a subscript in 26:46 resembling the subscript in 27:34, giving scholars the impression that chap. 27 is an appendix. Nevertheless Lev. 27 closes the overall structure of the book. Jacob Milgrom, *Leviticus 23–27: A New Translation with Introduction and Commentary*, AB 3B (New York: Doubleday, 2001), 2401–2, 2407–9.

6. The list of laws in Exod. 34:11–26 is often called the Ritual Decalogue.

voice and kept my charge, my commandments, my statutes, and my laws," implying that Abraham either received additional laws that are not recorded or kept principles that were later formulated as laws. In any case, it appears that laws were few and simple during the early periods when these individuals lived, but the emergence of the Israelite nation called for a radically expanded function of law to regulate a vastly more complex social system involving people with varying levels of experience with YHWH and loyalty to him.[7]

As the pentateuchal narrative continues, YHWH gave instructions concerning Passover and the Festival of Unleavened Bread (Exod. 12:1–20, 43–49; cf. vv. 21–27; 13:3–10) and consecration of the firstborn (13:1–2, 11–16) as the Israelites were about to depart from Egypt. In the wilderness he affirmed the need for Sabbath rest (16:5, 22–30). Then he proclaimed the Decalogue (20:3–17) from Mount Sinai a few months after the Israelites left Egypt (see 19:1–2), and it appears that he gave the Covenant Code (chaps. 21–23) to Moses shortly thereafter. Moses received Leviticus during a month in the Sinai desert at the beginning of the second year after the departure from Egypt (cf. Exod. 40:17 and Num. 1:1), and he presented the Deuteronomic laws in the land of Moab at the end of four decades of wilderness wandering (Deut. 1:3, 5). While the laws at Sinai were addressed to the generation of Israelites who left Egypt, Moses delivered the speeches/sermons recorded in Deuteronomy to the second generation, after the adults of the first generation had died (2:14–15).

During the wilderness period YHWH also gave new laws on several occasions to address particular situations and to provide guidance for the future regarding those and related cases (Lev. 10:8–11; 24:15–22; Num. 9:9–14; 27:6–11; 36:5–9). The close connections between these laws and their narrative contexts illustrate the fact that a law provides a kind of normative skeleton of a "story" that responds to a previous story and guides future stories.

For example, Num. 9 tells how some Israelites were disappointed because they were unable to keep the Passover at the appointed time, on the fourteenth day of the first month, because they were ritually impure (Num. 9:6–7). The Lord responded with a solution: A person with that problem (or on a journey) was to keep the Passover one month later (vv. 10–12). This law told the "story" of what an individual was to do whenever such a situation should arise. Although the Bible does not record stories/situations that created the need for all of its laws, it seems likely that real-life circumstances were behind many of them.

7. E.g., Moses, Aaron, Caleb, and Joshua versus Korah, Dathan, and Abiram. Exodus 12:38 reports that a "mixed multitude" departed from Egypt with the Israelites. Many of these people may have had no previous experience with YHWH.

Not surprisingly, the major law collections given at different times have different emphases. The Decalogue lays out basic moral principles governing divine-human and human-human relationships. The Covenant Code applies these and related principles to specific cases. Leviticus moves from concern with cultic holiness in chapters 1–7 and 11–16 to holy lifestyle in the Holiness Code (chaps. 17–26).[8] Much of the law collection in Deut. 12–26 expands on the principles of the Decalogue (cf. chaps. 11–12 of the present volume), and some of it parallels components of the Covenant Code (cf., e.g., Exod. 21:2–6 with Deut. 15:12–18).

The laws given to the first generation at Sinai contain a significant amount of repetition with variation. For instance, the Lord commands observance of the seventh-day weekly Sabbath in Exod. 20:8–11 (Decalogue); 23:12; 31:12–17; 34:21; 35:2–3; Lev. 19:3, 30; 23:3; and 26:2.[9] In the Holiness Code, a number of laws from Lev. 18 regulating sexual activity are reiterated in Lev. 20 with the addition of penalties.[10] There are plenty of new laws in Deuteronomy, but this book also contains a considerable amount of selective recapitulation and reinforcement of earlier laws, with varying degrees of differences.[11]

Other Pentateuchal Portions Related to Law

Outside the genre of ongoing laws, some other parts of the Pentateuch are related to or involved with law. First, there are narrative accounts of settings in which divine covenant formation and law-giving occur (e.g., Exod. 19; 24; 34:1–10; Lev. 24:10–12, 23), covenant blessings and curses for obedience or disobedience to YHWH's laws (Lev. 26; Deut. 27:11–26; chap. 28), and exhortations and warnings to encourage obedience (e.g., Lev. 20:22–26; Deut. 4; 29–30).

Second, the Pentateuch contains divine commands and instructions for particular occasions, which lack ongoing applicability. For instance, God directed the journeying of the Israelites after their departure from Egypt (e.g., Exod. 14:1–4; Num. 14:25; Deut. 2:2–7). Also, Exod. 25–31 and 40:1–15 provide instructions for onetime events: constructing and setting up the sanctuary,

---

8. However, Israel Knohl has proposed that materials from the same perspective as the Holiness Code appear elsewhere in the Pentateuch, such as Lev. 11:43–45 and 16:29–34. *The Sanctuary of Silence: The Priestly Torah and the Holiness School* (Minneapolis: Fortress, 1995), esp. 104–6.

9. In Deuteronomy for the next generation, see 5:12–15.

10. Mary Douglas finds this repetition to be a major key to the structure of Leviticus. "Poetic Structure in Leviticus," in *Pomegranates and Golden Bells: Studies in Biblical, Jewish, and Near Eastern Ritual, Law, and Literature in Honor of Jacob Milgrom*, ed. David P. Wright, David Noel Freedman, and Avi Hurvitz (Winona Lake, IN: Eisenbrauns, 1995), 251–53.

11. Cf., e.g., Exod. 21 and Deut. 15 regarding servitude; dietary rules in Lev. 11 and Deut. 14; cities of refuge in Num. 35 and Deut. 19.

making the priestly garments, and consecrating the priests and the sanctuary (fulfilled in Exod. 35–39; 40:16–33; Lev. 8).[12] This initial establishment of the sanctuary and its priesthood preceded the application of ongoing laws that regulated the cult (esp. Lev. 1–7, 11–16).

Third, some narratives show operation or violation (with penalties) of laws and legal principles in particular situations. After the Israelites defeated the Midianites, any Israelites who had contacted dead people were required to remain outside the camp and undergo purification (Num. 31:19) in accordance with laws presented earlier (5:1–4; 19:11–13, 16–20). When the Israelites worshiped a golden calf, they broke their covenant with YHWH (Exod. 32) by violating its first stipulations, consisting of the initial commandments in the Decalogue (Exod. 20:2–6). Idolatry and immorality resulted in disaster when Israelites were seduced by Moabite women into worshiping their gods (Num. 25) in blatant disregard of divine laws and warnings (e.g., Exod. 34:12–16). On various occasions the Lord ordered members of the community to execute some who committed serious wrongs (Exod. 32:27; Lev. 24:14; Num. 15:35; 25:4–5).

Law Materials outside the Pentateuch

The OT outside the Pentateuch introduces few laws per se. The only law collection elsewhere is in Ezek. 43:18–46:24, where cultic laws are presented within a framework of prophecy after directions for constructing an ideal temple (chaps. 40:1–43:17).[13] There are divine commands for particular situations (e.g., Judg. 4:6–7; 1 Sam. 13:13; 15:2–3; 1 Kings 13:21), and the term "torah" can refer to instruction through a prophet (Isa. 1:10), psalmist (Ps. 78:1), or wise person, such as a parent (Prov. 1:8). David initiated a rule of his own regarding distribution of spoil taken in war: "'For as his share is who goes down into the battle, so shall his share be who stays by the baggage. They shall share alike.' And he made it a statute [khoq] and a rule [mishpat] for Israel from that day forward to this day" (1 Sam. 30:24–25).

Outside the Pentateuch, mentions of laws in the sense of divinely instituted regulations or rules with ongoing applicability refer to pentateuchal laws, of which the priests should be the custodians and administrators (Jer. 2:8; 18:18; Ezek. 22:26).[14] These are the laws to which people are held accountable (Judg.

---

12. Cf. Num. 8, purifying the Levites and setting them apart for service at the sanctuary.

13. Ezekiel 45:9–12 diverges from cultic law to command ethical integrity, including by reiterating the requirement for just measures expressed in Lev. 19:35–36. Some cultic laws appear in Ezek. 42:13–14; 43:12 among directions for construction of the temple.

14. Cf. 2 Chron. 19:10, addressed by Jehoshaphat to "certain Levites and priests and heads of families of Israel, to give judgment for the LORD and to decide disputed cases" (v. 8).

3:4; Mal. 4:4 [3:22 MT]), whether they comply with them (e.g., Josh. 8:30–35; 2 Kings 14:6) or violate them (1 Kings 11:1–2; 2 Kings 17:34–41).

Law Concepts in Nonlegal Genres

The principles expressed in the laws of the Pentateuch are foundational for the lives of God's covenant people. Therefore concepts relating to those laws are plentiful in other genres of the Hebrew Bible. Following are a few examples in narrative, prophecy, and Psalms and Wisdom literature.

Narrative

Divinely instituted legal principles appear in narratives in several different ways, sometimes quite directly but often indirectly.[15]

Some narratives recount compliance with pentateuchal laws. For instance, the notice "These cities and their pasturelands the people of Israel gave by lot to the Levites, as the LORD had commanded through Moses" (Josh. 21:8) specifically indicates that the allocation of cities to the Levites, described in detail in Josh. 21, was in obedience to the instructions in Num. 35:2–8. Reforms at various points in Israelite history (e.g., Judg. 6:25–32; 10:15–16; 2 Kings 18:3–6; 22:2–23:25; 2 Chron. 29–31, 34–35) brought God's people back into a loyal covenant relationship with him, in which they once again obeyed his laws, especially against worship of other deities and idolatry (Exod. 20:3–6; Deut. 5:7–10). Narratives show that the prosperity of the Israelites depended on following the Lord's instructions (e.g., 2 Kings 18:3–8; 2 Chron. 14:1–7 [13:23–14:6 MT]; 24:18–20; 31:20–21; 32:27–30).

On the other hand, many narratives report violations of laws, as in Judg. 2:1–2, where the theophanic "angel of the LORD" reminded the Israelites that he had commanded them (through Moses in Exod. 23:32; 34:13; Deut. 7:2; 12:3) to "'make no covenant with the inhabitants of this land; you shall break down their altars.' But you have not obeyed my voice. What is this you have done?" The rest of the book of Judges and much of the books of Kings and Chronicles describe Israelite (and Judahite) transgression of YHWH's commands against assimilation to the idolatrous religious cultures of surrounding peoples that resulted from their failure to remove these influences from their midst. This constituted rebellion against YHWH, which caused

---

15. Gordon J. Wenham also demonstrates that biblical narratives themselves (using examples from Genesis and Judges) convey ethical values that can inform one's choices. *Story as Torah: Reading Old Testament Narrative Ethically* (Grand Rapids: Baker Academic, 2000).

all kinds of evil and suffering, as described in many narratives, and fulfilled the covenant curses, culminating in exile, of which the Torah warned (esp. Lev. 26; Deut. 28).

A key factor that planted idolatry in the Israelite nation during the monarchy period was the multiple marriages of Solomon to foreign, idolatrous women (1 Kings 11:1–10), which violated two pentateuchal prohibitions: against a king acquiring many wives for himself (Deut. 17:17, "lest his heart turn away") and against marrying women "from the nations concerning which the LORD had said to the people of Israel, 'You shall not enter into marriage with them, neither shall they with you, for surely they will turn away your heart after their gods'" (1 Kings 11:2, referring to Exod. 34:16; Deut. 7:3–4).

A narrative in 1 Kings 21 reports what appears to be compliance with laws of YHWH. Two witnesses charged: "'Naboth cursed [Heb. "blessed" as euphemism] God and the king.' So they took him outside the city and stoned him to death with stones" (v. 13). It is true that according to the Torah, "You shall not revile [or "curse"] God, nor curse a ruler of your people" (Exod. 22:28 [22:27 MT]), and "Whoever curses his God shall bear his sin. Whoever blasphemes the name of the LORD shall surely be put to death. All the congregation shall stone him" (Lev. 24:15–16). It is also true that at least two witnesses were necessary to condemn a person to death (Deut. 17:6; 19:15). However, the problem in this case was that Jezebel had set up false, lying witnesses to murder Naboth and steal his ancestral vineyard for her husband, Ahab, through abuse of the judicial process (1 Kings 21:1–16).

So under a veneer of legality, Jezebel through her accomplices was guilty of breaking Torah laws against false witness (Exod. 20:16 [Decalogue]; Deut. 19:16–21), slander (Lev. 19:16), murder (Exod. 20:13 [Decalogue]), and theft (Exod. 20:15 [Decalogue]; cf. Lev. 19:13) in order to deprive a man of his inviolable right to maintain ownership of his ancestral agricultural real estate (Lev. 25:23–24). When Ahab went to take possession of dead Naboth's vineyard, he accepted what Jezebel had done (1 Kings 21:16) and thereby incurred a divine sentence of death along with her (vv. 17–24).

Some narratives have more subtle connections to laws that illuminate our understanding of the stories when we recognize them. For instance, when the Israelites caught Adoni-bezek, a Canaanite king, they cut off his thumbs and big toes (Judg. 1:6). To a modern reader, this mutilation sounds utterly barbaric. However, according to the biblical text, the king confessed the justice of what was done to him: "Seventy kings with their thumbs and their big toes cut off used to pick up scraps under my table. As I have done, so God has repaid me" (v. 7).

It is doubtful that Adoni-bezek knew Israelite law, but his words, "As I have done, so . . ." show awareness of the lex talionis (law of retaliation) principle that appears in pentateuchal law regarding assault that results in permanent injury: "as he has done it shall be done to him" (Lev. 24:19–20).[16] According to this principle of justice, which was in ANE culture at least as early as the Old Babylonian Laws of Hammurabi §§196–97, 200 (eighteenth century BC), a person who cut off the thumbs and big toes of just one other individual would have the same done to him. But Adoni-bezek had maimed seventy kings in this way, and therefore he deserved a much more severe punishment. The Israelites were merciful to him, and he was surprised that they did not do more to him!

Jephthah vowed that if YHWH would give him victory over the Ammonites, he would offer "for a burnt offering" "whatever comes out from the doors of my house to meet me when I return" (Judg. 11:31). Archaeologists have discovered early Israelite two-story dwellings in which livestock was sheltered on the ground floor,[17] so it is plausible that Jephthah expected an animal to meet him first. However, to his horror, his daughter came out to meet him (vv. 34–35). With her consent (v. 36), he "did with her according to his vow that he had made" (v. 39).

The implication of what Jephthah did is clear. However, David Marcus has argued against a plain-sense reading, that Jephthah sacrificed his daughter, by recalling that the narrator of Judges "castigated Gideon for a much lesser crime with the Ephod (Judg. 8:27). Absence of condemnation is therefore significant in judging a character's action."[18]

However, Marcus misses the fact that the narrator of Judges does not need to condemn Jephthah or to point out his punishment (compare Judges 9:56, 57), because Jephthah's act directly accomplished its own punishment: not only the death of his daughter, but also the wiping out of his line of descendants. We see the seriousness of such a punishment in Leviticus 20, in which one of the punishments to come upon those who sacrifice their children to the god Molech is that the Lord "will cut them off from among their people" (verse 5; compare verse 3). Donald Wold has shown that this kind of penalty meant that an individual's line of descendants would die out, which is precisely what happened to Jephthah.

16. Cf. the fact that Samson invoked this principle to justify his revenge on the Philistines (Judg. 15:11, "As they did to me, so have I done to them"), although he probably was not think-ing of applying OT law.

17. Ehud Netzer, "Domestic Architecture in the Iron Age," in *The Architecture of Ancient Israel: From the Prehistoric to the Persian Periods*, ed. Aharon Kempinski and Ronny Reich (Jerusalem: Israel Exploration Society, 1992), 193–201.

18. David Marcus, *Jephthah and His Vow* (Lubbock: Texas Tech University Press, 1986), 48.

Now perhaps we can more fully appreciate the narrator's emphasis upon the virginity of Jephthah's daughter (Judges 11:37–39). As part of the tragedy of foregoing the personal fulfillment of family life that was so important to an Israelite woman, she had no opportunity to provide Jephthah with an heir so that his "name" could live on (compare Deut. 25:6, 7; Ruth 4:10).[19]

Prophecy

As early as Judg. 6:8–10 the Lord sent prophets to the Israelites to hold them accountable for covenant violations and to call them back to loyalty and cooperation with him. As recorded in narratives, preclassical prophets rebuked people for breaking YHWH's Decalogue commandments against having relations with deities other than himself (Judg. 6:10; cf. Exod. 20:3), idolatry (1 Kings 14:6–16; cf. Exod. 20:4–6), murder, and adultery (2 Sam. 12:1–12; cf. Exod. 20:13–14). Prophets also condemned priests for abusing their power, showing contempt for the Lord's sacrifices, and oppressing their people by misappropriating sacrificial portions belonging to YHWH and the offerers (1 Sam. 2:12–17, 27–36; 3:11–18; cf. Lev. 7:29–36).

Classical prophets encouraged, appealed to, and warned their people to be faithful to YHWH and his Torah and censured them for their failures, evil attitudes, hypocrisy, and false sense of security that treated the divine covenant (with God's protective presence in the temple) as if it were unconditional.[20] In the process, the prophets referred to and reused various kinds of OT laws and legal principles.[21] These include Decalogue commandments (e.g., Ezek. 22:6–9, 11; Hosea 4:2; cf. Exod. 20), related laws of holy living (e.g., Ezek. 22:9–11; cf. Lev. 18:7, 9, 15, 19; 19:16; 20:12, 17–18), and especially ethical principles of kindness and justice rather than oppression toward other members of society, particularly vulnerable ones, such as the poor, resident aliens, the fatherless, and widows (e.g., Isa. 3:14–15; Ezek. 22:7; Amos 2:6–8; 4:1; 5:11–12; 8:4–6; cf. Exod. 22:21–27 [22:20–26 MT]; Lev. 19:9–10, 13–15, 33–36; Deut. 24:10–15, 17–22).

The following divine message conveyed through Jeremiah exemplifies the wide range of prophetic concern for Torah principles, with application to circumstances in his day:

19. Roy Gane, *God's Faulty Heroes* (Hagerstown, MD: Review & Herald, 1996), 93, citing Donald J. Wold, "The Meaning of the Biblical Penalty *Kareth*" (PhD diss., University of California, Berkeley, 1978), 251–55. On the penalty of being "cut off," see chap. 5.

20. Cf. Roy Gane, "The End of the Israelite Monarchy," *JATS* 10, nos. 1–2 (1999): 345–47.

21. On issues involved with prophetic reuse of OT legal materials, see Kenneth Bergland, "Torah and Prophets: Case-Studies of Inner-Biblical Reuse and Appropriation between the Ethical Laws of the Torah and the Classical Prophets" (PhD diss., Andrews University, forthcoming).

Thus says the LORD of hosts, the God of Israel. "Amend your ways and your deeds, and I will let you dwell in this place. Do not trust in these deceptive words: 'This is the temple of the LORD, the temple of the LORD, the temple of the LORD.' For if you truly amend your ways and your deeds, if you truly execute justice one with another, if you do not oppress the sojourner, the fatherless, or the widow, or shed innocent blood in this place, and if you do not go after other gods to your own harm, then I will let you dwell in this place, in the land that I gave of old to your fathers forever. Behold, you trust in deceptive words to no avail. Will you steal, murder, commit adultery, swear falsely, make offerings to Baal, and go after other gods that you have not known, and then come and stand before me in this house, which is called by my name, and say, 'We are delivered!'—only to go on doing all these abominations? Has this house, which is called by my name, become a den of robbers in your eyes? Behold, I myself have seen it," declares the LORD. (Jer. 7:3–11)

Notice here the strong conditional element, "if," which appears in many other prophetic oracles (e.g., explicitly in Isa. 1:19–20; Jer. 17:21–27; Ezek. 18; Mal. 3:7–12). Thus prophets applied and amplified the conditional message of the covenant blessings and curses (esp. Lev. 26; Deut. 28).

The classical prophets were profoundly concerned with proper worship of YHWH. They reprimanded priests for drunkenness (Isa. 28:7, along with false prophets; cf. Lev. 10:8–11; Ezek. 44:21); not knowing the Lord (Jer. 2:8); unethical behavior (Jer. 6:13; 8:10; Hosea 6:9; Mic. 3:11); violating God's law and profaning his holy things; not making or teaching distinctions between holy, common, impure, and pure categories; and disregarding his Sabbaths (Ezek. 22:26; Zeph. 3:4; cf. Lev. 10:10–11; 19:3). However, the prophets almost never criticized sacrificial procedures at the Jerusalem temple for deviating from specific pentateuchal instructions. An exception is Malachi's rebuke of those who were offering defective sacrifices at the second temple (Mal. 1:6–14; cf. Lev. 22:17–25).

Prophetic critiques of legitimate Israelite worship practices generally were directed against hypocrisy at the legitimate temple in Jerusalem when people who were disobedient to YHWH's laws offered sacrifices and other forms of worship to him (Isa. 1:11–17; Jer. 6:19–20; 11:3–17; 14:10–12). Prophets often condemned illegitimate idolatry and worship of deities other than YHWH (e.g., Jer. 1:16; 7:9; 11:17; Ezek. 8, at the Jerusalem temple; Hosea 2:13 [2:15 MT]; cf. Exod. 20:3–6), including at unauthorized temples in northern Israel (e.g., Hosea 4:15–5:4; 8:5–6, 13; cf. Deut. 12:5–14)[22] and also child sacrifice (Isa. 57:5; Jer. 19:5; 32:35; Ezek. 23:37, 39; cf. Lev. 18:21; 20:1–5; Deut. 18:10).

22. First Kings 12:26–33 records the establishment of illicit cult sites in northern Israel by Jeroboam I.

Recognition of relationships between some prophetic passages and their pentateuchal backgrounds can illuminate the former. For example, in Isa. 58 the Judahites ask the Lord: "Why have we fasted, and you see it not? Why have we humbled ourselves [*piel* verb of *'-n-h* + direct object *nefesh*], and you take no knowledge of it?" (v. 3a). This fast was likely for the Day of Atonement, the only time when OT law required the Israelites to humble themselves by practicing self-denial (Lev. 16:29, 31; 23:27, 32; Num. 29:7, *piel* of *'-n-h* + direct object *nefesh*, as in Isa. 58:3), which included fasting (cf. Ps. 35:13).[23] The fact that Isa. 58 urges the people not to do their own pleasure on the S/sabbath (Isa. 58:13–14), by pursuing their own business (cf. v. 3b), reinforces the setting of the Day of Atonement. This great fast day was the only ceremonial sabbath when all work was forbidden (Lev. 16:29, 31; 23:28, 30–32), as on the weekly Sabbath (e.g., Exod. 20:10).[24]

In this light, the divine response to the Judahite query reveals something shocking: "Behold, in the day of your fast you seek your own pleasure, and oppress all your workers. Behold, you fast only to quarrel and to fight and to hit with a wicked fist" (vv. 3b–4). On this most solemn day of the year, when the high priest uniquely entered the holy of holies in the temple to ritually purge it from the sins of the people and thereby morally cleanse them (Lev. 16, esp. vv. 16, 30), they were vigorously adding to their sins (Isa. 58:1)! Although they were fulfilling the letter of the law to practice self-denial, they were showing disloyalty to YHWH by breaking his command to abstain from all work, thereby incurring his terminal condemnation to destruction (cf. Lev. 23:30). So it was remarkably merciful for the Lord to appeal to them to become faithful to him and enjoy his blessings by accepting into their lives the deeper meaning of the Day of Atonement fast (in harmony with social justice and kindness) and S/sabbath (Isa. 58:6–13).

Another prophetic passage in which pentateuchal legal background highlights divine mercy is Jer. 3: "If a man divorces his wife and she goes from him and becomes another man's wife, will he return to her? Would not that land be greatly polluted? You have played the whore with many lovers; and would you return to me? declares the LORD" (v. 1). This presents the relationship between YHWH and his covenant people, who had committed spiritual "adultery" against him (cf. 1:16; 2:8, 11, 20, 23–28, 32–33), in light of the law in Deut. 24:1–4 against a woman's remarriage to her original husband after

23. Ancient Israelites also fasted at other times of mourning, stress, or repentance, as in Judg. 20:26; 1 Sam. 7:6; 31:13; Ezra 8:21; Esther 4:3, 16; 9:31; Ps. 35:13; Dan. 10:2–3, 12; etc.

24. Cf. Shalom M. Paul, *Isaiah 40–66: Translation and Commentary*, ECC (Grand Rapids: Eerdmans, 2012), 493.

he has divorced her for "indecency" short of adultery (v. 1)[25] and she has been married to another man (vv. 2–3): "then her former husband, who sent her away, may not take her again to be his wife, after she has been defiled, for that is an abomination before the LORD. And you shall not bring sin upon the land that the LORD your God is giving you for an inheritance" (v. 4).[26]

Not only had YHWH found "indecency" in his chosen people for which he could have "divorced" them; they also had committed spiritual adultery, for which they deserved death (cf. Num. 25:1–5 of spiritual promiscuity; and Lev. 20:10; Deut. 22:22 of literal adultery). Not only had they gone to one other "husband"; they had hooked up with many paramours. So it appears that a fortiori YHWH would be even less able to take them back than a husband whose wife had been married to another man. They deserved no mercy. In spite of it all, YHWH appealed to his spiritually polluted people to acknowledge their guilt and return to him (Jer. 3:2–4:4). His mercy is not legislated. It does not follow strict rules of justice but overturns them. His grace is not merely amazing; it is also legally illogical and virtually indecent![27]

Psalms and Wisdom Literature[28]

The Psalms and Wisdom literature relate to the Torah from several angles. Some psalms extol the Lord's laws and the benefits of following them (e.g., Pss. 1; 19:7–8 [19:8–9 MT]; 37:30–31; 119; cf. Deut. 4:5–8). Others call on God to stop wicked people who oppress the poor and other socially vulnerable persons (Pss. 10:2, 9–10; 12:5 [12:6 MT]; 94:5–6; 109:16; cf. Exod. 22:21–27 [22:20–26 MT]; etc.),[29] despise and disregard God (Pss. 10:3–4, 11; 14:1–3; cf. Deut. 6:5), lie and deceive (Pss. 10:7; 12:2–4 [12:3–5 MT]; 31:18 [31:19 MT]; 109:2; cf. Lev. 19:11), bear false witness (Ps. 27:12; cf. Exod. 20:16); curse (Pss. 10:7; 109:17–18; cf. Exod. 21:17; 22:28; Lev. 19:14), and murder the innocent (Pss. 10:8; 94:6; cf. Exod. 20:13).

Psalm 15:2–5 describes the traits of a person who can dwell with God because he does what is right, as exemplified by the following (with references to some related pentateuchal laws in brackets):

25. An adulteress would be executed (Lev. 20:10; Deut. 22:22).
26. It seems clear that Jer. 3 refers to the law in Deut. 24 and not vice versa, with Kenneth Bergland, "Reuse of Deuteronomy 24:1–4 in Jeremiah 3:1–10: A Reexamination" (paper presented at the Annual Meeting of the Society of Biblical Literature, San Diego, November 24, 2014).
27. As dramatically illustrated in the life and message of Hosea.
28. Cf. Gordon J. Wenham, *Psalms as Torah: Reading Biblical Song Ethically*, STI (Grand Rapids: Baker Academic, 2012), esp. 97–118.
29. By contrast, see Ps. 41:1 (41:2 MT): "Blessed is the one who considers the poor! In the day of trouble the LORD delivers him."

> He who . . . speaks truth in his heart [Lev. 19:11];
> who does not slander with his tongue [Lev. 19:16]
>   and does no evil to his neighbor [Lev. 19:18],
>   nor takes up a reproach against his friend;
> in whose eyes a vile person is despised,
>   but who honors those who fear the LORD;
> who swears to his own hurt and does not change [Num. 30:2];
> who does not put out his money at interest [e.g., Exod. 22:25 (22:24 MT); Deut. 23:19]
>   and does not take a bribe against the innocent [Exod. 23:8; Deut. 16:19].

Some of the features of right living mentioned here in Ps. 15 do not appear as such in OT law, but they are logical extensions of Torah principles. For example, not taking up a reproach against one's friend could be derived from "You shall love your neighbor as yourself" (Lev. 19:18) and "You shall not go around as a slanderer among your people" (v. 16). Despising a vile person would be to treat an individual in accordance with his character as judged by the Lord, "condemning the guilty" (Exod. 23:7; 34:7; Deut. 25:1; cf. 1 Cor. 5:1–13), rather than subverting justice and misrepresenting God by treating him as though he were righteous (cf. Lev. 20:4–5). Conversely, honoring those who fear the Lord would mean treating them in harmony with God's assessment of them (cf. Exod. 23:7; Deut. 25:1).[30]

Perception of pentateuchal background can uncover nuances of a psalm that would otherwise be missed. Psalm 51, the penitential prayer of David when he was convicted of sin with Bathsheba, contains the acknowledgment: "For you will not delight in sacrifice [zevakh], or I would give it; you will not be pleased [qal of r-ts-h] with a burnt offering" (v. 16 [v. 18 MT]). Here David admitted that there was no form of sacrificial expiation that the Lord would accept (cf. niphal of r-ts-h in Lev. 1:4) to remedy the crimes of murder and adultery that he had committed, each of which incurred capital punishment (Exod. 21:12; Lev. 20:10; Deut. 22:22; Num. 35:31; Lev. 24:17).[31] He could

---

30. Cf. Ps. 101, in which David pledges to "walk with integrity of heart within my house" (v. 2) by shunning evil and evildoers (vv. 3–4), including those who are dishonest (v. 7), and by destroying slanderers (v. 5) and other wicked persons (v. 8), but by favoring those who are faithful (v. 6).

31. On the expiatory function of the burnt offering, see chap. 16. David did not mention the possibility of a purification offering, which was for lesser sins (Lev. 4:1–5:13), or a reparation offering, which expiated for sacrilege (Lev. 5:14–6:7 [5:14–26 MT]). For negation of expiation by a "sacrifice" (zevakh), such as a "sacrifice [zevakh] of well-being" (Lev. 7:11), cf. 1 Sam. 3:14. In Ps. 51:19 [51:21 MT] David speaks of God delighting in sacrifices after he receives mercy from God, but these are not to expiate his sin.

only hope for divine mercy to accept the sacrifice of his repentant heart (Ps. 51:17 [51:19 MT]).

David prayed: "Purge me with hyssop, and I shall be clean" (Ps. 51:7 [51:9 MT]). Hyssop is a small plant that was not used in any ritual for expiating a moral fault, but it was employed in rituals to remedy the physical ritual impurities of scaly skin disease (so-called leprosy, Lev. 14:4, 6)[32] and corpse contamination (Num. 19:6, 18). "In light of the intimate linkage between the two evils treated with hyssop, David portrays his moral state in physical terms that are strikingly appropriate: He is morally 'leprous' and deserved to die (become a corpse) for adultery and for having arranged for the death of Uriah, Bathsheba's husband" (2 Sam. 11–12).[33]

The book of Proverbs encourages a person to follow the teaching (torah, 1:8; 3:1; 4:2; etc.) or commandment (mitsvah, 2:1; 3:1; 4:4; etc.) of a wise mentor, such as a parent, because these instructions are wise in terms of cause and effect, serving as guides to success and happiness while preventing problems (cf. Deut. 10:13, "for your good"). Aside from issues of right and wrong, Proverbs has many helpful observations about life, including what works well and what does not in areas of human experience and relationships (e.g., Prov. 26:17).

Much of Proverbs encourages ethical rightness, with striking similarities between parental teaching here and divine instructions in the Pentateuch. First, both are referred to as torah (teaching) and mitsvah (commandment; cf., e.g., Deut. 30:10). Second, Prov. 6 urges a son to keep the commandment/teaching of his parents by metaphorically binding them on his heart and tying them around his neck (vv. 21–22). This echoes the exhortations in Deut. 6:6–9 and 11:18–20 to the Israelites, who are to treasure instructions from YHWH through Moses in their hearts and homes and teach them to their children. By employing the same kind of language to address a child as the recipient of parental teaching, Prov. 6 could be taken to imply that the ultimate source of this wise instruction is the Lord. Passing on this precious legacy from generation to generation in an unbroken chain depends not just on the faithfulness of parents in teaching their children; it also depends on the willingness of the children to accept the instruction so that they can in turn transmit it to *their* children.

Third, and most significant, Proverbs articulates, illustrates, applies, and extends Torah values and principles. For example, Prov. 6 warns that a person

32. See also Lev. 14:49, 51, 52 in the ritual for a house infected with fungus.
33. Roy Gane, *Leviticus, Numbers*, NIV Application Commentary (Grand Rapids: Zondervan, 2004), 594.

who "goes about with crooked speech, . . . with perverted heart devises evil, continually sowing discord" (vv. 12–14), will meet his demise with sudden calamity and "be broken beyond healing" (v. 15). The warning is based on the idea that an evil cause invariably produces a negative effect, but the text does not identify the specific agent of the calamity. Nevertheless, the following literary unit (vv. 16–19) introduces an agent, YHWH, who hates and no doubt punishes several unethical kinds of behaviors (pentateuchal laws cited in brackets), including sowing discord:

> There are six things that the LORD hates,
>   seven that are an abomination to him:
> haughty eyes, a lying tongue [cf. Lev. 19:11],
>   and hands that shed innocent blood [Exod. 20:13; Deut. 19:13],
> a heart that devises wicked plans [cf. Exod. 20:17, coveting],
>   feet that make haste to run to evil,
> a false witness who breathes out lies [Exod. 20:16],
>   and one who sows discord among brothers.

This list refers to some specific violations of pentateuchal laws (esp. the Decalogue) and other evils that are unloving, such as sowing discord, which exemplify violations of the overarching principle of loving one's neighbor (Lev. 19:18).

Elsewhere in Proverbs the same dynamics of causality apply to the crime of oppressing the poor, which results in the oppressor coming to poverty (22:16). Why does he come to poverty? "Whoever oppresses a poor man insults his Maker, but he who is generous to the needy honors him" (14:31). So consideration of cause and effect should take the Deity into major account, as the beginning of the book makes clear: "The fear of the LORD is the beginning of knowledge; fools despise wisdom and instruction" (1:7).

Also, positive actions carry consequences in relation to other humans and to God. Proverbs 25 urges: "If your enemy is hungry, give him bread to eat, and if he is thirsty, give him water to drink, for you will heap burning coals on his head, and the LORD will reward you" (vv. 21–22, cited in Rom. 12:20). Here kindness extends the principle of loving one's neighbor (Lev. 19:18) to a situation involving one's enemy (cf. Matt. 5:44), as in Exod. 23:4–5, which commands an Israelite to help an enemy with his animal.[34]

The Pentateuch condemns adultery as a crime against divine law (Exod. 20:14) that incurs capital punishment (Lev. 20:10; Deut. 22:22), but Prov. 6 discourages adultery from another angle: commonsense awareness of natural

---

34. For extended discussion of Exod. 23:4, see chap. 10.

dynamics in human social relationships. This chapter draws on vivid language and analogies to warn a son against a beguiling adulteress (vv. 24–31; cf. 7:5–27), concluding:

> He who commits adultery lacks sense;
>> he who does it destroys himself.
> He will get wounds and dishonor,
>> and his disgrace will not be wiped away.
> For jealousy makes a man furious,
>> and he will not spare when he takes revenge.
> He will accept no compensation;
>> he will refuse though you multiply gifts. (6:32–35)

These verses do not specify the husband's revenge, but the parallel passage in Prov. 7:22–27 indicates that yielding to the seduction of adultery leads to death.[35] So not only is adultery morally wrong because it breaks a divine principle; it is also incredibly stupid because it provokes against oneself a passionate human (husband) who will not rest until he gains justice.

Pentateuchal cultic law illuminates the opening words of the proposition by the brazen adulteress in Prov. 7:14: "I had to make a sacrifice of well-being; Today I fulfilled my vows" (NJPS). Leviticus 7:16 specifies regarding this kind of sacrifice: "But if the sacrifice of his offering is a vow offering or a freewill offering, it shall be eaten on the day that he offers his sacrifice, and on the next day what remains of it shall be eaten." The adulteress in Prov. 7 is saying that she has the luxury of plenty of meat at her house and needs help in eating it. She knows that the way to a man's heart is through his stomach (cf. Num. 25:1–2). Ironically and sacrilegiously, they would eat holy food and engage in morally unholy, impure conduct.[36]

Just as the conditional covenant blessings and curses present the choice between obedience and disobedience to YHWH's laws, with their corresponding consequences (Lev. 26; Deut. 28), Proverbs warns against adulterous wives but also describes in glowing detail a faithful, capable, and industrious wife

---

35. This could be death inflicted by the community if the husband presses charges, but reference to his jealous anger (Prov. 6:34) implies the possibility that he may personally finish off the adulterer before the latter can even stand trial. Cf. the "avenger of blood" in cases of murder: Num. 35:19, 21; Deut. 19:6, "in hot anger."

36. It was a terminal offense punishable by the divine penalty of being "cut off" to eat such holy food while in a state of physical ritual impurity (Lev. 7:20–21), including such impurity incurred through sexual intercourse (15:18) even with one's spouse. But perhaps the woman and her young paramour (in Prov. 7) would avoid this punishment by eating before having sex, while still ritually pure. For the fact that adultery is also *morally* impure, see Num. 5:11–31.

whom her husband praises (Prov. 31:10–31). Also encouraging marital fidelity in harmony with the Edenic "one flesh" ideal (Gen. 2:24) protected by the Torah (against adultery [see above]) is the Song of Songs (or Song of Solomon), a poetic rhapsody on the exquisite joys of marital intimacy that is beautiful, exciting, satisfying, and lasting.

5

How Does the Old Testament Law Genre Inculcate Values?

Old Testament law seeks to inculcate divine values by expressing and illustrating principles that flow from them and by providing motivation to live according to these principles and values.

Values before Laws

The values existed before the legal principles. Before God issued any law to inhabitants of planet earth, he valued as very good his creation of male and female humans, whom he created in his image, blessed with reproductive fruitfulness and dominion over other creatures, and to whom he gave food from plants and trees (Gen. 1:27–31). These elements show that God values the sanctity of life; social relationships, beginning with marriage; benevolent control of animals, implying care for the environment; and the ideal diet.

All of these values are for the well-being of God's creatures, whom he placed in a world that is perfectly suited to their needs (vv. 3–19). Therefore, the creation values are subsumed under the overarching value of love (1 John 4:8).

The fact that God established life in accordance with his values indicates that humans should simply conduct their lives in harmony with these values, as when he commanded faithful Abram: "Walk before me, and be blameless"

(Gen. 17:1). The Lord should not need to command: "You shall not murder [and thereby destroy life made in God's image]" or "You shall not commit adultery [and thereby disrupt the marriage union of male and female]" (Exod. 20:13–14).

According to the pentateuchal narrative, it was the fall into sin (Gen. 3) that resulted in violations of divine values and consequent suffering, as when Cain murdered his brother Abel (Gen. 4). Whether or not Cain had heard an explicit rule prohibiting murder, the created order told him that murder was wrong. In any case, God held him accountable and punished him because he knew better than to kill his brother.

Even after the fall, people should be able to discern moral values on the basis of divine natural law, and they are accountable for doing so (Rom. 1:18–32). However, the Bible records ways in which God has assisted weakened human perception by providing guidance in various literary genres to preserve and restore his values. The genre of OT law is especially helpful because it contains explicit statements and illustrations of principles.

Literary Expression of Principles to Inculcate Values

There is considerable variety in the ways that OT laws express their principles. A law can directly express a principle, such as "Honor your father and your mother" (Exod. 20:12). Alternatively, the principle may be illustrated by a case that can include description of a problematic fallen-life situation and the prescribed solution, as in "If a man has a stubborn and rebellious son who will not obey the voice of his father or the voice of his mother . . ." (Deut. 21:18–21). A law can articulate an overall principle (e.g., "You shall love the LORD your God," Deut. 6:5) or a narrower, more specific (sub)principle ("You shall rejoice before the LORD your God," Lev. 23:40). A law principle can correspond to a creation ideal ("You shall love your neighbor as yourself," Lev. 19:18) or accommodate to human fallenness (Deut. 24:1, divorce allowed for "some indecency").

Old Testament law consists of more than lists or examples of principles with stipulations of penalties for violations. It is literature in which laws are intentionally arranged and provided with elements such as introductions (e.g., Exod. 20:1–2; Lev. 18:1–5), summary statements (e.g., Lev. 7:37–38; 11:46–47), motive clauses (e.g., Exod. 20:5–6, 7, 11, 12), and exhortations accompanying groups of laws (e.g., Lev. 18:24–30; 20:22–26). Such elements show higher-level unity between related laws and seek to persuade hearers/readers to follow them in order to wisely enjoy positive outcomes in harmony with divine values rather than suffering negative results of noncompliance.[1]

The remainder of this chapter explores ways in which some literary features of the law genre in the OT contribute to inculcation of divine values. These features include positive and negative formulations, the manner of address, apodictic and casuistic formulations, recurring formulas expressing consequences, and motivational elements. Awareness of such elements is useful for interpreting the logic and meanings of different kinds of laws.

Positive and Negative Formulations

The OT laws can use positive or negative formulations to express a principle. Thus the positive "Honor your father and your mother" (Exod. 20:12) implies a prohibition against dishonoring them (cf. Exod. 21:15, 17; Deut. 21:18–21). Conversely, the negative "You shall have no other gods before me" (Exod. 20:3) implies the positive "It is the LORD your God you shall fear. Him you shall serve" (Deut. 6:13); and "You shall not murder" (Exod. 20:13) implies the imperative of positive respect for life.[2]

Prohibition of one behavior may sound less pleasant than permission of all the other activities that are allowed (an almost infinite variety), but the former can be more economical. A negative formulation does not unduly restrict freedom, as exemplified by the fact that when the Lord told Adam not to eat from "the tree of the knowledge of good and evil" (Gen. 2:17), he allowed him to "eat of every tree of the garden" (v. 16) except that one. God could have listed all the trees from which Adam was permitted to eat (apple, peach, pear, cherry, mango, guava, persimmon, pomegranate, durian, etc.), simply omitting "the tree of the knowledge of good and evil," but the meaning would have been the same, and it would have taken a lot longer.

We should not be turned off by the depressing and inaccurate notion that the purpose of OT law is to tie people up in a small box surrounded by "can't, shouldn't, mustn't, and oughtn't." Appropriate moral boundaries are essential to keep people from being hurt (cf. Deut. 10:13, "for your good"). So we need to know when to say no to things that God identifies as harmful,

---

1. Regarding such persuasion, see James W. Watts, *Reading Law: The Rhetorical Shaping of the Pentateuch*, BibSem 59 (Sheffield: Sheffield Academic, 1999).

2. Cf. Paul's explicit contrasts between corresponding negative and positive behaviors (e.g., Eph. 4:25, 28–29, 31–32).

but we should joyfully focus on the many more safe, enjoyable, and exciting yeses that he has provided for us.[3]

Manner of Address

Generic Address

Masculine is the prior/primary gender in the Hebrew language, so masculine grammatical forms can be used generically for persons, whether male or female.[4] Therefore OT laws addressing both men and women are formulated in masculine language. Some laws employ terms for persons such as *'adam* (man = human being/person) and *nefesh* (being, person) that can be generic in that they do not distinguish between male and female.[5] For example, "When a person [*nefesh*] presents an offering of meal to the LORD" (Lev. 2:1 NJPS); "When a person [*'adam*] has on the skin of his body a swelling or an eruption or a spot" (13:2).

Numbers 5:6 clearly demonstrates the generic nature of these terms by including both *'ish* (man) and *'ishah* (woman) within the semantic range of *'adam* and *nefesh*: "When a man [*'ish*] or woman [*'ishah*] commits any of the sins of mankind [*'adam*], acting unfaithfully against the LORD, and that person [*nefesh*] is guilty" (NASB). However, a given context may indicate that a masculine formulation specifically refers to a male (Exod. 20:17, "your neighbor's wife"; Lev. 6:18 [6:11 MT], "Every male"), and an exclusively feminine formulation occurs when the subject can only be female: "If a woman conceives and bears a male child . . ." (Lev. 12:2).[6]

Address to Male Heads of Households

Exodus 20:17 exemplifies address that is primarily to male heads of households: "You shall not covet your neighbor's house; you shall not covet your neighbor's wife, or his male servant, or his female servant, or his ox, or his donkey, or anything that is your neighbor's."[7] Here the "neighbor" is the social counterpart, who is a husband and can own major kinds of possessions.

---

3. Cf. "For all the promises of God find their Yes in him" (2 Cor. 1:20), in Christ.

4. On the priority of the masculine gender in Biblical Hebrew, see Bruce K. Waltke and M. O'Connor, *An Introduction to Biblical Hebrew Syntax* (Winona Lake, IN: Eisenbrauns, 1990), 108–9 (§6.5.3). See Num. 6:2, where "either a man or a woman" can make a special Nazirite vow, but the following verses refer to the Nazirite in masculine singular (vv. 3–21).

5. Cf. Gen. 1:27, where *'adam* includes both male and female.

6. Cf. feminine in Lev. 15:25; 20:16; Num. 30:3 (30:4 MT).

7. Cf. the Deut. 5:21 version, which places the wife first and separately. The fact that "house" appears before "wife" in Exod. 20:17 does not mean that the wife is mere chattel. Here it is quite clear that "house" means "household": The word "is used in its collective sense, in reference to

Indeed, Israelite heads of households were usually the chief owners and managers of possessions belonging to their families.[8]

The fact that only a man would covet his neighbor's wife[9] shows that the masculine verb in the second clause is not merely generic. However, the commandment logically implies that the principle applicable to the head of household extends to other members of his family by analogy, so it would be wrong for his wife, son, or daughter to covet the spouse of another person.

In light of this last commandment of the Decalogue (Exod. 20:17), it could be argued that the other commandments, including the prohibition of adultery (v. 14; see above), implicitly address male heads of households. In any case, the principles would also apply to their family members, for whose guidance they were responsible. Compare what YHWH said about Abraham, who was head of his household: "For I have chosen him, that he may command his children and his household after him to keep the way of the LORD by doing righteousness and justice, so that the LORD may bring to Abraham what he has promised him" (Gen. 18:19).

The heterosexual incest laws of Lev. 18:6–18 prohibit a male addressee from engaging in sexual activity with kin females other than his wife. The fact that some of these laws forbid sex with women of younger generations (vv. 10, 15) indicates that they target men who are relatively older and could be heads of their extended families. However, this does not mean that only such men are accountable for observing the sexual boundaries delineated in this chapter: The law against bestiality explicitly states that a woman must not "give herself to an animal to lie with it" (v. 23), and in chapter 20 any men or women who engage in forbidden sexual activities incur penalties (vv. 10–21).

Second- and Third-Person Address

Both second-person address and third-person address appear in OT law. Law collections of the ANE generally employ impersonal third-person (usually masc. sing.) address. For instance: "If a man accuses another man and charges him with homicide but cannot bring proof against him, his accuser shall be killed" (Laws of Hammurabi §1).[10] A significant number of OT laws

the 'neighbor's' entire family and his entire property, as for example in Gen 7:1 or Deut 11:6." John I. Durham, *Exodus*, WBC 3 (Waco: Word Books, 1987), 299.

8. But see Prov. 31:16 of a wife engaging in a real-estate transaction for her family: "She considers a field and buys it."

9. Lesbian attraction is not in view here.

10. Trans. Martha Roth, "The Laws of Hammurabi," *COS* 2.131:337; cf. Martha T. Roth, *Law Collections from Mesopotamia and Asia Minor*, SBL Writings from the Ancient World 6 (Atlanta: Scholars Press, 1995), 81.

are similarly addressed in the third person. For instance, "If a malicious witness arises to accuse a person of wrongdoing . . ." (Deut. 19:16). This is a conditional (casuistic/case law) formulation, but third-person address can also be used for an unconditional law (see below), as in "Whoever curses his father or his mother shall be put to death" (Exod. 21:17).

Unlike other ANE laws, many OT laws address Israelites more personally in second person, most often masculine singular. This is the case throughout the Decalogue (Exod. 20:3–17; Deut. 5:7–21) and in every other major law collection, both in unconditional and conditional formulations. Some unconditional examples are as follows: "You shall have no other gods before me" (Exod. 20:3); "You shall not uncover the nakedness of your father's wife" (Lev. 18:8); "You shall not eat any abomination" (Deut. 14:3). Some conditional cases include: "If you meet your enemy's ox or his donkey going astray . . ." (Exod. 23:4); "When you bring a grain offering . . ." (Lev. 2:4); "If your brother, a Hebrew man or a Hebrew woman, is sold to you . . ." (Deut. 15:12).

Second-person address establishes a direct link between the speaker and the hearer/reader. Third-person address allows hearers to decide whether or not a given law concerning "a man" or "a woman" or "whomever" relates to them or to someone else; second-person address makes it clear that the hearer is the one who is responsible for keeping the law. Therefore, second-person address plays an important rhetorical role in persuading people to pay attention to all of God's laws and follow them,[11] because each individual is his covenant vassal (cf. chap. 3 above).

The introduction to the Decalogue implies a reason for second-person singular address: "I am the LORD your God, who brought you [sing.] out of the land of Egypt, out of the house of slavery" (Exod. 20:2; cf. Deut. 5:6). Among divine-human connections in the ANE, it was unique that YHWH had a special covenant relationship with each Israelite because the Deity had delivered that person. Therefore the Lord could address commandments (including through Moses) to everyone individually. Bernard M. Levinson points out that this direct personal address by God transformed former slaves into moral persons with neighbors like themselves.[12]

YHWH also made a covenant with the Israelites as a group: "And Moses took the blood and threw it on the people and said, 'Behold the blood of the covenant that the LORD has made with you [plural] in accordance with all these words'" (Exod. 24:8). So the Lord could command the Israelites in

---

11. See James W. Watts, *Reading Law: The Rhetorical Shaping of the Pentateuch*, BibSem 59 (Sheffield: Sheffield Academic, 1999), 62–65.

12. Bernard M. Levinson, *"The Right Chorale": Studies in Biblical Law and Interpretation*, FAT 54 (Tübingen: Mohr Siebeck, 2008), 51.

second-person plural, as in these examples: "You [plural] shall not mistreat any widow or fatherless child" (Exod. 22:22 [22:21 MT]). "You [plural] shall be holy, for I the LORD your God am holy" (Lev. 19:2). "You [plural] are the sons of the LORD your God. You [plural] shall not cut yourselves or make any baldness on your foreheads for the dead" (Deut. 14:1).

Notice that this last law in Deut. 14 reminds the Israelites of their special connection with him as "sons" before prohibiting certain actions. The parent-child nature of the divine-human relationship indicates that it involves privilege but also accountability.

Second-person feminine-singular address appears in pentateuchal law only within part of a law in the priest's speech to the suspected adulteress in which he stipulates the wording of the oath that she takes (Num. 5:19–22). Second-person feminine-plural address does not occur in this corpus.[13]

Lack of such feminine address elsewhere in pentateuchal legal texts can be explained by two factors. First, masculine is the generic gender (see above), so in second person, "You [masc. sing.] shall not commit adultery" (Exod. 20:14) applies to women as well as men (cf. Lev. 20:10; Num. 5:11–31; Deut. 22:22). Second, some laws primarily address male heads of households.

Unconditional (Apodictic) and Conditional (Casuistic) Formulations

Albrecht Alt pointed out two basic kinds of formulation in OT legal texts: "apodictic" (or "apodeictic") and "casuistic."[14] An "apodictic" formulation is "an unconditional, categorical assertion" of something that is certainly right or wrong,[15] such as the commandment that states the principle "You shall not steal" (Exod. 20:15). On the other hand, a "casuistic" or "case" law is conditional, focusing on application of a principle if/when a kind of situation arises. It "defines a specific case, distinguishes it carefully from other similar cases, and stipulates the legal consequences."[16] For example, "If a man steals an ox or a sheep, and kills it or sells it, he shall repay five oxen for an ox, and four sheep for a sheep" (Exod. 22:1 [21:37 MT]).

The OT law texts do not indicate that apodictic laws, which are unconditional and categorical, carry greater divine authority than casuistic laws,

13. Second-person feminine address (singular or plural) does not appear in the laws of Ezek. 43:18–46:24.
14. Albrecht Alt, "The Origins of Israelite Law," in *Essays on Old Testament History and Religion*, trans. R. A. Wilson, BibSem (original German ed., 1934; Sheffield: JSOT Press, 1989), 88–132.
15. Dale Patrick, *Old Testament Law* (Atlanta: John Knox, 1985), 21.
16. Ibid.

which are circumstantial. According to the Pentateuch, both kinds came from YHWH, and he holds his people accountable for obeying all of his laws (e.g., Lev. 26:3, 14–15; Num. 15:22–23; Deut. 28:1, 15).

A casuistic law can carry the same principle as an apodictic law. For example, the casuistic law in Lev. 24:17 reads: "If anyone kills [lit., "strikes"] any human being, he shall be put to death" (NJPS). This reiterates the idea of the apodictic law in Exod. 20:13, "You shall not murder," except that Lev. 24:17 specifies a particular kind of murder, by striking, and stipulates capital punishment. Exodus 21:12, "Whoever strikes a man so that he dies shall be put to death," employs a kind of unconditional formulation (see below) to convey basically the same legal content as Lev. 24:17.

In general, OT law tends to employ apodictic formulations for relatively shorter, simpler laws, whatever their subject matter may be, and casuistic formulations for laws that include detailed specifications, especially if these include variable factors. Thus the apodictic commandment "You shall not murder" (Exod. 20:13) is extremely short, containing only two Hebrew words. However, the murder law of Exod. 21:20, with additional details that narrow the scope of application, is casuistic: "When a man strikes his slave, male or female, with a rod and the slave dies under his hand, he shall be avenged." This law contains the social status of the victim (here a slave), the instrument of striking (rod), the timing of death (during a beating), and the manner of punishment: vengeance, which is likely capital punishment (see chap. 9).

Apodictic Laws

Apodictic laws appear in all of the major biblical law collections (e.g., Exod. 20:3; 22:18; Lev. 2:13; 18:7; Deut. 16:19). The Decalogue (Exod. 20; Deut. 5), which represents the core of the covenant stipulations (Exod. 34:28; Deut. 4:13), consists entirely of apodictic commandments, two of which are stated in positive terms—remember/observe the Sabbath (Exod. 20:8; Deut. 5:12) and honor parents (Exod. 20:12; Deut. 5:16)—and the rest are negative ("You shall have no . . ." or "You shall not . . ."), allowing anything except the specified behavior (see above).

The unconditional "apodictic" category can be divided into two subcategories.[17] The first can be termed "addressed commandments," commands that are directly addressed to the hearer(s) in the second person, such as "You shall not murder" (Exod. 20:13), or the infinitive absolute functioning as an

17. Cf. Hans Jochen Boecker, *Law and the Administration of Justice in the Old Testament and Ancient East*, trans. Jeremy Moiser (Minneapolis: Augsburg, 1980), 192–201; Patrick, *Old Testament Law*, 23.

imperative, as in "Remember [*zakor*] the Sabbath day" (v. 8). In the second subcategory are "formulations in the third person that stipulate capital punishment or pronounce a curse," such as "Whoever strikes [*hiphil* participle of *n-k-h*] a man so that he dies shall be put to death" (21:12).[18] Like Exod. 20:13, the capital crime law of 21:12 forbids murder. However, there are three differences between these laws: the formulation (*lo'* + imperfect verb versus participle), 21:12 being limited to murder by striking, and the same law adding specification of capital punishment.

An apodictic-addressed commandment can be introduced in several ways:

1. Imperative verb, as in "Honor [*kabbed*] your father and your mother" (Exod. 20:12; Deut. 5:16).[19]

2. Infinitive absolute with an imperatival sense, as in "Remember [*zakor*] the Sabbath day" (Exod. 20:8).[20]

3. Second-person imperfect verb, as in "Above all you shall keep [*tishmoru*] my Sabbaths" (31:13). In a negative formulation the negative particle *lo'* precedes the verb, as in "You shall not [*lo'*] steal [*tignov*]" (20:15) and "You shall not [*lo'*] uncover [tegalleh] the nakedness of your father's wife" (Lev. 18:8).

Such a commandment can simply state what the addressed party is required or forbidden to do (e.g., Exod. 20:15). However, an apodictic-addressed commandment can expand in several kinds of ways, as illustrated in the Decalogue commandment concerning idolatry (vv. 4–6), which begins: "You shall not make for yourself a carved image." The following words emphasize the comprehensiveness of the prohibition by referring to the cosmic domains that ANE gods were believed to inhabit: "or any likeness of anything that is in heaven above, or that is in the earth beneath, or that is in the water under the earth." After forbidding manufacture of any new idol, the law adds a

18. A law can contain both kinds of formulation, as in Exod. 30:31–33, where the addressed commandment—"You shall make no other like it in composition" (v. 32)—is followed by a formulation stipulating a curse: "Whoever compounds any like it or whoever puts any of it on an outsider shall be cut off from his people" (v. 33).

19. The *piel* imperative form *kabbed* is identical to the form of the infinitive absolute (cf. Num. 22:17; 24:11, clearly infinitive absolute preceding and reinforcing the finite verb from the same root). So it is theoretically possible that *kabbed* at the beginning of the fifth commandment (Exod. 20:12; Deut. 5:16) could be understood as an infinitive absolute to match the infinitive absolute *zakor/shamor* at the beginning of the preceding fourth commandment, which is the only other commandment formulated in positive terms (Exod. 20:8; Deut. 5:12). Richard M. Davidson, personal communication.

20. Cf. the infinitive absolute in Deut. 5:12: "Observe [*shamor*] the Sabbath day." On use of the infinitive absolute for commands, see Waltke and O'Connor, *Introduction*, 593–94 (§35.5.1).

prohibition against use of such an object that is already in existence: "You shall not bow down to them or serve them" (v. 5a).

The law ends with a "motive clause" (vv. 5b–6) that expresses the reason why the addressee should comply with the law. In this instance the reason involves negative and positive aspects in relation to the jealous/zealous and loving character of YHWH, with warning of punishment for disloyalty, such as that which would be shown by making or worshiping an idol, and encouragement for loyalty.

A third-person formulation stipulating capital punishment or pronouncing a curse can be introduced as follows:

1. Active participle, as in "Whoever strikes [*makkeh*] his father or his mother shall be put to death" (Exod. 21:15).
2. Passive participle, as in "Cursed [*'arur*] be anyone who dishonors his father or his mother" (Deut. 27:16).
3. An expression denoting a person + relative pronoun + imperfect verb, as in "The man [*'ish*] who [*'asher*] lies [*yishkav*] with his father's wife has uncovered his father's nakedness; both of them shall surely be put to death. Their blood shall be upon them" (Lev. 20:11 NKJV).[21]

A law with this kind of formulation can stipulate a result other than capital punishment or a curse. For example, "Anyone [*kol*] in the open field who [*'asher*] touches [*yigga'*] a person slain by the sword, or who died naturally, or a human bone or a grave, will be unclean for seven days" (Num. 19:16 CEB). Here a corpse-contaminated person does not commit a crime and only incurs a temporary period of physical ritual impurity. So we can broaden this (sub)category of apodictic formulation to "formulations stipulating consequences."

By itself, a formulation stipulating a consequence is generally quite short because at least one effect or consequence (e.g., "has uncovered his father's nakedness," Lev. 20:11; "cursed," Deut. 27:16) is included in the same grammatical clause as identification of the subject's action. Such a formulation can constitute a self-standing law, as in "Whoever lies with an animal shall be put to death" (Exod. 22:19 [22:18 MT]). However, it can form part of a larger law, as in Exod. 21:12–14, where "Whoever strikes a man so that he dies shall be put to death" is followed by a casuistically formulated exception: "But if [*'asher*] he did not lie in wait for him . . ." This law ends with a

---

21. The ESV translates a number of laws in this category as if they were casuistic, introduced by "if" (Lev. 20:6, 10–18, 20–21).

casuistic contrast to the exception: "But if [*ki*] a man willfully attacks another to kill him by cunning, you shall take him from my altar, that he may die."[22]

Casuistic Laws

Casuistic laws appear in all of the major biblical law collections (e.g., Exod. 21:2–6; Lev. 1:3–9; 19:20–22; Deut. 21:15–17) except for the Decalogue. The first part of a casuistic law, which identifies the condition = circumstances/situation in view and thereby defines the law's scope of application, is called the "protasis." The second part, which stipulates the consequence, is termed the "apodosis." So the pattern is as follows:

> If/When so-and-so does such-and-such, (*protasis*)
> he shall be subject to such-and-such a result. (*apodosis*)

Dale Patrick has shown that the "casuistic" category can be subdivided into what he calls "casuistic remedial law" and "casuistic primary law": "One species of casuistic law is *remedial*—the case is described in the protasis (*if* clause), and the legal remedy (usually a penalty for violation of rights) is prescribed in the apodosis. The other species of casuistic law is *primary law*—the protasis describes a legal relationship, and the apodosis prescribes the terms of the relationship (rights and duties before violation)."[23] Here is an example of a "casuistic remedial law":

> If a man steals an ox or a sheep, and kills it or sells it, (*protasis*, case/crime)
> he shall repay five oxen for an ox, and four sheep for a sheep. (*apodosis*, legal remedy/penalty; Exod. 22:1 [21:37 MT])

Notice that the third-person address is impersonal. On the other hand, a "casuistic primary law" is as follows:

> If your brother becomes poor and cannot maintain himself with you, (*protasis*, legal relationship)
> you shall support him as though he were a stranger and a sojourner, and he shall live with you. (*apodosis*, terms of the relationship; Lev. 25:35)

22. In Exod. 30:31–33 the formulation stipulating a consequence (beginning "Whoever") comes at the end of the law, following introduction of the topic ("This shall be my holy anointing oil") and the addressed commands ("It shall not be poured, . . . and you shall make no other like it").

23. Patrick, *Old Testament Law*, 23, emphasis original.

This casuistic law is personally addressed in the second person.[24]

Ritual law contains another category of casuistic formulation, which we can term "casuistic procedural law." For instance, a pericope regarding grain offerings in Lev. 2:1–3 begins:

When [*ki*] anyone brings a grain offering as an offering to the LORD,
  (*protasis*)
his offering shall be of fine flour. (*apodosis*)

The protasis (v. 1aα) specifies the kind of procedure in view, in this instance a kind of sacrificial ritual, and the apodosis (vv. 1aβ–3) provides instructions for the procedure of preparing and offering the item to YHWH. This case does not fit in either of Patrick's categories, because the apodosis does not prescribe a legal remedy (the grain offering is not even expiatory) or terms of a relationship. Rather, it explains how to properly carry out a kind of worship.[25]

A casuistic formulation, whether it belongs to the remedial, primary, or procedural subcategory, begins with a conditional clause that constitutes or introduces the protasis. This clause commences with a word expressing a condition that can mean "when" or "if":

1. *ki*, as in "When [*ki*] you buy a Hebrew slave . . ." (Exod. 21:2).
2. *'im*, as in "If [*'im*] you lend money to any of my people with you who is poor . . ." (Exod. 22:25 [22:24 MT]).
3. *'asher*, as in "When [*'asher*] a leader sins . . ." (Lev. 4:22).[26]

A casuistic law can be short and simple:

"If [*ki*] anyone kills any human being, (*protasis*)
he shall be put to death." (*apodosis*; Lev. 24:17 NJPS)

However, this kind of law can be expanded by adding a series of subcases to deal with variable circumstances, as in the slave law of Exod. 21:2–6, which

24. Cf. ibid., 23–24.
25. Such a prescriptive procedural law can guide many performances of the procedure. By contrast, a descriptive narrative text recounts what happens during a single performance (e.g., Lev. 8–10, with chap. 8 fulfilling the instructions in Exod. 29). Regarding the distinction between prescriptive and descriptive ritual texts, see Baruch A. Levine, "The Descriptive Tabernacle Texts of the Pentateuch," *JAOS* 85 (1965): 307–18; Baruch Levine and William W. Hallo, "Offerings to the Temple Gates at Ur," *HUCA* 38 (1967): 17–58.
26. Here *'asher* is the functional equivalent of *'im*, "if," in Lev. 4:3, 13, 27.

is quoted below to show its format. As is common in Hebrew legal style, the main case is introduced by *ki*, "When/If," and the subcases begin with *'im*, "If."

Main Case:

> When [*ki*] you buy a Hebrew slave, (*protasis*)
>> he shall serve six years, and in the seventh he shall go out free, for nothing. (*apodosis*)

Subcases:

> If [*'im*] he comes in single, (*protasis*)
>> he shall go out single; (*apodosis*)
> if [*'im*] he comes in married, (*protasis*)
>> then his wife shall go out with him. (*apodosis*)
> If [*'im*] his master gives him a wife and she bears him sons or daughters, (*protasis*)
>> the wife and her children shall be her master's, and he shall go out alone. (*apodosis*)
> But if [*'im*] the slave plainly says, "I love my master, my wife, and my children; I will not go out free," (*protasis*)
>> then his master shall bring him to God, and he shall bring him to the door or the doorpost. And his master shall bore his ear through with an awl, and he shall be his slave forever. (*apodosis*)

In this law, the subcases define the man's marital situation when his period of servitude ends and he is free to "go out" from this arrangement. The final subcase indicates a circumstance under which the man chooses not to go out, even though the main case states that he has the right to do so.[27]

Properly recognizing the structure of a casuistic law can be crucial for grasping its intent. An important example is the law of Deut. 24:1–4:

> When [*ki*] a man takes a wife and marries her, if [*'im*] then she finds no favor in his eyes because he has found some indecency in her, and he writes her a certificate of divorce and puts it in her hand and sends her out of his house, and she departs out of his house, and if [supplied; no Heb. word for "if" here] she goes and becomes another man's wife,
>> and the latter man hates her and writes her a certificate of divorce and puts it in her hand and sends her out of his house, (*circumstance 1*)
>> or if [*ki*] the latter man dies, who took her to be his wife, (*circumstance 2, end of protasis*)

---

27. On the location of "bring him to God" in Exod. 21:6, which could refer to action at the sanctuary, see Thomas B. Dozeman, *Commentary on Exodus*, ECC (Grand Rapids: Eerdmans, 2009), 528–29.

> then her former husband, who sent her away, may not take her again
> to be his wife, after she has been defiled, (*apodosis*)
>
> for [*ki*] that is an abomination before the LORD. And you shall not bring
> sin upon the land that the LORD your God is giving you for an inheritance.
> (*motive*)

At first glance this appears to be a law about divorce. However, the reason
for and procedure of divorce are only mentioned in the protasis as part of
the overall scenario that is assumed, rather than stipulated in the apodosis,
which expresses the thrust of the law through what it stipulates. The apodosis,
reinforced by a motive clause, forbids a man to remarry his former wife after
he has divorced her and she has been married to another man. So the law
does not directly regulate divorce; it concerns a certain kind of remarriage
after divorce.[28] Nevertheless, by assuming that the divorce procedure involves
a certificate of divorce that the man gives to his wife, the law validates this
procedure as normative (cf. Matt. 5:31; 19:7).

Casuistic elements can structure and thereby reveal the logical trajectory of a sizable body of legal material that covers more than one chapter.
Leviticus 1:2 presents a main case introduced by *ki*: "When [*ki*] any of you
present a livestock offering [*qorban*] to the LORD, you can present it from
either the herd or the flock" (CEB).[29] This is followed by two subcases, each
introduced by *'im*, in which the long apodoses prescribe the procedures for
burnt offerings of herd animals (vv. 3–9) and flock animals (vv. 10–13). Additional subcases of (voluntary individual) livestock offerings, also introduced
by *'im*, appear in chapter 3, prescribing well-being offerings of herd animals
(vv. 1–5) and flock animals (vv. 6–16). Here the category of flock animals
is further subdivided into subsubcases, each introduced by *'im*, providing
instructions for sacrifices of sheep, which have fat tails (vv. 7–11), and goats,
which do not (vv. 12–16).

Between the subcases in Lev. 1:3–13 and those in chapter 3, there are intervening instructions regarding offering (*qorban*) categories that are not
subcases of livestock offerings. These are burnt offerings of birds (1:14–17)
and grain offerings (chap. 2).

---

28. Cf. Peter C. Craigie, *The Book of Deuteronomy*, NICOT (Grand Rapids: Eerdmans,
1976), 304–5; J. Carl Laney, "Deuteronomy 24:1–4 and the Issue of Divorce," *BSac* 149 (1992):
9; Daniel I. Block, *Deuteronomy*, NIV Application Commentary (Grand Rapids: Zondervan,
2012), 556–57.

29. This does not mean that every sacrificial offering (*qorban*) must be a livestock (herd
or flock) animal, because a sacrificial *qorban* could be a bird (Lev. 1:14–17) or grain (chap. 2).
Therefore "livestock" belongs not to the stipulation/apodosis (as in NKJV and ESV) but to the
condition/protasis (as correctly rendered by CEB).

Leviticus 1:2–13 (burnt offerings) and 3:1–16 (well-being offerings) belong together because they concern voluntary livestock offerings. So it is logical to ask why these units have been separated. The pericope regarding birds (1:14–17) supplements the prescriptions for burnt offerings to provide a less expensive option for the benefit of poor worshipers (cf. 5:7–10; 12:8). The instructions about grain offerings (chap. 2) logically follow those regarding burnt offerings according to an important organizing principle: "The progression of instructions for voluntary sacrifices (Lev. 1–3) moves from exclusive utilization by YHWH (Lev. 1, burnt offering) to increasing consumption by human beings (Lev. 2, grain offering eaten by priest [cf. 7:9–10]; Lev. 3, well-being offering eaten by priest and offerer [cf. 7:15–16, 31–36])."[30] The grain offering is "most holy" (6:17 [6:10 MT]), which explains why only a priest is permitted to eat from it (cf. 6:16–18 [6:9–11 MT]). Therefore the grain offering precedes the well-being offering, from which the offerer eats, which is not called "most holy."[31]

Recurring Formulas Expressing Consequences

Several recurring formulas in apodoses of casuistic laws indicate consistent consequences of circumstances described in protases. Use of the same formula, or variations thereof, by several laws implies that these laws are somehow related to each other. Following are introductions to three important formulas and the kinds of laws in which they appear:

1. *mot yumat*, "[he] shall surely be put to death" (e.g., Lev. 20:9).
2. *venikretah hanefesh hahi'*, "that person will be cut off" (e.g., Exod. 12:19).
3. *piel* of the root *k-p-r*, "expiate" + preposition *'al*, "on behalf of" + beneficiary, as in "Thus the priest shall make expiation [*vekipper*] for him [*'alayv*]" (e.g., Lev. 4:31 NJPS).

The first two of these state terminal penalties to be administered by the Israelite community (formula 1) or by YHWH himself (formula 2). The third expresses the redemptive goal of a sacrificial remedy that provides release

---

30. Roy Gane, "Didactic Logic and the Authorship of Leviticus," in *Current Issues in Priestly and Related Literature: The Legacy of Jacob Milgrom and Beyond*, ed. Roy E. Gane and Ada Taggar-Cohen, RBS (Atlanta: Society of Biblical Literature, 2015), 208.
31. The well-being offering is implicitly "holy" (although not "most holy") because a person in a state of physical ritual impurity is not permitted to eat it (Lev. 7:20–21).

from moral culpability or serious physical ritual impurity. Formulas 2 and 3 show considerable variation. We could legitimately represent their base forms in different ways, whether shorter and simpler (e.g., formula 3: simply *piel* of *k-p-r*, "expiate"), which takes supplementation, or longer and more complex (e.g., *vekipper ʿalayv hakohen mekhattaʾto*, "Thus the priest shall make expiation on his behalf from his sin"),[32] which can be abbreviated. For convenience and clarity, the base forms used here are those that most commonly occur.

Mot Yumat, "[He] Shall Surely Be Put to Death"

This formula of capital punishment appears in the law, "Whoever strikes a man so that he dies shall be put to death [*mot yumat*]" (Exod. 21:12).[33] The death penalty is to be administered by the Israelite community, as explicitly stated in Lev. 20:2; 24:16; Num. 15:35, which also specify stoning as the form of execution in these cases. However, in Num. 35:21 a highly motivated individual, a relative of a murdered person, is to administer the penalty on behalf of the community.

Most of the wrongs for which the penalty is *mot yumat* are clear violations of the Decalogue. The Ten Commandments themselves (Exod. 20; Deut. 5) do not indicate specific punishments,[34] but other laws in Exodus, Leviticus, and Numbers stipulate the *mot yumat* penalty for breaking principles expressed in the first eight commandments of the Decalogue (see chap. 14). For instance, the capital offenses of giving one's child to the pagan god Molech (Lev. 20:2) and practicing occult (Lev. 20:27) violate the first commandment: "You shall have no other gods before me" (Exod. 20:3).

Venikretah Hanefesh Hahiʾ, "That Person Will Be Cut Off"

In the canonical order of Scripture, this formula[35] first appears in the law of circumcision that YHWH gave to Abraham: "Any uncircumcised male who is not circumcised in the flesh of his foreskin, that person will

32. Basically Lev. 4:26 NJPS, but correcting "for his sin" to "from his sin." See Roy Gane, *Cult and Character: Purification Offerings, Day of Atonement, and Theodicy* (Winona Lake, IN: Eisenbrauns, 2005), 106–43.

33. The Hebrew construction is the *qal* infinitive absolute of *m-v-t* + *hophal* imperfect of *m-v-t*.

34. But the second and third commandments contain warnings of divine punishment (Exod. 20:5, 7; Deut. 5:9, 11).

35. *Niphal* perfect consecutive of *k-r-t* with *nefesh* as subject + third-person feminine-singular pronoun as a far demonstrative pronoun (as in Gen. 17:14).

be cut off [*venikretah hanefesh hahi'*][36] from his people [*me'ammeha*]; he has broken my covenant" (Gen. 17:14). Here the formula is followed by *me'ammeha*, "from his people," which refers to the group from which the violator is cut off.[37]

There are several variations on the formula.[38] Like the base form given here, most variations on it use passive *niphal* forms of the root *k-r-t*, and therefore they do not explicitly identify who administers the penalty. The implied agent is YHWH, as in other places where contexts indicate that he performs actions expressed by passive verbs (e.g., *venislakh lo*, "and he shall be forgiven," in Lev. 4:26, 31, 35). However, some variations of the *k-r-t* penalty formula make the agent explicit because the verb appears in the *hiphil* first-person singular with YHWH as subject, as in *vehikrati 'otah miqqerev 'ammah*, "and [I] will cut him off from among his people" (Lev. 17:10). In such instances, the modified formula follows the terrifyingly personal notice that YHWH will set his face against the person(s) who commit(s) the offense (cf. 20:3, 5, 6).[39]

The fact that the *k-r-t* penalty is directly administered by YHWH himself raises two questions: (1) What is the nature of the punishment? (2) Why doesn't the Deity have the community carry it out?

None of the laws in Exodus, Leviticus, and Numbers where the *k-r-t* formula appears describes the punishment. Nevertheless, there are some clues regarding its nature. First, the fact that the penalty is for grave wrongs suggests that it is terminal. Sacrificial expiation is available for inadvertent violations of divine commandments in Num. 15:22–29, but verses 30–31 simply condemn a defiant sinner to *k-r-t*, implying that he cannot gain absolution through a sacrificial remedy.

Second, a person who gives his child to the god Molech incurs two kinds of punishment: He is stoned to death by the community (Lev. 20:2), and YHWH adds that he will set his face "against that man and will cut him off

36. Modifying ESV, which does not translate *hanefesh hahi'* in order to avoid redundancy: "Any uncircumcised male . . . shall be cut off from his people."

37. This is the most common expression that follows the formula elsewhere (also in Lev. 7:20–21, 25, 27; 19:8; 23:29; Num. 9:13). Functionally equivalent expressions, also containing the preposition *min*, "from," + terminology referring to the covenant people, follow the formula in other passages: "from among his people" (Exod. 31:14; Num. 15:30); "from Israel" (Exod. 12:15; Num. 19:13); "from the congregation of Israel" (Exod. 12:19); "from the midst of the assembly" (Num. 19:20). A different kind of expression following the formula is "from my presence" (Lev. 22:3), which is appropriate here in a law for priests, who minister before YHWH.

38. See Exod. 30:33, 38; Lev. 17:4, 9, 14; 18:29; 20:18; 23:29; Num. 15:31.

39. Other instances of YHWH's threat to set his face against those who rebel against him occur in Lev. 26:17; Jer. 44:11; Ezek. 14:8; 15:7.

from among his people" (v. 3). This implies that the divine penalty goes beyond death; otherwise there would be no point in mentioning it, because the violator is already executed by human agency. It appears that a person who is "cut off" from (among) his people is further denied a place among them in an afterlife, which could happen if his line of descendants would cease.[40] Being "cut off" could not merely be banishment from the community, because in this case the individual is dead.

For an Israelite, forfeiture of an afterlife with his people would entail a catastrophically permanent and total loss of identity. His place in the tribal community was essential for his identity not only while he lived but also after he died. Concern for such identity after death is shown by the institution of levirate (brother-in-law) marriage to perpetuate the name, the remembered identity, of a childless dead man through a surrogate line of descendants (Gen. 38:7–11; Deut. 25:5–10; Ruth 4).[41]

Childlessness was a major problem for Israelites (cf. Gen. 15:2–3; 30:1–2; 1 Sam. 1:5–11), so it could function as severe punishment for moral crimes of incest (Lev. 20:20–21), for which the penalty in Lev. 18 is being "cut off" (vv. 14, 16, 29). The k-r-t penalty seems to mean that YHWH would see to it that the culprit's name would be extinguished in any case, sooner or later, which means that he will not even be history because there will be nothing and nobody to recollect or serve as a reminder of his name.[42]

Crimes punishable by being "cut off" tend to be especially against God himself, such as breaking his religious commandments, and/or committed in secret so that only the Deity can unerringly hold the perpetrators accountable (see chap. 14 below). Examples include failure of an Israelite male to undergo circumcision (Gen. 17:14); eating blood, meaning meat of an animal from which the blood is not drained out when it is slaughtered (Lev. 7:27; 17:10, 14); illicit (and undoubtedly secret) sexual activity (18:29); giving one's child to Molech (20:3) or failing to execute a person who does that (vv. 4–5); resorting

40. See Donald J. Wold, "The Meaning of the Biblical Penalty *Kareth*" (PhD diss., University of California, Berkeley, 1978), 251–55; Jacob Milgrom, *Leviticus 1–16: A New Translation with Introduction and Commentary*, AB 3 (New York: Doubleday, 1991), 457–60; Baruch J. Schwartz, "The Bearing of Sin in the Priestly Literature," in *Pomegranates and Golden Bells: Studies in Biblical, Jewish, and Near Eastern Ritual, Law, and Literature in Honor of Jacob Milgrom*, ed. David P. Wright, David N. Freedman, and Avi Hurvitz (Winona Lake, IN: Eisenbrauns, 1995), 13. Cf. Ps. 109:13, "May his posterity be cut off; may their names be blotted out in the next generation" (NJPS).

41. Cf. the petition of the daughters of Zelophehad that their father's name should live on in his clan by being attached to an inheritance in the promised land through an unbroken line of descendants, including through daughters in a generation that has no sons (Num. 27:1–4).

42. One variation on the k-r-t penalty formula specifies punishment sooner rather than later in a certain case of incest (Lev. 20:17).

to occult practitioners (20:6);[43] and defiant sins by which rebels cast off their allegiance to YHWH (Num. 15:30–31).

In light of the foregoing pentateuchal legal background, Dan. 9:26 is jarring: "the Messiah will be cut off [niphal of k-r-t]" (NASB). Here it appears that the Messiah (mashiakh, "Anointed One") suffers the divine penalty of forfeiting an afterlife, which would be a death beyond our ordinary death—in other words, a "second death" (cf. Rev. 2:11; 20:6, 14; 21:8). Indeed, if the Messiah in Dan. 9:26 is Christ (Greek for "Messiah/Anointed One"), it makes sense that on the cross he suffered the equivalent of the second death by being separated from his Father (Matt. 27:46) in order to bear for fallen humans the curse of sin (Gal. 3:13), which is (eternal) death (Rom. 6:23; contrasted to "eternal life"), not simply the first, temporary death that Jesus likened to sleep (John 11:11). Whereas there is no return from the second death in Rev. 20, Christ was innocent and bore the sins of others (1 Pet. 2:24; cf. Isa. 53:4–9; 2 Cor. 5:21). Therefore, he has risen from his second-death experience (Matt. 28; etc.; cf. Isa. 53:10–12).

Piel of K-P-R (Expiate) + Preposition 'Al (on behalf of) + Beneficiary

This formula appears in laws of ritual procedure, especially as the goal of expiatory sacrifices, which include burnt, purification, and reparation offerings.[44] Our concern here is with usage of the formula in clearing evils that are offensive to God from persons or things rather than with the precise semantic range of the profound and much-debated term kipper (piel of k-p-r).[45]

Most instances of the formula refer to the expiatory benefits that people receive from sacrifices offered on their behalf, which, according to the NT, prefigure salvation from sins and their results accomplished by Christ (e.g., Matt. 1:21; John 1:29; Heb. 10:1–18; 1 John 1:9). Unlike the formulas of punishment discussed above, this one expresses a merciful remedy gained through a ritual that God graciously offers in order to remove an impediment affecting the relationship between one or more faulty humans and himself. The element of mercy is especially clear in Lev. 5, where a person who commits

---

43. Cf. King Saul's secret visit to an occult medium (1 Sam. 28).

44. It is true that Lev. 17:11 refers to a kind of kipper that applies to a well-being offering, but in pentateuchal ritual law this sacrifice is not mandated in cases when persons have committed sins or incurred physical ritual impurities.

45. On kipper, see, e.g., Jay Sklar, Sin, Impurity, Sacrifice, Atonement: The Priestly Conceptions, Hebrew Bible Monographs 2 (Sheffield: Sheffield Phoenix, 2005); Milgrom, Leviticus 1–16, 1079–84; Gane, Cult and Character, 192–95; William K. Gilders, Blood Ritual in the Hebrew Bible: Meaning and Power (Baltimore: Johns Hopkins University Press, 2004), 28–29.

a certain sin "shall bear his iniquity," his culpability leading to punishment (v. 1).[46] If the individual confesses the wrong and offers a sacrifice, "the priest shall make expiation [*vekipper*] on his behalf [*'alayv*] for his sin" (v. 6 NJPS), freeing the person from condemnation and punishment (cf. v. 10, "and he shall be forgiven").

The formula appears by itself in a pericope regarding the burnt offering (Lev. 1:4),[47] without specifying (and therefore leaving open) the evil that the sacrifice removes. In prescriptions for the reparation offering, several elements can be added to the formula, including identification of the kind of victim (a ram) that serves as the instrument of expiation (5:16), the priest as the one who performs the expiation by officiating the sacrifice (5:16, 18; 6:7 [5:26 MT]), reference to the sin for which the sacrifice expiates (5:18), and the formula of divine forgiveness (*venislakh lo*, "and he shall be forgiven"; 5:16, 18; 6:7 [5:26 MT]) that is promised upon completion of the prerequisite sacrificial expiation.

Prescriptions for purification offerings on behalf of persons include the priest as subject of the verb in the *piel* of *k-p-r* + *'al* + beneficiary formula[48] plus the forgiveness formula (*venislakh lo*) if the sacrifice remedies a sin— that is, a moral fault that violates a divine command (e.g., Lev. 4:20, 31). If the sacrifice is to remove a severe physical ritual impurity—such as a male or female genital flow (Lev. 12, 15), surface disease (so-called leprosy; Lev. 14),[49] or corpse contamination (Num. 19)—the result is a state of purity (e.g., *ve-taharah*, "and then she shall be clean [pure]," Lev. 12:7, cf. v. 8)[50] rather than forgiveness. This indicates that physical ritual impurities themselves were not sins, although violations of divine commands concerning them were sins (e.g., 7:20–21; 22:3, 8–9; Num. 19:13, 20). Such impurities represented heightened manifestations of the birth-to-death cycle of mortality[51] resulting from sin (cf. Rom. 6:23), the state of sinfulness, which had to be kept separate from the pure sphere of holiness surrounding and associated with God (e.g., Lev. 7:20–21; 15:31), who is the eternally living life-giver (e.g., Gen. 1–2; Deut. 30:20; Dan. 5:23, "in whose hand is your breath"; 1 Tim. 6:16).[52]

46. Schwartz, "Bearing of Sin," 8–15.
47. With the *piel* of *k-p-r* as an infinitive: "to expiate for him" (Lev. 1:4, my trans.).
48. With the verb in perfect consecutive form.
49. On *tsara'at*, which is not leprosy (Hansen's disease), see Milgrom, *Leviticus 1–16*, 774–76, 816–26. Milgrom calls it "scale disease" when it appears on human skin (e.g., 768–71, 816). Because *tsara'at* can also refer to mold or fungus/mildew infestations of fabrics (Lev. 13:47–59) and walls of houses (14:33–53), it could be characterized more broadly as "surface disease."
50. Trans. ibid., 742.
51. Hyam Maccoby, *Ritual and Morality: The Ritual Purity System and its Place in Judaism* (Cambridge: Cambridge University Press, 1999), 49, cf. 31–32, 48, 50, 207–8.
52. Cf. Milgrom, *Leviticus 1–16*, 766–68, 1000–1003.

The *piel* of *k-p-r* + *'al* + beneficiary formula is often followed by one of two prepositions, *'al* or *min*, plus specification of the sin or impurity that is expiated. In this context, *'al* means "concerning/for," as in *'al-khatta'to 'asher-khata'*, "for [concerning] the sin which he has committed" (Lev. 4:35). The preposition *min*, "from" (privative usage), + term for evil (sin or impurity) indicates the evil impediment to the divine-human relationship that the expiation removes from the offerer, as in *mekhatta'to*, "from his sin" (4:26; 5:6, 10; my trans.).[53]

The beneficiary in the formula can also be an object or structure connected to humans from which evil is removed by a ritual. If this is part of God's sanctuary, which is polluted by faults and faultiness of the human community (e.g., Lev. 16:16b), it is purged by purification offerings. Parts of the sanctuary purged in this way are the outer altar (Exod. 29:36, 37; Lev. 8:15; 16:18); the altar of incense (Exod. 30:10); the outer sanctum (Lev. 16:16b); and the inner sanctum (vv. 14–16a).[54] In Lev. 14:48–53 an elimination ritual using two birds purges an ordinary house of impurity, analogous to human impurity, that is caused by a kind of surface disease (fungus/mildew).

Motivational Elements

The OT laws motivate their hearers/readers to comply with them in several ways, such as through statements of their divine origin and authority, explanations showing that they are reasonable and just, promises of divine blessings for obedience, and stipulations of punishments for violations. Such elements—which themselves inculcate values such as loyalty, accountability, and justice in the process of persuading people to keep laws based on a variety of values—are conveyed through "motive clauses" that express rationales behind laws, as in the following sections.[55] Such motive clauses can be distinguished from broader exhortations that summon people to obey groups of laws (e.g., Deut. 12:28; 13:4 [13:5 MT]).[56]

---

53. Cf. Gane, *Cult and Character*, 106–43; Gane, "Privative Preposition *min* in Purification Offering Pericopes and the Changing Face of 'Dorian Gray,'" *JBL* 127 (2008): 209–22.

54. When the beneficiary is nonhuman, the formula can be varied by using the direct object marker *'et* (Lev. 16:20, 33) instead of the preposition *'al* following the *piel* of *k-p-r*. Regarding ritual purgation of the sanctuary on the Day of Atonement and its theological significance, see Gane, *Cult and Character*, 217–41, 267–333.

55. Motive clauses are subordinate legal clauses, not limited to single grammatical clauses, that are attached to legal prescriptions. On motive clauses in OT law, see Rifat Sonsino, *Motive Clauses in Hebrew Law: Biblical Forms and Near Eastern Parallels*, SBLDS 45 (Chico, CA: Scholars Press, 1980), esp. 65–152; Watts, *Reading Law*, 65–67.

56. Sonsino, *Motive Clauses*, 66–69.

Attribution to YHWH

Old Testament laws are presented as addressed to Israel from YHWH, whether directly (e.g., Gen. 9:4–6; Exod. 20:1) or through his representative, Moses (e.g., Deut. 12:1). Some laws emphasize this divine authority by including the expression "I am the LORD (your God)," which appears as a refrain in the Holiness Code (Lev. 18:2, 4–6, 21, 30; 19:3–4; etc.). Such attributions to YHWH place the laws within the narrative framework of the Pentateuch, in which YHWH displays awesome power (e.g., Exod. 7–14, 19).

The connection to the narratives is reinforced by numerous references to Egypt, from which YHWH delivered the Israelites, as in the historical prologue to the Ten Commandments (Exod. 20:2) and the motive clause in Lev. 11:45: "For I am the LORD who brought you up out of the land of Egypt to be your God" (cf. 19:36; 22:33; 25:38; Deut. 13:5, 10; 20:1; etc.). Because of YHWH's power and beneficence on their behalf, his people should be grateful and loyal to him, ready to do his will, and they should also be afraid to disregard the commands of such a powerful being, who can use his superhuman abilities to hold them accountable (e.g., Num. 16).

The Lord's demonstration of grace for his people and his ongoing concern for afflicted or vulnerable individuals should motivate them to follow his example of justice and mercy. For example, if they take someone's "cloak in pledge," they should return it before nightfall so that the person can sleep in it, lest that person cry to the Lord, who promises, "I will hear, for I am compassionate" (Exod. 22:26–27 [22:25–26 MT]). In other words, Israelites should be compassionate like YHWH (cf. Deut. 10:18–19).

Explanation of Logical Justice

Some laws contain explanations of their logic and justice in terms of cause and effect, illustrating the claim that all of YHWH's commandments are wise, sensible, righteous, and for the good of his people (Deut. 4:6, 8; 10:13), so that those who keep them "shall live by them" (Lev. 18:5). Following are some examples.[57]

"You shall not wrong a sojourner or oppress him, for you were sojourners in the land of Egypt" (Exod. 22:21 [22:20 MT]). The motive clause, "for you were sojourners," reminds the Israelites to treat others as they wish to be treated when they are in a similar situation (cf. Lev. 19:34; Deut. 15:15; 24:22). This kind of empathetic justice is related to the ethic of reciprocity in Jesus's Golden Rule: "So whatever you wish that others would do to

---

57. Some other examples include Deut. 20:19; 22:8; 25:3.

you, do also to them, for this is the Law and the Prophets" (Matt. 7:12; cf. Luke 6:31).[58]

Exodus 22 stipulates that an outer garment (cloak/mantle) taken from a poor person as a pledge for a loan must be returned before nightfall (vv. 25–26 [vv. 24–25 MT]). The reason is logical in humanitarian terms: "for that is his only covering, and it is his cloak for his body; in what else shall he sleep?" (v. 27 [v. 26 MT]; cf. Deut. 24:13). Avoidance of physical discomfort for the borrower takes precedence over the financial right of the lender.

If an Israelite is unable to maintain an independent livelihood and sells himself to another Israelite or to a resident alien, the person who acquires his service is to treat him as a temporary hired worker, not as a slave (Lev. 25:39–41, 43, 47, 53–54).[59] YHWH states the reason: "For they are my servants, whom I brought out of the land of Egypt; they shall not be sold as slaves" (v. 42; cf. v. 55). Because the Lord redeemed the Israelites to freedom, they belong to him, and therefore he has the right to declare that they never will be slaves again. To be a servant of God is to be free!

In Deut. 15 a male or female Hebrew debt-servant is to be released in the seventh year after (presumably a maximum of) six years of service (v. 12). Verse 18 supplies a financial explanation to encourage the master's willingness to let the bond servant go: "It shall not seem hard to you when you let him go free from you, for at half the cost of a hired worker he has served you six years." In other words, you already have gotten a good deal, so be satisfied with it! Additionally, this law commands the master: "You shall furnish him liberally out of your flock, out of your threshing floor, and out of your winepress. As the LORD your God has blessed you, you shall give to him" (v. 14). The amount of this parting bonus, which would smooth the transition to independent life, is variable according to the master's assessment of what he can afford in accordance with God's blessing in the past. It is reasonable and just for God to ask his people to pass on some of the blessings that they have received from him.[60]

Divine Blessings

Some laws offer divine blessings to those who obey, including long life in the land of Israel for those who honor their parents (Exod. 20:12) and pursue

---

58. The Babylonian Talmud cites a similar concise summary by Hillel, an older contemporary of Jesus: "That which is hateful to you, do not do to your fellow. That is the whole Torah; the rest is the explanation; go and learn" (b. Shabbat 31a).

59. See further in chap. 13 below.

60. Cf. Matt. 10:8, "You received without paying; give without pay."

only justice in court (Deut. 16:20), and for a future king who follows God's instructions (Deut. 17:20). Deuteronomy 23:20 (23:21 MT) forbids an Israelite to charge his "brother" (fellow Israelite) interest "that the LORD your God may bless you in all that you undertake in the land that you are entering to take possession of it."

A farmer at harvesttime who forgets a sheaf in the field is to leave it for a needy resident alien, fatherless child, or widow so that the Lord will bless him in all the work of his hands (Deut. 24:19).[61] This blessing encourages the farmer to be generous in spite of the fact that the law cannot be enforced by human beings. Similarly, Deut. 15 promises divine blessing to creditors who freely loan and grant debt release and to masters who free debt-servants in accordance with YHWH's instructions (vv. 4, 6, 10, 18).

Deuteronomy 15 does not specify penalties for violation that are to be administered by the human legal system, perhaps because they would be difficult to enforce against socially powerful individuals who possess the means to lend and acquire slaves. Rather, these commands directly hold such people accountable to the Lord for compassionate treatment of their vulnerable neighbors. Verses 9–10 are a tour de force of persuasion concerning the most challenging aspect of YHWH's demands:

> Take care lest there be an unworthy thought in your heart and you say, "The seventh year, the year of release is near," and your eye look grudgingly on your poor brother, and you give him nothing, and he cry to the LORD against you, and you be guilty of sin. You shall give to him freely, and your heart shall not be grudging when you give to him, because for this the LORD your God will bless you in all your work and in all that you undertake.

Thus a person with means is to extend a loan to his poor fellow Israelite that would likely turn out to be an outright gift because it probably would be released by statute before it could be paid off. From a human financial standpoint, the law is impractical, and scholars tend to view it as utopian.[62] However, the fellow-Israelite borrower is called "your . . . brother," reminding the lender of his obligation to invest in someone who belongs to his extended

---

61. Cf. Deut. 14:28–29 of sharing tithe with landless Levites, resident aliens, fatherless children, and widows.

62. E.g., Walter J. Houston, *Contending for Justice: Ideologies and Theologies of Social Justice in the Old Testament*, LHBOTS 428 (London: T&T Clark, 2006), 174–75; Raymond Westbrook, *Law from the Tigris to the Tiber: The Writings of Raymond Westbrook*, ed. Bruce Wells and Rachel Magdalene, 2 vols. (Winona Lake, IN: Eisenbrauns, 2009), 1:158–59; Douglas A. Knight, *Law, Power, and Justice in Ancient Israel*, LAI (Louisville: Westminster John Knox, 2011), 221.

family. Moreover, the perspective of the law is not limited to ordinary human economics, because God promises to more than make up for loss of the loaned resources. So whether or not one grants such a loan depends upon trust, or lack thereof, in God's promise of blessing. The law is a test of faith.

The Sabbatical Year prohibition against sowing or reaping crops (Lev. 25:4–7) also presents a test of faith in God's blessing, which he specifies in this case: "And if you say, 'What shall we eat in the seventh year, if we may not sow or gather in our crop?' I will command my blessing on you in the sixth year, so that it will produce a crop sufficient for three years. When you sow in the eighth year, you will be eating some of the old crop; you shall eat the old until the ninth year, when its crop arrives" (vv. 20–22).

Such blessings promised in individual laws illustrate positive consequences of obedience to all of YHWH's directives, which he offers in the conditional covenant blessings (Lev. 26:3–13; Deut. 28:1–14).

Warnings

Many laws motivate by including warnings, including stipulations of punishments, on those who violate them. Thus the two legal formulas discussed above—*mot yumat* and *venikretah hanefesh hahi'*—state terminal punishments to be administered by the community (death, usually by stoning) and by YHWH, respectively. Examples of other kinds of penalties are retaliatory punishment (lex talionis, Lev. 24:19–20; Deut. 19:19–21); being burned (Lev. 20:14; 21:9); having one's hand cut off (Deut. 25:11–12); beating (Deut. 25:2–3); fines (Exod. 22:1, 4, 7, 9 [21:37; 22:3, 6, 8 MT]), with debt servitude for inability to pay a fine (22:3 [22:2 MT]); and divinely inflicted childlessness (Lev. 20:20–21).[63]

Implicit or explicit divine threats appear in some social-justice laws that would be difficult for the human community to adequately enforce, injustices caused by disparities in social and economic power between oppressors and the vulnerable persons whom they exploit.[64] In Exod. 22:27 [22:26 MT] the Lord warns a lender that if he keeps the outer garment of a poor person in pledge beyond nightfall, "if he cries to me, I will hear, for I am compassionate." This implies the possibility that divine aid for the borrower may have negative consequences for the lender. Such a possibility is stronger in Deut. 24:15, where the employer of a day laborer is warned to comply with the rule to pay him the same day, "lest he cry against you to the LORD, and you be guilty of sin." Exodus 22:22–24 (22:21–23 MT) leaves no shred of doubt regarding

---

63. On such punishments and divine justice, see chap. 14 below.
64. On social justice in OT law, see chap. 13 below.

divine punishment that fits social-justice crimes: "You shall not mistreat any widow or fatherless child. If you do mistreat them, and they cry out to me, I will surely hear their cry, and my wrath will burn, and I will kill you with the sword, and your wives shall become widows and your children fatherless."

Extended exhortations following series of laws in Lev. 18 and 20 warn the Israelites against violating these prohibitions by engaging in detestable behaviors (esp. sexual immorality and idolatry) practiced by the people of Canaan, whom the Lord was driving out before his people (18:24–30 and 20:22–26). If the Israelites would do these things, the promised land would "vomit" them out (18:28; 20:22) as it vomited out its previous inhabitants (18:25, 28). This is a conditional divine threat of corporate exile, the same punishment that figures prominently at the appalling climax of the covenant curses (26:33–35, 38–39, 41, 43–44; cf. Deut. 28:36, 41, 63–68). Thus, as with divine blessings (see above), divine punishments in individual laws illustrate and operate within the framework of total covenant accountability to God (e.g., Lev. 26; Deut. 28).

6

Historical Contexts Illuminating Old Testament Laws

Biblical laws express or encapsulate values and principles that transcend cultures, but God did not give them in a cultural vacuum. He communicated them to certain real ANE people within their life setting in order to address their needs in ways that they would understand. Their cultural environment was similar to ours in some ways but significantly different in others. Modern readers can easily comprehend laws such as the Ten Commandments (Exod. 20; Deut. 5), which express moral principles with only minor references to cultural elements (Exod. 20:10, 17, servants and livestock; cf. Deut. 5:14, 21). However, other laws are not so transparent if they involve situations, aspects of worldview, or cultural institutions (e.g., levirate marriage; see below) that were part of ancient life but are unfamiliar to us.

The present chapter facilitates understanding of biblical laws by introducing their historical background in terms of ancient Israelite social and legal culture, legal developments relating to changing circumstances, and some relationships between OT law and other ANE legal systems.

Ancient Israelite Social Culture

Tribal Society

The Israelite nation was composed of a hierarchical extended family of successive generations descended from Jacob/Israel, plus other people who joined it in various ways (see below). The structure of the hierarchy was based on genealogy, with tribes (*shevet/matteh*, the largest subdivisions) descending from Jacob's sons, and clans (*mishpakhah*, major subdivisions of tribes) stemming from Jacob's grandsons (Exod. 6:14–19; cf. 1 Sam. 10:21). The clans were composed of "father's house" (*bet 'av* or simply *bayit*, "[father's/ancestral] house") units, which were extended family "households" that contained nuclear families (see below).[1] Heredity, which determined tribal and clan affiliation, was patrilineal.

The process of elimination by which Achan was identified as the culprit who misappropriated spoil from Jericho that was devoted to sacral destruction (Josh. 7:1) illustrates the patrilineal tribal hierarchy: "Whichever tribe [*shevet*] the LORD indicates shall come forward by clans; the clan [*mishpakhah*] that the LORD indicates shall come forward by ancestral houses, and the ancestral house [*bayit*] that the LORD indicates shall come forward man by man" (v. 14 NJPS). When this procedure was carried out (vv. 16–18), it identified the tribe of Judah, the clan of Zerah (son of Judah; Num. 26:20), and the ancestral house of Zabdi (grandfather of Achan; Josh. 7:1).[2]

Affiliations within the Israelite tribal structure determined roles and responsibilities of individuals. Members of the same tribe were numbered together in military censuses (Num. 1, 26), camped and marched together in the wilderness (Num. 2–3), went to war together (e.g., Num. 31:4–6; 1 Chron. 12:23–37), and inherited territories in Canaan together (Num. 26:52–56; Josh. 13–19). The tribe of Levi, including the priests, was not included in the army and did not inherit a territory in Canaan (Num. 1:47–49; 18:20, 24; Josh. 14:3–4; 18:7),[3] but members of each Levite clan were to camp, march, and provide service to the sanctuary together (Num. 1:50–53; 3–4).

Leadership of the tribes and their subunits was hierarchical, with a representative head/chief (*ro'sh/nasi'*, Num. 1:4–16; 13:2–16; 17:2–6 [17:17–21 MT]) and several levels of judicial, army, and administrative officers serving each tribe (Exod. 18:21–26; Num. 31:14, 48, 52, 54; Deut. 1:9–15). Tribal elders (plural of *zaqen*) played important roles in representing, governing, advocating for, and administering justice to their people throughout ancient Israelite history (e.g., Exod. 3:16; Num. 11:16, 24–25; Deut. 19:12; 21:2–4; 1 Sam. 8:4; 2 Kings 23:1; Ezra 10:14). Cultic leadership was also linked to tribal hierarchy, with the high priest as the head of the tribe of Levi (Num. 17:2–3 [17:17–18 MT]),

---

1. Cf. Daniel I. Block, "Marriage and Family in Ancient Israel," in *Marriage and Family in the Biblical World*, ed. Ken M. Campbell (Downers Grove, IL: IVP Academic, 2003), 35–40.
2. Cf. identification of Saul in 1 Sam. 10:20–21.
3. Instead of a territory, the Levite tribe received sacred contributions and cities (Num. 18, 35; Josh. 21).

other descendants of Aaron assisting him as ordinary priests (e.g., Lev. 9), and the rest of the tribe of Levi assisting the priests (Num. 3:6–7; 8:19; 18:2–3).

Once the Israelite monarchy was established, the king, his family, nobles, and bureaucratic hierarchy dominated many aspects of Israelite society and weakened tribal leadership. During that time, the disparity between wealthy and poor Israelites greatly increased (see esp. the books of Kings and Chronicles).

The foundation of Israelite tribal society was the *bet 'av*, "father's house" (Num. 1:2, 4, 18, 20, etc.), or simply *bayit* (Josh. 7:14), "ancestral house" (NJPS; see above) or "household" (ESV), the lowest/smallest unit of extended family. It typically consisted of three to five generations, including the father of the family (paterfamilias), who was the oldest living male and served as the family head; his wife; their married sons and their wives; any unmarried children, along with married or unmarried grandchildren as well as great-grandchildren, and so forth.[4] Such a "household" could consist of "fifty to a hundred people living in close proximity" in compounds of dwellings around common courtyards, as shown by archaeological evidence at several sites.[5]

Family members were subject to the father's authority (e.g., Gen. 18:19), which explains why some OT laws are primarily addressed to such men (e.g., Exod. 20:17). The father, in turn, was responsible for the well-being of his family (e.g., Gen. 42:1–4),[6] including by providing its members with legal protection through his role as their representative elder in the village council, which governed local administrative and judicial matters (Deut. 21:19–20; 22:15–19; 25:7–9).[7] To supplement protection by the father, some OT laws supplied additional inner-family safeguards in potentially problematic areas, especially those in which the father himself could be at fault (Lev. 18, 20, against incest; Deut. 21:15–17, on preserving inheritance for his firstborn son by an unloved wife).

Tribal kinship constituted key background for several kinds of biblical laws, including some regarding inheritance within a given clan. Inheritance followed patrilineal heredity, but Zelophehad fathered only daughters. After he died, they petitioned to receive his inheritance in Canaan in order to maintain his identity through a land-owning line of descendants (Num. 27:1–4). YHWH granted their request (vv. 6–7) and issued the following law

4. Married daughters would have joined the families of their husbands.

5. Jacob Milgrom, *Leviticus 17–22: A New Translation with Introduction and Commentary*, AB 3A (New York: Doubleday, 2000), 1526.

6. Victor H. Matthews and Don C. Benjamin, *Social World of Ancient Israel, 1250–587 BCE* (Peabody, MA: Hendrickson, 1993), 8–10; Block, "Marriage and Family," 41–44, using the term "patricentrism" instead of "patriarchy" to describe the Israelite social structure.

7. Cf. Matthews and Benjamin, *Social World*, 122–4; Walter J. Houston, *Justice: The Biblical Challenge*, Biblical Challenges in the Contemporary World (London: Equinox, 2010), 22.

to cover this kind of case and related cases in the future: "If a man dies and has no son, then you shall transfer his inheritance to his daughter. And if he has no daughter, then you shall give his inheritance to his brothers. And if he has no brothers, then you shall give his inheritance to his father's brothers. And if his father has no brothers, then you shall give his inheritance to the nearest kinsman of his clan, and he shall possess it" (vv. 8–11). Notice the outward progression of kinship within the clan, with the nearest possible relatives receiving the inheritance. According to verse 9, if an Israelite has no (surviving) child at all to inherit his property, it goes to his brothers. However, the levirate marriage law of Deut. 25:5–10 provides a way for a brother (or presumably the nearest kinsman in lieu of a brother; cf. Ruth 4) to supply a deceased man with an heir of his own by marrying his widow, thereby redeeming her (cf. Ruth 3:13).

Leviticus 25 provides for retention of ancestral real estate within a clan, for the benefit of future generations of that clan, when an Israelite farmer encounters tough times. If he must sell part of his inherited land, "then his nearest redeemer [*qal* participle of *g-'-l*] shall come and redeem what his brother has sold" (v. 25). The "redeemer" is the nearest kinsman, who can buy the property back in order to keep it within the family (cf. Ruth 4:3–4).[8] If the farmer has nobody to redeem the land and is unable to redeem it himself, the land nevertheless reverts to his ownership in the year of Jubilee (Lev. 25:10, 13, 26–28), which is to occur every fiftieth year (vv. 8–11). Thus sale of such ancestral agricultural real estate is only temporary (vv. 23), like a lease (vv. 14–16),[9] and the farmer has another opportunity to maintain himself and his family independently on his own land.

Another area of biblical law affected by tribal kinship was financial dependence. In Lev. 25, if a man cannot survive (with his immediate family) on his own, his fellow Israelites are to help him without profiting by charging him interest on a loan (vv. 35–38). If he sells himself to another Israelite, the latter is to treat him as a hired worker or (non-Israelite) sojourner, not as a slave, to maintain him until the Jubilee, when he can start over on his land (vv. 39–43; cf. v. 10). A worse scenario would be for a poor Israelite to sell himself to a non-Israelite (v. 47), in which case his kinsfolk could redeem him, i.e., buy him back (vv. 48–49). If they do not and he does not acquire the means to redeem himself (cf. v. 49b), the Jubilee provides the redemption of last resort: "then he and his children with him shall be released in the year of jubilee" (v. 54).

---

8. Cf. Raymond Westbrook, *Property and the Family in Biblical Law*, JSOTSup 113 (Sheffield: JSOT Press, 1991), 58–62.

9. See Lev. 25:16, "For it is the number of the crops that he is selling to you."

Thus far we have seen three legal roles of a tribal kinsman as redeemer: to redeem ancestral land (Lev. 25:25; Ruth 4:3–4), a poor Israelite who has lost his independence (Lev. 25:48–49), and a childless widow by marrying her (Deut. 25:5–6; Ruth 3:13). A fourth role of such a redeemer was to receive a reparation to a (presumably deceased) kinsman who had been wronged (Num. 5:8; cf. Lev. 6:1–5 [5:20–24 MT]). A fifth role was to serve as a redeemer who is an avenger of blood, to gain justice for a murdered relative by hunting down and carrying out capital punishment on the murderer (Num. 35:16–21; cf. Exod. 21:12).[10]

Just as the custom of levirate marriage was present before the formation of the Israelite nation and its law collections (Gen. 38), it appears that the role of the kinsman-executioner preceded the laws that limited this practice by instituting cities of refuge to protect accidental manslayers (Num. 35; Deut. 19). The OT law worked with the existing tribal culture as much as possible by regulating its customs in order to mitigate or prevent problematic side effects rather than by replacing these customs with unfamiliar and unnatural alternatives.

Servitude

Israelite society included servants or slaves (same word *'eved*) of varying status. An Israelite could hold either fellow Israelites or foreigners as bonded laborers, but normally Israelites were to serve only temporarily. According to Exod. 21:2–6 and Deut. 15:12–17a, 18, a male Israelite was to be freed after six years unless he preferred life with his master and voluntarily chose to permanently work for him. Deuteronomy 15:17b applies the same regulations to a female servant. The OT law allowed a master to physically discipline his servant, but protected servants from excessive abuse (Exod. 21:20–21, 26–27).

Inability to pay debt due to hard times would have been the most likely reason for an Israelite to become a servant. This is illustrated by 2 Kings 4:1, where a widow's children who served as collateral were about to be seized when the creditor foreclosed on the unpaid loan. Servitude could also result from debt incurred by crime if the thief lacked the means to make reparation (Exod. 22:3 [22:2 MT]; cf. 22:1, 4 [21:37; 22:3 MT]). Presumably he would be set free when his debt was paid by his labor. Deuteronomy 15 shows the close relationship between debt and servitude by placing its servant release law (vv. 12–18) after laws concerning remission of debt (vv. 1–6; cf. chap. 13 below) and generous lending to the poor (vv. 7–11). Verse 18 indicates how a

10. Cf. Num. 35:12, 21, 24–25, 27; Deut. 19:6, 12; Josh. 20:3, 5, 9; 2 Sam. 14:11.

servant's debt could be amortized: "at half the cost of a hired worker he has served you six years."

The law of Exod. 21:7–11 protected an Israelite daughter whose father sold her as a servant wife/concubine. Because this arrangement involved a kind of marriage, it would be permanent unless she turned out to be displeasing to her master, in which case he was to allow her to be redeemed, or if he did not continue to properly provide for her when he took another wife, in which case he was to grant her freedom.[11] He was not permitted to sell her to a foreigner, which would remove her from the protection of her people.

In hard times, an Israelite struggling for survival could voluntarily sell himself to another Israelite, in which case he was to be treated as a hired worker or resident alien and released in the Jubilee Year (Lev. 25:39–43; see above). However, it was especially undesirable for an Israelite to become the servant of a non-Israelite, even temporarily. For one thing, the Israelites were meant to be free as servants of YHWH, who had brought them out of slavery to non-Israelites in Egypt (cf. Lev. 25:55). Moreover, Israelites would not be as safe under the control of foreigners as they would be in the service of fellow Israelites, who should have a vested interest in them due to a shared heritage. A resident alien to whom a poor Israelite had to sell himself was to treat him as a hired worker and allow him to be redeemed. If he was not redeemed, he was to go free in the Jubilee Year (Lev. 25:47–55).

On the other hand, Lev. 25 allowed Israelites to buy foreigners as permanent slaves, who would become part of their property that their children would inherit (vv. 44–46). Non-Israelites could also become permanent slaves if Israelites captured them in war (e.g., Num. 31:9–18; Deut. 20:10–14; 2 Sam. 12:31).[12] Such permanent slavery allowed by God is particularly problematic for modern readers (see chap. 14 below).

Foreigners Joining Israel

Individuals who were not descended from Jacob/Israel could join the nation in several ways. Due to the patrilineal nature of tribal affiliation, women could more easily be absorbed into Israel through marriage than men (e.g., Ruth 4:13; 2 Sam. 3:3; 1 Kings 14:21).[13] However, pentateuchal law prohibited Israelites from intermarrying with the idolatrous inhabitants of Canaan because they

---

11. See further on such servant marriage in chap. 14 below.
12. Cf. the Gibeonites, who deceived the Israelites and became their servants (Josh. 9) as if they had been captured in a distant war (Deut. 20:11), thereby avoiding death that was specified for such inhabitants of Canaan (Josh. 9:16–18).
13. Cf. Josh. 6:25 in light of Matt. 1:5 (Rahab).

would turn their Israelite spouses from YHWH to serve other gods (Exod. 34:11–16; Deut. 7:1–4). The same principle applied to other foreigners who did not worship YHWH (1 Kings 11:1–10; 16:31; Ezra 9:1; Neh. 13:23–27).

The cases of Rahab, a Canaanite prostitute from Jericho, and Ruth the Moabitess were exceptional. Although they came from idolatrous peoples, they could safely be assimilated into Israel (Josh. 6:25; cf. Matt. 1:5; Ruth 4, esp. v. 13) because they accepted YHWH as their God (Josh. 2:9–12; Ruth 1:16–17).

One law allowed an Israelite man to marry a foreign woman in a special kind of circumstance: if the Israelite army had captured her in war (Deut. 21:10–14). The law required her to "shave her head and pare her nails. And she shall take off the clothes in which she was captured and shall remain in your house and lament her father and her mother a full month" (vv. 12–13). It appears that in these ways she was to bring closure to her former identity and kinship so that she could be assimilated into Israelite society.[14] The fact that she was to mourn for her parents implies that she was a young virgin girl (cf. Num. 31:17–18). At this impressionable age, she could be expected to adopt the required religious culture of Israel.[15]

A non-Israelite could dwell among the Israelites as a resident alien (ger), who was protected by law (Exod. 22:21 [22:20 MT]; 23:9; Lev. 19:33–34).[16] He was responsible for obeying many laws required of the Israelites (e.g., Exod. 12:19; 20:10; Lev. 16:29; 24:22) and could participate in some religious practices like native Israelites (Exod. 12:48, Passover if circumcised; Lev. 17:8, offering sacrifices).[17] A resident alien could become prosperous, even more so than an Israelite (Lev. 25:47).

Children of the third generation born to an Edomite or Egyptian could be admitted into the assembly (qahal) of YHWH (Deut. 23:7–8 [23:8–9 MT]), thus having membership in the Israelite governing assembly of adult males, with full rights of citizenship.[18] However, descendants of an Ammonite or

14. Cf. Daniel I. Block, *Deuteronomy*, NIV Application Commentary (Grand Rapids: Zondervan, 2012), 496.

15. See further on this law in chap. 13 below.

16. When the Israelites departed from Egypt, "A mixed multitude also went up with them" (Exod. 12:38). It is not clear how or to what extent these people were eventually assimilated into the Israelite community. At least one individual of mixed ancestry (Israelite mother and Egyptian father) caused trouble and was executed (Lev. 24:10–14, 23). Later in Israelite history, Hiram of Tyre, an artisan in bronze with an Israelite mother and a father from Tyre (1 Kings 7:13–14), played a key role in construction of Solomon's temple (vv. 15–47).

17. A less integrated *toshav*, "sojourner," was not permitted to eat of the Passover sacrifice (Exod. 12:45).

18. On the Israelite "assembly," see Jeffrey H. Tigay, *Deuteronomy: The Traditional Hebrew Text with the New JPS Translation*, JPS Torah Commentary (Philadelphia: Jewish Publication

Moabite were permanently barred from such membership because of the way their ancestors treated the Israelites when they came from Egypt (vv. 3–6 [vv. 4–7 MT]).[19]

As mentioned above, Israelites could permanently keep non-Israelite slaves, who would remain lesser members of society (Lev. 25:44–46). However, 1 Chron. 2:34–35 records the rare and therefore noteworthy case of Sheshan, who had only daughters and gave one of them in marriage to his Egyptian slave in order to continue his family line (cf. vv. 36–41).

Corporate Identity and Motivation

As in Middle Eastern tribal societies today, the self-identity, rights, responsibilities, and well-being of an individual ancient Israelite largely depended on one's place within the corporate identity of the family, clan, tribe, and nation. Such a group was able to protect its people from other individuals or groups to the extent that its members kept it strong and cooperated to defend it from various threats. Maintaining one's place within the group, including after death (Num. 27:4; Deut. 25:6),[20] was existentially crucial, so it was a disaster to be ostracized or banished, even temporarily (e.g., Num. 12:14–15). Therefore, social groups could exercise a high degree of control over their members, who were expected to live up to corporate expectations.

Societies persuade their members to comply with their norms through several kinds of motivations. These include (1) honor versus shame (resulting in ostracism), (2) guilt (resulting in punishment) for violating a principle of right versus wrong, and (3) fear of retribution. The OT law utilizes all three social approaches in order to persuade people to comply with divine instructions.

Biblical laws addressed the robust honor-shame component of ancient Israelite culture in several ways.[21] First, people must show honor to their parents

Society, 1996), 209–10; cf. Jacob Milgrom, *Leviticus 1–16: A New Translation with Introduction and Commentary*, AB 3 (New York: Doubleday, 1991), 242–43.

19. This did not affect Ruth the Moabitess because she was a woman who was incorporated into Israel through marriage.

20. Cf. expressions for death: "gathered to his people" (Gen. 25:8, 17; 35:29; etc.; cf. Num. 27:13); "slept with his fathers" (1 Kings 2:10; 11:43; 14:20; etc.).

21. On the important factor of shame and honor in societies belonging to the world of the Bible, see, e.g., Saul M. Olyan, "Honor, Shame, and Covenant Relations in Ancient Israel and Its Environment," *JBL* 115 (1996): 201–18; T. R. Hobbs, "Reflections on Honor, Shame, and Covenant Relations," *JBL* 116 (1997): 501–3; Victor H. Matthews, "Honor and Shame in Gender-Related Legal Situations in the Hebrew Bible," in *Gender and Law in the Hebrew Bible and the Ancient Near East*, ed. Victor H. Matthews, Bernard M. Levinson, and Tikva Frymer-Kensky, JSOTSup 262 (Sheffield: Sheffield Academic, 1998), 97–112; Jiří Moskala, "Reflections on the Concept of Shame and Honor in the Biblical Creation and Fall Narratives," in *Shame & Honor: Presenting Biblical Themes in Shame & Honor Contexts*, ed. Bruce L. Bauer (Berrien Springs,

(Exod. 20:12; Lev. 19:3) and elderly folk (Lev. 19:32), and it is forbidden to curse God, a ruler, a deaf person, or one's parents (Exod. 22:28 [22:27 MT]; Lev. 19:14; 20:9). Notice that "honor and shame communicate relative social status, which may shift over time."[22]

Second, a number of laws use pejorative language to discourage prohibited behaviors. Leviticus characterizes serious sexual offenses as *to'evah*, "abomination," something abhorrent (18:22, 26–27, 29; 20:13).[23] "Abominations" in Deuteronomy include idolatrous images (7:25–26; 27:15), worship of deities other than YHWH (13:14 [13:15 MT]; 17:4), prohibited food (14:3), sacrificing a defective animal (17:1), practice of human sacrifice and the occult (18:9–12), wearing clothing pertaining to the opposite gender (22:5), using the fee of a prostitute to pay a vow to YHWH (23:18 [23:19 MT]), remarrying a woman after she has been married to someone else (24:4), and using false weights and measures (25:13–16). Leviticus 20 wields a rich vocabulary for the shamefulness of sexual violations: *tevel*, "perversion" (v. 12), *zimmah*, "depravity" (v. 14), *khesed*, "disgrace" (v. 17), and *niddah*, "impurity" (v. 21).

Third, some punishments specified by laws are shameful. A judge can make a condemned man lie down and have him beaten in his presence, but not with more than forty stripes, "lest . . . your brother be degraded in your sight" (Deut. 25:2–3). A bridegroom who slanders his bride by falsely alleging that he did not find her to be a virgin on their wedding night is to be disciplined/punished and fined "because he has brought a bad name upon a virgin of Israel" (22:18–19). On the other hand, if the groom's accusation is substantiated, the bride is to be stoned to death at the entrance to her father's house "because she has done an outrageous thing in Israel by whoring [*qal* infinitive of *z-n-h*, "committing promiscuity"] in her father's house" (v. 21). A woman convicted of adultery through the suspected adulteress ritual suffers gynecological pain, inability to conceive children, and consequent shame, so that she "shall become a curse among her people" (Num. 5:27, contrast v. 28). Some couples who contract forbidden, incestuous marriages are punished by the shame of childlessness (Lev. 20:20–21). Notice that honor and shame are public, and loss of honor that results in shame diminishes social status.[24]

In addition to the laws themselves, the covenant blessings and curses encourage obedience by promising honor (Lev. 26:13; Deut. 28:1, 13) and discourage disobedience by warning of shame (Lev. 26:32; Deut. 28:37, 43–44, 68).

MI: Department of World Mission, Andrews University, 2014), 23–28; Richard M. Davidson, "Shame and Honor in the Beginning: A Study of Genesis 4," in *Shame & Honor*, 43–46.

22. Olyan, "Honor, Shame," 204.

23. The summary in Lev. 18:26–27, 29 also includes Molech worship (v. 21) as an abomination.

24. Olyan, "Honor, Shame," 204.

The OT law also appeals to the motivation of guilt as complementary to that of honor-shame. It strongly expresses absolute divine principles of right and wrong (e.g., the Decalogue, Exod. 20; Deut. 5) and states that guilt (e.g., Lev. 5:1; 6:4–6 [5:23–25 MT]; Deut. 22:8) and punishments (e.g., Exod. 21:12, 14–17; 22:1, 4 [21:37; 22:3 MT]; 31:14), including some shameful public punishments (Lev. 20:2; 24:14, 16, 23; Num. 15:35–36; Deut. 22:18, 21; 25:2), would ensue from violating these principles. In biblical law, guilt resulting from wrongdoing and leading to punishment is self-defeating and shameful, and innocence in harmony with right is profitable and honorable (cf. Deut. 26:13–19; Ps. 15).

Additionally, OT law employs the incentive of fear. Several laws explicitly refer to the fear of God as the reason for obeying them (Lev. 19:14, 32; 25:17, 36, 43). Major punishments, such as death by stoning (e.g., Lev. 20:2) or the divine penalty of being cut off (v. 3; see chap. 5 above), undoubtedly would inspire fear. Deuteronomy repeatedly speaks of severe punishments as making examples of (and thereby implicitly shaming) those who commit serious offenses so that other Israelites would hear and fear and never repeat their offenses (13:8–11 [13:9–12 MT]; 17:12–13; 19:18–21; 21:21).

Ancient Israelite Legal Culture

Family Law and Beyond

Marriage and divorce in ancient Israel were mostly under family law administered by the male head of the household. Fathers normally contracted first marriages for their daughters (Exod. 21:7; 22:17 [22:16 MT]; Deut. 7:3; 22:16, 29) or sons (Exod. 34:16; Deut. 7:3).[25] Husbands could divorce their wives (Deut. 24:1, 3) without involving the court system.

Consensual sexual relations alone did not create a marriage in OT law: "If a man seduces a virgin who is not betrothed and lies with her, he shall give the bride-price [more accurately, "marriage present"][26] for her and make her his wife. If her father utterly refuses to give her to him, he shall pay money equal to the bride-price for virgins" (Exod. 22:16–17 [22:15–16 MT]). The

25. Cf. Gen. 24:50–51, where Laban participated with his father, Bethuel, in agreeing that his sister, Rebekah, could marry Isaac.

26. Rather than signifying a man's purchase of his wife like other property, this "probably represents the compensation to the father for the work the daughter would otherwise have contributed to her family, and probably ultimately belonged to the wife, not the father." Richard M. Davidson, *Flame of Yahweh: Sexuality in the Old Testament* (Peabody, MA: Hendrickson, 2007), 249.

transaction between the groom and the father was essential; without it there was no marriage. Jesus affirmed that sex does not establish a marriage when he said to a Samaritan woman, "You have had five husbands, and the one you now have is not your husband" (John 4:18). So if a modern couple is known to have engaged in premarital sex, it is incorrect to tell them that they must become officially married because according to the Bible they are already married in God's sight. It may be better for them to confess their sin to God, receive his forgiveness (1 John 1:9), and go their separate ways.

According to OT law, the Israelite community and its courts were to become involved in cases concerning marriage and sexuality when disputes arose or laws were possibly or clearly broken.[27] Thus city elders hear the complaint of a widow who has no son if her brother-in-law does not wish to perform his duty of levirate marriage for her (Deut. 25:7–10). The elders also judge a dispute over whether or not a bride has entered marriage as a virgin (Deut. 22:13–21). The residents of a town in which a betrothed virgin has sex with a man other than her fiancé are to stone the couple to death because she is already bound by a marriage contract (v. 24, "his neighbor's wife"), and therefore this is equivalent to the capital crime of adultery (cf. v. 22; Lev. 20:10). The community is responsible for judging and executing those who engage in homosexual practice (Lev. 20:13), bestiality (vv. 15–16), and some kinds of incest (vv. 11–12, 14). However, at his sanctuary YHWH himself judges the case of a suspected adulteress (Num. 5:11–31).

Inheritance was under family jurisdiction but subject to divine guidelines in certain cases. A man whose unloved wife bore his firstborn son must justly give him, not a son of his loved wife, the double inheritance of the firstborn (Deut. 21:15–17). A man's inheritance goes to his daughters if he has no sons and to his other closest relatives if he also has no daughters (Num. 27:7–11). Inheriting daughters must marry within their clan (36:6–9).

An Israelite clan took the responsibility to execute the murderer of one of its members through its delegated "redeemer/avenger of blood" (Num. 35), even if the murderer belonged to the family of the victim (2 Sam. 14:7, 11). So to this extent, a case of murder came under family and clan law. By contrast, cuneiform law elsewhere in the ANE indicates that the central government, within an urban and bureaucratically governed society, controlled the adjudication of homicide. This does not mean that the legal process in OT law was more primitive. Rather, it fit the nature of ancient Israelite society, which was rural and decentralized, with strong kinship ties and community-based

27. In the patriarchal period, cases of sexual misconduct were under the jurisdiction of the head of household (see Gen. 38:24).

justice, so associations of families were responsible for protection of family members.[28]

To safeguard the justice of its system of dealing with murder, OT law uniquely mandates establishment of cities of refuge at the national level to protect accidental manslayers from being executed by avengers (Num. 35; Deut. 19; Josh. 20–21).[29] A manslayer who fled to one of these cities was to receive a fair trial by the community, which would judge in accordance with criteria for establishing whether he lacked intent, in which case he could have continued asylum, or committed premeditated murder (Num. 35:12, 15–25; Deut. 19:4–6, 11–13), in which case the elders of his city of refuge were to hand him over to be executed by the avenger (Deut. 19:12).[30] Presumably, knowledge of this law would tend to discourage a first-degree murderer from fleeing to a city of refuge.

Israelites were not only to seek justice for their kinfolk but were to bring their relatives and countrymen to justice when they committed crimes. For instance, if an Israelite or resident alien in Israel gives any of his children to the god Molech, God holds the "people of the land" responsible for executing him by stoning (Lev. 20:2, 4–5). Deuteronomy 13 requires Israelites to execute family members or close friends who try to entice them into idolatry (vv. 6–10), and an Israelite city that is led into idolatry is to be utterly destroyed (vv. 12–17).[31]

Israelite Judiciary

Much of the administration of justice in ancient Israel was carried out privately within families and between primary parties (cf. above). Thus, for example, "Exod. 22:25–26 and Deut. 24:6, 10–13, 17 are appeals to the creditor's benevolence, necessary since no court was involved."[32]

---

28. Pamela Barmash, *Homicide in the Biblical World* (Cambridge: Cambridge University Press, 2005), 202.

29. Realistically, the redeemer/avenger of blood was like a force of nature in that his passion for bringing the killer to justice was not expected to distinguish between first-degree homicide and accidental manslaughter.

30. Partly implied by Num. 35:19, 21, 24–25, although this passage does not mention the role of the elders—who would have had knowledge of his relationship to the slain person—in taking him from the city of refuge.

31. The narrative of Judg. 19–20 recounts corporate accountability on an even higher level. The men of Gibeah, belonging to the tribe of Benjamin, gang-raped a Levite's concubine to death in lieu of raping the Levite himself (chap. 19). The other tribes demanded that the Benjaminites hand over the Gibeahite culprits to be executed, but the Benjaminites refused to give up their kinsmen and mustered their army instead (20:12–16). Consequently, the other tribes waged a war against Benjamin that destroyed Gibeah and almost wiped out the tribe (vv. 17–47; cf. 21:3, 6).

32. Ze'ev W. Falk, *Hebrew Law in Biblical Times: An Introduction*, 2nd ed. (Provo, UT: Brigham Young University Press; Winona Lake, IN: Eisenbrauns, 2001), 56.

According to the Pentateuch, Israelite public justice was to be administered by elders representing their households and clans, court judges, and priests. Exodus 18 recounts the origin of the judiciary shortly before the Israelites reached Mount Sinai: Moses followed the counsel of Jethro, his father-in-law (vv. 21–22), by appointing a hierarchy of men with authority to judge all but "the hard cases," which they reserved for Moses (vv. 24–26 CEB; cf. Deut. 1:13–17).

Later Moses instructed the Israelites that when they would settle in their land, they should appoint "judges and officers" in all their towns (Deut. 16:18). City elders could serve as local judges and official witnesses to legal transactions (21:19–20; 22:15–19; 25:7–9; cf. Ruth 4:1–12). If a case arose that was too difficult for the local judges, they were to consult "the Levitical priests" and "the judge who is in office in those days"[33] at the central sanctuary (Deut. 17:8–10), as earlier judges were to bring difficult cases to Moses (1:17; cf. Exod. 18:22). The decision of this high court (or "supreme court") was final. Anyone who failed to follow its decision was to die (Deut. 17:10–13).[34]

High-court judges were to work with the priests for at least two reasons. First, the priests were the primary custodians of the divine laws (Lev. 10:10–11; Deut. 17:18; 31:9–13, 24–26; 33:10). Second, an oracle from YHWH could be accessed through the sacred lot of Urim and Thummim worn by the high priest in the event that this was deemed necessary (Exod. 28:30; Lev. 8:8; Num. 27:21; 1 Sam. 14:41).

The OT law refers to priestly roles in certain kinds of cases. In Deut. 21 priests are to witness (v. 5) a ritual for corporate absolution from an unsolved murder, which is to be performed by the elders of the city closest to the location where the corpse was found (vv. 1–9). In this context, v. 5 indicates that the priests hold broad judicial authority: "By their word every dispute and every assault shall be settled." A priest alone was to officiate the suspected-adulteress ritual at the sanctuary (Num. 5:11–31) because of the cultic nature of this case judged by YHWH himself (see chap. 13).[35]

In addition to deciding verdicts, judges could preside over administration of punishments (Deut. 25:2–3). The narrative of Num. 25 records an extreme situation in which judges themselves were to serve as executioners (v. 5).

33. Cf. Deut. 19:17, "The priests and the judges [plural] who are in office in those days."
34. Cf. Hittite Laws §173a: "If anyone rejects a judgment of the king, his house will become a heap of ruins. If anyone rejects a judgment of a magistrate, they shall cut off his head" (trans. Harry A. Hoffner Jr., "Hittite Laws," COS 2.19:117).
35. Priests were also to diagnose and render judgments regarding cases of potential, actual, or abated ritually impure surface disease (so-called leprosy) in human bodies, garments, and houses (Lev. 13; 14:2–4, 34–48).

Normally, however, capital punishment was administered by the community (Lev. 20:2; 24:14, 16, 23; 15:35–36) or, in a case of murder, by the "redeemer/ avenger of blood" (Num. 35:19, 21; Deut. 19:12; see above).

Judicial Procedure

An Israelite legal case was decided by one or more judges, who reached their verdicts by weighing evidence.[36] Those who judged were to be fair and impartial (Exod. 23:3, 6–7; Lev. 19:15; Deut. 1:16–17; 16:18–20), without taking bribes (Exod. 23:8; Deut. 16:19; 27:25).

Other participants in a legal case, whether or not they actually stood in court, could include one or more individuals representing the prosecuting/ accusing side (Num. 35:24–25; Deut. 21:18–20; 22:13–14, 17), a defendant accused of a crime (Deut. 19:16; 22:13–14), two individuals who needed resolution of a dispute between them (25:1), and witnesses (e.g., Num. 35:30; see further below), who could support the prosecution or the defense. There was no public prosecutor, defense attorney, or trial by jury per se.[37] Courts generally convened at public places such as city gates (Deut. 21:19; 22:15; 25:7; Ruth 4:1–2), except in cases that involved the direct participation of YHWH, which were handled at the sanctuary (Exod. 22:8–9 [22:7–8 MT]; Num. 5:11–31).

Evidence presented in a court case could be material in nature (Exod. 22:13 [22:12 MT]; Deut. 22:15, 17; cf. Josh. 7:22–23),[38] but more often it consisted of testimony from witnesses.[39] In a murder trial, for example, witnesses played a crucial role in determining intentionality or its absence on the part of the killer by testifying concerning the circumstances of the death itself (Num. 35:16–18, 20–23; Deut. 19:5, 11) and whether or not the killer had previously hated the slain person (Num. 35:23; Deut. 19:4, 6, 11).

Some cases were problematic because available evidence was inadequate. Several strategies overcame this problem. When witnesses to a crime were

36. On legal procedures and terminology in ancient Israel, see Pietro Bovati, *Re-establishing Justice: Legal Terms, Concepts and Procedures in the Hebrew Bible*, trans. Michael J. Smith, JSOTSup 105 (Sheffield: JSOT Press, 1994); cf. Hans Jochen Boecker, *Law and the Administration of Justice in the Old Testament and Ancient East*, trans. Jeremy Moiser (Minneapolis: Augsburg, 1980), esp. 27–52.

37. However, when Jonathan was found guilty of violating a foolish oath that his father, King Saul, had laid on the Israelite army, the army (acting like a jury) ransomed Jonathan from death by protesting that he should not die because he had been instrumental in obtaining a great victory (1 Sam. 14:24–28, 43–45).

38. In Deut. 22:15, 17 the evidence consists of a garment that is bloodstained from the first intercourse of a virgin bride.

39. For detailed study of testimony in OT law against its ANE background, see Bruce Wells, *The Law of Testimony in the Pentateuchal Codes*, BZABR 4 (Wiesbaden: Harrassowitz, 2004).

needed for a trial, the community could employ a publicly proclaimed adjuration (*'alah*), a curse on anyone with knowledge of the circumstances who fails to come forward and testify (Lev. 5:1).[40] A case involving breach of trust could be brought before God, likely at his sanctuary (Exod. 22:8–9 [22:7–8 MT]). The text does not say how the omniscient Deity would adjudicate the case. Perhaps it would be decided through one or both parties swearing an oath in YHWH's name to confirm their innocence or through judgment administered by priests, who had access to a divine oracle (cf. Num. 27:21; Judg. 20:27–28; see also Exod. 28:30). The oath procedure is specified for a case involving loss of property: "an oath by the Lord shall be between them both to see whether or not he has put his hand to his neighbor's property" (Exod. 22:11 [22:10 MT]; Lev. 6:3, 5 [5:22, 24 MT]). A suspected adulteress, against whom there were no human witnesses (Num. 5:13), was to take an oath that functioned as a conditional curse, which called on YHWH to punish her if she was guilty (vv. 19–23).

Particularly problematic were cases in which evidence was deceptive. Material evidence could be manipulated (Gen. 37:31–35), or an accuser or witness could present lying testimony in order to harm an innocent defendant (Deut. 19:16; 22:13–19; cf. 1 Kings 21:13), in violation of the Decalogue (Exod. 20:16; Deut. 5:20; cf. Exod. 23:1–2). To counter this threat to justice, an individual shown to be a malicious false witness would receive the same punishment (by the lex talionis principle) that the innocent accused person would have received if he had been condemned as guilty (Deut. 19:16–21).[41] Such an outcome was not only to preserve justice in this case but also to dissuade anyone else from proffering false testimony in the future (v. 20).[42]

40. On this unique Israelite law of required testimony, see ibid., 54–82.

41. Cf. law §1 of the Laws of Hammurabi: "If a man accuses another man and charges him with homicide but cannot bring proof against him, his accuser shall be killed" (trans. Martha Roth, "The Laws of Hammurabi," COS 2.131:337; cf. Martha T. Roth, *Law Collections from Mesopotamia and Asia Minor*, SBL Writings from the Ancient World 6 [Atlanta: Scholars Press, 1995], 81). Roth points out that this formulation reveals "that a false accuser suffers the penalty he sought for his intended victim" and implies "that homicide demands the death penalty" (72).

42. A bridegroom who falsely accused his bride of not being a virgin was to be quite severely punished (Deut. 22:18–19). "The triple punishment is exceptional but, as noted by Maimonides and Abravanel, each element corresponds to a part of the husband's offense. He is flogged, and thereby degraded, . . . because he has defamed the girl and her family. He is fined because his accusation would have forced her father to return the bride-price. He loses the right to divorce her, which was probably his aim in slandering her. In this way the father is compensated for the harm attempted against him, and the girl is protected against divorce" (Tigay, *Deuteronomy*, 205). However, the groom was not to be stoned to death as the bride would if she were found guilty (vv. 20–21). This constitutes an exception to the rule regarding false witnesses in 19:16–21, perhaps because execution of the groom would further punish the bride by removing her means of support, especially because he had taken her virginity, without which it would be difficult

It was difficult for humans to apprehend someone who swore a false oath. However, such a person could experience guilt by suffering adverse circumstances, indicating that he was responsible to YHWH for making reparation to the wronged party and for sacrificing a reparation offering (Lev. 6:1–7 [5:20–26 MT]).[43]

Old Testament law requires a minimum of two or three witnesses to establish a case against a defendant (Deut. 19:15). This is designed to protect the accused in the event that testimony from one source is false or otherwise faulty or misleading, especially in a capital case (Num. 35:30; Deut. 17:6). Furthermore, when the community puts someone to death (by stoning), the witnesses must initiate the execution (Deut. 17:7). Knowledge of this solemn responsibility would tend to make witnesses serious about what they said against the defendant (cf. John 8:7–11).

Justice could be perverted if two or more false witnesses were set up by unjust higher authorities, as in the trials of Naboth (1 Kings 21:7–14), Jesus (Matt. 26:59–62; Mark 14:55–60), and Stephen (Acts 6:11–14). However, if properly applied, biblical law protected innocent people by upholding a high standard for conviction: certainty of guilt (e.g., Deut. 17:4).

Theocracy and Law

The Deity YHWH was the actual and functioning head of state in ancient Israel, according to the Bible (e.g., Exod. 15:18; Num. 23:21; Deut. 33:5; Judg. 8:23; 1 Sam. 8:7; Pss. 5:2; 44:4 [5:3; 44:5 MT]). Even when the Israelites chose to have a human king, he and his subjects remained accountable to the Lord (e.g., 1 Sam. 12:14). During the wilderness period, God communicated instructions for his people to Moses, his spokesman, at his sanctuary headquarters (Exod. 25:22; Lev. 1:1–2; Num. 7:89). "Moses was like God's Prime Minister in the sense that he was responsible for ensuring that the Lord's will got carried out and for arranging its details. But he was not in charge

---

for her to remarry. As it is, the groom is bound to support her for the rest of his life because he can never divorce her.

43. Bruce Wells explains the verb *'ashem*, "has realized his guilt" (e.g., Lev. 6:4 [5:23 MT]):
The idea that the word refers to psychological feelings of remorse or guilt, to pangs of conscience, is anachronistic. It is unlikely that the ancients conceived of guilt in this way. Rather, the notion of becoming guilty in the ancient Near East often meant that some tangible sign had arisen to indicate that a particular person was guilty of some wrongdoing and was suffering divine punishment. The person may have felt the guilt but in a very physical way. . . . A person becomes guilty by falling ill, losing a loved one, or suffering some other misfortune. It is the misfortune that makes a person think he or she is guilty. (*The Law of Testimony in the Pentateuchal Codes*, BZABR 4 [Wiesbaden: Harrassowitz, 2004], 67–69)

of formulating policy—that was the Lord's job."[44] Israel's government was a unique true theocracy, unlike later pseudotheocracies.

Old Testament law was affected by YHWH's dynamic theocratic rule in several ways. First, the Israelites were accountable to him as the one who brought them out of Egypt (e.g., Exod. 20:2; Lev. 11:45; 19:36; 22:33), owned the land of Canaan (Lev. 25:23), and promulgated his laws as stipulations of the covenant that he personally made with them (e.g., Exod. 19–24). Second, the Lord could make new laws or adjustments to existing laws in response to situations that arose (e.g., Num. 9:6–14; 27:1–11). Third, God set the penalties for violations of his laws in order to protect his covenant community from evil (e.g., Deut. 17:12; 19:19; 21:21), and he could determine punishments in specific instances (Lev. 24:14; Num. 15:35). Fourth, YHWH as king and therefore ultimate judge[45] was to try some cases, including breach of trust (Exod. 22:9 [22:8 MT]) and suspected adultery (Num. 5:11–31). If a suspected woman were guilty of adultery, the verdict would be manifested by divinely inflicted punishment (v. 27). Fifth, the Deity served as witness to the choice of an Israelite to permanently remain in servitude (Exod. 21:6). Sixth, God gave some laws that regulated thoughts (Exod. 20:17; Lev. 19:18), for which only he could hold people accountable. Seventh, only God could inflict the penalty of cutting off a violator, which deprived the person of afterlife (see chap. 5 above). Eighth, ritual laws regulated interactions with the Lord at his sanctuary headquarters (e.g., Lev. 1–16).

Legal Development

Laws are not given in a vacuum; they address real-life circumstances. So it is not surprising that we see considerable development in OT law over time as situations changed.

Early Laws

At the beginning of the biblical narrative, in the original perfect world, there was almost no need for law in the sense of externally imposed requirements. The first humans were to simply enjoy Sabbath (Gen. 2:2–3; cf. Mark 2:27), marriage (Gen. 2:18, 20–24), and (no doubt pleasant) work in their garden (v. 15) that the loving Creator had given them. When he informed them of

44. Roy Gane, *In the Shadow of the Shekinah: God's Journey with Us* (Hagerstown, MD: Review & Herald, 2009), 17.

45. Isaiah 33:22 explicitly affirms these roles of YHWH: "For the LORD is our judge; the LORD is our lawgiver; the LORD is our king; he will save us." For the role of a human king as judge, see, e.g., 2 Sam. 14:4–24; 15:2–4, 6; 1 Kings 3:16–28; Prov. 29:14.

their role, it was in the context of a blessing: "And God blessed them. And God said to them, 'Be fruitful and multiply and fill the earth and subdue it, and have dominion over the fish of the sea and over the birds of the heavens and over every living thing that moves on the earth'" (Gen. 1:28). The ways in which God set things up for Adam and Eve naturally represented profound normative values regarding relationships between God and humans, humans and each other, and humans and their environment.

The only external "law," YHWH's prohibition against eating fruit from one particular tree (Gen. 2:16–17; 3:1–3), served as a test of obedience in an area that was peripheral because the fruit of that tree was completely unnecessary for human life.[46] When Eve and Adam chose to experience evil by disobeying God's one commandment, curses because of sin affected the human experience of marriage and work (3:16–19) but not the Sabbath, which implicitly remains a piece of paradise.

God gave Noah a few laws for the entire postdiluvian human race. The human diet was originally vegetarian (Gen. 1:29; 2:9, 16; 3:17–19, 23), but now God permitted meat,[47] except with its lifeblood (9:3–4).[48] Then he addressed the matter of human lifeblood, for which he holds animals and humans accountable (9:5), and he issued a capital crime law that authorizes humans to inflict death for murder (v. 6).[49]

Confirming the ongoing validity of the Noachian laws, later biblical laws reiterate the prohibition of eating meat with its blood (Lev. 3:17; 7:26–27; 17:10–14; 19:26; Deut. 12:16, 23; 15:23; cf. Acts 15:20, 29) and the mandate to execute murderers (e.g., Exod. 21:12). Developments in OT law associated the Noachian laws with some other requirements (Lev. 3:17, also not eating fat; Lev. 17:11, putting sacrificial blood on the altar), specified ways in which they could be carried out (Lev. 17:13, pour out blood and cover it with earth; cf. Deut. 12:16; 15:23), set up a legal process and infrastructure to distinguish murderers from accidental manslayers (Num. 35; Deut. 19:1–13, 15), and identified legitimate executioners of murderers (Num. 35:19, 21; Deut. 19:12).

The Lord affirmed to Isaac that his father Abraham "obeyed my voice and kept my charge, my commandments, my statutes, and my laws" (Gen. 26:5). Genesis records only one ongoing law as such that God gave to Abraham:

---

46. Obviously this prohibition no longer applies after humans lost access to the garden of Eden (Gen. 3:24).

47. Apparently Noah and his family experienced a shortage of vegetarian food due to the devastation caused by the flood.

48. Cf. the fact that God's permission of food for Adam and Eve was also accompanied by an exception (Gen. 2:16–17).

49. The motive clause in Gen. 9:6 ("for God made man in his own image") implies that murder involves sacrilege because life is sacred.

the requirement of circumcision as the covenant sign (17:10–14). Unless God gave him other laws that the Bible does not record, the point seems to be that the patriarch lived in harmony with divine principles that were known to him, as YHWH commanded him in general terms: "Walk before me, and be blameless" (17:1).

Like the Noachian laws, the stipulation of circumcision continued into the covenant stipulations between YHWH and the Israelite nation (Lev. 12:3). A kind of legal development occurred when circumcision became a condition for males to eat the Passover meal (Exod. 12:44, 48).

Laws for the Israelite Nation

The need for laws greatly increased when the household of Jacob/Israel grew to be a nation.[50] Initially YHWH gave laws to the Israelite nation concerning Passover, the Festival of Unleavened Bread, firstborn, and the Sabbath (Exod. 12–13, 16). Subsequently he presented the Ten Commandments (Exod. 20; Deut. 5), which collected key moral principles already known and expressed them as externally imposed requirements,[51] as the unchangeable core of the stipulations governing the divine-human covenant that constituted the national charter. He also gave the Israelites many other laws, which they had no right to alter and for which he held them accountable (e.g., Lev. 26:3, 14–15; Deut. 28:1, 15). However, these laws reflected some historical developments as the Lord addressed changes in the circumstances of his people, of which the most important were transitions from tribal households to the theocratic nation, from Egypt or the wilderness camp to settled life in the land of Canaan, and from solely tribal leadership to monarchy, as well as some instances of failure to keep God's covenant stipulations.

First, OT laws regulate some aspects of households to promote holy living within the national theocracy governed by YHWH. For instance, incest laws explicitly exclude marriages and sexual relations between relatives (Lev. 18, 20). Among the forbidden unions are those between a man and his father's wife (Lev. 18:8; Deut. 22:30 [23:1 MT]; 27:20), which already was regarded as immoral when Reuben lay with Bilhah (Gen. 35:22; 49:4),[52] and some unions

50. Cf. O. Palmer Robertson, *The Christ of the Covenants* (Phillipsburg, NJ: Presbyterian and Reformed, 1980), 186–87.

51. Jo Ann Davidson shows that the principles of the Decalogue are already attested in the narratives of Genesis. "The Decalogue Predates Mount Sinai: Indicators from the Book of Genesis," *JATS* 19, nos. 1–2 (2008): 61–81.

52. Cf. the incest of Lot's daughters with their father (Gen. 19:30–38). For a man to have sex with his daughter, mother, or full sister was automatically forbidden by the prohibition in Lev. 18:6 concerning a man's closest blood relatives: "None of you shall approach any one of

that apparently were acceptable in earlier times: with one's half sister (Lev. 18:9; cf. Gen. 20:12, Abraham and Sarah), with one's father's sister (Lev. 18:12; cf. Exod. 6:20, Amram and Jochebed, parents of Moses!), and with two sisters (Lev. 18:18; cf. Gen. 29, Leah and Rachel with Jacob).

The fact that God blessed Jacob, whom he renamed Israel (Gen. 32), so that this man became the patronymic ancestor of the chosen nation by fathering many sons through his flawed multiple marriages (chaps. 29–30), illustrates wise, pastoral divine patience with human weakness.[53] Then Lev. 18:18, "You shall not take a woman as a rival wife to her sister," illustrates the Lord's revelation that leads his people to a higher ethic through which they can avoid the kind of stress experienced by Jacob and his primary wives, who were rival sisters (cf. Gen. 29–30).

Second, some OT laws recognize movement to settled life in the promised land. On the way to Canaan, God gave the Israelites a number of laws that would begin to apply "When you come into the land . . ." because they concern aspects of life there, such as houses (rather than tents; Lev. 14:34–53), land ownership (Lev. 25; Num. 27:1–11; 36), agriculture (Lev. 19:23–25; 23:10–11; 25:2–7; Num. 15:2–10, 18–21; Deut. 26:1–4), cities of refuge (Num. 35; Deut. 19), and rejection of Canaanite religious and occult practices (Deut. 18:9–14).

The first Passover celebration of national independence was carried out at individual homes in Egypt (Exod. 12) before the sanctuary was constructed (chaps. 35–40). When the sanctuary would be established at a location in Canaan where the Lord would "make his name dwell," the Passover was to be performed there (Deut. 16:2, 5–7; cf. 12:5–14, 17–18, 26–27).[54] The original Passover instructions called for accompanying unleavened bread (Exod. 12:8), but not wine. However, wine was to be added in Canaan when the Passover service moved to the sanctuary because a libation of wine was required with any *zevakh*, "sacrifice" from which the offerer(s) ate (Num. 15:5, 7, 10), and this rule applied to the Passover *zevakh* (Exod. 12:27; 34:25).[55]

There is a significant legal shift between Lev. 17 and Deut. 12. Leviticus 17:1–9 forbids the Israelites to slaughter any (domestic) sacrificable species

---

his close relatives to uncover nakedness" (cf. Lev. 21:2–3). "The purpose of the list of Leviticus 18 is to indicate *who else* is forbidden by extension from these basic relationships." Susan Rattray, "Marriage Rules, Kinship Terms and Family Structure in the Bible," in *Society of Biblical Literature 1987 Seminar Papers*, ed. Kent Richards, SBLSP 26 (Atlanta: Scholars Press, 1987), 542, emphasis original (quoted by Milgrom, *Leviticus 17–22*, 1527, cf. 1528).

53. Cf. William J. Webb, *Slaves, Women & Homosexuals: Exploring the Hermeneutics of Cultural Analysis* (Downers Grove, IL: IVP Academic, 2001), 57–60.

54. Cf. the Passovers in Jerusalem under Hezekiah and Josiah (2 Chron. 30:1; 35:1).

55. This appears to explain why wine was part of the Passover service in the Second Temple period (Matt. 26:27–29). Cf. rabbinic tradition regarding four cups of wine in *m. Pesahim* 10.1, 2, 4, 7.

of animal "in the camp" or "outside the camp" (v. 3) and commands them to offer it as a sacrifice at the sanctuary. Therefore the people could only eat meat from their flock or herd animals if they sacrificed them as well-being offerings (vv. 5–6; cf. Lev. 3; 7:11–36). This requirement of sacral slaughter would not be such a hardship because the explicit setting is the wilderness camp, where all the Israelites dwell together around and close to the sanctuary (cf. Num. 2–3). In a later context, Deut. 12, unlike Lev. 17, permits nonsacral (or "profane") slaughter of domestic sacrificable animals: "When the LORD your God enlarges your territory, as he has promised you, . . . if the place that the LORD your God will choose to put his name there is too far from you . . ." (vv. 20–21; cf. vv. 15–16, 22–25). There is no legal contradiction to Lev. 17 here; this is merely a concessive adaptation to a diachronic change of practical circumstances when many Israelites would dwell far from the location of the sanctuary in the promised land.

Third, the so-called Law of the King in Deut. 17:14–20 looks ahead to the possibility of a monarchy in the future if the people should choose such a form of leadership. However, the king's power would be limited: He would be selected by and subject to YHWH, and he should learn the divine law so that his heart would not "be lifted up above his brothers" (v. 20). He should be a countercultural king by not acquiring for himself many horses or wives or an overabundance of silver and gold.[56]

Fourth, some developments in biblical law respond to circumstances of human failure or problems that occurred on particular occasions. John H. Sailhamer points out that "the narrative of Exodus 32 (the incident of the golden calf and the people's 'running wild') helps to show clearly that the laws given to Israel at Sinai were not mere arbitrary restrictions but necessary controls on an otherwise desperate and helpless situation."[57] When the Israelites rebelled on the day after the Lord destroyed Korah and company, the divine response was a devastating plague (Num. 16:41–50 [17:6–15 MT]). Consequently, the people were terrified that they would die if they approached God's tabernacle (17:12–13 [17:27–28 MT]). In response, the Lord reassured them by making the priests and Levites responsible for any violation of a boundary that would incur his wrath when the people would come to the sanctuary (18:1, 3, 22–23).[58]

Failure by individuals generated some new laws. After YHWH executed Nadab and Abihu due to their failure to strictly follow his ritual instructions

---

56. Violated by Solomon (1 Kings 4:26 [5:6 MT]; 10:21–22, 26; 11:1–3) and subsequent kings.

57. *The Pentateuch as Narrative: A Biblical-Theological Commentary*, LBI (Grand Rapids: Zondervan, 1992), 312–13.

58. Cf. Jacob Milgrom, *Numbers*, JPS Torah Commentary (Philadelphia: Jewish Publication Society, 1990), 145–47, 155, 424.

(Lev. 10:1–2), he issued the following permanent rule to Aaron (their father, the high priest): "Drink no wine or strong drink, you or your sons with you, when you go into the tent of meeting, lest you die" (v. 9). Placement of this law in the narrative context of chap. 10 implies that it was at least partly intended to lessen the danger that such a tragedy would recur due to diminished cognition resulting from inebriation (cf. v. 10).[59] The Lord also gave new laws concerning blasphemy and assault (Lev. 24:15–22) in response to the incident of a brawling blasphemer (vv. 10–11).

Numbers 9:6–14 recounts a practical problem encountered by faithful Israelites and YHWH's response. Some men were unable to keep the Passover on the fourteenth day of the first month because they had incurred corpse contamination, no doubt due to the unavoidable need to bury their relatives. The Lord solved the dilemma by instituting an alternate Passover one month later for anyone in such a situation.

Relationships to Other Ancient Near Eastern Legal Systems

The major pentateuchal law collections came relatively late to the ANE legal environment. Even if they originated in the second half of the second millennium BC, they were preceded by the major Mesopotamian law collections in the Sumerian language of Ur-Namma (or Ur-Nammu; ca. 2100 BC) and Lipit-Ishtar (ca. 1930 BC); in Akkadian the Laws of Eshnunna (ca. 1770 BC) and Laws (Code) of Hammurabi (ca. 1750 BC); and the Hittite Laws (ca. 1650–1500 BC).[60] These collections appear to be legal treatises that provide models of judicial wisdom.[61] As such, they could be used by kings who sponsored them to demonstrate their judicial wisdom and thereby support the legitimacy of their reigns.[62]

Evidence is lacking that courts directly consulted and referred to the law collections.[63] We learn more about actual day-to-day legal and social practices in the ANE from other kinds of documents, such as records of court proceedings, contracts, and family records.[64] Nevertheless, the law collections are

---

59. This could be taken to imply that Nadab and Abihu were inebriated.

60. Roth, *Law Collections*, 13, 23, 57, 71, 213–14. Subsequent Akkadian collections are the Middle Assyrian Laws (ca. 1076 BC; ibid., 153) and the Neo-Babylonian Laws (ca. 700 BC; ibid., 143).

61. Cf. John H. Walton, *Ancient Near Eastern Thought and the Old Testament: Introducing the Conceptual World of the Hebrew Bible* (Grand Rapids: Baker Academic, 2006), 288–91.

62. Ibid., 291, 294–97. This is especially clear in the prologue and epilogue that frame the Laws of Hammurabi.

63. Roth, *Law Collections*, 5–7.

64. Ibid.; Walton, *Ancient Near Eastern Thought*, 70–71. Cf. Jeremiah's deed of purchase of a field (Jer. 32:10–14), but archaeologists have not yet discovered this inscription.

remarkably informative regarding the values and (often sophisticated) legal reasoning of their times.

Scholars have invested great effort in comparing the biblical laws with other ANE laws to ascertain relationships between them. There are some striking similarities, along with differences.

Similarities

The OT laws manifest the justice of their divine lawgiver (e.g., Deut. 10:17–19), just as the ANE collections can demonstrate the justice of the human rulers who sponsored them. There are also many points of contact between OT laws and other ANE laws in terms of contents, including the following examples of parallels that show similarities along with some differences. Notice that in the Laws of Hammurabi, an *awīlu* is an upper-class free man.

> *Laws of Ur-Namma §6*: If a man violates the rights of another and deflow-ers the virgin wife of a young man, they shall kill that male.[65]

> *Deut. 22:23–27*: If there is a betrothed virgin, and a man meets her in the city and lies with her, then you shall bring them both out to the gate of that city, and you shall stone them to death with stones, the young woman because she did not cry for help though she was in the city, and the man because he violated his neighbor's wife. . . . But if in the open country a man meets a young woman who is betrothed, and the man seizes her and lies with her, then only the man who lay with her shall die.

> *Laws of Lipit-Ishtar §b*: If a man dies without male offspring, an unmar-ried daughter shall be his heir.[66]

> *Num. 27:8*: If a man dies and has no son, then you shall transfer his in-heritance to his daughter.[67]

> *Laws of Eshnunna §53*: If an ox gores another ox and thus causes its death, the two ox-owners shall divide the value of the living ox and the carcass of the dead ox.[68]

---

65. Trans. Martha Roth, "The Laws of Ur-Namma (Ur-Nammu)," *COS* 2.153:409.
66. Trans. Martha Roth, "The Laws of Lipit-Ishtar," *COS* 2.154:411.
67. The fact that the daughters of Zelophehad were not yet married was legally important (cf. Num. 36).
68. Trans. Martha Roth, "The Laws of Eshnunna," *COS* 2.130:335.

Exod. 21:35: When one man's ox butts another's, so that it dies, then they shall sell the live ox and share its price, and the dead beast also they shall share.

Laws of Hammurabi §206: If an *awīlu* should strike another *awīlu* during a brawl and inflict upon him a wound, that *awīlu* shall swear, "I did not strike intentionally," and he shall satisfy the physician (i.e., pay his fees).[69]

Exod. 21:18–19: When men quarrel and one strikes the other with a stone or with his fist and the man does not die but takes to his bed, then if the man rises again and walks outdoors with his staff, he who struck him shall be clear; only he shall pay for the loss of his time, and shall have him thoroughly healed.

Hittite Laws §193: If a man has a wife, and the man dies, his brother shall take his widow as wife. (If the brother dies,) his father shall take her. When afterwards his father dies, his (i.e., the father's) brother shall take the woman whom he had.[70]

Deut. 25:5: If brothers dwell together, and one of them dies and has no son, the wife of the dead man shall not be married outside the family to a stranger. Her husband's brother shall go in to her and take her as his wife and perform the duty of a husband's brother to her.[71]

The distinctive lex talionis (law of retaliation) kind of penalty first appears in the Laws of Hammurabi (LH) and later shows up in OT law:

LH §196: If an *awīlu* should blind the eye of another *awīlu*, they shall blind his eye.

LH §197: If he should break the bone of another *awīlu*, they shall break his bone.

LH §200: If an *awīlu* should knock out the tooth of another *awīlu* of his own rank, they shall knock out his tooth.[72]

---

69. Trans. Roth, "Laws of Hammurabi," *COS* 2.131:348; cf. Hittite Laws §10: "If anyone injures a person and temporarily incapacitates him, he shall provide medical care for him. In his place he shall provide a person to work on his estate until he recovers. When he recovers, (his assailant) shall pay him 6 shekels of silver and shall pay the physician's fee as well" (trans. Hoffner, "Hittite Laws," *COS* 2.19:107).
70. *COS* 2.19:118.
71. Here the father does not perform this function if the widow's brother-in-law dies, but see Gen. 38.
72. Trans. Roth, "Laws of Hammurabi," *COS* 2.131:348.

Lev. 24:19–20: If anyone injures his neighbor, as he has done it shall be done to him, fracture for fracture, eye for eye, tooth for tooth; whatever injury he has given a person shall be given to him. (cf. Exod. 21:23–25; Deut. 19:19, 21)

It seems clear that OT laws were formulated with awareness of ANE legal traditions.[73] However, the Bible presents OT law as promulgated by and carrying authority from the Deity YHWH, whose distinctive set of values is represented by his commandments. Thus OT law has utilized and thereby affirmed some existing legal concepts that are in harmony with YHWH's values.

Differences

While OT law overlaps with other ANE legal traditions in many respects, it differs in significant ways, such as the following:

First, Shalom Paul has pointed out that "only in biblical compilations are moral exhortations and religious injunctions combined with legal prescriptions; elsewhere . . . these three distinct spheres are found in separate independent collections"[74]—namely, "law collections, wisdom literature, and priestly handbooks."[75] The uniquely holistic nature of OT law is due to the fact that "man's civil, moral and religious obligations all ultimately stem from God, and hence are interwoven within a single corpus of divinely given law."[76]

Second, OT law was given and intended to operate within the context of the unique covenant between Israel and the one Deity YHWH (Exod. 19:5; 24:7–8; 34:27–28; Lev. 26:3, 9, 14–15; Deut. 29:1), who instructed his people to emulate his holy character in how they relate to him and other human beings (Exod. 19:6; Lev. 11:44–45; 19:2, 18, 34; 20:26; Deut. 6:5). Outside Israel, laws were developed in cultures saturated with polytheism and idolatry, so they do not relate at all to commandments in the Decalogue or other OT laws regarding obligations to one true Deity (Exod. 20:3–11; etc.).

73. See, e.g., David P. Wright, *Inventing God's Law: How the Covenant Code of the Bible Used and Revised the Laws of Hammurabi* (Oxford: Oxford University Press, 2009).
74. Shalom Paul, *Studies in the Book of the Covenant in the Light of Cuneiform and Biblical Law*, VTSup 18 (Leiden: Brill, 1970; repr., Eugene, OR: Wipf & Stock, 2006), 43. Some laws of the ANE collections touch on religion, but only in a very limited sense. Thus the Laws of Hammurabi address an accusation of practicing witchcraft (§2) and stipulate punishments for stealing things belonging to a deity (or to the palace, §§6, 8). The Hittite Laws require proper disposal of remnants of a ritual for purifying a person "in the incineration dumps. But if he disposes of them in someone's house, it is sorcery (and) a case for the king" (§44b; trans. Hoffner, "Hittite Laws," COS 2.19:110; cf. §XXXIV [= late version of §44b?]).
75. Paul, *Studies*, 37.
76. Ibid.

Third, only OT law deals with underlying attitudes, such as love (Lev. 19:18, 34; Deut. 6:5) versus hatred and grudges (Lev. 19:17–18), covetousness (Exod. 20:17; Deut. 5:21), and generous versus selfish thinking (Deut. 15:9–10), which only God can detect and reward or punish.[77]

Fourth, unlike some ANE laws, OT law does not permit mere economic compensation for homicide or from physical loss resulting from assault, thereby placing a higher value on human life made in God's image (cf. Gen. 9:6; see chap. 3 above).[78] Like Exod. 21:12, the Laws of Ur-Namma §1 orders capital punishment for homicide.[79] However, the Hittite Telipinu Edict §49 allows for the possibility that a murderer can be ransomed if the heir of his victim says: "Let him make compensation."[80] By contrast, Num. 35:31 categorically prohibits a ransom payment in a case of murder, leaving no option but the death penalty (cf. v. 33; Lev. 24:17, 21). The Laws of Eshnunna §47A specifies a money payment for death resulting from a brawl: "40 shekels of silver,"[81] but OT law has no corresponding provision: Exod. 21:18–19 clears (apparently from capital punishment) a man who injures another in a quarrel only if the latter does not die.

The Laws of Hammurabi §198 indicates payment for injury resulting from assault of a lower-status person: "If he [an *awîlu*, referred to in §§196–97; see above] should blind the eye of a commoner or break the bone of a commoner, he shall weigh and deliver 60 shekels of silver."[82] This financial alternative to the lex talionis for assault is not available in biblical law, which mandates literal retaliatory punishment in such cases (Lev. 24:19–20), acknowledging the priceless nature of the human body, which is made in God's image (cf. Gen. 1:27; 9:6).

Fifth, unlike OT law, some other ANE laws punish individuals through the deaths of their family members, as in the following examples:

LH §229: If a builder constructs a house for a man but does not make his work sound, and the house that he constructs collapses and causes the death of the householder, that builder shall be killed.

77. For the idea that God knows human thoughts, see, e.g., 1 Sam. 16:7; 1 Chron. 28:9; Ps. 139:2, 4, 23–24; Jer. 11:20.
78. Concerning homicide, cf. Moshe Greenberg, "Some Postulates of Biblical Criminal Law," in *Yehezkel Kaufmann Jubilee Volume*, ed. Menahem Haran (Jerusalem: Magnes, 1960), 13–20; Greenberg, "More Reflections on Biblical Criminal Law," in *Studies in Bible*, ed. Sara Japhet, ScrHier 31 (Jerusalem: Magnes, 1986), 9–17.
79. Trans. Roth, "Laws of Ur-Namma," *COS* 2.153:409.
80. Trans. Hoffner, "Hittite Laws," *COS* 2.19:119.
81. Trans. Roth, "Laws of Eshnunna," *COS* 2.130:334.
82. Trans. Roth, "Laws of Hammurabi," *COS* 2.131:348, with supplied explanation in brackets. Cf. §201 regarding payment for the tooth of a commoner. Other law collections also prescribe monetary compensations for physical injuries: Laws of Ur-Namma §§15–17; Laws of Eshnunna §§42–46; Hittite Laws §§7–16.

LH §230: If it should cause the death of a son of the householder, they shall kill a son of that builder.[83]

Here LH §230 applies a kind of lex talionis to make the punishment fit the crime by causing loss to the offender that is equal to that which he brought upon the other person. However, the one who is physically affected (by death in this case) is someone other than the offender (cf. §§116, 210; Middle Assyrian Laws A §55).

This has been called "vicarious talion,"[84] which implies that the family member dies *in place of* the one who committed the crime. More precisely, however, it appears that the son in LH §230 dies because he *belongs to* his father, who is punished by losing his son. If so, this is a talionic instance of what David Daube has called "ruler punishment,"[85] so we could label it "talionic ruler punishment." In any case, Deut. 24:16 prohibits Israelites from putting one person to death when his relative has committed the crime: "Fathers shall not be put to death because of their children, nor shall children be put to death because of their fathers. Each one shall be put to death for his own sin" (cf. 2 Kings 14:6).[86] Thus, when an ox with a history of goring kills a man's son or daughter, it is the owner of the ox who is to be put to death unless he is ransomed (Exod. 21:31; cf. vv. 29–30), not the son or daughter of the owner.[87]

Sixth, there are no social class distinctions between free persons in OT laws against assault or murder.[88] This is in contrast to some ANE laws that assign more or less severe punishments to those who attack individuals of higher or lower rank, as in the Laws of Hammurabi §§196–98 (see above; cf. §§200–204, §§206–12).

Seventh, in OT law adultery is an absolute wrong that requires capital punishment for both parties (Lev. 20:10; Deut. 22:22), with no variations in penalties due to different kinds of intention. Circumstances can be relevant for determining whether an illicit sexual act involving a married (including betrothed) woman is regarded as (consensual) adultery or (nonconsensual)

---

83. Trans. Roth, "Laws of Hammurabi," *COS* 2.131:349.

84. Paul, *Studies*, 77.

85. David Daube, *Studies in Biblical Law* (Cambridge: Cambridge University Press, 1947; repr., New York: Ktav, 1969), 161–86, esp. 165: "A sinner might be punished by being deprived of human 'property' (his men if he was a king, his son if he was a father, his wife if he was a husband) just as well as by being deprived of any other goods."

86. Putting fathers to death because of their children would not be "ruler punishment." According to Ezek. 18, esp. v. 20, punishment by YHWH himself follows the same principle as in Deut. 24:16.

87. Daube, *Studies*, 167–68.

88. For laws against excessive discipline or assault against slaves by their masters, see Exod. 21:20–21, 26–27.

rape (Deut. 22:23–27). But if it is adultery, the circumstances, including lack of premeditation (vv. 23–24), do not alter the punishment. The offense is not only against the husband of the woman but also against God, who created marriage as the sacred foundation of the home and society (Gen. 2:18, 21–24), so the husband is not permitted to lighten the penalty.[89]

Extrabiblical ANE law is more subjective with regard to adultery.[90] The penalty can be death (Laws of Eshnunna §28; Laws of Hammurabi §133b; Middle Assyrian Laws A §§13, 15). But in other cases the punishments are influenced by degrees of intention indicated by circumstances, with the husband having jurisdiction over his adulterous wife and therefore determining her punishment, which the state matches for her paramour unless (in some instances) he can establish his inadvertence (Laws of Hammurabi §129; Middle Assyrian Laws A §§14–16, A §23; cf. Hittite Laws §§197–98).[91]

Eighth, OT law provides a major advance in jurisprudence by consistently treating an individual as innocent unless found to be guilty through an authorized procedure, as in United States law. Even in the unique suspected-adulteress ritual, through which YHWH himself delivers the verdict, the test involving a conditional curse and holy water only punishes a guilty woman by divine intervention; the procedure is otherwise physically harmless and does not affect an innocent woman (Num. 5:16–28; cf. chap. 13 below). This differs from other ANE trials by ordeal, in which an accused person, whether innocent or guilty, is subjected to real physical danger apart from any action by a deity.[92] For example,

> LH §132: If a man's wife should have a finger pointed against her in accusation involving another male, although she has not been seized lying with another male, she shall submit to the divine River Ordeal for her husband.[93]

The River Ordeal involved jumping or being thrown into the Euphrates River, which was regarded as a divine judge. A person who survived was presumed innocent, but one who drowned was regarded as guilty.

89. Greenberg, "Postulates," 12–13; Anthony Phillips, *Essays on Biblical Law*, JSOTSup 344 (London: Sheffield Academic, 2002), 74–93, repr. of "Another Look at Adultery," *JSOT* 20 (1981): 3–25.

90. Cf. Roy Gane, *Leviticus, Numbers*, NIV Application Commentary (Grand Rapids: Zondervan, 2004), 365–66.

91. Greenberg, "Postulates," 12; Jacob J. Finkelstein, "Sex Offenses in Sumerian Laws," *JAOS* 86 (1966): 355–72.

92. Herbert C. Brichto, "The Case of the *SŌṬĀ* and a Reconsideration of Biblical 'Law,'" *HUCA* 46 (1975): 64–66.

93. Trans. Roth, "Laws of Hammurabi," *COS* 2.131:344.

The present chapter has identified some key aspects of the historical backgrounds of OT laws, including the social and legal culture of ancient Israel, diachronic development of OT law, and relationships to other ANE laws. As the next chapters of the present volume demonstrate, before we can attempt to apply the laws to modern Christian life, we must understand OT laws within their ancient contexts in order to accurately identify their underlying principles.

PART 3

Applying Old Testament Laws

7

Introduction to Applying Old Testament Laws to Christian Life

Christians in general will be interested in OT laws to the extent that they can benefit by applying these teachings to their lives in valid, sensible, and practical ways. A significant number of the laws are clear, show good common sense, and are obviously transcultural and transtemporal. So it is easy to see that they can be just as helpful today as they would have been in ancient Israel if we will only read and follow them.

For example, the Ten Commandments call for fulfillment of basic duties: "Honor your father and your mother. . . . You shall not murder. You shall not commit adultery. You shall not steal. You shall not bear false witness against your neighbor. You shall not covet" (Exod. 20:12–17). The Covenant Code contains wise mandates: "You shall not mistreat any widow or fatherless child" (Exod. 22:22 [22:21 MT]). "You shall not revile God, nor curse a ruler of your people" (v. 28 [v. 27 MT]). "You shall not spread a false report" (23:1). Leviticus 19 instructs the people: "You shall not steal; you shall not deal falsely; you shall not lie to one another. . . . You shall do no injustice in court. . . . You shall not hate your brother in your heart. . . . You shall not take vengeance or bear a grudge against the sons of your own people, but you shall love your neighbor as yourself" (vv. 11, 15, 17–18).

Deuteronomy commands them: "You shall love the LORD your God with all your heart and with all your soul and with all your might" (6:5). "You shall not pervert justice. You shall not show partiality, and you shall not accept a bribe" (16:19). On quite a specific level, Deuteronomy requires a parapet (a low wall) around a flat roof to protect those who walk there from falling off (22:8).

If modern Christians were to fully implement only this small sampling of OT laws, which are straightforward but carry deep and broad implications (esp. Lev. 19:18, 34 and Deut. 6:5 regarding the overall value of love), how much better our lives and society would be! The benefit can radically expand if we recognize that each principle can be represented by the absence of its opposite. So we can logically take negatively formulated laws as protections of positive values.

For example, the negatively formulated commandments "You shall not murder. You shall not commit adultery. You shall not steal" (Exod. 20:13–15) protect life, marriage, and property from serious violations, implying that we should go the other direction—away from murder, adultery, and theft—to show respect for life, marriage, and property in as many ways as we can. Conversely, the positively formulated commandment "Honor your father and your mother" (Exod. 20:12) implies a prohibition against dishonoring them (cf. Exod. 21:15, 17; Deut. 21:18–21).

Remember that forbidding one behavior (e.g., murder) may sound less pleasant than permission of all the other activities that are allowed (almost infinite), but the former formulation may appear simply because it is more economical (Gen. 2:16–17). So we should not succumb to the depressing and debilitating notion that OT law and Christian life are all or mainly about what we cannot do (see chap. 5 above).

Unfortunately, it is easy to take the clear laws for granted and fixate on some of the more difficult ones. This can lead to neglect of some laws that we could readily keep, or even premature dismissal of the whole body of OT laws as too weird and fraught with complications. It would be better to follow the instructions that are immediately accessible to us while exploring the others, all under the guiding value of love. Love is not just a feeling: basically, love is an ethical imperative, something to do. We *should do love* (Lev. 19:18, 34; Deut. 6:5; cf. Matt. 22:37–40).

The present chapter of this volume introduces some key factors involved in application of OT laws to modern life. This introduction facilitates comprehension of the next chapter (8), which surveys and critiques some existing scholarly approaches to such application. Then chapter 9 builds on the two chapters before it to synthesize a holistic approach to application that is termed "Progressive Moral Wisdom."

Problems with Direct Application of Old Testament Laws

In our exploration of OT law, we encounter problems or even obstacles regarding direct application of many laws because of various issues, more than one of which can occur in connection with a given law. Here we will summarize categories of problems and point in the direction of solutions that will be further developed and exemplified in subsequent chapters of the present volume.

Exegetical Issues

Some laws are hard to comprehend because they include cultural elements that are foreign to us, such as usage of Hebrew terminology (e.g., *'el-ha'elohim*, "to God[?]," in Exod. 21:6; *biflilim*, "as the judges[?] determine," in v. 22) and reference to obsolete Israelite customs (e.g., "The right of the firstborn" in Deut. 21:17; "up to the gate to the elders" in 25:7; "and pull his sandal off his foot" in v. 9).

How can we apply a law if we don't fully grasp what it is about? The main solution is good exegesis, examining the language of the law and its referents within their linguistic and cultural contexts. Even if our own exegetical study and analyses found in scholarly secondary sources do not offer a definitive answer regarding every detail, we may be able to grasp the overall point of the law.

Clearer laws may shed light on unclear ones. For example, Lev. 19:19 appears strange because it includes no rationale for ruling out certain kinds of mixtures. However, the parallel law in Deut. 22:9–11 indicates that mixtures belong to the divine sphere of holiness (v. 9, lest the whole mixed harvest shall become holy [*qal* of *q-d-sh*], i.e., forfeited to the sanctuary),[1] and Exod. 30:22–38 forbids making things that especially pertain to the holy realm, thereby diminishing holiness by blurring its distinction from what is common.[2]

Legal Scope Issues

Many OT laws regulate situations that do not occur in our lives. For instance, some laws are for farmers, who kept animals for various purposes

---

1. Cf. mixtures in Exod. 26:31; 28:6; Ezek. 1:10.
2. Cf. Jacob Milgrom, *Leviticus 17–22: A New Translation with Introduction and Commentary*, AB 3A (New York: Doubleday, 2000), 1660–62.

(Exod. 21:28–22:1; 22:4–6 [21:28–37; 22:3–5 MT]; etc.). Such people con-stituted the majority of ancient Israelites. These laws may apply to some farmers today (including the Amish, who still use work animals), but they seem irrelevant or impractical for most of us because we are not involved in agriculture. Other laws regulate social and legal institutions in which we in the modern West are not involved, such as slavery (Exod. 21:2–11, 20–21, 26–27; Lev. 25:39–55; Deut. 15:12–18; 23:15–16), polygamy (Exod. 21:10–11; Lev. 18:18; Deut. 21:15–17), levirate marriage (Deut. 25:5–10), and ancestral ownership of Israelite agricultural land, which was protected by the Jubilee instructions (Lev. 25). Laws commanding circumcision as a sign of initiation into the covenant community (Gen. 17; Lev. 12:3) do not apply to Christians because the new covenant has become universal, without a distinction between Jews and Gentiles (Acts 15; cf. Gal. 3:28), and the NT has terminated this religious requirement.

Quite a number of laws regulated an institution that does not exist any-where in the world today: the Israelite sanctuary/temple with its ritual worship system (e.g., Lev. 1–7, 16), which required separation between the holy sphere and physical ritual impurities (e.g., Lev. 11:24–45; 12:1–15:33). Moreover, the ancient Israelite theocracy is gone, so its humanly administered penalties are not in force,[3] although God can still administer divine penalties (see chaps. 5, 14 of the present volume).

How can we follow instructions that don't relate to what we do? Obviously, we can't. If we are outside the scope of a law, it is not for us to directly keep. Nevertheless, we may be able to learn from valuable concepts represented in the law, such as principles concerning liability and theft (Exod. 21–22 in farming contexts), divine holiness in contrast to human faultiness (Lev. 1–16 in sanctuary and related contexts), and the importance of provision for independent living (Lev. 25, Jubilee).

Some laws partly apply to us. For example:

> Whoever strikes a man so that he dies shall be put to death. But if he did not lie in wait for him, but God let him fall into his hand, then I will appoint for you a place to which he may flee. But if a man willfully attacks another to kill him by cunning, you shall take him from my altar, that he may die. (Exod. 21:12–14)

This expands on the sixth of the Ten Commandments: "You shall not murder" (Exod. 20:13). The idea that someone who intentionally, not accidentally, kills

---

3. But a few modern governments outside the West still administer some punishments like those of ancient Israel.

another person by striking him should be severely punished as a murderer is a logical extension of the Decalogue commandment and therefore constitutes a moral principle that remains in force today. However, the details "I will appoint for you a place to which he may flee" (cf. Num. 35; Deut. 19, cities of refuge) and "You shall take him from my altar" (cf. altar asylum in 1 Kings 1:50–53; 2:28–29) are obsolete, and a modern state may choose not to administer capital punishment.

Theodicy Issues

Some laws seem clear enough, but aspects of them are offensive to people within modern Western culture. Embarrassingly, they appear to represent a lower level of ethics (esp. in terms of individual freedom and human dignity) than that which we find in secular society today. For example, some OT laws regulate but still tolerate slavery and polygamy (see refs. above), and some of the penalties for violating laws strike us as unduly harsh (e.g., Lev. 20:9; Deut. 21:21; 25:2–3, 12). Especially brutal are theocratic laws commanding corporate capital punishment of the Canaanites (Deut. 7:1–2; 20:16–18).

Why should we lower our moral values to that of such an OT law? To begin with, notice that the kinds of laws just mentioned cannot directly apply to modern Christians because we do not practice slavery or polygamy, and the Israelite theocracy came to an end long ago. So the question is not how we can literally keep these laws. Rather, the issue concerns theodicy: How could God tolerate evils such as slavery and polygamy and command cruel punishments, and yet still claim that his moral system is based on love (Lev. 19:18, 34; Deut. 6:5; cf. Matt. 22:37–40; John 13:34–35; 1 John 4:8) if such love includes concern for happiness? Isn't this hypocritical? How can God's moral authority be trusted for any ethical decisions, including those that affect the happiness of homosexual persons? The biblical prohibition of homosexual practice (Lev. 18:22; 20:13) is a special case because not only is it offensive to many in modern Western society, but it can also be applied today, although without the theocratic penalty (20:13).

This theodicy issue calls for exploration of further questions, such as these: On what basis do we think our ethics and definition of love are superior to those of God? Does our view of happiness in this life reliably define unselfish true love? Does the OT law represent a moral "halfway (or quarterway) house" on the way to a higher standard, more closely applicable to us, that is pointed out elsewhere in Scripture (e.g., Gal. 3:28, "There is neither slave nor free"; 1 Tim. 3:2, 12, "the husband of one wife")? Did God have loving reasons for accommodating to human weakness and seeking to eliminate evils from ancient Israelite society through means that would work in that context? These are big questions. We will attempt to address them to some extent later in the present volume.[4]

Indirect Application of Old Testament Laws

We can indirectly apply the teachings and implications of many OT laws to varying degrees, whether or not they also directly apply to us. Indirect application can fill some gaps when we are faced with situations that no laws directly address. Paul wrote to Timothy: "All Scripture is breathed out by God and profitable for teaching, for reproof, for correction, and for training in righteousness, that the man of God may be complete, equipped for every good work" (2 Tim. 3:16–17). "All Scripture" includes all OT laws, including those that directly apply to us and those that do not so apply, for reasons mentioned above. If we accept what Paul says here, there must be indirect ways in which even laws that are not directly applicable to us are "profitable" for guiding and equipping the people of God, filling gaps in our wisdom regarding how to live.

This does not mean that the Bible tells us how to do everything, even if we have a sophisticated understanding of its teachings and how to apply them in all sorts of ways. Many gaps inevitably remain. However, by absorbing biblical wisdom we can develop attitudes (esp. the humble, unselfish attitude of Christ; Phil. 2:5–8) and discernment in harmony with God's character and will that enable us to navigate the many challenging choices of our complex lives with moral integrity.

Filling Gaps between Laws

The OT law is comprehensive in its overarching value of love (Lev. 19:18, 34; Deut. 6:5; see further below). There are no gaps or loopholes in love, so it can supply general direction in every situation. However, we often need more specific guidance as well. Paradigmatic examples of love in OT law were not complete in their coverage of potential life situations in ancient Israel,[5] and they are even less complete today. In our complex modern lives, which involve many technologies, procedures, norms, and institutions that did not exist in biblical times, we encounter circumstances involving ethical choices (e.g., stem-cell research, termination of life support) to which no specific biblical laws directly apply.[6]

---

4. See esp. chap. 14 on theodicy.
5. E.g., no OT laws specifically address abortion, euthanasia, and sexual abuse of children.
6. For studies that grapple with modern ethical issues in light of biblical guidance, see, e.g., John Jefferson Davis, *Evangelical Ethics*, 4th ed. (Phillipsburg, NJ: P&R, 2015); John S. Feinberg

How can we know what is the right thing to do if OT law doesn't address the issue? Even if no law directly applies, one or more subvalues of love exemplified in OT law may provide indirect guidance. For example, "You shall not murder" (Exod. 20:13) prohibits wrongful (excluding just war or capital punishment), *active* taking of a human life, including one's own, which applies to suicide and euthanasia (cf. 1 Sam. 31:3–5; 2 Sam. 1:6–16). However, it does not rule out *passive* measures that mercifully (guided by Lev. 19:18, "Love your neighbor") allow a terminally ill person to die naturally (showing respect for mortal life) by removing an artificial life-support system.[7]

Jesus demonstrates a way to fill gaps between laws by penetrating to the inner motivations that lead to moral violations. Here is an example: "You have heard that it was said to those of old, 'You shall not murder; and whoever murders will be liable to judgment.' But I say to you that everyone who is angry with his brother will be liable to judgment; whoever insults his brother will be liable to the council; and whoever says, 'You fool!' will be liable to the hell of fire" (Matt. 5:21–22). In applying the Decalogue prohibition of murder (Exod. 20:13), Jesus reminds people that God holds a person accountable for the kind of hatred and anger that is behind murder, as revealed in OT narrative (Gen. 4:5–8) and prohibited by law (Lev. 19:17–18).[8] Because this kind of anger is wrong, other manifestations of it are also wrong, such as insulting a person with whom one is angry. We could legitimately add other sinful fruits of anger attested elsewhere in the Bible, including cursing other people or God (e.g., Exod. 21:17; 22:28 [22:27 MT]; Lev. 24:11), slandering individuals (Lev. 19:16), falsely accusing them in court (Exod. 20:16; Deut. 19:16–21), or causing physical injury (Lev. 24:10, 19–20). Modern life provides opportunities for outlets of anger not mentioned in the Bible, such as cutting off a driver who arouses road rage by driving too slowly in the fast lane or emailing a computer virus to someone who has provoked us in some way.

Jesus's condemnation of lustful intent that can lead to adultery (Matt. 5:27–28; cf. Exod. 20:14) also implicates other manifestations of lust, such as flirting between individuals who are married to others and viewing pornography. Again, Jesus's approach identifies mental activity behind a particular

---

and Paul D. Feinberg, *Ethics for a Brave New World*, 2nd ed. (Wheaton, IL: Crossway, 2010); John F. Kilner, ed., *Why the Church Needs Bioethics: A Guide to Wise Engagement with Life's Challenges* (Grand Rapids: Zondervan, 2011); Scott B. Rae, *Moral Choices: An Introduction to Ethics*, 3rd ed. (Grand Rapids: Zondervan, 2009).

7. Cf. Walter C. Kaiser Jr., "A Principlizing Model," in *Four Views on Moving beyond the Bible to Theology*, ed. Gary T. Meadors, Counterpoints (Grand Rapids: Zondervan, 2009), 27–30.

8. However, some anger is not sinful (Eph. 4:26). Moses experienced righteous indignation on a number of occasions (e.g., Exod. 16:20; 32:19; Num. 16:15), as did God himself (e.g., Exod. 4:14; Num. 11:1, 10, 33; 25:3–4; Deut. 9:8, 20).

action prohibited by a law, which can spread out to generate other actions. He was emphasizing and drawing attention to the important role of thoughts, already presented in OT law, as in the Decalogue commandment against coveting, which forbids lust for the wife of another (Exod. 20:17).[9]

Responsible Analogy: Continuity with Discontinuity

Indirect application of OT laws requires thought and allows for some creative freedom within the framework of biblical wisdom, which protects one from arbitrary conclusions resulting from insertion of human notions or rationalization, rather than faithfulness to divine leading. In the next two chapters (8–9) we will discuss the matter of methodology in much more detail while critiquing scholarly models and developing a holistic approach, but we can introduce the topic here by considering a case study in which Paul gives us a head start, providing an example of indirect application by analogy.[10] In 1 Cor. 9 he cites and discusses Deut. 25:4:

> Do we [Paul and Barnabas] not have the right to eat and drink? . . . Who plants a vineyard without eating any of its fruit? Or who tends a flock without getting some of the milk? Do I say these things on human authority? Does not the Law say the same? For it is written in the Law of Moses, "You shall not muzzle an ox when it treads out the grain." Is it for oxen that God is concerned? Does he not speak certainly for our sake? It was written for our sake, because the plowman should plow in hope and the thresher thresh in hope of sharing in the crop. . . . Do you not know that those who are employed in the temple service get their food from the temple, and those who serve at the altar share in the sacrificial offerings? In the same way, the Lord commanded that those who proclaim the gospel should get their living by the gospel. (1 Cor. 9:4–14)

Deuteronomy 25:4, "You shall not muzzle an ox when it is treading out the grain," does not state a penalty for violation, but it seeks to prevent something that God regards as wrong. Presumably the itinerant Paul did not own an ox, so the law did not directly apply to him, although it could have directly applied to some of the Christians to whom his epistle is addressed. In any case, Paul found in this culturally garbed instruction a paradigmatic example of the principle of justice, not merely kindness, that workers deserve material benefit from their labors, which Jesus also expressed: "The laborer

---

9. Cf. teaching of biblical Wisdom literature against lust, e.g., Job 31:1; Prov. 6:25.

10. On analogical reasoning as a necessary method for applying Scripture to modern moral issues, see Charles H. Cosgrove, *Appealing to Scripture in Moral Debate: Five Hermeneutical Rules* (Grand Rapids: Eerdmans, 2002), 51–89.

deserves his food/wages" (cf. Matt. 10:10, "food"; Luke 10:7, "wages"). Paul applies this principle to support for Christian ministers (cf. 1 Tim. 5:17–18). So Paul views the narrow law as a kind of "window" on a broader area of divine teaching, somewhat the way a grammatical paradigm serves as a pattern that applies to many other analogous instances.[11]

There is both continuity and discontinuity between a paradigm and other cases to which it applies by analogy. In application of a grammatical paradigm, an inflection remains while lexical items change. In Paul's example, the element of benefiting from one's labor remains while the specifics change from the paradigmatic example of an ox grinding grain to the application of a minister engaged in spiritual work.

Paul strengthens the persuasiveness of his application by narrowing the gap between the animal agricultural example and the human ministerial application in two ways. First, he bridges the animal-to-human difference by pointing out that a human is also entitled to the results of his agricultural labor: "Who plants a vineyard without eating any of its fruit? Or who tends a flock without getting some of the milk? . . . The plowman should plow in hope and the thresher thresh in hope of sharing in the crop" (1 Cor. 9:7, 10).

Second, Paul bridges the agricultural-ministerial difference by referring to the rights of nonagricultural workers to receive support, beginning with a soldier (v. 7) and concluding with a form of ministry for which OT law makes provision: "Do you not know that those who are employed in the temple service get their food from the temple, and those who serve at the altar share in the sacrificial offerings?" (v. 13; cf. Lev. 7:7–10, 14, 31–36; Num. 18; etc.).

Why doesn't Paul simply refer to the laws regarding portions for sanctuary/temple personnel, which are much closer to his target application situation than the ox law, since they benefit humans involved in ministerial work? Perhaps some could object that the laws on cultic perquisites involve special circumstances that do not apply to Christian ministers because they are not employed at the sanctuary/temple. Paul makes a stronger case by first invoking the ox law, which exemplifies the principle of benefiting from one's work at a more basic level. In fact, its level is so basic that any application to human work implies an a fortiori argument: If even an ox has this right, the more so should a human.[12]

11. For the analogy of paradigms in grammar, see Christopher J. H. Wright, *Old Testament Ethics for the People of God* (Downers Grove, IL: InterVarsity, 2004), 65–66.

12. However, here Paul does not explicitly frame his application in a fortiori terms. Rather, he says: "Is it for oxen that God is concerned? Does he not speak certainly for our sake?" (1 Cor. 9:9–10). Thus he emphasizes that the law speaks directly to Christians (cf. Richard B. Hays, *Echoes of Scripture in the Letters of Paul* [New Haven: Yale University Press, 1989], 165–66),

For at least some of our indirect application of OT law, we can learn from Paul's approach. It is true that he was an apostle who was gifted with special inspiration, and we are not, but he did not base the persuasiveness of his conclusion on his apostolic authority or his own special revelation. Rather, he relied on careful identification of commonality between the purpose of biblical laws in addressing a certain kind of justice and the needs of an analogous situation that affected him and his ministerial coworkers. This kind of approach could be viewed as "responsible analogy, with 'responsible' in a dual sense, namely responsibility to the textual material (control) and personal responsibility and accountability in the way we apply it (freedom under responsibility)."[13]

Paul recognized the paradigmatic power and scope of the ox example: "Is it for oxen that God is concerned? Does he not speak certainly for our sake?" (1 Cor. 9:9–10). Reference to the origin of the law from God indicates that it was never intended to be only about oxen but was presented as a paradigm from the time when it was promulgated. This implies that at least some other OT laws were meant to function similarly.

Why did God choose to communicate values in this way? Why not formulate a law in terms of a raw principle, unencumbered by situation-bound details, such as "Thou shalt allow any worker, whether human or animal, to benefit from his labor?" First, the ox provides a memorable illustration at a basic, earthy level to which people could relate. Engaging with real life in the world of the original hearer is more interesting than a dry statement of principle. Second, instruction through the illustration alone is economical, especially when the illustration is on a basic level from which multiple applications can be derived through a fortiori reasoning. Third, by giving the illustration alone, the law calls for the hearer/reader who wishes to follow God to expend effort in exercising wise reflection to gain the benefit. Thus the law sets up a test between the wise/obedient and the unwise/disobedient. For the same reason Jesus taught with parables, paradigmatic stories (Matt. 13:10–17; cf. 12:50; 13:44–46).

Vertical and Horizontal/Historical Perspectives

To gain perspective for directly or indirectly applying an OT law, it is helpful to gain perspective by locating its coordinates both "vertically" within a

---

as if the ox represents the minister (cf. Paul's allegorization of narrative Torah in Gal. 4:21–31). Kaiser recognizes the a fortiori logic in 1 Cor. 9 ("Principlizing Model," in Meadors, *Four Views on Moving beyond the Bible to Theology*, 25). He also points out that Paul could have cited Deut. 24:14–15, which requires an employer to pay a poor hired worker on the same day (24–25).

13. Kenneth Bergland (PhD candidate, Andrews University), personal communication.

hierarchy of moral values flowing from love, which is epitomized by Christ's sacrifice, and "horizontally" within the historical progression to restore creation ideals in the new creation. Doing this facilitates recognition of the role that the law plays in guiding moral growth. Moral growth can be defined as moving toward greater fulfillment of higher moral values in the hierarchy and toward restoration of creation ideals. These axes ultimately converge because it was at creation that the highest values reigned supreme. The highest value of all is love (e.g., 1 Cor. 13; see further below), the moral character of the eternal Deity (1 John 4:8), which serves as the perpetual North Star to orient our moral compass.[14]

Hierarchy of Values Flowing from Love

The scope of some broader commands in the OT includes that of narrower commands, which serve as examples. Thus in Lev. 19:13 the broader prohibition "You shall not oppress your neighbor or rob him" is directly followed by an injunction that forbids a certain kind of oppression: "The wages of a hired worker shall not remain with you all night until the morning." Similarly, verse 15 begins with the overall "You shall do no injustice in court" and then supplies a case in point: "You shall not be partial to the poor or defer to the great."

Verse 17 prohibits a very broad category of inner attitudes—"You shall not hate your brother in your heart"—and then provides a specific positive illustration of outward compliance that expresses lack of hatred or at least choice of movement away from it: "you shall reprove your neighbor" (NRSV). This is just one of many ways to show lack of hatred. Others could include abstaining from oppressing someone or treating anyone unjustly in court.

Thus far we have found evidence for a hierarchy of values and value-based principles within just a few verses:

---

14. On God's demonstration of steadfast love (*khesed*) along with his sovereignty in Gen. 1–3, see Kyle D. Fedler, *Exploring Christian Ethics: Biblical Foundations for Morality* (Louisville: Westminster John Knox, 2006), 72–75.

The beginning of the next verse (Lev. 19:18) forbids another kind of expression of hate: "You shall not take vengeance or bear a grudge against the sons of your own people." The following words articulate an overall value-based principle, "You shall love your neighbor as yourself," that positively expresses what was negatively formulated in verse 17: "You shall not hate your brother in your heart" (v. 17a). Love is a very broad value that contains and generates many others, with subvalues and sub-subvalues descending the hierarchy at various levels and moving from generality and broader scope toward specificity and narrower focus.

Jesus recognized that love is the paramount value and virtue. When he was asked which is the greatest commandment in the Torah (Matt. 22:36), he identified two commandments concerning love: First and greatest is "You shall love the Lord your God with all your heart and with all your soul and with all your mind" (v. 37, citing Deut. 6:5), and second is "You shall love your neighbor as yourself" (Matt. 22:39; quoting Lev. 19:18; cf. Luke 10:25–28). Then he summarized: "On these two commandments depend all the Law and the Prophets" (Matt. 22:40), including all of canonical Scripture to that point. The Bible teaches about God's kind of love, which is his moral character (1 John 4:8). We need a lot of instruction concerning love because we have departed so far from it since the fall into sin.

Jesus did not artificially impose a human priority on the OT but astutely recognized the strategic placement of love in Deut. 6:5 immediately after the basic call to acknowledge YHWH as the one God: "Hear, O Israel: The Lord our God, the Lord is one" (v. 4),[15] which he cited in Mark 12 as the beginning of the first, most important commandment to love the Lord your God (vv. 29–30). This identifies the one God as the object of love, just as Exod. 20:2 identifies "the Lord your God, who brought you out of the land of Egypt," which immediately precedes the first of the Ten Commandments, as the Deity before whom you are to "have no other gods" (v. 3). Love also strategically appears in Lev. 19:18 at the heart of chapter 19[16] in the middle book of the Pentateuch (Leviticus), which is the foundation of the whole Bible.

Jesus encapsulated a guide to love for others in what has come to be called his Golden Rule: "So whatever you wish that others would do to you, do also

15. Recited by observant Jews as a prayer (called "Shema Yisrael" ["Hear, O Israel"] or simply "Shema") every morning and evening.
16. Mary Douglas finds Lev. 19 to be the central turning point in a "ring composition" structure of Leviticus. "Poetic Structure in Leviticus," in *Pomegranates and Golden Bells: Studies in Biblical, Jewish, and Near Eastern Ritual, Law, and Literature in Honor of Jacob Milgrom*, ed. David P. Wright, David N. Freedman, and Avi Hurvitz (Winona Lake, IN: Eisenbrauns, 1995), 251–53.

to them, for this is the Law and the Prophets" (Matt. 7:12; cf. Luke 6:31). The fact that he summarized "the Law and the Prophets" both with love (see above) and the Golden Rule indicates that the latter also defines love.

Broad values, such as love for one's neighbor (Lev. 19:18), provide overall guidance for moral rightness that unifies and gives perspective for more specific values. The specific values, in turn, supply the higher values with content and definition, showing how they are useful. So values at all levels need each other, and the interpreter should look both up and down the hierarchy.

The Bible demonstrates how values are useful by providing specific illustrations of how they apply in life. In the case of love for one's neighbor, OT law and other biblical genres supply many other positively and negatively formulated expressions of this value in action (e.g., Lev. 19:9–11, 13–16, 25:35–43; Deut. 24:10–25:3; Ps. 112:4–5, 9; Prov. 14:21; Isa. 58:6–7) so that we can know what love is and how to live according to it. Jesus affirmed that much of the OT unpacks the principle of love for one's neighbor (Matt. 22:39–40; Mark 12:31; cf. Luke 10:27–28), whom Jesus defined as including even people among groups that we would tend to regard as our enemies (Luke 10:29–37).

Jesus's own life on earth, as described in the Gospel accounts, has given us the greatest dynamic paradigm of love for others (e.g., Matt. 4:23–24; Luke 7:21–23; John 11:5; 13:1; Acts 10:38). Some of the most important, helpful, and frequent questions we can ask ourselves in various situations are these: What would Jesus do? What would he see in someone else that I should recognize? What is the truly loving thing to do in this situation, defining love in his way according to biblical values and principles?

Above all, Christ demonstrated and defined God's kind of unselfish, sacrificing love through his sacrifice on the cross, the pivotal event of salvation history, which fulfilled OT messianic hope and sacrificial typology (e.g., Gen. 3:15; Ps. 22; Isa. 53; John 1:29; Heb. 10):[17] "For God so loved the world, that he gave his only Son, that whoever believes in him should not perish but have eternal life" (John 3:16). "But God shows his love for us in that while we were still sinners, Christ died for us" (Rom. 5:8). That love, the attitude of Christ that he shares with us (Phil. 2:5; cf. vv. 1–4, 6–8), is the pinnacle, fountainhead, and guiding light of all moral goodness.

In accordance with Jesus's summary in Matt. 22, the Ten Commandments express subprinciples of love for God (Exod. 20:2–11) and love for human beings (vv. 12–17). Paul explicitly refers to the fact that several commandments of the Decalogue are subsumed under love for one's neighbor, for other human beings (cf. Luke 10:29–37):

---

17. On OT laws regarding sacrifices that prefigured Christ's sacrifice, see chap. 16.

Owe no one anything, except to love each other, for the one who loves another has fulfilled the law. For the commandments, "You shall not commit adultery, You shall not murder, You shall not steal, You shall not covet," and any other commandment, are summed up in this word: "You shall love your neighbor as yourself." Love does no wrong to a neighbor; therefore love is the fulfilling of the law. (Rom. 13:8–10; cf. Gal. 5:14; James 2:8)

The following table and abstracted diagram show how the value-based principles of the Ten Commandments (Exod. 20:3–17; paralleled by Deut. 5:7–21), expressed in positive terms, come under the two subvalues of love: love for God and love between humans. Here and in the following chapters, I use the demarcation and division of the biblical text into Ten Commandments that is followed by the Reformed tradition.[18] The verse numbers given here are from Exod. 20.

The Ten Commandments Divided by the Two Subvalues of Love

Love God	Love Humans
1 Treat the Lord as the only Deity (v. 3).	
2 Worship the Lord as a transcendent personality, for whom nothing that he has created can substitute (vv. 4–6).	
3 Respect the name of the Lord (YHWH, which represents his authority, character, and reputation; v. 7).	
4 Honor God as the creator by ceasing from work on the seventh day as he did at the end of the creation week (vv. 8–11).	
5	Honor your parents (v. 12).
6	Guard against wrongful taking of human life (v. 13).
7	Preserve sexual boundaries of marriage (v. 14).

18. Jewish tradition interprets the prologue (Exod. 20:2) as the first commandment (or "word" of the "Ten Words"; 34:28; Deut. 4:13; 10:4) and combines Exod. 20:3 with vv. 4–6 as the second commandment. Roman Catholic and Lutheran traditions combine vv. 3–6 into the first commandment and divide v. 17 into the ninth and tenth commandments (see, e.g., Walter C. Kaiser Jr., *Toward Old Testament Ethics* [Grand Rapids: Zondervan, 1983], 82–83; Patrick D. Miller, *The Ten Commandments*, Interpretation: Resources for the Use of Scripture in the Church [Louisville: Westminster John Knox, 2009], 15). For a table showing the numbering of the Ten Commandments according to various traditions, see Yiu Sing Lúcás Chan, *The Ten Commandments and the Beatitudes: Biblical Studies and Ethics for Real Life* (Lanham, MD: Rowman & Littlefield, 2012), 241.

Love God	Love Humans
8	Preserve property rights of others (v. 15).
9	Be truthful in court (v. 16).
10	Be satisfied with what you can legitimately acquire (v. 17).

It is true that the first commandment is basic, but listing the Ten Commandments vertically is not meant to imply that they carry descending degrees of importance. The following diagram more clearly shows the commandments of the Decalogue on the same hierarchical level:

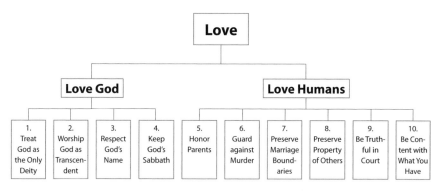

Commandments 1–4 and 5–10 are not as separate as they appear here. Love for other human beings (right column) shows love for God (left column) because humans bear his image (Gen. 1:26–27) and belong to him (e.g., Isa. 43:1). Jesus dramatically expressed the solidarity between love for others and love for God when he portrayed himself as the divine King who says to those who treat others with kindness, "As you did it to one of the least of these my brothers, you did it to me" (Matt. 25:40).

Another connection between love for God and love for humans is the fact that the Sabbath commandment includes both. The primary principle is to honor God as the creator (Exod. 20:11) or redeemer (Deut. 5:15), but a secondary principle is to allow others in one's household to enjoy the God-given benefit of Sabbath rest (Exod. 20:10), as emphasized in Moses's retelling of the commandment:

> On it you shall not do any work, you or your son or your daughter or your male servant or your female servant, or your ox or your donkey or any of your livestock, or the sojourner who is within your gates, that your male servant and your female servant may rest as well as you. (Deut. 5:14)

Work animals are included here along with humans. Love for them does not come under the heading of love between humans, but love for God as the Creator includes respect for everything he has created, including animals and the environment (cf. Sabbatical Year rest for the land in Exod. 23:10–11; Lev. 25:1–7). This includes respect for animal life, paralleling respect for human life (commandment 6), which needs rest.

As is well known, many instructions in the pentateuchal law collections are based on and apply the subprinciples of love articulated in the Decalogue (see chaps. 11–12 below).[19] A couple of the more obvious examples are these: "Whoever strikes a man so that he dies shall be put to death" (Exod. 21:12; cf. 20:13, "You shall not murder") and "If a man steals an ox or a sheep, and kills it or sells it, he shall repay five oxen for an ox, and four sheep for a sheep" (Exod. 22:1; cf. 20:15, "You shall not steal").

It is important to understand and keep in mind that the Ten Commandments are not comprehensive. Rather, they are prominent examples of broader moral areas. For instance, "You shall not murder" (Exod. 20:13), which can be positively expressed as "6: Guard against wrongful taking of human life" (see above), represents the broader principle to "respect life," which also includes principles such as guarding against wrongful infliction of permanent physical defects in another human being (Lev. 24:19–20). "You shall not commit adultery" (Exod. 20:14) expressed as "7: Preserve sexual boundaries of marriage" represents a broader principle to "maintain sexual purity." This kind of moral purity is biblically defined as limiting sexual expression to legitimate heterosexual marriage, in accordance with the creation ideal (Gen. 1–2; see further below). Elsewhere in OT law, maintaining sexual purity is also exemplified by laws against premarital sex (Exod. 22:16–17 [22:15–16 MT]), rape (Deut. 22:25–29), incest (Lev. 18:6–18; 20:11–12, 14, 17, 19–21; Deut. 22:30 [23:1 MT]), homosexual activity (Lev. 18:22; 20:13), and bestiality (Lev. 18:23; 20:15–16), plus restrictions on polygamy (Exod. 21:10–11; Lev. 18:18) and divorce (Deut. 24:1–4).

We have found a hierarchy of principles flowing from love. "Hierarchy" in this context refers to the concept in General Systems Theory of a structure in which larger items contain smaller items, and in these smaller items yet smaller items are embedded/nested, and so on through any number of levels. There is no suggestion that smaller items are unimportant and therefore dispensable. The larger items would not be what they are without the smaller items,

---

19. Stephen A. Kaufman has argued that the Deuteronomic law collection expands on and is structured according to the Decalogue. "The Structure of the Deuteronomic Law," *Maarav* 1, no. 2 (1978–79): 105–58.

just as an organism dies without an essential small organ. Thus violation of a biblical command that is small in the sense that its scope is narrow automatically violates the larger principle of love in which the small command is embedded (cf. James 2:10). It would be illogical and unbiblical to assert that only love matters now, so I am free to break a smaller divine command. Such an approach certainly would not help a marriage, in which true love must be demonstrated in all kinds of little ways, none of which are trivial because they seem small.

Ephesians 5:1–4 shows how the moral hierarchy flowing from love works in Christian life:

> Therefore be imitators of God, as beloved children. And walk in love, as Christ loved us and gave himself up for us, a fragrant offering and sacrifice to God. But sexual immorality and all impurity or covetousness must not even be named among you, as is proper among saints. Let there be no filthiness nor foolish talk nor crude joking, which are out of place, but instead let there be thanksgiving.

Here love guides the overall Christian "walk" (cf. 1 Cor. 13:13; Gal. 5:6). This is God's kind of unselfish love: "as Christ loved us and gave himself up for us." Love includes positive elements such as thanksgiving but excludes behaviors characterized as sexually immoral, impure, and covetous. Moral "impurity" could be regarded as including "foolish talk" and "crude joking," which are fairly specific kinds of activities. If so, we can identify one branch of a positive hierarchy of values from broad and general at the top to more narrow and specific lower down: love → purity → pure speech. We need both the general and specific perspectives, with the former (the "forest") providing an overall guide, within which the latter (the "trees") provides examples to help us with application in real life, without attempting to exhaustively prescribe each detail of our conduct.

Love is associated with holiness in both Testaments. The Lord's first and overall command in Lev. 19 is "You shall be holy, for I the LORD your God am holy" (v. 2). Within this framework are a variety of instructions regarding interactions with God and other humans, and at the center of the chapter is the command "You shall love your neighbor as yourself" (v. 18). It is not surprising that emulating God's holiness would involve love, because God's holy character is love (1 John 4:8). In 1 Thess. 3:12–13 increase of love is paralleled by growth of holiness (= sanctification), indicating that the more loving God's people become, the closer they approach him in character: "May the Lord make you *increase and abound in love* for one another and for all, as we do for you, so that he may *establish your hearts blameless in holiness* before our God and Father, at the coming of our Lord Jesus with all his saints" (emphasis added).[20]

If all of God's instructions are subsumed under love, which is the holy divine character that we are to emulate, and if Christ is divine (e.g., Luke 1:35; John 8:58; 10:30, 36–38), then obedience to all of God's instructions is imitation of Christ. Paul indicates this in Eph. 5:2: "Walk in love, as Christ loved us and gave himself up for us." In addition to imitation of Christ, scholars have labeled two other kinds of ethical bases as "deontological," because a course of action is right as one's duty (e.g., Eph. 6:1, "Children, obey your parents in the Lord, for this is right"), and "teleological," because it reaches a goal with a good result (v. 3, "that it may go well with you and that you may live long in the land").[21]

Old Testament law is right because it flows from love, teaches holy living that emulates God's character, and has a good result. This affects our understanding of specific laws and our attitude toward them. Consider an extreme and currently controversial example: "If a man lies with a male as with a woman, both of them have committed an abomination; they shall surely be put to death; their blood is upon them" (Lev. 20:13). How is this loving? In light of our discussion above, this law fits into the hierarchy of values and value-based principles as follows:

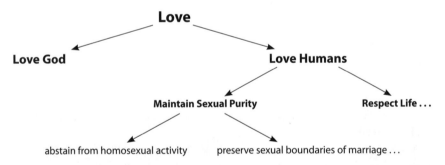

Abstaining from homosexual activity, like preserving the sexual boundaries of marriage and a number of other values (see above), comes under and serves the purpose to "maintain sexual purity," which is necessary to fulfill the principle to "love humans." The fact that several principles on the same hierarchical level as "abstain from homosexual activity" are also protected by capital punishment, administered under the Israelite theocracy (gone now),

20. Paul goes on to specify some aspects of a holy and loving life in 1 Thess. 4:1–12.
21. E.g., John Barton, *Understanding Old Testament Ethics: Approaches and Explorations* (Louisville: Westminster John Knox, 2003), 52–53.

for violation of them (adultery, Lev. 20:10; Deut. 22:22; rape, Deut. 22:25; incest, Lev. 20:11–12, 14; bestiality, Lev. 20:15–16) indicates the importance of maintaining sexual purity for truly loving human beings. If the penalty sounds harsh, it is because these principles are so crucial and consequences of violating them are so serious for individuals and society that God lovingly seeks to prevent and root out the causes of such harm (cf. Deut. 10:13, commandments "for your good").

Many people today suppose that the principle to "love humans" includes homosexual marriage, which they view as a valid expression of love. However, they overlook the fact that any legitimate sexual expression must come under the rule to "maintain sexual purity," a principle under the value calling us to "love humans," which delineates human love in the area of sexuality, limiting it to heterosexual marriage (also excluding adultery, etc.). We may not understand why, but the wise and loving Creator has made it that way (Gen. 1–2) and has never changed it. Humans lack the authority to revise the divine pattern for sexual intimacy or the power to alter its results.[22] To attempt a change in this regard is to usurp the place of God.

There can be strong and loyal pure love between members of the same gender, such as Jacob and his son Joseph; Naomi and her daughter-in-law Ruth; David and his brother-in-law, friend, and comrade Jonathan; and Jesus and his beloved disciple (John), but not pure sexual love.[23] Biblically speaking, homoerotic love is not pure love that God accepts. Likewise, although there can be pure love between members of the opposite sex who are not married to each other, such as Jephthah and his daughter, Mordecai and his cousin Esther, and Jesus and his friends Mary and Martha, there is no such thing as pure sexual love outside marriage. Amnon, a son of David, "loved" (*qal* of *'-h-b*) his half sister Tamar (2 Sam. 13:1, 4), leading to his incestuous rape of her (v. 14; incest prohibited in Lev. 18:9; 20:17), but this was not pure love any more than was David's adulterous lust for Bathsheba (2 Sam. 11:2–4) or a Corinthian Christian's undoubted liking for his stepmother with whom he was cohabiting (1 Cor. 5:1).

Progression in Restoration of Creation Ideals

Paul uses creation language to describe converted people whom God has regenerated to produce good works: "For we are his workmanship, created [*ktizō*] in Christ Jesus for good works, which God prepared beforehand, that

22. On homosexual activity and "marriage," see chap. 15 below.
23. On modern application of this principle, see Wesley Hill, *Spiritual Friendship: Finding Love in the Church as a Celibate Gay Christian* (Grand Rapids: Brazos, 2015).

we should walk in them" (Eph. 2:10; cf. v. 15). Paul uses the same Greek word in Eph. 3:9 to speak of "God, who created [*ktizō*] all things" (cf. Rev. 10:6), referring to the original creation described in Gen. 1–2. He joins the two kinds of creation in Eph. 4:23–24, where he reminds the Ephesian believers that they had been taught "to be renewed in the spirit of your minds, and to put on the new self, created [*ktizō*] after the likeness of God in true righteousness and holiness." In ESV the phrase "after the likeness of God" (cf. similarly in NRSV; CEB) interprets *kata theon*, "according to God" (NKJV). That is, converted Christians are re-created "to be like God in true righteousness and holiness" (NIV). This fulfills God's OT call to emulate him in holy living (Lev. 11:44–45; 19:2; 20:7, 26), which Peter applies to Christians (1 Pet. 1:15–16).

Reference to creation according to God, to be like God, also strongly alludes to Gen. 1:26–27: "Then God said, 'Let us make man in our image, after our likeness.' . . . So God created man in his own image, in the image of God he created him; male and female he created them." Therefore, re-creation in Christ (cf. 2 Cor. 5:17) restores believers to the ideal of righteousness and holiness that God had for them in the beginning.

The portions of Gen. 1–2 describing the creation of human life could appear to be slender evidence for an ideal system of moral values. However, the brief accounts of what God set up in a perfect world provide remarkably rich conceptual DNA that implies values in a positive way without expressing them as commandments. Regarding the "creation ordinances," Walter C. Kaiser Jr. observes,

> These ordinances reflect the work of God in creation and depict "the constitution of things" as they were intended to be from the Creator's hand. They cover and regulate the whole gamut of life: bearing children, superintending the earth as a responsible steward before and under God, responsibly ruling the creatures of all creation, finding fulfillment and satisfaction in work labor, resting on the Sabbath, and enjoying marriage as a gift from above.[24]

Most significant are marriage and Sabbath, the two original human institutions.

First, God created male and female humans as equal partners in his image (i.e., like him in important ways) to govern the other creatures on planet Earth (Gen. 1:26–27) and to cultivate and keep the garden of Eden (2:15). He created man and woman for each other to be joined in the union of marriage as "one flesh" (2:20–24), and he blessed them and their capacity for continuing creation by producing new human lives (1:28). This one-flesh covenant bond between Adam and Eve (Gen. 2:23–24) informs our understanding of ideal

24. Kaiser, *Toward Old Testament Ethics*, 31.

love between all members of the human family, who have issued from that first marriage. Marriage is the basic human social relationship. While other relationships are less intimate, the value of belonging to one another to varying degrees so that we are each other's "keepers" (contra Cain in 4:9) has great relevance for ethics in many areas of life.

Second, on the seventh day of the creation week, God ceased (*qal* of *sh-b-t*) from his creative work (2:2) and "blessed the seventh day and made it holy" (v. 3). By bringing the creation days to a close in this way, God created the ongoing weekly cycle[25] that would structure human life throughout the future,[26] and by making the seventh day holy he established holy time (cf. Lev. 23). What God did during the creation week was for the benefit of human beings, who would follow his example because they were made in his image.[27] So the "Sabbath was made for man" (Mark 2:27), as Jesus explicitly affirmed. By emulating God on the Sabbath, humans participate in his holiness, as he is holy (cf. Lev. 19:2), which explains why the Sabbath serves as the sign that God sanctifies his people (Exod. 31:13). Preserving a sense of holy time ordained as such by the Creator can greatly encourage holy living, in which believers are grateful for and accountable to his unique lordship.

Marriage and Sabbath are prominent and unique in several ways. First, God explicitly blessed only these elements of the created world (1:28; 2:3). Second, marriage and Sabbath were not just for Adam and Eve, but for the whole human race. Regarding marriage, this is shown by the fact that they would need the assistance of their descendants in carrying out the blessing to "multiply and fill the earth" (Gen. 1:28). Sabbath rest delineated the weekly cycle and set a pattern for the benefit of anyone on planet Earth (cf. Mark 2:27), just as "signs" and "seasons" and "days and years" (Gen. 1:14) would be for everyone. Third, marriage and Sabbath encapsulate divine example: procreation within marriage continues God's creation, and Sabbath

25. Delineation of the week by the Sabbath explains why the plural of *shabbat*, "S/sabbath," can refer to "weeks," i.e., periods from one Sabbath to the next (Lev. 23:15; cf. 25:8, "weeks [lit., sabbaths] of years").

26. Until today even for atheists, agnostics, and adherents of religions that do not accept the Lord (YHWH) as their deity. Other cycles of time—days, months, and years—are signified by movements of earth, the moon, and the sun (cf. Gen. 1:14), but not the Israelite week, which "is entirely independent of the movement of celestial bodies. The Sabbath thus underlines the fundamental idea of Israelite monotheism: that God is wholly outside of nature" (Nahum M. Sarna, *Genesis: The Traditional Hebrew Text with the New JPS Translation*, JPS Torah Commentary [Philadelphia: Jewish Publication Society, 1989], 15). Because the existence of the week depends on the word and example of YHWH, all who structure their time in weeks implicitly acknowledge his authority.

27. Cf. Gordon J. Wenham, *Story as Torah: Reading Old Testament Narrative Ethically* (Grand Rapids: Baker Academic, 2000), 27.

rest emulates God's cessation of work (2:2; Exod. 20:11; 31:17). Fourth, the Bible repeatedly protects marriage and Sabbath for humans by categorical divine commandments, including the Decalogue (Exod. 20:8–11, 14; Deut. 5:12–14, 18).[28] Fifth, Sabbath and marriage exemplify God's kind of loyal love in the two overall areas of love for him (Deut. 6:5) and love for other human beings (Lev. 19:18), which are represented in the Decalogue (Exod. 20; Deut. 5) and cover all of God's revealed will (Matt. 22:37–40).

Genesis does not directly state that God created humans and other creatures to love them, but this is abundantly clear from the care that he lavished on them by creating a perfect world, with everything they need for their well-being and happiness. God brought his character of love (1 John 4:8) to planet Earth and applied this greatest of all values to the setting here, where he established marriage and Sabbath. Shining through these two institutions the way light passes through a prism to refract light, love generates a hierarchy of moral values to be cherished, maintained, and applied by human beings. This hierarchy includes love between humans ("You shall love your neighbor as yourself"; Lev. 19:18; Matt. 22:39), first exemplified by marriage, which produces all subsequent human life. It also includes love for God ("You shall love the LORD your God"; Deut. 6:5; Matt. 22:37), first exemplified by the Sabbath, which acknowledges the one God, whose personal name is YHWH (usually translated "the LORD"),[29] as the Creator (Exod. 20:11; 31:17) and deliverer (Deut. 5:15). From these two categories of love, the value-based principles exemplified in the Decalogue radiate (see the table earlier in this chapter).

If conversion involves divine restoration to original values of righteousness and holiness, it follows that creation ideals can inform Christian life. Jesus showed the way when he was asked: "Is it lawful to divorce one's wife for any cause?" (Matt. 19:3), "for any reason at all?" (NASB).[30]

He answered, "Have you not read that he who created them from the beginning made them male and female, and said, 'Therefore a man shall leave his father and his mother and hold fast to his wife, and the two shall become one flesh'? So they are no longer two but one flesh. What therefore God has joined together, let not man separate." They said to him, "Why then did Moses command one to give a

28. See elsewhere regarding marriage: Lev. 18:20; 20:10; Num. 5:11–31; Deut. 22:22. Regarding Sabbath: Exod. 23:12; 31:13–17; 35:2–3; Lev. 23:3; etc.
29. Usually transliterated as Yahweh (formerly Jehovah).
30. It appears that Jesus was being asked to register his opinion regarding a disagreement between two rabbinic traditions: that of the House of Shammai, which interpreted the ground for divorce in Deut. 24:1—lit., "the indecency of a thing/matter"—as "a thing/matter of indecency" (possibly indecent exposure), and that of the House of Hillel, which said that a man could divorce his wife even if she spoiled a dish of food that she cooked for him (m. Gittin 9.10).

certificate of divorce and to send her away?" He said to them, "Because of your hardness of heart Moses allowed you to divorce your wives, but from the beginning it was not so. And I say to you: whoever divorces his wife, except for sexual immorality [*porneia*], and marries another, commits adultery." (Matt. 19:4–9)

Jesus's answer to the question is clear: no, it is not lawful to divorce one's wife for just any reason at all. He interprets Deut. 24:1, which allows a man to divorce his wife if he finds "some indecency" (*'erVat davar*, lit., "nakedness of a thing"; cf. Deut. 23:14 [23:15 MT]) in her, in light of the creation ideal of permanent marital union.[31] In this verse, "he has found some indecency in her" apparently refers to some kind of behavior that the husband regards as intolerable and claims as his justification for terminating the marriage.[32] Jesus acknowledges that this is the law delivered through Moses but points out that it was a concession due to the Israelites' "hardness of heart." His own ruling, which excludes anything but sexual immorality (*porneia*) as the ground for expelling one's wife,[33] moves in the direction of the creation ideal by affirming the strength of the marriage bond and making its dissolution more exceptional. The result still falls short of the ideal, but allowing (although not requiring) divorce for sexual immorality is the best option in a fallen world.

Matthew 19:3–9 refers to four different positions regarding divorce, three of which are divine in origin (including that of Christ). The four include the creation ideal for marriage, a fallen human approach, and two levels of divine accommodation below the ideal that nevertheless move back toward it from the fallen human approach:[34]

31. Jesus's statements on "divorce" (Matt. 5:31–32; 19:3–9; Mark 10:2–12; Luke 16:18), including the exception clause allowing divorce on the ground of sexual immorality (Matt. 5:32; 19:9), concern the situation addressed in Deut. 24:1, where one spouse expels/sends (*piel* of *sh-l-kh*) the other from the marriage. The scope of Jesus's statements does not include termination of a marriage through one spouse abandoning the other, which can leave the remaining spouse free to remarry even if the departed spouse does not commit sexual immorality (1 Cor. 7:15); cf. Roy Gane, "Old Testament Principles Relating to Divorce and Remarriage," *JATS* 12, no. 2 (2001): 54–55nn37, 41.

32. Cf. Jeffrey H. Tigay, *Deuteronomy: The Traditional Hebrew Text with the New JPS Translation*, JPS Torah Commentary (Philadelphia: Jewish Publication Society, 1996), 221. The ground for divorce here does not include major sexual immorality such as adultery, for which a woman would be executed under OT law (e.g., Lev. 18, 20), thus with no opportunity for remarriage following divorce (Deut. 24:2).

33. Under OT law, sexual immorality would have incurred capital punishment (Lev. 20, esp. v. 10; Deut. 22:22) rather than divorce. Jesus's exception of divorce for immorality in Matt. 5:32; 19:9 was needed after the death penalty was abolished in Israel in AD 30. Cf. Richard M. Davidson, *Flame of Yahweh: Sexuality in the Old Testament* (Peabody, MA: Hendrickson, 2007), 655.

34. This makes Matt. 19 a good example of a biblical passage with what Webb calls "a multilevel ethic." William J. Webb, *Slaves, Women & Homosexuals: Exploring the Hermeneutics of Cultural Analysis* (Downers Grove, IL: IVP Academic, 2001), 41–43.

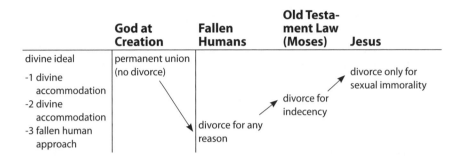

	God at Creation	Fallen Humans	Old Testament Law (Moses)	Jesus
divine ideal	permanent union (no divorce)			
-1 divine accommodation				divorce only for sexual immorality
-2 divine accommodation			divorce for indecency	
-3 fallen human approach		divorce for any reason		

This table shows relationships between the creation ideal, human views that depart far from it, OT law that accommodates to human fallenness but steps back in the direction of the ideal, and continuation of that positive trajectory under the leadership of Christ. God promises to fully restore ideal life in a re-created new earth,[35] where there will be no suffering or sorrow (Rev. 21:4)[36] or sinners to cause it (20:7–10, 15; 21:8, 27; 22:15).

Other NT passages also point to recovery of true and fuller fulfillments of the law of love that are in closer harmony with ideals already revealed, at least by implication, in the OT. Jesus pointed in this direction in a striking series of statements in his Sermon on the Mount ("You have heard that it was said . . . But I say to you . . ."; Matt. 5:21–48).[37] He even expanded on "You shall love your neighbor as yourself" (Lev. 19:18) to show that it means harmony with the character of God, who shows love to all rather than excluding enemies (Matt. 5:43–45).

Jesus's response to a wealthy young man who had kept all the commandments and wondered what he lacked in order to have eternal life (Matt. 19:16–20) offers a radical fulfillment of unselfish love: "If you would be perfect, go, sell what you possess and give to the poor, and you will have treasure in heaven; and come, follow me" (Matt. 19:21).

James includes as an essential element of pure and undefiled religion: "to visit orphans and widows in their affliction" (James 1:27). The OT laws help orphans and widows by prohibiting mistreatment of them (Exod. 22:22–24 [22:21–23 MT]; Deut. 24:17–18) and by requiring others to leave food for

35. This does not mean that the new creation will be exactly like the original creation in all respects. For example, Jesus said, "For in the resurrection they neither marry nor are given in marriage, but are like angels in heaven" (Matt. 22:30).

36. Including sorrow caused by divorce (cf. Mal. 2:13–16).

37. John R. W. Stott points out that Jesus was seeking to correct traditional misinterpretations of OT laws and to bring out their true meanings and implications. *The Message of the Sermon on the Mount (Matthew 5–7)*, The Bible Speaks Today (Downers Grove, IL: InterVarsity, 1978), 76–81.

them to glean at harvesttimes (Deut. 24:19–22), to give them a tithe of produce every three years (Deut. 14:28–29), and to include them in religious feasting at the Festivals of Weeks and Booths (Deut. 16:10–15). But Christians are to take social justice to a higher level by more closely following God's example (Deut. 10:18) to go out of our way to actively assist them (visiting to help, not just to greet or chat) when they are in need. This implies sensitivity and awareness of their situation. Of course, the ancient Israelites already had God's example and the general principle to love one's neighbor as oneself (Lev. 19:18), so they could have deduced that it was in accordance with the divine will for them to actively care for orphans and widows, and perhaps many of them did. However, James explicitly states this.

We have been finding that the NT relates to OT laws and their values in various ways, which can facilitate our progress toward application (including modified application) or nonapplication in Christian life:

1. The NT reiterates and reaffirms our need to observe a number of laws, especially from the Ten Commandments, and identifies love as the overarching value (e.g., Matt. 19:18–19; 22:37, 39; Rom. 13:8–10; Gal. 5:6).

2. The NT encourages more complete fulfillment of the law of love, in closer harmony with the creation ideal ("You have heard that it was said . . . But I say to you," Matt. 5:21–48; cf. 19:3–9).

3. The NT describes ways in which humans depart from the creation ideal and violate divine values presented in OT law (e.g., Matt. 19:3–9; Rom. 1:18–32; 1 Cor. 5:1; James 4:1–4).

4. The NT shows links between OT laws that we could otherwise miss (e.g., "covetousness, which is idolatry," Col. 3:5; cf. Eph. 5:5).

5. The NT applies OT law values to Christian life in ways that we may not think of but which generate further reflection on our part ("'You shall not muzzle an ox when it treads out the grain.' . . . Does he not certainly speak for our sake?" 1 Cor. 9:9–10; cf. 1 Tim. 5:17–18).

6. The NT identifies some OT laws that Christians are not required to keep (Acts 15, circumcision; Col. 2:16–17, religious rituals prefiguring Christ's sacrifice).

8

Approaches to Applying
Old Testament Law

Through the centuries, Christians have held a wide range of opinions regarding the extent to which OT laws apply to Christian life.[1] This chapter first surveys some current approaches that see either radical continuity between OT law and applicability to Christians or sharp discontinuity between them. Then the bulk of the chapter introduces some of the more balanced approaches that find both continuous and discontinuous elements and contribute methodological tools for distinguishing between them.[2]

Radical Continuity: Christian Reconstructionism = Theonomy

"Christian Reconstructionism" originated among Reformed (Calvinistic) Christians, although most Reformed Christians do not accept it, and it

1. See, e.g., David A. Dorsey, "The Law of Moses and the Christian: A Compromise," *JETS* 34, no. 3 (1991): 321–24, including a summary of six approaches to the applicability of OT law to Christians, beginning with that of Marcion (second century AD), who rejected the entire OT, including its law. Cf. Christopher J. H. Wright's survey of historical Christian approaches to OT law (*Old Testament Ethics for the People of God* [Downers Grove, IL: InterVarsity, 2004], 387–99). Minnie Warburton observes that many Christians followed a simplistic approach for centuries: "The early Church Fathers dealt with Leviticus, Numbers, Deuteronomy, and chunks of Exodus very simply: We keep the Ten Commandments, and the rest of the Law and Commandments do not apply to Christians." "Letting the Voice of Leviticus Speak," *STRev* 37 (1994): 164.

2. For summaries and critiques of various contemporary approaches, including some that I do not cover in the present chapter, cf. C. Wright, *Old Testament Ethics*, 399–412; Joe M. Sprinkle, *Biblical Law and Its Relevance: A Christian Understanding and Ethical Application for Today of the Mosaic Regulations* (Lanham, MD: University Press of America, 2006), 1–25.

has spread to a wider circle of American evangelicals and fundamental-
ists. The defining characteristic of this school of thought is its emphasis
on the OT law of God, so it refers to its approach as "theonomy" (the law
of God). A leading proponent explains, "Theonomists are committed to
the transformation or reconstruction of every area of life, including the
institutions and affairs of the socio-political realm, in accordance with the
holy principles of God's revealed Word (theonomy). It is toward this end
that the human community must strive if it hopes to enjoy true justice and
peace."[3]

Theonomists believe in salvation through faith in Christ rather than through
law-keeping. However, they maintain that the OT laws, including not only the
moral laws but also the judicial/civil laws with their penalties, are permanently
applicable everywhere and continue to be binding on Christians unless the NT
explicitly sets them aside. For theonomists, the judicial law not only governed
ancient Israel under the direct rule of God but also applies to Gentile nations,
including modern countries such as the United States, which should enforce
it and carry out its penalties. Nevertheless, reconstructionists recognize that
much of OT law cannot be literally observed today, so its principles must be
applied in adapted ways.[4]

How to understand the OT laws and implement them in politics, government, and lawcourts today is complicated, so theonomists have produced a
large amount of published material to work out the details.[5] In the process,
a number of differences of opinion have developed between them concerning
ways in which particular OT laws should be applied today.

The Christian reconstructionist movement does not advocate coercion,
violence, or political revolution to rapidly advance its cause. Rather, theonomists seek to influence society through lawful, peaceful means of influence and

3. Greg L. Bahnsen, "The Theonomic Reformed Approach to Law and Gospel," in *Five
Views on Law and Gospel*, by Greg L. Bahnsen et al., Counterpoints (Grand Rapids: Zondervan, 1999), 118. This essay concludes with a helpful summary of the theonomic approach to
God's law (141–43).
    4. On cultural and redemptive-historical discontinuities between OT law and modern society,
see ibid., 100–108.
    5. Some of their most prominent books include Rousas J. Rushdoony, *The Institutes of
Biblical Law* (Nutley, NJ: Presbyterian and Reformed, 1973); Rushdoony, *Law and Society*,
vol. 2 of *The Institutes of Biblical Law* (Vallecito, CA: Ross House, 1982); Rushdoony, *The
Intent of the Law*, vol. 3 of *The Institutes of Biblical Law* (Vallecito, CA: Ross House, 1999);
Greg L. Bahnsen, *Theonomy in Christian Ethics*, 3rd ed. (Nacogdoches, TX: Covenant Media,
2002); Bahnsen, *By This Standard: The Authority of God's Law Today* (Tyler, TX: Institute for
Christian Economics, 1985; repr., Powder Springs, GA: American Vision; Nacogdoches, TX:
Covenant Media, 2008); Gary North, *Tools of Dominion: The Case Laws of Exodus* (Tyler,
TX: Institute for Christian Economics, 1990).

education over time,[6] encouraged by their postmillennial eschatology to strive toward establishment of Christ's kingdom on earth during the present era.

Theonomists have made a positive contribution by drawing attention to OT law and ways in which modern Christians can appreciate and benefit from its wisdom. They point out some advantages of OT law over the modern criminal justice system, such as the facts that OT law provided for restitution to victims of theft and did not employ a costly prison infrastructure. However, biblical alternatives to incarceration, including death for a number of crimes in addition to murder, tend to seem harsh to modern people (cf. chap. 14). Theonomists respond that contemporary Christians need to get used to God's true justice, which is superior to that which human minds can devise.[7]

Theonomists are right that God's laws were not only for individuals but also for society and its leaders. So those who possess authority and shape our society today, as well as those who elect and appoint them, can (and should if they are Christians) gain much wisdom from principles in OT law. However, the theonomist agenda encounters some major problems, such as the following.[8]

First, judicial/civil aspects of OT laws, including prescribed punishments (mostly in casuistic formulations), were given within the context of the ancient Israelite theocracy, which was unique in redemption history.[9] According to the pentateuchal narrative, the Israelite nation was centered around the presence of God, whose glory was visibly manifest at his sanctuary. He ruled the Israelites from a sanctuary on earth because they were bound to him in a unique national covenant relationship, and they could seek guidance and judgments from him through priests at his sanctuary (Deut. 17:8–12). No other nation has ever enjoyed the privilege of such intimate proximity to God on earth, which carried with it a high level of responsibility and accountability to his laws.

It is true that Israel was a paradigm for other nations, ancient and modern (see below), but the OT civil regulations were specifically addressed to the Israelites, not directly to other peoples. In the Bible, other nations are held

6. Bahnsen, "Theonomic Reformed Approach," 139–41.

7. Ibid., 132–35.

8. I refrain from undertaking a critique of postmillenial eschatology here because this would go beyond the scope of the present book. Bahnsen et al., *Five Views on Law and Gospel*, presents responses from different perspectives to Bahnsen, "Theonomic Reformed Approach," 93–143: response by Willem A. VanGemeren, 144–49; by Walter C. Kaiser Jr., 150–57; by Wayne G. Strickland, 158–64; and by Douglas Moo, 165–73. For a Reformed response, which views theonomy as a distorted interpretation of the continuity and discontinuity between OT law and modern life, see William S. Barker and W. Robert Godfrey, eds., *Theonomy: A Reformed Critique* (Grand Rapids: Academie Books, 1990).

9. Cf. Tremper Longman III, "God's Law and Mosaic Punishments Today," in Barker and Godfrey, *Theonomy*, 47.

accountable for basic justice and morality (e.g., Amos 1:3–2:3), including sexual morality (Lev. 18), but not for implementation of civil ordinances given to Israel.

Under the new covenant, God's community on earth is a church, not a civil state. Like ancient Israel, the church has boundaries of membership and discipline for those who violate covenant stipulations. However, whereas a number of severe penalties administered to Israelites were physical, and purging their community of grave wrongdoing was accomplished through execution of the offenders (e.g., Deut. 13:5; 17:7, 12; see chap. 14 below), the NT does not sanction physical punishment carried out by believers, and expulsion from fellowship effects elimination from the church community. In 1 Cor. 5, for example, Paul calls for the Corinthian church to disfellowship a man whose sexual immorality would be punishable by death according to Lev. 20:11. If Paul were a theonomist, his statement regarding this case would be a golden opportunity for him to add that if Christians were in charge of the local civil court, the sinner should be put to death. But neither Paul nor any other NT writer ever expresses such a sentiment, because Christ's kingdom is "not of this world" (John 18:36; cf. Phil. 3:20, "Our citizenship is in heaven"), so its manifestation on earth is in a spiritual rather than civil community.[10]

A second problem is that specifics of the OT legal system were designed for people in a certain culture at a particular stage of redemption history. Israelite administrators of justice included not only court judges but also male heads of households, clan leaders, and priests (see chap. 6 above), but no women, except for Deborah, whose judicial authority was based on her special prophetic gift (Judg. 4:4–5). Modern Western society is not organized by clans, and we have no priests with access to a living divine oracle, but we do have women in positions of social leadership. Therefore, implementing administration of OT law in the biblical way would require massive social engineering, reinstitution of the theocracy, which only God could accomplish, and banning female nonprophets from the judiciary.

Theonomists are not so concerned with what modern people perceive to be just; what matters to them is fulfillment of God's blueprint for justice. However, while the God of the Bible is countercultural in some ways (e.g., Deut. 23:15–16, protecting fugitive slaves), he is concerned that people within their own cultural context should view him as just so that they will be attracted to his beneficent rule (4:5–8). Therefore he does not engage in wholesale social engineering to effect radical change in ways that could cause unnecessary

10. Christ had the support of people who wanted to set him up as ruler of an earthly kingdom, but he rejected their initiative (John 6:15).

damage, as shown by his pragmatic patience with slavery, polygamy, and some aspects of male-dominated Israelite society that arguably were less than ideal.[11]

Justice is a crucial part of God's character (e.g., Ps. 89:14 [89:15 MT]). As our Creator and Redeemer, he has the moral authority to determine what is just for us, but his justice operates within social-historical contexts, not in a cultural vacuum. Thus some adjustment of details may be necessary to accomplish the same level of justice for different groups of people, just as a parent must be sensitive to differences between children in order to be fair.

According to the Pentateuch, the Israelites had just come out of harsh Egyptian slavery when they received God's law. Severe physical punishments were common in those days, and rebellions against divine rule, to which the Israelites had voluntarily pledged their lives (Exod. 24:3–8), threatened to tear the fledgling community apart (e.g., Num. 14, 16). It appears that milder legal consequences would have been inadequate for curbing evil in order to maintain the corporate divine-human relationship, which was a matter of survival for the Israelites, as shown by the disastrous results of the Baal Peor apostasy (Num. 25).

By contrast, at a later time and in a setting that much more closely approximates the modern context, the divinely inspired apostle Paul ordered a radically different penalty than the capital punishment that OT law prescribed for the same offense (1 Cor. 5; see above). The Christian punishment of disfellowshipping was not physical, and its purpose was redemptive ("so that his spirit may be saved"), but its effectiveness should not be underestimated in view of Paul's injunction "to deliver this man to Satan for the destruction of the flesh" (1 Cor. 5:5).[12]

Which of the punishments, OT or NT, was just? Both were, within their respective contexts, according to the wisdom of God. Neither penalty was ideal, because there is no such thing as an ideal penalty, given that all penalties address nonideal situations.

A third problem involves authority in modern implementation. The OT laws served as paradigms to instruct all Israelites, including those who administered justice, regarding divine principles and their application. The law collections were exemplary rather than comprehensive. Judges were informed by the laws and bound by them in some ways, such as the rule that ransom was not

---

11. E.g., the option for fathers or husbands to annul vows by their daughters or wives, which called for statutory divine forgiveness of these females (Num. 30).

12. On the meaning of these words, see Gordon D. Fee, *The First Epistle to the Corinthians*, NICNT (Grand Rapids: Eerdmans, 1987), 208–14. Fee concludes that the man "is being excluded from the Christian community with its life in the Spirit. The inevitable consequence is that he is back out in Satan's domain, where, Paul hopes, his 'flesh' may be destroyed so that he may be saved on the Day of the Lord. . . . What Paul does not tell us is *how* he perceived this 'destruction' of his flesh to take place" (213, emphasis original).

allowed in cases of murder (Num. 35:31, 33). However, the specifics of their decisions were to take into account the complexities of real life, which can present aggravating or mitigating factors.[13] In actual practice, King David as judge granted amnesty to a murderer (who was fictitious, although he didn't know it), due to the extenuating circumstance that the criminal was the only surviving child of a widow (2 Sam. 14:4–11).

Translating such a legal system into a modern law code, which judges would be expected to follow much more closely, would be a monumental task and require filling in many gaps and making numerous choices regarding appropriate (but inevitably inconsistent) levels of literalness versus adaptation to the modern context. Who should possess the authority to make these choices, which are literally matters of life and death when they involve capital punishments? According to Bahnsen, Christian Reconstructionism calls for implementation of OT law only within the scope of its actual coverage,[14] but who decides how far its application extends?

Realistically, fulfillment of the theonomic vision will never be carried out by modern secular governments. This vision requires establishment of a church-state pseudotheocracy controlled by a cadre of scholarly clerics, analogous to the mullahs and ayatollahs of Islam, whose subjective interpretations and applications of Scripture are regarded as the Word of God.[15] Pseudotheocratic power during the centuries of "Christendom" has already resulted in untold misery, and there is little doubt that another manifestation of it would continue the gruesome legacy, casting the reputation of Christ into further disrepute.

Radical Discontinuity

At the other extreme from theonomy, several approaches to OT law hold that none of it governs the lives of NT Christians.

Practical Impossibility: Cyril Rodd

Cyril Rodd concludes that modern application of biblical law is practically impossible for Christians because he regards cultural differences between ancient Israelite society and modern Christian life as insurmountable barriers.[16]

13. Cf. chap. 2 on the nature of OT law.
14. Bahnsen, "Theonomic Reformed Approach," 127–28.
15. Cf. Longman, "God's Law," 49–51.
16. Cyril S. Rodd, *Glimpses of a Strange Land: Studies in Old Testament Ethics*, OTS (Edinburgh: T&T Clark, 2001), esp. 301–29. For a more extensive summary of Rodd's approach, see C. Wright, *Old Testament Ethics*, 439–40.

He is right that the cultural differences pose significant challenges, and modern interpreters should beware of reading their concerns back into the biblical texts.[17] However, NT use of OT law and teaching regarding it (see chap. 1), including Paul's assertion that "All Scripture is . . . profitable" (2 Tim. 3:16), encourage us in the modern world to persist in seeking some kind of authoritative guidance from the venerable divinely revealed laws.

Dispensationalism

Dispensationalists believe that God's administration of the church by grace is completely separate from his administration of Israel by the law.[18] Wayne G. Strickland explains,

> The Mosaic law naturally ended when God suspended his program with Israel (Rom. 9–11) and inaugurated his program with the church. God's moral law in and of itself does not change, but its specific application and structure in the Mosaic code ended with the repeated violations of the Mosaic covenant and the beginning of the church dispensation. . . . The law of Christ is the new covenant counterpart to the Mosaic law. . . . Both are specific applications of God's eternal moral standard.[19]

However, Strickland denies that dispensationalists teach two ways of salvation: Mosaic law for God's OT people, and grace through faith for NT Christians.[20] God has only ever justified people by grace. However, whereas God has used the Mosaic law to regulate his covenant relationship with Israel, which will find literal future fulfillment for the nation of Israel in the messianic millennial kingdom of Christ, now he governs Christians by the law of Christ, which is fulfilled by loving others (Gal. 5:14; 6:2).[21]

> The dispensationalist approach to OT law interprets passages such as Romans 6:14 ("For sin will have no dominion over you, since you are not under law but under grace"), 10:4 ("For Christ is the end of the law for righteousness to everyone who believes"), and Galatians 5:18 ("But if you are led by the Spirit,

---

17. Rodd, *Glimpses of a Strange Land*, 1, 3, 304, 307–8, 314, 321–23; cf. Matthew J. M. Coomber, "Introduction," in *Bible and Justice: Ancient Texts, Modern Challenges*, ed. Matthew J. M. Coomber (London: Equinox, 2011), 3–4.

18. Cf. Bruce K. Waltke, "Theonomy in Relation to Dispensational and Covenant Theologies," in Barker and Godfrey, *Theonomy*, 60.

19. Wayne G. Strickland, "The Inauguration of the Law of Christ with the Gospel of Christ: A Dispensational View," in Bahnsen et al., *Five Views on Law and Gospel*, 276–77.

20. Ibid., 235–36.

21. Ibid., 278–79.

you are not under the law") to mean that Christ has ended the applicability of
the law of Moses as a whole, including the Ten Commandments, for Christians.
Christians are accountable for keeping "the law of Christ" (Gal. 6:2), which has
some points of contact with Mosaic law, but the latter has lost its authority.
So if an OT law carries over into the New Covenant era, it is only because it is
specifically identified by the NT as part of the law of Christ.[22]

Dispensationalists overlook, or at least do not adequately take into account, several lines of biblical evidence that affect the theological contexts
within which their prooftexts should be understood.[23] First, the new covenant,
under which the "law of Christ" operates, is in direct continuity with the OT
covenant's phases, including the covenant at Sinai, under which the so-called
Mosaic law functioned. Inauguration of a new-covenant phase does not establish an alternative (e.g., for Christians) to an earlier phase (e.g., for Jews),
but builds upon it, incorporating and adapting features to a new situation.[24]
Thus the law that God writes on the hearts of his people in Jer. 31:33 is OT
law, which in this context is the law of the promised "new covenant" (vv.
31–34).[25] The NT builds on and shows fulfillment of the gospel message of
the OT, including in OT law, regarding the character of God and the coming
of Christ. The NT does not abrogate this message, although performance
of ritual activities prescribed by pentateuchal laws is no longer necessary

22. Charles C. Ryrie, "The End of the Law," *BSac* 124 (1967): 239–47; cf. Strickland, "Inauguration," 229–79. Strickland disputes use of Matt. 5:17–19; Rom. 7; 1 Tim. 1:8 to support
continuity of the Mosaic law (256–60) and presents arguments for basic discontinuity between
the OT and NT, including interpretations of Rom. 6:14–15; 10:4; 2 Cor. 3:3, 6–18 (262–75).
His essay is followed by responses from other perspectives by VanGemeren (280–89), Bahnsen
(290–301), Kaiser (302–8), and Moo (309–15).

23. Sprinkle (*Biblical Law*, 9–11) points out alternative interpretations of some of the key
prooftexts (Rom. 6:14; 10:4; Gal. 5:18), which can be interpreted in ways that do not require the
conclusion that the Mosaic law is completely abrogated for Christians. Cf. Joseph A. Fitzmyer,
who interprets "you are not under law but under grace" in Rom. 6:14 as follows:

> Where the Christian lives by faith that works itself out through love, that Christian is
> living by grace, and life is no longer viewed as existence "under law," even the possibility
> of it (5:20). This attitude does not imply that the Mosaic law has been abolished or has
> no validity, for Paul does not say that Jewish Christians need not observe it. His point is
> rather that "in Christ Jesus" even their perspective is that of "grace." What was demanded
> by the law is now attained through grace. In chap. 8 Paul will relate this concept to life
> in the Spirit. (*Romans: A New Translation with Introduction and Commentary*, AB 33
> [New York: Doubleday, 1993], 447–48)

24. On the unity of the divine covenants, see O. Palmer Robertson, *The Christ of the Covenants* (Phillipsburg, NJ: Presbyterian and Reformed, 1980), 27–52.

25. Willem A. VanGemeren, "Response to Wayne G. Strickland," in Bahnsen et al., *Five
Views on Law and Gospel*, 285–86; Walter C. Kaiser Jr., "Response to Wayne G. Strickland,"
in Bahnsen et al., *Five Views on Law and Gospel*, 304.

because Christ has fulfilled their prophetic typology (Col. 2:16–17; cf. Heb. 7–10), and legal elements that were specific to theocratic civil governance do not apply within a church context.

Second, the new covenant is universal for all people on earth, inviting both Jews and Gentiles to join it so that together as a church community, a spiritual "Israel," they can enjoy the covenant promises given to Abraham and his descendants (Gal. 3:26–29; 1 Pet. 2:9; cf. Exod. 19:5–6).[26] The new covenant does not bracket out the Jewish people for divine governance under a separate program.

Third, the same holy God of love (1 John 4:8, 16) gave both the OT law of love (Matt. 22:37–40) and the NT "law of Christ," which is also love (e.g., Gal. 5:14; 6:2). So rather than replacing OT law, the "law of Christ" continues OT law both in terms of authority and also content as a guide to sanctification, which is growth in love (1 Thess. 3:12–13). The expression "Mosaic law" emphasizes the human medium of revelation, but the biblical narrative indicates that this law, like the "law of Christ," is of God.

Fourth, NT passages explicitly affirm the ongoing value of the laws given through Moses (e.g., Matt. 5:17–20; Rom. 3:31; 7:12, 14; 2 Tim. 3:16–17), and NT writers apply specific OT laws to Christian life[27] simply because they are ongoing divine standards, without pausing to explain that they are being reinstituted under the new covenant after having been abrogated. "Even when Christ or the apostles explicitly cite the Old Testament and they say they are repeating what is found in the 'Scripture' or the 'Law and the Prophets' (Matt. 22:37–40; Rom. 13:8–10; Gal. 5:14; James 2:8–12), the position Strickland adopts in his essay flatly denies it!"[28]

Lutheran Theology

Traditional Lutheran theology, as represented by the Book of Concord (1580), holds that the law serves several purposes: to maintain external discipline, to show people that they are sinners who need gospel grace, and to guide the lives of Christian believers. In this context the "law" is defined as God's unchangeable will (not the law of Moses), moral law as presented in the Ten Commandments, and natural law. The judicial/civil laws of Moses applied only to the Jews, claims the Book of Concord, except to the extent

26. Cf. Hans K. LaRondelle, *The Israel of God in Prophecy: Principles of Prophetic Interpretation*, Andrews University Monographs, Studies in Religion 13 (Berrien Springs, MI: Andrews University Press, 1983).

27. Sprinkle, *Biblical Law*, 7–9.

28. Kaiser, "Response to Wayne G. Strickland," 302.

that they represent natural law, so Christians should obey the civil laws of the states in which they live.[29]

This approach avoids problems of legalism, letterism, and antinomianism. However, biblical evidence does not support such a radical separation of the Decalogue from the other OT laws. As we will see in chapters 11 and 12 of this book, the Ten Commandments are inextricably linked to the other laws, which also came from God and exemplify moral principles in many ways.

Another issue is the relationship between Mosaic and natural laws. What methodological controls guide identification of elements in Mosaic law that coincide with natural law and therefore continue for Christians?[30] Prerequisite to such identification is definition of what is "natural" according to natural law.[31]

Advocating a "modified Lutheran view," Douglas Moo maintains that "the Mosaic law is tied firmly to the Sinaitic covenant, now abrogated in Christ. . . . The Mosaic law is not a *direct* and *immediate* source of guidance to the new covenant believer."[32] However, the law of Moses is profitable to Christians (2 Tim. 3:16) in at least three ways.[33]

First, while the Mosaic law as such is not binding on Christians, individual commandments in the law may be binding because the NT reapplies them. Moo contrasts his view that Christians "are bound only to that which is clearly repeated within New Testament teaching" with the Reformed approach, according to which we are obliged to keep everything in OT law that the NT has not clearly repealed.[34] Second, the detailed requirements of Mosaic law contribute to understanding principles that belong to both old and new covenant law. Third, although OT law lacks authority of law in the new-covenant era, it carries authority as a prophetic witness to the fulfillment of the divine plan in Christ.

Like dispensationalism, the Lutheran approach suffers from inadequate recognition of continuity between the OT and NT phases of divine covenant law (cf. above). Kaiser objects to the way in which Moo "separates Law from Gospel, demanding that they be two *successive* eras in salvation history and

29. Summarized by Sprinkle, *Biblical Law*, 11–12.
30. Ibid., 11–13.
31. Ibid., 12–13.
32. Douglas Moo, "The Law of Christ as the Fulfillment of the Law of Moses: A Modified Lutheran View," in Bahnsen et al., *Five Views on Law and Gospel*, 375 (emphasis original), followed by responses from VanGemeren (377–82), Bahnsen (383–92), Kaiser (393–400), and Strickland (401–5).
33. Ibid., 376.
34. Ibid.

not two constant aspects in God's Word."[35] Thus Kaiser points out that OT people possessed the gospel call for faith, as affirmed by NT passages such as Gal. 3:8: "The Scripture, foreseeing that God would justify the Gentiles by faith, preached the gospel beforehand to Abraham, saying, 'In you shall all the nations be blessed'" (cf. Rom. 1:1–2; Heb. 4:2).[36]

Both Continuity and Discontinuity

Many current interpreters, including myself, take moderate positions because we find both continuity between OT law and modern life in terms of shared values and principles or ethical paradigms as well as discontinuity of many details.[37] Methodology for identifying such values, principles, or paradigms and ways in which they can transfer to modern life has been debated for centuries and is still developing, with considerable variety of perspectives and conceptual models. Following is a selective survey of some of these different approaches.[38]

Categories of Laws (Reformed Theology)

"Of the Law of God," chapter 19 of the Westminster Confession of Faith (1646), divides biblical laws into moral, ceremonial, and judicial (i.e., civil) categories. According to this document, which is still influential, *moral law* consists of the principles articulated in the Ten Commandments and is the only category that continues to directly apply to Christians. *Ceremonial laws,*

35. Walter C. Kaiser, "Response to Douglas Moo," in Bahnsen et al., *Five Views on Law and Gospel*, 393, emphasis original.

36. Ibid., 393–94.

37. E.g., William J. Webb, *Slaves, Women & Homosexuals: Exploring the Hermeneutics of Cultural Analysis* (Downers Grove, IL: IVP Academic, 2001); C. Wright, *Old Testament Ethics*; Sprinkle, *Biblical Law*; Jonathan Burnside, *God, Justice, and Society: Aspects of Law and Legality in the Bible* (New York: Oxford University Press, 2011); Coomber, *Bible and Justice*.

38. Cf. the discussion by Walter C. Kaiser Jr. of hermeneutical issues such as the traditional threefold division of OT law into civil, ceremonial, and moral categories. He surveys six contemporary hermeneutical stances and offers seven guidelines for interpreting OT moral instructions (*Toward Old Testament Ethics* [Grand Rapids: Zondervan, 1983], 41–56). Gary T. Meadors, ed., *Four Views on Moving beyond the Bible to Theology*, Counterpoints (Grand Rapids: Zondervan, 2009), presents essays by four authors on their respective approaches to application of OT laws and responses to them. The essays are by Walter C. Kaiser Jr., "A Principlizing Model" (19–50); Daniel M. Doriani, "A Redemptive-Historical Model" (75–120); Kevin J. Vanhoozer, "A Drama-of-Redemption Model" (151–99); and William J. Webb, "A Redemptive-Movement Model" (21–48). The present chapter summarizes and critiques the approaches of Kaiser and Webb.

which regulated ordinances that prefigured Christ, are abrogated for Christians. *Judicial* (= *civil*) *laws*, which God gave the Israelites to govern them, expired when their state came to an end.[39]

Bruce K. Waltke affirms the tripartite division of OT law by the Westminster Confession on the basis of ways in which the Pentateuch gives priority to the Decalogue and separates collections of laws belonging to the three categories.[40] Sprinkle regards the Reformed approach as strong in two areas. First, it recognizes that some biblical laws are more important than others (cf. Matt. 23:23, "the weightier matters of the law"). Walter C. Kaiser Jr. qualifies this by pointing out that distinctions between weightier and lighter commandments are in terms of relative significance, without indicating that the lighter ones do not need to be observed.[41] Second, Sprinkle finds that the Reformed approach takes into account NT indications that the ritual laws temporarily foreshadowed Christ and have finished serving their purpose (Heb. 7–10).[42]

The Reformed distinctions between moral, civil, and ceremonial laws are not stated in the Bible but are later Christian analytical constructs.[43] We will find that they can be helpful (see below), but J. Daniel Hays views them as inadequate for three reasons.[44] First, he regards them as arbitrary. Many laws that are supposed to belong to different categories appear together, yet with no textual indicators of distinctions between them (e.g., Lev. 19:18–19). Also, it is often difficult to identify the category into which a law fits. "Because the Mosaic Law defined the covenant relationship between God and Israel, it was

39. The last vestiges of theocratic nationhood were terminated in AD 70 when the Romans destroyed Jerusalem and its second temple. Note that according to Willem A. VanGemeren, the ceremonial laws applied the first four commandments of the Decalogue to the Israelite nation and the judicial laws applied the last six commandments to that same context. "The Law Is the Perfection of Righteousness in Jesus Christ: A Reformed Perspective," in Bahnsen et al., *Five Views on Law and Gospel*, 53.

40. "Theonomy in Relation to Dispensational and Covenant Theologies," 70–72.

41. *Toward Old Testament Ethics*, 312.

42. Sprinkle (*Biblical Law*, 4) refers to the following to exemplify the abrogation of the ritual laws: "Christ indicated that food laws are no longer obligatory (Mark 7:19, 'Thus he declared all foods clean')." However, this is not a good example. The Greek of this verse does not include "Thus he declared," which is supplied by the translator. The NKJV more accurately renders verses 18b–19: "Do you not perceive that whatever enters a man from outside cannot defile him, because it does not enter his heart but his stomach, and is eliminated, thus purifying [participle of *katharizō*] all foods?" That is, the process of elimination purifies foods (see further in chap. 15 below).

43. J. Daniel Hays points out that the distinction between moral laws, which continue to apply to Christians, and ceremonial laws, which the gospel has canceled, dates back to John Calvin's *Institutes of the Christian Religion*. "Applying the Old Testament Law Today," *BSac* 158 (2001): 22n3.

44. Ibid., 22–30.

by nature theological. All of the Law had theological content. Can a law be a theological law but not a moral law?"[45]

The OT law does not make sharp distinctions between "moral" and other categories, or even between religious and secular categories, because every aspect of life as the people of God came under his jurisdiction. All of the laws were "moral" in the sense that Israelites were morally obligated to keep all of them, and laws belonging to what we would classify as the religious and secular domains often appear together.

In addition, the category of a law is complicated by the fact that some legal requirements have to do with more than one category. In fact, the Sabbath commandment came to involve all three categories. Basic Sabbath rest, which is independent of Israel's worship system,[46] is part of the Decalogue, which exemplifies principles governing basic divine-human and human-human relationships (Exod. 20:8–11; Deut. 5:12–15). Later the ceremonial worship system honored the Sabbath with extra sacrifices (Num. 28:9–10) and with changing the "bread of the Presence" on that day (Exod. 25:30; Lev. 24:7–8). Sabbath rest was enforced by the penalty of death under Israelite theocratic civil law (Exod. 31:14–15; 35:2; Num. 15:32–36). The requirement for ceasing work on the Sabbath could even be regarded as a health law (a fourth category) because it provides for physical rest that refreshes humans and work animals (Exod. 23:12).[47]

The second objection given by Hays is the fact that all of the Mosaic legal material is embedded in narrative texts, so the law is part of the pentateuchal narrative. "Is not narrative in the Scripture as authoritative as Law? To give the Mosaic Law a greater authority over the Christian's moral behavior than that of the other parts of the Old Testament narratives is to create a canon within a canon."[48] To illustrate the importance of narrative, Hays points out that in Mark 2:23–28 Jesus answers an accusation of violating a Sabbath law (Exod. 34:21) by citing a narrative passage (1 Sam. 21:1–6).

We could add that if there are no degrees of authority between OT law as a whole and biblical narrative, it is difficult to argue for degrees of authority between moral, civil, and ceremonial laws. However, there are other issues aside from authority, such as clarity and applicability. Law tends to serve as a clearer source of moral guidance than narrative because laws often (but not always) communicate principles more directly and transparently. Regarding

---

45. Ibid., 23.

46. Not understood by Hays, in ibid., 24.

47. On OT laws relating to health, see Roy Gane, *Leviticus, Numbers*, NIV Application Commentary (Grand Rapids: Zondervan, 2004), 209–10, 212–13.

48. Hays, "Applying the Old Testament Law Today," 26.

applicability, even if moral, civil, and ceremonial laws carried equal authority under the Israelite covenant theocracy in that they were given by the same Deity, who required obedience to all of them, the ongoing force of the laws belonging to these categories is affected to varying degrees by the extent to which the conditions (including institutions) that they were designed to regulate have continued.

Hays's third point is the way in which the traditional approach overlooks the theological context of OT law. That law is part of the Mosaic covenant, which involved Israel's possession of the promised land, the divine presence in the tabernacle/temple, and conditional blessings and curses for obedience or disobedience to the law. This covenant no longer functions now that Jesus has come as "the mediator of a new covenant" (Heb. 8:13; 9:15). So all of the laws that made up the Mosaic covenant, without any distinctions between moral, civil, and ceremonial categories, no longer function under that covenant. Now "the meaning of the Law must be interpreted in light of His coming and in light of the profound changes introduced by the New Covenant."[49]

Hays goes on to advocate an approach that he labels "principlism," which is identified with "principlizing" and "paradigmatic" approaches (see further below). He asserts that principlism allows for consistent interpretation of biblical passages without the need to arbitrarily separate the laws into categories that are applicable or not.[50] According to Hays, principlism involves five steps: (1) Identify what the particular law meant to the initial audience. (2) Determine the differences between the initial audience and believers today. (3) Develop universal principles from the text. (4) Correlate a principle with NT teaching. (5) Apply the modified universal principle to life today.[51]

Hays's critique of the traditional categories and proposed alternative of looking for principles are instructive. However, we can suggest two changes to his approach. First, "modified universal principle" sounds like an oxymoron. If a principle is really universal, why would it need to be modified? Any aspects that are modified when moving from the OT to the NT, such as elements belonging to the OT ritual system, are not part of the universal principle. It is true that Christians are now under the new covenant, which has introduced profound changes that make some aspects of the OT laws obsolete for Christian

49. Ibid., 29. Douglas Moo agrees with Reformed theologians that "the Mosaic law, especially the Ten Commandments, contains principles and requirements that reflect God's eternal moral will," but he maintains that "the Mosaic law is not identical with this eternal moral law. It is part of a covenant document entered into with the nation Israel and is therefore specifically addressed to Israel—and not to the new covenant community" ("Response to Willem A. VanGemeren," in Bahnsen et al., *Five Views on Law and Gospel*, 84).
50. Hays, "Applying the Old Testament Law Today," 30.
51. Ibid., 31–35.

practice, most notably those regulating activities belonging to the typological ritual system and Israelite civil governance, neither of which has continued to exist. But Jesus and the NT writers affirmed the ongoing applicability of universal principles in OT law (see chap. 1 above), which carry over to the new covenant. The fact that Christ's grace has eclipsed Moses's law as a glorious revelation of God (John 1:17; Rom. 6:14; 2 Cor. 3) does not mean that the new covenant has abrogated the universal principles of OT law, only to pick them up again. Rather, the one eternal Deity gave universal principles to ancient Israel that remain under the new covenant precisely because they are universal.

Second, if we abandon a simplistic attempt to place each OT law as a whole in one category that is either applicable (moral law) or not applicable (civil and ceremonial law) to Christians, we nevertheless can find it useful to employ the terms "moral," "civil," and "ceremonial" in revised ways.[52] "Moral law" can refer to universal principles applicable to Christians, whether these are stated outright, as in the Ten Commandments, or lie under the surface of elements in laws that apply them to limited situations. "Civil" and "ceremonial" are major categories of such limiting elements, referring to features pertaining to and dependent on the function of the Israelite civil theocracy (with its penalties) and the ritual system, respectively.

We can speak of "civil" and "ceremonial" laws that no longer can be literally applied because the behaviors that they regulate on the surface involve now-defunct civil and ceremonial institutions. However, we should acknowledge that such laws are also moral in the general sense that the Israelites were morally obliged to literally keep them under their covenant with God, and Christians should keep any universal principles that underlie them. More specifically, we can refer to a particular law as "moral" if it is simply stated in terms of a universal principle, without elements that are limited to the OT era. Whether or not it is stated as a universal moral principle must be determined through contextual exegesis on a case-by-case basis.

For example, Lev. 18:20 ("And you shall not lie sexually with your neighbor's wife and so make yourself unclean with her"), which reiterates the Decalogue commandment against adultery (Exod. 20:14), is easy to recognize as a "moral law" because it expresses only a transcultural universal principle.[53] On the

---

52. Cf. my earlier discussion in Gane, *Leviticus, Numbers*, 209–10, 306–9.

53. It is true that, in general, sexual intercourse would cause Israelites to incur physical ritual impurity (Lev. 15:18). However, the defilement in view in 18:20, for which no ritual remedy is provided, is irremediable moral impurity, which could also result from bestiality (v. 23) or resorting to occult practitioners (19:31; cf. Jacob Milgrom, *Leviticus 17–22: A New Translation with Introduction and Commentary*, AB 3A [New York: Doubleday, 2000], 1551). Adultery also causes moral uncleanness in Num. 5:13–14, 20, 27–29; Ezek. 18:6, 11, 15; 33:26. While physical ritual impurity was connected to the Israelite ritual system, moral impurity was not. Thus this

other hand, Lev. 20:10 adds a civil penalty to violation of the universal moral principle, thereby making an Israelite "civil law": "If a man commits adultery with the wife of his neighbor, both the adulterer and the adulteress shall surely be put to death." Returning to Lev. 18, verse 19 states: "You shall not approach a woman to uncover her nakedness while she is in her menstrual uncleanness." Does this formulation simply refer to something universal, or does it apply a universal principle in a way that limits the literal requirement to ancient Israelites? We will examine this law in chapter 15.

Principlizing Approach

Raymond Westbrook has argued that Babylonian law "dealt in principles but could only express them as cases. The principles can be extracted, but [only] by applying the *native* cultural and social concepts."[54] Similarly, several scholars maintain that an interpreter of OT laws should look for underlying principles.[55] Joe Sprinkle holds that we can safely abstract moral and religious principles from biblical laws if we view them (1) within their system of law, (2) in light of biblical, cultural, and social concepts, and (3) against their ANE background—applying what Westbrook would call their native cultural and social concepts.[56] "We ask the question, 'What principle led God through the writer to say this under those circumstances?' Once the principle is derived, then we can apply that same principle to analogous situations today."[57]

To identify and apply abstracted principles, Kaiser employs a model that he calls "the Ladder of Abstraction," which he defines as "a continuous sequence

---

category applies to Christians, as shown by NT texts referring to sexual immorality as defiling (Matt. 15:19–20; Mark 7:20–23; 2 Pet. 2:10; Rev. 17:4). But moral impurity of Christians does not defile the land of Israel so that they will be exiled from it, as the Israelites would within the OT covenant context (cf. Lev. 18:24–30).

54. Raymond Westbrook, *Studies in Biblical and Cuneiform Law*, CahRB 26 (Paris: Gabalda, 1988), 77n156, emphasis original.

55. E.g., Kaiser, *Toward Old Testament Ethics*; Kaiser, "Principlizing Model"; Sprinkle, *Biblical Law*; Dorsey, "Law of Moses," 324–34; Hays, "Applying the Old Testament Law Today," 30–35. Cf. Gane, *Leviticus, Numbers*, regarding OT law: "*A law should be kept to the extent that its principle can be applied unless the New Testament removes the reason for its application*" (310, emphasis original).

56. Sprinkle, *Biblical Law*, 25.

57. Ibid., 21; cf. Kaiser, "Principlizing Model," 22, quoting from his book, *Toward an Exegetical Theology: Biblical Exegesis for Preaching and Teaching* (Grand Rapids: Baker, 1981), 152. Kaiser outlines steps in finding principles in biblical passages of various genres: First ascertain the topic/subject of its focal point, then identify its emphasis and ways in which it is connected, and finally "see how each paragraph (in prose genres), scene (in narratives), or strophe (in poetical passages) can be expressed in propositional principles" ("Principlizing Model," 22–23). On strengths of the principlizing method, see Sprinkle, *Biblical Law*, 22–24. He points out that this method is compatible with the Reformed approach in some ways (21).

of categorizations from a low level of specificity up to a high point of generality in a principle and down again to a specific application in the contemporary culture."[58] He takes the law in Deut. 25:4 that a farmer should not muzzle an ox treading out grain as an illustration of how the "ladder" works:

> From the *ancient specific situation* (oxen that tread out grain) we move up the ladder to *the institutional or personal norm* (animals are God's gifts to humanity and should be treated kindly), to the top of the ladder, which gives to us *the general principle* (giving engenders gentleness and graciousness in those mortals who care for and can minister back to those who serve them as well, whether they are animals or people). As we descend the ladder on the other side, we meet *the theological and moral principle* behind our general principle ("love your neighbor" or just the injunction in the ninth commandment), to the contemporary or New Testament *specific situation* (pay those pastors ministering to you, including Paul, 1 Cor. 9:9–12).
>
> In this movement on the Ladder of Abstraction, we must move from the ancient specificity of the text (taking pity on those muzzled oxen who are going crazy walking round and round over top of grain they long to take a swipe at) up to the overarching general principle that applies and generalizes the particularity of the Scripture before we can once again apply that abstracted general principle in a new contemporary specific situation. Paul's point is not only one of being kind to animals; rather, it is about the special work of grace and generosity that takes place in the hearts and lives of those who express special concern and love for those who are ministering to them (whether as oxen threshing out the grain or as ministers of the gospel feeding the people the Word of God).[59]

The principlizing approach has much to commend it if movement on the Ladder of Abstraction is biblically controlled rather than skewed by cultural biases of the interpreter.[60] For example, the pentateuchal laws against eating blood, meat from which the blood is not drained out at the time of slaughter (Lev. 3:17; 7:26–27; 17:10–14; Deut. 12:16, 23–25; 15:23), are explicitly based on the concept that "the life of the flesh is in the blood" (Lev. 17:11; cf. Gen. 9:4, "flesh with its life, that is, its blood"). So behind draining the blood is the moral principle of profound respect/reverence for life that God has created, as exemplified in the Decalogue command "You shall not murder" (Exod. 20:13; cf. Gen. 9:5–6).[61] According to the pentateuchal narrative, the blood

58. Kaiser, "Principlizing Model," 24. See below on the relationship between the "Ladder of Abstraction" and the hierarchy of moral values discussed in chap. 7 above.

59. Ibid., 25–26, emphasis original.

60. Cf. ibid., 22, quoting his *Toward an Exegetical Theology*, 198.

61. Note the close connection between the blood prohibition in Gen. 9:4 and the prohibition against murder in the next two verses (vv. 5–6).

prohibition originated just after the flood (Gen. 9:4), long before the Israelite ritual system came into existence. So its applicability does not depend on the functioning of that system, which came to an end in the first century AD.

Are Christians accountable for observing the blood prohibition, or can we ascend the ladder of abstraction to the principle of respect for life and then just reapply the principle in other ways?[62] Since hardly any meat-eating Christians observe the prohibition today, it could be argued that the literal biblical requirement lacks a place in today's world. However, this inserts a modern cultural interpretive bias in a circular way: We don't observe the law, so we don't need to. Acts 15 shows that this approach is mistaken: By contrast with the abrogation of circumcision as a religious requirement (vv. 1–19, 28), even Gentile Christians must "abstain from [eating] what has been sacrificed to idols, and from blood, and from what has been strangled [i.e., killed in such a way that the blood has not drained out]" (v. 29; cf. v. 20).[63] Whether or not Christians themselves do the slaughtering is irrelevant; what matters is how the animals that they eat have been slaughtered. So the blood prohibition continues in force for all Christians, with no need to indirectly reapply it through the ladder of abstraction.

The example just presented begins to reveal some limitations of the principlizing method. First, principlization does not determine whether a biblical law remains directly applicable for modern Christians or not, although it can assist with recognition of ways in which a principle indirectly applies.

Second, the principlizing method by itself deals with one biblical passage at a time within its context without seeking to discern possible movement from one level of moral quality (not to be confused with levels of abstraction) to another. Such a multilevel moral trajectory is found in biblical texts regarding diet. According to the creation account, the original and ideal human and animal diet was vegetarian (Gen. 1:29–30; 2:9; cf. 3:17–19, continuing after the fall), which completely respected animal life. Only after the flood did God permit humans to eat meat (9:3), but not its lifeblood (v. 4). So the dietary blood prohibition, which maintains respect for life at an inferior level, applies to the less-than-ideal diet of meat. A vegetarian diet could be restored in the eschatological new creation,[64] and in the

---

62. Kaiser does not loosely reapply like this. Rather, he includes the original biblical situation (ox treading grain in his example) with the extended application of a principle ("Principlizing Model," 25–26).

63. Cf. application of the blood prohibition to Gentile resident aliens dwelling in the land of Israel in Lev. 17:10, 12–13. So this requirement simply continues for Gentile Christians who belong to God's community of faith. On the issue of eating food sacrificed to idols, see 1 Cor. 8; 10:14–31.

64. Cf. cessation of predation and death presented as ideal in Isa. 11:6–9; 65:25; Rev. 21:4.

meantime, people can voluntarily reach this superior level of respect for life by choosing this diet (cf. the multilevel ethical trajectory regarding divorce in Matt. 19:3–9).

A third limitation of the principlizing method is its loss of specificity, and therefore control, as it ascends the ladder of abstraction.[65] It is precisely this decontextualization that gives the method flexibility for recontextualization in other situations, but at what cost in accuracy and perspective, particularly if it is necessary to go up the ladder of abstraction several rungs before reaching a universal and permanent level?

Paradigmatic Approaches of Waldemar Janzen and Christopher J. H. Wright

Modern "positive law" attempts to explicitly regulate all kinds of cases in detail, but "both biblical and ancient Near Eastern laws represent paradigmatic law, giving illustrations of justice and providing examples to inform judges when they dealt with analogous cases."[66] Waldemar Janzen and Christopher J. H. Wright have developed quite different paradigmatic approaches to application of OT laws. In his *Old Testament Ethics: A Paradigmatic Approach*, Janzen seeks to develop a comprehensive understanding of OT ethics that takes multiple literary genres into account.[67] Beginning with narratives and then moving to other genres, he finds several paradigms/models for good ethical living, including the familial paradigm, the priestly paradigm of holy life, the wisdom paradigm, the royal paradigm of just life, and the prophetic paradigm of serving and suffering. He links these to roles of Jesus as priest, sage, king, prophet, and especially as God-imaging human.

Janzen reacts against reductionistic approaches that limit God's ethical requirements to the Ten Commandments or to decontextualized abstract principles, such as a general concept of justice or love. He points out that the corpus of biblical laws only presents samples of the good life, encapsulating concepts that are fleshed out in narratives, supplemented by other genres. He argues that stories, which describe life in its complexity for the benefit of the reader's character formation, are the primary source of ethical guidance and that the laws are secondary.

65. C. Wright is concerned that, by itself, the approach of abstracting principles "can lead to the eventual discarding of the specific realities of the Old Testament text" (*Old Testament Ethics*, 70). He prefers to view the texts regarding Israel as a more complex paradigm that "preserves their historical particularity" (71). See further below.

66. Sprinkle, *Biblical Law*, 25.

67. *Old Testament Ethics: A Paradigmatic Approach* (Louisville: Westminster/John Knox, 1994).

Janzen's points are important. Indeed, according to Paul, the purpose of studying all Scripture (2 Tim. 3:16), including teachings in all of its genres, is for holistic character development, "that the man of God may be complete, equipped for every good work" (v. 17). Values and principles in OT law should be understood within the totality of biblical revelation, recognizing that the various genres need each other to effectively convey God's moral instructions.

Jesus and Paul did summarize God's law in terms of the overarching principle of love (Matt. 22:37–40; Rom. 13:8–10), but they did not view it as a decontextualized abstraction. Rather, they saw it as containing and therefore defined by the content of "all the Law and the Prophets" (Matt. 22:40), including the other commandments (Rom. 13:9). This does not leave it up to human imagination to figure out how to love or allow Christians to disregard the rest of biblical teaching because they suppose that Christ commanded them only to love (John 13:34–35; 15:12, 17; but see Matt. 28:20, "teaching them to observe all that I have commanded you"). If love embraces everything, it cannot negate what it summarizes![68]

Jesus placed the command for his disciples to love in the context of his story: "just as I have loved you" (John 13:34). To comprehend love, look at how Jesus treated his disciples. To identify the neighbor whom you are to love as yourself (Matt. 22:39; Rom. 13:9; citing Lev. 19:18), listen to Jesus's story of the good Samaritan (Luke 10:29–37). You will gain far more ethical wisdom from reading the Gospel narratives than you can from contemplating the summary injunction to love by itself. Similarly, the narratives of salvation history in the OT provide a richer and more nuanced view of God's character and many aspects of his will than the laws in the Pentateuch.

Nevertheless, summary statements and laws are important for several reasons. First, they show the dynamic unity of God's revelation and will so that we can grasp his values and principles as a package of complementary, interactive, and mutually informing elements rather than as stand-alone concepts. The fact that they function as a unit in relation to him as a person, whose character and law is love, explains why Moses repeatedly exhorted the Israelites to follow all of God's instructions (e.g., Deut. 6:2; 10:12; 12:28; 13:18 [13:19 MT]). It also explains why breaking any part of the law violates the law as a whole (James 2:8–11) in the sense that it transgresses the law of love and thereby negatively affects the divine-human relationship.

---

68. However, John C. Peckham points out that "the biblical conception of love is quite different than the classical tradition claims. This points to the further danger of abstracting a principle that is itself understood in an unbiblical manner (without recognizing it as such)" (personal communication). On the concept of God's kind of love, see Peckham's *The Love of God: A Canonical Model* (Downers Grove, IL: IVP Academic, 2015).

Second, laws are useful for analyzing and evaluating situations in life or biblical narratives that convey wisdom through recounting past life because the laws single out morally relevant elements, just as breakdowns of body parts in an anatomy and physiology textbook assist a physician-in-training to recognize individual factors in the complex and dynamically interactive human organism. This function of law is especially clear in the Pentateuch where divine law directly follows and responds to a situation in a narrative unit (Lev. 10:1–11; 24:10–23; Num. 9:6–14; 27:1–11).[69]

Third, laws are abstractions from situations that could be recounted as narratives.[70] The fact that they lack all the details of stories makes their abbreviated form much more concise. Therefore the Bible can and does speak to many more kinds of value-related situations in the law genre than it can through narratives.

Fourth, while a story can demonstrate complex interactions between multiple kinds of values, isolation of values in laws facilitates recognition of affinities between related values. For example, the lists of prohibited sexual relations in Lev. 18 and 20 include homosexual activity (18:22; 20:13), an intended offense of the men of Sodom for which they were guilty and suffered divine punishment as though they actually had succeeded in doing it (Gen. 19:4–11, 13, 24–25, 28; Jude 7; cf. Ezek. 16:50).[71] Leviticus 18 and 20 also include sins of incest (Lev. 18:6–18; 20:11–12, 14, 17, 19–21), which Reuben committed (Gen. 35:22), in the same series of laws against various forms of categorically forbidden sexual behaviors. This invites some kind of comparison between the stories of Reuben and of the men of Sodom.

Fifth, relationships between laws (including in series) and summary statements of overall principles of law (e.g., Matt. 22:37–40, citing Deut. 6:5 and Lev. 19:18; Matt. 7:12, so-called Golden Rule) assist us in extending love, as biblically defined in several genres, to situations regarding which we do not find directly relevant biblical teaching. There are no gaps or loopholes in love, which is exhaustively comprehensive in scope (cf. Rom. 13:8–10; Gal.

---

69. Bernon P. Lee shows how some pentateuchal laws interact with surrounding narratives to enhance awareness of certain themes. *Between Law and Narrative: The Method and Function of Abstraction*, Gorgias Dissertations, Biblical Studies 51 (Piscataway, NJ: Gorgias, 2010).

70. On narrative reading of OT casuistic laws, which reveals aspects of their effectiveness in encouraging obedience to their norms, see Assnat Bartor, *Reading Law as Narrative: A Study in the Casuistic Laws of the Pentateuch*, Society of Biblical Literature Ancient Israel and Its Literature 5 (Atlanta: Society of Biblical Literature, 2010). "Despite the rigid framework, the set patterns, the brief format, and the sparse details, the laws manage to leave us with a powerful impression of reality" (184).

71. They were prevented only by the intervention of two angels (Gen. 19:9–11).

5:14; Col. 3:14), so fully illustrating it would require an infinite number of examples, whether in narratives, laws, or other genres. The examples we have in the Bible serve as signposts to guide the trajectories of our moral journeys, the details of which are largely up to our choices.

Christopher J. H. Wright accepts the validity of Janzen's approach[72] and proposes another, complementary way in which the idea of a paradigm can be employed by treating ancient Israel's entire society and body of laws as a paradigm. He explains his use of the term "paradigm" in this context:

> A paradigm is a model or pattern that enables you to explain or critique many different and varying situations by means of some single concept or set of governing principles. To use a paradigm you work by analogy from a specific known reality (the paradigm) to a wider or different context in which there are problems to be solved, or answers to be found, or choices to be made. Or a paradigm may provide criteria by which you evaluate or critique some set of circumstances or proposals, positively or negatively. So a paradigm may function descriptively or prescriptively or critically.[73]

Wright lists some important features of the revolutionary Israelite worldview that constitute a paradigm in the broad sense of a system of beliefs and values. These include monotheism; YHWH as Lord of creation who acts in history; values such as concern for those who are vulnerable and oppressed, justice, and rejection of idolatry, which YHWH demonstrated through the exodus and incorporated in Israel's law; a covenantal approach to social structure (with YHWH as king); the concept that YHWH owns the land of Israel; and the belief that the divine creator sustains the natural order.[74]

In a narrower sense, "Israel itself was a paradigm" in that "they constituted a concrete model, a practical, culturally specific, experimental exemplar of the beliefs and values they embodied."[75] For a while Israel demonstrated such things as how theocracy could function without a human king, that land could

---

72. C. Wright, *Old Testament Ethics*, 70.

73. Ibid., 63–64.

74. Ibid., 67–68.

75. Ibid., 68. C. Wright also finds that the way God related to Israel in their land was a paradigm for his redemptive purpose for fallen humanity in the cursed earth. Complementing this paradigmatic approach are typological and eschatological levels of interpreting and applying OT material relevant to ethics (182–98). Wright takes the Jubilee instructions (Lev. 25) as a case study to show how various angles of perspective (social, economic, theological) and levels of interpretation and application (typological, paradigmatic, eschatological) can work (198–210). For paradigmatic interpretation, he views the Jubilee regulations from the economic, social, and theological angles in order to see how the paradigm of Israel speaks to modern Christians through this institution (206–9).

be used without absolute ownership of it, and how a basically egalitarian, family-based society could prevent or remedy poverty, debt, and servitude.[76] "By seeing how *they* addressed, within *their* cultural and historical context, problems and issues common to humanity in principle or practice, we are helped to address (if not always to solve) the ethical challenges *we* face in our different contexts."[77] The details of their context are not obstacles for us to overcome, but important aids for the process of dealing with our specific contexts.[78]

Wright finds evidence in Exod. 19:4–6 that God designed Israel to serve as a paradigm of a priestly, holy people whose compliance with covenant law would distinguish them *from* other nations. "But at the same time, as a priesthood, they were to be teacher, model and mediator *for* the nations. Keeping the law, then, was not an end in itself for Israel, but related to their very reason for existence—God's concern for the nations."[79] Thus the paradigmatic function of Israel, including to enlighten modern people, is expressed in the biblical text; it is not merely an artificial scholarly construct. The Israelites "render to us a paradigm, in one single culture and slice of history, of the kinds of social values God looks for in human life generally."[80]

Rather than abstracting generalized principles from laws, Wright seeks to identify the coherent, paradigmatic system of principles on which laws (or institutions that they regulate) are based and that they exemplify.[81] He lists four steps for moving from an OT law to our current world, of which the first three steps evaluate the law within the context of ancient Israel and the fourth transitions to modern relevance:[82]

1. "Distinguish the different kinds of law in the text," such as criminal law, case law, family law, cultic law, and compassionate law.[83]
2. "Analyze the social function and relative status of particular laws and institutions."[84]

76. Ibid., 68.
77. Ibid., 69; cf. 66.
78. Ibid., 65, 69, 320; cf. John Barton, *Ethics and the Old Testament*, 2nd ed. (London: SCM, 2002), 14–18.
79. C. Wright, *Old Testament Ethics*, 64, cf. 65.
80. Ibid., 65; cf. 74, 320–21.
81. E.g., ibid., 71; cf. 206–7.
82. Ibid., 321–4.
83. Cf. ibid., 288–301. "It is immediately clear that we do not find a separate, textually isolated, category of 'moral law' as such. But we do find moral motivation, rationale, objectives and values, sometimes expressed and sometimes implied, in every category of law we identify" (321).
84. "When dealing with any particular law, we need to ask how it related to and functioned within the overall social system of Israel. Is it central or peripheral to the dominant themes and social objectives we find in the rest of the material? Is it a primary expression of key values

3. "Define the objective(s) of the law in Israelite society."[85]
4. "Preserve the objective but change the context."

So Wright moves from OT law to modern Christian life by way of analogy, with the objective providing the continuity.[86] Paul exemplified the way this kind of transfer works by transferring the objective of the threshing ox law (Deut. 25:4), support for a worker, to the Christian context in his argument for support of another kind of worker: the Christian minister (1 Cor. 9:8–12).[87]

In addition to laws, Wright sees other particular aspects of ancient Israel serving as paradigms, such as events, especially the exodus,[88] and narratives, such as Nathan's juridical parable to David (2 Sam. 12:1–10).[89] In the NT the accounts of the life of Jesus are paradigmatic.[90]

Wright provides a holistic framework for moving from the OT to modern life, considering not only ethical applications but also implications within the full canonical and modern contexts. His four-step approach to a given law (see above) supplies greater control than isolation and application of highly abstract principles would. However, rather than eliminating use of principles, Wright refines it by (1) implicitly defining the principle(s) in a law in terms of its objective(s), and (2) pointing out that the principle(s) in a law must be understood within the context of the principles underlying

---

and priorities, or does it reinforce other such primary legislation? Or is it a modification or a secondary application?" (ibid., 322).

85. C. Wright lists questions that could be addressed to determine the purpose of the law, such as these:

What kind of situation was this law trying to promote, or prevent? Whose interests was this law aiming to protect? Who would have benefited from this law and why? Whose power was this law trying to restrict and how did it do so? What rights and responsibilities were embodied in this law? What kind of behaviour did this law encourage or discourage? What vision of society motivated this law? What moral principles, values or priorities did this law embody or instantiate? What motivation did this law appeal to? What sanction or penalty (if any) was attached to this law, and what does that show regarding its relative seriousness or moral priority? (ibid., 323)

86. "We can ask a parallel set of questions about our own context. . . . We can seek to identify comparable situations, interests, needs, powers, rights, behaviours . . . that need to be addressed in our own society. Then in that new context (our own contemporary world) we ask how the objectives of Old Testament laws can be achieved. Or we ask how we can bring our own social ethical objectives to point in the same direction" (ibid., 323).

87. Ibid., 73.

88. Ibid., 69, 71–72.

89. See also "one of the most powerful narrative paradigms ever created—Jesus' parable of the good Samaritan (Luke 10:30–39) . . . 'Go and do *likewise*' (v. 37 [emphasis added]). . . . Jesus' words did not mean 'Go and do *exactly the same*.' They meant 'Go and live your life in a way which expresses the same costly and barrier-crossing neighbourliness that my story illustrates—that is what it will mean to obey the law (since you asked)'" (ibid., 72).

90. Ibid., 73.

it within the total paradigmatic package of biblical Israel. He cannot avoid some subjectivity, because defining the objective(s) of a law involves a kind of interpretive abstraction that at least resembles identification of a principle within the principlizing approach (see above), provided that the latter takes all contextual factors into account.

It would be helpful if Christopher Wright were to provide some case studies that could test and demonstrate the usefulness of his four-step approach for obtaining answers to questions and solving problems regarding applications of specific laws.[91] Such case studies could also clarify relationships between his method and the principlizing approach.

Redemptive-Movement Model of William J. Webb

In *Slaves, Women & Homosexuals*, William J. Webb pursues in greater detail than other scholars the question of why modern Christians should continue to apply some parts of biblical teaching but not others.[92] He makes clear that Scripture determines the outcome of analysis that leads to application. Culture itself—whether ANE (in OT times), GR (= Greco-Roman during the NT period), or modern—does not decide between what is cultural and what is transcultural in Scripture.[93] However, assessment of culture is a vital part of the hermeneutic of application because "the Bible represents God's communication to human society through cultural forms."[94] God's people are to move with changes in their surrounding culture unless it conflicts with biblical values, in which cases they should act counterculturally.[95]

In support of Webb's point here, consider the following law: "A woman shall not wear a man's garment, nor shall a man put on a woman's cloak, for whoever does these things is an abomination to the LORD your God" (Deut. 22:5). The biblical value is for men and women to wear apparel that pertains to their respective genders, apparently to avoid gender-identity confusion.[96] But the Bible does not contain prescriptions of male and female attire, which must be defined (not just conditioned) by cultural norms.

Webb further points out (1) that decisions regarding questions of whether biblical requirements are transcultural or culturally bound are most solidly

91. C. Wright's case study on the Jubilee (ibid., 198–210) does not show how to use his four-step approach.
92. William J. Webb, *Slaves, Women & Homosexuals: Exploring the Hermeneutics of Cultural Analysis* (Downers Grove, IL: IVP Academic, 2001), 16.
93. See, e.g., ibid., 245–46.
94. Ibid., 245.
95. Ibid., 22.
96. See further on this law in chap. 12 below.

developed through coordinated use of multiple criteria, (2) specific biblical commands that can involve cultural elements express higher-level transcultural principles, and (3) biblical texts can show redemptive movement pointing to higher ethics than God could require in biblical times.

Using texts relating to slaves, women, and homosexuals for his primary case studies, Webb develops sixteen intrascriptural and two extrascriptural criteria to be used together in a balanced way in biblical texts for distinguishing between cultural components that do not carry over to modern life and transcultural elements that do still apply today.

For example, Webb's "Criterion 1: Preliminary Movement" is as follows:

> A component of a text may be culturally bound if Scripture modifies the *original* cultural norms in such a way that suggests further movement is possible and even advantageous in a *subsequent* culture. Two questions bring this criterion into focus: (1) Has Scripture modified the original cultural norms? (2) If so, is the movement an "absolute movement" or a "preliminary movement"?[97]

Webb goes on to define his terms:

> *Absolute movement:* the biblical author has pushed society so far and that is as far as it is supposed to go; further movement is not desired.
> *Preliminary movement:* the biblical author pushed society as far as it could go at that time without creating more damage than good; however, it can and should ultimately go further.[98]

He identifies three measures for such movement:

> (1) "foreign movement"—change relative to ANE/GR cultures, (2) "domestic movement"—change compared to what was currently happening within the covenant community itself and (3) "canonical movement"—change across broad redemptive epochs, such as from the Old Testament to the New Testament.[99]

Webb finds that the Bible does not simply present static truth that always should be applied today exactly according to the wording of the text. Rather,

---

97. Webb, *Slaves, Women & Homosexuals*, 73.
98. Ibid.
99. Ibid., 74; cf. 82 for Webb's suggested guidelines to assess redemptive movement: "(1) the ANE/GR *real* world must be examined along with its *legal* world, (2) the biblical subject on the *whole* must be examined along with its *parts*, (3) the biblical text must be compared to a number of other ANE/GR cultures which themselves must be compared with each other and (4) any portrait of movement must be composed of broad input from all three streams of assessment—foreign, domestic and canonical."

its historically embedded teaching often presents a spirit and direction pointing toward an ideal that goes beyond what God could constructively require of his people in ancient times.[100] We should identify this redemptive movement and follow its trajectory in order to apply the biblical message as close to the ideal as possible, even beyond the requirements explicitly articulated in the Bible itself.

For instance, slaves suffered many abuses in the original culture of the biblical world, to which OT law responded in a culturally bound way by requiring fewer abuses and better conditions. The NT continued the upward trajectory (Gal. 3:28; Philemon; etc.) yet did not abolish slavery due to cultural limitations. Our modern culture has continued progress from the *preliminary movement* begun by the Bible but has gone beyond its literal wording, with slavery abolished and working conditions generally improved. However, there is still room for improvement toward an "ultimate ethic," which would include "wages maximized for all, and harmony, respect and unified purpose between all levels in an organizational structure."[101]

Webb broadly addresses the vital question of how to determine whether something is better within redemptive movement by referring to "biblical, theological, logical, sociological, ethical, canonical, empirical, even practical" factors established in his detailed analyses.[102] He also summarizes his hermeneutic of redemptive movement toward an ultimate ethic:

> The Christian seeking to apply Scripture today should examine the movement between the biblical text and its surrounding social context. Once that movement has been discovered, there needs to be an assessment of whether the movement is preliminary or absolute (see criterion 1). If it is preliminary and further movement in the direction set by the text would produce a more fully realized ethic, then that is the course of action one must pursue. The interpreter extrapolates the biblical movement toward a more just, more equitable and more loving form. If a better ethic than the one expressed in the isolated words of the text is possible, and the biblical and canonical spirit is headed that direction, then that is where one ultimately wants to end up.[103]

By contrast with slavery, Webb finds that although homosexual practice was widely accepted in ANE culture, as in our modern culture, the Bible negatively

---

100. "Biblical texts often represent pastoral letters, written with the tenderness of a pastor's heart. Their words are designed to 'stretch' the covenant people as far as they could go, like an elastic band, but not to cause them to 'snap'" (ibid., 58).

101. Ibid., 37.

102. Ibid., 48.

103. Ibid., 36.

assessed and banned it, stopping redemptive movement there. So this is an example of *absolute movement*, in which the explicit biblical prohibition is transcultural and should be applied today.[104]

In his discussion of Criterion 17: "Pragmatic Basis between Two Cultures,"[105] Webb incorporates the principlizing "ladder of abstraction," which moves from broad, abstract, transcultural principles to more particular and concrete expressions that often include "culture-based pragmatic factors."[106] His illustration of such a ladder has the command "Love your neighbor" (Lev. 19:18, cited in Matt. 22:39) at the top. This encapsulates an abstract, transcultural principle that has its ultimate basis in the "character and will of God" and the "value of people created in God's image." Lower down on the ladder is the transcultural subprinciple: "Help/feed the poor." Still lower, pragmatic factors, such as a "high percentage of population involved in farming" and "close proximity between population and farms," shape a particular cultural form of the subprinciple in the command "Leave the corners of your fields unharvested" (for the poor and the resident alien; Lev. 19:9–10).[107] If such a law is impractical in a modern setting, where locations of farms at a distance from the urban poor makes it impossible for them to glean, we can nevertheless learn something if we "move up the ladder of abstraction to discover what is transcultural in this biblical command."[108]

We can add that other laws also carry out the subprinciple "Help/feed the poor" (e.g., Deut. 14:28–29; 15:13–14; 26:12–13), and other subprinciples, such as "Provide justice for the vulnerable" (e.g., Exod. 23:6; Deut. 24:17; cf. 27:19), also come under the overarching principle "Love your neighbor." Therefore, a particular "ladder of abstraction" reaching down to one law belongs to a larger hierarchy of moral values and subvalues/principles that generate and unite many laws (see chap. 7 above), just as a specific directory path identifies the location of a document on a computer (e.g., Documents/Current Projects/

104. Ibid., 39–40. Webb also describes an "ultimate ethic" that not only regards homosexual practice as negative and completely restricts it but also includes "greater understanding and compassion, utilization of a sliding scale of culpability, and variation in the degree of negative assessment based on the type of same-sex activity" (40). See further on homosexual practice in chap. 15 of the present book.

105. Webb introduces this criterion as follows: "A component of a biblical imperative may be culturally relative if the pragmatic basis for the instruction cannot be sustained from one culture to another. The converse is that a biblical command is more likely to be transcultural in its articulated form to the extent that the pragmatic factors are themselves sustainable across various cultures" (209).

106. Ibid., 210. Regarding the "ladder of abstraction," see above on Kaiser, "Principlizing Model," 24–26.

107. Webb, *Slaves, Women & Homosexuals*, 210.

108. Ibid., 211; cf. 180–81.

Writing Projects/Old Testament Law for Christians folder/Old Testament Law for Christians manuscript.docx) represents a hierarchically organized collection of documents.

Webb recognizes that placement of biblical imperatives within the broad framework of salvation history provides an important macroperspective for assessment of redemptive movement.[109] For instance, according to Gen. 1–2 the transcultural ideal of loving harmony between humans created in the divine image and full provision for their needs and happiness was not radical in the beginning; it was the norm, simply the way God created things to be. The fall into sin (Gen. 3) is what made the ideal radical and generated the need for redemptive movement toward restoration of the ideal in the "new earth" (Rev. 21–22).

Some scholars have questioned Webb's claim that in some instances an ultimate ethic should be found even beyond the NT because its writers belonged to and were to some extent constrained by their culture.[110] They have pointed out the inadequacy of Webb's methodological control, and therefore potential for subjectivity, in defining what is a better or ultimate ethic.[111] However, it appears to me that further consideration of the hierarchy of moral values and the creation (Gen. 1–2) and new creation (Rev. 21–22) ideals could assist Webb in meeting these objections.[112] The high-level ideal values that originally governed and will again govern a sinless planet Earth can provide a framework for delineation of ultimate ethics that is found within the Bible rather than beyond it.

For example, OT laws that protect slaves come under the overall transcultural principle "Love your neighbor." Webb finds that the ultimate basis

109. Several of Webb's criteria relate to this framework: "Criterion 5: Basis in Fall or Curse," "Criterion 6: Basis in Original Creation, Section 1: Patterns," "Criterion 7: Basis in Original Creation, Section 2: Primogeniture," and "Criterion 8: Basis in New Creation" (ibid., 110–52).

110. Mark L. Strauss, "A Reflection by Mark L. Strauss," in Meadors, *Four Views on Moving beyond the Bible to Theology*, 282.

111. E.g., ibid., 287–89; Al Wolters, "A Reflection by Al Wolters," in Meadors, *Four Views on Moving beyond the Bible to Theology*, 306–7.

112. Webb focuses his "Criterion 8: Basis in New Creation" on the NT "in Christ" community in Pauline writings (esp. 1 Cor. 12:13; Gal. 3:28; Eph. 2:15; 4:22–24; Col. 3:9–11), in which fulfillment of redemptive elements of the eschatological age to come is already taking place (Webb, *Slaves, Women & Homosexuals*, 145–52). He finds that "the closer the new-creation community moves toward the eschaton, the more likely it will engage transcultural perspectives" (146). This makes sense, given that unification is a process that brings multicultural Christians together. Here Webb does not discuss the ultimate new creation described at the end of the book of Revelation (Rev. 21–22), although he does include Rev. 21:8 and 21:15 (surely meaning 22:15), which exclude various categories of sinners from the new creation and the holy new Jerusalem, among transcultural vice and virtue lists (194). However, restoration of ideal life at the end of the Bible surely carries greater implications for ultimate ethics than Webb's presentation indicates.

for this principle is found in the "character and will of God" and the "value of people created in God's image."[113] I would emphasize that God originally created free people (Gen. 1–2), not slaves, and he liberated the Israelites from slavery to freedom when he created their nation (Exod. 1–15).[114] Moreover, those who inherit the new creation, because they are "in Christ Jesus," "are all sons of God, through faith" (Gal. 3:26). As God's sons, they are not slaves: "There is neither Jew nor Greek, there is neither slave nor free, there is no male and female, for you are all one in Christ Jesus. And if you are Christ's, then you are Abraham's offspring, heirs according to promise" (vv. 28–29). This statement was already true in a spiritual sense in Paul's day, but its complete social implementation was constrained by the harsh realities of the Roman Empire.

By using the word "heirs," Gal. 3:29 recognizes the present limitations and promises fulfillment in the future. So our quest for an ultimate ethic should press on to find that time of fulfillment. When "the kingdom of the world has become the kingdom of our Lord and of his Christ" (Rev. 11:15), Christ's people will inherit his eternal domain under his benevolent rule (cf. Dan. 7:27; Matt. 25:34). Then unity and equality in Christ will finally prevail, along with restoration of other creation ideals such as full intimacy with God and freedom from physical suffering (Rev. 21:3–4). God says that anyone who "will have this heritage" "will be my son" (v. 7), in agreement with Gal. 3:26, but now unfettered by the faultiness of fallen human society, and ruling out slavery in any sense. Therefore, although because of cultural limitations the OT and NT do not explicitly outlaw slavery, there is no need to go outside the Bible to identify and define the ultimate ethic of freedom for everyone, which complete fulfillment of the command "Love your neighbor" implies.

Two components of the prefall Eden scenario are especially promising guides for development of biblically controlled ultimate ethics: the permanent, transcultural institutions of (inherently heterosexual) marriage (Gen. 1:27–28; 2:18, 21–24) and Sabbath (2:2–3). Webb loses an opportunity to strengthen his case for redemptive movement leading to ultimate ethics by missing the full extent to which the creation marriage and Sabbath serve as persuasive transcultural paradigms that can shape ultimate ethics. He discusses issues involved with marriage, as well as Sabbath and the related length of a

113. Webb, *Slaves, Women & Homosexuals*, 210.
114. The exodus is "a paradigm of hope for all oppressed peoples, assuring them they have not been created to be slaves but to be free in a society that should protect and practice justice." Enrique Nardoni, *Rise Up, O Judge: A Study of Justice in the Biblical World*, trans. Seán Charles Martin (Peabody, MA: Hendrickson, 2004), 62. On formation of the Israelite nation as a creation, cf. chap. 11 below.

workweek,[115] under his "Moderately Persuasive" "Criterion 6: Basis in Original Creation, Section 1: Patterns . . . A component of a text may be transcultural if its basis is rooted in the original-creation material."[116] He recognizes that the creation of lifelong marriage itself "carries a strong transcultural force,"[117] but by focusing on departures from it (divorce, polygamy, singleness), rather than on marriage itself and its implications, he compromises the transcultural persuasiveness of the creation-pattern criterion.

Webb also compromises on the Sabbath:

> While affirming transcultural components to Sabbath (worship of the Creator God, a work-and-rest rhythm, etc.), most Christians today depart from the sabbath pattern in significant ways. For example, most have changed the sabbath day from Saturday to Sunday and many have softened the work prohibitions and penalties. Further, many Christians, while accepting various underlying Sabbath principles, do not prescribe any specific day of the week for its fulfillment. Although I will not attempt to prove the case here, Sabbath offers a good example of a creation pattern with a significant cultural component. Though the approaches differ, there is general Christian consensus that this aspect of creation pattern should be modified to *some* extent.[118]

Here Webb's assessment is shaped by factors other than Scripture, such as consensus and tradition regarding practice. These are cultural elements, which he appears to treat as a kind of authority, departing from his assertion that Scripture should always be the authority (see above). Then he concludes that Sabbath is an example of a creation pattern "with a significant cultural component." This is circular reasoning: Evaluating the biblical Sabbath requirement in terms of cultural practice, he naturally finds that some aspects of it are culturally bound.[119]

---

115. Webb, *Slaves, Women & Homosexuals*, 124–27.

116. Ibid., 123.

117. Ibid., 124.

118. Ibid., 125–26.

119. Webb states: "Developments in salvation history (along with a movement away from an agrarian culture) have helped bring about a relinquishing or reworking of the Sabbath pattern. Cf. Galatians 4:10; Colossians 2:16" (ibid., 126n5). However, he does not explain how Gal. 4:10 and Col. 2:16 support his statement. Later he states: "The sabbath laws would appear to no longer apply *literally* because of the change in covenants, old to new, the corresponding change in covenant symbols, and the New Testament repeal of cultic days" (175). However, God made basic Sabbath rest for human beings (Gen. 2:2–3; Mark 2:27) before the fall into sin (Gen. 3) and subsequent institution of the temporary typology of redemption in the Israelite cultic system. Practices that functioned as typological shadows of coming events became obsolete when Christ fulfilled "the substance" (Col. 2:16–17; see chap. 15, below, on this passage). But basic Sabbath rest was never a temporary "type" of things to come and could not be cultic in the

Another aspect of Webb's approach that has attracted criticism is the prominent role that ethical movements from ancient cultures to biblical teachings play in his model.[120] Daniel M. Doriani questions whether we are sufficiently certain about other ANE cultures to adequately assess relationships between them and the Bible.[121] Al Wolters raises additional issues: Webb's model "treats 'ancient Near Eastern' culture as an ethically monolithic entity," and movements between the ANE and the Bible may not always have been improvements.[122]

Kevin J. Vanhoozer finds it more precise to speak of "contrast" rather than "movement": "Synchronic contrast highlights how viewing things biblically is a change for the better vis-à-vis the ancient Near East; diachronic contrast highlights change for the better within the Bible itself."[123] Wolters further objects to viewing the synchronic contrast between ethical teaching in the Bible and that of neighboring pagan cultures along with diachronic contrast between the OT and NT "as part of the same 'redemptive' trajectory that leads from ancient pagan culture to a postcanonical ultimate ethic that bears a close resemblance to contemporary Western values."[124] Moreover, although contemporary Western values appear superior in some ways, such as through abolition of slavery and greater rights for women, they may show regression from ancient ethics in other ways, such as in the areas of family values, sense of community, hospitality, and distribution of wealth.[125]

No doubt Webb is right that ethical values in the Bible are often superior to those of non-Israelite cultures, as Scripture itself affirms (Lev. 18:3–5, 24–30; 20:22–26; Deut. 4:5–8). However, given that adequately precise relationships between particular non-Israelite and biblical ethical norms are often difficult to establish, it would appear safest to base our understanding of the cultural/

---

sense that it was an integral part of the cultic system, depended on it, and became obsolete with it when Christ inaugurated the new covenant, because Sabbath rest preceded the need for the cult and commemorated something more basic and enduring than the process of redemption: God's resting from the work of creation (Gen. 2:2–3; Exod. 20:11; 31:17); cf. Gane, *Leviticus, Numbers*, 391–95, 754–56.

120. E.g., Webb, *Slaves, Women & Homosexuals*, 82.

121. Daniel M. Doriani, "A Response to William J. Webb," in Meadors, *Four Views on Moving beyond the Bible to Theology*, 260.

122. Wolters, "Reflection," 304–5. See, e.g., the fact that law §117 of the Laws of Hammurabi requires manumission of debt-servants after only three years, but according to OT law, an Israelite debt-servant was to be freed after six years (Exod. 21:2; Deut. 15:12).

123. Kevin J. Vanhoozer, "A Response to William J. Webb," in Meadors, *Four Views on Moving beyond the Bible to Theology*, 265, cf. 264; Wolters, "Reflection," 305–6.

124. Wolters, "Reflection," 306.

125. Paolo Esposito (my student), review of Webb's *Slaves, Women & Homosexuals* for my Andrews University course "Seminar in Old Testament Theology," fall semester 2015.

social situations addressed by OT laws on exegesis of biblical data, which (as in any good OT exegesis) can be illuminated by judicious consideration of available and relevant ANE background materials. As to Wolters's objection concerning "a postcanonical ultimate ethic," see above regarding the alternative of inner-biblical evidence for ultimate ethics (hierarchy of values and creation/new creation ideals) that are independent of "contemporary Western values."

The moderate methods for applying OT law to modern life critiqued in this chapter contain many helpful insights.[126] In the next chapter, we will attempt to synthesize their strong points, avoid their weaknesses, and build on them (along with factors identified in chap. 7) to develop an approach that I call "Progressive Moral Wisdom."

---

126. Especially the principlizing model of Walter C. Kaiser Jr., the paradigmatic approaches of Waldemar Janzen and Christopher J. H. Wright, and the redemptive-movement model of William J. Webb.

9

Progressive Moral Wisdom

Second Timothy 3:15–17 provides a framework for the process of developing an approach to application of OT law. Here Paul affirms to Timothy the ongoing worth of "the sacred writings, which are able to make you wise for salvation through faith in Christ Jesus. All Scripture is breathed out by God and profitable for teaching, for reproof, for correction, and for training in righteousness, that the man of God may be complete, equipped for every good work." These verses contain the following concepts regarding the appropriate Christian attitude toward and use of "the sacred writings," which primarily refer to the OT here.

Introduction to Progressive Moral Wisdom

The "sacred writings" have the ability to make a Christian who receives them "wise for salvation through faith in Christ Jesus."[1] Neither the Scriptures themselves (including law portions) nor adherence to them (including obedience to laws) *provide* salvation, but the Scriptures do supply wisdom regarding salvation that is received through faith in Christ (cf. John 5:39–40).[2]

---

1. Cf. Eccles. 7:12, "The advantage of knowledge is that wisdom preserves the life of him who has it."
2. Cf. Luke 24:27, "in all the Scriptures the things concerning himself."

All Scripture by God for Teaching

"All Scripture is breathed out by God." Every portion of Scripture (including OT law) conveys thoughts that come from God himself, although they are conveyed through human instruments. Therefore no biblical passage is left behind because it lacks a contribution to our understanding of the divine will.

"All Scripture is . . . profitable for teaching."[3] Paul does not single out any particular biblical genre or section, such as historical narrative, law, prophecy, or Wisdom literature. Every part of the Bible is valuable for Christian teaching, which therefore should draw on Scripture as a whole, with understanding of one part (such as OT law) both informed by and illuminating comprehension of other parts.

Progressive Training in Moral Wisdom

The categories "teaching . . . reproof . . . correction, and . . . training in righteousness" overlap. Teaching can involve reproof (refuting error), which can play a role in restorative correction (e.g., 1 Cor. 5). These can contribute to "training in righteousness," which enables Christians to develop strong moral character by progressively bringing them from ignorance and moral faultiness into harmony with wise divine perspectives and values. So Paul advocates what could be termed "progressive training in moral wisdom," which we can abbreviate to "progressive moral wisdom."

The Greek word for "training" in 2 Tim. 3:16 is *paideia*, which refers to "the act of providing guidance for responsible living, *upbringing, training, instruction*," including "as it is attained by *discipline, correction*."[4] In Heb. 12:5–11 God is portrayed as a father who disciplines the child he loves. Verse 11 observes: "For the moment all discipline [*paideia*] seems painful rather than pleasant, but later it yields the peaceful fruit of righteousness to those who have been trained by it." This concept of discipline yielding righteousness as its "fruit," its result, complements the expression "training [*paideia*] in righteousness" in 2 Tim. 3:16.

Goal: Moral Maturity and Positive Empowerment

Receiving biblical "teaching, . . . reproof, . . . correction, and . . . training in righteousness," including from OT law, is not an end in itself. Rather, it serves

---

3. Paul's corpus of canonical "Scripture" was not identical to ours, at least because not all NT books had been written yet. But the Pentateuch, which is the primary focus of the present study, was firmly established as Scripture by Paul's day.
4. BDAG 748, emphasis original.

the purpose of moral character development toward the goal "that the man of God may be complete, equipped for every good work." Such good works are not the basis of salvation, but result from acceptance of and cooperation with God's free gift of salvation through Christ (e.g., Eph. 2:4–10). Elsewhere in the NT, including in the example of Christ's life, good works are portrayed as loving service to others (e.g., Matt. 25:34–36; Luke 7:21–22; Gal. 5:6; James 2:14–17).

If we focus on the OT law portions of Scripture, we see that, according to Paul, all of this material is divine teaching and contributes to wisdom for salvation for the purpose of developing a complete character as a person of God who is equipped for useful service in harmony with the divine will. The way to achieve this goal of moral maturity is progressive training in biblical wisdom.

Deuteronomy 4:5–8 reveals the purpose of progressive moral wisdom for serving others. Here Moses exhorts the Israelites, as Paul advised Timothy. Moses reminds his people that he has taught them God's laws, which they should keep, "for that will be your wisdom and your understanding in the sight of the peoples, who, when they hear all these statutes, will say, 'Surely this great nation is a wise and understanding people'" (v. 6). The Israelites are so wise and understanding because they have the Lord near them whenever they call on him (v. 7) and because they have such righteous laws (v. 8). When God's people follow his righteous instructions within the context of his intimate covenant relationship with them, they become wise in the way they live, so that others are drawn to him and his ways. Thus progressive moral wisdom is not only for the benefit of God's special people. Rather, they also serve as a channel of true wisdom and blessing to the world (cf. chap. 3 above).

"Progressive moral wisdom" has the potential to serve as a rich methodological model. "Progressive" involves discipline that moves one from a lower level of capability to higher levels in pursuit of an ideal. Paul refers to competitive runners as a helpful analogy for spiritual and moral training (1 Cor. 9:24–27; cf. Phil. 3:12–14; 2 Tim. 4:7–8; Heb. 12:1–2), training "for godliness" (1 Tim. 4:7), recognizing that "while bodily training is of some value, godliness is of value in every way, as it holds promise for the present life and also for the life to come" (v. 8).

However, our hope for success is not based on the principle that practice makes perfect or that our own godliness saves us. Rather, "To this end we toil and strive, because we have our hope set on the living God, who is the Savior of all people, especially of those who believe" (v. 10). Paul also says regarding resurrection from the dead, "I press on to make it my own, because Christ Jesus has made me his own" (Phil. 3:12).

Following Paul's example of drawing on a physical analogy for a parallel logical structure, we can learn from comparison with another activity: progressive weight training, in which a person keeps increasing the weights lifted over a period of time to increase strength and musculature. I started this from the low level of a scrawny teenager after my father observed: "Son, you're more fearfully than wonderfully made!" (cf. Ps. 139:14). That assessment gave me little hope of attracting a beautiful woman to be my wife. So when my college required me to take a physical education course, I chose bodybuilding. This was in the 1970s, so posted on the wall of the weight room at the gym was a picture of our hero, Arnold Schwarzenegger, who represented the ideal of the physically "perfect man" (cf. Eph. 4:13 KJV, NKJV) toward which my classmates and I aspired.

We had no hope of ever coming close to the physique of Mr. Olympia, but seeing the ideal provided inspiration, and we made considerable progress from where we had begun. Our starting points and progress varied because we were different individuals. Unlike some others who succeeded in building considerable bulk, I remained thin but became wiry, with almost as much "definition" as a concise dictionary, so that my classmates dubbed me "Mighty Mouse" when they saw my spindly legs doing squats with 300 lbs.

Despite the differences between us, the instructions provided by our teacher helped all of us because they were based on sound physical principles that were applicable to the body of any healthy human being. These principles are hierarchical. Most basically, all skeletal muscles gain strength when they are subjected to increasing levels of exertion between periods of rest. This principle of the body as a whole operates on the level of individual muscles belonging to various parts of the body.

When progressive training is "moral," rather than physical, musical, financial, or something else, it is concerned with developing wisdom in dealing with principles of right versus wrong. Our training, enabled and empowered by God (Phil. 2:13), takes us from moral weakness that originated with the fall (Gen. 3) and has grown to permeate our surrounding cultures, toward a divinely defined ideal of moral maturity that is capable of doing all kinds of good works. The picture on the wall of our moral weight room is that of Christ, who perfectly embodies and lavishly demonstrates the overarching ideal of love, which is the holy divine character (1 John 4:8, 16).[5]

A Progressive Moral Wisdom Model

A holistic progressive moral wisdom (PMW) approach is relevant for gaining wisdom for salvation from any biblical passage, but here we are focusing on OT

---

5. Cf. spiritual and moral (in love) "body-building" of the church as the "body of Christ" in Eph. 4:11–16.

law. When the object of inquiry is a particular law, it is necessary to begin by analyzing the function of this instruction, which reveals the value that it represents.

The procedure is to examine the law by itself and then to broaden the scope of investigation to progressively larger synchronic and diachronic contexts: the OT system of laws, including its hierarchy of moral values; the Israelite setting revealed by the Bible within its ANE background, to the extent that this is available, clear, and relevant; and the process of redemption history, including restoration of the creation ideal.[6] Then conclusions regarding the paradigmatic function/value of the law can be applied by analogy (or extended implication) to the modern life situation.[7]

While decisions regarding how to make such application are reached through an intellectual process, the purpose of OT law only reaches fulfillment when decisions are lived out by a whole person, who consequently grows in moral character. True service to God is not by behavior alone, but "with all your heart and with all your soul" (e.g., Deut. 10:12; 11:13 cf. 6:5), with the whole being, including the emotions.

The PMW approach is progressive in several ways. First, it develops enhanced understanding of God's instructions. Second, it facilitates more complete, beneficial, and satisfying fulfillment of God's will for one's life. Third, it fosters growth in strength of moral character and relationship to God as a person orients responses to all life situations (including challenging ones) toward love, continually looking up the moral hierarchy and especially contemplating divine love as supremely manifested in Christ and his sacrifice. Fourth, it moves toward restoration of creation ideals.

All four of these ways are involved in individual sanctification: Followers of God progress in sanctification as growth in character through divinely empowered adherence to God's wise and righteous principles brings them into closer harmony with his holy character. There is also a corporate aspect: Within the context of salvation history, progressive moral wisdom moves God's people as a group, in accordance with further revelation, understanding, and obedience, toward fulfillment of his wise moral ideals for human beings, which in significant ways restore the ideals that he established at creation (see chap. 7).[8]

---

6. Cf. "A Reflection by Christopher J. H. Wright," in *Four Views on Moving beyond the Bible to Theology*, ed. Gary T. Meadors, Counterpoints (Grand Rapids: Zondervan, 2009), on "Biblical Ethics and the Biblical Story Line," 331–39, with the important observation that "Creation provides our foundational values and principles" (337).

7. On steps and criteria for contextualization, see Mark L. Strauss, "A Reflection by Mark L. Strauss," in Meadors, *Four Views on Moving beyond the Bible to Theology*, 293–98.

8. This use of the term "progressive" is not meant to imply that the moral principles taught by the OT are primitive, outmoded, inferior, or irrelevant. Rather, people belonging to cultures possess limited understanding and need moral uplifting over time.

Keep in mind that the purpose of progressive moral wisdom is to grow in wisdom from God as we continue to receive his gifts of knowledge, grace, and love provided through Christ. This is not about works righteousness, self-help, or knee-jerk obedience to rules that govern every detail of our lives. The success of any work that we do (Phil. 2:12) depends on "God who works in you, both to will and to work for his good pleasure" (v. 13).

The following is an outline of a suggested PMW model, which is followed by explanation and illustration of its components.

Progressive Moral Wisdom

Analyze the Law by Itself

1. What is the topic of the law in terms of the kind of life situation that it addresses?
2. What is the scope of the law in terms of the boundaries of its direct application?
3. Who is responsible for keeping the law?
4. What is the goal of the law?

Analyze the Law within the System of Old Testament Laws

1. Does the law coordinate with any other laws in its immediate literary context?
2. Are there topically related laws in more distant literary contexts within the same or another pentateuchal law collection?
3. How does the law function within the hierarchy of moral values?

Further Analyze the Law within the Context of Its Ancient Life Situation

1. How do biblical texts shed light on the ancient life situation that the law sought to affect?
2. How do extrabiblical materials supplement our understanding of the ancient life situation?

Analyze the Law within the Process of Redemption

1. How does the law relate to creation and new-creation ideals?
2. How does the law seek to remedy something faulty that results from the fall into sin?
3. Does the OT indicate moral growth beyond the stage represented by the law?

4. Does the NT indicate moral growth beyond the stage represented by the law?

Relate Findings regarding the Function of the Law to Modern Life

1. Does the law, or at least some element of it, directly apply to modern life now, or could it do so in the future?
2. Whether or not a law directly applies today, how does it serve as a paradigmatic example of higher-level values that still apply to analogous modern circumstances?
3. Does biblical development of the value exemplified by the law show a trajectory that moves beyond the law itself to a higher moral level that should be applied in the modern life situation?

Analyze the Law by Itself

After the prerequisite step of determining the boundaries of the legal literary unit in the biblical text,[9] try to understand the function or purpose of this law in terms of what it is commanding, encouraging, or forbidding a person to do or think, and why. In the process, formulate answers to the following questions to the best of your ability. Your answers may be adjusted later as you consider the law in its various contexts (see below).

1. *What is the topic of the law in terms of the kind of life situation that it addresses?* Ask what category(ies) of activity or thought is regulated by the law. For example, does it provide directions for a proper way to interact with God, such as through ritual worship, or does it have to do with treatment of family members, a person outside the family, or a work animal? Identifying the topic category facilitates comparing with and learning from other laws that are similar to it in this regard (see below).[10]

2. *What is the scope of the law in terms of the boundaries of its direct application?* The overall values of love for God (Deut. 6:5) and one's neighbor

---

9. For assistance with delineation of such boundaries, see chap. 5 on elements of individual laws, such as ways in which apodictic and casuistic formulations can be introduced, and the protasis, apodosis, and possible subcases of a casuistic law. Connections between pronouns and their antecedents contribute to unification of individual laws. For example, Exod. 20:5 continues the second commandment of the Decalogue, rather than beginning another commandment, because its pronouns ("You shall not bow down to *them* or serve *them*") refer to the "carved image, or any likeness" in v. 4. Cf. the law of Lev. 20:1–5, in which "that man" in vv. 3–5 refers to the person identified in v. 2a.

10. Cf. Walter C. Kaiser Jr. on identifying a topic/subject in a biblical passage ("A Principlizing Model," in Meadors, *Four Views on Moving beyond the Bible to Theology*, 22–23) and Christopher J. H. Wright on different kinds of law (*Old Testament Ethics for the People of God* [Downers Grove, IL: InterVarsity, 2004], 288–301).

(Lev. 19:18) have unlimited scope; they apply at all times and everywhere for everyone. The Ten Commandments (Exod. 20; Deut. 5) have broad scope in that they apply anytime when and anyplace where anyone faces choices regarding their principles (e.g., respecting God's name, keeping Sabbath, honoring parents, respecting life). Anyone can be confronted with these choices, but not necessarily at all times. For instance, Sabbath keeping pertains to only one day of the week, and not every life situation deals with the issue of honoring parents or respect for life or protecting sexual boundaries of marriage, and so forth.

The scope of a more specific law is narrower. For instance, a law that concerns a marriage relationship (e.g., Num. 5:11–31) would not directly apply to an unmarried person, although that could change in the future if the individual marries, and the law could be helpful in preparing for marriage or indirectly providing guidance regarding other relationships. A law or legal provision that regulates or establishes an Israelite cultural custom or institution (e.g., levirate marriage, Deut. 25:5–10; cities of refuge, Num. 35; the sanctuary/temple, Lev. 1–7, 16; etc.; theocratic jurisprudence with its penalties) would directly apply to that custom or institution while it existed.

The scope of direct application can include categories that the explicit formulation of the law only refers to by example. For instance, "If you meet your enemy's ox or his donkey going astray, you shall bring it back to him" (Exod. 23:4). What about a sheep, goat, or some other kind of domesticated animal, which could also go astray (cf. Matt. 18:12)? "Ox" and "donkey" are just examples of the larger category of domesticated animals, as in Exod. 20:17: "his ox, or his donkey, or anything that is your neighbor's."

3. *Who is responsible for keeping the law?* Many laws are primarily addressed to male Israelite heads of households, who are also responsible for seeing that the divine instructions are carried out by other members of their families. Some laws or portions thereof primarily or exclusively regulate certain other members of society, such as women (e.g., Lev. 12; 15:19–30; 20:16), priests and/or Levites (Lev. 6:8–7:10 [6:1–7:10 MT]; 21:1–22:16; Num. 18), or a future king (Deut. 17:14–20).

4. *What is the goal of the law?* That is, what does the law seek to accomplish in affecting the life situation that it addresses, whether in countering something negative or encouraging something positive? For instance, Lev. 25:36 commands an Israelite regarding a poor fellow Israelite: "Take no interest from him or profit, but fear your God, that your brother may live beside you." Here the last clause expresses the goal: to assist a poor person's economic survival (cf. vv. 35, 37). However, a law by itself may not indicate its goal: "You shall not

boil a young goat in its mother's milk" (Exod. 23:19). In such a case, further investigation within the system of laws is necessary.[11]

While many laws are preventive in that they prohibit and thereby warn and seek to protect against behaviors that are harmful according to God (see, e.g., Lev. 18, 20), other laws provide remedies when things go wrong. Remedies can include sacrificial expiation leading to divine forgiveness (e.g., Lev. 4:1–6:7 [4:1–5:26 MT]), punishments that purge and thereby safeguard the covenant community by removing people who violate terms of the divine-human covenant (e.g., Deut. 13:5; 17:7, 12; 19:12–13), and reparation to victims by those who have wronged them (e.g., Exod. 21:33–34, 22:1 [21:37 MT]; Lev. 6:1–5 [6:20–24 MT]). Regarding nonideal practices such as slavery, polygamy, and divorce, certain laws seek to prevent some aspects and effects of these institutions (e.g., Exod. 21:1–11, 20–21, 26–27; Lev. 18:18; Deut. 21:15–17; 24:1–4), but in a higher sense these laws could also be regarded as providing partial remedies for situations that God tolerated because of the hardness of human hearts (cf. Matt. 19:3–12).

Analyze the Law within the System of Old Testament Laws

The function of a given law can be illuminated by its relationships to other laws. At this stage of investigation, it is helpful to address the following questions.

1. *Does the law coordinate with any other laws in its immediate literary context?* If so, what can you learn from this? Leviticus 19:27 commands: "You shall not round off the hair on your temples or mar the edges of your beard." The reason for these prohibitions is not specified, but the surrounding laws provide important clues. Immediately preceding and following are prohibitions against pagan practices: "You shall not interpret omens or tell fortunes" (v. 26b), and "You shall not make any cuts on your body for the dead or tattoo yourselves: I am the LORD" (v. 28). Thus, from cutting hair in verse 27, verse 28 continues the topic of cutting, but now the object of cutting is the body and the reason is given: "for the dead," as a pagan mourning custom (cf. 1 Kings 18:28).[12] Deuteronomy 14:1 explicitly links making baldness (by cutting hair) to mourning: "You are the sons of the LORD your God. You shall not cut yourselves or make any baldness on your foreheads for the dead."

---

11. On this law, see chap. 12 below.

12. Cf. the mourning of the god 'Ilu (El) for the dead deity Ba'lu (Baal) in an Ugaritic myth, which includes these lines: "With a stone he scratches incisions on (his) skin, with a razor he cuts cheeks and chin. He harrows his upper arms, plows (his) chest like a garden" (trans. Dennis Pardee, "The Ba'lu Myth," COS 1.86:268).

So it appears that the short laws in Lev. 19:26–28 should be read together, and certain kinds of haircutting are prohibited because of their association with pagan mourning practices (cf. Isa. 15:2; Jer. 47:5; 48:37; Ezek. 27:31).[13] Knowing this can affect one's assessment regarding possible application of verse 27 to modern life.

2. *Are there topically related laws in more distant literary contexts within the same or another pentateuchal law collection?* If so, what light do they shed on the law? For example, Lev. 19:19 does not provide a reason for its prohibitions against certain kinds of mixtures. However, as pointed out in chapter 7 above, the related laws against mixtures in Deut. 22:9–11 provide an important hint: "You shall not sow your vineyard with two kinds of seed, lest the whole yield be forfeited" (v. 9). The word translated "be forfeited" in ESV is the *qal* of the root *q-d-sh*, which means "become holy."[14] A mixture becomes holy, which means that ordinary people are not permitted to use it because it belongs to God, who is represented by his priests at the sanctuary.[15]

3. *How does the law function within the hierarchy of moral values?* This hierarchy, which reaches up to love as epitomized by Christ's sacrifice and points to restoration of creation ideals in the new creation, was discussed in chapter 7 with examples. Keep in mind two points. First, if goals of other laws reveal related values or value-based principles at the same hierarchical level, they are united by a higher-level value. Second, higher and lower values are mutually informative. Higher values, which provide an overall framework, illuminate and are in turn defined by lower values.

As a further example of an Israelite law within the context of the moral hierarchy, consider Lev. 25:36, which prohibits an Israelite from taking interest or profit from a poor fellow-Israelite, "but fear your God, that your brother may live beside you." Not financially exploiting the poor person in these specific ways clearly contributes to the goal of helping him to maintain his existence in the community. This goal represents an important social principle, as shown by the way verse 36 continues the emphasis of the previous verse: "You shall support him as though he were a stranger and a sojourner, and he shall live with you" (v. 35). Such assistance for people in hard times, along with aid for chronically poor and vulnerable resident aliens (mentioned in v. 35), widows, and orphans (e.g., Exod. 22:21–24 [22:20–23 MT]), as well as protection of blind and deaf persons (Lev. 19:14), logically represent some subprinciples of a higher level, a more general principle: treat needy people with kindness,

13. Jacob Milgrom, *Leviticus 17–22: A New Translation with Introduction and Commentary*, AB 3A (New York: Doubleday, 2000), 1684–95, esp. 1690–91.
14. NKJV, NIV, and NASB mistranslate this word in Deut. 22:9 as "defiled."
15. Cf. Milgrom, *Leviticus 17–22*, 1660–62.

which in turn is a subprinciple of "You shall love your neighbor as yourself" (Lev. 19:18). Recognizing the operation of the paramount value of love in relatively small acts of kindness puts the importance of these acts in perspective (cf. Matt. 25:31–46) and encourages the doer to continue and expand them.

In the absence of a penalty for noncompliance, the words "but fear your God" in Lev. 25:36 indicate that God also places obedience to the law under the value of loyalty to himself, so that he personally holds an Israelite accountable for the way he treats his poor neighbor (cf. "I am the LORD" at the end of 19:18). In this sense, the principle of helping someone else to maintain an independent existence also comes under another higher-level principle: "You shall love the LORD your God" (Deut. 6:5).

Further Analyze the Law within the Context of Its Ancient Life Situation

Seeking to ascertain the function of a law by itself and within the context of the OT system of law involves some consideration of the ancient life situation (see above). The present step broadens the scope of source materials to include any OT texts, along with any relevant ANE materials that illuminate them. In the process, it is helpful to answer the following questions.

1. *How do biblical texts shed light on the ancient life situation that the law sought to affect?* For instance, Deut. 23:15–16 (23:16–17 MT) commands: "You shall not give up to his master a slave [*'eved*] who has escaped from his master to you. He shall dwell with you, in your midst, in the place that he shall choose within one of your towns, wherever it suits him. You shall not wrong him." The narrative in 1 Kings 2:39–40 recounts an incident that exemplifies the kind of circumstances to which the law responded: "But it happened at the end of three years that two of Shimei's servants [plural of *'eved*] ran away to Achish, son of Maacah, king of Gath. And when it was told Shimei, 'Behold, your servants are in Gath,' Shimei arose and saddled a donkey and went to Gath to Achish to seek his servants. Shimei went and brought his servants from Gath."

The text does not say that Shimei had mistreated his servants, but this would be the most likely reason that they would run away. In any case, it appears that the Philistines at Gath did what was expected in the ANE by handing Shimei's servants/slaves over to him, prioritizing his right of ownership over the slaves' well-being. On the other hand, Deut. 23 is radically countercultural by reversing the priorities and thereby seriously undermining slavery.

2. *How do extrabiblical materials supplement our understanding of the ancient life situation?* The idea that returning fugitive slaves to their masters

was the norm, so that the law of Deut. 23 was countercultural, is supported by the fact that this injunction was unique in the ANE; there was nothing like it outside the Bible. This is an argument from silence, but it is somewhat reinforced by indirect evidence from an earlier period and from outside the immediate geographic environment of Israel. In Mesopotamia during the Old Babylonian period, §§15–19 of the Laws of Hammurabi express a standard of justice that strongly supports the rights of slave owners to control their human property (1) by calling for the death penalty on anyone who assists a fugitive slave or otherwise fails to return that slave and (2) by rewarding anyone who returns such a slave.

Analyze the Law within the Process of Redemption

This stage places the law within the trajectory of redemption revealed in the entire Bible, including the NT, to see where its function fits in the process of directing humans from faultiness toward moral wholeness. The following are questions to consider.

1. *How does the law relate to creation and new-creation ideals?* For example, Lev. 18:18 seeks to prevent contention that is likely to arise when a man marries "a woman as a rival wife to her sister, uncovering her nakedness while her sister is still alive," as Jacob discovered when he married both Leah and Rachel (Gen. 29–30). Preservation of marital harmony by avoiding this kind of bigamy points in the direction of the perfect unity such as that which Adam and Eve enjoyed (Gen. 2:23–25). However, while the law reflects the underlying value of the monogamous ideal, its explicit formulation only represents a stage on the way to restoration of happiness because it accommodates to human weakness by not forbidding bigamy with women who are not sisters, who also could become rivals (e.g., 1 Sam. 1:1–2, 4–8, esp. vv. 6–7).[16] The promise that in the ultimate new creation, God "will wipe away every tear from their eyes, neither shall there be . . . crying" (Rev. 21:4) suggests that human relations will be restored to full happiness in the future (contrast Gen. 29:30–30:20; 1 Sam. 1:7–8, 10).[17]

2. *How does the law seek to remedy something faulty that results from the fall into sin?* Just after Adam and Eve sinned by eating from the forbidden tree, the first note of relational discord appeared when Adam blamed both his fellow human being and God, who had given her to him (Gen. 3:12), thereby violating the principles of love for God and for other humans. This was the origin of

---

16. On polygamy and the law in Lev. 18:18, see further in chap. 13 below.
17. Although Jesus stated, "In the resurrection they neither marry nor are given in marriage, but are like angels in heaven" (Matt. 22:30).

distrust between marriage partners (Gen. 3:12), which can grow to the point that one suspects the other of adultery. The suspected adulteress law in Num. 5:11–31 provides a remedy for such suspicion by petitioning God through a ritual at the sanctuary to show whether such a woman is guilty or innocent. If she is innocent, the marriage can be healed because her husband can rest assured that his wife is faithful to him.[18] Of course, this is only a Band-Aid for the ongoing possibility of distrust on the way to full restoration of trust in the new creation, when nobody will be sexually immoral (Rev. 21:8; 22:15) or untrustworthy (21:27).

3. *Does the OT indicate moral growth beyond the stage represented by the law?* Moral growth is movement toward greater fulfillment of higher values in the moral hierarchy and restoration of the creation ideal (cf. chap. 7). For instance, in pentateuchal law, Israelites are commanded to treat a non-Israelite resident alien (*ger*) with kindness and love rather than oppression (Exod. 22:21 [22:20 MT]; 23:9; Lev. 19:33–34; Deut. 10:19) because such a person is allotted no inheritance of ancestral land on which to make an independent living by farming (cf. Deut. 14:29, like the Levite). However, the instructions for an ideal future in Ezek. 47 radically upgrade the status and life situation of such non-Israelites by allotting land as an inheritance for resident aliens in the territories of the tribes in which they reside (vv. 21–23). In this respect, "They shall be to you as native-born children of Israel" (v. 22).[19] This upgrade demonstrates greater love for one's neighbor (Lev. 19:18) and restoration of the prefall situation, in which one family of humans created in God's image were to share the dominion of planet Earth (Gen. 1:26–28).

4. *Does the NT indicate moral growth beyond the stage represented by the law?* For example, the law of Ezek. 47 calls for equality between Israelites and non-Israelite resident aliens and includes the latter among beneficiaries of the divine promise of the land of Canaan to Abraham and his descendants (Gen. 12:1, 7; 13:14–15, 17; 15:7, 18–21). However, Ezekiel still recognizes that the non-Israelites are a distinct group. In Gal. 3:28–29 Paul goes further by erasing this distinction and incorporating non-Israelites into one new-covenant group of those who inherit all of the divine promises to Abraham: "There is neither Jew nor Greek, . . . for you are all one in Christ Jesus. And if you are Christ's, then you are Abraham's offspring, heirs according to promise."[20]

18. See further on this law in chap. 13 below.

19. Cf. Exod. 12:48, where a circumcised resident alien is to be treated as a native of the land in that he is permitted to participate in the Passover celebration. This similarity to Israelite citizens does not mean that aliens at that time (when the Israelites were departing from Egypt) possessed all other rights of Israelites, including the right to inherit land within tribal territories when the Israelites would conquer Canaan.

20. See other promises to Abraham in Gen. 12:2–3; 22:17–18.

Relate Findings regarding the Function of the Law to Modern Life

Equipped with an understanding of how the law functions within its various ancient contexts, one is prepared to bring at least some aspect of its paradigmatic teaching into modern life by pondering the following questions.

1. *Does the law, or at least some element of it, directly apply to modern life now, or could it do so in the future?* This involves comparison between the scope and goal of the law and the modern life situation. If the modern situation falls within the scope of direct application of the law, *and* if modern direct application would accomplish the same goal as in the ancient setting to which the law was originally addressed, the law should be literally observed today. For example, if you have a flat roof on which people walk, you should install a railing/parapet around it, in accordance with the law in Deut. 22:8, for the same reason as in ancient times: to prevent injury or death that could occur if someone were to fall off. Providing for the safety of others is an important part of loving one's neighbor as oneself.

Just because observance of a law would not be convenient, within our ideological "box," or in harmony with our traditional ways of doing things does not mean that we are not responsible for keeping it. The Bible continues to be countercultural. Culture itself is not a moral norm, although cultural contexts affect ways in which we can live out moral norms.

Direct application of some OT laws would not accomplish their goals in our society because we lack essential elements of the cases that they address. For instance, the protasis that commences the case law in Deut. 25:5–10, specifying the situation to which the stipulations in the subsequent apodosis are directed, is as follows: "If brothers dwell together, and one of them dies and has no son" (v. 5a). In terms of these words alone, such a tragedy could befall a modern family. However, the rest of the law regulates the ancient Israelite custom of levirate marriage, which, according to the pentateuchal narrative, existed before this law (Gen. 38:8). The custom was intended to provide the dead brother with a surrogate son through union of his widow with his surviving brother in order to preserve his name/identity attached to his inheritance of ancestral land in Israel (cf. Num. 27:3–4; Ruth 4) by providing him with a line of descendants (Deut. 25:6).[21]

21. On the levirate marriage law of Deut. 25:5–10, see Richard M. Davidson, *Flame of Yahweh: Sexuality in the Old Testament* (Peabody, MA: Hendrickson, 2007), 465–76, including the interpretation that the man who marries the widow most likely would be an unmarried younger brother living in the home of his married older brother ("If brothers dwell together . . .") before the older brother dies (469), following Anthony Phillips, *Deuteronomy*, CBC (Cambridge: Cambridge University Press, 1973), 168; Phillips, *Essays on Biblical Law*, JSOTSup 344 (London: Sheffield Academic, 2002), 204–5, repr. of "The Book of Ruth—Deception and Shame," *JJS* 37 (1986): 3–4.

Therefore, in Deut. 25 the nature of the remedy specified in the apodosis informs our understanding of the circumstance described in the protasis: "If brothers dwell together, and one of them dies and has no son" (v. 5a), the name/identity of the deceased brother will "be blotted out of Israel" (v. 6b) unless levirate marriage is performed. Such a situation does not occur in our modern Western society. Loss of a childless brother and husband is still heartbreaking and causes hardship, but it does not result in loss of identity in the nation of Israel and its land. Thus levirate marriage today cannot fix the problem targeted by the OT law. For this reason, and not because levirate marriage is simply foreign to our way of doing things, the law of Deut. 25:5–10 does not directly apply to us.

Laws that articulate high-level, general values, such as love for God (Deut. 6:5) and for one's neighbor (Lev. 19:18) and the Ten Commandments (Exod. 20; Deut. 5), clearly have ongoing direct application for us because they carry out the same goals in modern life. Other laws that encapsulate principles exemplified in the Decalogue, such as "You shall not deal falsely; you shall not lie to one another" (Lev. 19:11; cf. Exod. 20:16, honesty about one another in judicial context), can directly apply today when they are relevant to choices that we make. However, even in the Decalogue, some details from the ancient Israelite life situation (Exod. 20:10, "your male servant, or your female servant, or your livestock"; v. 17, "his male servant, or his female servant, or his ox, or his donkey") do not directly apply to us if we do not keep servants/ slaves or work animals.

A considerable number of OT laws no longer apply because the ancient Israelite customs or institutions that they regulated and/or on which their function depended have ceased to exist (cf. chap. 7). Customs such as levirate marriage (Deut. 25:5–10; cf. Gen. 38) and execution of a murderer by a kinsman-avenger (Num. 35:19; Deut. 19:12) have disappeared. God did not create these customs, but OT law presupposed and addressed their operation within Israelite culture. Therefore, there is no valid reason to resurrect them within our culture. Ancestral ownership of land in Israel, cities of refuge in the land of Israel, and the theocracy with its administration of judicial penalties are all gone, so laws regarding these institutions are obsolete in terms of direct applicability to modern Christians, who constitute a new-covenant church rather than a civil state.

The earthly sanctuary/temple with its rituals and rules for ritual purity (esp. Exod. 25–Lev. 16) is also gone, and it is no longer needed under the new covenant. Since the death, resurrection, and ascension of Christ, new-covenant Christian worship is focused toward the heavenly temple, where he has been ministering for us (Heb. 7–10). Circumcision as a religious requirement for

Abraham and the chosen nation that came from him predated the sanctuary/ temple (Gen. 17) and did not depend upon its function. However, Christians no longer need this ritual because the new covenant originally promised to the Israelites (Jer. 31:31–34) now transcends ethnic boundaries (Acts 15).

2. *Whether or not a law directly applies today, how does it serve as a paradigmatic example of higher-level values that still apply to analogous modern circumstances?* This relates conclusions regarding placement of the law within the hierarchy of values to modern life. The values or value-based principles that an OT law exemplifies as a paradigm logically apply not only to the same situation if it occurs but also by analogy to related situations from which additional examples could be taken. For instance, the requirement to construct a parapet around a flat roof (Deut. 22:8) exemplifies the ongoing principle of preventing dangerous conditions that can result in injury or death. Other examples/applications of this principle could be found in ancient life, such as responsibility to restrain one's dangerous ox (Exod. 21:29–32, 36).[22] The need for a parapet continues into modern life wherever there is a flat roof on which people walk, but technology has greatly multiplied the number of other kinds of situations in which the principle of preventing danger should function, which explains why we have government inspectors to check the safety of many types of construction and products. Whether or not one has a flat roof, there are many areas where it is necessary to maintain safe conditions.

The full importance of preventing danger appears when we see that it is located on the hierarchy of values under respect for life, which is exemplified by the Decalogue commandment "You shall not murder" (Exod. 20:13). This connection explains the language of the motive clause in Deut. 22:8, which characterizes responsibility for accidental death resulting from negligence in failing to build a parapet as blood-guilt, associated with guilt for murder: "that you may not bring the guilt of blood [*damim*] upon your house, if anyone should fall from it."[23] By analogy, someone who fails to prevent the death of another person by neglecting to provide another kind of protection on property that they control (e.g., a house, factory, or construction site) is also guilty of a kind of murder.

If a given OT law is obsolete in terms of direct application, it nevertheless can exemplify ongoing values and principles that have other specific modern applications. For instance, the law of levirate marriage (Deut. 25:5–10) confirmed a custom that sought to perpetuate the remembered identity of a person

---

22. Cf. responsibility for death to an animal by making a dangerous condition (Exod. 21:33–34).

23. For the plural of *dam* referring to guilt incurred by committing murder, see, e.g., Exod. 22:2–3 (22:1–2 MT); Deut. 19:10.

within the community of Israel. Not explicitly mentioned in the law is the obvious fact that providing the widow with a child would also make provision for her welfare in old age (1 Tim. 5:4). Modern Christians can preserve two values exemplified by the levirate marriage law—respectful preservation of memory of the dead (cf. Rev. 14:13) and care for widows (1 Tim. 5:3–16; James 1:27)—that flow from the higher value of love for one's neighbor (Lev. 19:18).

Observance of laws concerning sacrifices and purity at the sanctuary/temple cannot be required for modern people, but these instructions teach valuable concepts regarding worship of God, his nature and character in relation to fallen humanity, and his provision for redemption from sin and mortality through the ultimate sacrifice of Christ (see further in chap. 16). The theocracy with its judicial system for administering penalties has also ended, but from the relative gravity of these penalties we can learn degrees of importance attached to the values that they protected. Thus, according to Lev. 20:11, if a man has sexual relations with his father's wife, both of them should be put to death (cf. the curse in Deut. 27:20). In light of the seriousness of this kind of offense, Paul called for the highest level of church discipline, expulsion from fellowship as a member of the church community, when a man in the church at Corinth was committing it (1 Cor. 5).

3. *Does biblical development of the value exemplified by the law show a trajectory that moves beyond the law itself to a higher moral level that should be applied in the modern life situation?* This step draws on analysis of the law within its ancient context and in the process of redemption. Webb has identified a powerful example: slavery.[24] The OT law regulated this institution to mitigate its harshness (cf. chaps. 13–14), but the law that protected fugitive slaves (Deut. 23:15–16) rather than the rights of their owners seriously undermined slavery. From the OT system of laws we could derive the principle that slavery is allowed only if the master does not treat his slave(s) with excessive harshness. However, the NT further undermined slavery by excluding the distinction between slaves and free persons in the new-covenant community of Christ: "There is neither . . . slave nor free, . . . for you are all one in Christ Jesus" (Gal. 3:28). The ground is level at the foot of the cross. This equality points to the creation and new-creation ideal, in which all humans are free.

The NT writers lacked the civil authority to abolish slavery within the context of the Roman Empire, so they endeavored to promote harmonious relations between slaves and their masters in order to make the best of the situation (Eph. 6:5–9; Col. 3:22–4:1; 1 Tim. 6:1–2; Titus 2:9–10; Philemon;

24. William J. Webb, *Slaves, Women & Homosexuals: Exploring the Hermeneutics of Cultural Analysis* (Downers Grove, IL: IVP Academic, 2001), 37–38, 44–45, 74–76, 84, etc.

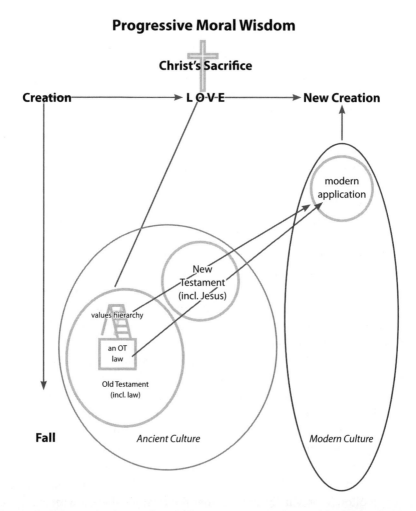

1 Pet. 2:18–20). However, if a modern society is informed by biblical values (not dependent on a modern Western worldview), there is no valid reason for it not to move further toward the creation and new-creation ideal by abolishing slavery.

In light of the outline of PMW methodology presented above, we can diagram the conceptual dynamics of this approach as shown above.

Profiles of Progressive Values Exemplified by Old Testament Laws

The following table can be useful for tracing trajectories of values exemplified by OT laws from the creation ideal through progressive phases of restoration between creation and new creation in order to identify appropriate modern application. Restoration can pass through multiple levels of divine accommodation: -1 acc. (accommodation) and so forth, with numbers up to -3 acc., indicating relative distance from the creation ideal.

The first example here adapts and expands the table in chapter 7 by showing three different divine positions regarding the ground for divorce in the divorce and remarriage law of Deut. 24:1–4 (esp. v. 1) that are stated in Matt. 19:3–9 (creation, OT Law, and NT), plus suggested modern application and the apparent new-creation ideal, moving in relative chronological order from left to right. The position in the column "Modern" is based on the fact that Christians today have no reason to move from Jesus's ruling: "And I say to you: whoever divorces his wife, except for sexual immorality, and marries another, commits adultery" (v. 9; cf. 5:32). In our broken world, we are unfortunately not yet ready for no divorce at all.

Ref. and Law	Moral Level	Creation	OT Law	NT	Modern	New Creation
	ideal	permanent union (no divorce)				(no divorce)[a]
Deut. 24:1–4, limitation of divorce	-1 acc.			divorce for sexual immorality	divorce for sexual immorality	
	-2 acc.		divorce for indecency			
	-3 acc.					

[a]However, Jesus also indicated that in the new creation following the resurrection there will be no marriage as we know it (Matt. 22:30).

A second example shows a different kind of relationship between the NT and modern levels. Here the modern level should move above the level that could be implemented in NT times, although the NT itself points to this higher level:

The law is as follows: "When a man strikes his slave, male or female, with a rod and the slave dies under his hand, he shall be avenged. But if the slave survives a day or two, he is not to be avenged, for the slave is his money" (Exod. 21:20–21). In light of the overarching principle of love for one's neighbor (Lev. 19:18), as illustrated throughout the Bible, it is clear that Exod. 21:20–21 delineates only a minimum standard of respect for a bonded worker: respect for the person's life.

Although the standard is a minimum, it is enforced by severe punishment. If a master beats his slave to death, the slave "shall be avenged" (v. 20, verbal

Ref. and Law	Moral Level	Creation	OT Law	NT	Modern	New Creation
	ideal	egalitarian society				egalitarian society
Exod. 21:20–21, prohibition of beating slave to death	-1 acc.				respect well-being of employee	
	-2 acc.			respect well-being of slave		
	-3 acc.		respect life of slave			

forms of the root *n-q-m*), which means that the master would suffer capital vengeance.[25] The seriousness of this penalty could serve as a deterrent against beating that could get anywhere close to immediately taking the life of a servant. However, the law allows for the possibility that if the slave doesn't die right away, something other than the beating could be the cause of death. In

---

25. For possible interpretations of the verb from the root *n-q-m*, "avenge," see, e.g., William H. C. Propp, *Exodus 19–40: A New Translation with Introduction and Commentary*, AB 2A (New York: Doubleday, 2006), 218–19; Thomas B. Dozeman, *Commentary on Exodus*, ECC (Grand Rapids: Eerdmans, 2009), 534. Indications that *n-q-m* refers to inflicting death appear, e.g., in 2 Kings 9:7 and YHWH's command in Num. 31:2, "Avenge [verb of *n-q-m*] the people of Israel on the Midianites," i.e., for their destructive deception of the Israelites (25:17–18). The result of this command was a war against the Midianites in which many of them were killed (chap. 31). David P. Wright suggests that choice of the nonspecific verb *n-q-m* here (rather than *mot yumat*, "[he] shall surely be put to death," on which see chap. 5 above) may allow for variable punishment due to mitigating factors (possibly allowing for compensation in some cases) and inclusion of both Hebrew debt-servants (who would have kin to avenge their murders) and foreign chattel-slaves (who may not have kin) in the scope of the law (*Inventing God's Law: How the Covenant Code of the Bible Used and Revised the Laws of Hammurabi* [Oxford: Oxford University Press, 2009], 175–76). Earlier, Moshe Greenberg had proposed that the verb *yumat* "is used for 'normal' execution of a slayer by the victim's next of kin (Num. 35:19; cf. Deut. 19:12), but because a slave might not have a family in the neighborhood of his death, whether because he was foreign or because though Israelite he lived away from his native place, the law used the term נקם [*nqm*] for punishment implying death by extraordinary procedure. There is, in sum, no ground for the notion that נקם here (or anywhere) can mean a monetary payment" ("More Reflections on Biblical Criminal Law," in *Studies in Bible*, ed. Sara Japhet, ScrHier 31 [Jerusalem: Magnes, 1986], 13–14, transliteration in brackets added). Bernard S. Jackson maintains that *n-q-m* refers to vengeance carried out by the kin of the deceased slave, and he does not find convincing the explanation that a slave may be far removed from his or her family (*Wisdom-Laws: A Study of the Mishpatim of Exodus 21:1–22:16* [Oxford: Oxford University Press, 2006], 246–48). Gregory C. Chirichigno, *Debt-Slavery in Israel and the Ancient Near East*, JSOTSup 141 (Sheffield: JSOT Press, 1993), 149–69, adds another possible dimension: "If the community or the court failed to prosecute the guilty party, then they became accountable for the crime," and "God himself will execute vengeance against the owner if he is not discovered by the community" (168–69).

the absence of a modern medical diagnosis, the master is given the benefit of the doubt, regarded as innocent because he cannot be proved guilty, and loss of his economic investment in the slave constitutes his punishment.[26] He is permitted to physically discipline his slave up to a point but must respect the slave's life rather than regarding himself as possessing the right to do anything he wishes to his human property.

In the NT, Paul seeks to prevent escalation of tensions between Christian slaves and masters so that they will not reach the point of beating:

> Bondservants, obey your earthly masters with fear and trembling, with a sincere heart, as you would Christ, . . . knowing that whatever good anyone does, this he will receive back from the Lord, whether he is a bondservant or is free. Masters, do the same to them, and stop your threatening, knowing that he who is both their Master and yours is in heaven, and that there is no partiality with him. (Eph. 6:5–9; cf. Col. 3:22–4:1; 1 Tim. 6:1–2; Titus 2:9–10; 1 Pet. 2:18–20)

Here Paul's counsel to masters that they stop threatening indicates his desire that these individuals respect the well-being of their slaves so that the slaves will not serve their masters merely out of fear of punishment. This would significantly improve the conditions of slaves above the minimum standard mandated by Exod. 21:20–21. In the process of urging both parties to get along with each other as best they can, Paul undermines the social stratification thinking that supports slavery by telling both slaves and masters that they are equal under God (cf. Gal. 3:28). Thus, Paul points to restoration of the creation ideal: a fully egalitarian human society. There is no evidence that in the new creation (esp. Rev. 21–22) there will be bonded or even contractual workers who will be subservient to others.

Paul's NT teaching showed progress, but he lacked the power to abrogate the institution of slavery in the Roman Empire. Nevertheless, he implicitly expressed the desire for its abolition. So modern Christians should not rest with the NT position of respecting the well-being of a slave. Rather, we should continue in the egalitarian direction that Paul emphasized by not keeping bonded workers at all. This is not going beyond NT teaching to a superior postcanonical level but implementing a higher moral standard that is represented in the NT itself.

In fact, our modern Western society has outlawed slavery.[27] So now the OT and NT instructions regarding slavery are technically obsolete for us. However,

---

26. Cf. Nahum M. Sarna, *Exodus: The Traditional Hebrew Text with the New JPS Translation*, JPS Torah Commentary (Philadelphia: Jewish Publication Society, 1991), 124.

27. Although there are illegal sex slaves and many millions of slaves elsewhere in the world.

we still have plenty of room for progress toward the fully egalitarian ideal. Now those who need respect for their well-being are contractual employees. We are not ready to dispense with unequal employer-employee relationships, but we can improve them, pending full restoration of the creation ideal.

A third example of the trajectory of a value-based principle represented by an OT law shows a flatline profile, in which there is no accommodation from the ideal because the high-level principle is absolute (see above), although Jesus clarified its definition in the NT (Luke 10:27–37):

Ref. and Law	Moral Level	Creation	OT Law	NT	Modern	New Creation
Lev. 19:18, Love your neighbor as yourself	ideal	love neighbor	love neighbor	love neighbor	love neighbor	love neighbor
	-1 acc.					
	-2 acc.					
	-3 acc.					

This chapter has developed a methodological model for applying OT laws to modern Christian life, which I have termed "Progressive Moral Wisdom." The model contains five main steps toward application of a given law: (1) analyze the law by itself, (2) analyze the law within the system of Old Testament laws, (3) further analyze the law within the context of its ancient life situation, (4) analyze the law within the process of redemption, and (5) relate findings regarding the function of the law to modern life. The final section of this chapter has illustrated the fact that within the Bible as a whole, values exemplified by various OT laws appear with different trajectories, some of which move beyond the laws themselves to a higher moral level that guides modern conduct. Application of OT laws should take all relevant Scripture passages into account so that we can enjoy the maximum benefits of divine wisdom.

10

Case Study of Progressive Moral Wisdom

Lost and Profound in Exodus 23:4

This chapter explores one OT law as a case study to demonstrate how the suggested steps of the progressive moral wisdom (PMW) approach can uncover wise values that are useful for modern Christian life. It is not necessary to go into this much detail in every exploration of an OT law. Usually such an investigation only focuses on selected aspects that are particularly interesting, disturbing, or relevant in the context of a larger discussion, as in the remaining chapters of the present volume. The purpose here, however, is to provide a thorough (although not exhaustive) illustration of how the elements of the proposed PMW method can work together.

The law considered here is: "If [*ki*] you meet your enemy's ox or his donkey going astray, you shall bring it back to him" (Exod. 23:4). The boundaries of the legal unit in the text are clear because it is a simple casuistic formulation (case law) introduced by the conditional word *ki*, "When/If," and the next verse (5) begins another law in the same way (cf. chap. 5 above). This instruction seems noncontroversial to a Christian, but its significance is considerably richer than one may suppose at first glance, particularly because it stipulates a duty to assist a person who is explicitly identified as an enemy.

Analyze the Law by Itself

1. *What is the topic of the law in terms of the kind of life situation that it addresses?* Like the Decalogue commandment "You shall not steal" (Exod. 20:15), the topic of the law in Exod. 23:4 involves a relationship between two people involving property. In this case, it has to do with one's responsibility to an enemy regarding his lost property. The property is mobile, an animal, and has gone out of the owner's control, but it has come to the attention of the addressee of the law. The key element is the fact that there is a hostile relationship between the addressee and the owner of the property.

Like other legal units, the law in Exod. 23:4 encapsulates a story in skeletal form, which could be fleshed out in many ways and presents a test of character for the one(s) to whom the law is addressed. For example, you could be trudging home to your village from your barley field in the evening, exhausted from a long day of harvesting. As you round a bend in the path, you see a young ox plodding toward you by himself, heading away from the village. He should be in his stall by this time, but obviously his owner has not adequately secured him, and he has gotten loose. Then you recognize that this ox belongs to a certain man who lives in your village. That scoundrel! Nine years ago he cheated you out of seventy shekels of silver and then blamed you, convincing others that he was in the right. Now his carelessness has cost him his prize ox, which he uses as his "tractor" to plow his fields and pull his wagon. Hah! Serves him right! Now let's see who gets the last laugh!

In whatever way real life fills in the details, the situation poses an awkward choice that tests your character. The fact that the owner is your enemy naturally tends to make you indisposed to help him, especially if you are tired and don't feel like going out of your way for anyone, let alone someone who has "done you dirty." You can avoid helping by simply doing nothing, in which case your enemy could permanently suffer the loss of the animal, and nobody, except God, could blame you.

The fact that only God would know[1] explains why the law lacks a clause specifying a penalty for violation administered by the community. It also explains why the law is needed in response to the inclination of fallen human nature: Including it in covenant instructions for which the Deity makes his people accountable to himself (cf. Exod. 19:5; 21:1; 24:3–4, 7–8) is intended to motivate you to do the right thing even when you don't feel like doing so.

2. *What is the scope of the law in terms of the boundaries of its direct application?* The law directly applies to a person having an enemy who owns

---

1. Cf. other laws regarding problems of lost things, which implicitly recognize that only God would know: Exod. 22:9 (22:8 MT); Lev. 6:3–4 (5:22–23 MT).

animals such as oxen and donkeys if such an animal wanders off and the addressee comes across it. Ancient Israelites could also own other kinds of animals that could go astray, such as sheep (e.g., Deut. 22:1; Matt. 18:12), so it seems clear that the ox or donkey mentioned in the law are only examples of domesticated animals in general. In fact, it appears that the law chooses domesticated animals to represent the larger category of an enemy's property in general (cf. Deut. 22:3), perhaps because an animal is capable of going off by itself, thereby setting up a scenario that especially tests the finder's character.

3. *Who is responsible for keeping the law?* Like many other Torah laws, Exod. 23:4 explicitly addresses males, with masculine-gender verbs and pronouns, but it could also apply to females. For one thing, masculine was the generic gender in the Hebrew language. Moreover, male heads of households represented their families, so laws addressed to them were also directed to any other members of their households for whom the instructions were relevant (see chap. 5 above).

4. *What is the goal of the law?* The law at least seeks to constrain results of hostility between two parties by forbidding willful neglect to assist another person with regard to their property on the basis that the owner is an enemy. According to the law, such a relational problem is irrelevant for guiding action in this kind of circumstance. Prejudice is ruled out of court in favor of benefit for the stray animal and its owner.

The strong formulation of the injunction shows recognition of the need for persuasion: The Hebrew behind the translation "you shall bring it back to him" is an emphatic positive command, reinforced by an infinitive absolute, that could be rendered, "You shall surely return it to him" (NASB; cf. NKJV), "Be sure to take it back to him" (NIV), or "You must take it back to him" (NJPS). This means (in negative terms) that you should not even consider ignoring the animal. Simply doing nothing could result in harm to it or its complete loss to your enemy. So you are to take the trouble, and perhaps some risk because an ox can gore (Exod. 21:28–32) and a donkey can kick, to gain control of the animal and go out of your way to return it to the owner, seeking your enemy's benefit rather than your own convenience.

The law does not stipulate a penalty for noncompliance. You should return such an animal even when you cannot be held accountable by the human community in the likely event that there are no human witnesses to your discovery of it. The emphatic formulation adds force to this, partly compensating for lack of a statement specifying punishment for violation (cf. Deut. 15:8, 10, 11, 14). It would be pointless for a secular state to make such a law because people would not bother complying if there were no penalty. However, the fact that this law is part of the covenant stipulations promulgated by the Deity

YHWH implies that he will hold his people accountable (cf. Exod. 22:22–24 [22:21–23 MT]). The issue is not merely about treatment of an enemy but also about loyalty to YHWH.

Returning lost property to its owner is simply common decency, but in the context of an otherwise hostile relationship, such an act would carry far greater significance. Requiring people to perform what would be perceived as gestures of kindness to their enemies would foster reconciliation and peace between them. Peace between God's people, in spite of irritations and faults that threaten to drive them apart and make them hostile to one another, powerfully testifies to the uniquely wise value system of the divine lawgiver. His instructions promote well-being in life and society so that when foreigners "hear all these statutes," they "will say, 'Surely this great nation is a wise and understanding people'" (Deut. 4:6).

The famous prophecy of Isa. 2:2–4 and Mic. 4:1–3 (remarkably in parallel between the two prophets) expands on the idea in Deut. 4: YHWH's law and word go out from Jerusalem and attract peoples of other nations, who come to his temple because they want to learn his superior ways and follow them. He alone is able to satisfactorily settle disputes and bring peace.

Jesus developed the same concept when he told his followers, "By this all people will know that you are my disciples, if you have love for one another" (John 13:35), and when he prayed for them "that they may all be one, just as you, Father, are in me, and I in you, that they also may be in us, so that the world may believe that you have sent me" (John 17:21; cf. vv. 22–23). This kind of unity in unselfish love is impossible for fallen humans to achieve on their own without divine assistance.

It is nothing for people to love those who love them (Matt. 5:46–47; Luke 6:33–34). But loving even enemies (Matt. 5:44–45; Luke 6:27–29, 35–36), whether inside or outside the same community, testifies to one's connection with divine power and wisdom, which makes the influence of such an individual distinctly positive (cf. Matt. 5:13, "salt of the earth"). Love for enemies and harmony among believers who resolve their differences are among the most effective missiological ways in which they can let their "light shine before others, so that they may see" their "good works and give glory to" their "Father who is in heaven" (v. 16).

Analyze the Law within the System of Old Testament Laws

1. *Does the law coordinate with any other laws in its immediate literary context?* The law in Exod. 23:4 appears among a series of laws about justice (vv. 1–8):

You shall not spread a false report [*shema' shav'*]. You shall not join hands with a wicked man [*rasha'*] to be a malicious witness (v. 1).

You shall not fall in with the many to do evil, nor shall you bear witness in a lawsuit, siding with the many, so as to pervert justice (v. 2),

nor shall you be partial to a poor man [*dal*] in his lawsuit [*riv*] (v. 3).

If you meet your enemy's ['*oyev*] ox or his donkey [*khamor*] going astray, you shall bring it back to him (v. 4).

If you see the donkey [*khamor*] of one who hates you [participle of *s-n-'*] lying down under its burden, you shall refrain from leaving him with it; you shall rescue it with him (v. 5).[2]

You shall not pervert the justice due to your poor ['*evyon*] in his lawsuit [*riv*] (v. 6).

Keep far from a false charge [*devar-sheqer*], and do not kill the innocent and righteous, for I will not acquit the wicked [*rasha'*] (v. 7).

And you shall take no bribe, for a bribe blinds the clear-sighted and subverts the cause of those who are in the right (v. 8).

The way in which Hebrew terms and expressions, some of which are synonymous, are arranged in the series shows that it is structured as a chiasm:

A Do not subvert impartial legal justice (vv. 1–2).

  B Do not be partial to *the poor in his lawsuit* (v. 3).

    C Return *your enemy's* lost animal to him (v. 4).

    C' Assist *your enemy* in helping his animal (v. 5).

  B' Do not subvert impartial justice against *the poor in his lawsuit* (v. 6).

A' Do not subvert impartial legal justice (vv. 7–8).

This unit is unified by the theme of impartial justice. The framing verses 1–2 and 7–8 prohibit practices that subvert full justice, especially by people in positions of relative social power (v. 2, "with the many"; v. 8, with enough wealth to give a bribe). Verses 3 and 6 forbid judicial partiality regarding a poor, socially weak person, whether in his favor (v. 3) or against him (v. 6). At the heart of the chiasm, verses 4–5 command (in positive terms) an Israelite to provide assistance to his enemy regarding the latter's animal in two ways (paralleled in Deut. 22:1–3, 4).

---

2. Alternatively, "lying under its burden and would refrain from raising it, you must nevertheless raise it with him" (NJPS).

At first glance, the brief laws in these verses appear to interrupt the theme of legal justice to put an anticlimax in the center of the chiasm, dealing with relatively trivial matters about animals. However, the point is not about the animals but about the enemies who own them. The issue is still impartial justice, but in an even more challenging form: away from judicial accountability and involving the choice to help or not help a person whom one could regard as having forfeited their right to receive aid. Just as witnesses and judges in court must discipline themselves to ignore extraneous factors, an Israelite who witnesses (v. 4, "meet"; v. 5, "see") an animal with a problem must judge rightly by bracketing out the fact that it belongs to an enemy, justly treating an enemy no differently than a friend.

2. *Are there topically related laws in more distant literary contexts within the same or another pentateuchal law collection?* There is a parallel law in Deut. 22:1–3:

> You shall not see your brother's ox or his sheep going astray and ignore them. You shall take them back to your brother. And if he does not live near you and you do not know who he is, you shall bring it home to your house, and it shall stay with you until your brother seeks it. Then you shall restore it to him. And you shall do the same with his donkey or with his garment, or with any lost thing of your brother's, which he loses and you find; you may not ignore it.

In some respects, this law confirms the above analysis of Exod. 23:4. First, Deut. 22 also refers to a sheep, which agrees with the assessment that the ox and donkey in Exod. 23 are just examples of animals that could wander off. Second, by adding "or with his garment, or with any lost thing of your brother's, which he loses and you find," Deut. 22 explicitly broadens the scope to any lost thing belonging to another person. Third, Deut. 22, like Exod. 23, emphasizes the obligation to return the lost thing but does not state a penalty for violation of the law. Deuteronomy 22 gives the positive formulation ("You shall take them back")[3] with the infinitive absolute reinforcing the main verb (NASB, "You shall certainly bring them back"), but it also includes the negative formulation "You shall not . . . ignore them" at the beginning of the law (v. 1) and at the end (v. 3): "You may not ignore it" (cf. v. 4).[4] Indeed, the principle of not ignoring another person's need is the main thrust of this law (Deut. 22:1–3, paralleling Exod. 23:4) and the next (Deut. 22:4, paralleling Exod. 23:5).

---

3. *Hiphil* infinitive absolute and imperfect of *sh-v-b*, as in Exod. 23:4.

4. "Ignore" in Deut. 22:1, 3, 4 renders the *hithpael* of *'-l-m*, which literally means "hide oneself," as in Isa. 58:7, "when you see the naked, to cover him, and not to hide yourself from your own flesh?"

The law in Deut. 22 differs from that of Exod. 23 in three major ways. First, whereas Exod. 23 describes the owner of the lost animal as "your enemy," Deut. 22 uses the neutral expression, "your brother." This must be a wider meaning of "brother" than "male sibling" or even "member of the same clan" because it can include someone who lives far away or whom you do not even know (v. 2). Presumably, "brother" here simply means "fellow Israelite" (cf. Exod. 2:11; Lev. 19:17; Deut. 15:12; 17:15). Of course, a fellow Israelite could be a friend or an enemy. So the scope of the Deut. 22 law includes the case of the enemy in Exod. 23. Nevertheless, while the explicit scope of Deut. 22 is considerably broader than that of Exod. 23, the implicit force of the latter narrows the gap. If you return your enemy's animal, you will certainly also return your friend's animal (a fortiori you will be more inclined to do so!); it goes without saying, and a law to that effect should not really be necessary.

Second, the Deut. 22 law is formulated differently and is more complex. Exodus 23:4 simply begins with a conditional clause ("If you meet") followed by a positive command ("you shall bring"), but Deut. 22:1–3 begins with negative and positive commands ("You shall not see" and "You shall take," v. 1). These are followed by a conditional clause introducing a subcase ("And if he does not live near you") containing positive stipulations ("you shall bring it home . . . ," v. 2). Finally, in verse 3 a series of positive commands ("And you shall do the same") and a negative command ("You may not ignore it") extend the instructions of verses 1–2 to "any lost thing of your brother's, which he loses and you find."

Third, the subcase in Deut. 22:2 answers a possible excuse for ignoring a stray animal: you don't know the owner, and he lives too far away for you to bring the animal to him without undue hardship to you.[5] This at least partly explains why Deut. 22 must inclusively describe the owner as "your brother" rather than "your enemy": if you don't even know who the owner is, how could you know that he is your enemy? Thus Deut. 22 uses the broad designation "your brother" to cover all kinds of relationships to the owner, even as it broadens the scope of the lost object (but not including slaves; 23:15–16 [23:16–17 MT]).

---

5. ESV translates "And if he does not live near you *and* [*vav* conjunction] you do not know who he is" (emphasis added). Other versions (NKJV, NRSV, NJPS, NASB, NIV, CEB) render the *vav* conjunction "or." In any case, the lost animal is to remain in the care of the finder until the owner comes looking for it. This implies that the finder is obligated to expend resources, time, and energy for the animal by giving it food, water, shelter, and protection. However, there is no restriction on using the animal for work before the owner shows up, so this could supply some compensation. By taking care of the animal, the finder fulfills his obligation. If the owner never comes or sends for the animal, it presumably belongs to the finder.

Returning to Exod. 23:4, it is important not to read concepts into this law from another law, even one that is in parallel, in this case Deut. 22:1–3. However, in light of comparison between the two laws, we can sharpen our understanding of the value-based principle exemplified in Exod. 23:4: "You must return, to the extent of your ability, any lost thing that you find, even if it belongs to your enemy."

3. *How does the law function within the hierarchy of moral values?* The topic of the law in Exod. 23:4 concerns return of another person's property. Therefore, it primarily represents the value behind the Decalogue commandment "You shall not steal" (Exod. 20:15), which can be positively formulated: Preserve property rights of others. This is a subprinciple of love for humans (Lev. 19:18; cf. chap. 7). Plugging the law of Exod. 23:4 into Jesus's Golden Rule of love (Matt. 7:12) results in the following: Just as you would wish that another person, even your enemy, would return a lost thing of yours that is found, do also to such a person.

Viewed under the overall value of love, the law of Exod. 23:4 also relates to some other values. For one thing, concern for the life of a lost domestic animal (cf. Deut. 22:1–3) exemplifies the value of respect for life that includes the subvalue of guarding against wrongful taking of human life, which is expressed in the Decalogue commandment "You shall not murder" (Exod. 20:13). It is true that OT law mainly expresses ways in which humans are to show love for God and each other, and an ancient Israelite most likely would regard kindness to an animal belonging to someone else as kindness to its owner. Nevertheless, we can see that humane treatment of animals for their own sake comes under the overarching principle of love. Love includes treating all that God has created, animals as well as humans, with kindness and respect (cf. chaps. 12–13 below).

Helping an enemy as one would assist a friend (cf. Deut. 22:1–3, "brother") demonstrates a kind of justice, which explains placement of the law in Exod. 23:4 among laws regarding this value (see above). A person of such integrity that he exercises justice by voluntarily helping his enemy can be counted on to show justice in other areas of life, including in court. In a discourse on love (Luke 6:27–36), Jesus points out that treating one's enemies with love, seeking their good and expecting nothing in return, is an excellent form of genuine, unselfish love that emulates God's character (cf. Matt. 5:43–48).

The laws in Exod. 23:4–5 rightly constitute the center of a chiasm (see above) because they call for a high degree of justice, which belongs to love. These verses are united by the value of helping others, even enemies, with regard to their property, doing so to the extent of one's ability. A more general value of helping others would include assistance not only with property but also with preservation of someone's life (cf. Decalogue commandment in Exod. 20:13), marriage (v. 14), or reputation (v. 16).

Recognizing how the values exemplified by the law in Exod. 23:4 fit within the hierarchy of love, as we have done here, benefits understanding in several ways. First, it puts apparently insignificant actions into a larger perspective that invests them with profound significance (cf. Matt. 25:31–46). Just returning a straying animal is a gesture of the value of love, whether or not one feels a loving emotion, and if the animal belongs to your enemy, this action can change two lives: yours and your enemy's. Positive emotions will likely ensue, but the guide for choices and actions is the imperative to do the right thing.

Second, placement within the hierarchy reveals logical relationships between actions that can assist one in making decisions. For example, if you assist your enemy by returning his stray animal (Exod. 23:4), it makes sense that you would also help him get his donkey back on its feet (v. 5) because both scenarios are governed by the same loving value of helping others, even enemies, with regard to their property.

Third, when a situation in life arises that no law specifically addresses, one can identify the kind of value under love that could govern the situation, look for one or more laws that exemplify this value, and see what light the law(s) could shed on an appropriate response. This process can also assist with situations that would uniquely confront a modern person (see below), but here we are still working with circumstances that could occur in the ancient world that was addressed by the formulations of OT law.

Suppose, for example, that a young adult is becoming rebellious against his parents and is as stubborn as a donkey. In spite of their discipline, the rebel does not listen to the parents and has a tendency to gluttony and bouts of inebriation. It is clear that this course is leading to a tragic end if the rebel does not change.[6] But as a friend of the wayward youth, you have some influence, even though these parents have seriously hostile feelings toward you.

There is no OT law that directly tells you if or how you should act under such circumstances, but you know that you should "love your neighbor as yourself" (Lev. 19:18). What does love do in such a situation? Perhaps love should avoid interfering, which would involve interaction with the young man's parents that could increase their resentment toward you. However, further thought shows that the parents, your enemies, are losing their child, who is going astray morally. Is there any law that is relevant to a situation in which someone/something belonging to one's enemy/ies is going astray and you are

---

6. For the tragic end under the Israelite theocracy, see the law of the rebellious son in Deut. 21:18–21, which results in permanent removal of the son from the community by stoning.

in a position to help? "If you meet your enemy's ox or his donkey going astray, you shall bring it back to him" (Exod. 23:4). Your responsibility is now clear: If this is what you should do with an animal of your enemy that is straying to an uncertain fate, a fortiori you should use all the influence at your disposal to help a straying human who is lurching toward a certainly disastrous fate to turn around and be reconciled to his parents, in spite of their past animosity against you. Thus a seemingly mundane law about an ox or (literal) donkey implies a profound message relevant to human redemption!

Further Analyze the Law within the Context of Its Ancient Life Situation

1. *How do biblical texts shed light on the ancient life situation that the law sought to affect?* "There was a man of Benjamin whose name was Kish . . . a Benjaminite, a man of wealth. . . . Now the donkeys of Kish, Saul's father, were lost. So Kish said to Saul his son, 'Take one of the young men with you, and arise, go and look for the donkeys'" (1 Sam. 9:1, 3). Then Saul (later the first king of Israel) and his servant went on quite a long expedition to locate the missing animals, which turned out to be unsuccessful (vv. 4–5).[7] The text does not say how many donkeys were gone, but the fact that a wealthy family would be so concerned about retrieving them indicates the value of such animals to ancient Israelites. So "your enemy's ox or his donkey going astray" (Exod. 23:4) refers to a significant item of property, roughly equivalent to a motor vehicle belonging to a modern person. Neglecting to return such property could result in major loss to the owner. If the owner is one's enemy, naturally such neglect would be all the more attractive, but the law counters this inclination with concern for the enemy.

2. *How do extrabiblical materials supplement our understanding of the ancient life situation?* A stray animal can encounter various dangers if someone does not return it to its owner. One hazard could arise from the fact that a domestic animal would be attracted to other animals. The Middle Kingdom Egyptian narrative of Sinuhe employs a simile referring to such a scenario: "I am indeed like a stray bull in a strange herd, whom the bull of the herd charges, whom the longhorn attacks."[8] Law §66 of the Hittite Laws also recognizes that a stray animal could end up in the wrong place with other animals, but here the issues are the right of the stray's owner to take it back and protection of the pen's owner from prosecution as a thief.

7. However, Samuel subsequently informed Saul: "As for your donkeys that were lost three days ago, do not set your mind on them, for they have been found" (9:20).
8. Trans. Miriam Lichtheim, "Sinuhe," *COS* 1.38:79.

Hittite Laws §71 allows the finder of a stray ox, horse, or mule to harness (and use) it while it is in his custody, but only after he has had it presented to the elders in the event that he found it in the country. If he does not duly notify the elders in this way, he is treated as a thief, apparently because it is assumed that he is trying to avoid the return of the animal to its owner.[9] By permitting the finder to use the animal, the law implicitly and fairly reimburses the finder for his output of energy and resources in caring for and feeding the animal until the owner turns up. Compare Deut. 22:2, which does not state that the finder may use the animal, but this can be understood.

Hittite Laws §71 does not consider the possibility implicit in Exod. 23:4 and explicit in Deut. 22:1, 3 that someone could come across a stray animal and ignore the situation, simply letting it go on its way, whether out of animosity toward the owner or unwillingness to undergo inconvenience. Apparently the Hittite law assumes that an individual who sees a stray work beast would view it as an opportunity to utilize it temporarily (like an extra tractor or pickup), or even permanently if the owner fails to appear. In any case, the Hittite law does not hold someone accountable for simply ignoring a stray animal, thereby choosing not to "find" it. Such an offense generally would be impossible for humans to detect. The biblical laws, which hold God's people directly accountable to him, not only to human jurisprudence, are unique in this regard.

Like the later Hittite Laws, law §50 of the Mesopotamian Laws of Eshnunna delineates boundaries of theft when someone finds a stray animal. However, this law includes the factor of abuse of power by a person in authority and treats fugitive slaves together with stray animals as two kinds of lost property: "If a military governor, a governor of the canal system, or any person in a position of authority seizes a fugitive slave, fugitive slave woman, stray ox, or stray donkey belonging either to the palace or to a commoner, and does not lead it to Eshnunna but detains it in his house and allows more than one month to elapse, the palace shall bring a charge of theft against him."[10]

Unlike this law, OT law separates fugitive slaves from stray animals. Whereas an Israelite must actively return an animal to its owner, even if he is an enemy (Exod. 23:4; Deut. 22:1–3), Deut. 23:15–16 (23:16–17 MT) prohibits an Israelite from even surrendering a fugitive slave to his master. Thus Deut. 23 does not regard such slaves as mere property and prioritizes their rights above those of their masters.

---

9. Cf. OT laws dealing with theft that can occur when someone claims that lost property that he has found actually belongs to him (Exod. 22:9 [22:8 MT]; Lev. 6:3–4 [5:22–23 MT]).
10. Trans. Martha Roth, "The Laws of Eshnunna," COS 2.130:334–35.

Analyze the Law within the Process of Redemption

1. *How does the law relate to creation and new-creation ideals?* The creation and new-creation settings do not include enemies and stray animals or danger to them, and there is no evidence for other kinds of lost property in those contexts. In the fallen world between those ideal environments, humans cannot avoid the possibility of losing things, including animals. Neither can they prevent unreasonable hostility of others toward them. However, the Bible encourages people to pursue restoration toward the ideal by treating others with kindness, including by returning any lost property of theirs that they find (Deut. 22:1–3), even if the owners have regarded them as enemies (Exod. 23:4).

2. *How does the law seek to remedy something faulty that results from the fall into sin?* Cain murdered his brother Abel (Gen. 4), taking the recent fall into sin (Gen. 3) to an unprecedented depth of unloving behavior. When the Lord asked Cain where Abel was, he retorted: "I do not know; am I my brother's keeper?" (Gen. 4:9). Cain's implied answer to this rhetorical question was no, in opposition to the principle of love for other humans, which would answer yes. Aside from lying to God about his knowledge of Abel's whereabouts, Cain treated his brother as his enemy, showing no concern for any aspect of Abel's welfare.

To prevent the kind of selfish attitude and action displayed by Cain, OT law leads people back to harmony with each other through kindness as a matter of principle: "If you meet your enemy's ox or his donkey going astray, you shall bring it back to him" (Exod. 23:4). This may seem like a minor matter, but it signifies much more. One who helps his enemy with his animal, thereby showing respect for its life, a fortiori will not take the life of the enemy as Cain did, but at least implicitly acknowledges that the hostile person is still his brother (cf. Deut. 22:1–3, "your brother's ox or his sheep").

3. *Does the OT indicate moral growth beyond the stage represented by the law?* Exodus 23:4 and its parallel in Deut. 22:1–3 specify neither a penalty for violation nor a reward for compliance.[11] The finder of a lost item, such as a stray animal, is to do the right thing because it is right and the covenant Deity has commanded it. It is not only right; it is also wise. Who knows when your enemy may find something of yours that is lost and return the favor? Moreover, by doing your enemy an unsolicited favor, that enemy may become a valuable friend. Enemies are liabilities, but friends are valuable.

Proverbs 25 recognizes and expands on the wisdom of helping an enemy: "If your enemy is hungry, give him bread to eat, and if he is thirsty, give him

---

11. So in this case we cannot place a penalty for violation within the system of penalties in OT law to weigh the relative seriousness of the moral fault (cf. chap. 14 below).

water to drink, for you will heap burning coals on his head, and the LORD will reward you" (vv. 21–22; cited in Rom. 12:20). There is no law in the Pentateuch that explicitly commands a person to feed or give drink to an enemy, but this wisdom instruction in Proverbs sounds like a law. It goes beyond the law of Exod. 23:4 in that it urges one to be aware of an enemy's personal needs (exemplified by food and drink) and meet them by giving from one's own resources, which involves more intimate interaction and greater cost than simply handing over a lost item.

The proverb explicitly offers two types of motivation that are not articulated in Exod. 23:4, although they could also apply there. First, "You will heap burning coals on his head" (Prov. 25:22). This metaphorical consequence sounds vengeful and cruel rather than loving, but the enemy internally experiences your kind act this way only because they harbored animosity. One's responsibility is to carry out the positive deed and "let the chips fall where they may." The proverb employs a brilliantly persuasive irony: Even if you lack a feeling of love toward your enemy, returning good for evil is the sweetest, most satisfying, and most effective form of revenge because it embarrasses the hostile person in a totally unexpected way (cf. 2 Kings 6:18–23). The biblical way to destroy your enemy is to turn him into a friend!

The second motivation in the proverb is the promise that "the LORD will reward you" (Prov. 25:22). Don't worry about the awkwardness or expense of assisting your enemy; God will compensate you. He blesses "peacemakers" (Matt. 5:9) who act in accordance with his character of love and resulting initiative of reconciliation, which he has carried out for us through Christ even though we have been his enemies (Rom. 5:1–11).

4. *Does the NT indicate moral growth beyond the stage represented by the law?* Paul further develops the value of helping an enemy, which the laws in Exod. 23:4–5 represent and on which Prov. 25:21–22 expands, by quoting the latter passage in Rom. 12 to support a broader principle: A Christian should always seek to overcome evil with good, leaving the vengeance of retributive justice up to God (citing Deut. 32:35), who can do the job much better than we can.

> Repay no one evil for evil, but give thought to do what is honorable in the sight of all. If possible, so far as it depends on you, live peaceably with all. Beloved, never avenge yourselves, but leave it to the wrath of God, for it is written, "Vengeance is mine, I will repay, says the Lord." To the contrary, "if your enemy is hungry, feed him; if he is thirsty, give him something to drink; for by so doing you will heap burning coals on his head." Do not be overcome by evil, but overcome evil with good. (Rom. 12:17–21)

Jesus provided the supreme example of this value (overcoming evil with good) during his ministry on earth and especially when he was abused and crucified on our behalf: "When he was reviled, he did not revile in return; when he suffered, he did not threaten, but continued entrusting himself to him who judges justly. He himself bore our sins in his body on the tree, that we might die to sin and live to righteousness. By his wounds you have been healed" (1 Pet. 2:23–24).[12]

Paul did not mention rescue of an animal in Rom. 12, but Jesus did when he used an analogy to justify deliverance of a human being. He entered a synagogue on the Sabbath,

> And a man was there with a withered hand. And they asked him, "Is it lawful to heal on the Sabbath?"—so that they might accuse him. He said to them, "Which one of you who has a sheep, if it falls into a pit on the Sabbath, will not take hold of it and lift it out? Of how much more value is a man than a sheep! So it is lawful to do good on the Sabbath." Then he said to the man, "Stretch out your hand." And the man stretched it out, and it was restored, healthy like the other. But the Pharisees went out and conspired against him, how to destroy him. (Matt. 12:10–14; cf. Luke 14:1–6)

Here Jesus declared that any of those watching would not hesitate to save his sheep from a pit on the Sabbath.[13] This circumstance resembles that of Exod. 23:5 and Deut. 22:4 in that it involves lifting a fallen animal, but three factors are different: the item of property is a sheep in a pit, not a work animal on or by a path/road; the person in question rescues his own animal rather than assisting someone else; and the incident occurs on the Sabbath.

Nevertheless, the pentateuchal laws inform the case cited by Jesus. Neither Exod. 23:5 nor Deut. 22:4 contains an exception that prohibits an Israelite or someone helping him from lifting his fallen animal on the Sabbath, nor is there a Sabbath exception in Exod. 23:4 or Deut. 22:1–2 with regard to returning a stray animal. This implies that such emergency aid would not be viewed as work (*mela'kah*) that is forbidden on the Sabbath (Exod. 20:10; etc.). Therefore, it is entirely permissible to rescue one's sheep from a pit on the Sabbath. By referring to a sheep, which is not a work animal, rather than a "donkey . . . lying down under its burden" (Exod. 23:5) or a "donkey or . . . ox fallen down by the way" (Deut. 22:4), Jesus avoided confusing the issue

---

12. When Jesus was crucified, he prayed, "Father, forgive them, for they know not what they do" (Luke 23:34). Cf. Isa. 53:3–12 and Rom. 5:10, "While we were enemies we were reconciled to God by the death of his Son."

13. But see CD (Cairo Genizah copy of the *Damascus Document*) 11.13–14, which prohibits lifting an animal out of a well or pit on the Sabbath.

at hand by preempting the possibility that the emergency occurred while the owner was working his animal, which would be forbidden on the Sabbath (Exod. 20:10, "or your livestock").

It appears that Jesus's opponents correctly understood an application of laws regarding rescue of animals. However, they had missed the next logical step: "Of how much more value is a man than a sheep!" (Matt. 12:12). Thus Jesus made an unassailable a fortiori argument: If you may preserve animal life on the Sabbath, you are surely allowed to do something for human life on this holy day. In fact, healing of a withered hand restores life to a condition that is closer to the holy ideal of creation, which the Sabbath commemorates (Gen. 2:2–3; Exod. 20:11; etc.), so this kind of activity would be especially appropriate on the Sabbath.[14] As Jesus observed on another occasion, "The Sabbath was made for man, not man for the Sabbath" (Mark 2:27).

A key component of Exod. 23:5 and Deut. 22:4 implicitly condemns those who were looking for a way to accuse Jesus. These laws command one person to aid another with an animal in distress. Jesus was ready to help the man with the withered hand, instead of an animal, while the onlookers failed to offer any assistance and even opposed Jesus's humane activity. In this way they were violating the principle "You shall love your neighbor as yourself" (Lev. 19:18), which includes the subprinciple that you must help anyone, even your enemy (see above). Like Cain, they refused to be their "brother's keeper" (Gen. 4:9). On Sabbath they would not hesitate to rescue their own animal, which was their property, but not another human being, who was not their property. Also like Cain, their rebellion against the law of love grew to murderous hatred: After Jesus healed the man, "the Pharisees went out and conspired against him, how to destroy him" (Matt. 12:14). In their encounter with Jesus, we see the clash between creation values and fall vices in microcosm.

By applying the value exemplified in Exod. 23 and Deut. 22 to deliverance of a human being, Jesus pointed to the wider and higher value of helping anyone at any time and in any way to the extent of our ability. Obviously our ability to help others is limited, but the responsibility to do what we can transcends situational and cultural boundaries or even barriers, as Jesus illustrated in his parable of the good Samaritan (Luke 10:30–37).

In his parable of Luke 15:4–7, Jesus drew an analogy between the physical lostness of a sheep and the spiritual lostness of a human being. To save the spiritually lost, Christ himself, "the good shepherd" (John 10:11, 14), came down into our fallen world, and he commissioned his disciples to assist him:

---

14. If a physical defect (*mum*) diminishes holiness (see chap. 3 above on Lev. 21, 22, 24), healing it would restore holiness.

"Go into all the world and proclaim the gospel to the whole creation. Whoever believes and is baptized will be saved" (Mark 16:15–16). This is cooperation with God in rescue on a cosmic scale.

Relate Findings regarding the Function of the Law to Modern Life

1. *Does the law, or at least some element of it, directly apply to modern life now, or could it do so in the future?* People in some parts of the world today could literally experience the same situation addressed in Exod. 23:4, an enemy's ox or donkey going astray, or any of the related scenarios in verse 5 or Deut. 22:1–4. This would be highly unlikely for most modern Westerners and probably would be even less likely in the future, but we do keep other kinds of animals, mainly as pets, and occasionally they go astray. On several occasions my wife and I have returned lost animals to their owners, and we have been grateful when neighbors or strangers have reunited our wandering dogs with us. Like ancient or non-Western folk, we can also have enemies, so that complicating factor can continue to test characters.

2. *Whether or not a law directly applies today, how does it serve as a paradigmatic example of higher-level values that still apply to analogous modern circumstances?* In Exod. 23:4 and Deut. 22:1–2, restoring a straying animal to its owner serves as a paradigmatic example of returning anything belonging to the larger category of lost property, as acknowledged in Deut. 22:3: "And you shall do the same with his donkey or with his garment, or with any lost thing of your brother's, which he loses and you find; you may not ignore it." The principle of returning "any lost thing" to your "brother," which we can understand more broadly as referring to any other person,[15] has many more applications today than in ancient times because we have more things to lose (including data in electronic devices) and more ways to lose them.

We also have plenty of ways to help our enemies in addition to returning lost items (including pets). You may not come across "the donkey of one who hates you lying down under its burden" (Exod. 23:5), but you could encounter an individual who has been antagonistic toward you struggling with another kind of vehicle or work instrument, such as a truck, car, computer, or smartphone. If so, you have an opportunity to implement a high-level principle articulated by Jesus: "Love your enemies, do good to those who hate you, bless those who curse you, pray for those who abuse you" (Luke 6:27–28).

15. Cf. Jesus's account of the good Samaritan (Luke 10:29–37), where Jesus expanded the concept of "neighbor" to include even a member of an enemy group.

3. *Does biblical development of the value exemplified by the law show a trajectory that moves beyond the law itself to a higher moral level that should be applied in the modern life situation?* As discussed above, Exod. 23:4 and laws related to it could be applied today, whether directly (although rarely) or by close analogy to innumerable other situations that call for helping others, including enemies, with their property. Proverbs 25:21–22 extends the value of helping one's enemy to situations calling for more intimate and costly assistance, and Rom. 12:17–21 further expands to repaying evil with good at all times. These instructions for God's people continue to be valuable today for the same reasons, especially including opportunities for relational reconciliation.[16]

Jesus shifted the focus of the object of rescue from animals (Matt. 12:11; 18:12–13; Luke 15:4–6) and other kinds of property (Luke 15:8–9) to humans in need of physical healing (Matt. 12:12–13) and redemption (Luke 15:7, 10–32). Just as his people are to help each other with lost or fallen animals (Exod. 23:4–5; Deut. 22:1–4), Christ makes his followers responsible for assisting him with his "lost" and "fallen" human beings (Matt. 28:19–20; Mark 16:15–16). If we should aid even an enemy with his beast, should we not the more so (a fortiori) help our greatest friend with precious people so that they too can enjoy reconciliation with him through Jesus's sacrifice and be "in Christ," a "new creation" (2 Cor. 5:17–21)?

---

16. On the importance of relational reconciliation in later times, see Mal. 4:5–6 (3:23–24 MT).

PART 4

Values in Old Testament Law

11

Ten Commandments and Related Laws, Part One

The Ten Commandments or Decalogue (Exod. 20:3–17; Deut. 5:7–21), which Exod. 34:28; Deut. 4:13; 10:4 literally call "the ten words," are the best known of all OT laws. They are unique in that YHWH proclaimed them directly to the Israelite community (Exod. 19:9; 20:19–22; Deut. 5:4, 22–26). They represented the core of the covenant stipulations, as shown by Exod. 34:28 ("the words of the covenant, the Ten Commandments") and Deut. 4:13 ("his covenant, which he commanded you to perform, that is, the Ten Commandments"). Therefore, they were recorded on two tablets as the primary covenant document, the "witness/testimony" to the covenant (Exod. 31:18; 32:15; 34:29),[1] and deposited in the ark of the covenant (25:16; Deut. 10:1–5; cf. 1 Kings 8:9).

The Ten Commandments are apodictic statements that serve as paramount examples of key moral principles governing divine-human and human-human relationships. The first four commandments focus on obligations to God and the last six on duties to human beings. However, the fourth commandment regarding the Sabbath serves as a transition to the last six commandments in that it requires people to allow subordinate

---

1. That the commandments were inscribed on both surfaces of the tablets (Exod. 32:15) suggests that each tablet contained all of the commandments. The usual modern depictions that show bifurcation in two columns (as if they are two tablets) on one surface of a tablet are inaccurate.

members of their households to rest.[2] Furthermore, the last six commandments also express duties to God because he holds people accountable for
how they treat each other.

In terms of their explicit legal scope, the Ten Commandments do not cover
every divine moral requirement, but they implicitly represent broader values
(cf. chap. 7).[3] For instance, "You shall not commit adultery" (Exod. 20:14;
Deut. 5:18) explicitly prohibits married people from having sexual relations
with persons other than their spouses, without referring to other kinds of
sexual offenses. Not committing adultery exemplifies the larger value of preserving sexual purity, which also excludes a number of other kinds of sexual
practices that God rules out in other laws (e.g., Lev. 18, 20). Thus, the range
of morality underlying the Decalogue is vast.

It is the purpose of this chapter and the next to explore the values that are
exemplified by the Ten Commandments, under headings that express their
principles in positive terms,[4] in synchronic relation to some other OT laws that
flesh them out and expand on them.[5] The fact that OT laws supplement the
Decalogue is especially clear in Deuteronomy. Stephen A. Kaufman's analysis
has supported the idea that the Deuteronomic laws of Deut. 12:1–25:16 are
structured around the Ten Commandments (as stated in Deut. 5:7–21) as
an expanded Decalogue.[6] The Ten Commandments and the other laws are

2. "With the Sabbath Commandment, we come to the end of the first table of the Decalogue,
that is, those commandments that focus on the proper worship and love of God. At the same
time . . . this commandment is a crucial bridge connecting to the commandments having to
do with love of neighbor and the protection of our neighbor's well-being." Patrick D. Miller,
The Ten Commandments, Interpretation: Resources for the Use of Scripture in the Church
(Louisville: Westminster John Knox, 2009), 117.

3. On the sampling nature of the OT law collections, including the Decalogue, see Waldemar Janzen, *Old Testament Ethics: A Paradigmatic Approach* (Louisville: Westminster/John
Knox, 1994), 87–96.

4. Cf. the way in which Yiu Sing Lúcás Chan interprets the Ten Commandments as expressions of positive ethical virtues (*The Ten Commandments and the Beatitudes: Biblical Studies
and Ethics for Real Life* [Lanham, MD: Rowman & Littlefield, 2012], 43–140). Note that I follow
the Reformed delineation and numbering of the Ten Commandments (cf. chap. 7).

5. Cf. parallels to the first nine of the Ten Commandments (not including the commandment against coveting; Exod. 20:17; Deut. 5:21) in other parts of the Pentateuch pointed out by
Moshe Weinfeld, "The Decalogue: Its Significance, Uniqueness, and Place in Israel's Tradition,"
in *Religion and Law: Biblical-Judaic and Islamic Perspectives*, ed. Edwin B. Firmage, Bernard G.
Weiss, and John W. Welch (Winona Lake, IN: Eisenbrauns, 1990), 4–9. For detailed exposition
of the Ten Commandments and relationships between them and other parts of the Bible, see
esp. Miller, *Ten Commandments*.

6. "The Structure of the Deuteronomic Law," *Maarav* 1, no. 2 (1978–79): 105–58. For
example, according to Kaufman, Deut. 12 calls for eradicating pagan cults and centralizing
YHWH worship. This concern for right worship relates to the first two commandments of
the Decalogue (113, 118–22). Kaufman explains that in the Deuteronomic Law, "provisions

inseparable, so it is a misunderstanding of OT law for Christians to retain the former but simply dismiss the latter (cf. introduction and chap. 8).[7]

The present chapter covers commandments 1–4 (obligations to God) and laws that are conceptually associated with them, and the following chapter deals with commandments 5–10 (duties to humans) and related laws. Our quest is for progressive moral wisdom (PMW) through understanding biblical values and how to apply them to Christian life. So in this and the following chapters, we will flexibly draw on conceptual elements of the PMW methodology outlined in chapter 9 and illustrated by the case study in chapter 10 without labeling them as such. There is insufficient space in this volume for step-by-step PMW analysis of each law.

God introduced the Ten Commandments as a whole with the words "I am the LORD [YHWH] your [sing.] God, who brought you [sing.] out of the land of Egypt, out of the house of slavery" (Exod. 20:2; cf. Deut. 5:6). Like the historical prologue of an ANE treaty formulation, this introduction identifies the superior party to the covenant (YHWH) and what he has graciously done for the lesser party (the Israelites). His merciful and miraculous deliverance was to call forth their profound gratitude, from which their loyal obedience to his covenant stipulations/commandments could be expected to naturally flow (cf. chap. 3 above). The singular address indicates that YHWH related to Israel not only as the national covenant Deity but also as the covenant Lord of every individual within the nation, so that each of them was a vassal, an underlord, with primary responsibility for compliance and direct accountability to him.[8] Jacqueline E. Lapsley makes a crucial observation:

> The prologue is, then, intimately connected to the first commandment ("You shall have no other gods before me"). Based on the truth of the prologue, of who this God is, the people are not to have any other gods. And the first commandment, together with the prologue, serves as the foundation upon which all the others stand. They affirm unequivocally that the vertical, divine-human relationship is prior to, and sustaining of, all horizontal relationships among human beings.[9]

---

flow smoothly and logically from one to the other while the sequence of its major topical divisions consciously reflects the order of the Decalogue" (125). The point that Deuteronomy expands on the Ten Commandments stands even if not all details of Kaufman's analysis are accepted.

7. For example, Lev. 19:11 contains the comprehensive law against lying, but it is outside the Decalogue.

8. Unlike an ANE treaty in which only the vassal ruler had such a direct relationship with the suzerain (overlord) and was responsible for the compliance of his subjects.

9. "Ten Commandments," in *Dictionary of Scripture and Ethics*, ed. Joel B. Green (Grand Rapids: Baker Academic, 2011), 773.

First Commandment: Relate to the Lord (YHWH) Alone as the Deity

The first commandment affirms YHWH's absolute sovereignty and makes the divine-human relationship exclusive: "You [sing.] shall have no other gods before me" (Exod. 20:3; cf. Deut. 5:7). This rules out treatment of anyone as a deity aside from YHWH, who uniquely created the world (Exod. 20:11), delivered the Israelites from Egypt (v. 2; Deut. 5:6, 15), and was giving them the land of Canaan (Exod. 20:12; Deut. 5:16). The Hebrew expression '*al-panay*, rendered "before me," does not indicate that it is permissible to have other gods as long as they are not ranked higher than the Lord. Rather, '*al-panay* means "in front of my presence," anywhere within God's field of perception (cf. Jer. 6:7; Ps. 9:19 [9:20 MT]), which is limitless (Ps. 139:7–12). Only YHWH is to be God to his people, which means that all reverential awe, worship, and submission to divine authority are to be directed to him alone. Attention to any other "deity" is spiritual promiscuity (e.g., Exod. 34:16; Lev. 17:7; 20:5).

Such monotheism greatly simplifies, economizes, and de-stresses human life. Polytheistic ANE peoples felt obliged to invest vast resources of energy and materials in temples and offerings for many gods. By contrast, normative Israelite worship as prescribed in the Bible was much more economical, with infrastructure and offerings required for only one Deity. An Israelite aware of having fallen out of divine favor, perhaps because of an offense committed without realizing it (e.g., Lev. 5:17), knew what deity to approach in order to make amends (cf. vv. 18–19). The offender was not left in uncertainty.

Laws Related to the First Commandment

Corollaries of the first commandment appear in other laws:

1. Acknowledge and pay tribute to YHWH as the divine overlord, including by appearing before him at festivals with offerings (Exod. 23:14–17) and paying tithes (Lev. 27:30–32; Num. 18:21, 24, 26, 28; Deut. 12:6, 11; etc.). But do not sacrifice to any deity other than YHWH (Exod. 22:20 [22:19 MT]). Treating him as the overlord includes adherence to all of his ritual instructions (e.g., Lev. 1–7, 12–16) and rules out offering one's child to Molech (18:21; 20:1–5).

2. Do not make material gods to be "with me" (Exod. 20:23; cf. v. 3, "before me") or set up symbols of other gods (Deut. 16:21–22). These prohibitions rule out idols or symbols of any deity other than YHWH, overlapping the scope of the second commandment (see below).

3. Have nothing to do with the polytheistic, idolatrous Canaanites and their culture, but drive them out (Exodus) or destroy them (Deuteronomy), obliterate their religious infrastructure, and do not worship YHWH as they serve their gods—including by child sacrifice (Exod. 23:23–24, 31–33; 34:11–16; Deut. 7:1–5; 12:2–4, 29–31; 18:10; 20:16–18).[10]

4. Do not cause the names of other gods to be remembered or speak of them (Exod. 23:13)—that is, in reverential terms.[11]

5. Destroy any individual or group in Israel that worships other gods or attempts to turn others from YHWH to service of other gods (Deut. 13; 17:2–5).

6. Shun occult practices and put occult practitioners to death (Exod. 22:18 [22:17 MT]; Lev. 19:26, 31; 20:6, 27; Deut. 18:9–14).

Second Commandment: Relate to the Lord Only as a Transcendent Personality

The second commandment prohibits idolatry, including manufacture or worship of any material representation that is treated as a deity:

> You shall not make for yourself a carved image, or any likeness of anything that is in heaven above, or that is in the earth beneath, or that is in the water under the earth. You shall not bow down to them or serve them, for I the LORD your God am a jealous God, visiting the iniquity of the fathers on the children to the third and the fourth generation of those who hate me, but showing steadfast love to thousands of those who love me and keep my commandments. (Exod. 20:4–6; cf. Deut. 5:8–10)

Notice that the law does not condemn art that is not worshiped. The first commandment already forbids interaction with any deity but YHWH (Exod. 20:3), which as a corollary excludes idols of other gods (see above). The second commandment reinforces and makes explicit the ban on such idolatry and additionally rules out idolatrous portrayals of YHWH himself, such as the golden calves set up by Aaron (Exod. 32:2–5) and Jeroboam (1 Kings 12:26–29). Because YHWH rejects idols of himself as valid representations (e.g., Exod. 32:8; cf. v. 31; Deut. 4:15–18), they too could be regarded as other gods, which can be taken to indicate that the first commandment implicitly prohibits them as well.

10. On theodicy and this destruction of nations, see chap. 14 below.
11. The Bible and its prophets mention names or titles of a number of deities other than YHWH in order to speak against them (e.g., Lev. 20:2–5; Judg. 8:33; Isa. 46:1; Jer. 50:2; Ezek. 8:14).

Thus we find that there is a close connection between the first and second commandments. If people were to grasp the full implications of the first commandment, they would not really need the second. But faulty humans can miss these implications because they tend to want the security of relating to divinity through something that they can see, control, and own, without the need to adequately exercise faith in and acknowledge complete account-ability to the unseen, transcendent YHWH. So the second commandment specifically rules out material representations, even if they ostensibly serve as crutches for worship of himself.

There are three major problems with any material image of the Lord, even if it is intended to honor him. First, it is impossible to accurately depict him because not even the Israelites who heard his voice at Mount Sinai saw his form (Deut. 4:12, 15–18). Fallen humans cannot see his unveiled glorious face and live (Exod. 33:20). Their condition of mortality that results from sin (Gen. 3; Rom. 6:23), which separates them from holy YHWH, was represented in the Israelite ritual system by physical ritual impurities, regarding which a number of laws provide regulations and remedies (esp. Lev. 12–15; Num. 19).[12]

Second, a material representation substitutes for YHWH a lesser likeness, such as a figure of something created by him, and thereby diminishes his greatness and glory (cf. Rom. 1:22–23, 25), which no material rendition can capture (Deut. 4:16–18; contrast Isa. 40:12–18; Ezek. 1:26–28; Dan. 7:9–10; Rev. 4:2–3). Humans are made in God's image (Gen. 1:26–27), so lowering him in this way has the effect of diminishing them, including in terms of their moral worth (cf. Rom. 1:24, 26–32). The problem of a lesser likeness would be serious enough in a perfect world, but in our broken world such a material substitute is devalued by the fact that it is imperfect.

Third, those who make or worship a material representation thereby deny God's real, immanent presence with his people (e.g., Deut. 4:7). When the Lord was with the Israelites in a pillar of cloud (Exod. 13:21–22) and at his sanctuary (25:8), he was there as a living personality who could see (14:24), hear (Num. 11:1), speak (7:89), and act (Exod. 14:24–25; Lev. 9:24; 10:2; Num. 11:1). He moved to his sanctuary by himself (Exod. 40:34–35) rather than in the usual ANE form of an idol or symbol carried by cultic functionaries, and he could also move out by himself (Ezek. 10–11).[13] There was no need to approach him indirectly through a material surrogate as other peoples inter-

---

12. On the concept of mortality underlying Israelite physical ritual impurities, see Hyam Maccoby, *Ritual and Morality: The Ritual Purity System and its Place in Judaism* (Cambridge: Cambridge University Press, 1999), 49, cf. 31–32, 48, 50, 207–8.

13. Roy E. Gane, "Leviticus," in *Zondervan Illustrated Bible Backgrounds Commentary*, ed. John H. Walton, 5 vols. (Grand Rapids: Zondervan, 2009), 1:298–99.

acted with the deities (really demons; Deut. 32:16–17; 1 Cor. 10:20) whom they believed inhabited the regions of their cosmos: "heaven, . . . earth, . . . the water under the earth" (Exod. 20:4).

Invocation of YHWH through an idol would exhibit faithless rejection of his self-revelation and rebellious denial of his transcendent nature and beneficent character. In fact, such idolatry would constitute breach of the divine-human covenant, as the Lord's reaction to the golden calf at Mount Sinai dramatically illustrated (Exod. 32–34).

In the NT, Paul identifies covetousness as idolatry (Col. 3:5). He thereby links the first and last (tenth) commandments of the Decalogue and expands the scope of idolatry to include illegitimate desire for anything, because it displaces God in the heart just as a material image denies his presence.

William Barclay points out that idolatry is a present threat to modern people:

(i)   Idolatry means making *means into ends*. In the beginning an idol was . . . a means towards making memory and worship easier; in the end it became itself the object of worship. The means had become the end.

      This is constantly happening in the Church. A liturgy is a means of worshipping God; but an elaborate liturgy can become an end in itself, so that the means and the method of worship end by becoming more important than the worship itself. . . .

(ii) The second danger of idolatry is even more obvious. *Idolatry substitutes the thing for the person*. . . . The dead idol has taken the place of the living God.

      A man's god is that which he thinks to be the most important thing in life. His god is that to which he is prepared to give his whole time, his whole thought, his whole strength. Whenever things become more important than persons to us, then idolatry has entered into life.[14]

Due to the seriousness of idolatry, the second commandment includes a major motive clause, beginning with the words "for I the LORD your God am a jealous [*qanna'*] God" (Exod. 20:5–6; cf. 34:14; Deut. 4:24; 6:15), a Deity who is zealous to guard the exclusiveness of his covenant relationship with Israel.[15] This links to the idea of the first commandment (cf. Exod. 34:14), on which the second commandment builds.

---

14. *The Ten Commandments* (Louisville: Westminster John Knox, 1998), 11–12, emphasis original.

15. Cf. use of words from the same root *q-n-'* with reference to jealousy that a husband experiences if he suspects that his wife may have violated their exclusive marital relationship by committing adultery (Num. 5:14, 30).

The rest of the motive clause indicates punishment versus reward for those who disobey or obey not only the second commandment but other commandments (plural) as well (20:5–6). The warnings here and in the third commandment (v. 7) are as close as the Decalogue gets to indicating punishment for violation, without specifying the penalty. Punishment is extended to "the third and the fourth generation of those who hate me" (Exod. 20:5), thus limited to generations who could be included in a living extended family, not because they would inherit guilt (cf. Ezek. 18), but if they have the same attitude of hatred toward God as their parents. By contrast, God's "steadfast love [*khesed*]" extends to "thousands" (ESV, NKJV, NASB 1995; or "the thousandth generation," NJPS, NRSV, CEB; or "a thousand generations," NIV 2011) of those "who love" him and show it by their obedience (Exod. 20:6).

Laws Related to the Second Commandment

Some other pentateuchal laws reiterate the second commandment by forbidding manufacture of metal gods (Exod. 20:23; 34:17; Lev. 19:4) or making or setting up material objects of worship in other forms (Lev. 26:1).[16] Leviticus 19:4 prohibits turning to idols as objects of worship, and Deut. 12:2–4 commands the Israelites to destroy the idolatrous places and objects of the Canaanites from their land because they are not to worship YHWH in that manner.

Third Commandment: Treat the Lord's Name (Identity and Reputation) with Respect

The third commandment requires respect for YHWH's uniquely holy and exalted name: "You shall not take the name of the Lord your God in vain, for the Lord will not hold him guiltless who takes his name in vain" (Exod. 20:7; cf. Deut. 5:11). The motive clause, "for the Lord will not hold him guiltless," warns of punishment that is not specified (cf. above).

The third commandment does not prohibit taking the Lord's name at all, but only in vain.[17] Speech characterized as vain is deceitful, dishonest, false,

---

16. On the "figured stone" in Lev. 26:1, see Victor Hurowitz, "Wish upon a Stone: Discovering the Idolatry of the *Even Maskit*," *BRev* (October 1999): 51.

17. Cf., e.g., Ruth 2:4, where Boaz and his reapers use the name of YHWH respectfully in common greetings: "YHWH be with you!" and "May YHWH bless you!" (my trans.). However, people in later times moved away from saying the divine name aloud in order to avoid the danger of showing disrespect. According to the Mishnah, the name was still spoken aloud by the high priest on the Day of Atonement during the Second Temple period (*m. Yoma* 6.2), but after the Romans destroyed the temple, pronouncing the name fell into disuse.

and evil (Pss. 12:2; 41:6 [12:3; 41:7 MT]; 144:8, 11; Isa. 59:4; Ezek. 13:8). In a court setting, testimony characterized by vanity (Deut. 5:20) is false witness that is a lie (Exod. 20:16). A vain report is a false report, devoid of substance but damaging in effect (Exod. 23:1). Therefore the primary sense of uttering the name of YHWH in vain is to use it for a deceitful or evil purpose, which thereby diminishes and falsifies his reputation for having the ultimate holy character and disregards his power and status as the origin of all being: "I AM WHO I AM" (Exod. 3:14).

Laws Related to the Third Commandment

Some other laws indicate ways in which the divine name could be abused: by swearing a false oath (Lev. 19:12),[18] including to commit fraud (6:2–5 [5:21–24 MT]); by making a promise through an oath or vow to the Lord or in his name that one does not fulfill (Lev. 5:4; Num. 30:2 [30:3 MT]; Deut. 23:21–23 [23:22–24 MT]);[19] or by cursing or blaspheming God (Exod. 22:28 [22:27 MT]; Lev. 24:15–16).[20]

Any use of YHWH's name that is not in harmony with his exalted nature and character is deceitful at least in the sense that it misrepresents his incomparable identity, just as idolatry fails to do justice to his form (see above). Thus, for example, punctuating speech with empty and therefore profane references to God would falsely trivialize him. However, it is entirely appropriate to reverently utter his name in settings such as prayer, worship, or an honest judicial oath.[21]

The Hebrew word *shem*, "name," can also mean "reputation" of a human being (e.g., Deut. 22:14, 19; Prov. 22:1; Eccles. 7:1) or of the Lord (e.g., Exod. 9:16; 1 Sam. 12:22; Ezek. 20:9). His name is on his people (Num. 6:27), who belong to him because of their covenant with him (e.g., Exod. 19:4–6); and his name is at the place of his sanctuary, where his presence is among them (Deut. 12:5, 11, 21; 14:23–24; etc.).[22] Therefore, the people's behavior can affect his reputation, through which he seeks to draw other nations to himself (e.g., Deut. 4:5–8). This radically expands the scope of the third commandment,[23]

18. Cf. Ps. 24:4; Mal. 3:5.
19. Cf. Ps. 15:4; Matt. 5:33–37; James 5:12.
20. Exodus 22:28 (22:27 MT) adds "nor curse a ruler of your people," apparently because a ruler is to serve as God's representative.
21. Leviticus 19:12 prohibits only a *false oath* in YHWH's name, implying that there is no problem with an honest oath.
22. Cf. Lev. 26:2, "reverence my sanctuary." Contrast Deut. 12:3, where the Israelites are to destroy the "name" of the Canaanite gods from their cult places (cf. v. 2).
23. Cf. Dale Patrick, *Old Testament Law* (Atlanta: John Knox, 1985), 49.

which in a broad sense calls God's people to lives of comprehensive holiness in accordance with his principles so as to properly represent him in the world for a missiological purpose.[24]

Fourth Commandment: Celebrate God as the Creator-Redeemer on the Sabbath

The fourth commandment concludes the pattern of protection for YHWH's unique holiness in terms of his divinity (first commandment), form (second commandment), name/reputation (third commandment), and now his day, the Sabbath (fourth commandment). The Sabbath is external to himself, but it signifies his unique activity in the history of planet Earth for the benefit of human beings: creation (Exod. 20:11) and deliverance of Israel from Egypt (Deut. 5:15). These unique acts demonstrate his unique nature and holiness. Therefore, the fourth commandment reinforces the basis for the first three commandments.

The fourth and fifth commandments (cf. v. 12), at the center of the Decalogue and transitioning from duties toward God to responsibilities toward other humans, are similar in that they begin with positive address, by contrast to the negative formulation of the other eight commandments. In the fourth, however, with the positive injunction to keep the weekly Sabbath holy comes a prohibition that defines how it is to be kept holy: by not working. Refraining from work does not mean that observance of the Sabbath requires no effort; it is a significant change of daily routine that calls for prior preparation.[25]

The Exodus version of the fourth commandment is as follows:

> Remember the Sabbath day, to keep it holy. Six days you shall labor, and do all your work, but the seventh day is a Sabbath to the LORD your God. On it you shall not do any work, you, or your son, or your daughter, your male servant, or your female servant, or your livestock, or the sojourner who is within your gates. For in six days the LORD made heaven and earth, the sea, and all that is in them, and rested on the seventh day. Therefore the LORD blessed the Sabbath day and made it holy. (Exod. 20:8–11)

Moses's homiletical presentation of this commandment in Deuteronomy includes some substitutions and additions:

---

24. Some narratives illustrate how seriously the Lord guards his name/reputation from misrepresentation by his leaders (e.g., Lev. 10:1–3; Num. 20:10–13).
25. Cf. Exod. 16:22–24; Mark 15:42; Luke 23:54; John 19:31.

Observe the Sabbath day, to keep it holy, as the LORD your God commanded you. Six days you shall labor and do all your work, but the seventh day is a Sabbath to the LORD your God. On it you shall not do any work, you or your son or your daughter or your male servant or your female servant, or your ox or your donkey or any of your livestock, or the sojourner who is within your gates, that your male servant and your female servant may rest as well as you.

You shall remember that you were a slave in the land of Egypt, and the LORD your God brought you out from there with a mighty hand and an outstretched arm. Therefore the LORD your God commanded you to keep the Sabbath day. (Deut. 5:12–15)

Differences include the following:

1. Exodus begins "Remember" (*qal* infinitive absolute of *z-k-r*), but Deuteronomy begins "Observe," meaning "keep/guard" (*qal* infinitive absolute of *sh-m-r*).

2. Deuteronomy adds "as the LORD your God commanded you," emphasizing that this commandment was given in the past (cf. Exod. 20:8, "Remember").

3. Deuteronomy specifies the two main work animals: "your ox or your donkey or any of your livestock."

4. Deuteronomy adds: "that your male servant and your female servant may rest as well as you."

5. Most significantly, whereas the motive clause in Exodus bases the rationale for the Sabbath on the creation of the world, the Deuteronomy motive clause grounds it in redemption from Egypt, through which Israel was created as YHWH's covenant nation: "You shall remember that you were a slave in the land of Egypt, and the LORD your God brought you out from there with a mighty hand and an outstretched arm."[26] This is the same event to which the Lord refers in the introduction to the Decalogue, both in Exodus and Deuteronomy, as the reason for the Israelites' special relationship to himself and the reason why they should obey his covenant stipulations (Exod. 20:2; Deut. 5:6).

26. "The divine proclamation of covenantal law is as much a moment of creation as when God spoke to bring the world into being in Gen. 1. It is through the Sinai covenant that the nation gains its identity and history, both its past as a people redeemed from slavery and its future, which is given in the mandate to minister to the world: 'You shall become for me a kingdom of priests and a holy nation' (Exod. 19:6, my trans.)." Bernard M. Levinson, *"The Right Chorale": Studies in Biblical Law and Interpretation*, FAT 54 (Tübingen: Mohr Siebeck, 2008), 48.

The Exodus version begins with the word "Remember" (*qal* infinitive absolute of *z-k-r*; v. 8)—that is, call to mind something in the past or that already exists (cf. Gen. 40:14; Deut. 5:15; 24:9). This indicates that the Sabbath was instituted before God proclaimed the Decalogue at Mount Sinai. Indeed, the regular cycle of six work days followed by Sabbath was already regulating the weekly routine of the Israelites since he first miraculously provided them with manna on six days of each week (with a double portion on the sixth day) and commanded them to rest on the Sabbath (Exod. 16, esp. vv. 22–30).[27]

According to Gen. 2, the Sabbath originated long before the miracle of the manna. God ceased (*qal* of *sh-b-t*) from his work of creation on the seventh day of the creation week (v. 3). "So God blessed the seventh day and made it holy, because on it God rested from all his work that he had done in creation" (v. 3). This is not a direct command for humans to keep the Sabbath (noun *shabbat*, time of cessation). However, that God blessed and consecrated a day in earth time during the creation week, when he was setting up patterns for all human life, including cyclical time (1:14), indicates that he intended for all humans, made in his image (vv. 26–27), to follow his example by enjoying Sabbath rest to celebrate his creation. Jesus affirmed that the Sabbath was intended for humans from the beginning when he stated, "The Sabbath was made for man, not man for the Sabbath" (Mark 2:27).[28]

God made the Sabbath holy (*piel* of *q-d-sh*; Gen. 2:3), so its sanctity is independent of anything that human beings do. It is fixed in time like a birthday because its essence is cyclical commemoration of an event in the past: God's cessation from completion of creation on the seventh day of the creation week (Gen. 2:2–3; Exod. 20:11; 31:17).

27. Earlier, while the Israelites were still in Egypt, the pharaoh had complained to Moses and Aaron, "You make them rest [*hiphil* of *sh-b-t*] from [*min*] their burdens!" (Exod. 5:5). This combination of the *qal* of *sh-b-t*, "cease/rest" + preposition *min* + a term for work also appears in Gen. 2:2, 3 of God ceasing his work on the seventh day of the creation week, which he consecrated as the Sabbath. So perhaps Moses and Aaron were inciting the Israelites to rest on the Sabbath, just as they demanded from the pharaoh that the Israelites should be able to worship YHWH through a feast in the wilderness with sacrifices (Exod. 5:1, 3). Cf. Mathilde Frey, "Sabbath in Egypt? An Examination of Exodus 5," *JSOT* 39 (2015): 249–63.

28. How could the Sabbath be "made for man" if the first human beings were to keep working in the garden (Gen. 2:15) on the Sabbath while God rested, as if they were his slaves? In the Old Babylonian Epic of Atraḫasis, humans were created to be slaves for the gods (see trans. Benjamin R. Foster, "Atra-ḫasis," *COS* 1.130:451), but there is no indication in Genesis that YHWH designed for humans to fulfill this function. Rather, he made them in his image to have dominion over earth (1:26–28). Jesus also proclaimed himself "lord of the Sabbath" (Matt. 12:8; cf. Mark 2:28) and reaffirmed the Sabbath in the NT in the same way that God had instituted it: by his own example, including by regularly participating in worship "on the Sabbath day" (Luke 4:16, "as was his custom").

While the Sabbath is objectively holy, the Lord requires people to keep it holy (*piel* of *q-d-sh*; Exod. 20:8) in the sense that they treat it as holy and thereby participate in its holiness by abstaining from work (v. 10; cf. Jer. 17:22, 24, 27).[29] Thus Israel's observance (*qal* of *sh-m-r*) of YHWH's Sabbaths is a sign of the covenant relationship between the Israelites and YHWH, who sanctifies (*piel* of *q-d-sh*) them (Exod. 31:13; cf. vv. 16–17; Ezek. 20:12, 20). The holy covenant people (cf. Exod. 19:5–6) keep the holy covenant day.

Work (*mela'kah*) is prohibited on the Sabbath (Exod. 20:10) because this day commemorates God's cessation of his finished creation work (*mela'kah*; Gen. 2:2–3). The word *mela'kah*, "work," has a broad meaning. It can refer to all kinds of tasks, such as those involved with making things (Exod. 31:3–5); doing the occupation by which one earns a livelihood (Lev. 23:7), including agriculture (1 Chron. 27:26); and engaging in trade, including business travel (Ps. 107:23).[30] When the Lord instructed the Israelites how to keep the Sabbath in their wilderness camp, he told them: "Remain each of you in his place; let no one go out of his place on the seventh day" (Exod. 16:29). They did not have a concept of recreational walking to enjoy nature, which would have been appropriate on the Sabbath. If they had gone out, it would have been to work (cf. Num. 15:32), so God told them to stay home in order to rest.

The responsibility for resting on the Sabbath is not onerous. This day is intended to be "a delight" (Isa. 58:13),[31] an easy yoke and a light burden (cf. Matt. 11:30).[32] It is a gift from God, just as he gave manna to the Israelites to sustain them: "See! The LORD has given [*qal* of *n-t-n*] you the Sabbath; therefore on the sixth day he gives [*qal* of *n-t-n*] you bread for two days" (Exod. 16:29).

Exodus 20:10 makes the head of an Israelite family responsible for ensuring that others enjoy Sabbath rest as he does. These include members of his

29. Cf. the *piel* of *q-d-sh* in Lev. 21:8 of treating as holy a priest who was already consecrated.

30. Service for YHWH performed by the priests on the Sabbath (e.g., Lev. 24:8; Num. 28:9–10) was exempt from the prohibition of work on the Sabbath (cf. Matt. 12:5).

31. Isaiah 58:13 could simultaneously apply to the Day of Atonement Sabbath (Lev. 16:29, 31; 23:28, 30–32) in the context of Isa. 58, which refers to self-denial through fasting, etc. (vv. 3, 5), a practice that OT law required only on the Day of Atonement (Lev. 16:29, 31; 23:27, 29, 32). Cf. Shalom M. Paul, *Isaiah 40–66: Translation and Commentary*, ECC (Grand Rapids: Eerdmans, 2012), 493.

32. "When Adam and Eve sinned by showing disloyalty to God (Gen. 3:6), their marriage and work suffered from the curse of evil (3:16–19), but the Sabbath institution remains unaffected by the Fall—a little piece of Paradise." Roy Gane, *Leviticus, Numbers*, NIV Application Commentary (Grand Rapids: Zondervan, 2004), 392.

household—his children, servants, and working animals—and also his resident aliens, meaning those under his protection, who reside within the gates of his town.[33] This gives Sabbath a social-justice dimension as everyone receives the same needed benefit.

The Deut. 5 version of the fourth commandment (vv. 12–15) emphasizes the social-justice aspect in two ways. First, after the list of household members it adds, "that your male servant and your female servant may rest as well as you" (v. 14). This highlights the fact that these vulnerable persons need and deserve rest just as much as the family head, who could be tempted to exploit them by making them continue to work on the Sabbath (cf. Isa. 58:3). Exodus 23:12 conveys the same concern with addition of explicit reference to work animals and resident aliens: "that your ox and your donkey may have rest [*qal* of *n-v-kh*], and the son of your servant woman, and the alien, may be refreshed [*niphal* of *n-p-sh*]."[34]

Second, the motive clause in Deut. 5:15 expresses the reason for keeping the Sabbath in social-justice terms: "You shall remember that you were a slave in the land of Egypt, and the LORD your God brought you out from there with a mighty hand and an outstretched arm" (Deut. 5:15). Here in Deuteronomy the Sabbath celebrates God's deliverance of the Israelites from oppression by his awesome creative power (cf. Exod. 7–15).[35] Their freedom from work on the Sabbath signifies their freedom from slavery to perpetual work.[36]

The words "You shall remember that you were a slave in (the land of) Egypt" appear elsewhere in Deuteronomy to urge Israelites to empathize with disadvantaged members of their society and treat them well in gratitude for what YHWH had done for all of his people (15:15; 16:12; 24:18, 22). Therefore, remembrance of past slavery supports the command to allow subordinate members of the family, including servants, to rest as well.

33. The list does not include his wife, so presumably she is included with him.

34. Exodus 31:17 says that YHWH "was refreshed" (*niphal* of *n-p-sh*) when he rested on the seventh day of creation, but this is anthropomorphic language, apparently to emphasize that his rest served as an example to humans. Other biblical passages affirm that the Deity does not grow weary (Ps. 121:4; Isa. 40:28).

35. Some regard the exodus as a paradigm of social-justice liberation; e.g., John R. Donahue, *Seek Justice That You May Live: Reflections and Resources on the Bible and Social Justice* (New York: Paulist Press, 2014), 35–38.

36. Contrast the man in Num. 15:32–36 who gathered (*poel* of *q-sh-sh*) pieces of wood on the Sabbath as the Israelite slaves had been forced to gather (*poel* of *q-sh-sh*) straw to make bricks for the pharaoh in Egypt (Exod. 5:7, 12). Thus the wood gatherer, as a microcosm of the rebellious Israelite community that had wished to return to Egypt (Num. 14:3–4), rebelliously rejected the freedom that God had graciously provided. Mathilde Frey, "The Sabbath in the Pentateuch: An Exegetical and Theological Study" (PhD diss., Andrews University, 2011), 119–20, 124–25, 130–31.

Laws Related to the Fourth Commandment

Some other pentateuchal laws highlight aspects of the fourth commandment or expand on it. There is no exception to Sabbath rest even at the busiest times of the year: "In plowing time and in harvest you shall rest" (Exod. 34:21). "You shall kindle no fire in all your dwelling places on the Sabbath day" (35:3) rules out the household chore of cooking.[37] Profaning the holy day by working on it incurs capital punishment (31:14–15; 35:2) and the terminal divine penalty of being "cut off" (31:14).

Two verses in Leviticus contain the wording: "You shall keep my Sabbaths and reverence my sanctuary: I am the LORD" (19:30; 26:2). In 26:2 this law requiring God's people to respect his holy time and place on earth is strategically placed immediately before the covenant blessings for obedience and curses for disobedience to all of his commands (vv. 3–45). Indeed, reverence for divine holiness is foundational for living in harmony with him and his values. Those who do not grasp the meaning of holiness, with its boundaries between what is common and what is sacred, do not adequately comprehend the difference between themselves and the holy God, who is vastly superior to them and to whom they owe loyalty and obedience. Even when the physical sanctuary of God on earth is gone, the Sabbath remains as his temple in time[38] to illustrate holiness in a dimension to which all human beings have access.

Exodus 23:10–11 and Lev. 25:1–7 extend the sabbatical principle of rest during holy time from weeks to years: a Sabbath rest for the land every seventh year, when regular agricultural work of sowing, reaping, and tending is to be suspended. The Sabbatical Year fallow, which benefits the productivity of the land, acknowledges that it ultimately belongs to God and therefore he controls it (cf. Lev. 25:23). This principle becomes a crucial element in the covenant blessings and curses in Lev. 26: The Lord will bless his people on the land if they obey him, but he will curse them and exile them from the land if they persist in rebelling against him.[39]

---

37. The *piel* of *b-ʿ-r* refers to starting a fire (Jer. 7:18) or maintaining it by adding wood (Lev. 6:12 [6:5 MT]). See Num. 15:32–36, where a man was gathering sticks, no doubt to cook, on the Sabbath. This law would not appear to rule out minimum activity necessary for maintaining a fire for warmth in a cold climate, which was not an issue for the Israelites in the wilderness.

38. Abraham Heschel wrote, "Six days a week we live under the tyranny of things of space; on the Sabbath we try to become attuned to *holiness in time*. It is a day on which we are called upon to share in what is eternal in time, to turn from the results of creation to the mystery of creation; from the world of creation to the creation of the world." *The Sabbath: Its Meaning for Modern Man* (New York: Farrar, Straus & Young, 1951), 10, emphasis original.

39. See esp. Lev. 26:34–35, 43, where the land enjoys its Sabbaths, i.e., Sabbatical Years, when the Israelites have gone into exile.

As evidence of YHWH's control over the land, he promises a special blessing on the crop of the sixth year to sustain the Israelites during the fallow year until they will reap their next crop (Lev. 25:20–22).[40] This parallels the double portion of manna on the sixth day of the week to carry over the Sabbath (Exod. 16:5, 22, 29). God used his distribution of manna to test the people's faith in his ongoing creative ability to provide for them, especially over the Sabbath day (vv. 4–5, 22–29; cf. vv. 19–20), which commemorates his initial creation (see above), when he first gave food to human beings (Gen. 1:29; 2:16). Similarly, but to a much greater degree, the Sabbatical Year tests the Israelites' faith in the divine pledge that if they will be faithful to him, the land will yield its fruit and they will eat their fill (Lev. 25:18–19).

So the concept of Sabbath not only points back to the onetime event of creation but also reminds humans that the Creator-God continuously sustains their lives (cf. Ps. 145:15–16; Dan. 5:23, "the God in whose hand is your breath"). This idea is reinforced by placement of fresh bread of the Presence on the golden table in the sanctuary each Sabbath (Lev. 24:7–8) as a token of gratitude for divine provision of basic food.[41]

When the land returns to its natural state in the Sabbatical Year, property boundaries do not govern benefit from it. Thus these fallow years facilitate a kind of social justice in that whatever grows on the land without agricultural work belongs to everyone alike, including the poor and the wild animals (Exod. 23:11; Lev. 25:6–7).

After each super-sabbatical forty-ninth year (seventh Sabbatical Year = 7 × 7 years), the Israelites are to consecrate the fiftieth year as the Jubilee and proclaim liberty (Lev. 25:8–12). In addition to another fallow year for the land (vv. 11–12), YHWH grants two kinds of liberty in the Jubilee Year, taking social justice to a high level: "Each of you shall return to his property and each of you shall return to his clan" (v. 10). That is, Israelites repossess their ancestral agricultural property if they have been forced to sell it (i.e., sell the use of it until the next Jubilee) due to hard times (vv. 13–17, 23–34), and those who have sold themselves into service for others in order to survive reclaim their freedom so that they can return to their own clans (vv. 39–55; see further in chap. 13 below).

The Jubilee Year is proclaimed, and therefore begins, on the Day of Atonement, which appears strange because this is "the tenth day of the seventh month" (v. 9). However, the Jubilee is not a basic calendar year: it is an overlying functional year during which a certain set of conditions apply.

---

40. On the sequence of years in these verses, see Gane, *Leviticus, Numbers*, 434–35.
41. Roy Gane, "'Bread of the Presence' and Creator-in-Residence," *VT* 42 (1992): 179–203.

There are two additional connections between the Jubilee and the Day of Atonement, which is a ceremonial Sabbath.[42] First, the Day of Atonement is the most sacred day of each year, when the high priest uniquely enters the holy of holies in the sanctuary and purges the sanctuary with applications of sacrificial blood (Lev. 16:14–16, 18–19)[43] and when YHWH judges between those who are loyal and those who are disloyal to him (23:26–32).[44] Correspondingly, the Jubilee Year following forty-nine years is the most sacred year of each half century (25:10, "You shall consecrate the fiftieth year").

Second, the special rituals at the sanctuary on the Day of Atonement purge it from effects of human faultiness to restore the cult to its pristine state.[45] Similarly, the Jubilee Year "resets" society by liberating the land and its people from negative effects of life in an imperfect world.

42. Isaiah 58 links the themes of Day of Atonement (vv. 3, 5), liberation (v. 6), and Sabbath (vv. 13–14).

43. These applications of purification offering blood—from the bull for the priests and the goat for the nonpriestly community—in the inner sanctum and outer sanctum and on the outer altar total forty-nine (7 × 7) if applications to the four horns of the inner and outer altars are counted separately, once for each horn. First, the high priest sprinkles the blood of each animal once on the ark and seven times in front of the ark (Lev. 16:14–15). Then he performs similar blood applications in the outer sanctum (v. 16b), which means that he puts blood on each of the four horns of the incense altar (cf. Exod. 30:10) and sprinkles blood seven times in front of that object. Finally, he puts the mixed bloods of both animals on the four horns of the outer altar in the courtyard and sprinkles blood on it seven times (Lev. 16:18–19). So the number of blood applications at each part of the sanctuary is as follows:

inner sanctum: bull 1 + 7; goat 1 + 7
outer sanctum: bull 4 + 7; goat 4 + 7
outer altar: bull and goat 4 + 7

See Jacob Milgrom, *Leviticus 1–16: A New Translation with Introduction and Commentary*, AB 3 (New York: Doubleday, 1991), 1038–39; Roy Gane, *Cult and Character: Purification Offerings, Day of Atonement, and Theodicy* (Winona Lake, IN: Eisenbrauns, 2005), 224–29.

44. On the Day of Atonement as Israel's judgment day, when YHWH's people were to demonstrate their continuing loyalty to him, see Gane, *Cult and Character*, 305–16.

45. See, e.g., Lev. 16:19 regarding the outer altar: "and cleanse it and consecrate it from the uncleannesses of the people of Israel."

12

Ten Commandments and Related Laws, Part Two

This chapter continues exploration of values that the Ten Commandments exemplify by discussing commandments 5–10, which focus on duties to human beings, along with other laws that are related to them.

Fifth Commandment: Respect Parents

The fifth commandment is similar to the fourth in that it is positively formulated: "Honor your father and your mother, that your days may be long in the land that the LORD your God is giving you" (Exod. 20:12). The Deuteronomy version slightly expands this: "Honor your father and your mother, as the LORD your God commanded you, that your days may be long, and that it may go well with you in the land that the LORD your God is giving you" (5:16).

Deuteronomy adds two elements. First, "as the LORD your God commanded you" repeats the reminder that appears in the Deuteronomy version of the fourth commandment (5:12; cf. v. 15). The fact that this supplementation occurs only in the fourth and fifth commandments augments their affinity of formulation, reinforcing the possibility that there is a special connection between them. Indeed, just as the fourth commandment requires people to honor their divine creator (Exod. 20:11), the fifth commandment calls for them to honor the human beings (parents) who continued God's creative work by making them through procreation. Thus, after the Lord told the

Israelites to "be holy" as he is "holy" (Lev. 19:2), he reiterated the fifth and fourth commandments (in reverse order) together: "Every one of you shall revere his mother and his father, and you shall keep my Sabbaths: I am the Lord your God" (v. 3).[1] Holy living includes respect for the human and divine originators of our lives.[2]

Second, the insertion "and that it may go well with you" motivates the Israelites by promising them that if they obey the Lord, they will not only live long in the promised land; they will also enjoy a quality life there (Deut. 5:16).[3] The same motivation, with some variation of wording in Hebrew, also appears a number of times elsewhere in Deuteronomy (4:40; 5:33; 6:3, 18; 12:25, 28; 22:7).

Continued quality life in the land is a consequence of divine covenant blessing (cf. Lev. 26:3–13; Deut. 28:1–14), yet it also results from cause and effect as people keep laws that inherently are for their good (Deut. 10:13). In the case of the fifth commandment, respect for parents is crucial for maintaining the health and longevity of the society (see further below).

Laws Related to the Fifth Commandment

Some other laws show what it means to "honor" (*piel* of *k-b-d*) one's parents. According to Lev. 19:3, a person is to "revere/fear" (*qal* of *y-r-'*) "his mother and his father."[4] Notice placement of "mother" first here, affirming her importance as an equal parent with the father. Elsewhere this verb (*y-r-'*) is used for fear of God, the great respect that is manifested in obedience (e.g., Exod. 14:31; Deut. 4:10; 5:29; 6:2).[5] The nature of obedience changes as a

1. Note the chiastic citation, also including the reversal "his mother and his father." On such citations, see Pancratius C. Beentjes, "Discovering a New Path of Intertextuality: Inverted Quotations and their Dynamics," in *Literary Structure and Rhetorical Strategies in the Hebrew Bible*, ed. L. J. de Regt, J. de Waard, and J. P. Fokkelman (Assen, Netherlands: Van Gorcum, 1996): 31–50.

2. Thus Philo grouped the fifth commandment with the first four commandments, dividing the Decalogue into commandments 1–5 and 6–10. *The Decalogue*, ed. and trans. F. H. Colson, Loeb Classical Library (London: Heinemann, 1968), 106–21.

3. Cf. Eph. 6:2–3, "'Honor your father and mother' (this is the first commandment with a promise), 'that it may go well with you and that you may live long in the land'" (including the Deut. 5:16 addition).

4. The book of Proverbs emphasizes respect for one's parents and the need for children and young people to hear and follow instruction that they provide in harmony with divine wisdom (e.g., 1:8–9, following the statement "The fear of the Lord is the beginning of knowledge," v. 7).

5. Cf. Mal. 1:6, where the two Hebrew roots appear together in a divine speech that parallels honor for one's father with honor of a servant for his master, whom he must obey: "A son honors [*piel* of *k-b-d*] his father, and a servant his master. If then I am a father, where is my honor [noun *kabod*]? And if I am a master, where is my fear [noun *mora'* from the root *y-r-'*]?"

child develops into an independent adult,[6] but even an adult should respect and follow the wishes of the parents insofar as they are in harmony with God and divine principles (as in Gen. 42:1–3, but not 27:5–19; 1 Sam. 14:27–30). Loyalty to family members is subordinate to the primary obligation of loyalty to God (Deut. 13:6–11 [13:7–12 MT]; cf. Matt. 10:35–37). So the parental claim to honor comes with responsibility to be worthy of honor, and Paul adds: "Fathers, do not provoke your children to anger" (Eph. 6:4).

In the Bible, respect for parents includes listening to their guidance with regard to selection of a marriage partner, which is not only for the happiness of their child but also allies their family with another family.[7] Thus Isaac accepted the guidance of his father in this regard. Although Isaac's marriage to Rebekah was arranged for him, in accordance with the custom of the times, the arrangement was not based on parental whim, nor was it coercive. Rather, Abraham and his servant Eleazar relied on divine wisdom to find a suitable wife for Isaac (Gen. 24:7, 12–14, 21, 26–27, 40, 42–48), and Rebekah was allowed to choose whether to accept the marriage proposal (vv. 5, 8, 39, 41, 57–58).

In the case of Jacob, his specific selection of Rachel was sparked by love (Gen. 29:10–11, 17–18a, 20), and marriage arrangements with her father Laban followed (vv. 18b–22, 27–30). However, Jacob followed the instruction of his father, Isaac, by taking a wife from one of the daughters of his kinsman Laban rather than from among the Canaanites (28:1–2; cf. 24:3–4). It seems clear that this instruction was not arbitrary but was at least partly intended to protect Jacob from the corrupting influence of the inhabitants of Canaan (cf. Gen. 19; Exod. 34:16) so that he could enjoy the covenant blessings promised to Abraham and his descendants (Gen. 28:3–4).

Honor for parents includes properly burying them when they die. This is not stated in a law, but it is exemplified in narratives (e.g., Gen. 25:8–10; 35:29; 49:33–50:14).

Some OT laws exclude certain behaviors that dishonor parents. Whereas striking another person ordinarily incurs capital punishment only if the victim dies (Exod. 21:12), punishment for striking one's father or mother is death even if the parent survives (v. 15). Just as it is forbidden to curse God or a human ruler (22:28 [22:27 MT]), "Whoever curses his father or his mother shall be put to death" (21:17; cf. Lev. 20:9).[8]

---

6. Cf. Dale Patrick, *Old Testament Law* (Atlanta: John Knox, 1985), 51–52.

7. Cf. Raymond Westbrook and Bruce Wells, *Everyday Law in Biblical Israel: An Introduction* (Louisville: Westminster John Knox, 2009), 55.

8. Such cursing (*piel* of *q-l-l*) in the Bible is intended to bring about harm (e.g., Deut. 23:4 [23:5 MT]; 2 Kings 2:24), so it is much more serious than common cussing.

Notice that OT law allows freedom of speech except when speech is harmful, as with the kinds of curses just mentioned and also lying (Lev. 19:11), false oaths (19:12; cf. 6:3 [5:22 MT]), false witness (Exod. 20:16; Deut. 19:16–21), and leading people away from loyalty to YHWH (Deut. 13).

The most detailed law that protects honor for parents is also the most disturbing to modern readers:

> If a man has a stubborn and rebellious son who will not obey the voice of his father or the voice of his mother, and, though they discipline him, will not listen to them, then his father and his mother shall take hold of him and bring him out to the elders of his city at the gate of the place where he lives, and they shall say to the elders of his city, "This our son is stubborn and rebellious; he will not obey our voice; he is a glutton and a drunkard." Then all the men of the city shall stone him to death with stones. So you shall purge the evil from your midst, and all Israel shall hear, and fear. (Deut. 21:18–21)

This appears to be shockingly harsh treatment of a child. However, several important factors emerge from careful reading. First, although the son is still in the home of his parents, he is a grown man, or at least old enough to be characterized as "a glutton and a drunkard." Therefore he is fully accountable for his uncooperative and disrespectful behavior. Second, this is an extreme case of an incorrigible individual, as emphasized by repeated reference to his stubbornness, rebellion, and disobedience, in spite of repeated appeals from both of his parents. Third, the parents do not have the right to simply execute their son; they must submit their complaint to the city elders. If the elders concur with their judgment (assumed in the text), the son is executed by the entire community.

Presumably, the law and its procedure would be intended to bring the young man to his senses before it was too late. In any case, the fact that he is judged by the community implies that allowing a persistently rebellious individual to live is a threat to society. Egregious violation of the divine command to honor parents terminates one's right to live in the Israelite covenant community. Remember that ancient Israel had no prison system to protect society by incarcerating dangerous people at great expense, as we do today.

According to the analysis of Stephen A. Kaufman, the laws of Deut. 16:18–18:22 relate to the fifth commandment. These laws concerning appointing judges (16:18–20), the judicial system (17:2–13), the king (vv. 14–20), the priesthood (18:1–8), and prophets (vv. 9–22) "proclaim the authority figures of the nation just as the Fifth Commandment proclaims the authority of the parents within the family."[9]

Sixth Commandment: Respect Life

The sixth commandment is short: "You shall not murder" (Exod. 20:13; Deut. 5:17). Each of the following commandments in Deuteronomy begins with the conjunction *vav* (vv. 18–21), thereby connecting commandments 6–10. These commandments concern ethical interactions between human beings who are on the same social level ("neighbor" in vv. 20–21), not including parents, who can be regarded as superior in the sense that they originate life (see above).

The sixth commandment prohibits the illegal, unjustifiable taking of life. The verb is the *qal* of *r-ts-kh*, which refers (including in participial forms) to premeditated homicide (e.g., Num. 35:16–19, 21, 31) or involuntary (accidental) manslaughter (e.g., vv. 11, 25–28).[10] Premeditated homicide is first-degree murder, but unpremeditated manslaughter is not. While the language of the commandment forbids all homicide, obeying it or not involves choice, which is lacking in cases of accidents. Prohibiting an accident can only mean that one must be careful to avoid it.

The familiar KJV rendering "Thou shalt not kill" is misleading because the sixth commandment does not forbid all killing. According to OT law, justifiable killing includes slaughter of animals for food (e.g., Deut. 12:15–16, 21–24) or sacrifice (e.g., Lev. 1–9);[11] legally mandated execution of criminals convicted of capital offenses (e.g., Lev. 20:2, 27; 24:16; Num. 35:19, 21);[12] justifiable war (e.g., Num. 31; Deut. 20);[13] and self-defense killing of a person who invades one's home at night (Exod. 22:2–3 [22:1–2 MT]), implying the right to protect the lives of oneself and family members with deadly force if necessary when evidence for the intent of such an invasion is concealed by darkness.

Justifiable killing does not include suicide or active euthanasia (e.g., 1 Sam. 31:3–5; cf. 2 Sam. 1:6–16), both of which would come under the category of

9. Stephen A. Kaufman, "The Structure of the Deuteronomic Law," *Maarav* 1, no. 2 (1978–79): 133. Kaufman explains Deut. 16:21–17:1 as playing a transitional role (133–34).

10. In Num. 35:30 the *qal* of *r-ts-kh* is exceptionally used for legal execution of a murderer, making the punishment fit the crime.

11. Narratives also include justifiable killing of dangerous wild animals (e.g., Judg. 14:5–6; 1 Sam. 17:34–36).

12. Including animals that commit crimes, such as an ox that gores someone to death (Exod. 21:28–29, 32) and an animal involved in bestiality (Lev. 20:15–16; cf. under some circumstances in the Hittite Laws §199, but not in §200a).

13. But avenging a wartime death during peacetime is murder (1 Kings 2:5).

murder. However, allowing life to naturally terminate by withdrawing artificial life support is not killing; therefore it is not murder.[14]

Laws Related to the Sixth Commandment

A number of other laws are related to the sixth commandment in that they concern respect for human or animal life.[15] Already in Gen. 9, God informed Noah and his sons: "And for your lifeblood I will require a reckoning. . . . From his fellow man I will require a reckoning for the life of man. Whoever sheds the blood of man, by man shall his blood be shed, for God made man in his own image" (vv. 5–6). Murdering a human being, who is sacred because the person was created in the divine image, forfeits one's right to live on planet Earth.[16]

Notice the reason for capital punishment here: Human life is sacred because it is created in God's image, so murder is a serious form of sacrilege.[17] Thus first-degree murder is an absolute crime in OT law. Circumstances can play a role in determining whether or not it has occurred (Num. 35:16–23; Deut. 19:4–6, 11), but if it is murder, the culprit must die (Exod. 21:12, 14, 20; Lev. 24:17; Num. 35:16–21, 30; Deut. 19:11–13), with no ransom permitted (Num. 35:31, 33).[18] However, OT law mandates places of refuge for Israelites whose homicide is unpremeditated (Exod. 21:13; Num. 35:1–15, 22–29; Deut. 19:1–10)[19] and prescribes a ritual for absolution from collective responsibility for an unsolved murder case (Deut. 21:1–9).[20]

---

14. With Walter C. Kaiser Jr., "A Principlizing Model," in *Four Views on Moving beyond the Bible to Theology*, ed. Gary T. Meadors, Counterpoints (Grand Rapids: Zondervan, 2009), 27–30.

15. Kaufman ("Structure of the Deuteronomic Law," 134–37) regards the laws of Deut. 19:1–22:8 as relating to the sixth commandment in that they are concerned with taking life, under the main subtopics of homicide; war and criminal justice, "the only legitimate procedures for taking a human life"; and "the prevention of unnecessary loss of life through intentional oversight" or negligence.

16. Patrick, *Old Testament Law*, 54.

17. The prohibition of murder (Gen. 9:6) is immediately followed by the divine blessing to be fruitful and multiply (v. 7), which murder would compromise.

18. On the contrast with ANE law in this regard, see chap. 6.

19. Exodus 21:14 stipulates, "But if a man willfully attacks another to kill him by cunning, you shall take him from my altar, that he may die." This indicates that YHWH's sacred altar could be a place of asylum (cf. 1 Kings 1:50; 2:28, grasping the horns of the altar), presumably because it represented the divine realm, and executing someone who was holding it would defile the altar with corpse impurity. However, a deliberate murderer was not eligible for such protection and was to be removed from the altar to receive capital punishment (cf. 1 Kings 2:29–34, but not referring to removal from the altar).

20. On this ritual, see David P. Wright, "Deuteronomy 21:1–9 as a Rite of Elimination," *CBQ* 49 (1987): 387–403. For an extensive discussion of collective/communal responsibility, see

Respect for life requires taking safety measures to prevent accidental injury or death at one's house (by making a parapet for the roof; Deut. 22:8) or by one's powerful and aggressive animal (Exod. 21:29–31), for which the owner would be culpable. Whereas a home-invading thief can be killed at night, when victims are especially vulnerable and visibility for recognizing and disabling an attacker is poor (22:2 [22:1 MT]), even the life of such a criminal is protected by law if his attempt occurs during daylight (22:3 [22:2 MT]).

Physical assault short of homicide manifests culpable disrespect for life by endangering or partially destroying a life made in God's image. It is especially serious, incurring the death penalty, when the victim is a parent who originated the life of the assailant (Exod. 21:15). Assault is also serious when it inflicts permanent injury (*mum*), in which case literal physical talionic punishment applies: "as he has done it shall be done to him, fracture for fracture, eye for eye, tooth for tooth; whatever injury he has given a person shall be given to him" (Lev. 24:19–20; cf. chap. 3 above). When a slave loses an eye or tooth due to assault by the master, the master loses the slave, who must be set free (Exod. 21:26–27).

Temporary physical injury caused during a quarrel or brawl can incur lesser consequences. If a man is laid up in bed after being struck during a quarrel (Exod. 21:18) but subsequently "rises again and walks outdoors with his staff, he who struck him shall be clear; only he shall pay for the loss of his time, and shall have him thoroughly healed" (v. 19).

In the unusual case that brawling men knock a pregnant woman,[21] causing her to prematurely give birth[22] without a further problem, the penalty is a fine (Exod. 21:22), perhaps because premature birth could compromise the health of the baby (in the absence of modern neonatal care). However, "if there is harm [*'ason*]" to the baby or the mother or both, the lex talionis applies: "life for life, eye for eye, tooth for tooth" (vv. 23–25).[23]

David Daube, *Studies in Biblical Law* (Cambridge: Cambridge University Press, 1947; repr., New York: Ktav, 1969), 154–89.

21. Cf. the way the Laws of Hammurabi "refer to many situations that require resolution, often expressed as a complicated or hard case, by analogy to which the simpler case is readily resolved," and such a formulation (as in law §1) can reveal several points regarding the legal system. Martha T. Roth, *Law Collections from Mesopotamia and Asia Minor*, SBL Writings from the Ancient World 6 (Atlanta: Scholars Press, 1995), 71–72.

22. Rendered literally by ESV "so that her children come out [*qal* of y-ts-']," which NIV, NKJV, and NASB interpret: "she gives birth prematurely." This does not appear to be a miscarriage in this context (against NJPS, NRSV, NJB, and CEB), for which a verbal form from the root *sh-k-l* most likely would be used (Gen. 31:38; Exod. 23:26; Job 21:10; Hosea 9:14; cf. Walter C. Kaiser Jr., *Toward Old Testament Ethics* [Grand Rapids: Zondervan, 1983], 170–71), although the *qal* of y-ts-' for miscarriage does appear in Num. 12:12.

23. Elsewhere the word *'ason* only appears in Gen. 42:4, 38; 44:29 with reference to some kind of serious "harm" that could come upon Benjamin if he went to Egypt, thereby causing

At first glance the lex talionis formulation in Exod. 21:23–25 appears to call for infliction of physical damage corresponding to that which the culprit caused. However, "you shall give [qal of n-t-n]" (lit., as in NKJV; cf. CEB) in v. 23 most likely means "you shall pay" (ESV), like "he shall pay" (also qal of n-t-n) in the context of v. 22. That is, a fixed money penalty must be paid to the victim in place of variable (and probably higher) ransom money that could be demanded for loss of a life, eye, tooth, and so forth, or from an injury such as a burn or wound.[24] So "life for life" means "payment for a life in place of the life that was taken"; it does not specify capital punishment for accidental death in this case. Therefore the law does not conflict with verse 13, which indicates that the death penalty does not apply to inadvertent manslaughter.[25]

This law does not distinguish between harm to the mother and harm to the baby, nor does it specify that the fetus must have reached a certain age or stage of development in order for the fine to apply. Thus the child is regarded

loss to his father, Jacob. Bernard S. Jackson interprets 'ason, "harm," in Exod. 21:23 as miscarriage, which would provide additional support for the idea that lack of harm in verse 22 indicates live birth (Wisdom-Laws: A Study of the Mishpatim of Exodus 21:1–22:16 [Oxford: Oxford University Press, 2006], 216–18). However, it is not clear that 'ason is necessarily fatal or that it could not apply to the mother, thereby causing loss to her husband. In any case, the penalty for the loss of the baby is not simply a monetary fine, as in the Laws of Lipit-Ishtar §d and §f. It could be argued that monetary ransom is possible in Exod. 21:23–25 because it is not explicitly forbidden, as it is in a case of murder (Num. 35:31; so Kaiser, Toward Old Testament Ethics, 104). However, neither is it explicitly allowed, as it is for the owner of an ox that gores someone to death (Exod. 21:30), and Lev. 24:19 disallows ransom in application of the lex talionis by specifying: "If anyone injures his neighbor, as he has done it shall be done to him" (cf. vv. 20–21). David Daube (Studies in Biblical Law, 146) has pointed out regarding the lex talionis, "Punishment constitutes compensation in both directions: the criminal, by suffering punishment, is making restitution to the offended party, and again, in suffering punishment, receives his due." Jackson (Wisdom-Laws, 232–33) argues that the talionic expression "life for life" (nefesh takhat nefesh, i.e., person for person) refers to substitution, whether by death of the offender or by giving a live person to replace the dead one. Cf. Lev. 24:18, where "life for life" qualifies restitution (piel of sh-l-m) to indicate restitution in kind for taking the life of an animal, i.e., apparently giving a live animal in place of the dead one. However, in Exod. 21:23–24 and Deut. 19:21, "life for life" is directly followed by "eye for eye, tooth for tooth." Live substitution could not apply to eyes and teeth, etc., in an age before the possibility of transplants. Furthermore, Deut. 19:21 reads: "Your eye shall not pity. It shall be life for life," with lack of pity implying death rather than substitution.

24. Cf. Raymond Westbrook, Law from the Tigris to the Tiber: The Writings of Raymond Westbrook, ed. Bruce Wells and Rachel Magdalene, 2 vols. (Winona Lake, IN: Eisenbrauns, 2009), 2:352–58. Westbrook interprets the shift to second-person address in Exod. 21:23 ("You shall pay") as indicating that the community, addressed as "you" (as in v. 14; 22:18 [22:17 MT]), pays the compensation because the brawler who accidentally inflicted damage on a passerby is not caught, which would explain why that individual cannot be made to pay ransom as in 21:30 (here ransom for life).

25. Cf. Umberto Cassuto, A Commentary on the Book of Exodus, trans. Israel Abrahams (Jerusalem: Magnes, 1967), 276.

as a person, just as the mother is a person, throughout the pregnancy. Neither this nor any other OT law directly addresses abortion,[26] which would be unthinkable for ancient Israelites, who generally wanted as many children as possible. However, the value of the life of an unborn baby during the entire time of pregnancy rules out deliberate abortion, counting it as murder.[27]

God also holds animals accountable for killing humans (Gen. 9:5), so an ox that gores a person to death is to be stoned (Exod. 21:28–29, 32). Its owner is free from culpability unless he knows that his ox has a history of goring in the past and he has not properly restrained the animal, in which case he is to be put to death for culpable negligence that is regarded as a kind of murder (vv. 28–29). However, if he is allowed to give a ransom to save his life, he must pay whatever is demanded of him (v. 30). The fact that the law explicitly allows for this option, which is forbidden for direct murder in Num. 35:31, appears to acknowledge that the owner did not directly kill the victim.

Thus the law reflects the seriousness but limits of culpability for negligence. This balanced approach carries modern implications for the level of responsibility borne by pet owners or parents if they fail to restrain their animals or children, respectively, that are prone to violence.

Exodus 21:32 is disturbing at first glance. The verse reads: "If the ox gores a slave, male or female, the owner shall give to their master thirty shekels of silver, and the ox shall be stoned." Does this mean that a slave is not fully regarded as a person because a mere money payment can compensate for that life?

No, the difference between a slave and a free person here is not in terms of relative personhood but concerns the kind of relationship between the victim and the one(s) compensated. The relative(s) of a free person can also receive a money payment, but it is potentially much more because it is ransom for the life of the person indirectly responsible for their loss of a priceless family member. However, a master's legal vested interest in his slave is economic: the slave's capacity for labor. The fact that the master receives a

---

26. But see the Middle Assyrian Laws A §53: "If a woman aborts her fetus by her own action and they then prove the charges against her and find her guilty, they shall impale her, they shall not bury her. If she dies as a result of aborting her fetus, they shall impale her, they shall not bury her" (trans. Martha Roth, "The Middle Assyrian Laws," COS 2.132:359).

27. Richard M. Davidson, *Flame of Yahweh: Sexuality in the Old Testament* (Peabody, MA: Hendrickson, 2007), 493–97; cf. Kaiser, *Toward Old Testament Ethics*, 103, 168–72; in disagreement with interpretations such as that of Joe M. Sprinkle (*Biblical Law and Its Relevance: A Christian Understanding and Ethical Application for Today of the Mosaic Regulations* [Lanham, MD: University Press of America, 2006], 69–88), who concludes that the entire case likely assumes the death of the fetus and the law allows for the possibility that the unborn child was regarded as subhuman (88).

fixed amount of thirty shekels, apparently the price of a replacement slave, indicates that he does not own the person of a slave; he only owns the slave's work. The fact that the murderer, the ox, is to be stoned (v. 32), as it would be if the victim were a free person (cf. v. 29), acknowledges the absolute value of the slave's life.[28]

A number of laws require humans to show respect for the lives of animals, even when they kill them for food. Most prominent is the repeated and emphasized prohibition against eating meat with its blood, representing its life, which is to be drained out at the time of slaughter (Gen. 9:4; Lev. 3:17; 7:26–27; 17:10–14; 19:26; Deut. 12:16, 23–25; 15:23; cf. Acts 15:20, 29). Abstinence from consumption of the lifeblood acknowledges that humans do not have absolute control over animal life, which God alone can create. Moreover, draining the blood ensures that an animal is actually dead before part of it is eaten.[29]

Leviticus 24:17–18, 21 stipulate consequences of striking dead a human versus an animal. If the victim is a human, the penalty is death, but if it is an animal, it is to be replaced "life for life" by a similar live animal (cf. Exod. 21:36). Replacement of an animal obviously provides economic compensation for its owner, but the context here, which juxtaposes killing of a human and an animal, also indicates concern for the value of the animal's life.

Several laws maintain respect for life by regulating utilization of a young animal with its parent:[30]

> Whenever an ox or a sheep or a goat is born, it shall remain seven days with its mother, and from the eighth day on it will be acceptable as a food-gift offering to YHWH. However, no animal from the herd or from the flock shall be slaughtered on the same day as its young. (Lev. 22:27–28)[31]

> If you come across a bird's nest in any tree or on the ground, with young ones or eggs and the mother sitting on the young or on the eggs, you shall not take the mother with the young. You shall let the mother go, but the young you

28. Mesopotamian laws require money payments from owners of fatally goring oxen, with lesser payments if the victims are slaves (Laws of Eshnunna §§54–55; Laws of Hammurabi §§251–52), but there are no requirements to kill the oxen.

29. According to Lev. 3:17, it is also forbidden to eat animal fat (suet), which belongs to YHWH (v. 16). Leviticus 7:23–25 limits this dietary prohibition to fat of sacrificable species of animals, even if they died a natural death or were killed by wild animals and so were ineligible to serve as sacrificial victims, which were to be unblemished, live animals (cf. 22:18–25).

30. On treatment of animals, see further in chap. 13 below.

31. Trans. Jacob Milgrom, *Leviticus 17–22: A New Translation with Introduction and Commentary*, AB 3A (New York: Doubleday, 2000), 1304. Generic masculine forms in 22:28 include both the father and mother of the animal (cf. ibid., 1884).

may take for yourself, that it may go well with you, and that you may live long. (Deut. 22:6–7)

You shall not boil a young goat in its mother's milk. (Exod. 23:19; 34:26; Deut. 14:21)[32]

Seventh Commandment: Respect Marriage

The seventh commandment is "You shall not commit adultery" (Exod. 20:14; cf. Deut. 5:18). Adultery (here *qal* of *n-'-p*) is defined as voluntary extramarital sexual relations. However, the ancient understanding of adultery differed from our modern one in two respects, due to cultural factors. First, the fact that ancient betrothal was more binding than modern engagement affected the definition of "extramarital." When a betrothal process reached the stage that the man had given the marriage present (cf. Gen. 34:12; Exod. 22:16b [22:15b MT]), his fiancée was considered his "wife" so that her voluntary sexual relations with any other man was treated as adultery (Deut. 22:23–24, "his neighbor's wife"). The Bible does not institute this kind of betrothal but assumes it, so there is no reason for modern Christians to adopt it.

Second, ancient toleration of polygamy resulted in a double standard regarding the working definition of adultery: Culpable adultery was limited to sexual relations between a married woman and any man other than her husband.[33] But a married man could take another wife or concubine, so he could get away with extending the scope of his sexual activity to an additional woman if she was not already married to someone else. Polygamy was a nonideal aspect of ancient culture that God did not initiate, so modern Christians should not take it as license for married men to engage in extramarital affairs with unmarried women.

Like murder, adultery is an absolute crime in OT law. Circumstances can be cited to determine whether an illicit sexual encounter involving a married

---

32. On possible rationales for this law, including prohibition of a Canaanite practice, for which there is no evidence, and the suggestion by some medieval Jewish exegetes that the motivation is humanitarian, see, e.g., Nahum M. Sarna, *Exodus: The Traditional Hebrew Text with the New JPS Translation*, JPS Torah Commentary (Philadelphia: Jewish Publication Society, 1991), 147; William H. C. Propp, *Exodus 19–40: A New Translation with Introduction and Commentary*, AB 2A (New York: Doubleday, 2006), 285–86. Repetition of the prohibition in the Pentateuch, which raises its prominence, suggests that it was intended to end a well-known practice. For the rabbinic generalization of the prohibition to cooking the meat and milk of any clean cattle together, see *m. Hullin* 8.4.

33. Anthony Phillips points out that paternity was a major concern. *Essays on Biblical Law*, JSOTSup 344 (London: Sheffield Academic, 2002), 79.

or betrothed woman was voluntary (adultery) or forced (rape), but if the offense is adultery, the penalty can only be death (Lev. 20:10; Deut. 22:22) if the act was apprehended by humans.[34] This is unlike some ANE laws outside the Bible, in which the husband of an adulteress has the right to decide her punishment and the state applies equivalent punishment to her paramour.[35]

Suspected adultery is exceptional. If there are no human witnesses, but God himself convicts the woman through a ritual at the sanctuary (Num. 5:11–31), she suffers severe physical consequences and shame (v. 27), but not death. This may be to make her an ongoing example.

Laws Related to the Seventh Commandment

The prohibition of adultery in the seventh commandment exemplifies the imperative of sexual purity.[36] Other laws further protect sexual purity by reiterating this prohibition, assigning penalties, and forbidding other kinds of behaviors, as shown in the following table.[37] The relative seriousness of a penalty indicates the gravity of a given offense.

This table raises some questions for modern readers, such as the following:

1. Why does a promiscuous daughter of a priest receive such a harsh penalty (Lev. 21:9)?

34. Under OT law, even the husband of an adulteress could not lessen her punishment or that of her lover, because their offense was not only a wrong against the husband, but it was also a great sin against the Lord. Moshe Greenberg, "Some Postulates of Biblical Criminal Law," in *Yehezkel Kaufmann Jubilee Volume*, ed. Menahem Haran (Jerusalem: Magnes, 1960), 12–13; Greenberg, "More Reflections on Biblical Criminal Law," in *Studies in Bible*, ed. Sara Japhet, ScrHier 31 (Jerusalem: Magnes, 1986), 2–4; Phillips, *Essays on Biblical Law*, 74–93.

35. Laws of Hammurabi §129; Middle Assyrian Laws A §§14–15, 23a; Hittite Laws §§197–98. By contrast to OT law, Mesopotamian law was subjective concerning adultery: While adultery could automatically incur capital punishment (e.g., Middle Assyrian Laws A §13), penalties for adultery in some kinds of circumstances were affected by degrees of apparent intention. Greenberg, "Some Postulates," 12; Jacob J. Finkelstein, "Sex Offenses in Sumerian Laws," *JAOS* 86 (1966): 355–72.

36. Kaufman ("Structure of the Deuteronomic Law," 113, 138) sees Deut. 22:9–23:18 (22:9–23:19 MT) as relating to the seventh commandment. This section includes the law against mixtures (22:9–11), the requirement to make tassels on garments (v. 12), rules about illicit sexual relations (22:13–30 [22:13–23:1 MT]), sexual "wholeness and genetic purity as requirements for membership in God's community" (23:1–8 [23:2–9 MT]), sexual "purity and cleanliness in the military camp" (23:9–14 [23:10–15 MT]), escaped slaves (23:15–16 [23:16–17 MT]; transitional), and prohibitions against Israelite women becoming cult prostitutes or bringing the fee of a prostitute into the temple to fulfill a vow (23:17–18 [23:18–19 MT]).

37. A negative confession in the Egyptian Book of the Dead refers to a kind of sexual activity that is not mentioned in the Bible: "I have not masturbated" (trans. Robert K. Ritner, "Book of the Dead 125," *COS* 2.12:61).

Violations of Sexual Purity in Old Testament Law

Reference	Behavior	Penalty
Exod. 20:14; Lev. 18:20, 29; 20:10; Deut. 5:18; 22:22	adultery involving married woman	death of both and "cut off"
Deut. 22:23–24	adultery involving betrothed woman	death of both by stoning
Num. 5:11–31	adultery by married woman convicted through suspected adulteress ritual	"bitter pain, and her womb shall swell, and her thigh shall fall away, and the woman shall become a curse among her people" (v. 27)
Lev. 21:9	promiscuity of priest's daughter	burning (presumably after death)
Deut. 22:20–21	promiscuity of daughter before marriage	death by stoning at the door of her father's house
Deut. 22:25–27	rape of betrothed woman	death of rapist
Deut. 22:28–29	rape of unbetrothed virgin	"fifty shekels of silver, and she shall be his wife. . . . He may not divorce her all his days"
Exod. 22:16–17 (22:15–16 MT)	seduction of unbetrothed virgin	"he shall give the bride-price for her and make her his wife. If her father utterly refuses to give her to him, he shall pay money equal to the bride-price for virgins"
Lev. 19:20–22	illicit sex with assigned slave woman	sacrifice ram for reparation offering
Lev. 19:29	prostitution	(none)
Lev. 18:19, 29; 20:18	intercourse during menstruation	"cut off"
Lev. 18:6–18, 29; 20:11–12, 14, 17, 19–21; Deut. 22:30	various kinds of incest[a]	all "cut off" (divine penalty); varying additional penalties, including death, burning (presumably after death), and childlessness
Lev. 18:22, 29; 20:13	homosexual activity	death and "cut off"
Exod. 22:19 (22:18 MT); Lev. 18:23, 29; 20:15–16	bestiality	death and "cut off"; animal killed

a. On the kinds of relationships defined as incest in Lev. 18 and 20, as well as the Laws of Hammurabi and the Hittite Laws, see Roy E. Gane, "Leviticus," in *Zondervan Illustrated Bible Backgrounds Commentary*, ed. John H. Walton (Grand Rapids: Zondervan, 2009), 1:310–11. For detailed discussion of the incest laws in Lev. 18, see Milgrom, *Leviticus 17–22*, 1523–49; Susan Rattray, "Marriage Rules, Kinship Terms and Family Structure in the Bible," in *Society of Biblical Literature 1987 Seminar Papers*, ed. Kent Richards, SBLSP 26 (Atlanta: Scholars Press, 1987), 542. Incest laws implicitly include prohibition of child abuse within extended families (cf. Roy E. Gane, *Leviticus, Numbers*, NIV Application Commentary [Grand Rapids: Zondervan, 2004], 331). Note that uncovering (*piel* of g-l-h) nakedness is a euphemism for sexual relations in Lev. 18 and 20.

Her crime is especially serious because, according to this verse, she profanes her father, who is consecrated to God. On severe punishments, see chapter 14 below.

2. Why does a man who rapes an unbetrothed virgin get to marry her (Deut. 22:28–29)? Doesn't this punish the woman instead of the man?

     In ancient Israelite society, marriage in cases of rape or seduction of unbetrothed virgins protected them from lack of support that would almost inevitably result if no other man would want to marry them because they had lost their virginity.

3. Why is a man who engages in illicit sex with a servant woman designated for marriage to another man merely required to sacrifice a ram as a reparation offering (Lev. 19:20–22)?

     Illicit sex between a man and a consenting, free, betrothed woman is treated as adultery, with both parties subject to capital punishment (Deut. 22:23–24). However, a designated/betrothed servant woman is not held accountable for adultery because she lacks the legal ability to consent and the culpability that would come with it. She is protected, apparently due to her social vulnerability to pressure, including sexual harassment. Because she is not treated as an adulteress, her lover is technically not an adulterer and cannot be put to death either. However, he must offer a sacrifice because he has sinned against God.[38] This shows that the socially stronger person is primarily responsible, a principle that can apply today to illicit relationships between teachers and students, employers and employees, and so forth.[39]

4. Why is there no punishment for prostitution (Lev. 19:29)?

     This verse prohibits fathers from making their daughters serve as prostitutes. The law does not specify a penalty for violation, but the fact that YHWH forbids it implies that he would hold fathers accountable. While OT law clearly disapproves of prostitution, it does not call for punishment on prostitutes themselves, likely because such single women were often victims of unfortunate circumstances, such as extreme difficulty of surviving in other ways and/or male chauvinist abuse.

---

38. Milgrom, *Leviticus 17–22*, 1665–66, 1672–75. Milgrom points out that the man who has sex with her is not required to compensate her owner, because she is betrothed to another man (1665).

39. An extreme case is King David's adultery with his young subject Bathsheba, for which David received all the blame from God, as communicated through the prophet Nathan, and Bathsheba and her husband were regarded as victims (2 Sam. 11–12).

5. What is the problem with sex during menstruation (Lev. 18:19, 29; 20:18)?
   See chapter 15 below.
6. Why is polygamy not in the above list as a violation of sexual purity according to OT law?[40]
   See chapter 13 below.

Deuteronomy 22:5 raises another issue related to sexual purity: "A woman shall not wear a man's garment,[41] nor shall a man put on a woman's cloak, for whoever does these things is an abomination to the LORD your God." Scholars have debated the reason for this law, but in any case, it clearly rules out deliberate attempts to switch or blur gender identities through cross-dressing.[42] In the Bible there are two genders, male and female, as defined by their distinctive physical characteristics, and the differences between these genders are to be recognized in society, apparently to avoid confusion and temptations to engage in immoral behavior. Such temptations would not only be to homosexual activity. Heterosexuals could come into closer contact than they would otherwise if one is mistaken to belong to the same gender.

The law does not directly address transgender individuals, but it seems relevant to a significant aspect of their lives. There is no question that such persons suffer due to real dissonance, beyond their control, between their perceived (mental and emotional) gender identities and their biological sexual makeup. Discussion of this sensitive dilemma is beyond the scope of the present volume, but it appears that Deut. 22:5 would encourage a transgender person to prioritize physical gender as the factor that determines one's place in society, as indicated by what one wears.

Eighth Commandment: Respect Property Rights of Others

The eighth commandment is "You shall not steal" (Exod. 20:15; cf. Deut. 5:19). This prohibits the wrongful (without permission or right) misappropriation

40. Leviticus 18:18 does prohibit marriage to two sisters at the same time, because it is regarded as incestuous.
41. Hebrew *keli*, which has a much broader meaning than clothing and could refer here to anything normally worn by a man, including a decoration or piece of equipment. Jeffrey H. Tigay, *Deuteronomy: The Traditional Hebrew Text with the New JPS Translation*, JPS Torah Commentary (Philadelphia: Jewish Publication Society, 1996), 200; Daniel I. Block, *Deuteronomy*, NIV Application Commentary (Grand Rapids: Zondervan, 2012), 512.
42. See, e.g., Tigay, *Deuteronomy*, 200; Block, *Deuteronomy*, 512.

of something that belongs to someone else.[43] The basic meaning is clear and simple, but its application varies because there are many ways to steal.

The OT law prescribes economic penalties for theft, such as restitution or fines, except when that which is stolen is a human (kidnapped), in which case the punishment is death (Exod. 21:16; Deut. 24:7; cf. Laws of Hammurabi §14). Thus the Bible clearly prioritizes the value of a human being above that of nonhuman property. The Laws of Hammurabi reflect a different value system, calling for capital punishment in some cases when nonhuman property is stolen (§§6–7, 9–10, 22, 25).[44]

Laws Related to the Eighth Commandment

Other OT laws illustrate ways to justly protect property rights. A number of these laws concern elements of the ancient agricultural subsistence economy that modern Western people do not experience in their home countries. Nevertheless, we can see transferable principles of honest dealing, equitable ownership, and circumstantially conditioned degrees of responsibility in treatment of property.

Leviticus 19:11 reiterates the prohibition against stealing (but in plural address), followed by other kinds of dishonesty: "You shall not deal falsely; you shall not lie to one another." Indeed, deception and lying are often involved with stealing. Three ways to steal through deception that are forbidden in OT law are by using dishonest measures in trade (Lev. 19:35–36; Deut. 25:13–16), moving a landmark to gain some of a neighbor's ancestral real estate (Deut. 19:14), and defrauding another person through swearing a false oath (Lev. 6:1–5 [5:20–24 MT]).[45]

43. In some other contexts the Hebrew verb used here, *qal* of *g-n-b*, can refer to secret but justifiable movement, such as recovering the bones of Saul and Jonathan from the Philistines (2 Sam. 21:12) and rescuing Joash from Athaliah (2 King 11:2; 2 Chron. 22:11).

44. On the contrast between the biblical and ANE value systems regarding life and property, see Moshe Greenberg, "Some Postulates," 13–20. Greenberg observes that "in biblical law life and property are incommensurable; taking of life cannot be made up for by any amount of property, nor can any property offense be considered as amounting to the value of a life. Elsewhere the two are commensurable: a given amount of property can make up for life, and a grave enough offense against property can necessitate forfeiting life" (18–19). Greenberg defends his assessment of these value systems in "More Reflections," 4–17.

45. Jacob Milgrom comments on Lev. 6:3 (5:22 MT), "Not only has the offender wronged his fellow but he has denied it under oath. Assumed is that in the ancient Near East the plaintiff could always demand that the unapprehended but suspected criminal be put under oath" (*Leviticus 1–16: A New Translation with Introduction and Commentary*, AB 3 [New York: Doubleday, 1991], 337). Note that the words "You shall not swear by my name falsely, and so profane the name of your God" in Lev. 19:12 immediately follow the prohibition against stealing and lying in v. 11.

It is particularly serious to steal from God by not fulfilling a vow to him (Deut. 23:21–23 [23:22–24 MT]) or by sacrilegiously misappropriating something holy that belongs to him (Lev. 5:15–16), such as a tithe (e.g., 27:30, 32).[46] The divine execution of Ananias and Sapphira in Acts 5:1–11 dispels any doubt as to the ongoing need for complete honesty toward God. Another kind of sacrilege is to misuse God's land by not allowing it to lie fallow during a sacred Sabbatical or Jubilee Year (Lev. 25:1–7, 10–12; 26:34–35, 43).

The penalty for theft of a domestic animal is multiple restitution, with the amount (double, fourfold, fivefold) depending on the kind/value of the stolen animal and whether it is recovered from the thief (Exod. 22:1, 4 [21:37; 22:3 MT]). If the thief lacks the means to pay, he is sold as a slave to repay the debt (22:3 [22:2 MT]). Presumably similar principles would apply to theft of inanimate property. Notice that these remedies for theft directly compensate the victims, by contrast to modern law that treats theft as a crime against the state, so that the victims may receive no restitution even if the thief is caught.

Theft can occur when a person entrusts an object to another for safekeeping (Exod. 22:7–9 [22:6–8 MT]). If it is lost to the owner, did the trusted party take it, or did something else happen? If a third-party thief is caught, he must pay double (v. 7 [v. 6 MT]). If such a thief is not found, a kind of legal procedure before God (an oath or judgment by priests, possibly involving the divine oracle?), probably at his sanctuary, can clear suspicion from the trusted person or condemn him (vv. 8–9 [vv. 7–8 MT]). Such a procedure can also settle cases in which two parties claim a lost item (v. 9 [v. 8 MT]).

When property entrusted for safekeeping is an animal, possible reasons for loss increase to include its death or injury, or it "is driven away, without anyone seeing it" (Exod. 22:10 [22:9 MT]).[47] These are circumstances that the person responsible could not prevent, so he must only swear an oath to the effect that he did not steal the animal (v. 11 [v. 10 MT]). However, he is responsible for negligence if someone simply steals the animal from him, so he must make restitution (v. 12 [v. 11 MT]). Nevertheless, he owes no restitution if the animal is torn apart by a wild creature and he presents its carcass as evidence (v. 13 [v. 12 MT]). This implies that he is not required to risk his life to save the animal from a vicious beast.[48]

If a borrowed animal is injured or dies when its owner is not with it, the borrower must make restitution (Exod. 22:14–15a [22:13–14a MT]). Thus, a

46. Leviticus 5:15–16 provides a remedy that leads to forgiveness for such sacrilege if it is inadvertent, but not for deliberate sacrilege.

47. This is "cattle rustling, . . . not the same as ordinary theft mentioned in verse 11 [12 Eng.]." Sarna, *Exodus*, 133.

48. As young David did (1 Sam. 17:34–35).

borrower who has received free use of an animal for his benefit logically has greater responsibility than an individual to whom an owner has entrusted his animal for the owner's benefit.

A person must make restitution or payment when he indirectly causes loss to another person's property (Exod. 21:33–36; 22:5–6 [22:4–5 MT]). However, the owner of an ox that unexpectedly kills someone else's ox bears minimal responsibility (Exod. 21:35) in the absence of the aggravating factors that his ox has a past history of such behavior and he has been negligent in restraining it (v. 36).

A man who seduces and has sex with an unbetrothed virgin causes economic damage to her family (among other things). Once she has lost her virginity, another man who might want to marry her will not pay the bride-price for virgins. Therefore the man who took away her virginity must "give the bride-price for her and make her his wife" (Exod. 22:16 [22:15 MT]); if her father refuses to allow the marriage, the man must make restitution by paying "money equal to the bride-price for virgins" (v. 17 [v. 16 MT]).

Several laws protect rights of inheritance. In the event that the unloved wife of a man having two wives bears his firstborn son (cf. Gen. 29:31–32), he is not permitted to unjustly bypass this son and confer the rights of the firstborn on the son of his beloved wife (Deut. 21:15–17). So inheritance rights are to be shielded from marital favoritism. Although modern Christians do not practice bigamy or assign double portions to their firstborn, the overall principle of insulating inheritance rights from marital favoritism can apply in modern culture to protect inheritance rights of older children produced by a previous marriage that ended in divorce.

Two laws concern female roles in protecting inheritance. First, the inheritance of a man whose surviving children include only daughters is to pass through them (Num. 27:7–8). Second, levirate marriage produces a surrogate heir for a childless man through the union of his widow and his surviving brother (Deut. 25:5–10).

A number of social-justice measures protect poor persons and even animals from exploitation that would cause them hardship through a form of stealing from them. Poor day laborers have the right to receive their wages at the end of the work day (Lev. 19:13; Deut. 24:14–15), and an ox has the right to eat from the grain that it threshes (Deut. 25:4). A garment taken in pledge (collateral) for a loan must be returned by nightfall so that its owner can keep warm through the night (Exod. 22:26–27 [22:25–26 MT]; Deut. 24:12–13), and it is forbidden to take a widow's garment in pledge at all (Deut. 24:17). It is also forbidden to take an essential tool for survival (hand mill or even an upper millstone) in pledge (v. 6).[49] Charging interest on a loan to a poor Israelite is not permitted (Exod. 22:25 [22:24 MT]; Lev. 25:36–37; Deut. 23:19–20 [23:20–21 MT]).[50]

Laws that regulate various forms of servitude protect vulnerable Israelites from exploitation by placing limits on the period and/or conditions of service and by providing opportunity for their redemption under some circumstances (Exod. 21:2; Lev. 25:39–55; Deut. 15:12, 18). However, Exod. 21:4 also protects the rights of the master: "If his master gives him a wife and she bears him sons or daughters, the wife and her children shall be her master's, and he shall go out alone."

Several laws go beyond the negative concept of prohibiting stealing (including exploitation) to the corresponding positive idea of providing assistance to those in need. Thus an Israelite should help another (even his enemy) with his animal or lost property (Exod. 23:4–5; Deut. 22:1–4), allow a neighbor to eat (but not harvest) from his vineyard or field of grain (Deut. 23:24–25 [23:25–26 MT]), leave remnants of his harvest for poor gleaners (Lev. 19:9–10; Deut. 24:19–21), and allow anyone (including the poor and wild animals) to eat what grows by itself on his land during a Sabbatical or Jubilee Year (Exod. 23:10–11; Lev. 25:5–7, 11–12). Because nobody works to plant, prune, or harvest in a Sabbatical or Jubilee Year, nobody can claim exclusive ownership of what comes up from the land, which ultimately belongs to God (Lev. 25:23).

Some laws are designed to assist Israelites in supporting themselves independently. These include the injunction to help (lit., "strengthen") one's countryman if he is in financial difficulty (Lev. 25:35) and provisions for cyclical debt release (Deut. 15:1–3; but not for foreigners), redemption of real estate (Lev. 25:24–27, 29, 31–33),[51] and the automatic, cyclical release of ancestral real estate in the Jubilee Year that restores equitable land distribution (Lev. 25:13–16, 28, 31, 33; see chap. 13 below).

Ninth Commandment: Tell Only the Truth about Others

The ninth commandment logically belongs near the end of the Decalogue, concluding the commandments that can be enforced by the human legal system (at least in some cases), because it concerns misuse of that system to accuse

---

49. On different kinds of loans and pledges in ancient Israel and elsewhere in the ANE, see Westbrook and Wells, *Everyday Law*, 112–16.

50. Although it is permitted to charge a foreigner interest (Deut. 23:20 [23:21 MT]).

51. However, redemption was intended to keep land in the extended family (cf. Jer. 32:8), not necessarily to restore it to the original owner. Westbrook and Wells, *Everyday Law*, 122.

and condemn individuals for violations of any of the earlier commandments or laws related to them. The tenth commandment, against coveting (Exod. 20:17; Deut. 5:21), is separate from the first nine commandments since it is a thought process that only God can judge (see below).

The ninth commandment prohibits a false (lying or deceptive) legal testimony against another person: "You shall not bear false witness against your neighbor" (Exod. 20:16; cf. Deut. 5:20). A testimony of accusation can precipitate a court case that results in condemnation and punishment of a person who is found to be guilty, and testimony can play a key role in determination of the verdict. Therefore, a false accusation or court testimony can lead to unjust punishment. It can even result in death of an innocent person for a capital crime, which brings the guilt of murder on those who are guilty of perpetrating the lethal lie (cf. Exod. 23:7; 1 Kings 21; cf. Matt. 26:60–66).

Ancient Israelite courts mostly relied on testimony from witnesses as evidence for reaching verdicts.[52] This set a high standard of evidence for conviction, which protected innocent defendants,[53] but such testimony could be easily corrupted from various motivations, with major consequences. So it was imperative that the people should be God-fearing, knowing that they were accountable to the omniscient and omnipotent Deity even when they could get away with fooling humans. Individuals who are not God-fearing cannot be trusted, but the Lord holds them accountable anyway (1 Kings 21).

The ninth commandment rules out a certain kind of dishonesty: using falsehood to harm another person by making them vulnerable to unfair negative consequences through legal action. This is not a comprehensive prohibition against all lying, which is found outside the Decalogue. The fact that the important general injunction "You shall not lie to one another" (Lev. 19:11) appears in another law collection (the so-called Holiness Code) illustrates the error of the common notion that "Mosaic" laws outside the Ten Commandments are irrelevant or peripheral for Christians.

Laws Related to the Ninth Commandment

Lying about someone else to harm their reputation in any context, including with legal implications, is slander, which Lev. 19:16 forbids: "You shall not go around as a slanderer among your people." This law rules out damaging speech, including gossip (cf. Rom. 1:29–30; 2 Cor. 12:20; 1 Tim. 5:13).[54]

52. Bruce Wells, *The Law of Testimony in the Pentateuchal Codes*, BZABR 4 (Wiesbaden: Harrassowitz, 2004), esp. 1.
53. Cf., e.g., Gane, *Leviticus, Numbers*, 802–3.
54. For some ANE texts that discourage slander, see Gane, "Leviticus," 313.

Exodus 23 juxtaposes and thereby implicitly associates the spreading of a false report with an agreement to be a malicious witness (lit., "witness of violence"), and it warns against siding with the majority to pervert justice (vv. 1–2). Legal proceedings are to be conducted with complete impartiality (Exod. 23:6; Lev. 19:15; Deut. 16:19), including without reverse discrimination (Exod. 23:3; Lev. 19:15), and of course without bribery (Exod. 23:8; Deut. 16:19). "Justice, and only justice, you shall follow" (Deut. 16:20). The prohibition against falsely swearing by YHWH's name (Lev. 19:12), which would violate the third commandment (Exod. 20:7; see above), could also apply to a court situation when a false oath by a witness could reinforce false testimony.

Truth can be compromised by nonverbal means, such as gestures and facial expressions, or by simply doing nothing. Thus a person who "hears a public adjuration to testify, and though he is a witness, whether he has seen or come to know the matter, yet does not speak, he shall bear his iniquity" (Lev. 5:1).[55] Not only shall you "not go about as a slanderer among your kin; you shall not stand aloof beside the blood of your fellow" (19:16)[56] if you could say or do something to save the innocent person from conviction and punishment resulting from a slanderous false charge (cf. Exod. 23:7).[57] Notice here the strong connection to the principle of respect for life represented by the sixth commandment, against murder. Of course, the same principle of rescuing someone from injustice would also apply when life is not threatened.

Some trial-and-punishment procedures provide partial insulation against dishonesty or undue subjectivity on the part of witnesses. A minimum of two witnesses is necessary to convict a defendant of wrongdoing (Deut. 19:15), especially in a capital case (17:6). This reduces risk from a personal grudge or inadequate perspective of one individual, but it does not eliminate the possibility of collusion between two or more witnesses to testify falsely (cf. Exod. 23:1; cf. 1 Kings 21:10, 13; Matt. 26:60–61). To ensure that witnesses in a capital case take their role seriously, they are to initiate the execution process if the defendant is condemned (Deut. 17:7; cf. Lev. 24:14).

Deuteronomy 19:16–21 directly targets malicious false witnesses. If they are caught through judicial inquiry, they are subjected to the lex talionis: The same penalty that the wrongly accused person would have received

55. "The wrongdoing referred to in verse 1 has to do with a potential witness, who is required to give testimony in a particular case but who fails to come forward and make a statement." Wells, *Law of Testimony*, 56.

56. Trans. Milgrom, *Leviticus 17–22*, 1298.

57. Ibid., 1645. Thus Lev. 19:16 continues the theme of justice in court that v. 15 introduces.

if condemned is inflicted on the witness.[58] This is intended as a serious deterrent to anyone else contemplating the nefarious strategy of false witness (v. 20).

In Lev. 19, immediately following laws against injustice in court, slander, and standing by while your neighbor dies (vv. 15–16), vv. 17–18 seek to prevent the underlying causes behind false witness: "You shall not hate your brother in your heart, but you shall reason frankly with your neighbor, lest you incur sin because of him. You shall not take vengeance or bear a grudge against the sons of your own people, but you shall love your neighbor as yourself: I am the LORD."

Tenth Commandment: Be Content with What You Can Rightfully Have

The tenth commandment (Exod. 20:17; Deut. 5:21) is unique in the Decalogue in that it forbids a kind of attitude: coveting, a strong desire/greed to own something that belongs to someone else.[59] Only God can detect such evil before it is manifested in outer behavior, because he alone can read thoughts (e.g., Ps. 139:1–2, 4, 23–24).[60] This and other laws regulating thoughts that can lead to actions (Lev. 19:17–18; Deut. 15:9–10) reflect the OT claim that its law is divinely mandated and enforced.

Such laws challenge God's people to nip temptations in the bud by choosing to reject sins while they are still only potentialities in the mind, without allowing them to bear evil fruit as actions or words that cause external damage.[61] This is Jesus's point in his Sermon on the Mount discourse regarding the sins of anger and lust in relation to murder and adultery, respectively (Matt. 5:21–30). People are guilty of sins that they decide they would commit if they

58. Cf. Laws of Hammurabi §1, "If a man accuses another man and charges him with homicide but cannot bring proof against him, his accuser shall be killed" (trans. Martha Roth, "The Laws of Hammurabi," COS 2.131:337).

59. On the importance of this commandment and the question of whether it constitutes one commandment (Jewish and Reformed numbering) or two commandments (Catholic and Lutheran numbering), see Patrick D. Miller, *The Ten Commandments*, Interpretation: Resources for the Use of Scripture in the Church (Louisville: Westminster John Knox, 2009), 388–89. Kaufman ("Structure of the Deuteronomic Law," 142–43) relates to the tenth commandment the laws in Deut. 25:5–16, including the law of levirate marriage (vv. 5–10, "the property of his brother, no matter how desirable in his own eyes, remains in his brother's estate"), the prohibition against a wife seizing the genitals of a man fighting her husband (vv. 11–12), and having honest measures (vv. 13–16).

60. Cf. Jesus's reading thoughts (Luke 7:39–48).

61. Cf. the trajectory described by James, "But each person is tempted when he is lured and enticed by his own desire. Then desire when it has conceived gives birth to sin, and sin when it is fully grown brings forth death" (1:14–15).

have the opportunity. Jesus was not creating a new area of ethics here; he was simply drawing out implications in OT law.

The principle of Jesus's words regarding lust, "Everyone who looks at a woman with lustful intent has already committed adultery with her in his heart" (Matt. 5:28), would apply to viewing pornography, whether of females, males, or both. Lust for those to whom one is not married, involving covetousness and desire to participate in illicit sex, is what pornography is all about.

The Exod. 20:17 version of the tenth commandment is as follows: "You shall not covet your neighbor's house; you shall not covet your neighbor's wife, or his male servant, or his female servant, or his ox, or his donkey, or anything that is your neighbor's." Here "house" is placed separately before repetition of the verb "covet," followed by examples of persons and other things that also belong to the male head of household, whom the formulation addresses.

At first glance this could be taken to demean the wife as a mere possession of her husband, even less important than his house. However, it seems clear that "house" refers to the house and everything included in or connected with it, thus a man's "household." So this logically appears first as a kind of summary, with itemized contents following, including the wife, who is an important member of the household, not her husband's chattel.[62]

The Deut. 5:21 version reflects a somewhat different perspective regarding objects of coveting: "And you shall not covet your neighbor's wife. And you shall not desire your neighbor's house, his field, or his male servant, or his female servant, his ox, or his donkey, or anything that is your neighbor's." Here the wife appears separately at the beginning before another (synonymous) verb, followed by "house . . . field," and so on. In this context, the wife is implicitly superior to everything else, and the "house" is only an item of real estate along with the "field" (added here).

Laws Related to the Tenth Commandment

The tenth commandment implicitly relates to many other OT laws because covetousness is a root of evil (Isa. 14:13–14) that can sprout into adultery (breaking Decalogue commandment 7), theft (commandment 8), murder (6) if one or more people get in the way of what one wants, and false witness (9) if it facilitates acquisition of an illicitly desired object. Coveting can also lead to dishonoring parents (5) by taking what rightfully belongs to them or is due to them.

One who yields to the temptation of coveting may even break the first four commandments, which concern obligations to God, in the following ways: by

---

62. Cf. R. Davidson, *Flame of Yahweh*, 249.

swearing a false oath in YHWH's name (3) in order to defraud, working on the Sabbath (4) to (therefore illicitly) acquire something, making or worshiping an idol (2) for (therefore illicit) profit or benefit, or in any of the above ways by treating an object of greed as a god that is more important than the Lord (1).[63] So observance of the tenth commandment protects people by preventing a plethora of troubles.

The opposite of covetousness and greed is contentment with what one rightfully possesses or can acquire. Paul testified concerning himself: "I have learned in whatever situation I am to be content. I know how to be brought low, and I know how to abound. In any and every circumstance, I have learned the secret of facing plenty and hunger, abundance and need. I can do all things through him who strengthens me" (Phil. 4:11–13; cf. 1 Tim. 6:6–8; Heb. 13:5). For Paul, as for other people in our fallen world, contentment was not automatic or easy; he learned it and needed divine strength to achieve and maintain it.

63. Cf. Luke 12:13–21; Col. 3:5, "covetousness, which is idolatry."

13

Social Justice
in Old Testament Law

God's Character and Social Justice

Underlying OT law is the character of God, which the beloved disciple John expressed as the fundamental assertion of the entire Bible: "God is love" (1 John 4:8, 16). God's love is the motivation for his initiative to save human beings through the gift of his Son (John 3:16; Eph. 2:4–9; 1 John 4:9–10). His love is reflected by his revealed will in Scripture, including OT law, which teaches people to respond to and emulate that love (Matt. 22:37–40; Rom. 13:8–10; 1 John 4:7–8, 11–12).[1] "We love because he first loved us" (1 John 4:19).

God's love is a broad concept,[2] as shown, for example, by the wide semantic range of the Hebrew word *khesed*, which can be rendered "love." This term in various contexts can refer to "loyalty, faithfulness, kindness, love, mercy, pl. mercies, (deeds of) kindness."[3] We tend to think of God's love primarily in terms of his mercy, as in David's penitential psalm: "Have mercy on me, O God, according to your steadfast love [*khesed*]; according to your abundant mercy blot out my transgressions" (Ps. 51:1 [51:3 MT]).[4] However, divine love

---

1. For the idea of emulating God in character, cf. Lev. 19:2, "You shall be holy, for I the LORD your God am holy," followed in v. 18 by "You shall love your neighbor as yourself."
2. For a detailed theological study of God's love, see John C. Peckham, *The Love of God: A Canonical Model* (Downers Grove, IL: IVP Academic, 2015).
3. *DCH* 3:278; cf. H.-J. Zobel, *ḥesed*, *TDOT* 5:44–64.
4. Examples of other verses where *khesed* is associated with mercy are Pss. 25:6; 69:16 (69:17 MT); Lam. 3:22. For *khesed* with the idea of forgiveness, see, e.g., Num. 14:19; Ps. 86:5; cf. Ps. 25:7.

can also be manifested in his justice (*mishpat*), as shown by parallelism in some psalms: "He loves righteousness and justice [*mishpat*]; the earth is full of the steadfast love [*khesed*] of the LORD" (Ps. 33:5); "Righteousness and justice [*mishpat*] are the foundation of your throne; steadfast love [*khesed*] and faithfulness go before you" (89:14 [89:15 MT]); "Hear my voice according to your steadfast love [*khesed*]; O LORD, according to your justice [*mishpat*] give me life" (119:149).[5]

So God's love/kindness involves justice as well as mercy.[6] His justice is loving because it protects people and saves them from oppressors, as in Ps. 76:9 (76:10 MT): "God arose to establish judgment [*mishpat*], to save all the humble of the earth" (cf. 36:6 [36:7 MT]; 119:84).

Because God's love includes both justice and mercy, human emulation of his love requires these values: "Thus says the LORD of hosts, Render true judgments [*mishpat*], show kindness [*khesed*] and mercy to one another, do not oppress the widow, the fatherless, the sojourner, or the poor, and let none of you devise evil against another in your heart" (Zech. 7:9–10).[7] Here justice, kindness, and mercy are associated with social justice (not oppressing the widow, etc.) and rejection of negative attitudes toward others. In carrying out social justice, people follow the example of God, "who is not partial and takes no bribe. He executes justice for the fatherless and the widow, and loves the sojourner, giving him food and clothing. Love the sojourner, therefore, for you were sojourners in the land of Egypt" (Deut. 10:17–19).

Social justice has to do with fairness in relationships between individuals and their society in areas such as distribution of resources, social status and privileges, and opportunities for activity. Various ANE texts show concern for socially marginalized persons from early times.[8] Uniquely in the ANE,

---

5. Cf. Jer. 9:24 (9:23 MT), "I am the LORD who practices steadfast love, justice, and righteousness in the earth."

6. On the importance of justice to God, see, e.g., Ps. 99:4.

7. Cf. Hosea 12:6 (12:7 MT); Mic. 6:8.

8. The Sumerian king Uru-inimgina of Lagash (ca. 2351–2342 BC) instituted the first known systematic legal reforms (see trans. William W. Hallo, "Reforms of Uru-Inimgina," COS 2.152:407–8), which pioneered the tradition of ANE social justice. His reforms include the following: "A citizen of Lagash living in debt, (or) who had been condemned to its prison for impost, hunger, robbery, (or) murder—their freedom he established. Uru-inimgina made a compact with the divine Nin-Girsu that the powerful man would not oppress the orphan (or) widow" (ibid., 408). Later law collections, such as those of Ur-Namma, Lipit-Ishtar, and Hammurabi, echoed these ideals, as did other literature (e.g., the Nanshe Hymn: see trans. Wolfgang Heimpel, "To Nanshe," COS 1.162:526, 529–30). Gudea, the ruler of Lagash (ca. 2100 BC), claimed that he put into effect a number of social (including social justice) and ritual regulations during the inauguration of the Eninnu temple:

He cancelled debts (and) cleared the hands (of criminals). When his king entered into the temple, for seven days the slave girl did become equal with her mistress; the slave

however, the Israelites were to kindly assist and protect disadvantaged individuals (including resident aliens) in specific ways as part of their covenant obligations to the Deity, for which he held them accountable. Consequently, their treatment of such people was to affect their own well-being and destiny as individuals and as a nation.[9]

Contemporary social-justice movements are pushing against the social status quo and seeking to overcome its implicit barriers in order to gain equality of rights and economic and social benefits. However, social justice in biblical times was not about class struggle, ending ethnic discrimination, women trying to break through a "glass ceiling," family members seeking parity with the representative head of the household, entitlements to public wealth, or creation of economic safety nets, such as welfare programs. In a tribal society with a predominantly agrarian subsistence economy, there was no public wealth or welfare as we know it today. Individuals survived by belonging to and carrying out their cooperative duties within extended families. Failure to cooperate was not a viable option (cf. Deut. 21:18–21).

Social-justice measures in OT law had the purpose of preserving the status quo by maintaining or restoring the preexisting socioeconomic opportunities of individuals so that they could receive what was reasonably due to them when they fulfilled their expected roles within the society as it was.[10] "Social

---

did walk beside the master; in his city the unclean one did sleep on its outside edge(?). He removed speaking(?) from the evil tongue; turned back anything evil from that(?) house. To the laws of Nanshe and Ningirsu he paid close attention. He did not deliver the orphan up to the rich man; he did not deliver the widow up to the powerful man. In the house that had no male heir, he installed its daughter as the heir. A day of majestic justice arose for him; he put his foot on the neck of (the) evil one(s) and complainer(s). (trans. Richard E. Averbeck, "The Cylinders of Gudea," *COS* 2.155:432)
On social justice in ancient Mesopotamia and Egypt, cf. Enrique Nardoni, *Rise Up, O Judge: A Study of Justice in the Biblical World*, trans. Seán Charles Martin (Peabody, MA: Hendrickson, 2004), 1–41.

9. Jeremiah Unterman, *Justice for All: How the Jewish Bible Revolutionized Ethics* (Philadelphia: Jewish Publication Society; Lincoln: University of Nebraska Press, 2017), 41–84, esp. 83–84.

10. Raymond Westbrook, *Law from the Tigris to the Tiber: The Writings of Raymond Westbrook*, ed. Bruce Wells and Rachel Magdalene, 2 vols. (Winona Lake, IN: Eisenbrauns, 2009), 1:143–44, 160. Moshe Weinfeld has argued that the biblical ideal of doing justice and righteousness (*mishpat utsedaqah*) "implies maintaining social justice" (*Social Justice in Ancient Israel and in the Ancient Near East* [Jerusalem: Magnes, 1995], 5). This includes carrying out responsibilities to put things right by helping the needy and oppressed (Bruce V. Malchow, *Social Justice in the Hebrew Bible: What Is New and What Is Old* [Collegeville, MN: Michael Glazier, 1996], 16–17), with emphasis on equity of responsibilities rather than rights or benefits (Joe M. Sprinkle, *Biblical Law and Its Relevance: A Christian Understanding and Ethical Application for Today of the Mosaic Regulations* [Lanham, MD: University Press of America, 2006], 16; Joshua A. Berman, *Created Equal: How the Bible Broke with Ancient Political Thought* [Oxford: Oxford University Press, 2008], 175). Berman points out that in the Pentateuch, "equality is born

justice is a high priority in biblical law, but it did not mandate revolutionary social engineering. Rather, it outlined a blueprint for an existing society to undergo moral transformation by moving its people along the road of social justice at a pace that they could be expected to handle if they were loyal to YHWH and exercised faith in him."[11]

The remainder of this chapter will explore values of social justice in OT law[12] by considering its provisions in five areas: (1) assistance for Israelites to preserve their socioeconomic independence, including through debt release; (2) protection for several kinds of Israelite bonded servants, with requirements for their recovery of independence in most cases; (3) protection and assistance for chronically vulnerable free persons, such as widows, orphans, and non-Israelite resident aliens, meaning immigrants;[13] (4) treatment of women, including regarding vows by women, divorce, suspected adultery, marriage of a captive woman, and polygamy; and (5) protection of the environment and animals. The chapter will conclude with a summary of basic human rights in OT law. The next chapter will grapple with the topic of divine justice in OT law from another angle, that of theodicy (lit., "justifying God"): How could a just God permit permanent slavery, stipulate harsh punishments, and mandate destruction of entire nations?

Assistance for Israelites to Remain Independent

The Lord had delivered his people from Egypt—accomplishing the paradigmatic social-justice revolution—in order for them to be free and independent (cf. Lev. 26:13) on their own land.[14] Their use of the land was crucial because it

---

of a communitarian ideal. The equality between members of the Israelite polity is granted to them in order that they should collectively answer the higher calling of serving as subordinate kings in covenantal partnership. Individual rights exist, but they exist essentially to advance a collective good" (174).

11. Roy E. Gane, "Social Justice," in *The Oxford Handbook of Biblical Law*, ed. Pamela Barmash (Oxford: Oxford University Press, forthcoming).

12. For fuller treatment of the first three subtopics below, see ibid.

13. A resident alien (*ger*) was a man who moved (by himself or with his family) from his home territory for some reason, usually an extenuating circumstance, to another place where he could reside, although he lacked full rights of belonging to the majority group there. Resident aliens did not include non-Israelites such as the Gibeonites, whose ancestors had preceded the Israelites in the land of Canaan and who were allowed to remain (but as servants to the Israelites; Josh. 9:27), or Rahab, who was a woman assimilated into Israel through marriage (Josh. 6:25; Matt. 1:5).

14. Cf. Nardoni, *Rise Up, O Judge*, 42–62. Having provided a powerful example by freeing his people from Egypt, he expected them to treat one another with similar kindness and justice (Lev. 25:35–38; Deut. 10:17–22; 15:13–15; 24:17–22); cf. Christopher J. H. Wright, *Old*

was their most basic and essential resource. YHWH provided for its equitable distribution among the Israelite tribes and clans when they conquered Canaan (Num. 26:52–56; 33:54; Josh. 13–19, 21). This land was to be passed on to subsequent generations within the same clans[15] so that all Israelite families could have the opportunity to independently support themselves and prosper on their own ancestral properties.

All could go well until a negative circumstance disrupted the ability of Israelite farmers to gain the benefits of their labors. Such a circumstance could be crop failure due to drought, plant disease, storms, or pests; interference from warfare or raiding; or illness or death of one or more family members who had provided essential farm labor.

Such setbacks could necessitate economic assistance for survival, requiring not only food but also seed to plant in the following year. But such aid could only come from private individuals with limited resources. The best-case scenario was to receive temporary support by a more fortunate Israelite (e.g., Lev. 25:35), with whom a needy Israelite would share kinship ties. Even then, economically dependent individuals could be vulnerable to exploitation (vv. 36–37). In many cases it would be necessary for the head of household to take out a secured loan, with his possessions and family members (valued for their potential labor) as collateral. At this point, a creditor could take advantage of him by charging interest, which would worsen his situation.

If hard times forced the head of household to sell his possessions, especially his land, or if he lost them through default on a loan, there would be no remaining collateral aside from himself and his family members. So further inability to repay debt would result in pressure for at least some individuals in his family to serve as bonded workers in order to work off the amount owed (2 Kings 4:1; Neh. 5:3–5; cf. Isa. 50:1).[16]

A second way to fall into debt servitude was to be caught stealing something but not possess the means to make reparation for it (Exod. 22:3 [22:2 MT]; cf. 22:1 [21:37 MT]): The thief would be sold to pay off this obligation so that the victim of his crime would be fully compensated. Not having the amount

---

Testament Ethics for the People of God (Downers Grove, IL: InterVarsity, 2004), 253–65; 459–60. Not surprisingly, YHWH's deliverance often appears in motive clauses of social-justice laws (Exod. 22:21 [22:20 MT]; 23:9; Lev. 19:34; 25:42, 55; Deut. 5:15; etc.).

15. As in Lev. 25:13–16, 23–24, 34; Num. 36; cf. 1 Kings 21:3.

16. Raymond Westbrook and Bruce Wells, *Everyday Law in Biblical Israel: An Introduction* (Louisville: Westminster John Knox, 2009), 113–14. For detailed investigation of debt servitude, including its social background and laws relevant to it in Israel and Mesopotamia, see Gregory C. Chirichigno, *Debt-Slavery in Israel and the Ancient Near East*, JSOTSup 141 (Sheffield: JSOT Press, 1993).

to pay was not an acceptable excuse.[17] A third path to servitude would be to sell oneself and/or family members simply to stay alive if there were no other choice. This could be called "famine servitude" (see below). A fourth way to turn an Israelite into a slave was to kidnap and sell him.

Once people lost their economic and social independence in any of the above ways, they were at the mercy of their masters. So in practical terms it was possible for an unscrupulous master to keep them indefinitely (cf. Jer. 34:8–11).

A number of OT laws aim to forestall the loss of independence and to protect vulnerable individuals from suffering. Kidnapping an Israelite to sell or enslave him incurs the death penalty (Exod. 21:16; Deut. 24:7). Israelites are commanded to aid those who have become poor to the point that they cannot maintain themselves (Lev. 25:35). If possible, a relative is to "redeem," to buy back, property that a poor person is forced to sell, in order to keep it in the family (v. 25; cf. chap. 6 above). It is forbidden to profit from a needy person by charging him interest (Exod. 22:25 [22:24 MT]; Lev. 25:36–37; Deut. 23:19–20 [23:20–21 MT]). There are restrictions on creditors regarding essential personal belongings that they can take as collateral (Exod. 22:26–27 [22:25–26 MT]; Deut. 24:6, 12–13, 17) and the way in which they can collect pledges (Deut. 24:10–11). An employer must pay a poor day laborer (lacking his own land) on that same day (Lev. 19:13; Deut. 24:14–15).

Debt Release

To keep debts from piling up and dragging Israelites down to servitude, Deut. 15 mandates a release of all Israelite debts at the end of every seven years (vv. 1–3). The fact that this release is regular and does not depend on the will of a human ruler (unlike similar measures in Mesopotamia) makes it a more reliable mechanism for resetting the economy.[18]

However, as with most other OT social-justice laws, including those cited above (except for kidnapping), no humanly administered penalties are specified for violation, which in this case would involve refusal to grant release of a debt at the appointed time. Nevertheless, motivational elements in the text point to stronger reasons for compliance than human beings could provide:

17. Cf. the Laws of Hammurabi §8, which harshly stipulates thirtyfold reparation for theft of something belonging to a deity or to the palace and tenfold reparation in a case of theft from a commoner, and "if the thief does not have anything to give, he shall be killed" (trans. Martha Roth, "The Laws of Hammurabi," COS 2.131:337).

18. Jeffries M. Hamilton, *Social Justice and Deuteronomy: The Case of Deuteronomy 15*, SBLDS 136 (Atlanta: Scholars Press, 1992), 48–56, 71–72; Westbrook, *Law from the Tigris to the Tiber*, 1:151–60. On occasional and unpredictable releases from debts and other obligations and manumission of slaves by some Mesopotamian kings, see Weinfeld, *Social Justice*, 75–96.

YHWH himself promises to bless those who obey and hold accountable those who do not (e.g., vv. 4–6, 9–11; see further below). Humanly imposed penalties could be ineffective, especially in the area of social justice, because courts would tend to be controlled by men with greater socioeconomic power, precisely the group from which the OT laws sought to protect those who were socially and economically weak, poor, and vulnerable. So YHWH made those with greater means and authority directly accountable to himself, the higher power who played a very real role in Israelite life.[19]

The reliability and predictability of the seventh-year debt release causes a major problem, as verse 9a recognizes: "Take care lest there be an unworthy thought in your heart and you say, 'The seventh year, the year of release is near,' and your eye look grudgingly on your poor brother [fellow Israelite], and you give him nothing." Why would people grant loans that almost certainly could not be repaid, so that a loan could be regarded as a gift from the outset?[20] From the standpoint of economics governed by natural human impulses, this is an unworkable, fatally flawed law, which a number of scholars consequently regard as utopian.[21] However, the problem would only grow to be severe when the year of release is approaching. Otherwise, Israelites would be more likely to grant loans with the expectation that they would be paid off before the end of the seventh year.

Moreover, the Lord supplies some powerful negative and positive motivation: "and he [the poor brother] cry to the LORD against you, and you be guilty of sin. You shall give to him freely, and your heart shall not be grudging when you give to him, because for this the LORD your God will bless you in all your work and in all that you undertake" (vv. 9b–10). Results of divine blessing will be worth more than the value of the loan/gift (cf. Matt. 6:19–21; Luke 12:33–34). So investing in your poor brother is a wise investment. Obviously, this is a test of faith.

---

19. In the ANE there was no dichotomy between the natural and supernatural domains. "In the end, there is a distinction between the heavenly realm and the earthly one, but events in the two were often intertwined or parallel. It would be difficult to discuss with ancients the concept of divine intervention, because in their worldview deity was too integrated into the cosmos to intervene in it. For the most part, deity is on the inside, not the outside." John H. Walton, *Ancient Near Eastern Thought and the Old Testament: Introducing the Conceptual World of the Hebrew Bible* (Grand Rapids: Baker Academic, 2006), 87.

20. Westbrook, *Law from the Tigris to the Tiber*, 1:159.

21. E.g., Walter J. Houston, *Contending for Justice: Ideologies and Theologies of Social Justice in the Old Testament*, LHBOTS 428 (London: T&T Clark, 2006), 174–75, 179, 183–84; Westbrook, *Law from the Tigris to the Tiber*, 1:158–59; Douglas A. Knight, *Law, Power, and Justice in Ancient Israel*, LAI (Louisville: Westminster John Knox, 2011), 221. To circumvent the debt release, Hillel invented the *prosbol*, by which a declaration before a court allowed a creditor to collect an unpaid debt that was otherwise canceled at the Sabbatical Year (*m. Shevi'it* 10.3–4).

Protection for Temporary Bonded Servants

Old Testament law regulates bonded servitude to protect individuals and in most cases to provide for the release of Israelites within a reasonable period of time.[22] Hebrew terminology does not distinguish between servant/servitude and slave/slavery (esp. words from the root '-b-d'), so the following discussion uses them interchangeably. It was not necessarily shameful to be called a "slave" in ancient Israel:

> As has often been noted, the term for slave, male or female, was used indiscriminately in ancient Near Eastern languages to refer to any hierarchical inferior, for example, a subject before a sovereign, a king before an emperor, or an emperor before a god, without necessarily implying the strict legal relationship of ownership of the former by the latter. In introducing oneself, the expression "Your slave" was commonly used as a formula of polite self-abasement.[23]

Modern readers of the Bible, whose perspectives on bonded servitude are shaped by their knowledge of the unconscionably degrading racist slavery practiced in the Americas before the Civil War, understandably tend to be offended by the fact that the Lord did not simply abolish servitude altogether. However, such readers would do well to remember that there are different kinds and degrees of servitude-slavery (see further below). For example, it is well known that many poor white persons, who could not afford passage across the Atlantic Ocean, came to America on voluntary loans and agreed to pay off the loans through their labor as "indentured servants." This is much closer to the bonded servitude of ancient Israelites than the oppressive chattel slavery of millions of African-Americans.

Debt Servitude

An Israelite who contracted a loan did so voluntarily and agreed to pay it back, with his assets, including his family's capacity for labor, serving as collateral. So a voluntary loan carried with it the risk of servitude/slavery. When servitude resulted from default due to depletion of the borrower's tangible possessions, it was economically reasonable, although it was far from ideal.

God and the Bible did not originate servitude yet allowed and regulated some forms of it in a broken world to prevent something worse: starvation.[24]

22. On cases of permanent servitude, see chap. 14.
23. Westbrook, *Law from the Tigris to the Tiber*, 2:166.
24. Cf. the progression of events in Egypt during Joseph's time as people were desperate to avoid death by starvation during a severe famine (Gen. 47:13–26).

In an agrarian subsistence economy without lending institutions or other public financial infrastructure, potential lenders were individuals who generally could not afford to loan something without collateral and the expectation of repayment.[25] If OT law had summarily abolished all servitude, individuals with nothing to offer as collateral but their own labor would not have been able to obtain loans to procure food in order to live.

Thus the ethics of OT law contain a realistic, pragmatic element. To keep indigent people alive, it is necessary to gain the cooperation of those who possess the resources to help them by safeguarding their interests as well (Deut. 15:7–11). Therefore Israelite creditors can receive human labor as collateral, a master who gives a wife to a bonded servant can retain her and the children she bears when the servant is released (Exod. 21:4), and a master may discipline his servant within limits (vv. 20–21, 26–27) because the master owns the servant's labor.

Aside from limits on discipline, servants were protected by two additional factors. First, they lived with the households of their masters and shared at least some of its benefits (Deut. 15:16), including Sabbath rest (Exod. 20:10; Deut. 5:14) and some festive cultic occasions (Deut. 12:12, 18; 16:11, 14). Second, their economic value consisted of the work that they produced, so it was in their masters' interests to preserve their well-being in order to maintain their ability to work effectively (cf. Exod. 21:21b, for "the slave is his money"). Servitude was not necessarily so bad, as indicated by the fact that OT law envisages the possibility that an individual could view the quality of dependent life as superior to independence, with its cares and vicissitudes, and choose to remain a servant for the rest of his/her life (Deut. 15:16–17; cf. Exod. 21:5–6).

The OT law puts a six-year limit on the period that a "Hebrew," an Israelite,[26] can be required to serve, "and in the seventh he shall go out free, for nothing" (Exod. 21:2; cf. Deut. 15:12, 18).[27] In context, the instructions in Deut. 15 that include the six-year limit (vv. 12–18) appear to primarily concern debt servitude, as shown by the fact that they immediately follow the provision for debt release (vv. 1–11). Thus the motivational explanation in verse 18a—"It shall not seem hard to you when you let him go free from you, for at half the

25. Granting a loan as a virtual gift shortly before the year of release (see above) would be exceptional.

26. On "Hebrew" as Israelite, see David P. Wright, *Inventing God's Law: How the Covenant Code of the Bible Used and Revised the Laws of Hammurabi* (Oxford: Oxford University Press, 2009), 126; against C. Wright, *Old Testament Ethics*, 158n8.

27. This is reminiscent of the sabbatical principle of rest on the seventh day after six days of work (Exod. 20:8–11). "The association of God's seventh day with 'ceasing' or 'resting' helps to explain why the Hebrew slave is released on the seventh year (Exod. 21:2), not on the third year as in the Laws of Hammurabi (§117)." Sprinkle, *Biblical Law*, 59–60.

cost of a hired worker he has served you six years"—can be taken to imply that profit from the servant's labor would have amortized his debt.

Close parallels between Exod. 21:2–6 and Deut. 15:12–18 and the fact that bonded service for debt was a common problem in the ANE indicate that the former law also concerns release from debt servitude after a maximum of six years. It appears that this six-year period for an individual would be independent of the cyclical year of national debt release for the nation every seven years (Deut. 15:1–3).[28]

Famine Servitude

Leviticus 25 prescribes a different time limit for servitude: up to a maximum of forty-nine years until the next Jubilee Year, which was to occur every fiftieth year (vv. 8–10, 39–43, 47–55).[29] This apparent radical extension of servitude in the "Holiness Code" has disturbed scholars.[30]

However, the key is to recognize that Lev. 25 concerns a different kind of servitude: "If your brother becomes poor beside you and sells himself to you, you shall not make him serve as a slave ['eved, the term for a bonded servant in Exod. 21:2, 5; Deut. 15:17]: he shall be with you as a hired worker and as a sojourner. He shall serve with you until the year of the jubilee" (Lev. 25:39–40). This is not debt servitude[31] to pay off a previous financial obliga-

28. Daniel I. Block, *Deuteronomy*, NIV Application Commentary (Grand Rapids: Zondervan, 2012), 371.

29. On the chronology of successive Jubilee cycles, with integration of Sabbatical Years, see Roy E. Gane, *Leviticus, Numbers*, NIV Application Commentary (Grand Rapids: Zondervan, 2004), 432–34.

30. E.g., Raymond Westbrook, *Property and the Family in Biblical Law*, JSOTSup 113 (Sheffield: JSOT Press, 1991), 51–52; Richard H. Hiers, *Justice and Compassion in Biblical Law* (New York: Continuum, 2009), 198–99; D. Wright, *Inventing God's Law*, 153. Ayala Levy views Lev. 25 as an attempt to improve debt servitude in a way that would be palatable to creditors by increasing the maximum time limit to 49 years but also raising the status of the bonded individual to that of a hired servant or resident alien, as specified in vv. 39–43 ("Aspects of Bondage and Release in the Bible: Comparative Studies of Exod. 21:2–6; Lev. 25:25–55; Deut. 15:12–18" [in Hebrew] [PhD diss., Jewish Theological Seminary of America, 1981]). Adrian Schenker has proposed that the longer period of service until the Jubilee is for married men who have (male) children before they enter slavery (not covered in Exod. 21) and therefore are more costly to maintain than individuals without children. *Recht und Kult im Alten Testament: Achtzehn Studien*, OBO 172 (Freiburg, Schweiz: Universitätsverlag; Göttingen: Vandenhoeck & Ruprecht, 2000), 142–43, 145, in the chapter titled "The Biblical Legislation on the Release of Slaves: The Road from Exodus to Leviticus," reprinted from JSOT 78 (1998): 23–41.

31. Against, e.g., Levy, "Aspects of Bondage"; Tikva Frymer-Kenski, "Israel," in *A History of Ancient Near Eastern Law*, ed. Raymond Westbrook, Handbook of Oriental Studies, Section 1, The Near and Middle East 72 (Leiden, Brill, 2003), 1023–24; Westbrook, *Law from the Tigris to the Tiber*, 1:159, 195–96; D. Wright, *Inventing God's Law*, 153. Westbrook (*Property and the Family*, 51) does acknowledge that "release of debts is not mentioned in the Jubilee legislation."

tion by providing labor "at half the cost of a hired worker" (Deut. 15:18), but another category that Raymond Westbrook has identified in Mesopotamian texts, which he terms "famine slavery."[32]

"Famine slavery/servitude" would originate when a poor man who could no longer support himself and his family during hard times would sell himself and possibly his family into servitude to stay alive. The desired outcome for the poor man was not to keep the period of service as short as possible, but to prolong it through the time of difficulty until he could make an independent living.[33] This is exactly what happens in Lev. 25. If a poor man must sell the use of at least part of his ancestral farmland, cannot redeem it (vv. 25–28), and "cannot maintain himself with you" (v. 35) but "sells himself[34] to you" (v. 39), most likely he would be unable to support himself and his family until he recovers his land.[35]

This maintenance is a matter of survival. At the end of verse 35, "and he shall live with you" refers to living (*qal* of *kh-y-h*) rather than dying, not living simply as residing. So it is completely logical that his dependent arrangement ends at the Jubilee Year, so that he and any family members with him are released (vv. 40–41, 54) when his land reverts to his control and he can make a new start (vv. 13, 28).[36]

Famine servitude was a contractual obligation from which a person could not simply walk away, but Lev. 25 regulates it by allowing redemption from it (vv. 48–52), automatically releasing people from it at the Jubilee Year (vv. 40–41, 54), and requiring that a person in this state was to be treated like a free hired worker or resident alien rather than a forced worker (vv. 39–40, 53).

The OT law provides for some welfare in the form of gifts and concessions to disadvantaged persons, including the (second) tithe of every third year and the right to glean (see below), and it encourages Israelites to assist

32. Westbrook, *Law from the Tigris to the Tiber*, 1:178–80, 189–92. For identification of the servitude in Lev. 25 as famine slavery, see Gane, "Social Justice" (moving away from agreement with Levy published in Gane, *Leviticus, Numbers*, 437–39), agreeing with concepts articulated by Chirichigno, *Debt-Slavery*, 335–36.

33. Cf. that Deut. 15 calls for the Israelite master to provide his departing debt-servant with a gift of food and drink to help the person make the transition back to independent life (vv. 13–14).

34. *Niphal* of *m-k-r* interpreted as a reflexive. The *niphal* can also be passive, "is sold," as in the ESV rendering of Deut. 15:12.

35. But Lev. 25:49–52 allows for the possibility that an Israelite could redeem himself from a foreigner before the Jubilee Year.

36. The land could "not be sold in perpetuity" (v. 23), so only the temporary use of the land for growing crops was sold until the Jubilee Year (vv. 13–16). The introduction to the Jubilee Year refers to the two kinds of releases—of land and people—for which this institution was intended to provide: "It shall be a jubilee for you, when each of you shall return to his property and each of you shall return to his clan" (v. 10).

the poor among them (Lev. 25:35). These measures would mitigate the difficulty of poverty, but they would not guarantee full, ongoing support for an extended period of time as the famine servitude and Jubilee provisions of Lev. 25 would do.

The Lev. 25 plan offers the most thorough OT law solution to poverty during temporary hard times, but it does not tax the fruits of labor from those who possess them in order to distribute them to those in need, thereby tending to reduce the incentive of both parties. Rather, the have-nots are to be sustained by the haves in a mutually beneficial relationship, although it is not ideal, until the poor recover the essential resource, land, through which to gain the fruits of their own labor in a better situation.

The resource of land that is equitably distributed provides opportunity; it is not the outcome of other people's success, nor does it guarantee success (cf. Deut. 15:11). Thus, although the system outlined in Lev. 25 could be regarded as a major form of welfare, it would preserve incentive to work (cf. 2 Thess. 3:10).[37] It is true that the ancient setting greatly differed from ours, but before modern people dismiss the biblical laws as irrelevant or utopian,[38] perhaps we can learn something!

As with laws regarding loans (see above), laws that stipulate release from servitude and return of ancestral land in the Jubilee Year come with no humanly enforced penalties. However, YHWH claims ownership of the land (Lev. 25:23) and of the Israelites as his servants (v. 55), so he has the right to determine what is done with them.

Jeremiah 34 demonstrates the gravity of accountability to YHWH, who takes social justice seriously. When Judah was about to fall to the Babylonians (vv. 6–7), King Zedekiah made a covenant with the people of Jerusalem to

37. "In contrast to both capitalism and Marxism, biblical law presents a third way; access to the means of production *and* incentives to work hard. Whereas modern Western approaches to social welfare favor a system of redistributive taxation *after* the process of wealth creation, biblical law provides for a roughly equitable distribution of productive assets that can be maintained over a lifetime. To put it another way, biblical law addresses the question of social welfare by giving as many people as possible the capacity to produce and hence to look after themselves." Jonathan Burnside, *God, Justice, and Society: Aspects of Law and Legality in the Bible* (New York: Oxford University Press, 2011), 251, emphasis original; cf. 249–50.

38. A number of scholars regard the Jubilee regulations as impractical and utopian (e.g., Westbrook, *Property and the Family*, 38–56; Westbrook, *Law from the Tigris to the Tiber*, 1:159; Houston, *Contending for Justice*, 189–91, 197–99, 201). Part of their support for this conclusion is the fact that they have found no clear description of Jubilee observance in other biblical texts to attest that it was ever implemented. But see the attempt of Lisbeth S. Fried and David N. Freedman, "Was the Jubilee Year Observed in Preexilic Judah?," in *Leviticus 23–27: A New Translation with Introduction and Commentary*, by Jacob Milgrom, AB 3B (New York: Doubleday, 2001), 2257–70.

proclaim "liberty" (*deror*, vv. 8–9, 15; cf. Lev. 25:10) so that they should release
their male or female "Hebrew" slaves (Jer. 34:9; cf. Deut. 15:12), in accordance
with previously ignored OT law (Jer. 34:14, citing Deut. 15:1, 12), which they
did (Jer. 34:10, 15). Soon thereafter, however, they undid their last-ditch gesture
of repentance and reclaimed their slaves (vv. 11, 16), resulting in the divine
sentence of destruction by the Babylonians (vv. 17–22), which subsequently
occurred (Jer. 39; cf. 2 Kings 25; 2 Chron. 36).

Jeremiah 34 illustrates the fact that unhealthy socioeconomic stratification,
which developed during the monarchy, gave rise to a selfish, oppressive elite,
who disregarded ethical principles expressed in OT laws (e.g., Jer. 34:14).
YHWH's prophets aggressively countered them (e.g., Isa. 3:14–15; 10:1–2;
Ezek. 22:27–29; Amos 2:6–7; 8:4–6), but it took the Babylonian exile to end
the problem.[39]

Jeremiah 34 also shows that the "impracticality" of the instructions in Deut.
15, as well as Lev. 25, was not inherent. These social-justice measures could
be implemented if the people chose to unselfishly help their needy kinsmen,
as Walter Houston has recognized: "The impracticality is not a matter of
physical impossibility but of motivation."[40]

Protection and Assistance for Socially Vulnerable Free Persons

Socioeconomic independence in ancient Israel required two things: agricultural
land and the labor to farm it. Thus OT law sought to keep ancestral property
and farming families together and to reunite the land and people when they
became separated (see above). However, some kinds of individuals tended to
be chronically poor, dependent, and socially vulnerable because they lacked
either ancestral land (even the right to reclaim it at the Jubilee) or the ability
to work it, or both. These included widows, orphans (or fatherless children),
and non-Israelite resident aliens, who did not belong to families with Israelite
heads of households.

In some cases, a childless widow could marry her brother-in-law or another kinsman (Deut. 25:5–6; cf. Gen. 38; Ruth 4). But if her male relatives
refused or neglected this responsibility (Deut. 25:7–10; cf. Gen. 38:11, 14; Ruth
4:5–6), she would need another means of support, as would a widow lacking
a close relative to marry, or with children and therefore ineligible for levirate

39. At this time the upper classes were removed (2 Kings 24:14–16; 25:6–7, 11–12), but oppression resurrected after the exile (Neh. 5). For the ultimate end of oppression, see Rev. 18–20,
where 18:13 mentions trafficking in "slaves—and human lives" (NRSV).
40. Houston, *Contending for Justice*, 194.

or kinsman-redeemer marriage. If she had sons who were old enough, they could do the farmwork or at least help her with it. But she would be legally vulnerable without a male head of household, and if she had no children or her children were small, she could not manage the farm and would be dependent on others for support. Ideally, she would receive some assistance from her extended family members, but these could be absent or unable to help, in which case her situation could be a desperate fight for survival.

Young orphans or fatherless children (Heb. *yatom*) could be destitute even if they inherited land because, like widows, they did not have the strength to cultivate it by themselves. Without an adult male to represent them, they would also be vulnerable to legal exploitation.

Foreigners residing in Israel were not permitted to permanently own ancestral property at all, although they could purchase the use of farmland until the Jubilee Year as a kind of leasehold.[41] Resident aliens could be economically independent and prosperous (Lev. 25:47). Without ongoing land tenure, however, it appears that they tended to be dependent on the hospitality of Israelite communities and households, whose workforces they augmented, likely as day laborers. It is likely that their legal vulnerability was even greater than that of widows and orphans because they had no Israelite relatives, not even distant kinsmen, to represent them in court.

In addition to the general social-justice protections of the Decalogue (cf. chap. 12 above), OT law protects and assists vulnerable persons, including widows, orphans, and resident aliens, in more specific ways. Several OT laws prohibit injustice in lawcourts, especially against poor persons, resident aliens, orphans/fatherless, and widows (Exod. 23:6; Deut. 24:17; cf. 27:19). The law that an employer must pay a day laborer on the same day (Lev. 19:13; Deut. 24:14–15) would benefit resident aliens as well as poor Israelites.

Poor people, including resident aliens, orphans, and widows, possess the legal right to glean from the harvests of Israelite farmers (Lev. 19:9–10; 23:22; Deut. 24:19–21), pick what grows by itself on farmland during fallow Sabbatical and Jubilee Years (Exod. 23:11; Lev. 25:6, 11–12), and eat from agricultural (second) tithes every third year, along with (landless) Levites (Deut. 14:28–29; 26:12–13).[42] Notice that only the tithes, which belonged to God, could be eaten without any work. There were no handouts from what belonged to other humans.

41. But YHWH somewhat leveled the difference between Israelites and resident aliens by reminding the former that because he ultimately owned the land, "you are strangers and sojourners with me" (Lev. 25:23); Burnside, *God, Justice, and Society*, 220.

42. On tithes, see further in chap. 15 below. Also, Deut. 16:11, 14 directs Israelites to include disadvantaged persons in their festival celebrations. Levites lacked a territory, but they were to be supported in their cities by tithes (Num. 18:21–24; 35:1–8).

The provisions just mentioned would not be sufficient to fully support the poor,[43] but they would provide some assistance and inclusion in the community and could bring these socially marginal individuals to the attention of those who could further help them (cf. Ruth 2). Thus OT law does not provide solutions to all problems, but it does encourage community members to generously and compassionately alleviate suffering (Lev. 25:35; Deut. 15:7–11, 13–15).[44] The perpetual presence of the poor among them (Deut. 15:11; cf. Matt. 26:11; etc.) would call for their best character and faith, with individual commitment to the value of outgoing unselfishness, which goes beyond what can or should be legally enforced.[45] As James put it, "Religion that is pure and undefiled before God, the Father, is this: to visit orphans and widows in their affliction, and to keep oneself unstained from the world" (James 1:27).[46]

The OT law benefits two categories of vulnerable individuals in addition to those discussed above: It protects handicapped persons (deaf and blind) from harassment (Lev. 19:14; Deut. 27:18) and mandates respect for the elderly (Lev. 19:32). In fact, OT law even provides social justice for the dead, whose names/identities are to live on through their heirs and inheritances (Num. 27:1–11; Deut. 25:5–10).[47]

Immigration

Concern for the poor, widows, and the fatherless, as well as debtors and debt-servants, had a long history in the ANE before Israel came on the scene.[48] However, laws against oppressing resident aliens (Exod. 22:21 [22:20 MT]; 23:9; Lev. 19:33), laws to provide economic aid for them, and the remarkable

43. Houston, *Contending for Justice*, 115–16.

44. Deuteronomy 15 articulates the ideal that poverty would be erased among the Israelites, whom God would bless if they would obey him (vv. 4–5). However, the same chapter acknowledges the reality that there would always be poor persons (v. 11), perhaps because the Israelites would not adequately obey YHWH. Houston, however, argues for a real paradox here: "The utopian object of the programme, an undivided society of equal 'brothers,' is for ever to be out of reach. The text recognizes this, but urges the hearers to constantly act *as though it were true*: the moral appeal of vv. 7–11 is based on the perception of the poor man as a brother" (ibid., 184, emphasis original).

45. Ibid., 107, 117, 131–32, 187, 230.

46. The NT church emphasized the need to care for truly needy widows (Acts 6:1–4; 1 Tim. 5:3–16). Cf. Jesus's concern for needy people, making practical kindness the criterion of his eschatological judgment (Matt. 25:31–46).

47. Therefore a person could be punished after death by loss of his family members (2 Sam. 21, Saul punished after his death for attempting genocide on the Gibeonites).

48. Malchow, *Social Justice*, 1–5; Westbrook and Wells, *Everyday Law*, 119–21; OT law adapted and developed aspects of existing ANE social-justice concepts (Malchow, *Social Justice*, 76–77; D. Wright, *Inventing God's Law*, esp. 121–53).

divine command for citizens to love these foreigners as themselves (Lev. 19:34; cf. Deut. 10:19) were unique to Israel. YHWH's country was to be the most hospitable and socially just on earth, drawing people into association with the covenant community through which all nations were to be blessed (cf. Gen. 12:3; 22:18; Deut. 4:5–6; Isa. 2:2–3; Mic. 4:1–2).

Here is a model for treatment of immigrants, including people displaced by warfare. Israelites were to generously assist resident aliens so that they could survive and thrive throughout the land. These immigrants would not displace the Israelites. They were to assimilate into Israelite culture as minority members of many villages rather than establishing enclaves of their own subculture that would spread to progressively take over the country. The foreigners were to live by the laws of the land, which included respect for YHWH.[49] They were not required to convert to the Israelite religion, although they were welcome to participate in it (e.g., Exod. 12:48, if males were circumcised; Lev. 17:8–9; 22:18; Num. 9:14; 15:14–16), but they were forbidden to engage in practices that were contrary to YHWH's laws, such as sexual immorality (Lev. 18:26), idolatry (20:2), blasphemy (24:16), murder, and assault (v. 22).

The progressive trajectory of God's plan for absorbing immigrants is nowhere clearer than in the remarkable instructions of Ezek. 47:22–23 for an ideal future. Here, when Israel is strong and pure, immigrants are to be elevated to the status of people of Israelite descent in that they are to receive land as an inheritance among the Israelite tribes.

Treatment of Women

Modern Western culture is concerned with equal rights for women in society. This is good and has biblical support in the fact that God created men and women in his image as equal partners to have benevolent dominion over planet Earth (Gen. 1:26–28). Yet OT law was designed to work with an imperfect, postfall society that already included female inequality, divorce, and polygamy along with servitude. It sought to move people back in the direction of creation ideals by strategically correcting and preventing the most important problems without generating worse results (cf. chaps. 7–9 above).

We have found that OT law permitted servitude as a way for desperate people to survive, but it regulated and limited such servitude in order to protect those individuals from abuse (see above and further in chap. 14 below). Similarly, the divine laws allowed nonideal female inequality, divorce,

---

49. E.g., the resident alien (*ger*) was to rest on the weekly Sabbath (Exod. 20:10) and to practice self-denial and rest on the Day of Atonement (Lev. 16:29).

and polygamy rather than precipitating the more damaging consequences of abolishing them. If YHWH had engaged in extensive social engineering by simply eliminating these, no doubt Israelite women would have suffered more due to factors such as power clashes with men, especially those who had been heads of their households; conflicts in unworkable marriages that could not be ended; and frustration of a man with a barren wife, which could lead to his abusing her if he could not take another wife to provide a line of descendants.

Additional laws attempting to suppress such collateral damage, especially by controlling male attitudes and behaviors, would have been ineffective and impossible for the community to enforce. Widespread social progress is deep and lasting only if the members of a society voluntarily implement it. This explains the incremental nature of the changes demanded by OT law, including regulations to protect women from abuse (see below) and the extent to which it employs persuasive strategies (cf. chap. 5 above). It is easy to criticize the ancient Israelites for their unreadiness to give up servitude and polygamy, which we view as unacceptable. However, our rampant divorce and remarriage rate, with multiple marriages in succession (serial monogamy) rather than at the same time (polygamy); domestic abuse; and growing pains in reaching female equality remind us that positive transformation of a society is a challenging business.

There is no clear evidence that ancient Israelites regarded equality of women with the male heads of their households as a social-justice issue. It appears that social leadership by the heads of households (cf. chap. 6 above) was accepted by women and also by subordinate males.[50] A free woman, especially the wife of a head of household, possessed greater social power than male servants of the household, whom she could command (1 Sam. 25:19). The role of an Israelite woman was mainly in the home (e.g., Prov. 31:10–31) rather than in the public sphere,[51] but she could engage in activities such as business (vv. 16, 18, 24), serving as a witness in a legal case (Lev. 5:1), making a legal appeal (2 Sam. 14:4–11; 1 Kings 3:16–22; 2 Kings 6:26–29; 8:5–6), and participating in worship at the sanctuary (1 Sam. 1).

Regarding worship at the sanctuary, only men were required to attend the three annual pilgrim festivals (Exod. 23:14–17; 34:22–24), but women could

50. "Male dominance was assumed: it was part of the social order of the world that the Bible did not question. The Bible has a new religious vision, but it is not a radical *social* document." Tikva Frymer-Kensky, *In the Wake of the Goddesses: Women, Culture, and the Biblical Transformation of Pagan Myth* (New York: Free Press, 1992), 128, cf. 119–20, emphasis original.

51. Walter J. Houston, *Justice: The Biblical Challenge*, Biblical Challenges in the Contemporary World (London: Equinox, 2010), 22.

accompany them to the sanctuary (cf. 1 Sam. 1:3–7).[52] No doubt men generally offered sacrifices for their families (vv. 4–5, 21), but ritual law gave women rights with nonpriestly men to engage in sacrificial activities as offerers,[53] as shown by use of the generic terms *'adam* (man = human being/person) and *nefesh* (being, person) with reference to lay offerers of sacrifices in Leviticus (*'adam*, Lev. 1:2; *nefesh*, 2:1; 4:27; etc.).[54]

Women were required to offer sacrifices in some cases (12:6–8; 15:29–30). Like men, women could choose to take the Nazirite vow that consecrated a person to a temporary state of holiness, at the end of which the one vowing was obliged to offer several sacrifices (Num. 6). So already the Lord's ritual worship system in the holy domain under his full control pointed forward to the ideal: "There is no male and female, for you are all one in Christ Jesus" (Gal. 3:28).[55]

Old Testament law granted women most of the same rights as men.[56] "Special rules applied to women in areas of law like marriage and inheritance and for certain sexual offenses, such as adultery. Otherwise, laws were not

52. It could be difficult for women to travel with babies (e.g., 1 Sam. 1:22).

53. Mayer I. Gruber, "Women in the Cult according to the Priestly Code," in *Judaic Perspectives on Ancient Israel*, ed. Jacob Neusner, Baruch Levine, and Ernest Frerichs (Philadelphia: Fortress, 1987), 35–48; cf. Jacob Milgrom, *Leviticus 1–16: A New Translation with Introduction and Commentary*, AB 3 (New York: Doubleday, 1991), 759. Officiating priests, who were exclusively authorized to come in contact with the altar and to enter the sacred tent, could only be male descendants of Aaron (Exod. 28–29; Lev. 8–9; Num. 18:1–7). On possible reasons for this, see Gane, *Leviticus, Numbers*, 375–77.

54. See confirmation of the generic nature of these terms in Num. 5:6, "When a man [*'ish*] or woman [*'ishshah*] commits any of the sins of mankind [*'adam*], acting unfaithfully against the LORD, and that person [*nefesh*] is guilty . . ." (NASB).

55. It is true that the Aaronide priests had to be male, but they typified Christ himself in his role as priest (Heb. 7–10; etc.) rather than representing human leaders of the Christian church, all members of which constitute "a royal priesthood" (1 Pet. 2:9). Note that some sacrificial animals, which typified Christ in his role as sacrificial victim, were female (Lev. 3:1, 6; 4:28, 32; 5:6; Num. 15:27; 19:2).

56. Richard H. Hiers, *Women's Rights and the Bible: Implication for Christian Ethics and Social Policy* (Eugene, OR: Pickwick, 2012), xv–xvi; for exceptions, see 53–55. On the complex issue of defining and assessing patriarchy in ancient Israel, see Carol Meyers, *Discovering Eve: Ancient Israelite Women in Context* (New York: Oxford University Press, 1988), 24–46. Meyers corrects some modern misconceptions, pointing out, among other things, that the OT provides an incomplete record of patriarchy, and evidence is lacking that ancient Israelite women "felt oppressed, degraded, or unfairly treated in the face of cultural asymmetry. Gender differences that appear hierarchical may not have functioned or been perceived as hierarchical within Israelite society" (34). Richard M. Davidson finds in the OT that the husband's servant leadership in the home "does not override the basic equality between the marriage partners or imply the husband's ownership, oppression, domination, or control over the wife. . . . There is no biblical legislation indicating a punishment for a wife's rebelling against her husband's leadership." *Flame of Yahweh: Sexuality in the Old Testament* (Peabody, MA: Hendrickson, 2007), 222.

gender-specific."⁵⁷ Like men, women were protected by OT law from many crimes, including murder, assault, adultery by their spouses, theft, malicious accusations, and so on (see chap. 12 above). Several laws guarded and aided widows along with other socially weak and poor individuals, such as orphans and resident aliens (see above), and the garment of a widow, uniquely, could not be taken as a pledge (Deut. 24:17).

Other laws specifically benefited women in cases of rape (Deut. 22:25–29), seduction (Exod. 22:16–17 [22:15–16 MT]),⁵⁸ and a false accusation of non-virginity by a bridegroom (Deut. 22:13–19). A couple of laws assisted women in preserving the lines of inheritance of their deceased fathers or husbands by providing for daughters to inherit when their father died, if he had no sons (Num. 27:8), and by encouraging (although not forcing) a brother-in-law to take his widowed and childless sister-in-law in levirate marriage (Deut. 25:5–10).

Readers who view the biblical laws from their modern perspective usually misinterpret a number of laws as representing a male chauvinist perspective when in fact they protected women within the ancient cultural context. The following sections briefly explore these laws.

Vows by Women

The father of an unmarried woman or the husband of a married woman could annul her vow when he first heard it (Num. 30). This protected a woman from guilt in the event that she was unable to fulfill her promise to YHWH because of resistance from the man of the house (vv. 5, 8, 12 [vv. 6, 9, 13 MT], "The Lord will forgive her"),⁵⁹ since what she bound herself to do could negatively affect him. For example, if she vows to sacrifice an animal (Lev. 7:16) or otherwise dedicate an item to YHWH (Lev. 27), this would reduce the family assets that were managed by her father or husband, so his agreement was needed to preserve harmony in the family.⁶⁰ It appears that Num.

57. Westbrook and Wells, *Everyday Law*, 54. Cf. Frymer-Kensky (*In the Wake of the Goddesses*, 118–43) regarding conceptions of gender in the Bible and ancient Israel. Frymer-Kensky points out that the Bible presents a unified picture of human beings, influenced by monotheism, in which women share the same intrinsic characteristics as men (esp. 120–21, 142–43).

58. Obligatory marriage in cases of rape or seduction of unbetrothed virgins could protect them from lack of support that would result if nobody else wanted to marry them because they had lost their virginity.

59. "But if he makes them null and void after he has heard of them, then he shall bear her iniquity" (Num. 30:15 [30:16 MT]), in which case she is still protected from guilt.

60. Another kind of vow would be to practice self-denial (Num. 30:13 [30:14 MT]), which could involve abstinence from sexual relations that would affect the husband. Cf. 1 Cor. 7:5 regarding the need for mutual consent regarding such abstinence.

30 implies the relative importance of divine values: God gives up his right to receive sacrifices vowed by women in order to maintain family unity.[61] This testifies to the remarkably (in the ANE) unselfish character of Israel's Deity.

Divorce

The divorce law in Deut. 24:1–4 refers to a man divorcing his wife, but there is no corresponding law permitting a woman to divorce her husband. However, this law does not have the purpose of allowing divorce; it only regulates a kind of second remarriage if divorce should occur. The protasis in verses 1–3 describes existing circumstances involving divorce and remarriage, and the apodosis in verse 4 presents what is stipulated in response to that scenario: remarriage to one's original spouse after an intervening marriage following divorce is forbidden. That is what the law is about. Nevertheless, by assuming divorce under certain conditions, as on the serious ground of indecency and with the husband giving his wife a written notice of divorce, the law implicitly permits divorce under these conditions (cf. Matt. 5:31; 19:7; Mark 10:4).

Both of these conditions and the prohibition against remarriage to the original spouse protect women in ways that men probably would not need, due to their stronger position in ancient Israelite society.[62] Limitation of divorce to "indecency" ('ervat davar, lit., "nakedness of a thing," Deut. 24:1) appears to rule out frivolous reasons for ending a marriage, provided that "indecency" is interpreted as something serious.[63] A written document, indicating or at least implying the reason for the divorce, protects a woman in case she is subsequently suspected or blamed for the much more serious capital offense of adultery.

The explicit reason for the prohibition against remarriage to the original spouse after an intervening marriage is that the first husband may not take her back after she has been caused (by her first husband) to defile herself (rare hotpa'al passive reflexive form of the root t-m-', Deut. 24:4). Although the law tolerates divorce by the first husband, he lacks full divine approval because

---

61. Cf. Roy Gane, In the Shadow of the Shekinah: God's Journey with Us (Hagerstown, MD: Review & Herald, 2009), 146–47.

62. There is no clear OT evidence that wives could divorce their husbands in ancient Israelite society, although Jesus refers to this possibility in Mark 10:12 during the period of Greco-Roman influence.

63. As Shammai (m. Gittin 9.10) and Jesus (Matt. 5:32; 19:9; etc.) did, but not Hillel (m. Gittin 9.10, even if she ruined the dish of food that she was preparing for him). On 'ervat davar, see R. Davidson, Flame of Yahweh, 390–92, who concludes that this phrase "describes some type of serious, shameful, and disgraceful conduct of indecent exposure probably associated with sexual activity but less than illicit sexual intercourse" (392).

he caused his wife to defile herself by uniting with another man, similar to committing adultery.[64] "If the woman were then to remarry her first husband, after divorcing the second, the analogy with adultery would become even more complete; the woman lives first with one man, then another, and finally returns to the first."[65] The fact that violation of the prohibition is labeled an "abomination" (v. 4), as the sexual offenses in Lev. 18 are "abominations" both for Israelites and non-Israelites (vv. 26–27, 29), indicates that it carries permanent and universal moral force.[66]

Modern readers need to understand that Deut. 24:1–4 does not cover all kinds of dissolution of marriage, which we call "divorce." This law, which defined the scope of Jesus's discussion (Matt. 5:31–32; 19:3–9; Mark 10:2–12; cf. Luke 16:18), including his identification of sexual immorality (*porneia*) as the only legitimate ground for divorce (only in Matt. 5:32; 19:9), involves only expulsion of a spouse from a marriage for a particular cause, as indicated by the *piel* form of the verb *sh-l-kh*, "send out" (Deut. 24:1, 3–4; cf. Mal. 2:16). The Bible also recognizes dissolution of marriage when an unbelieving spouse abandons a Christian partner, who then "is not bound," which means that the person who has been abandoned is free to remarry (1 Cor. 7:15 NIV).[67] In OT law, concubinage could be terminated due to active physical abuse (Exod. 21:26–27, servant freed even if she is a concubine; cf. vv. 7–11) or passive abuse by neglect (vv. 10–11).

Suspected Adultery

Numbers 5:11–31 allows a man who suspects his wife of adultery to bring her and a small offering for YHWH to the sanctuary, where she undergoes a ritual that requires her to assent to a conditional curse pronounced by a priest and to drink holy water containing some dust from the floor of the sanctuary and the curses that the priest has washed off from a document on which he has written it (vv. 23–24). The brew functions as a kind of litmus (and perhaps lie-detector) test: If the woman is morally pure, she experiences nothing, but if she is morally impure, the holy substance and conditional curses that she has taken into her body causes gynecological damage resulting in sterility and severe social stigma. The punishment manifests the verdict.

---

64. R. Davidson, *Flame of Yahweh*, 395–98; cf. Matt. 5:32; 19:9; Mark 10:11.

65. Peter C. Craigie, *The Book of Deuteronomy*, NICOT (Grand Rapids: Eerdmans, 1976), 305. On possibilities regarding the overall purpose of the law in Deut. 24:1–4, see R. Davidson, *Flame of Yahweh*, 398–405.

66. R. Davidson, *Flame of Yahweh*, 397–98.

67. Cf. 1 Tim. 5:8, "But if anyone does not provide for his relatives, and especially for members of his household, he has denied the faith and is worse than an unbeliever."

The law presupposes that YHWH controls the outcome because only he has the knowledge to differentiate between a guilty or innocent woman. This use of a ritual resulting in a miracle or its absence to reach a decision is unique in OT law.[68]

The fact that there is no corresponding suspected-adulterer ritual to which a man must submit if his wife suspects him causes modern readers, especially feminists, to view the law as sexist. However, Jacob Milgrom has pointed out that the law protected an innocent woman from the danger of being unjustly sentenced to death for adultery by an all-male court (as courts were in ancient Israel) that would tend to sympathize with her husband's suspicion.[69] It would also protect her from being unjustly divorced on the ground of indecency (Deut. 24:1). YHWH preempted such miscarriages of justice against women by giving only women the right to a unique "supreme court" trial by himself. If the Lord indicated that the wife was innocent, her husband could rest assured that this was so, and the marriage could be healed.[70]

Marriage of a Captive Woman

Deuteronomy 21:10–14 permits an Israelite man to bring a non-Israelite woman captured in war (cf. 20:14) to his house with the intent to marry her, provided that he followed a certain protocol: "She shall shave her head and pare her nails. And she shall take off the clothes in which she was captured and shall remain in your house and lament her father and her mother a full month. After that you may go in to her and be her husband, and she shall be your wife" (21:12–13). The process, which involves sensitivity to her feelings as she sheds her former identity, provides a liminal period in a kind of "rite of passage"[71] by which she transitions from being an unmarried non-Israelite captive girl[72] to living as a free married woman belonging to the Israelite community.

The idea that a man could obtain a wife in this way is disturbing at first glance, but the law mandates a vast improvement over the common fates of

---

68. Although cf. legal decisions by God in Exod. 22:8–9 (22:7–8 MT).

69. Jacob Milgrom, "A Husband's Pride, A Mob's Prejudice," *BRev* 12 (1996): 21.

70. Roy E. Gane, "Innovation in the Suspected Adulteress Ritual (Num. 5:11–31)," in *Ritual Innovation in the Hebrew Bible and Early Judaism*, ed. Nathan MacDonald, BZAW 468 (Berlin: de Gruyter, 2016), 113–27. Even if the wife was guilty, YHWH punished her himself (not with death in this case) because he and not humans had apprehended her.

71. Cf. the classic work by Arnold van Gennep, *The Rites of Passage* (Chicago: University of Chicago Press, 1960).

72. Presumably young and unmarried because she mourns her parents, whether or not they are dead, rather than her husband.

females captured in war throughout history, including modern times: rape (Lam. 5:11; Zech. 14:2), enslavement (Lev. 25:44–46), or even death (Num. 31:17). An Israelite could have a captured girl only if he made a commitment to care for her with the plan to make her his wife. Delay in consummation of the marriage additionally protected the girl by allowing her some time to grieve and adjust and by giving the man an opportunity to deal with any second thoughts while she lived in his house without her full head of beautiful hair.[73]

Further protection applied after the marriage was consummated if the man no longer wanted her as his wife. He was prohibited from selling her or retaining her as his slave but instead was required to treat her as a free wife undergoing divorce by letting "her go where she wants" (v. 14), in which case she could return to her original nation or remarry if she wished (cf. Deut. 24:1–2).

Polygamy

The protasis of the law in Deut. 21:15–17 begins: "If a man has two wives, the one loved and the other unloved . . ." (v. 15). Thus OT law clearly tolerated but regulated multiple marriages, which obviously lowered the status of women.[74]

Israelite culture inherited the ancient institution of polygamy, more precisely polygyny, a kind of polygamy in which a man has more than one wife. Biblical narratives portray such arrangements in a consistently negative light. The first bigamist was a murderer (Gen. 4:19–24), and multiple marriages gave rise to

73. Cf. Jeffrey H. Tigay, *Deuteronomy: The Traditional Hebrew Text with the New JPS Translation*, JPS Torah Commentary (Philadelphia: Jewish Publication Society, 1996), 194.

74. Cf. toleration of divorce in the protasis of the law against remarriage to the first spouse after an intervening marriage (Deut. 24:1–4). Some scholars argue that "if a man has two wives" in Deut. 21:15 could mean that he has had two wives in succession, having married the second after the first died (Walter C. Kaiser Jr., *Toward Old Testament Ethics* [Grand Rapids: Zondervan, 1983], 186–87; R. Davidson, *Flame of Yahweh*, 201). However, two wives in succession is not the plain sense of the text. First, other instances in which a certain number of entities belong to something/someone, expressed by *qal* verb of *h-y-h* + possessive preposition *l*, indicate that they belong at the same time, as in Gen. 47:24; Exod. 28:7; 1 Kings 10:26; 11:3, Solomon's 700 wives and 300 concubines, not in succession!; Job 42:13; 1 Chron. 2:22; etc. See also 1 Sam. 1:2 of Elkanah, in a verbless clause without the *qal* of *h-y-h*: "He had two wives" at the same time. Second, just as the law in Lev. 18:18 rules out rivalry between two sisters who are simultaneously married to one man, such as was manifested between Rachel and Leah during the patriarchal period (Gen. 30), Deut. 21:15–17 also addresses a situation that parallels that of Rachel and Leah: Jacob loved Rachel but not Leah, who bore his eldest son (Gen. 29:30–32), and Jacob favored Joseph, a younger son by Rachel (30:22–24; 37:3), to whom he ultimately gave a double inheritance by adopting Joseph's two sons as his own (48:5).

jealousy, rivalry, and strife between wives (Gen. 16, 21, 29–30; 1 Sam. 1:2–7) and their children (Gen. 37; Judg. 8:30–31; 9:1–6).

Ze'ev W. Falk points out that most ancient Israelites were monogamous. The main motivation for taking a second wife would have been childlessness of the first wife. Also, rich and royal persons multiplied wives and children to show their wealth and status.[75]

So why didn't God simply abolish polygamy in OT law? The Bible doesn't say, but perhaps this could have caused a serious problem for some women in the ancient cultural context. Most significantly, there was an overwhelming drive for a man to have children (esp. sons) to assist his labor-intensive agricultural endeavors (e.g., Gen. 37:12), enhance his social standing and protection (Ps. 127:3–5), provide for him in old age and bury him (Gen. 25:9), and inherit his property in order to carry on his identity through a line of descendants (Num. 27:1–11; Deut. 25:5–10). Therefore a man with a barren wife would view himself as having a serious difficulty that could be resolved in one of two ways: (1) divorce his wife and remarry, although "indecency" as the assumed ground for divorce in Deut. 24:1 (see above) does not include barrenness; or (2) take a second wife (Gen. 16:1–4; 30:3–13; cf. 1 Sam. 1:2).[76] If he chose the first option, it could be difficult for his divorced wife to remarry because she was known to be barren,[77] so she could be forced to live without male support, like a widow.

In any case, it appears that the Lord regarded polygamy as the lesser of two evils, so he did not try to move his people back to the creation ideal of monogamy (Gen. 1–2) faster than they could handle (cf. Matt. 19:8). However, he regulated several aspects of polygamy to avoid some of its negative effects.

First, OT law prohibited a man from taking "a woman as a rival wife to her sister, uncovering her nakedness while her sister is still alive" (Lev. 18:18).[78]

75. *Hebrew Law in Biblical Times: An Introduction*, 2nd ed. (Provo, UT: Brigham Young University Press; Winona Lake, IN: Eisenbrauns, 2001), 127.

76. In the absence of modern fertility techniques such as artificial insemination. Additional wives taken by patriarchs in Gen. 16 and 30 were maidservants serving as surrogate mothers.

77. Apparently ancient Israelites did not adequately understand the possibility of male infertility.

78. Some have argued that "sister" here broadly refers to any other woman, so that this is a blanket prohibition of polygamy (Angelo Tosato, "The Law of Lev. 18:18: A Reexamination," *CBQ* 46 [1984]: 202–8; Gordon P. Hugenberger, *Marriage as a Covenant: A Study of Biblical Law and Ethics Governing Marriage Developed from the Perspective of Malachi*, VTSup 52 [Leiden: Brill, 1994], 115–18; R. Davidson, *Flame of Yahweh*, 193–98; cf. the *Temple Scroll* [11QT] 57.17–18 and the *Damascus Document* [CD] 4.21). They take Lev. 18:17 to be the last of the incest laws (vv. 6–17), which have a distinctive pattern of formulation, and view v. 18 as belonging to the next group of laws (vv. 18–23), which are formulated differently and (with the possible exception of v. 18) do not concern incest. They also interpret *'ishah 'el-'akhotah*, lit.,

This would prevent sisters, such as Leah and Rachel (Gen. 29–30; before the law was given), from becoming hostile competitors.[79] It would also serve as a warning that marriage to more than one woman at the same time, whether or not they are sisters, likely will result in unhealthy rivalry (1 Sam. 1:4–8).[80]

Second, a husband was not permitted to downgrade the entitlements of his servant concubine if he took another wife (Exod. 21:10–11).

Third, a man with two wives, one of whom he preferred over the other, with the latter producing his firstborn son, was not allowed to give the privileges of the firstborn to a younger son by his preferred wife (Deut. 21:15–17).

Fourth, while prominent and wealthy men were tempted to multiply wives in order to increase their children and therefore their power and, of course, to satisfy their sexual appetites (Judg. 8:30–31; 2 Sam. 3:2–5; 1 Kings 11:1–3), OT law discouraged this: A king "shall not acquire many wives for himself, lest his heart turn away" (Deut. 17:17).[81] The Israelite high priest, whose life was to exemplify holiness, was to have only one wife (Lev. 21:13–14).

The NT moved the Christian faith community away from polygamy by specifying that church leaders, who should be examples to others (1 Tim. 4:12; 1 Pet. 5:3), must be monogamous (1 Tim. 3:2, 12; Titus 1:6). However, there is no blanket prohibition of polygamy in the NT, undoubtedly to allow

---

"a woman to her sister," in v. 18 as the general expression for a connection between two grammatically feminine entities (cf. Exod. 26:3, 5, 6, 17; Ezek. 1:9, 23; 3:13, but none of these refer to women), comparable to the masculine expression *'ish 'el-'akhiv*, "a man to his brother," which can be rendered "to one another" (e.g., Exod. 16:15; 25:20; 37:9). However, *'ish 'el-'akhiv* can refer to literal brothers, i.e., male siblings (Gen. 37:19; 42:21, 28), and the immediately preceding context in Lev. 18 concerns incest, in which the word *'akhot*, "sister," unambiguously refers to a female sibling rather than to just any woman (vv. 9, 11–13; cf. Jacob Milgrom, *Leviticus 17–22: A New Translation with Introduction and Commentary*, AB 3A [New York: Doubleday, 2000], 1548–49). Cf. the Hittite Laws §192, "If a man's wife dies, [he may take her] sister [as his wife.] It is not an offence" (trans. Harry A. Hoffner Jr., *COS* 2.19:118). Here "sister" is the sibling of a man's wife, whom he may marry after his wife's death, in agreement with Lev. 18:18. This factor in Lev. 18:18 can explain placement of this verse within Lev. 18. Unlike the incest prohibitions in vv. 6–17, that of v. 18 lasts only "while" [preposition *b*] a relative "is still alive," just as the following prohibition in v. 19 lasts only "while" [preposition *b*] a woman "is in her menstrual uncleanness." For such pairing between laws, see vv. 20–21, both of which involve illicit giving (*qal* of *n-t-n*) and seed (*zera'*, semen/children). Note that if Lev. 18:18 were a blanket prohibition of polygamy, it would irreconcilably conflict with Deut. 21:15–17, which regulates inheritance in an explicitly bigamous household, showing that Deuteronomy tolerates rather than prohibits multiple marriages.

79. It is the reference to rivalry between two women in Lev. 18:18 that calls for the expression *'ishah 'el-'akhotah*, "a woman to her sister," with the preposition *'el* rather than simply the conjunction, as in v. 17, "a woman and her daughter."

80. Cf. Gane, *Leviticus, Numbers*, 320.

81. According to 1 Kings 11, Solomon's multiple marriages to foreign women led him into idolatry.

polygamous families to join the church. This indicates that modern Christian missionaries to polygamous people groups (e.g., in Africa) should receive members of such families into full church fellowship when they are converted to Christ rather than breaking up the families to enforce monogamy. If God could grant centuries of grace for this change, we should allow one generation.[82]

There is no excuse for people who are already part of the Christian church to take additional spouses. The Bible never encourages polygamy but only discourages it. We know enough to follow the biblical trajectory back to the creation ideal, which is reinforced by the OT and NT rules regarding exemplary religious leaders (see above). Although we may have some practical needs for children that coincide with those of ancient Israelites, we have other strategies (medical and financial, etc.) for dealing with infertility and its results. More importantly, because Christians belong to Christ, we are all "heirs according to promise" (Gal. 3:29). So we know that our success and security depend on God's Son rather than on our own sons, and our hopes are invested in his heavenly country (cf. Matt. 6:19–21; Heb. 11:16) rather than in our earthly enterprises.

Protection of Animals and the Environment

Not only does OT law look out for the welfare of vulnerable humans, but it also protects animals and the environment, including the land and its fruit trees. Work animals, like humans (including servants and resident aliens), have the right to rest on the weekly Sabbath (Exod. 20:10; 23:12; Deut. 5:14). That which grows on uncultivated land during fallow Sabbatical Years can be freely eaten by wild animals, along with needy humans (Exod. 23:11; cf. Lev. 25:6–7). A working animal should be permitted to enjoy some results of its labor (Deut. 25:4), and a smaller animal should not be unduly taxed by making it pull equal weight with a larger and stronger animal (22:10).[83]

Some laws benefit animals along with their owners. A stray animal should be returned to its owner, even if the individual is an enemy (Exod. 23:4; Deut. 22:1–3), and a person who sees another's fallen animal should assist him to lift it to its feet (Deut. 22:4). The fact that someone who makes a pit into which an animal falls and dies must make restitution to the owner would encourage

82. Roy E. Gane, "Some Biblical Principles Relevant to Evangelism among Polygamous Peoples," *Journal of Adventist Mission Studies* 2, no. 1 (2006): 29–43, esp. 43. Note that polygamous marriages are real marriages, not simply common-law arrangements that could more easily be terminated.
83. Cf. Prov. 12:10, "The righteous care for the needs of their animals, but the kindest acts of the wicked are cruel" (NIV).

Israelites to prevent such harm (Exod. 21:33–34). Similarly, it would be wise for the owner of an ox with a history of goring to keep it restrained in order to protect another animal from being killed by it, in which case he would be obliged to make compensation (21:35–36).

Even when humans kill animals for food, they must treat the lives of these creatures with respect by draining out their blood at the time of slaughter (esp. Gen. 9:4; Lev. 17:10–14; Deut. 12:16, 23–25; 15:23; Acts 15:20, 29), not boiling a baby animal (kid goat) in its mother's milk (Exod. 23:19; 34:26; Deut. 14:21),[84] and not taking a mother bird (to eat) along with its young or its eggs (Deut. 22:6–7). Also showing respect for life, a baby animal could not be sacrificed before it was eight days old (Lev. 22:27), and it was forbidden to slaughter a parent animal (father or mother) from the herd (bovines) or flock (sheep or goats) and its young on the same day (v. 28).[85]

Concerning the environment, human beings live in an interdependent relationship with it. If people damage their land and its productivity, they harm not only their own ability to gain sustenance from this fundamental resource but also that of others, including members of their households and those who inherit the land after them. So in this sense, not only allocation of land but also the way it is used can be regarded as a social-justice issue. The Bible teaches that everything we have, including our land and all that comes from it, is a gift from our creator (Gen. 1; cf. Deut. 8:18). It follows that we should manage these resources responsibly, taking into account impacts of our actions on all forms of life that God has made.

The OT law promotes the health of agricultural land by stipulating that it rest from cultivation every seventh year (Exod. 23:10–11; Lev. 25:2–5) and additionally during the Jubilee Year every half century (Lev. 25:11). These fallow periods would allow the soil to recover its depleted nutrients. In addition, OT law protects fruit trees belonging to any city, including outside the land of Israel, by forbidding Israelite armies to cut them down to make siege works during time of war (Deut. 20:19–20). They are vulnerable trees, not human enemies, so it is unjust to destroy them (v. 19b).

Leviticus 19:23–25 instructs Israelites regarding care of young fruit trees in the land of Israel. For the first three years, they are to treat its fruit as a foreskin (Hebrew *qal* of '-*r*-*l* + noun *'orlah*) by removing "the incipient fruit inside its bud."[86] This would be a beneficial horticultural practice, allowing

---

84. On the prohibition of boiling a young goat in its mother's milk, see chap. 12, n. 32.

85. Milgrom, *Leviticus 17–22*, 1884, following the Hebrew text with generic masculine forms that include the father of the animal, which Lev. 22:28 ESV ("But you shall not kill an ox or a sheep and her young in one day") does not accurately represent here.

86. Milgrom, *Leviticus 17–22*, 1679.

the immature tree to become established before putting its energy into developing fruit.[87] Only in the fourth year are the Israelites to allow the fruit to ripen and to pick it, but this first harvest is holy, which means that it belongs to YHWH and is to be given to him as an offering of praise.[88] Finally, in the fifth year the people are permitted to eat of the fruit. This procedure, with the delay of four years, is "to increase its yield for you" (v. 25).[89] Thus God will bless the productivity of the tree if the Israelites will acknowledge that its value for them, like that of the land that he gives them to use, depends on him and following his principles.[90]

Basic Human Rights

In Paris on December 10, 1948, the United Nations General Assembly adopted the Universal Declaration of Human Rights (resolution 217A) that belong equally to every person in the world.[91] This document, which contains a preamble and thirty articles, is a major milestone in the history of basic human rights and is generally regarded as the foundation of international human rights law.

Most of the articles in the Universal Declaration of Human Rights (UDHR) have antecedents in OT law, a much earlier milestone originally given to one nation—ancient Israel—that was to serve as a model for other nations (e.g., Deut. 4:5–8; Isa. 2:2–4; Mic. 4:1–3).[92] In light of what we have learned about OT law thus far, we can see that it affirmed equal dignity and rights of Israelite families, whose members were "endowed with reason and conscience

87. Ibid., 1679, 1684, citing Philo, *Virtues* §§157–59.

88. Presumably by giving it to the priests at the sanctuary for them to eat after an initial offering to YHWH on the altar (Milgrom, *Leviticus 17–22*, 1681, in agreement with Qumran texts: 11QT^a 38.1–7; 4QD^c 2.ii.6). Cf. other firstfruits offerings (cf. Exod. 23:19; 34:26; Lev. 2:14; 23:17, 20; Num. 18:13; Deut. 18:4; 26:1–11). Note that in Exod. 13:13; 34:20 the firstling of a donkey could not be offered to God, because it was impure, just as the fruit of the first three years of a tree could not be offered to God.

89. Cf. the Laws of Hammurabi §60, where the owner of a Babylonian date orchard and the gardener who develops it begin to utilize the fruit in the fifth year.

90. Cf. covenant blessings and curses involving dependence on God and the rain that he gives for productivity of the land and its trees (Lev. 26:4, 19–20). On the close connection between the Lord, Israel, and the land, see C. Wright, *Old Testament Ethics*, 19, 76–99. The law concerning young fruit trees in the land of Israel does not apply today as a religious requirement, because we can no longer "turn fourth-year fruit over to the domain of the sanctuary/temple, which no longer exists. Nevertheless, modern horticulture identifies an ongoing and universal practical benefit" (Gane, *Leviticus, Numbers*, 340).

91. See http://www.un.org/en/universal-declaration-human-rights/.

92. Cf. C. Wright, *Old Testament Ethics*, 62–74.

and should act towards one another in a spirit of brotherhood" (UDHR §1). The principles exemplified in OT law entitled individuals to "life . . . and security" (§3); "recognition . . . as a person before the law" (§6); "the right to an effective remedy by the competent national tribunals for acts violating the fundamental rights granted him by the constitution or by law" (§8); freedom from "arbitrary arrest, detention or exile" (§9); the right to "full equality to a fair and public hearing by an independent and impartial tribunal, in the determination of his rights and obligations and of any criminal charge against him" (§10); and "the right to be presumed innocent until proved guilty according to law in a public trial" (§11).

The OT law did not allow for a person to "be subjected to arbitrary interference with his privacy, family, home . . . nor to attacks upon his honour and reputation" (§12), but gave Israelites "the right to freedom of movement and residence within the borders of each state" (§13).[93] Everyone in Israel possessed "the right to a nationality" (§15), "the right to marry and to found a family" (§16),[94] and "the right to own property. . . . No one shall be arbitrarily deprived of his property" (§17). Israelites enjoyed "freedom of opinion and expression" (§19), except for certain damaging forms of speech, such as taking God's name in vain (Exod. 20:7), cursing God or a ruler (22:28 [22:27 MT]) or their parents (21:17), lying (Lev. 19:11), slander (v. 16), or false witness (Exod. 20:16; Deut. 19:16–21). They had the rights "to freedom of peaceful assembly and association" (§20), "to work" (§23), "to rest and leisure, including reasonable limitation of working hours and periodic holidays" (§24; although the holidays would not necessarily be "with pay"), and "freely to participate in the cultural life of the community" (§27).

The OT law would affirm that "everyone has duties to the community in which alone the free and full development of his personality is possible" (§29). However, OT law did not include all of the ideals set forth in the UDHR, which are not yet realized in our world today. Ancient Israel was a theocracy, not a democracy, and OT law recognized only YHWH worship as legitimate in Israel. It pragmatically accepted but regulated male social leadership and servitude (see above), pending further progress in restoring the creation ideal of full equality (Gen. 1; §1, "All human beings are born free and equal in dignity and rights") under YHWH (Gen. 1–2). These constraints limited OT law in relation to at least some components of the UDHR articles §§1–4, 7, 16, 18, 21, 23. Nevertheless, our current belief "that all men are created equal, that

93. Israelites generally resided within the inherited territories of their clans, but they could move around in Israel.
94. Israelites could even marry while they were debt-servants, but with constraints if their masters provided servants as their spouses (Exod. 21:4).

they are endowed by their Creator with certain unalienable Rights" (United States Declaration of Independence) is indebted to our cultural heritage, including concepts of equality that go back to the Pentateuch.[95]

Article §5 of the UDHR reads: "No one shall be subjected to torture or to cruel, inhuman or degrading treatment or punishment." Old Testament law expresses this concern by limiting punishment by flogging: "Forty stripes may be given him, but not more, lest, if one should go on to beat him with more stripes than these, your brother be degraded in your sight" (Deut. 25:3). However, OT punishments such as the lex talionis ("eye for eye, tooth for tooth") and stoning to death, which were aimed at achieving full justice and completely deterring violation of covenant principles within the ancient context (see chap. 14 below), may not have passed the standard set by modern interpretation of the principle embodied in §5.

Without a state public welfare system, an ancient Israelite did not have "protection against unemployment" (§23) or "the right to a standard of living adequate for the health and well-being of himself and of his family" (§25).[96] However, OT law does encourage society to "make resources available to as many as possible so that they can at least have a fair opportunity to thrive independently."[97] Israelites did not have "the right to education" provided by the state (§26), but they were supposed to have education in the form of homeschooling in practical skills, common wisdom, ethical values, and religious tradition that parents were to provide for their children (e.g., Exod. 12:26–27; 13:8–9; Deut. 6:6–7; Prov. 1:8; 4:1–5).

---

95. Berman, *Created Equal*, 174–75.
96. Cf. §22, which partly depends on state resources that the ancient Israelites did not possess: "Everyone, as a member of society, has the right to social security and is entitled to realization, through national effort and international co-operation and in accordance with the organization and resources of each State, of the economic, social and cultural rights indispensable for his dignity and the free development of his personality."
97. Gane, "Social Justice."

14

Old Testament Law
and Theodicy

In the preceding chapter, we found that God's justice is a positive and constructive part of his love. It is manifested in protecting people by providing them with fair treatment and eliminating oppression. Modern Christians can quite readily appreciate the social-justice elements of OT law when they understand them (see chap. 13). However, it is more difficult to grasp the justice of God in some other aspects of his laws where he permits Israelites to keep permanent slaves, stipulates harsh punishments for violations of his commandments, and mandates destruction of entire nations inhabiting the land of Canaan. These raise issues of theodicy (justifying God), which involves the question of why God allows evil. If God is omnipotent, so that he can prevent evil, why does he permit or even cause it if his character is really good?[1]

The present chapter attempts to wrestle with the issues just mentioned in order to suggest possible explanations on the basis of biblical evidence. However, at the outset it should be acknowledged that such an exercise in theodicy is tentative because God and his knowledge, perspective, and ways exceed human understanding (cf. Deut. 29:29), as Job and his friends discovered (Job 38–42).

---

1. Note that Isa. 45:7 says that YHWH creates *ra'*, which some older English versions render as "evil" (KJV), but the previous words say that he makes *shalom*, "well-being." So the meaning of *ra'* in this context is not evil in a moral sense but the opposite of well-being (NKJV, NASB, and ESV: "calamity").

Permanent Servitude

As discussed in chapter 13, debt and famine servitude in OT law were by no means ideal, but they originated from voluntary decisions, were temporary, and served useful economic purposes for all parties concerned within the existing ancient society. So they do not pose real problems of theodicy, nor does the choice of an Israelite bonded servant to permanently remain with his master because he prefers life as a member of his household (Exod. 21:5–6; Deut. 15:16–17, also female servant). Here we discuss more challenging cases of permanent servitude: servant marriage (Exod. 21:7–11) and servitude of foreigners (Lev. 25:44–46).

Servant Concubinage

Exodus 21:7–11 regulates a category of permanent servitude of an Israelite young woman (probably a teenage girl) that involves a kind of concubinage.[2] The law reads as follows:

> When a man sells his daughter as a slave ['*amah*, "maidservant"], she shall not go out as the male slaves [plural of '*eved*] do. If she does not please her master, who has designated her for himself [or "who has not designated her"],[3] then he shall let her be redeemed. He shall have no right to sell her to a foreign people, since he has broken faith with her. If he designates her for his son, he shall deal with her as with a daughter. If he takes another wife to himself, he shall not diminish her food, her clothing, or her marital rights ['*onah*, alternatively, "oil" or "habitation/dwelling"].[4] And if he does not do these three things for her, she shall go out for nothing, without payment of money.

2. On this and related cases, see Raymond Westbrook, *Law from the Tigris to the Tiber: The Writings of Raymond Westbrook*, ed. Bruce Wells and Rachel Magdalene, 2 vols. (Winona Lake, IN: Eisenbrauns, 2009), 2:149–74, chapter titled "The Female Slave," reprinted from *Gender and Law in the Hebrew Bible and the Ancient Near East*, ed. Victor H. Matthews, Bernard M. Levinson, and Tikva Frymer-Kensky, JSOTSup 262 (Sheffield: Sheffield Academic, 1998), 214–38; Raymond Westbrook and Bruce Wells, *Everyday Law in Biblical Israel: An Introduction* (Louisville: Westminster John Knox, 2009), 64–65; Bernard S. Jackson, *Wisdom-Laws: A Study of the Mishpatim of Exodus 21:1–22:16* (Oxford: Oxford University Press, 2006), 93–102. Jackson concludes that "the object here is not to produce heirs for the purchaser. . . . It is not inappropriate to use here language which would fail the standards of precision of a modern lawyer: she has a 'quasi-servile' status and a relationship 'somewhat akin' to marriage" (102, cf. 100).

3. English versions, including ESV, render the *qere* (scribal emendation) and Septuagint reading *lo* (preposition *l* + third-person masculine-singular pronominal suffix), "for himself." The *ketiv* (consonantal Masoretic text) reading *lo'* (particle of negation), "not," expresses the idea that the master has not designated her.

4. Regarding alternatives for '*onah*, see, e.g., Shalom Paul, *Studies in the Book of the Covenant in the Light of Cuneiform and Biblical Law*, VTSup 18 (Leiden: Brill, 1970; repr., Eugene,

We know that the woman is Israelite because "she shall not go out as the male slaves do," and the male slaves are "Hebrew" (v. 2). Her father sells her from free status into that of a female slave: *'amah*. According to Deut. 15:12, a Hebrew woman who is simply a slave would go free after six years of service, as a male slave would. However, Exod. 21:7–11 addresses a different kind of case that involves an additional factor: The servant woman is intended for a sexual relationship, as shown by the words "If he takes [*qal* of *l-q-kh*] another wife[5] to himself" (v. 10), indicating that he has taken the first woman. The expression "take [*qal* of *l-q-kh*] + woman" in this kind of context, referring to her change of status, refers to taking a wife or concubine (e.g., Gen. 4:19; Judg. 19:1; 2 Sam. 5:13).[6]

The woman in Exod. 21 is a concubine rather than a full-status wife, as indicated by the following factors:[7] She is sold as an *'amah*, not given in marriage (v. 7); she is entitled to rations as a servant (v. 10);[8] and termination of the relationship with her master would be accomplished through her manumission rather than divorce (v. 11). Other references to women with *'amah* status serving or having served sexual/childbearing functions appear in Gen. 20:17 (female servants of Abimelech); 21:10, 12–13 (Hagar); 30:3 (Bilhah).

After the young woman is sold (Exod. 21:7), there are three possibilities that the law regulates: (1) It turns out that the master does not like her and does not wish to keep her (v. 8). (2) He keeps her for his son (v. 9). (3) He keeps her for himself but takes an additional woman (vv. 10–11). The woman's concubinage is permanent unless one of two things happen.

First, if the master does not like her and chooses to break his agreement regarding her, he must let her be redeemed so that she can go back to her family (represented by her father). The cost of redemption no doubt would include a refund to the master for the price he has given for her, which could have paid a debt that her family owed him. This redemption occurs whether

---

OR: Wipf & Stock, 2006), 59–61; Richard M. Davidson, *Flame of Yahweh: Sexuality in the Old Testament* (Peabody, MA: Hendrickson, 2007), 192–93.

5. "Wife" is supplied in the translation; it is not in the Hebrew.

6. Gregory C. Chirichigno observes that the preceding law about the male servant (Exod. 21:2–6) is also concerned about marital rights. *Debt-Slavery in Israel and the Ancient Near East*, JSOTSup 141 (Sheffield: JSOT Press, 1993), 246, 255.

7. Carolyn Pressler, "Wives and Daughters, Bond and Free: Views of Women in the Slave Laws of Exod. 21:2–11," in *Gender and Law in the Hebrew Bible and the Ancient Near East*, ed. Victor H. Matthews, Bernard M. Levinson, and Tikva Frymer-Kensky, JSOTSup 262 (Sheffield: Sheffield Academic, 1998), 163–64. "The slave wife of a free man does not have the status of a free wife, but neither is she merely a chattel" (172).

8. Westbrook, *Law from the Tigris to the Tiber*, 2:173.

the master has designated her for himself or (alternative reading) has not designated her (v. 8) as a concubine.

The second scenario that can terminate the maidservant's relationship to the master is the alternative that he keeps her but takes another woman (concubine or wife) to himself and gives the second preferential treatment by cutting back on provisions to the first, thereby passively abusing her. In this case, he must simply let her go free without receiving financial compensation from her family (vv. 10–11). This part of the law clearly allows but regulates a bigamous arrangement.[9]

A modern reader is understandably disturbed by the idea that OT law would allow a father to sell his daughter as a concubine. Like debt and famine servitude, however, this could help a family, including the young woman, to survive in desperate circumstances. If she was of marriageable age and her family could no longer feed her, and if for some reason a normal marriage could not be arranged for her, she could gain permanent support by becoming a concubine, and her family would benefit by receiving the price for her, which could pay off an existing debt. The lasting nature of this solution could make it preferable to temporary debt or famine servitude, and it was certainly far better than making her a prostitute, which Lev. 19:29 forbids.

At first glance, the words "She shall not go out as the male slaves do" (Exod. 21:7) appear to represent blatant gender discrimination. But the agreement between the father of the girl and the master to whom he sells her is for her to be a permanent concubine. She is not to be temporarily used. By taking her, the master is required to make a long-term commitment. This is confirmed by the rule that he may not save expenses and downgrade her status by cutting down on her provisions if he takes another woman without altogether losing her (vv. 10–11). Her freedom could put her in the difficult position of supporting herself, but the master is discouraged from precipitating this circumstance by the fact that he would lose his investment in her along with her services ("She shall go out for nothing, without payment of money," v. 11).

The law of Exod. 21:7–11 protects the servant concubine in three ways. First, if the master finds her to be displeasing (ra'ah, "bad"), he must permit her to be redeemed, and he may not "sell her to a foreign people" (v. 8). This allows for

9. Some scholars avoid bigamy here by interpreting the law as follows: The master does not designate the maidservant for himself (ketiv in v. 8). So if he takes "another" to himself (v. 10), this second woman is instead of, rather than in addition to, the maidservant, and therefore no bigamy is involved (Walter C. Kaiser Jr., *Toward Old Testament Ethics* [Grand Rapids: Zondervan, 1983], 184–85; R. Davidson, *Flame of Yahweh*, 192). In v. 8, however, whether or not the master designates her for himself, he must let her be redeemed. If that happens, she leaves his household rather than remaining dependent on the master's provisions along with another woman, as v. 10 says that she does.

the possibility that if she is not redeemed, he could sell her to another Israelite, who would be obligated to observe the rest of this law, but foreigners in another country would not be bound by Israelite law and therefore would likely treat her as a chattel slave.[10] Second, if she is intended for the son, the master "shall deal with her as with a daughter" (v. 9),[11] in this case as if she were his (free) daughter (which she is not), until the couple is ready to consummate the marriage. This implies that he may not have sexual relations with her (cf. Lev. 18:15).[12] Third, if the master neglects her, he is not permitted to retain her, even as an ordinary slave,[13] but must free her without receiving a redemption price (Exod. 21:11).

As with other kinds of servitude discussed in chapter 13 above, servant concubinage was an existing customary arrangement that OT law regulated to protect the servant. The OT law did not engage in social engineering by abolishing the institution itself, because it could contribute to maintaining life within its cultural context and abolishing it could cause more harm than good. So this appears to resolve the problem of theodicy while exemplifying divine patience with imperfect social conventions and concern for protecting vulnerable individuals. The law provides no support for resurrecting servant concubinage, which is not an accepted part of modern Western culture, although some men do keep mistresses.

Servitude of Foreigners

A serious question of theodicy arises from Lev. 25:44–46a, which permits Israelites to hold non-Israelite servants in perpetuity:

> As for your male and female slaves whom you may have: you may buy male and female slaves from among the nations that are around you. You may also buy from among the strangers who sojourn with you and their clans that are with you, who have been born in your land, and they may be your property. You may bequeath them to your sons after you to inherit as a possession forever. You may make slaves of them.[14]

Why would God allow this? Of course, this was nothing new. Abraham had owned permanent servants from various nations (Gen. 12:16; 15:2; 16:1).

10. Westbrook, *Law from the Tigris to the Tiber*, 2:155–56.
11. Literally, "according to the custom [*mishpat*] of daughters" (21:9 NKJV, NASB).
12. Dale Patrick, *Old Testament Law* (Atlanta: John Knox, 1985), 71.
13. Joe M. Sprinkle, *Biblical Law and Its Relevance: A Christian Understanding and Ethical Application for Today of the Mosaic Regulations* (Lanham, MD: University Press of America, 2006), 136–37.
14. Cf. Lev. 22:11, "But if a priest buys a slave as his property for money . . ."

They were required to obey and work for him, of course, but this does not necessarily mean that their status was degraded. Abraham entrusted management of all his possessions to his senior servant (Gen. 24:2)[15] and designated Eliezer of Damascus, a member of his household and apparently his chief servant, as his heir in the absence of offspring (15:2–4). In later biblical history, "Sheshan had no sons, only daughters, but Sheshan had an Egyptian slave whose name was Jarha. So Sheshan gave his daughter in marriage to Jarha his slave, and she bore him Attai" (1 Chron. 2:34–35). These were exceptional cases, yet they show the extent to which slaves could be valued and respected.

The point of Lev. 25 is not to downgrade non-Israelites but to contrast with their ongoing status the new status of the Israelites, whom God had liberated from slavery in Egypt to be his own servants (vv. 42–43, 46b). "Without the release legislation, the default situation would have allowed perpetual slavery for Israelites. What is exceptional is not that non-Israelites could be held in perpetuity, but that Israelites could not. God elevated their status in accordance with their election and redemption. They had already served their time in Egypt (Lev. 25:42; Deut. 15:15)!"[16] This was not yet the ultimate ideal of freedom for all, but it represented an important first step[17] by using one nation as a model of freedom, which others could wish to emulate or join.

Notice that the legal differentiation between Israelites and non-Israelites was based on YHWH's covenant with Israel, not on skin color. There was no hint of the kind of racism that was inextricably linked with American slavery, which its supporters regarded as justified by the notion that a human being with dark skin color was inferior.

By contrast with treatment of non-Israelite slaves, Lev. 25:43, 46b, 53 prohibit "ruthlessly" (preposition *b* + *perek*) ruling over an Israelite servant. In this context, the prohibition means that Israelites who sold themselves into famine servitude could not be held in permanent servitude; they were to be treated as hired workers or sojourners and released in the Jubilee Year if they could not be redeemed before that (vv. 39–42, 47–54). This protected Israelites but implies that it was permissible to treat non-Israelite slaves ruthlessly, which means here that because they lacked the special rights of Israelites, they could be held as permanent slaves who were not treated as hired workers (vv. 44–46); their masters could force them to work.[18] However,

---

15. Cf. Joseph as a slave managing Potiphar's household in Egypt (Gen. 39:4).

16. Roy Gane, *Leviticus, Numbers*, NIV Application Commentary (Grand Rapids: Zondervan, 2004), 441.

17. Cf. chaps. 7–9 above on movement toward ideals.

18. In Exod. 1:13–14, *b* + *perek* refers to forcing slaves to work. Cf. Ezek. 34:4, where *b* + *perek* parallels *b* + *khazekah*, "with force."

Lev. 25 does not approve of cruel treatment of slaves (see further below on Exod. 21:20–21, 26–27).

The fugitive slave law of Deut. 23:15–16 (23:16–17 MT) puts a limit on harsh treatment: "You shall not give up to his master a slave who has escaped from his master to you. He shall dwell with you, in your midst, in the place that he shall choose within one of your towns, wherever it suits him. You shall not wrong him." So all that a slave must do to get away from an overly harsh master would be to flee. The law could apply to any slave, but the provision that such an individual can live as a free person "within one of your towns, wherever it suits him" would especially apply to non-Israelites.[19]

This radical law in Deuteronomy was unique in the ANE[20] and opposite to the Laws of Hammurabi, which rewarded a person who returned a fugitive slave to the owner (§17) but mandated the death penalty for someone who failed to do so (§§15–16, 19).[21] If the OT law were implemented, it would undermine the entire institution of slavery by removing its involuntary component,[22] and slaves from various nations could flock to Israel for freedom and safe haven, without fear of extradition.

So why would YHWH allow Israelites to buy and permanently own non-Israelite slaves at all? The Bible does not say, so we can only point to some relevant factors and trust that God was leading people toward a higher ideal— "There is neither slave nor free" (Gal. 3:28)—at a pace that they could handle[23] without causing excessive collateral damage. It is clear that God does not like slavery, just as he does not like polygamy (1 Tim. 3:2, 12, "husband of one wife") or divorce (Matt. 19:8), which he also permitted to avoid greater

---

19. Israelites presumably would tend to return to the villages of their clans (cf. Lev. 25:10, 41).

20. Westbrook, *Law from the Tigris to the Tiber*, 1:211–14.

21. Cf. the Laws of Ur-Namma §17, which specifies a reward for someone who returns a slave to the master, and the Laws of Lipit-Ishtar §§12–13, which stipulate economic penalties (slave for slave or 15 shekels of silver) for someone who harbors a female or male slave. See also 1 Kings 2:39–40, where Shimei retrieves his servants who have fled to the Philistine city of Gath, directly against what God had instructed the Israelites to do. Note that Paul did not disregard the fugitive slave law when he sent Onesimus back to Philemon, his master, because Onesimus voluntarily returned. Paul undermined slavery by encouraging Christian brotherly love as the basis of their relationship (Philemon, esp. v. 16).

22. Jeffries M. Hamilton, *Social Justice and Deuteronomy: The Case of Deuteronomy 15*, SBLDS 136 (Atlanta: Scholars Press, 1992), 119–20.

23. Cf. William J. Webb, *Slaves, Women & Homosexuals: Exploring the Hermeneutics of Cultural Analysis* (Downers Grove, IL: IVP Academic, 2001), 37–38, 58, 74–76, 84. Already within the Pentateuch we see advancement in the requirements for humane treatment of servants. By comparison with Exod. 21, Deut. 15 introduces the command for a master when he frees a servant: "Supply him liberally from your flock, from your threshing floor, and from your winepress" (Deut. 15:14 NKJV).

damage, but with regulation to prevent their worst effects (Exod. 21:10–11; Lev. 18:18; Deut. 21:15–17; 24:1–4).

Slavery in Israel, as elsewhere in the ANE, could be an alternative preferable to death by starvation when people were not able to support themselves (cf. Gen. 47:13–26). It was also an alternative to death when one group captured prisoners from another during warfare rather than killing them (e.g., 2 Sam. 12:31). Thus Deut. 20 regulates conflict between Israelites and a city not located in the land promised to them (v. 15):

> When you draw near to a city to fight against it, offer terms of peace to it. And if it responds to you peaceably and it opens to you, then all the people who are found in it shall do forced labor for you and shall serve you. But if it makes no peace with you, but makes war against you, then you shall besiege it. And when the LORD your God gives it into your hand, you shall put all its males to the sword, but the women and the little ones, the livestock, and everything else in the city, all its spoil, you shall take as plunder for yourselves. (vv. 10–14)

This looks brutal from our modern perspective, but we take a lot for granted, including the United Nations, international law, and strong countries that value justice and may deter one nation from preying on another. In the absence of such protections, the Israelites were on their own (with God) when they faced enemies who wanted to destroy them (e.g., Exod. 17:8–16; Num. 21–22, 25, 31). The stern reality on the ground was that YHWH's nation could survive only by eliminating threats from enemy males of fighting age by killing them if they chose to fight or, if they chose peace, by keeping them under control as slaves.

Thus the Lord allowed the Israelites to fight just wars and deal with their consequences within rules of engagement that recognized ANE realities but excluded simply killing the inhabitants of a city without giving them an opportunity to surrender and live. According to the Pentateuch, these contextually conditioned rules came from YHWH, who possesses the wisdom and authority to justly arbitrate between nations (Isa. 2:4; Mic. 4:3); they were not humanly devised military doctrines that make the end justify the means. We can learn from Deut. 20:10–14 that victorious military forces should preserve life as much as possible, and changed modern circumstances should allow for more favorable outcomes than in ancient times.

By permitting Israelites to acquire and keep foreigners as slaves, whether their status of servitude originated in Israel or in other countries, OT law allowed for their survival in conditions that were better than elsewhere.[24] The

---

24. Léon Epsztein, *Social Justice in the Ancient Near East and the People of the Bible*, trans. John Bowden (London: SCM, 1986), 119.

quality of life for foreign slaves held by Israelites would be enhanced by several factors if God's people observed the OT laws.

First, if the laws in Exod. 21:20–21, 26–27, which represent minimum standards applicable to extreme situations, apply to any slaves, they protect both Israelite debt-servants and non-Israelite permanent slaves from death or permanent physical damage inflicted by a master administering excessively harsh discipline.[25] In fact, verses 26–27 stipulate that a slave should receive the compensation of freedom for loss of an eye or tooth at the hands of the master. There is no analogous protection of slaves from their masters in ANE law. Law §199 of the Laws of Hammurabi does specify monetary compensation for blinding an eye or breaking a bone of a slave, but only when the injury is caused by a third party, and presumably it is the master who receives the restitution (half of the slave's value). Gregory C. Chirichigno points out that many Old Babylonian and Middle Assyrian private documents indicate that owners of chattel slaves could mutilate them, although masters who killed or seriously injured their slaves would suffer financial loss.[26]

Second, OT law provides for slaves to gain the major benefit of rest on the weekly Sabbaths (Exod. 20:10; 23:12; Deut. 5:14). Third, slaves are to enjoy some festive religious occasions, which involve special meals and time off from work, along with other members of the households to which they belong (Deut. 12:12, 18; 16:11, 14).

William J. Webb has pointed out that the Bible shows clear redemptive movement from slavery toward freedom, even though the ultimate ethic could not be realized in biblical (including NT) times, and Christians have been responsible for rightfully continuing the movement to abolition of servitude.[27] We know that liberty for all is the ideal not because of human subjective and therefore unreliable wisdom or culturally accepted norms that go beyond the Bible, but because it restores the freedom with which

---

25. The laws of Exod. 21:20–21, 26–27 do not specify that they apply only to Hebrew persons (cf. v. 2), and they are separated from the earlier pericopes regarding Israelite servants (vv. 2–6, 7–11). That God did hold Israel responsible for Saul's treatment of one group of permanent non-Israelite servants, i.e., the Gibeonites (cf. Josh. 9), is recounted in 2 Sam. 21:1–14. On treatment of slaves in Mesopotamia and improvement made by OT law regarding assault of slaves (Exod. 21:20–21, 26–27), raising chattel slaves to the same level as debt-servants in this regard, see Chirichigno, *Debt-Slavery*, 146, 176–77. However, some scholars maintain that these verses (Exod. 21:20–21, 26–27) apply only to Israelite debt-servants, as in vv. 2–11. Jackson, *Wisdom-Laws*, 249; cf. Raymond Westbrook, *Studies in Biblical and Cuneiform Law*, CahRB 26 (Paris: Gabalda, 1988), 90; Sprinkle, *Biblical Law*, 87.

26. *Debt-Slavery*, 146.

27. Cf. Webb, *Slaves, Women & Homosexuals*, 37–38, 74–76, 84, etc.

humans were originally endowed when they were created in the image of God (Gen. 1–2).[28]

Since we do not practice slavery,[29] what practical wisdom can we take away from studying the biblical laws that regulate it? For one thing, we can apply a fortiori logic: Since even an ancient bonded servant was protected from excessive discipline by his Israelite master, the more so should modern Christian employers abstain from excessive punishment of their contractual employees. This does not tell us exactly what to do in a given situation, but the Bible provides a framework for wise decisions and actions.[30]

For instance, a Christian employer who contemplates (nonphysical) discipline of a problematic worker[31] and yet pauses to read Exod. 21:20–21 and other relevant OT and NT passages can be reminded of several factors that could influence a decision: First, what is to be gained by harsh punishment, given that this could negatively affect the worker's future productivity for the employer?[32] Second, the employee has relatives, to whom the person is valuable and who are protective of that person. Third, in light of Lev. 19:17–18, is there another way to resolve the situation through clear communication and reconciliation that would result in less damage? Fourth, is the contemplated punishment fair in God's sight (cf. Eph. 6:9; Col. 4:1)? Fifth, seek wisdom from all available human sources and from God (cf. Prov. 2:1–15; James 1:5).

Severity of Punishments

Punishments Reflecting Values of Justice

In a fallen world, establishing justice and eliminating oppression can require a sterner side of justice, as revealed by Jer. 30:11: "For I am with you to

28. Among other things, forcing someone to serve as a slave could be regarded as robbing them of the right to what they could acquire and hold as a free person, against the Decalogue principle "You shall not steal" (Exod. 20:15). Related to this is the following law: "If a man is found stealing one of his brothers of the people of Israel, and if he treats him as a slave or sells him, then that thief shall die. So you shall purge the evil from your midst" (Deut. 24:7; cf. Exod. 21:16). Here "treats him as a slave" refers to keeping the stolen "property" to illicitly benefit from his labor.

29. Although millions of people are enslaved in the world today and need to be liberated.

30. If the Bible told us what to do in every situation, as in "positive law," its complexity and length would be incredible, and copying it by hand and preserving it through the centuries would have posed an insurmountable challenge.

31. Nonphysical discipline could involve a fine deducted from pay, withholding vacation time, withdrawal of certain privileges, etc.

32. The clause "for he [the worker] is his money" (Exod. 21:21 KJV) could discourage an employer from getting rid of a worker after making a certain investment, such as paying training costs.

save you, declares the LORD; I will make a full end of all the nations among whom I scattered you, but of you I will not make a full end. I will discipline you in just measure [preposition *l* + *mishpat*], and I will by no means leave you unpunished." Here God carries out justice on two groups: his erring people, who have departed from his principles of justice, and the nations that he uses to discipline them. This process is redemptive for his people, but he must eliminate some nations to end their oppression (cf. Dan. 7–8, 11; 2 Thess. 1:5–10; Rev. 18–20). God judges according to his values of justice, which prioritize the lives of victims above the lives of those who persist in trying to destroy them.

The words in Jer. 30:11—"I will by no means leave you unpunished" (ESV; *piel* infinitive absolute of *n-q-h* + negative particle *lo'* + *piel* imperfect of *n-q-h*)—echo the same expression (except in third person) found in Exod. 34:7, where ESV provides a valid alternative rendering: "but who will by no means clear the guilty." This is part of YHWH's proclamation of his own character while he passed before Moses:

> The LORD, the LORD, a God merciful and gracious, slow to anger, and abounding in steadfast love and faithfulness, keeping steadfast love for thousands, forgiving iniquity and transgression and sin, but who will by no means clear the guilty, visiting the iniquity of the fathers on the children and the children's children, to the third and the fourth generation. (Exod. 34:6–7)

This important statement in Exod. 34, to which several other biblical passages refer (e.g., Num. 14:18; Ps. 86:15; Joel 2:13), indicates the two sides of the divine character of love: mercy and justice (although *mishpat* does not appear here), including retributive justice. In light of Jer. 30:11, even God's punishments are part of his love because they discipline wrongdoers to motivate them to repent so that they can be saved and/or stop them from causing further harm to others. The question to ponder here is why some of the punishments specified in OT law seem so severe and therefore apparently unjust from a modern Western perspective.

We can learn a lot about the values behind OT law from the penalties that it stipulates. As could be expected of any rational legal system, the severity of a penalty for breaking a given OT law is proportional to the degree of negativity attached to the forbidden behavior, which corresponds to the magnitude of the perceived gap between the normative value underlying the law and violation of it.

For example, a farmer who indirectly steals by carelessly allowing his animals to feed on someone else's field or vineyard is subject to the light requirement to simply restore the amount of food that the animals ate (Exod. 22:5 [22:4 MT]; see above). However, direct and intentional theft and killing or selling of an animal carries a stiff penalty in addition to restoration: "He shall repay five oxen for an ox, and four sheep for a sheep" (22:1 [21:37 MT]). In a case of intentionally killing (murdering) or stealing (kidnapping) a human being, the penalty is radically more severe: death (Exod. 21:12, 16; Num. 35:30–31; Deut. 24:7).

From this gradation of penalties, we learn that intentional stealing departs from the value of respect for another person's property (e.g., Exod. 20:15) to a greater degree than indirect stealing through negligence. Furthermore, a human is valued above an animal, which is worth more than food that animals can eat.

Some other ANE legal systems allowed economic penalties in some cases of first degree homicide,[33] but OT law permitted no alternative to capital punishment for murder (esp. Num. 35:31). This difference does not mean that the OT legal system reflects a more primitive, barbaric worldview in which life is cheap. Rather, OT law reflects a different conceptual system in which human life is of supreme value, beyond price (cf. Ps. 49:7–8 [49:8–9 MT]), and its value would be diminished if monetary compensation could be made for it.[34]

Kinds of Penalties in Old Testament Laws

Penalties administered by the human community according to OT laws are of several kinds:

1. *Economic*, including reparation (e.g., Exod. 21:32; 22:1, 4, 7, 9, 16–17 [21:37; 22:3, 6, 8, 15–16 MT]; Deut. 22:29),[35] payment of a fine (Exod. 21:22–25; Deut. 22:19),[36] and loss of a servant who must be freed (Exod. 21:11, 26–27).

2. *Relational*, including public shaming (Deut. 25:9–10)[37] and permanent loss of the right to divorce (Deut. 22:19, 29).

33. E.g., Hittite Laws §§5–6; Middle Assyrian Laws A §10.
34. Moshe Greenberg, "Some Postulates of Biblical Criminal Law," in *Yehezkel Kaufmann Jubilee Volume*, ed. Menahem Haran (Jerusalem: Magnes, 1960), 13–17. In this light, the lex talionis penalty of absolute justice for permanent physical loss from assault (Lev. 24:19–20) as partial murder (see chap. 3 above) fits even more tightly within the biblical conceptual framework than in the earlier context of the Laws of Hammurabi (§§196–97, 200).
35. A person who lacks the means to make reparation can be sold into slavery to pay this debt (Exod. 22:3 [22:2 MT]).
36. On application of the lex talionis in Exod. 21:23–25 as a fine, see chap. 12 above. In Deut. 22:19 the fine is not payment of the marriage present or its equivalent (cf. Exod. 22:17 [22:16 MT]; Deut. 22:29), which already would have been paid.
37. Shaming was more serious in this ancient honor-shame society (cf. chap. 6 above) than in our culture. On the purpose of such shaming in the Bible (including in Lev. 20 and 1 Cor. 5)

3. *Physical*, including flogging (Deut. 22:18; 25:2–3),[38] an injury equivalent to that which the wrongdoer inflicted on the victim (literal lex talionis; Lev. 24:19–20; Deut. 19:19–21),[39] cutting off a hand (Deut. 25:11–12), death (e.g., Exod. 21:12, 14–17; 22:19 [22:18 MT]),[40] specifically death by stoning (e.g., Lev. 20:2, 27; 24:14, 16; cf. Num. 15:35–36),[41] death plus shaming by hanging up the corpse (Deut. 21:22–23; cf. Num. 25:4),[42] and burning (Lev. 20:14; 21:9).[43]

Additionally, some penalties are directly inflicted by God himself, including gynecological damage, sterility, and consequent shame (Num. 5:27; cf. v. 28), childlessness (Lev. 20:20–21), and being "cut off" (*k-r-t* = losing an afterlife; e.g., Lev. 7:20–21, 25, 27; 18:29).[44]

The economic and relational OT penalties look reasonable to us, as does capital punishment for murder (Exod. 21:12; Num. 35:16–21, 30–31; Deut. 19:11–12), which is still carried out today in some places. It is not difficult to grasp the rationales for flogging (Deut. 22:18; etc.), retaliatory punishment (lex talionis; Lev. 24:19–20; Deut. 19:19–21), and death for kidnapping (Exod. 21:16) and rape (Deut. 22:25), although modern Western countries do not administer these penalties and we may not feel comfortable with them.[45]

---

for warning and redemption, see Gane, *Leviticus, Numbers*, 363–64. Of course, all penalties administered by humans or by God would involve shame to some degree.

38. With a maximum of forty stripes, lest the individual be "degraded in your sight" (Deut. 25:3). Cf. the Laws of Hammurabi §202, "If an *awîlu* should strike the cheek of an *awîlu* who is of status higher than his own, he shall be flogged in the public assembly with 60 stripes of an ox whip" (trans. Martha Roth, "The Laws of Hammurabi," *COS* 2.131:348). The harshness of this Babylonian penalty was no doubt due to the fact that striking the cheek of another would inflict intolerable shame in that ANE culture, in addition to the physical pain.

39. The fact that the lex talionis formulations in Lev. 24 and Deut. 19 refer to literal physical retaliatory punishment is indicated by the words "as he has done it shall be done to him" and "whatever injury he has given a person shall be given to him" (Lev. 24:19–20) and "Then you shall do to him as he had meant to do to his brother" and "Your eye shall not pity" (Deut. 19:19–21).

40. See chap. 5 above on the capital punishment formula *mot yumat*.

41. Exodus 19:13, recounting preparations for YHWH's theophany on Mount Sinai, specifies that anyone who touches the mountain on that occasion "shall be stoned or shot" (with an arrow).

42. Cf. such exposure of corpses in Josh. 8:29; 10:26; 1 Sam. 31:10, 12 (attached to city wall by Philistines); 2 Sam. 4:12; 21:6, 9.

43. Cf. Gen. 38:24; Josh. 7:15, 25; Judg. 14:15; 15:6.

44. On the formula for the divine penalty of being "cut off," see chap. 5 above.

45. Gane, *Leviticus, Numbers*, 425–27, points out several factors relevant to retaliatory punishment: (1) Early Israel had no prisons, so incarceration was out of the question. (2) OT law tended to make punishments fit crimes if possible. (3) Literal application of the lex talionis was 100 percent justice. (4) Assault causing permanent damage was regarded as partial murder. (5) The primary concern in OT law was justice for the victim rather than protection of the criminal. (6) Ancient Israelites lacked our medical solutions and conveniences for permanently damaged victims of assault. (7) The lex talionis would have enhanced justice by stopping excessive

The divinely inflicted punishments of gynecological damage and sterility for adultery (Num. 5:27; cf. v. 28) and childlessness for incest (Lev. 20:20–21) are serious, but at least they do not involve capital punishment.

The OT penalties that most likely raise questions regarding justice, and therefore theodicy, for a modern reader are the nontalionic removal of a woman's hand (Deut. 25:11–12), the terminal penalties of death by the human community, and being "cut off" by God for a number of offenses that seem less serious to us than murder, kidnapping, and rape. Some of these are not even regarded as crimes in modern Western societies.

If penalties reflect the importance of the values behind them, perhaps our discomfort indicates that our assessment of values is partly out of alignment with God's. Therefore, the biblical system of penalties is worth exploring so that we can better understand his values. However, the physical punishments themselves should not be applied today under a kind of Christian theonomic "Taliban," because the only legitimate civil theocracy in history, that of ancient Israel, is gone (cf. chap. 8).

Physical Penalty for Sexual Assault

We will begin by considering the cutting off of a woman's hand and then turn to cases that call for terminal penalties. A casuistic law in Deut. 25 prohibits a wife from intervening in a brawl to help her husband in a certain way: "When men fight with one another and the wife of the one draws near to rescue her husband from the hand of him who is beating him and puts out her hand and seizes him by the private parts, then you shall cut off her hand. Your eye shall have no pity" (vv. 11–12).

A wife is permitted to intervene in all kinds of other ways that do not cause lasting damage,[46] but absolutely not this one. In another situation, an Israelite could lose a hand as retaliatory punishment for destroying another person's hand (cf. Lev. 24:19–20). However, Deut. 25:11–12 specifies the only nontalionic removal of a body part as a punishment in OT law.[47] Why is the penalty so harsh in this case?[48] To put the problem in perspective, however, it

retaliation (e.g., Gen. 4:23–24) and by mandating equal punishment without discrimination according to class or economic status (cf. Paul, *Studies*, 76). (8) When Jesus ruled out application of the lex talionis to personal vengeance (Matt. 5:38–39), he did not revoke it as a judicial penalty administered by a court, as it is in OT law.

46. If she inflicts permanent damage (*mum*), the lex talionis applies (Lev. 24:19–20).

47. Genesis 17:10–14 calls for removing the male foreskin in circumcision, but this is not a punishment.

48. Some scholars have tried to lessen the penalty by interpreting the *qal* of *q-ts-ts*, "cut off," with the direct object *kaf*, "palm, hand," as something other than amputating the hand (see

is remarkable that such punishment is so rare in OT law, given the frequency with which other ANE law systems specify physical mutilations.[49]

In the event that the wife were to crush and thereby cause the destruction (whether immediate or through subsequent infection) of one or both of the man's testicles, this would be a highly significant injury that would compromise or terminate his ability to procreate in order to have or increase a line of descendants.[50] A man who lacked reproductive capacity because his testicles were crushed was incomplete, and he was barred from belonging to the Israelite governing assembly (Deut. 23:1 [23:2 MT]).[51] If an Israelite woman permanently damaged a man, the lex talionis should ordinarily apply (Lev. 24:19–20). However, if his loss was a male organ, she would have no corresponding organ to forfeit as punishment. Therefore it would make sense that instead she should lose her offending hand, which had caused the injury.

The problem is that Deut. 25:11 only says that the wife seizes the other man's genitals; it does not say that she causes any damage at all, and we should not read this assumption into the text.[52] Obviously she would cause shame and pain to the man and threaten his procreative ability, thereby showing disrespect for life. The context here, following the law of levirate marriage (vv. 5–10), highlights the concern for "a threat to procreation that would lead to

---

review of proposals in R. Davidson, *Flame of Yahweh*, 477–80; cf. 249), such as talionic removal of the woman's genitals, probably a clitoridectomy (Lyle Eslinger, "The Case of an Immodest Lady Wrestler in Deuteronomy XXV 11–12," *VT* 31 [1981]: 269–81) or the hair of her groin (Jerome T. Walsh, "'You Shall Cut Off Her . . . Palm'? A Reexamination of Deut. 25:11–12," *JSS* 49 [2004]: 47–58). However, there is no convincing evidence to regard *kaf* here as anything other than the whole hand in this context, as in 1 Sam. 5:4: "The head of Dagon and both his hands [*kapot yadayw*, the palms of his hands] were lying cut off [*qal* passive participle of *k-r-t*] on the threshold." Neither does Deut. 25:12 indicate that anything other than the hand is cut off (*q-ts-ts*), such as hair (as in Jer. 9:26 [9:25 MT]; 25:23; 49:32). For references to interpretations that maintain the traditional hand-amputation view, see William J. Webb, *Corporal Punishment in the Bible: A Redemptive-Movement Hermeneutic for Troubling Texts* (Downers Grove, IL: IVP Academic, 2011), 100n4.

49. Webb, *Corporal Punishment*, 103–11.

50. A partial parallel to Deut. 25:11–12 is found in the Middle Assyrian Laws A §8, which does not mention that the woman is a wife trying to rescue her husband from another man: "If a woman should crush a man's testicle during a quarrel, they shall cut off one of her fingers. And even if the physician should bandage it, but the second testicle then becomes infected(?) along with it and becomes . . . , or if she should crush the second testicle during the quarrel—they shall gouge out both her [. . .]-s" (trans. Martha Roth, "The Middle Assyrian Laws [Tablet A]," *COS* 2.132:354).

51. A descendant of Aaron with at least one crushed testicle was disqualified from officiating as a priest (Lev. 21:20) and an animal with crushed testicles was unfit to serve as a sacrificial victim (Lev. 22:24), so it appears that such a defect diminished the holiness that an Israelite man should have. Cf. Jeffrey H. Tigay, *Deuteronomy: The Traditional Hebrew Text with the New JPS Translation*, JPS Torah Commentary (Philadelphia: Jewish Publication Society, 1996), 210–11.

52. Webb (*Corporal Punishment*, 101–2) assumes this on contextual grounds.

childlessness."[53] But why should her hand be cut off?[54] In this law the opposite gender of the individuals involved is clearly significant. The point seems to be that it is indecent and immoral for a woman to sexually assault a man (to whom she is not married) by grasping his genitals,[55] even in the extenuating circumstance that she is a wife who is trying to save her husband. A fortiori it would be even less justifiable for her to do it in another situation.[56]

There is no corresponding OT law against a man grabbing the private body parts of a woman to whom he is not married. However, from Deut. 25:11–12 it is easy to deduce that if it is wrong for a woman to seize a man by his genitals, it would be immoral for a man to sexually assault a woman by groping her under any circumstances.[57] This is distressingly relevant in our modern world! Deuteronomy 25 indicates that sexual assault is not a trivial offense: From God's point of view, a person who does this deserves to have a hand cut off, even though such a punishment will not be carried out under the laws of modern Western states and certainly should not be implemented by the church, which is a spiritual rather than civil community.

Capital Punishment

It is significant that most of the offenses for which OT law prescribes death are violations of principles exemplified by the first eight of the Ten Commandments (cf. chap. 5).[58] Zero tolerance for breaking these commandments accords with the fact that they constituted stipulations of the covenant between YHWH and Israel, which had to be preserved for the well-being of all Israelites (cf. Lev. 26; Deut. 28).

53. R. Davidson, *Flame of Yahweh*, 480, cf. 477.
54. Here OT law is tougher than the Middle Assyrian Laws, in which a woman forfeits a body part only if she causes damage (see law A §8, above). If an Assyrian woman only lays a hand upon a man, "she shall pay 1,800 shekels of lead; they shall strike her 20 blows with rods" (MAL A §7; trans. Roth, "The Middle Assyrian Laws," COS 2.132:354).
55. Cf. Walsh, "'You Shall Cut Off Her . . . Palm'?," 49.
56. Cf. the Laws of Hammurabi §195, "If a child should strike his father, they shall cut off his hand" (trans. Roth, "The Laws of Hammurabi," COS 2.131:348). There is no mention of permanent physical damage to the father here. The offense is physical expression of extreme disrespect, which in OT law would break the fifth commandment of the Decalogue (Exod. 20:12) and would incur the death penalty for striking either parent (Exod. 21:15). As in Deut. 25:11–12, the culprit's hand, the body part that committed the offense, is cut off.
57. Also elsewhere there are laws to one gender that have implications for the other gender, e.g., the tenth commandment of the Decalogue (against coveting) and the laws in Lev. 18:22 and 20:13 against male homosexual activity (cf. Rom. 1:26–27, including lesbian sex).
58. An exception is the death penalty for not obeying the verdicts of the central judicial authorities (Deut. 17:12). Notice that the Ten Commandments themselves do not specify any humanly administered penalties.

Capital Crime	Decalogue Commandment Violated
Sacrificing to any god other than YHWH (Exod. 22:20 [22:19 MT]); giving one's child to the god Molech (Lev. 20:2); worshiping other gods (Deut. 17:5); enticing Israelites to serve other gods (Deut. 13:10 [13:11 MT]); practicing occult (Lev. 20:27)	1. "You shall have no other gods before me" (Exod. 20:3)
Giving one's child to the god Molech (Lev. 20:2) and other forms of idolatrous worship of other gods (see above)	2. "You shall not make for yourself a carved image. . . . You shall not bow down to them or serve them" (Exod. 20:4–6)
Blaspheming the name of YHWH (Lev. 24:16)	3. "You shall not take the name of the LORD your God in vain" (Exod. 20:7)
Profaning the Sabbath by working on it (Exod. 31:14–15; 35:2; cf. Num. 15:35)	4. "Remember the Sabbath day, to keep it holy" (Exod. 20:8–11)
Striking one's parents (Exod. 21:15); cursing one's parents (Exod. 21:17; Lev. 20:9);[a] rebelling against one's parents (Deut. 21:21)	5. "Honor your father and your mother" (Exod. 20:12)
Murder (Gen. 9:6; Exod. 21:12; Lev. 24:17; Num. 35:16–18, 21, 31)	6. "You shall not murder" (Exod. 20:13)
Adultery (Lev. 20:10; Deut. 22:22–24) and other forms of sexual impurity:[b] promiscuity by daughter (Lev. 21:9; Deut. 22:21); rape (Deut. 22:25); incest (Lev. 20:11–12, 14), homosexual activity (Lev. 20:13), and bestiality (Exod. 22:19 [22:18 MT]; Lev. 20:15–16)	7. "You shall not commit adultery" (Exod. 20:14)
Kidnapping, stealing a human (Exod. 21:16).	8. "You shall not steal" (Exod. 20:15)

a. A curse was not merely bad language that expressed a malevolent wish; it actually invoked supernatural power as a weapon (cf. Num. 22–24).

b. Consensual sex of a betrothed woman with a man who is not her fiancé is treated as adultery (Deut. 22:23–24).

Notice that capital punishment is stipulated for violation of the eighth commandment only in a case of kidnapping. Penalties for other violations of this commandment are economic (e.g., Exod. 22:1–4 [21:37–22:3 MT]).[59] Thus OT law makes a clear distinction between human life and nonhuman possessions.

The last two commandments of the Decalogue, which are not always punishable by death, are set apart from the other commandments by the fact that they relate to several of the earlier commandments. The ninth commandment, "You shall not bear false witness against your neighbor" (Exod. 20:16), protects people from false accusations that they have violated one or more of commandments 1–8. Deuteronomy 19 specifies retaliatory punishment (vv.

59. "If he has nothing, then he shall be sold for his theft" (Exod. 22:3 [22:2 MT]) is an economic penalty: the thief must work off his reparation debt.

19, 21) for a false witness (vv. 16–18) that fits the crime and can include the loss of the culprit's life ("life for life," v. 21).

The tenth commandment, "You shall not covet" (Exod. 20:17), forbids the thought process that can lead to violations of other commandments, such as by stealing another person's possessions ("your neighbor's house") or committing adultery ("your neighbor's wife").[60] Because coveting is thought, it cannot be adequately detected and judged by human beings. So the community does not administer capital punishment for this wrong, which must be directly prosecuted by YHWH himself.

Terminal Divine Penalty of "Cutting Off"

As pointed out in chapter 5, the penalty of "cutting off" (*k-r-t*), which denies the offender an afterlife, is directly administered by God. Like the death penalty carried out by the human community, it is terminal punishment. Wrongs for which individuals are "cut off" generally involve violation of YHWH's religious (including ritual) commandments, committing offenses against him that are difficult or impossible for the human community to detect (e.g., secret sexual sins), or both.[61] These wrongs relate to principles exemplified by the Ten Commandments, to God's covenant with Israel, or to the Israelite ritual system as follows:

Violation Incurring "Cutting Off"	Violation of a Commandment
Giving one's child to the god Molech (Lev. 20:3, 5); utilizing occult mediums (v. 6)[a]	Decalogue 1. "You shall have no other gods before me" (Exod. 20:3)
Giving one's child to the god Molech (Lev. 20:3, 5)	Decalogue 2. "You shall not make for yourself a carved image. . . . You shall not bow down to them or serve them" (Exod. 20:4–6)
Working on the Sabbath (Exod. 31:14)	Decalogue 4. "Remember the Sabbath day, to keep it holy" (Exod. 20:8–11)
Eating meat with its blood, showing disrespect for life (Lev. 7:27; 17:10, 14)	Decalogue 6. "You shall not murder" (Exod. 20:13)
Any sexual activities forbidden in Lev. 18, including incest, sex during menstruation, adultery, homosexual activity, and bestiality (v. 29)	Decalogue 7. "You shall not commit adultery" (Exod. 20:14)
Defiantly ("with a high hand") breaking any of YHWH's commandments (Num. 15:30–31)[b]	Any of YHWH's commandments

60. As the tragic account of David and Bathsheba illustrates, coveting can also lead to murder (2 Sam. 11–12; cf. James 4:2).

61. Cf. Jacob Milgrom, *Leviticus 1–16: A New Translation with Introduction and Commentary*, AB 3 (New York: Doubleday, 1991), 457–58, 460.

Violation Incurring "Cutting Off"	Violation of a Commandment
Failure of an Israelite to be circumcised (Gen. 17:14)	Ritual initiation into divine covenant with Abraham and his descendants
Eating fat of a sacrificable animal (Lev. 7:25); eating meat from a well-being offering as late as the third day after it is slaughtered (19:7–8); eating from a well-being offering while ritually impure (7:20–21); a priest encroaching on holy things while ritually impure (22:3);ᶜ eating leavened bread during the Festival of Unleavened Bread (Exod. 12:15, 19); failing to keep the Passover in the first month when one is not ritually impure or on a journey (Num. 9:13); failing to undergo ritual purification from corpse impurity (19:13, 20); or failing to practice self-denial (by fasting, etc.) on the Day of Atonement (Lev. 23:29).	Israelite ritual system centered at the sanctuary

a. Notice the secret nature of Saul's visit to the female medium at Endor (1 Sam. 28, esp. v. 8).

b. For the idea that *beyad ramah*, "with a high hand," signifies defiance, see Exod. 14:8 ESV, KJV.

c. On the *qal* of *q-r-b* + preposition *'el* here with the meaning "encroaches upon" (i.e., illegitimately uses), see Jacob Milgrom, *Leviticus 17–22: A New Translation with Introduction and Commentary*, AB 3A (New York: Doubleday, 2000), 1850.

Some violations of the Ten Commandments that are direct offenses against YHWH are punishable both by the human community through execution if its members apprehend the crime and by YHWH through cutting them off. These violations are Molech worship (Lev. 20:2–3) and working on the Sabbath (Exod. 31:14). This dual punishment is possible because being "cut off" is a fate that goes beyond death (see chap. 5).

Terminal penalties (death and/or being "cut off") for violations of the Ten Commandments show that the Lord was serious about their principles, which were not merely Ten Recommendations. He had proclaimed them from Mount Sinai with the utmost clarity and emphasis as the paramount stipulations of his covenant with his people (Exod. 20; Deut. 5). The Israelites had voluntarily accepted YHWH's covenant stipulations (including the laws in the Covenant Code; Exod. 21–23) with their words of commitment to obey everything he had said, and with a blood ritual that emphasized the life-and-death consequences of obedience versus disobedience (24:3–8).

The Ten Commandments, along with the Lord's other stipulations, including regarding the covenant sign of circumcision (Gen. 17) and his ritual rules for maintaining his presence at the sanctuary, were absolute, nonnegotiable requirements for remaining in and enjoying the benefits of the covenant community and the promised land. Those who violated them were to be treated as rebels and permanently removed from the community by execution under the theocratic judicial system and/or condemned to losing a place among their people in the afterlife. If Israel as a whole persisted in widespread violation of divine laws, especially against idolatry, murder, and sexual offenses that morally polluted the land that YHWH gave to his chosen people (Lev. 18; 20; Num. 35:31, 33), he would punish them and exile them from the land (Lev. 26; Deut. 28).

Additional Factors Relevant to Old Testament Penalties

Consideration of the OT penalties should take into account some additional factors. First, an important reason for serious punishments was to deter Israelites from ever committing grave wrongs that would damage the community and for which there was zero tolerance (Deut. 13:11 [13:12 MT], "all Israel shall hear and fear"; 17:13; 19:20; cf. 21:21).[62] People could easily avoid the penalties by abstaining from such behaviors.

At least from a modern perspective, the punishment of being burned would pack the strongest punch in terms of deterrence. This penalty is stipulated if a man sexually takes both a woman and her mother (Lev. 20:14) or if a priest's daughter is sexually promiscuous, thereby profaning her consecrated father (21:9). The purpose of the punishment is explicit in Lev. 20:14: "that there may be no depravity among you." The penalty should never be implemented because the offense should never occur. Another wrong that should never occur is worshiping any god other than YHWH or influencing others to do this, which incurs the consequence of sacral devotion to utter destruction (verb *kh-r-m*; Exod. 22:20 [22:19 MT]; Deut. 13:15 [13:16 MT]; cf. Lev. 27:28–29), the same punishment to be inflicted on the idolatrous inhabitants of Canaan (see further below).

Second, stoning (e.g., Lev. 20:2, 27; 24:16) was a shocking process, but it served the purpose of involving the members of the community, beginning with the witnesses (Deut. 17:7), to enact their repudiation of the crime by

62. Not stipulated by OT law are several kinds of severe physical punishments prescribed by the Laws of Hammurabi (LH) and the Middle Assyrian Laws (MAL), although some of these consequences could result from operation of the lex talionis in OT law (Lev. 24:19–20; Deut. 19:19, 21). The ANE laws include casting a person into the water, presumably drowning them (e.g., LH §§108, 143), impaling (LH §153; MAL A §53), cutting out the tongue (LH §192), cutting off the nose (MAL A §§4–5), plucking out an eye (LH §193), cutting off one or both ears (e.g., LH §205; MAL A §§4–5), cutting off a breast (LH §194), and turning a man into a eunuch (MAL A §20). In this last law there is also a retaliatory punishment that would be unthinkable in Israel: "If a man sodomizes his comrade and they prove the charges against him and find him guilty, they shall sodomize him and they shall turn him into a eunuch" (MAL A §20; trans. Roth, "The Middle Assyrian Laws," COS 2.132:355). On physical mutilation in Sumerian, Egyptian, Babylonian, Assyrian, and Anatolian (Hittite) laws, see Webb, *Corporal Punishment*, 103–9.

carrying out the execution together. Thus YHWH instructed regarding a brawling blasphemer: "Bring out of the camp the one who cursed, and let all who heard him lay their hands on his head, and let all the congregation stone him" (Lev. 24:14, carried out in v. 23; cf. Num. 15:35–36).

Participation in such a stoning, which inflicted shameful rejection as well as pain and death, would powerfully reinforce the importance of maintaining the value(s) that had been violated and discourage contemplation of behavior that could lead to a similar fate. Like capital punishment by a firing squad, stoning also had the advantage that responsibility for the death of the criminal was widely spread, so nobody could subsequently blame just one or two individuals.

Third, biblical law calls for no jail sentences. Incarceration is the common modern punishment for crime, but it has massive problems that are well known, including the billions of taxpayer dollars required annually to house millions of prisoners and the fact that many prisoners become more hardened and dangerous while serving time. In early Israel a suspect could be held in custody, under guard pending trial (Lev. 24:12; Num. 15:34), but there was no prison infrastructure.[63] Neither were there facilities to hold the criminally insane, for whom OT law offers no legal defense on account of their mental condition. Wrongdoers were simply to be condemned for what they had done if there was clear evidence, punishment was to be quickly carried out, and life was to move on, without a huge bureaucracy, expensive lawyers, and backlogs of cases that keep unconvicted people in jail for extended periods of time while they await trial.

Fourth, several procedural aspects of OT law were designed to prevent miscarriage of justice in capital cases. David Llewellyn has listed five of these:

The five procedural items are: 1) Absolute certainty of guilt was required for conviction (Deut. 17:4). . . . 2) Conviction required the testimony of more than one witness (Deut. 19:15; Num. 35:30). Given the need for certain proof, most likely those witnesses were to be eyewitnesses. Moreover, since stoning to death was to be done by the witnesses (Deut. 17:7), one might suspect reticence to cast the first stone unless one was an eyewitness. 3) To discourage attempts to "frame" someone for a crime, witnesses who committed perjury in capital cases were themselves to be executed (Deut. 19:16, 19). 4) In difficult cases the

63. Prisons were present in Egypt (Gen. 39:20–23; 40:3–5; Exod. 12:29), Philistia (Judg. 16:21, 25), Assyria (2 Kings 17:4), and Babylon (2 Kings 25:27; Jer. 52:11, 31). During the period of the monarchy, they also existed in northern Israel (1 Kings 22:27) and Jerusalem (2 Chron. 16:10; Jer. 37:15–16, 18). A number of these prisons appear to have had the primary function of incarcerating those who had wronged or offended monarchs, as explicitly in Gen. 39:20.

verdict was deferred to judicial experts (Deut. 17:8, 9). . . . 5) If the verdict was "guilty," the death penalty was mandatory (Lev. 27:29; Num. 35:31). Lighter sentences could not be adopted. This made discriminatory application of the death penalty impossible; i.e., all people, regardless of social standing, etc., were treated equal if deemed guilty.[64]

Old Testament law provided a sixth safeguard in a case of adultery: Both the man and the woman were to be put to death (Lev. 20:10; Deut. 22:22–24; ignored in John 8:3–5). This protected women, who otherwise could be convicted of adultery simply because they were pregnant.[65]

Accountability under the New Covenant

Modern Christians are living under the new covenant (Luke 22:20; 1 Cor. 11:25; Heb. 8:8, 13; 9:15; 12:24; cf. Jer. 31:31–34), which constitutes a church community rather than a civil-religious nation. Now God leaves enforcement of law and order in society in the hands of the state. The state is authorized to administer penalties, including with "the sword," referring to its ability to carry out capital punishment (Rom. 13:1–7). This accords with the witness of Gen. 9:6 that God mandated the death penalty for murder in the Noachian laws for all humanity, long before the Israelite theocracy was established, indicating that justification for such punishment is permanent and universal, provided, of course, that it is justly administered.[66]

Some modern Western countries still execute murderers, who violate the sixth of the Ten Commandments, but they do not inflict capital punishment on those who commit other wrongs that coincide with violations of Decalogue commandments that were punishable by death under the Israelite theocracy. Nevertheless, this does not mean that obedience to the divine principles is less important than in ancient times or that God ultimately holds members of his Christian covenant community less accountable than the ancient Israelites.

In his Sermon on the Mount (Matt. 5:1), Jesus affirmed:

> Do not think that I have come to abolish the Law or the Prophets; I have not come to abolish them but to fulfill them. For truly, I say to you, until heaven and earth pass away, not an iota, not a dot, will pass from the Law until all is accomplished. Therefore whoever relaxes one of the least of these

64. David Llewellyn, "Restoring the Death Penalty: Proceed with Caution," *Christianity Today* 19 (May 23, 1975): 10–11.
65. On a modern example of this in Nigeria, see Gane, *Leviticus, Numbers*, 802–3.
66. On capital punishment in the Bible, cf. ibid., 799–806.

commandments and teaches others to do the same will be called least in the kingdom of heaven, but whoever does them and teaches them will be called great in the kingdom of heaven. For I tell you, unless your righteousness exceeds that of the scribes and Pharisees, you will never enter the kingdom of heaven. (Matt. 5:17–20)

Thus the moral standard for new-covenant Christians is higher, not lower, than it was for ancient Israelites under their earlier covenant phase.

Now that the new covenant is directly open to all peoples, Christians are no longer required to practice the Abrahamic covenant ritual of circumcision (Acts 15).[67] Nor are we obliged to observe the ritual rules connected with the ancient Israelite sanctuary/temple, because that institution is gone and we have direct access to God through Christ's priestly ministry in his heavenly sanctuary (Heb. 4:14–16; chaps. 7–10 above). However, Paul upheld the divine moral law as important and good (Rom. 3:20b; 31; 7:7, 12, 14, 22) and called on Christians: "Put to death therefore what is earthly in you: sexual immorality, impurity, passion, evil desire, and covetousness, which is idolatry. On account of these the wrath of God is coming" (Col. 3:5–6). Although Christians are not to execute other people, we are to put something to death: the sins in our own lives that would incur condemnation to eternal death that will be inflicted on the unrepentant when God's wrath comes (cf. Rev. 20:12–15; 21:8, 27; 22:15).

The NT provides evidence that affirms ongoing accountability to the major moral values represented in the Decalogue within the context of the Christian church. Paul called on the church community in Corinth to remove from its fellowship a member who was violating the incest law (related to the seventh commandment, against adultery, Exod. 20:14) against sex with one's stepmother, for which the OT penalty was death (1 Cor. 5; cf. Lev. 20:11; cf. 18:8; Deut. 22:30 [23:1 MT]).

Paul's ruling establishes an important precedent: Within the church context, the equivalent of removing a person who has committed a capital crime law by executing them is to remove them by disfellowshipping them. This protects the reputation of God, who is represented on earth by his true church, of which Christ is the head (1 Cor. 12:27; Eph. 4:15–16; 5:23). The church is not a civil theocracy, but it is a spiritual theocracy with authority to govern the boundaries of its community of faith in accordance with the divine will (cf. Matt. 16:19; 18:18; John 20:22–23).

67. But circumcision may continue to be desirable for hygienic reasons, and spiritual "circumcision" of the heart (Deut. 10:16; 30:6; Rom. 2:29) is experienced by a Christian at conversion (Col. 2:11–12), when a person accepts the new covenant.

Divinely Mandated Destruction of Nations

For many modern Christian readers of OT law, the single most disturbing feature is YHWH's repeated command to utterly exterminate all of the previous inhabitants of the land of Canaan, which he was giving to the Israelites (Deut. 7:1–5; 20:16–18).[68] He decrees in Deut. 20:16: "You shall save alive nothing that breathes." What this means is explicit in Josh. 6:21, which reports what the Israelites did to Jericho when they captured it: "Then they devoted all in the city to destruction, both men and women, young and old, oxen, sheep, and donkeys, with the edge of the sword."[69]

When the Israelites eradicated all people and domestic animals here and in other places, they were carrying out the divine orders given through Moses, as Josh. 10:40 and 11:12, 20 make explicit. So God was in charge of this, which explains why people and things that were dedicated/devoted (verbs from the root *kh-r-m* and noun *kherem*) could not "be sold or redeemed; every devoted thing is most holy to the LORD. No one devoted, who is to be devoted for destruction from mankind, shall be ransomed; he shall surely be put to death" (Lev. 27:28–29). Such devoted things were regarded as "most holy" because ownership of them had been irrevocably transferred to the domain of the holy Deity, who consequently governed their fate (Josh. 6:18–19, 24; 7:1).[70]

The Lord's instructions for taking Jericho reinforce the fact that this first conquest in Canaan was a sacral event under his control: "Seven priests shall bear seven trumpets of rams' horns before the ark. On the seventh day you shall march around the city seven times, and the priests shall blow the trumpets" (Josh. 6:4; cf. vv. 6, 8–9, 12–13, 16).

Lest we are still inclined to simply blame the Israelites, Josh. 11:20 also claims responsibility for God after an event of destruction: "For it was the LORD's doing to harden their hearts that they should come against Israel in battle, in order that they should be devoted to destruction and should receive no mercy but be destroyed, just as the LORD commanded Moses."

Some modern interpreters reject the possibility that the Lord could have commanded such destruction. They argue for radical discontinuity between the God of the OT and the God of the NT and/or view the OT as misrepresenting

---

68. On this, including modern implications, see Gane, *Leviticus, Numbers*, 771–77.

69. See further reports of extermination in Josh. 8:26; 10:28, 35, 37, 39–40; 11:11–12, 20–21; and destruction of enemies in Transjordanian cities, which were not part of Canaan (Deut. 2:34; 3:6).

70. Cf. Israel's vow to YHWH to devote Arad to destruction if he would enable its conquest (Num. 21:2), which he did so that the vow was fulfilled (v. 3).

the true divine character.[71] However, the most natural reading of the biblical text indicates that the one God of both Testaments sometimes gives up on groups of people and destroys them (e.g., Gen. 6–7, 19; Rev. 14:9–10, 17–20; 19:17–21; 20:9–10, 15).[72] In the case of the Canaanites, "during a certain phase of history he *uniquely* delegated *a carefully restricted part* of his destructive work to his chosen nation of ancient Israel, *which he tightly controlled and held accountable under theocratic rule.*"[73] Israel serves as a model/paradigm for the nations in other ways (cf. chap. 3 above) but not this one.

It is important to point out that the pentateuchal commands to destroy the Canaanites are not ongoing, permanent laws at all. Rather, they applied only to a certain temporary ancient Israelite historical situation, and their application was to cease when the job was done.[74] In this grim work, the Israelites were to go exactly as far as God commanded but no farther.[75] This does not justify destruction of nations or ethnicities at any other time or place.[76] The sacred writings of Judeo-Christian religion do not mandate violence throughout history and anywhere in the world to propagate the faith.[77] After the ancient Israelite theocracy ended, there can be just war but not holy war. Indiscriminate slaughter in God's name is unconscionable and blasphemous because it usurps the uniquely divine prerogative of corporate destruction

71. C. S. Cowles, "The Case for Radical Discontinuity," in *Show Them No Mercy: Four Views on God and Canaanite Genocide*, by C. S. Cowles et al., Counterpoints (Grand Rapids: Zondervan, 2003), 13–44; John J. Collins, "The Zeal of Phinehas: The Bible and the Legitimation of Violence," *JBL* 122 (2003): 3–21.

72. Divine retributive justice as depicted in Rev. 14:20, which sheds a far greater quantity of blood than in the entire OT put together, and the universal destruction of all who are unfaithful to God in Rev. 20 tend to neutralize the supposed dichotomy between a God of justice in the OT versus a God of mercy in the NT.

73. Gane, *Leviticus, Numbers*, 772, emphasis original. Cf. Eugene H. Merrill, "The Case for Moderate Discontinuity," in Cowles, *Show Them No Mercy*, 63–94; Daniel L. Gard, "The Case for Eschatological Continuity," in Cowles, *Show Them No Mercy*, 113–41; Tremper Longman III, "The Case for Spiritual Continuity," in Cowles, *Show Them No Mercy*, 161–87.

74. Cf. "Other Pentateuchal Portions Related to Law" in chap. 4 of the present volume.

75. God told the Israelites that if they did not obey him by driving out the Canaanites, "I will do to you as I thought to do to them" (Num. 33:55–56). However, the Israelites were not to exterminate people outside the promised land (Deut. 20:10–15) unless they had initiated hostile action against Israel (Exod. 17; Num. 21, 31; Deut. 2–3; 1 Sam. 15). The Lord held King Saul accountable for failing to completely destroy the Amalekites (1 Sam. 15), but God also punished him and his family (after his death) for breaking Israel's sworn treaty with the Gibeonites by attempting to wipe them out (2 Sam. 21; cf. Josh. 9).

76. Cf. William S. Brewbaker III and V. Philips Long, "Law and Political Order: Israel's Constitutional History," in *Law and the Bible: Justice, Mercy and Legal Institutions*, ed. Robert F. Cochran Jr. and David VanDrunen (Downers Grove, IL: IVP Academic), 56–59, citing Tremper Longman III and Daniel G. Reid, *God Is a Warrior* (Grand Rapids: Zondervan, 1995), 31–60.

77. Reuven Firestone, "Conceptions of Holy War in Biblical and Qur'ānic Tradition," *JRE* 24 (1996): 105–7, 111–18.

of the wicked, which is only justifiable if the Lord, the divine warrior, actually performs or theocratically controls it.[78] Only God possesses the requisite knowledge to determine what is just in such cases. Paul stated: "Beloved, never avenge yourselves, but leave it to the wrath of God, for it is written, 'Vengeance is mine, I will repay, says the Lord'" (Rom. 12:19).

How could a loving and just God be so heartlessly ruthless as to condemn all those Canaanite people, including women and children, to death along with even their animals? What was their crime?

The crimes of the Canaanites are clear: Their culture was permeated with abominable practices, including idolatrous worship of deities other than YHWH (Exod. 23:24, 32–33; 34:13, 15–16; Deut. 7:4–5; 20:18), as well as sexual perversions (Lev. 18, 20) and a variety of occult activities, which Deut. 18 lists along with child sacrifice as Canaanite practices prohibited for Israelites: "anyone who burns his son or his daughter as an offering, anyone who practices divination or tells fortunes or interprets omens, or a sorcerer or a charmer or a medium or a necromancer or one who inquires of the dead" (vv. 10–11; cf. Lev. 19:31; 20:6, 27).[79]

Israelites who did such things were to be treated similarly. Exodus 22:20 (22:19 MT) states the penalty for worship of other gods that applied to Israelites: "Whoever sacrifices to any god, other than the LORD alone, shall be devoted to destruction [hophal of kh-r-m]" (cf. the death penalty in Lev. 20:2; Deut. 17:5; see above). Israelites were to kill their family members (brother, son, daughter, wife) and close friends who encouraged them to serve other gods (Deut. 13:9–10 [13:10–11 MT]). If it was proved that a group of Israelites was committing the abomination of leading the inhabitants of their town toward worshiping other gods (vv. 12–14 [vv. 13–15 MT]), the nation was told,

> you shall surely put the inhabitants of that city to the sword, devoting it to destruction [hiphil of kh-r-m], all who are in it and its cattle, with the edge of the sword. You shall gather all its spoil into the midst of its open square and burn the city and all its spoil with fire, as a whole burnt offering to the LORD

78. "Israel's wars—insofar as they were waged in direct obedience to God's commands—were acts of worship, but they are not capable of being repeated outside of ancient Israel's specific theocratic context." Brewbaker and Long, "Law and Political Order," 58.

79. Deuteronomy 12:31 states: "every abominable thing that the LORD hates they have done for their gods, for they even burn their sons and their daughters in the fire to their gods." Cf. Lev. 18:21 and 20:1–5 against offering children to Molech. On the depravity of the Canaanites, see, e.g., Barna Magyarosi, *Holy War and Cosmic Conflict in the Old Testament from the Exodus to the Exile*, Adventist Theological Society Dissertation Series 9 (Berrien Springs, MI: Adventist Theological Society Publications, 2010), 33–37. To witness the remarkable extent to which a culture can be saturated with idolatry even today, one can visit India and Nepal.

your God. It shall be a heap forever. It shall not be built again. (vv. 15–16 [vv. 16–17 MT])

Therefore, the Canaanites' idolatrous worship of other gods constituted a capital crime, for which they were to be destroyed in the same way that Israelites guilty of the same crime were to be destroyed. This shows that the Lord's "vendetta was against wickedness, not ethnicity. Those who rebel against him are subject to 'equal-opportunity punishment.'"[80]

Because of the Canaanites' impure sexual practices (incest, adultery, homosexual activity, bestiality, prohibited in Lev. 18, 20), which YHWH regards as abominations, he expelled them from their land (Lev. 18:3, 24–25, 27–30; 20:23).[81] Concurrently with their expulsion, the Lord gave their land to the Israelites, whom he had separated from the peoples to belong to himself. However, he would also expel the Israelites if they followed the ways of the Canaanites (18:28; 20:22, 24, 26).[82] So there was no double standard: God held both the Canaanites and his own people accountable for the same crimes.

The Lord himself was in charge of the execution of the Canaanites (cf. Exod. 23:23, "I blot them out"), just as he was responsible for the destruction of every living thing on earth (except for those in the ark) by the great flood (Gen. 7) and in Sodom and Gomorrah by fire (Gen. 19), and just as he will ultimately annihilate the wicked by fire (Rev. 20).[83] The difference is simply the instrument of destruction: Rather than using water or fire, God deployed the Israelites to remove the Canaanites, thereby morally cleansing the land, which he repopulated with his people, who were to maintain the moral purity of the land by living in accordance with his values. God did not suspend the sixth commandment of the Decalogue, allowing the Israelites to temporarily sin by murdering the Canaanites. Rather, the Israelites served as the Lord's executioners to legitimately carry out justice on people whom he had condemned to capital punishment.

Why did the Lord require the Israelites to destroy the Canaanite women and children? Apparently he knew that the entire population of Canaan was irredeemably tainted by their evil culture, as in the cases of the antediluvian world (Gen. 6:5) and Sodom and Gomorrah (18:20–21; 19:4–11; Ezek.

---

80. Gane, *Leviticus, Numbers*, 773.

81. On Ugaritic and Canaanite sexual practices involved in fertility cults, see R. Davidson, *Flame of Yahweh*, 92–97.

82. Cf. exile threatened in the covenant blessings and curses (Lev. 26:33–39; Deut. 28:63–68). Eventually God did expel the Israelites through the destruction and exile of the kingdoms of Israel and Judah (2 Kings 17, 24; 2 Chron. 36).

83. Cf. Meredith Kline, *The Structure of Biblical Authority* (Grand Rapids: Eerdmans, 1972), 163.

16:49–50). If the Canaanites were allowed to remain, they would turn the Israelites from YHWH to serve other gods, resulting in the destruction of God's people (Exod. 23:33; 34:12, 15–16; Deut. 7:4; 20:18). Not only the Canaanite males would exert corrupting influences; the females also would be especially effective in leading God's people into idolatry if the Israelites allowed themselves to be enticed into pagan worship (Exod. 34:15; cf. Num. 25, including through sexual seduction; Num. 31:15–17)[84] or intermarried with them (Exod. 34:16; Deut. 7:3–4; cf. Ezra 9–10).

Why kill the animals of the Canaanites? They were not morally culpable,[85] but they were possessions of the condemned people that were disposed of, along with everything else that pertained to them, in order to erase memory of them. The animals could not be kept alive as spoil by the Israelites because they belonged to God alone (cf. 1 Sam. 15:3, 9, 14–22; see above on *kh-r-m* dedication).[86]

Why didn't the Lord simply destroy or drive out the Canaanites by himself? His original plan was to drive them out before the Israelites (Exod. 23:23, 27–30; 33:2), but he expected his people to cooperate with him: "I will give the inhabitants of the land into your hand, and you shall drive them out before you" (23:31; cf. Deut. 7:2). In this process, they were to show and grow their faith in God and obedience to him. However, due to their lack of faith, God made them fight in order to eradicate the Canaanites from the land.[87] When the Israelites neglected completion of this task (Judg. 1:27–2:3) and turned to worshiping Canaanite gods (2:10–19), YHWH left his people to their own efforts in order to test them by making them face more dangers of warfare (2:1–3, 20; 3:1–4). The Israelites' role as God's instrument was for their benefit, but they failed, and the miserable period of the judges ensued (3:5–6; etc.).

Granted that YHWH held the Canaanites and Israelites similarly accountable, how could he be justified in destroying the Canaanites when they had not entered into a covenant with him and did not have his OT laws, which he gave within the framework of that covenant? Paul explains in Rom. 1 that all human beings, not only God's covenant people, are responsible for basic knowledge of him and corresponding basic morality:

> For what can be known about God is plain to them, because God has shown it
> to them. For his invisible attributes, namely, his eternal power and divine nature,

84. The Moabites and Midianites in Num. 25 and 31 were Transjordanian, but they showed the danger of seduction into idolatry that would exert a powerful influence in Canaan.

85. Unless the people had committed bestiality with them (Lev. 20:15–16).

86. Cf. destruction of possessions of condemned Israelites in Num. 16:32–33; Deut. 13:15–17; Josh. 7:15, 24–25.

87. On this change of strategy, see Magyarosi, *Holy War*, 109–11.

have been clearly perceived, ever since the creation of the world, in the things that have been made. So they are without excuse. For although they knew God, they did not honor him as God or give thanks to him, but they became futile in their thinking, and their foolish hearts were darkened. (vv. 19–21)

It is because people reject the universally accessible, public-domain truth that they receive from contemplation of the Lord's creation (cf. Ps. 19:1–6 [19:2–7 MT]) that they turn to idolatry (Rom. 1:22–23, 25) and therefore also to sexual immorality (vv. 24–27, including homosexual activity) and all kinds of other sins (vv. 28–32).[88]

The inhabitants of Canaan had not been left without other sources of truth, such as influences from Melchizedek (Gen. 14:18–20), as well as Abraham and other patriarchs who were worshipers of the true God. Furthermore, the Lord gave the people of Canaan centuries to repent (15:13–14, 16; while his people waited in Egypt), much longer than the 120 years that he allowed for the entire antediluvian world (6:3).

This amazingly gracious patience with people engaged in disgusting be- haviors that continually insulted him demonstrates the fact that the Lord is "not wishing that any should perish, but that all should reach repentance" (2 Pet. 3:9; cf. Ezek. 18:32). Destroying sinners is a strange deed for YHWH (Isa. 28:21), but to eradicate evil and make the world safe again, he must let sinners go when there is nothing more that he can do to persuade them to allow him to separate them from their sins (cf. Isa. 5:4).

---

88. The basic need for awareness of creation highlights the importance of the Sabbath as the weekly reminder of creation (Gen. 2:2–3; Exod. 20:11; 31:17).

15

Questions about Keeping Old Testament Laws Today

Previous chapters of this book have answered many questions regarding whether or not certain OT laws or categories of laws continue to apply to Christians today. For example, we have found that moral and ethical principles exemplified in the Ten Commandments and many other divine instructions can still guide us to the extent that they are relevant to our life situations (see chaps. 11–12).

However, Christians are not required to keep cultic laws that regulated or depended on the Israelite sanctuary/temple system of ritual worship because (1) that system no longer exists, and (2) the sacrificed and risen Christ has transferred our focus of worship to God's temple in heaven, where he ministers as our great high priest (Hebrews, esp. chaps. 7–10). Therefore, we do not need to offer animal sacrifices (Lev. 1–7; etc.) or observe rules concerning physical ritual impurities or remedies for them (esp. Lev. 12–15; Num. 19) in order to keep them from the holy sphere centered at the earthly sanctuary, which is gone (see further in chap. 16 below).

Nor is it necessary for Christians to celebrate the Israelite annual festivals (Lev. 23). These required animal sacrifices at the sanctuary on behalf of all Israelites (Num. 28–29), and all Israelite men were required to attend three of the festivals at the sanctuary with offerings for YHWH (Exod. 23:14–17; 34:18, 22–24; Deut. 16:16–17). After the destruction of the Second Temple in AD 70, Jewish tradition developed elements of the festivals that could be performed without a sanctuary/temple into adapted festival observances. These practices do not fulfill the biblical requirements, because they lack the essential ritual components that involve a functioning sanctuary/temple authorized by the Lord. Nobody keeps or can keep the festivals in the biblical way today, and there is no biblical support for requiring Christians to observe any adapted festival, except for the Last Supper/Communion service that Jesus himself adapted from a Passover celebration (Matt. 26:26–29; Luke 22:14–20; 1 Cor. 11:23–26).[1]

The present chapter addresses a few residual questions about whether or how modern Christians should keep particular OT laws, or what the biblical laws have to say concerning issues that we face today. Questions regarding the applicability of prohibitions against certain kinds of mixtures and cutting one's hair and flesh in certain ways arise from uncertainty regarding the purposes of these laws. Tithing was a way to provide for the Israelite priests and Levites, but can it be used to support Christian ministers, and if so, how would it work? Do dietary restrictions and the prohibition of sexual intercourse during menstruation simply belong to the system of laws that regulated physical ritual impurity, or do they still apply? Can a biblical case be made for the moral acceptability of homosexual activity and the legitimacy of gay marriage?

This chapter does not engage in thorough application of the relevant OT laws by going through all the steps of progressive moral wisdom (PMW; see chaps. 9–10). Rather, the concern here is to target and resolve particular interpretive sticking points that are involved in questions of whether or not or how certain OT laws continue to apply today.

Forbidden Mixtures

Laws against mixtures appear in Lev. 19:19 and Deut. 22:9–11:

> You shall keep my statutes. You shall not let your cattle breed with a different kind. You shall not sow your field with two kinds of seed, nor shall you wear a garment of cloth made of two kinds of material. (Lev. 19:19)

> You shall not sow your vineyard with two kinds of seed, lest the whole yield be forfeited, the crop that you have sown and the yield of the vineyard. You shall not plow with an ox and a donkey together. You shall not wear cloth of wool and linen mixed together. (Deut. 22:9–11)

1. Roy Gane, *Leviticus, Numbers*, NIV Application Commentary (Grand Rapids: Zondervan, 2004), 393–95, 757–59.

Most of us are not farmers who own cattle, plow with animals, or sow fields or vineyards. However, we do wear clothes, and many of these contain mixed fibers, including cotton, wool, polyester, rayon, and polyethylene terephthalate (brand name, Dacron). Is it wrong to wear such mixed cloth?

As pointed out in chapters 7 and 9 of the present volume, Deut. 22:9 provides a key to the purpose of these laws in the conditional consequence of violating the prohibition against sowing a second kind of seed in a vineyard: The whole mixed harvest would "be forfeited"—literally, "become holy" (*qal* of *q-d-sh*). What was mixed belonged to the sacred domain; therefore it was forfeited to ownership by the sanctuary.[2]

Other biblical passages also connect mixtures to the holy sphere of God. Several items belonging to the Israelite sanctuary included mixtures of wool and linen, including the fabrics of the tabernacle, the inner veil, and the screens for the entrances to the sacred tent and to the courtyard (Exod. 26:1, 31, 36; 27:16; 36:8, 35, 37; 38:18); the high priest's ephod (an apron-like priestly garment) and breastpiece (28:6, 8, 15; 39:2–3, 5, 8); the sashes of the high priest and ordinary priests (39:29); the anointing oil (30:23–33); and the incense (vv. 34–38). The winged golden cherubim on the ark of the covenant (25:18–20; 37:7–9) and cherubim woven into the tabernacle fabrics and the inner veil (26:1, 31; 36:8, 35) represented mixed beings.

Ezekiel 1:5–11 and 10:8, 14–15, 20–22 describe the four living creatures (= cherubim) under the movable throne of YHWH's glory as having a human resemblance, plus four wings each, under which were human hands, foot soles like those of a calf, and four faces each, from a mixture of beings: human, lion, ox/cherub, and eagle.[3] These exotic subdivine creatures clearly belonged to the heavenly realm, which transcends the earthly domain. Ezekiel's description correlates with a plethora of ANE art and literature in which gods and other superhuman beings are depicted as composite creatures.[4]

2. On the concept that mixtures were to exclusively belong to the sacred sphere, see Jacob Milgrom, *Leviticus 17–22: A New Translation with Introduction and Commentary*, AB 3A (New York: Doubleday, 2000), 1659–65.

3. Cf. Rev. 4:7, "The first living creature like a lion, the second living creature like an ox, the third living creature with the face of a man, and the fourth living creature like an eagle in flight."

4. "In Mesopotamia, demons, monsters, and minor protective deities were depicted as bulls and lions with human heads, lion-centaurs, snake-dragons, goat-fish, bird-men, scorpion-people, and so on." Roy E. Gane, "Leviticus," in *Zondervan Illustrated Bible Backgrounds Commentary*, ed. John H. Walton (Grand Rapids: Zondervan, 2009), referring to Jeremy Black and Anthony Green, *Gods, Demons, and Symbols of Ancient Mesopotamia: An Illustrated Dictionary* (Austin: University of Texas Press, 1992), esp. 64–65. Cf. Constance E. Gane, "Composite Beings in Neo-Babylonian Art" (PhD diss., University of California, Berkeley, 2012).

The instructions regarding the anointing oil in Exod. 30 conclude: "It shall not be poured on the body of an ordinary person, and you shall make no other like it in composition. It is holy, and it shall be holy to you. Whoever compounds any like it or whoever puts any of it on an outsider shall be cut off from his people" (vv. 32–33). Similarly, verses 37–38 say that duplication of the incense for secular use incurs the divine penalty of being "cut off." These passages indicate the importance of maintaining clear distinctions between the sacred sphere centered at God's sanctuary on earth and the common domain of everyday life, in order not to diminish the special nature of that which is holy.

Now God has no sanctuary/temple on earth, so if we happen to make oil or incense like that which belonged to the ancient Israelite sanctuary, we will not duplicate and thereby remove the uniqueness of a presently existing holy substance. Similarly, the injunction against wearing mixed cloth in Lev. 19:19 and its parallel in Deut. 22:11, which limits the prohibition to wool and linen, have lost their purpose now that the special fabrics of the sanctuary and its priests are gone. Therefore the ban on wearing mixed cloth no longer applies.

The prohibitions against sowing a field or vineyard with more than one kind of seed and breeding or plowing with different kinds of animals extend the principle of avoiding holy mixtures explained above, even though there was no sowing, breeding, or plowing in the sacred sanctuary precincts. Today the produce of mixed seeds in a vineyard could not be holy in the sense that it would belong to the sanctuary (Deut. 22:9), which no longer exists, so this aspect of the ban on mixed sowing is no longer in force. However, following the biblical instructions could result in some ongoing practical benefits for the land and the quality of its produce. Scientific investigation of such possibilities is beyond the scope of the present book.

Mixed breeding of cattle (Lev. 19:19) is indirectly linked to the sanctuary in the sense that the cherubim on the ark and portrayed in the fabrics of the tabernacle and the inner veil were heavenly composite creatures (see above). In addition to this sanctuary connection, God originally created distinct species of land creatures on planet Earth "according to their kinds" (Gen. 1:24–25; cf. vv. 11–12, 21), rather than hybrid creatures that belong to the heavenly realm (cf. Ezek. 1, 10). Since the rationale of maintaining creation distinctions is independent of the sanctuary, it appears that mixed breeding would still be out of harmony with the divine plan.[5]

5. Again, compliance could also provide some ongoing agricultural benefits, which we cannot explore here.

The injunction against "plowing with an ox and a donkey together" (Deut. 22:10) has an implicit practical rationale involving treatment of animals that would apply today: Yoking work animals of such unequal size and strength would put undue strain on the smaller, weaker one.

Prohibitions regarding Cutting One's Hair and Flesh

Leviticus 19:27 forbids cutting one's hair in certain ways: "You shall not round off the hair on your temples or mar the edges of your beard." Verse 28 prohibits cutting one's flesh in certain ways: "You shall not make any cuts on your body for the dead or tattoo yourselves: I am the LORD."

To ascertain whether these prohibitions apply to modern Christians, we need to comprehend their purpose. Verse 28 supplies a key: Forbidden cuts on one's body are "for the dead"—that is, as a mourning practice. A law in Deut. 14 refers to this motivation both for cutting flesh and cutting hair (making baldness) and provides a reason why Israelites should not do these things:

> You are the sons of the LORD your God. You shall not cut yourselves or make any baldness on your foreheads for the dead. For you are a people holy to the LORD your God, and the LORD has chosen you to be a people for his treasured possession, out of all the peoples who are on the face of the earth. (vv. 1–2)

The Israelites were YHWH's "holy nation" (cf. Exod. 19:6), but dead bodies were ritually impure (Num. 19:11–22). Ritual impurity, which represented the birth-to-death cycle of mortality[6] that results from sin (Gen. 3; Rom. 6:23), was to be kept separate from holy things as much as possible (e.g., Lev. 7:20–21; 15:31) or removed from them (16:16, 19) because they were associated with the immortal Deity (cf. 1 Tim. 6:16), who is the source of life (cf. Gen. 1–2).[7] Therefore, although the Israelites were allowed to become impure through contact with or proximity to corpses, which was necessary in order to bury them, they were required to undergo ritual purification (Num. 19) and were forbidden to compromise their holiness by engaging in excessive mourning that affected their bodies.

Priests were especially holy, so their funerary activities were further restricted: They were not allowed to become impure from the dead at all, except

---

6. Hyam Maccoby, *Ritual and Morality: The Ritual Purity System and Its Place in Judaism* (Cambridge: Cambridge University Press, 1999), 49, cf. 31–32, 48, 50, 207–8.

7. On the rationale for biblical impurity, which is based on opposition between life-holiness versus death-impurity, see Jacob Milgrom, *Leviticus 1–16: A New Translation with Introduction and Commentary*, AB 3 (New York: Doubleday, 1991), 766–68, 1000–1004.

for their closest relatives (Lev. 21:1–4), and in this context, "They shall not make bald patches on their heads, nor shave off the edges of their beards, nor make any cuts on their body" (v. 5; cf. 10:6). The high priest was forbidden to incur corpse impurity at all, even from his father or mother (21:11).

In Israel and other parts of the ANE, inflicting lacerations on oneself and cutting one's hair and/or beard demonstrated extreme sorrow (Jer. 16:6; 41:5; 48:37, Moabites).[8] God's people naturally grieve for their departed loved ones, but because of their connection with him, the life-giver, they need not "grieve as others do who have no hope" (1 Thess. 4:13).

Returning to application of Lev. 19:27–28 today in light of this discussion, cutting/trimming one's hair or beard in the ways referred to here or getting a tattoo would not break the principle behind these laws within the context of contemporary culture unless the actions would be motivated by or interpreted as extreme mourning for the dead. Of course, if modern Christians mourn excessively in other ways that also affect their bodies, these practices would violate the principle in Lev. 19 because Christians, like the ancient Israelites, are "a holy nation" (1 Pet. 2:9). Such mourning would not accompany a physical ritual impurity that requires a remedy to protect an earthly sanctuary (cf. Num. 19:13, 20), but it would express lack of faith and undue distance from our holy God, who gives us hope of resurrection through Christ (John 11; 1 Cor. 15; 1 Thess. 4:13–18).[9]

Tithing

Some modern Christians practice tithing, giving a tenth of one's income to support a religious cause. This practice is based on the OT; the NT does not mention the matter of tithing by Christians.[10] So it can be helpful for Christians to examine tithing in the OT to learn about its purpose and how it worked.

Tithing first appears in the Bible in narratives about Abram (Abraham) and Jacob. From the spoils of his victory over several kings, Abram gave "a tenth

8. In the Ugaritic myth of Ba'lu (Baal), when the chief god 'Ilu (El) learns that Ba'lu (Baal) is dead, he expresses his grief as follows: "He pours dirt of mourning on his head, dust of humiliation on his cranium, for clothing, he is covered with a girded garment. With a stone he scratches incisions on (his) skin, with a razor he cuts cheeks and chin. He harrows his upper arms, plows (his) chest like a garden, harrows (his) back like a (garden in a) valley" (trans. Dennis Pardee, "The Ba'lu Myth," COS 1.86:267–68).

9. Of course, images in modern tattoos can be morally problematic if they are pornographic, contain occult symbolism, or otherwise send signals that are out of harmony with divine values (cf. 1 Pet 3:3–4 regarding inner rather than external adornment).

10. Although Jesus referred to tithing by scribes and especially Pharisees (Matt. 23:23; Luke 11:42; 18:12), and Hebrews (7:5–6, 8–9) mentions that the Levites and Melchizedek received tithes.

of everything" to Melchizedek, king of Salem and "priest of God Most High" (Gen. 14:18–20). At Bethel, Jacob vowed that if God would be with him, he would give to the Lord a tenth of all that God would give him (28:20–22). These patriarchal tithes were voluntarily given and promised, respectively, and they were a percentage of income that was not limited to agricultural produce.

Old Testament law required Israelites to pay tithes to God as a kind of religious tax. Leviticus 27 states that two kinds of agricultural tithes are holy, belonging to the Lord: "Every tithe of the land, whether of the seed of the land or of the fruit of the trees" (v. 30) and "every tithe of herds and flocks, every tenth animal of all that pass under the herdsman's staff" (v. 32). For an Israelite farmer, produce from seed and trees and from animal offspring represent his gross income. This passage does not articulate the purpose of these tithes, but the fact that they are holy means that they belong to the sanctuary, implying that the priests can use them.

In Num. 18 YHWH provides for support of the priests and Levites who serve him because they have no ancestral agricultural territory on which to support themselves (vv. 20, 23–24), and even if they did, presumably they would not have time to farm it. God assigns to the priests a variety of sacred contributions that the people bring to him (vv. 8–19), gives the tithes to the Levites (vv. 21–24), and instructs the Levites to give a tithe of the tithes that they receive to the priests (vv. 25–28).[11]

Deuteronomy presents another system of tithing. For two out of every three years,[12] the Israelites with their households and invited Levites from their towns are to joyfully eat their own agricultural tithes at the central sanctuary when they are settled in the land of Canaan (12:6–7, 11–12, 17–19; 14:22–27).[13] These tithes are specified as "all the yield of your seed that comes from the field" and "the tithe of your grain, of your wine, and of your oil, and the firstborn of your herd and flock" (12:17; 14:22–23). People who live too far from the sanctuary to carry their tithe there can convert it into money, which they take to the place where the sanctuary is located and buy there the food and drink that they eat before the Lord (14:24–26). The meal is sacred because the tithes belong to the Lord, and they eat as privileged persons virtually at the table

11. The priests were not required to pay a tithe.

12. With J. Christian Wilson, "Tithe," *ABD* 6:579; now correcting Gane, *Leviticus, Numbers*, 655, "If the Israelites gave 10 percent to the Levites every year, ate another 10 percent or its equivalent at the sanctuary every year, and gave another 10 percent every third year . . ."

13. "The second tithe was really a mandatory 'celebration account' to ensure that the people would have the means for a first class occasion of thanksgiving at the Lord's sanctuary. The spiritual, culinary, social, and emotional highlight of the year was all wrapped up in the same event. Needless to say, this would tend to encourage a positive attitude toward God and recognition of his gifts." Gane, *Leviticus, Numbers*, 655.

of the divine king.[14] Because the sacred meal is to be joyful, an individual is not permitted to eat it while mourning, and because the tithe is holy, those who handle it must be ritually pure (26:14).

Every third year, however, the Israelites are to keep the tithes in their towns (Deut. 14:28) and give them there to disadvantaged, landless classes of persons: "the Levite, because he has no portion or inheritance with you, and the sojourner, the fatherless, and the widow" (v. 29; cf. 26:12–13).

The fact that OT law prescribes two different tithing systems—that of Leviticus-Numbers and that of Deuteronomy—presents a major interpretive conundrum.[15] What is the relationship between these systems? It is difficult to argue that one system was intended to supersede the other, as when common slaughter of sacrificable animals at a distance from the sanctuary in the land of Canaan (Deut. 12:15, 20–22) would replace sacral slaughter at the sanctuary in the wilderness (Lev. 17:1–9), because both tithing systems dealt with agricultural produce in the land.[16]

Theoretically, the two systems could operate concurrently, so that the Israelites would give both kinds of tithes to YHWH, for a total of 20 percent of their agricultural income. This would not be as onerous as it could appear at first glance, because the Deuteronomy system would have the people eat most of their own tithes, with Levites as their guests, for two out of every three years. Thus the total of their income that would be used by others would be 13.33 percent plus whatever the Levite guests ate.[17]

The Leviticus-Numbers system already provides a tithe for the Levites as their "inheritance" from the Lord instead of agricultural territory (Num. 18:24). So why would they need additional "charity" provided to them by the Deuteronomy system? The answer can be found in the fact that Numbers

14. Cf. the honor of receiving food from a human king: 2 Sam. 9:7, 10–11; 1 Kings 2:7; 2 Kings 25:28–30; Dan. 1:5.

15. Old Testament narrative texts record implementation of only the Leviticus-Numbers system that provided support for Levites and priests (2 Chron. 31:4–12; Neh. 10:37–39; 12:44; 13:5, 12–13).

16. Historical-critical scholars maintain that the two tithing systems represent distinct perspectives of different pentateuchal sources: The P = Priestly approach of Leviticus-Numbers mandates support for the priests and Levites; and D = Deuteronomy is concerned for the people as a whole, including disadvantaged individuals (e.g., Wilson, "Tithe," 579). Jacob Milgrom has suggested a diachronic solution according to which one system replaced the other for a historical reason: The tithe in Deuteronomy preserved the institution of tithing after the Deuteronomic reform abolished the need for tithe to support Levite cultic personnel at regional sanctuaries. *Numbers: The Traditional Hebrew Text with the New JPS Translation*, JPS Torah Commentary (Philadelphia: Jewish Publication Society, 1990), 434–35.

17. However, implementation of both tithes together during the Second Temple period was problematic (ibid., 436).

and Deuteronomy refer to Levites in different situations. In Num. 18:21 God gives the tithes to the Levites as remuneration for their service at his sanctuary. However, Deut. 14:27 expresses concern for "the Levite who is within your towns, for he has no portion or inheritance with you" (cf. v. 29). Such Levites, who were distributed among the Israelite tribes and thus away from the sanctuary, would not receive the Leviticus-Numbers tithes because they did not serve at the sanctuary. They could come to the sanctuary and serve there if they wished, in which case they would have the right to eat from the sacred contributions (18:6–8), but otherwise they would be partially dependent on assistance from other Israelites where they lived.[18]

So should Christians practice tithing today, and if so, how? When Jesus sent disciples out to minister, he instructed them to "remain in the same house, eating and drinking what they provide, for the laborer deserves his wages" (Luke 10:7; cf. Matt. 10:10). Similarly, Paul makes the case that Christian ministers deserve material support for their spiritual labor (1 Cor. 9:4–14). His concluding argument refers to remuneration for temple workers, which was based on Leviticus and Numbers: "Do you not know that those who are employed in the temple service get their food from the temple, and those who serve at the altar share in the sacrificial offerings? In the same way, the Lord commanded that those who proclaim the gospel should get their living by the gospel" (vv. 13–14). Paul does not explicitly mention tithing, but this would have been a key way in which religious workers "get their food from the temple."

New Testament Christianity has no human cultic officials to mediate for the "laity." Christ is the only priest who mediates for us (1 Tim. 2:5; Hebrews), and all Christians are ministers (1 Pet. 2:9, "a royal priesthood"). However, some Christians are engaged in full-time ministry, so they cannot make a living for themselves and their families through other kinds of employment. Such individuals need support from the Christian community. They do not "serve at the altar," so they cannot "share in the sacrificial offerings" (1 Cor. 9:13) or most other kinds of sacred gifts that Israelites brought to the Lord at his sanctuary/temple, which Christians do not contribute. However, tithing of income remains a convenient and consistent way for God's people to support full-time ministers, as in the Leviticus-Numbers system.

Most Christians, at least in the developed world, are not farmers, so our incomes are money rather than agricultural produce. If we choose to adopt

---

18. On the intended religious leadership role of the Levites distributed throughout Israel in their cities, see Daniel I. Block, "'The Meeting Places of God in the Land': Another Look at the Towns of the Levites," in *Current Issues in Priestly and Related Literature: The Legacy of Jacob Milgrom and Beyond*, ed. Roy E. Gane and Ada Taggar-Cohen, RBS (Atlanta: Society of Biblical Literature, 2015), 93–121.

the Leviticus-Numbers mode of tithing, we can easily adapt it by giving to God's work 10 percent of our incomes.[19] If this seems like a lot, no doubt the divine promise of Malachi 3 is for modern Christians, as it was for ancient Israelites: "Bring the full tithe into the storehouse, that there may be food in my house. And thereby put me to the test, says the LORD of hosts, if I will not open the windows of heaven for you and pour down for you a blessing until there is no more need" (v. 10).

The needs addressed by the Deuteronomy system of tithing are also still with us. So Christians can regularly set aside a portion of their income to assist people who are less well-off than themselves (cf. Deut. 14:28–29; 26:12) and to pay expenses of generous religious-social rejoicing with their families and needy guests (12:17–19; 14:22–27). The latter is a novel idea for Christians. "It would be fascinating to experiment with application of this concept . . . and see what happens to attitudes toward God."[20]

Dietary Restrictions

In OT law the Lord restricted his people's consumption of meat in several ways, including by forbidding them to consume blood or to eat meat of "impure" species of animals. Some aspects of these prohibitions no longer apply because they were involved with the ritual system, which is gone. Other elements were not dependent on the existence of the sanctuary/temple and its regulations, so they remain relevant for Christians. The key to the question of application is to sort out which parts of the divine instructions are cultic and which are not.

Eating Meat with Its Blood

Leviticus 17 states the rationale for the ban on eating meat from which the blood is not properly drained out at the time of slaughter (vv. 10–14; cf. 3:17; 7:26–27; Deut. 12:16, 23–25; 15:23): "For the life of the flesh is in the blood, and I have assigned it to you on the altar to ransom your lives; for it is the blood that ransoms by means of life."[21] There is a clear cultic consideration here: "on the altar to ransom your lives."[22] However, the deeper reason, which underlies

19. Previously I referred to "net money income" equivalent to "net agricultural produce (not including seed for replanting)" (Gane, *Leviticus, Numbers*, 656), but now I think it is more accurate to say that tithe is based on gross income, which for farmers would not include seed retained for replanting, because this is not income/profit in economic terms.
20. Ibid.
21. Trans. Milgrom, *Leviticus 17–22*, 1295.
22. Cf. the prohibition against eating fat/suet (Lev. 3:16–17; 7:22–25).

the ransom-for-life function of blood in animal sacrifices, is the principle that "the life of the flesh is in the blood." Therefore, the blood prohibition has its basis in the ongoing value of respect for life, which is exemplified by the sixth of the Ten Commandments: "You shall not murder" (Exod. 20:13).

The basis on respect for life is confirmed by the context of the first canonical appearance of the ban on eating blood in laws that YHWH gave to Noah after the flood:

> Every moving thing that lives shall be food for you. And as I gave you the green plants, I give you everything. But you shall not eat flesh with its life, that is, its blood. And for your lifeblood I will require a reckoning: from every beast I will require it and from man. From his fellow man I will require a reckoning for the life of man. Whoever sheds the blood of man, by man shall his blood be shed, for God made man in his own image. (Gen. 9:3–6)

Here God allowed humans to eat meat of various (nonhuman) creatures, but he withheld permission to eat their blood, and nowhere else in the Bible has he ever reversed this exception. Genesis 9 closely connects treatment of animal lifeblood (v. 4) with accountability for shedding human lifeblood, which is murder (vv. 5–6). The fact that the latter obviously concerns respect for life indicates that abstinence from eating animal blood involves the same enduring value.

Several biblical factors support the continuing applicability of the blood prohibition, including for modern Christians (cf. chap. 8). First, the rule does not depend on the Israelite sanctuary system. For one thing, in the biblical narrative the prohibition to Noah appears long before the sanctuary was constructed. Furthermore, when the sanctuary was operating, the requirement to drain the blood was in effect when slaughter was done anywhere, not only at the sanctuary, and it applied to any animal or bird, not only to a sacrificial species (Lev. 3:17; 7:26, including birds; 17:13–14; Deut. 12:15–16, 21–25; 15:22–23; cf. 1 Sam. 14:32–34).[23]

Second, the ban on blood is not only for Israelites/Jews. The Lord gave it to Noah and his children for them and their descendants, thus meaning the entire postdiluvian human race, many centuries before the formation of the Israelite nation. Leviticus 17 requires non-Israelite resident aliens to observe the blood prohibition (vv. 10, 12–13). Acts 15:29 instructs Gentile Christians to "abstain . . . from blood, and from what has been strangled" (cf. v. 20)—that is, from meat that has not been slaughtered in such a way that its blood drained out.

---

23. However, the rule did not apply to fish.

Third, eating meat with its blood is listed among moral prohibitions in Ezek. 33:25–26 (with idolatry, murder, adultery) and in Acts 15 it is forbidden for Christians: "abstain from what has been sacrificed to idols, and from blood, and from what has been strangled, and from sexual immorality" (v. 29; cf. v. 20).[24] These contexts support the idea that the ban on blood is based on a moral issue: respect for life.

The fact that no Christian denomination, to my knowledge, observes the neglected blood prohibition affirmed in Acts 15 is irrelevant to the conclusion reached here: The biblical evidence clearly shows that the basic requirement of abstaining from eating meat from which the blood has not been properly drained applies to Christians today.[25]

Permitted and Forbidden Meats

Leviticus 11 and Deut. 14:3–20 distinguish between "pure" (*tahor*) land, sea, or flying creatures, which are fit to eat, and "impure" (*tame'*) or "detestable thing" (*sheqets*) creatures, which are unfit to eat.[26] In Lev. 12–15 words from the Hebrew root *t-m-'*, "be impure," refer to persons and things affected by physical ritual impurity, which should be kept away from the holy domain centered at the sanctuary (esp. 15:31), and which can be remedied by ablutions and expiatory sacrifices. Such physical ritual impurity appears in part of Lev. 11, where carcasses of impure or pure animals convey impurity that must be remedied, including by ablutions when persons are affected (vv. 24–40).

However, the basic distinction between creatures that are fit or unfit, thus permitted or forbidden by God, to eat does not relate to the holiness of the sanctuary. Rather, according to the rationale explicitly stated at the end of Lev. 11, it has to do with the holiness of God's people themselves: They are to emulate his holiness, and therefore, they must not defile themselves or make themselves detestable by eating meat that he categorizes as unfit (vv. 43–45; cf. 20:24–25).[27] The fact that the difference between pure and impure creatures

---

24. The same practices—idolatry, consumption of blood, and sexual immorality—are forbidden to both Israelites and non-Israelite resident aliens (Gentiles) in Lev. 17–18.

25. The biblical requirement to drain the blood (cf. 1 Sam. 14:32–34 in a narrative) does not include postbiblical traditional practices for koshering meat, such as roasting and salting to remove more blood, on which see Harry Rabinowicz and Rela Mintz Geffen, "Dietary Laws," in *EncJud* 5:651.

26. Cf. Deut. 14:3, "You shall not eat any abomination [*to'evah*]."

27. On theories regarding the rationale for these instructions, see Gane, *Leviticus, Numbers*, 206–8. Jiří Moskala makes a plausible case for impure creatures departing from the creation ideal of life (linked to holiness) because they are associated with death (reflected by impurity) in various ways, including their carnivorous diets, function in war, and negative effects on human health. *The Laws of Clean and Unclean Animals of Leviticus 11: Their Nature, Theology, and*

does not depend on the sanctuary is supported by the fact that it goes back to the time of Noah (Gen. 7:2–3, 8–9; 8:20), long before the Israelite sanctuary and its purity system were founded.

Defilement that a person would contract from eating unfit meat is a forbidden impurity (cf. Lev. 11:43–44).[28] Other forbidden impurities apply to consecrated priests and temporary Nazirites, who are forbidden to contract impurity from corpses (e.g., 21:1, 4, 11; Num. 6:6–7).[29] This corpse contamination is clearly physical ritual impurity because those who are permitted to incur it must undergo ritual purification (Num. 19:11–22) so that they do not defile the sanctuary (vv. 13, 20), and a Nazirite who accidentally becomes impure through an unexpected death must also undergo ritual purification (6:9).[30] Furthermore, the special holiness of priests and Nazirites, which should not be disrupted by corpse impurity, is linked to the sanctuary: Priests serve there, and a Nazirite concludes the votive period with a complex of offerings at the sanctuary, including sacrifices and one's own consecrated hair (Num. 6:13–21).

Nevertheless, while it is true that eating impure meat is a physical act that affects the body, there is no evidence that this forbidden impurity is physical ritual impurity. The biblical text does not say that a person who eats an impure animal becomes impure for a stated length of time and must undergo a ritual process to become pure, as with the permitted cases of touching or carrying an impure carcass (Lev. 11:24–25, 27–28, 31) or touching, eating, or carrying the carcass of a pure animal that has died of itself (vv. 39–40). Furthermore, the holiness that would be affected if the prohibition is violated is that of any Israelite, which derives not from the person's connection to the sanctuary, but from one's covenant connection with YHWH (Exod. 19:5–6), who separated the Israelites from among the peoples so that they should belong to him (Lev. 20:24–26).

The importance of personal dietary holiness is illustrated by Daniel's covenant commitment to God: As a captive in Babylon, far from the sanctuary, he risked his life to avoid defiling himself with the food or drink of his royal host

---

Rationale (An Intertextual Study), Adventist Theological Society Dissertation Series 4 (Berrien Springs, MI: Adventist Theological Society Publications, 2000).

28. On tolerated versus prohibited impurities, see David P. Wright, "Two Types of Impurity in the Priestly Writings of the Bible," *Koroth* 9 (1988): 180–93; D. Wright, "The Spectrum of Priestly Impurity," in *Priesthood and Cult in Ancient Israel*, ed. Gary Anderson and Saul M. Olyan, JSOTSup 125 (Sheffield: JSOT Press, 1991), 150–81.

29. With some exceptions for ordinary priests (Lev. 21:2–3).

30. The Nazirite must also receive sacrificial expiation for the moral faults of inadvertently violating the prohibition against coming in contact with a corpse and desecrating their own consecrated hair and vow (Num. 6:10–12); Gane, *Leviticus, Numbers*, 534; Milgrom, *Numbers*, 47; Milgrom, *Leviticus 1–16*, 357–58.

and captor, and the Lord richly rewarded him and his companions (Dan. 1, esp. v. 8).[31]

If defilement from eating unfit meat is not physical ritual impurity, what kind of impurity is it? Some scholars have identified a category of moral impurity that results from very serious violations of certain divine prohibitions, including regarding sexual behavior (Lev. 18), idolatry (18:21; cf. v. 24), and murder (Num. 35:31–34).[32] These sins break divine moral principles (cf. Exod. 20:3–6, 13–14) and generate permanent impurity that is unlike temporary physical ritual impurity in that it defiles not only the person (in this case the sinner) but also the land, which ultimately results in exile (Lev. 18:25, 27–28; Num. 35:33–34). Furthermore, such moral impurity is neither contracted nor secondarily passed on by mere physical contact.[33] Like deliberate contraction of a prohibited physical ritual impurity, moral impurity cannot be remedied by ritual means.

Impurity from consuming unfit meat is similar to the kind of moral impurity just described in that it does not convey secondary contamination to other persons or things by mere contact. However, there is no evidence that it defiles the land, so it is not as serious as a sexual wrong, idolatry, or murder. Although not even a person who inadvertently eats unfit meat could shed the impurity through a physical ritual mode of purification, including ablutions, presumably the inadvertent violation of the divine command could be expiated through a purification offering, prerequisite to forgiveness by God (Lev. 4). Also presumably, this sacrificial remedy for the morally defiling sin would take care of the impurity, which is moral rather than physical ritual in nature.

Therefore, the lesser moral defilement incurred by eating unfit meat is somewhat in a class by itself, pointing from Lev. 11 toward moral impurity in chap. 18, which belongs to the Holiness Code. This correlates with the literary relationship between 11:43–45 and chaps. 18–26, which exemplifies a didactic strategy that I have labeled "Introducing Concepts for Later Development": "In 11:43–45, the call for Israel to be holy because YHWH is holy and the divine self-identification ('I am YHWH') supply motivation for observance of dietary distinctions. These verses preview the literary style and content of

31. Daniel 1:8 does not say that the issue was impure meat or identify the problem with the wine, but it appears that impure meat could have been part of the problem.
32. Milgrom, *Leviticus 17–22*, 1326; Jonathan Klawans, *Impurity and Sin in Ancient Judaism* (Oxford: Oxford University Press, 2000), 21–31; Jay Sklar, *Sin, Impurity, Sacrifice, Atonement: The Priestly Conceptions* (Sheffield: Sheffield Phoenix, 2005), 139–53.
33. Contrast physical ritual impurities conveyed by contact in Lev. 11:24–28, 31–40; 12:4; 13:45–46; 15:4–12; etc.

later chapters of the book, which extensively develop the theme of Israel's holiness (esp. Lev. 18–26; cf. emulation of divine holiness in 19:2; 20:26)."[34]

The NT indicates that God's new-covenant people are also holy because of their connection with him: "But you are a chosen race, a royal priesthood, a holy nation, a people for his own possession" (1 Pet. 2:9, referring to Exod. 19:5–6). Peter cites Lev. 11:44–45, from the conclusion to the OT instructions on pure versus impure meats, to call Christians to holy living that abstains from morally defiling sins: "As obedient children, do not be conformed to the passions of your former ignorance, but as he who called you is holy, you also be holy in all your conduct, since it is written, 'You shall be holy, for I am holy'" (1 Pet. 1:14–16). "Thus, the objective of holiness for God's people is the same as it has always been (cf. Exod. 19:6; Deut. 7:6; 14:2, 21)."[35]

All things considered, the relevance of distinctions between pure/fit and unfit meats continues for Christians.[36] Some NT passages seem to contradict this conclusion, but on closer examination, they do not.

Jesus said, "Do you not perceive that whatever enters a man from outside cannot defile [*koinoō*, "make common"] him, because it does not enter his heart but his stomach, and is eliminated, thus purifying all foods?" (Mark 7:18–19 NKJV). At the end of Mark 7:19, ESV and most other English versions (e.g., NRSV, NIV, NJB, NASB) add the commonly accepted notion that by saying what he did, Jesus was declaring all foods clean, implying that he was abrogating the distinctions between pure/clean and impure/unclean meats in Lev. 11 and Deut. 14.

Aside from the fact that there is no Greek original behind the addition of "declared" in English translations, this interpretation is mistaken for four reasons. First, the context concerns the extrabiblical tradition of washing hands in a certain way before eating food that is fit to eat (Mark 7:1–5), not the OT instructions concerning permitted versus forbidden meats.

Second, when food (that is fit to eat, which would include only pure meat) is touched by unwashed hands, it is made "common" (adjective *koinos*; verb *koinoō*) in verses 2, 5, 15, 18. This extrabiblical category is not "impure,"

34. Gane, "Didactic Logic and the Authorship of Leviticus," in Gane and Taggar-Cohen, *Current Issues in Priestly and Related Literature*, 207–8. Cf. Israel Knohl, *The Sanctuary of Silence: The Priestly Torah and the Holiness School* (Minneapolis: Fortress 1995), 69, 182–84. Knohl views Lev. 11:43–45 as an editorial addition by the author(s) (which he calls the "Holiness School") that produced the Holiness Code. In any case, I see these verses exemplifying a literary strategy that is also found elsewhere in the canonical form of Leviticus.

35. Gane, *Leviticus, Numbers*, 215.

36. Cf. Jiří Moskala, "The Validity of the Levitical Food Laws of Clean and Unclean Animals: A Case Study of Biblical Hermeneutics," *JATS* 22, no. 2 (2011): 3–31.

as implied by the ESV translation "defile(d)" in these verses.[37] "Common" animals were pure according to Lev. 11, but tradition regarded them as less than pure, unfit to eat because they had associated with impure animals.[38]

Third, Jesus's statement, "There is nothing outside a person that by going into him can defile him [koinoō, "make common"], but the things that come out of a person are what defile [koinoō] him" (v. 15), was a "parable" (v. 17). This parable concerned the moral effect of evil things that come from a person's heart (vv. 20–23), by contrast with morally benign bodily processes of eating, digesting, and eliminating food that is eaten with unwashed hands (cf. Matt. 15:10–11, 17–20).

Fourth, the Greek text of Mark 7:19b says only katharizōn [present participle] panta ta brōmata, "purifying all foods," continuing Jesus's sentence in direct speech, rather than beginning a new sentence to explain what he taught. This is accurately rendered by NKJV, which supplies "thus" before these words. In the context of Jesus's speech, such purifying of all foods, which are fit to eat but eaten with unwashed hands, is simply due to the digestive and eliminatory physical processes. He said nothing here about pure meat versus impure meat, which his audience would not likely have regarded as food.[39]

Acts 10 describes Peter's experience with a paradigm-shattering vision:

[Peter] saw the heavens opened and something like a great sheet descending . . . In it were all kinds of animals and reptiles and birds of the air. And there came a voice to him: "Rise, Peter; kill and eat." But Peter said, "By no means, Lord; for I have never eaten anything that is common [koinos] or unclean [akathartos]." And the voice came to him again a second time, "What God has made clean, do not call common [koinoō]." (vv. 11–15)

The NIV incorrectly renders the second command of "the voice" in verse 15: "Do not call anything impure that God has made clean" (cf. "impure" in v. 14 NIV), which can be taken to imply that now God has made all impure creatures

37. On the "common" category here, see Colin House, "Defilement by Association: Some Insights from the Usage of Κοινός/Κοινόω in Acts 10 and 11," AUSS 21 (1983): 152–53.
38. Ibid., 143–53. Cf. Rom. 14:14, "Nothing is common [koinon] in itself, but it is common [koinon] for anyone who thinks it common [koinon]" (my trans., correcting ESV "unclean" to "common"). Verse 20 is to be understood in this context: "Do not, for the sake of food, destroy the work of God. Everything [including that which is "common"] is indeed clean."
39. Eike Mueller has shown that in Mark 7 neither Jesus nor Mark puts an end to the distinction between "clean" and "unclean" meats in Lev. 11. Rather, Jesus opposes extrabiblical traditions originating during the Second Temple period, which go beyond the divine requirements. "Cleansing the Common: A Narrative-Intertextual Study of Mark 7:1–23" (PhD diss., Andrews University, 2015).

fit to eat. But it is the extrabiblical "common" category that is to be regarded as "clean" here (with ESV); the biblical "impure" category is unaffected.

Peter's vision was not really about animals; it was a visual parable about people. The point was that Jewish Christians were not to regard any Gentiles as analogous to the "common" category of animals and therefore unfit for social interaction as believers share the gospel with them (see the rest of Acts 10, esp. vv. 34–35).[40] The metaphor of food was effective because in the cultural environment of Jesus and his apostles, social boundaries were indicated by those whom one accepted or rejected for table fellowship (e.g., Matt. 9:10–11; 1 Cor. 5:11; Gal. 2:11–14).

In Col. 2 Paul draws a logical conclusion based on what Christ's victory on the cross has accomplished for Christians: "So let no one judge you in food or in drink, or regarding a festival or a new moon or sabbaths, which are a shadow of things to come, but the substance is of Christ" (vv. 16–17 NKJV). Here "food" and "drink" do not concern dietary rules such as differences between pure and impure meats (Lev. 11; Deut. 14) or draining blood at the time of slaughter (e.g., Gen. 9:4; Lev. 17:10–14; Acts 15:20, 29), which were not associated with restrictions regarding drink, nor did they function as typological shadows of what was to come—that is, foreshadowing Christ's sacrifice. The context in Col. 2 indicates food and drink that belonged to the ritual system.[41]

It appears more accurate to render Col. 2:16–17: "Therefore, do not let anyone judge you in eating and drinking, *either* [particle *ē*] as part of a festival, or [*ē*] of a new moon, or [*ē*] of Sabbaths, which is a shadow of things to come, but the body is of Christ" (emphasis supplied).[42] This translation interprets the Greek particle *ē . . . ē* in sequence as "either . . . or," as in Matt. 6:24; 12:33; Luke 16:13; 1 Cor. 14:6 (cf. BDAG 432). Thus, Col. 2:16–17 does not downgrade requirements for Jewish dietary practices *and* sacred times, but dietary practices *at* sacred times: festivals, new moons, and Sabbaths.[43]

40. Notice that just as the portion of Mark 7 concerning defilement (vv. 1–23) is followed by a narrative about a Gentile, the Syro-Phoenician woman (vv. 24–30), so also in Acts 10 Peter's vision of all kinds of creatures (vv. 9–16) is followed by a narrative about Gentiles (Cornelius and others, vv. 17–48). Abstaining from unfit meats is not mentioned in Acts 15:29 (cf. v. 20) as a lifestyle requirement for Gentile Christians in addition to abstaining from improperly slaughtered meat. It appears that the distinctions between meats simply did not constitute an issue that had to be addressed at the Jerusalem Council.

41. Against James D. G. Dunn, who misses these contextual factors. *The Epistles to the Colossians and to Philemon: A Commentary on the Greek Text*, NIGTC (Grand Rapids: Eerdmans; Carlisle, UK: Paternoster, 1996), 172–73.

42. Translation from Bradford Maris, "The Case for a New Translation of Colossians 2:16–17: Dispelling a Theological Eclipse of Christianity's Central Truth" (unpublished paper).

43. Cf. Hosea 2:11 [2:13 MT]; Ezek. 45:17 ("the burnt offerings, grain offerings, and drink offerings, at [preposition *b*] the feasts [pilgrim festivals], the new moons, and the Sabbaths"), and

However Col. 2:16 is translated, it seems clear that the "food" and "drink" in this context refer to sacral meals connected with the ritual system, which common people (not only priests) could consume on certain special days of the calendar, such as Passover (Exod. 12:8–11; Deut. 16:2–8).[44] Israelites ate from well-being offerings for thanksgiving, fulfillment of vows, or as free-will offerings (Lev. 7:15–16; Deut. 12:6–7); they consumed (second) tithes of grain, wine, and oil; and they ate the meat of animal firstborn at the sanctuary/temple "before the LORD" (Deut. 12:6–7, 11–12, 17–18; 14:23–26; 15:19–20). While these activities were permitted on any day, the people would tend to come to the sanctuary/temple with their offerings on special days, especially the three mandatory pilgrim festivals (Exod. 23:14–17; 34:22–24; Deut. 16:16–17). That they were required to rejoice there during the Festival of Weeks (Deut. 16:10–11) and the Festival of Booths (16:13–15) implies that they would eat and drink on those occasions (cf. 12:7, "you shall eat . . . you shall rejoice").

Prohibition of Sexual Intercourse during Menstruation

Sexual behaviors that are categorically forbidden in Lev. 18 and 20 include incest (18:6–18; 20:11–12, 14, 17, 19–21), adultery (18:20; 20:10), homosexual activity (18:22; 20:13), bestiality (18:23; 20:15–16), and another one that most Christians do not know about:

> You will not approach a woman during her menstrual impurity to sexually uncover her nakedness. (18:19)

---

the reverse order in 2 Chron. 8:13 ("the Sabbaths, the new moons, and the three annual feasts"), following the order in Num. 28–29 but focusing on the three pilgrim festivals (Exod. 23:14–17; etc.). In Col. 2:16 the term "Sabbaths" could refer either to weekly or ceremonial S/sabbaths. However, in this context it appears that ritual activities of eating and drinking (participating in typological shadows) performed on weekly Sabbaths are in view (Lev. 23:3; Num. 28:9–10; cf. Paul Giem, "*Sabbatōn* in Col 2:16," *AUSS* 19 [1981]: 195–210) because ceremonial sabbaths were included in the "festivals" (Lev. 23:7–8, 21, 25, 28–32, 35–36, 39; cf. 23:38, "besides the Lord's [weekly] Sabbaths"; Num. 28:18, 25–26; 29:1, 7, 12, 35). In any case, Col. 2:16–17 certainly does not address abrogation of basic weekly Sabbath rest itself, which never served as a temporary type. It originated before the fall for the benefit of humans (Gen. 2:2–3; Mark 2:27), before the need for typology of redemption from sin, and it did not depend on the ritual system (Gane, *Leviticus, Numbers*, 393–95). Israelite festivals, on the other hand, did function as typological shadows (e.g., Passover: 1 Cor. 5:7; cf. Exod. 12:3–11; elevated/raised [so-called wave] sheaf of firstfruits: 1 Cor. 15:20; cf. Lev. 23:10–11; Festival of Weeks/Pentecost: Acts 2; cf. Lev. 23:16–21).

44. Wine was added to the Passover liturgy at least by the Second Temple period (Matt. 26:27), perhaps due to the requirement that when the Israelites would come into the promised land, they should provide drink offerings to accompany *zevakh* sacrifices (Num. 15:2, 5, including the Passover *zevakh*; Exod 12:27), from which offerers could eat.

If there is a man who has sexual intercourse with a woman having her menstrual condition, sexually uncovering her nakedness, he has exposed the source of her flow and she has uncovered the source of her blood. Both of them will be cut off from the midst of their people. (20:18)[45]

These prohibitions of sexual intercourse during a woman's menstrual period (18:19) or when she has any genital flow (20:18), including her regular period or discharge following childbirth (12:2) or resulting from an abnormal condition (15:25),[46] are included in Lev. 18 and 20 among absolute moral stipulations. They are based on the value of sexual purity exemplified by the seventh of the Ten Commandments (Exod. 20:14), as reinforced by the fact that Ezek. 18:6 and 22:10 also include the ban on sex during menstruation among moral issues.

Deliberate violations of any of the laws in Lev. 18, including the one under discussion, are abominations (vv. 26–27, 29) that generate irremediable moral impurity (see above; not physical ritual impurity) that defiles not only the sinners (vv. 24, 30) but also the land (vv. 25, 27–28; 20:22) and incurs the terminal divinely administered penalty of being "cut off" (18:29), which is specified in 20:18 for intercourse during menstruation. The rationale for the prohibition, "he has exposed the source of her flow and she has uncovered the source of her blood" (20:18), concerns the woman's body and does not involve the sanctuary.

Therefore we cannot escape the conclusion that the prohibition is permanent and applies to modern Christians as part of a holy lifestyle (20:7–8, 26; cf. 1 Pet. 1:15–16). The fact that Christians have not observed the ban on sex during menstruation is irrelevant. No OT law is ever abrogated by mere ignorance, oversight, or neglect.

We have found that deliberately violating the prohibition causes moral impurity, but Lev. 15 indicates that a man who has sex with a menstruant incurs temporary physical ritual impurity, for which there is a ritual remedy: "And if any man lies with her and her menstrual impurity comes upon him, he shall be unclean seven days, and every bed on which he lies shall be unclean" (v. 24). Thus he contracts her seven-day impurity through intercourse with her. This relatively mild consequence seems to conflict with the terminal penalty of being "cut off" for deliberate violation in 18:19 and 20:18.

Jacob Milgrom addresses the problem as follows:

It might be thought that the reason that P (15:24) prescribes seven days of impurity, whereas H (20:18) prescribes *kārēt*, is that P deals with inadvertences and H

45. Both verses are from the translation by Roy E. Gane and William K. Gilders, prepublication draft translation of Leviticus for the CEB.
46. Cf. Milgrom, *Leviticus 17–22*, 1754.

deals with advertences (R. Gane). It is more likely, however, following Abravanel (see NOTE on 15:24), that P is concerned with the nature of the generated impurity, not with its penalties. Indeed, certain acts described in chap. 15 are clearly deliberate (e.g., sex! v. 18). Indeed, intention plays no part whatsoever in chap. 15; whether advertent or inadvertent, they generate impurity. Chap. 20, however, focusing solely on sexual intercourse, is limited to advertences.[47]

Milgrom is right that Lev. 15 is not concerned with intention or penalties resulting from wrongdoing. For instance, sexual intercourse causes the man and woman to have physical ritual impurity (v. 18), without specifying that they are married to each other. Adultery would also generate such impurity, but it would be eclipsed by far more serious moral impurity resulting from the same act (Lev. 18:20; 20:10; cf. Num. 5:13–14, 20), for which there is no ritual remedy. So there would be no point in formulating a law that says: "And if a man other than her husband lies with her and her menstrual impurity comes upon him, he shall be unclean seven days." Clearly the case in Lev. 15:18 is primarily directed toward marital relations.

A man who has intercourse with a menstruant contracts physical ritual impurity in any case (Lev. 15:24), whether or not he additionally bears moral impurity (along with her) for deliberately violating the prohibitions in 18:19 and 20:18. However, as with 15:18 and adultery, 15:24 would be virtually super-fluous if it covered only deliberate sex with a menstruant. If a person is subject to a terminal penalty, how do seven days of physical ritual impurity matter?

Therefore, it appears that the main reason for the provision in 15:24 is a situation in which the couple does not incur moral impurity because their violation is accidental rather than deliberate. The language of the verse, "and her menstrual impurity comes [imperfect of *h-y-h*, "is"] upon ['*al*] him," refers to the physical phenomenon of menstrual blood on the man's penis, without indication of intention. He clearly intended to have intercourse with her but was not aware that she was menstruating. This scenario includes the possibility that the couple discovers during or just after intercourse that the woman has begun to menstruate.[48] Compare the similar language of 15:17, regarding purification from accidental contact with semen from a nocturnal emission: "Any cloth or skin on ['*al*] which there is [imperfect of *h-y-h*] an emission of semen will be laundered in water and be impure until evening."[49]

47. Ibid., 1756.

48. Milgrom refers to this possibility in *Leviticus 1–16*, 940, and in *Leviticus 17–22*, 1756, citing a suggestion that I offered in his seminar. My answer to the problem here in the present work is a nuanced version of that seminar comment that takes Milgrom's points into account.

49. Trans. Gane and Gilders. Notice that both in 15:17 and v. 24, the Hebrew word order is *h-y-h* + '*al*, although translation of the relative clause "on which there is" (lit., "which there is

The physical ritual impurity element is irrelevant for modern Christians because the earthly sanctuary is gone. But deliberate violation is still sin that generates moral defilement, damaging the divine-human relationship, although defilement of the literal land of Israel that results in exile from it is no longer an issue.

The explicit reason for the prohibition of sex during a woman's period is to avoid exposing the source of her flow of blood by sexual contact (20:18). Intercourse would open what should remain closed during that time. Whatever abstract concept may be behind this, it makes perfect gynecological sense because the female reproductive system is vulnerable while menstrual blood is flowing from it: The OB/GYN physician Daniel C. Oliver, MD, FACOG, reports that sexual intercourse during menstruation leads to an increased risk of some sexually transmitted diseases, which can involve complicated pelvic infections commonly called PID (pelvic inflammatory disease).[50]

As with other OT laws in which we can recognize health benefits, including the prohibitions of dietary blood and unfit meat, the health aspect is secondary to the stated rationale. However, YHWH did correlate the health of his people with their obedience to all of his instructions (Exod. 15:26; Deut. 7:12, 15).[51]

Leviticus 20:18 hints at another secondary benefit of abstinence from intercourse during a woman's period or other genital flow. Here the Hebrew term for her condition is the adjective *daveh*, "faint" (cf. 15:33; Lam. 1:13; 5:17).[52] This can be taken to imply a women's rights issue: The OT law protects "the woman from unwanted advances by her husband during her period of weakness (R. Gane)."[53]

Homosexual Activity and "Marriage"

Leviticus 18 and 20 address homosexual activity as follows:

You shall not lie with a male as with a woman; it is an abomination. (18:22)

If a man lies with a male as with a woman, both of them have committed an abomination; they shall surely be put to death; their blood is upon them. (20:13)

---

on it") in v. 17 changes the order in English. Cf. Lev. 11:34, "Any food in it that could be eaten, on ['al] which water comes [impf. of b-v-'], shall be unclean."

50. Personal communication.

51. On the so-called health laws, see Gane, *Leviticus, Numbers*, 209–10, 212–13.

52. See also the *qal* infinitive of the same root *d-v-h* in Lev. 12:2.

53. Milgrom, *Leviticus 17–22*, 1755. For a concise and helpful discussion of the laws concerning menstruation and references to secondary literature, see Richard M. Davidson, *Flame of Yahweh: Sexuality in the Old Testament* (Peabody, MA: Hendrickson, 2007), 332–34.

It is crucial to point out that the Bible, including in these laws, never condemns anyone for simply being homosexual in the sense of having homosexual tendencies, just as it never condemns any heterosexuals merely for their attractions. A homosexual person can be a Christian in the fullest sense of the word. The problem comes when heterosexual or homosexual people carry out forbidden acts by giving in to temptations that arise from their propensities (cf. Matt. 5:27–28; James 1:14–15).

There are no real interpretive difficulties in Lev. 18:22 and 20:13. The sticking point is not in these laws but in the minds of people who do not want to accept their clear meaning and try to invent all kinds of creative ways to get around it. I have addressed a number of those failed strategies elsewhere[54] and will not repeat all of that discussion here; instead I confine the present comments to a few key clarifications.

Leviticus 18:22 and 20:13 refer to male homosexual activity as (lit.) "lie [verb sh-k-b][55] a male the lyings down [plural of mishkav] of a woman." "Lie down" covers the whole process of going to bed and having sex with someone, including any foreplay, penetration, and ejaculation.[56] The expression "the lyings down of a woman" characterizes what a man would experience while having sex with a woman, just as "the lying down of a male" describes the sexual experience of a woman with a man (Num. 31:17, 18, 35; Judg. 21:11, 12).[57] Therefore, Lev. 18 and 20 forbid a male to have the kind of sexual experience with another male that he would otherwise have with a woman.

Genesis 49:4 provides further insight regarding the meaning of mishkav, "lying down" or "place of lying down," meaning couch/bed. Here Jacob speaks to his son Reuben regarding his incest with Bilhah, Jacob's concubine, (lit.): "You went up [onto] the beds [plural of mishkav] of your father." The problem was the fact that Reuben usurped Jacob's exclusive prerogative to bed down with Bilhah. This right is expressed by the (probably abstract) plural of mishkav, the same word used in Lev. 18:22 and 20:13. In these verses,

54. Gane, Leviticus, Numbers, 325–30; Gane, "Some Attempted Alternatives to Timeless Biblical Condemnation of Homosexual Acts," in Homosexuality, Marriage, and the Church: Biblical, Counseling, and Religious Liberty Issues, ed. Roy E. Gane, Nicholas P. Miller, and H. Peter Swanson (Berrien Springs, MI: Andrews University Press, 2012), 163–74.

55. It appears that the Hebrew 'et here is the direct object marker, but it may be the preposition "with," resulting in the translation "lie with a male."

56. For penetration by itself, Hebrew employs another expression: verb n-t-n + noun shekovet + preposition b, lit., "put (one's) penis in" (Lev. 18:20, 23; 20:15; Num. 5:20). For the translation "penis" for shekovet, see Harry Orlinsky, "The Hebrew Root ŠKB," JBL 63 (1944): 40. English versions do not really translate this word.

57. "Lying down" translates the singular of mishkav, "bed" or place of lying down.

"the lyings down [also plural of *mishkav*] of a woman" rightfully belong to a woman, never to a man.

The verb *sh-k-b*, "lie down," in Lev. 18:22 and 20:13 is masculine singular, and the word *'ishah*, "woman," in these verses can also mean "wife" in Hebrew. However, these laws do not only forbid a married man, such as the male head of a household, to engage in homosexual activity that violates his wife's right to exclusive sexual intimacy with him, interpreting "the lyings down of a woman" as "on the beds of a wife."[58] First, there is no indication that "a woman" here is married at all, just as "the lying down of a male" in Num. 31:17, 18, 35; Judg. 21:11, and 12 does not say whether "a male/man" (*zakar*) is married or not, because *zakar* by itself does not mean "husband."

Second, even if "a woman" in Lev. 18:22 and 20:13 is "a wife," these verses do not say that she is the wife of the man who engages in the homosexual activity, or of any other man, for that matter, by contrast with other verses in chaps. 18 and 20 that identify wives belonging to certain men (18:8, 11, 14–16, 20; 20:10–11, 20–21). Therefore, the *'ishah* in 18:22 and 20:13 refers to any woman, and the prohibition against homosexual activity applies to any male. In fact, this and the other laws in Lev. 18 apply not only to Israelites but also to non-Israelite resident aliens (18:26), and YHWH held the inhabitants of Canaan accountable for breaking their principles (vv. 24–25, 27–28; 20:23).

There is no law in Leviticus against lesbian sex. However, the idea that such a deviation from the heterosexual norm is unacceptable, as Paul makes explicit in Rom. 1:26, could be inferred from the prohibition of male homoerotic activity in Lev. 18:22; 20:13 within the context of the general warnings in Lev. 18:3, 24–30; 20:23 against perpetrating the abominable practices of the Egyptians and Canaanites.[59]

As mentioned above, homosexual activity is included in Lev. 18 and 20 among categorically forbidden sexual behaviors, along with incest, sexual intercourse during menstruation, adultery, and bestiality. All of these are characterized as abominations, incur the terminal penalty of being "cut off," generate irremediable moral impurity, and the prohibitions against them continue to apply to Christians today (see above).[60] However, the death penalty specified in Lev. 20:13, which was to be administered under the theocracy,

---

58. This interpretation has been proposed by Bruce Wells, "The Grammar and Meaning of the Leviticus Texts on Same-Sex Relations Reconsidered" (paper presented at the annual meeting of the Society of Biblical Literature, San Diego, November 24, 2014), http://www.acad emia.edu/11958189/The_Grammar_and_Meaning_of_the_Leviticus_Texts_on_Same-Sex_Re lations_Reconsidered.

59. Cf. R. Davidson, *Flame of Yahweh*, 150.

60. Among the prohibited sexual activities, only homosexual activity is labeled as an abomination within the individual laws (Lev. 18:22; 20:13).

would not apply today. Instead, removal from the Christian community is accomplished by putting violators outside the circle of fellowship among members (1 Cor. 5).

Notice that the ongoing force of the command against sex during menstruation (see above) removes the argument that because Christians are not required to keep that law, they do not need to observe the ban on homosexual activity either.[61]

The Bible consistently maintains a negative stance toward homosexual activity.[62] Like OT law, the NT condemns it along with other sins (Rom. 1:26–27, including lesbian sex; 1 Cor. 6:9; 1 Tim. 1:10; cf. Jude 7), but it also provides hope for redemption and transformation through Christ and the Holy Spirit:

> Or do you not know that the unrighteous will not inherit the kingdom of God? Do not be deceived: neither the sexually immoral, nor idolaters, nor adulterers, nor men who practice homosexuality, nor thieves, nor the greedy, nor drunkards, nor revilers, nor swindlers will inherit the kingdom of God. And such were some of you. But you were washed, you were sanctified, you were justified in the name of the Lord Jesus Christ and by the Spirit of our God. (1 Cor. 6:9–11)

So what about gay "marriage," which involves homosexual activity in the context of a loyal, committed, monogamous relationship? Nowhere, including in Lev. 18 and 20, does the Bible provide exceptions to sexual prohibitions on the basis of such criteria. The activities are simply forbidden, regardless of any circumstantial factors or intentions. The member of the church in Corinth who was living in a sexual relationship with his stepmother may have been very fond of her, committed, and exclusively loyal, but none of that was relevant because his incest was wrong according to Lev. 18:8 and 20:11 (cf. Deut. 22:30 [23:1 MT]; 27:20).

In the Bible, marriage is only between a man and a woman. Homosexual "marriage" is an oxymoron. No amount of social or state recognition can invest gay "marriage" with moral legitimacy for Christians whose guide is Scripture. The value of equality is a legitimate modern concern in many areas of life, but not "marriage equality" that includes homosexual unions at the expense of the value of sexual purity.

---

61. Gane, *Leviticus, Numbers,* 324–26, responding to William J. Webb, *Slaves, Women & Homosexuals: Exploring the Hermeneutics of Cultural Analysis* (Downers Grove, IL: InterVarsity, 2001), 168–70.

62. Cf. Webb, *Slaves, Women & Homosexuals,* 39–40, 81–82, etc. For thorough discussion of the biblical approach to homosexual practice, see Robert A. J. Gagnon, *The Bible and Homosexual Practice: Texts and Hermeneutics* (Nashville: Abingdon, 2001).

The solution for homosexuals is not to seek legitimate ways to act on their tendencies, of which there are no such ways to act, but to rely on the mighty power of Christ and the Spirit in order to live in sexual purity.[63] Members of the church community have a special responsibility to reach out to them and assist their journey with Christ as they struggle against powerful physical and social forces, including feelings of hopelessness, alienation, loneliness, and suicidal depression. We should include them in our friendship, listen to their stories, pray with them and for them, and draw on their talents.

Leviticus 18:22 and 20:13 are not the only OT laws that speak to the situations of homosexuals, along with bisexual individuals. As we ponder how to relate to them, we will do well to remember and implement a towering principle of OT law and wisdom in the chapter between Lev. 18 and 20: "You shall love your neighbor as yourself" (19:18). Paul expressed a relevant corollary: "Bear one another's burdens, and so fulfill the law of Christ" (Gal. 6:2; cf. v. 1).[64]

63. Cf. Wesley Hill, *Spiritual Friendship: Finding Love in the Church as a Celibate Gay Christian* (Grand Rapids: Brazos, 2015).

64. Cf. Roy E. Gane, "Old Testament Principles Relevant to Consensual Homoerotic Activity—Part 3," *Ministry: International Journal for Pastors* 88, no. 1 (January 2016): 12–13.

16

Values Reflected in Ritual Laws

The importance of the ritual laws in the OT is shown by the sheer volume of these materials and the extent to which they are interspersed among other kinds of OT laws as well as narratives.[1] It is also indicated by the canonical placement of Leviticus, where the core instructions regarding sacrificial worship are found at the center of the Pentateuch. This literary placement could be regarded as corresponding to the physical location of YHWH's sanctuary at the center of the Israelite camp (see below).

The present chapter begins by identifying laws concerning aspects of the normative Israelite ritual system[2] throughout the Pentateuch to show what kinds of Israelite rituals were to be performed and where the regulations about them are located. The remaining sections of the chapter explore the question of how Christians can appropriate values reflected in the ritual laws as they seek to have God at the center of their lives, approach him in worship, ask him to remove their sins, gain assurance of reconciliation with him, and grow in holiness.[3]

The ritual laws are profound and complex. Therefore this chapter provides only a brief overview of some major topics, overlapping to some extent, that can be especially valuable for Christians. Thorough exegesis and progressive moral wisdom (PMW) analysis of a fraction of any of the points addressed

---

1. See also ritual laws in Ezek. 43:18–46:24 (except 45:6–12) within a framework of prophecy after directions for constructing an ideal temple (40:1–43:17).
2. Not including laws against pagan cultic practices.
3. I endeavor to draw concepts from the OT through exegesis, but it is difficult to know how much of the typological meaning of rituals the ancient Israelites understood.

here would consume an entire chapter; hence much of what I present here summarizes conclusions that I have reached through investigations already published elsewhere.[4]

Identification of Ritual Law Topics in the Pentateuch

Chapter 4 of the present book identifies locations of law collections, lesser clusters or series of laws, and some isolated laws in the OT. There two collections devoted to ritual laws are identified: Lev. 1–7, 11–16; and Ezek. 43:18–46:24. However, many ritual laws in the Pentateuch appear elsewhere, including in other law collections and series.

Genesis–Exodus

According to the pentateuchal narrative, God gave some ritual laws before the Israelite sanctuary was established. He commanded Abraham and his line of descendants to perform circumcision of males as the sign that they belonged to the covenant community (Gen. 17:9–14). As the Israelites were about to depart from Egypt, the Lord instituted the Festivals of Passover and Unleavened Bread (Exod. 12:3–27, 43–49; 13:3–10; cf. 34:18) and the requirement to sacrifice male firstborn animals but to redeem nonsacrificable male animals and humans (13:11–16).

Following the Decalogue and immediately preceding the so-called Covenant Code, Exod. 20:24–26 instructs the Israelites to make local sacrificial altars of earth or stone in order to worship YHWH. The Covenant Code (Exod. 21–23) and the so-called Ritual Decalogue (34:11–26) command Israelite males to observe three annual pilgrim festivals (23:14–17; 34:18, 22–24), issue some rules regarding sacrifices (23:18; 34:25), and require firstfruits offerings (23:19; 34:26). Exodus 34:19–20 reiterates the requirement to sacrifice firstborn animals but to redeem nonsacrificable species and humans. The narrative of Exodus also describes the sacrificial ceremony by which the nation of Israel entered the covenant with YHWH at Mount Sinai (24:4–8).

Texts regarding the Israelite ritual system centered at the sanctuary begin with divine instructions for constructing and setting up the sanctuary infrastructure (including making the priestly garments) in Exod. 25–31, followed by narrative fulfillment of those directions in chaps. 35–40. Interspersed among

4. Esp. Roy Gane, *Leviticus, Numbers*, NIV Application Commentary (Grand Rapids: Zondervan, 2004); Gane, *Cult and Character: Purification Offerings, Day of Atonement, and Theodicy* (Winona Lake, IN: Eisenbrauns, 2005); cf. Gane, *Altar Call* (Berrien Springs, MI: Diadem, 1999).

the instructions are some ritual prescriptions/laws for ritual activities and priestly roles that utilize the items to be made, including the golden table (25:29–30), lamps on the lampstand (v. 37; 27:20–21; 30:7–8), priestly garments (28:29–30, 35, 38, 43),[5] outer altar (29:36–42), incense altar (30:7–10), basin (vv. 19–21), anointing oil (vv. 26–33), and incense (vv. 36–38).[6] Related to the ritual system, Exod. 30:11–16 also requires a half-shekel offering from each Israelite when there is a census.

Development of the sacrificial system involved a transition from patriarchal worship to worship at the sanctuary. The first sacrifices recorded in canonical Scripture are those of Cain and Abel, which they presented as homage to YHWH. Each of these sacrifices is called a *minkhah*, "offering," even though Cain's was from the ground and Abel's was from the flock (Gen. 4:3–5). Thus the term *minkhah* here is used in a general sense rather than referring to a specific kind of sacrifice. Later in the pentateuchal narrative flow, *minkhah* is used more specifically in the Israelite cult for homage in the form of a "grain offering" that could be independent (Lev. 2; 6:14–23 [6:7–16 MT]) or could accompany an animal sacrifice along with a libation (e.g., Exod. 29:41; Lev. 23:13, 18; Num. 15:4–5).

Two specific kinds of animal sacrifices are attested during the postdiluvian patriarchal era, before the Israelite sanctuary was established: *'olah*, "burnt offering," and *zevakh*, "sacrifice" (Exod. 10:25; 18:12). The burnt offering, which was wholly consumed by the fire on an altar and ascended to the Deity in the form of smoke, served as a basic ritual instrument of sacrificial worship that invoked the Lord.[7] Its first attestation is the sacrifice of Noah (Gen. 8:20). Subsequently the burnt offering was not restricted to the covenant line of patriarchs: It was offered not only by Abraham (22:13) but also by Job and his friends to expiate for sins (Job 1:5; 42:7–9, commanded by YHWH).

The *zevakh* type (Gen. 46:1), imprecisely translated simply as "sacrifice," included the "(sacrifice of) well-being offering" (*zevakh shelamim*, Exod. 20:24;

---

5. Cf. Exod. 29:1–35: instructions for the onetime consecration of the priests with their garments.

6. Cf. some ritual activities in Exod. 40: reiteration of instructions concerning the anointing oil (vv. 9–15) and priestly garments (vv. 12–15), and narrative description of actions involving the table (v. 23), incense altar (v. 27), outer altar (v. 29), and basin (vv. 30–32).

7. Cf. Baruch A. Levine, *Leviticus: The Traditional Hebrew Text with the New JPS Translation*, JPS Torah Commentary (Philadelphia: Jewish Publication Society, 1989), 5–6. The basic function of this sacrifice is reflected by the facts that its procedural outline comes first in Leviticus (chap. 1), the outer altar is called the "altar of burnt offering" (Exod. 30:28; 31:9; 35:16; etc.), probably at least partly because burnt offerings were always to be burning on it (Lev. 6:9, 12–13 [6:2, 5–6 MT]), and the morning and evening sacrifices every day were burnt offerings (Exod. 29:38–42; Num. 28:1–8).

24:5) and the Passover sacrifice (*zevakh pesakh*, Exod. 12:27). This kind of sacrifice was eaten by the offerer, which he could share with other people in a communal meal (Gen. 31:54; Exod. 12:3–4, 8–9).

With the institution of the sanctuary, burnt and well-being offerings came under regulation by ritual law because now they were officiated at the sanctuary altar by Aaronic priests, whose ritual roles and portions from the sacrifices had to be specified (Lev. 1, 3; 6:8–13 [6:1–6 MT]; 7:8, 14, 28–36). Leviticus begins by presenting the burnt offering as a voluntary sacrifice (chap. 1), presumably because it continued to serve as a basic instrument of worship, which explains why the (required) regular morning and evening sacrifices and many festival sacrifices for the entire Israelite community were burnt offerings (Exod. 29:38–42; Num. 28–29). Because the function of the burnt offering continued to include expiation (Lev. 1:4), as in the book of Job (1:5; 42:8), it could be required in some situations when certain kinds of expiation were needed: for physical ritual impurities (Lev. 12:6, 8; 14:19, 22, 31; 15:15, 30) and on the Day of Atonement (16:24).

Two kinds of mandatory expiatory sacrifices performed at the sanctuary, the purification offering (*khatta't*, so-called sin offering) and the reparation offering (*'asham*, so-called guilt offering), were added to the Israelite ritual system to remedy certain kinds of evils.[8] Purification offerings remedied inadvertent sins (Lev. 4; Num. 15:22–29), sins of omission (Lev. 5:1–13) through forgetfulness (vv. 2–4) or deliberate neglect to offer testimony regarding a crime (v. 1),[9] and severe physical ritual impurities (Num. 19:9, 17; usually accompanied by burnt offerings: Lev. 12:6, 8; 14:19; etc.). Reparation offerings dealt with sins of sacrilege, including misuse of holy things or fraud against a fellow Israelite that was facilitated by a false oath in YHWH's name (Lev. 5:14–6:7 [5:14–26 MT]).

Leviticus

The core of instructions regulating ritual procedures is found in Lev. 1–16. Leviticus 1:1–6:7 (1:1–5:26 MT) outlines activities included in five major kinds of sacrifices: burnt offering (chap. 1), grain offering (chap. 2), (sacrifice [*zevakh*] of) well-being offering (chap. 3), purification offering (4:1–5:13), and

8. The purification offering first appears in Exod. 29:14, 36 in the prescription for the complex of rituals by which the Israelite sanctuary and its priesthood are to be consecrated (29:1–37). Performance of the consecration service is described in Lev. 8. The reparation offering is introduced as a specific kind of sacrifice in Lev. 5:15–16, 18–19.

9. Jacob Milgrom, *Leviticus 1–16: A New Translation with Introduction and Commentary*, AB 3 (New York: Doubleday, 1991), 228–29, 242, 294–95, 298–300; Bruce Wells, *The Law of Testimony in the Pentateuchal Codes*, BZABR 4 (Wiesbaden: Harrassowitz, 2004), 63–82.

reparation offering (5:14–6:7 [5:26 MT]). Then 6:8–7:38 (chaps. 6–7 MT) provides additional instructions, especially for priests, concerning the various kinds of sacrifices, including the burnt offering (6:8–13 [6:1–6 MT]; 7:8), grain offering (6:14–18 [6:7–11 MT]; 7:9–10), high priest's regular grain offering (6:19–23 [6:12–16 MT]), purification offering (vv. 24–30 [vv. 17–23 MT]), reparation offering (7:1–7), and well-being offering (vv. 11–36), concluding with a summary statement (vv. 37–38).[10]

Leviticus continues with a narrative description of two closely related and juxtaposed ritual events: the onetime consecration (Lev. 8; fulfilling instructions in Exod. 29:1–35; cf. 40:9–15) and inauguration (Lev. 9–10) of the sanctuary and its priests, with the latter recounting a fatal ritual mistake of two priests at the end of the inauguration (Lev. 10). Laws resume in Lev. 11 with nonritual distinctions between animals that are pure/fit versus impure/unfit to eat (vv. 1–23, 41–47; cf. Deut. 14:3–20) and identification of animals whose carcasses convey physical ritual impurity by contact (Lev. 11:24–40). The laws in the following chapters concern physical ritual impurities resulting from childbirth (Lev. 12), surface disease (*tsara'at*, commonly rendered "leprosy"; chaps. 13–14),[11] and genital flows (chap. 15). Purification from such impurities (including with sacrifices in severe cases) is required, especially before contact with holy things (see, e.g., 7:20–21).

Leviticus 16 requires ritual purification of the sanctuary once per year on the Day of Atonement to remove defilements from physical ritual impurities and sins that have accumulated there. This is the only occasion when the high priest is permitted to enter inside the inner veil into the holy of holies (called simply *qodesh*, "holy place" in Lev. 16). On this day all Israelites are required to practice physical self-denial (including fasting) and to abstain from all work (vv. 29, 31; 23:26–32).

The so-called Holiness Code (Lev. 17–27) includes some ritual laws that reiterate earlier instructions and/or provide additional information about sacrificial slaughter (17:1–12); physical ritual impurity (vv. 15–16); well-being

10. On didactic logic involved in the order of ritual instruction units in this part of Leviticus, see Roy E. Gane, "Didactic Logic and the Authorship of Leviticus," in *Current Issues in Priestly and Related Literature: The Legacy of Jacob Milgrom and Beyond*, ed. Roy E. Gane and Ada Taggar-Cohen, RBS (Atlanta: Society of Biblical Literature, 2015), 208, 211.

11. The same term for the disease (*tsara'at*) on skin of humans also refers to fungous infections on garments (Lev. 13:47–59) and walls of houses (14:33–53). The symptoms of *tsara'at* on humans described in Lev. 13 are not identical to those of modern leprosy (Hansen's disease), but the chronic form of the disease may have at least included an ancient form of leprosy. Gane, *Leviticus, Numbers*, 235, referring to Milgrom, *Leviticus 1–16*, 817; R. K. Harrison, "Leper; Leprosy," *ISBE* 3:103–6; cf. Harrison, *Leviticus: An Introduction and Commentary*, TOTC (Leicester, UK: Inter-Varsity, 1980), 136–45, 241–46.

(including thanksgiving) offerings (19:5–8; 22:29–30); a case requiring a reparation offering (19:20–22); rules for priests regarding prohibited impurities, holy living, acceptable officiation (with no blemish or impurity), and use of holy food (21:1–22:16); acceptable sacrificial animals (22:17–28); annual festivals (23:4–44);[12] lamps on the lampstand (24:1–4); and the "bread of the Presence" to be placed on the golden table (vv. 5–9). Leviticus 27 involves the ritual system in that it provides directions for dedications of various items to the sanctuary.

Numbers

The book of Numbers contains narrative interwoven with laws, which include ritual laws regarding serious impurities (5:1–3); restitution with reparation offerings and donations belonging to priests (vv. 5–10); a ritual concerning a suspected adulteress (vv. 11–31); rituals (including sacrifices) performed by Nazirites (6:9–21); lamps on the lampstand (8:1–2); ritual purification (including sacrifices) of the Levite workforce (8:5–19); Passover (9:1–4, 9–14); blowing trumpets on festival occasions (10:10); grain and drink accompaniments to sacrifices (15:1–16); contribution of first dough (15:17–21); purification offerings (vv. 22–29); purification from corpse impurity (chap. 19); and the calendar of public sacrifices to be offered every day, on Sabbaths, at new moons, and at annual festivals (chaps. 28–29).

Other passages in Numbers that are relevant to the ritual system concern responsibilities of the Levites (1:50–51, 53; 3:5–10, 25–26, 31–32, 36–37; 4:1–33; 8:23–26; 18:1–6), prohibitions of encroachment on priestly prerogatives by unauthorized nonpriests (1:51; 3:10, 38; 18:7), placement of the sanctuary in the middle of the Israelite camp (2:17; 3:23, 29, 35, 38), the redemption price of Israelite firstborn "over and above the number of male Levites" (3:46–51), gifts of tribal chieftains for the service of the sanctuary when it was consecrated (chap. 7), summary description of purification of the Levite workforce (8:20–22), Aaron's rod that budded in the sanctuary (17:1–11 [17:16–26 MT]), portions from consecrated offerings and contributions for support of priests and Levites (18:8–32), purification from corpse impurity of Israelite soldiers and Midianite captives and spoils (31:19–24), and an offering of gold from the Midianite spoils given by the Israelite army officers (vv. 48–54).

---

12. The first introduction in Lev. 23 (vv. 1–2) introduces the sacred times as a whole, followed by reaffirmation of the weekly Sabbath (v. 3), which is the foundation of sacred time. However, the Sabbath is not an inherently ritual occasion, since its observance consists simply of abstaining from work, and according to the Pentateuch, its origin preceded the need for a ritual system (Gen. 2:2–3).

Deuteronomy

Ritual laws in the so-called Deuteronomic Code (Deut. 12–26) have to do with sacrifices and eating of tithes at the central sanctuary (12:5–14, 17–19, 26–27; 14:22–27), sacrifice of firstborn male animals (15:19–21), reiteration of Passover (now at the central sanctuary) and three annual pilgrim festivals (16:1–17), prohibition of sacrificing blemished animals (17:1), portions of offerings and contributions for priests and Levites (18:1–8), a ritual for an unsolved murder (21:1–9), exclusion of a soldier with a nocturnal emission from his war camp (23:10–11), a reminder to follow directions of priests in cases of leprosy (24:8), firstfruits offerings at the central sanctuary (26:1–11), and a declaration of obedience every third year regarding proper handling of the sacred tithe (26:13–14).

Christian Appropriation of Values Reflected in Ritual Laws

Christians cannot directly keep the OT laws that regulated the Israelite ritual system, because that system no longer exists, and it has been replaced by Christ's priestly ministry in the heavenly temple (e.g., Heb. 7–10).[13] Nevertheless, while the ritual laws are obsolete in that sense, they encapsulate enduring values that inform the Christian understanding of the Lord's presence, sovereignty, and character; worship; salvation from sin through Christ; divine judgment; assurance; sanctification; and ministry. These concepts assist us in receiving and cooperating with God's work in our lives as we interact with him by faith through Christ, our high priest, in the heavenly temple (e.g., Heb. 4:14–16). Moreover, since the Israelite sanctuary was patterned after the temple in heaven and ritual offerings at the earthly sanctuary served as "a copy and shadow of the heavenly things" (Heb. 8:5), the OT information regarding the sanctuary and its services provides essential background to the NT books of Hebrews and Revelation, where Christ's ministry in God's heavenly temple is prominent.

It makes sense that the OT ritual laws have been preserved in "the sacred writings, which are able to make you wise for salvation through faith in Christ Jesus" (2 Tim. 3:15). These laws teach people how to "love the LORD your God with all your heart and with all your soul" (Deut. 6:5), which Jesus identified as "the great and first commandment" (Matt. 22:37–38). Love for God provides perspective that is foundational to biblical morality, including

---

13. Some laws discussed in chap. 15 above are related to the ritual system, and there the question was whether or not Christians should keep them today. In the present chapter, there is no question of Christians keeping any of the laws discussed here.

love for one's fellow human being (Lev. 19:18, 34; Matt. 22:39), the principles exemplified by the Ten Commandments, and all values reflected in OT laws that concern relationships with God and humans. Lest there is any doubt regarding the integral connection between ritual laws and other OT laws, some important OT rituals expiated moral faults (e.g., Lev. 4:1–6:7 [4:1–5:26 MT]), pointing to the remedy of Christ's sacrifice for human violations of divine commandments (e.g., 1 John 1:7, 9). In fact, YHWH himself rendered a judicial decision regarding one kind of case involving morality through a ritual at his sanctuary (Num. 5:11–31).

God at the Center of Human Life

Ritual laws regulated activities at the sanctuary, where the Lord's living presence resided. Therefore these laws are closely tied to other kinds of texts about the sanctuary, including instructions and narrative descriptions regarding its infrastructure (Exod. 25–31, 35–40).

The sanctuary was placed at the center of the Israelite camp in the wilderness (Num. 2:17; 3:23, 29, 35, 38). This was a constant reminder that YHWH was central to the worship and lives of his people as their divine Creator, deliverer, ruler, provider, and protector, not only on the Sabbath but also every day. Although the sanctuary is now gone, Christians continue to need God at the center of our lives.

Divine Presence

According to Exod. 25, YHWH articulated the basic purpose of the sanctuary: "that I may dwell in their midst" (v. 8). Despite human fallenness, God has promised to be with those who accept a relationship with him (e.g., Gen. 26:3; 31:3; Exod. 3:12; Judg. 6:16; Isa. 43:2; John 14:16–17; cf. Ps. 23:4). YHWH fulfilled that promise at the sanctuary by residing with a privileged chosen people as close as he could get to them. Their access to him was restricted in order to protect them (Num. 17:12–18:7 [17:27–18:7 MT]), but they could interact with YHWH through rituals that he established. His desire for restoration of intimacy with them, in spite of all their faultiness (e.g., Lev. 16:16b), testified to his incomparable grace.

The presence of God in the Israelite camp dramatically demonstrated the "Immanuel" = "God is with us" (cf. Isa. 7:14)[14] aspect of the divine

14. This Hebrew name is a nominal (verbless) sentence in which the verb "to be" should be supplied: "God *is* with us." It is an assertion of divine presence, not merely a description. The Greek of Matt. 1:23 simply renders the Hebrew word for word as "God with us."

covenant phases, by which the Lord narrows the gap between himself and human beings by dwelling among them.[15] Sacrifices at the sanctuary pointed ahead to the incarnate Immanuel, who would "save his people from their sins" (Matt. 1:20–23). He would provide for us a way of direct access to the throne of God by faith (Heb. 4:14–16; 6:19–20; 10:19–22) and ultimate deliverance to a new creation, in which full access to God will be restored (Rev. 21:3, 22).

Now that Christ has offered up himself as the once-for-all truly atoning sacrifice (Heb. 7:27; 9:26–28; 10:12, 14) and is ministering for us in God's temple in heaven (esp. chaps. 8–9), Christians can make the most of the access that we presently enjoy by often directing our thoughts into the presence of God in heaven through faith as we pray and worship. We can have confidence that because Jesus, our great high priest, has opened a way of access for us, we can "draw near to the throne of grace, that we may receive mercy and find grace to help in time of need" (Heb. 4:16).

The structure of the sanctuary and rituals performed there highlighted the reality of YHWH's resident presence. The sanctuary was configured like a portable palace, with a courtyard, living room, and throne room. The living room (holy place) contained items that could be in the residence of a human king, including a table for bread and drink (Exod. 25:23–30), a lampstand with seven lamps for light (vv. 31–39), and an incense burner/altar (30:1–10).[16] Priests maintained the components in the living room through regular rituals (25:29–30, 37; 27:20–21; 30:7–8; Lev. 24:1–9).

Although the sanctuary was a residence, several aspects of its furnishings and rituals showed that YHWH is suprahuman. He did not sit on a throne in his throne room (holy of holies), but his glorious presence hovered above the ark of the covenant between (and above) the cherubim on it (Exod. 25:22; Num. 7:89; 1 Sam. 4:4; 2 Sam. 6:2). YHWH received food at the outer altar in the courtyard in the form of smoke from burning sacrifices (Num. 28:1–8), and he did not eat the bread on the golden table in his living room but assigned it to his priests while they burned for him the incense that had been placed on top of it (Lev. 24:5–9).[17] Furthermore, his lamps remained lit all through the night "from evening to morning before the LORD" (Exod. 27:21), showing that "he who keeps Israel will neither slumber nor sleep" (Ps. 121:4).

---

15. O. Palmer Robertson, *The Christ of the Covenants* (Phillipsburg, NJ: Presbyterian and Reformed, 1980), 49–52, discussing the biblical theme, "I shall be your God and you shall be my people."

16. On the function of incense in providing a pleasant odor in a dwelling, see Kjeld Nielsen, *Incense in Ancient Israel*, VTSup 38 (Leiden: Brill, 1986), 90.

17. Roy Gane, "'Bread of the Presence' and Creator-in-Residence," *VT* 42 (1992): 194–98.

This is the kind of God we need: one who is with us but greater than we are. This is the kind of divine-human Savior we have: one who as the Word "became flesh and dwelt among us" but who also possesses divine "glory as of the only Son from the Father" (John 1:14).

The sanctuary on earth was patterned after the heavenly sanctuary (Heb. 8:5; cf. Exod. 25:9), which is God's headquarters (e.g., Rev. 4–5), and the two sanctuaries were associated with each other. The smoke from the fire on the altar in the Israelite sanctuary's courtyard (Lev. 6:9, 12–13 [6:2, 5–6 MT]) ascended like incense (*qetoret*, from the root *q-t-r*) when the priests burned (*hiphil* of *q-t-r*, lit., "make smoke") sacrifices as pleasing aromas to YHWH in heaven (e.g., Lev. 1:9, 13, 17), affirming the continual nexus between the two sanctuaries. Thus Solomon prayed that when he and his people would pray (horizontally) toward the temple, their prayers would go (vertically) from there up to God, who would listen in heaven, his dwelling place (1 Kings 8:28–30). But now that Christ is ministering for us in the heavenly temple, we can pray anytime directly up to God, without the help of mediation by ordinary human priests on earth. Christ himself is our nexus, our ladder between heaven and earth (John 1:51; cf. Gen. 28:12–17).

The fire on the altar at the sanctuary was lit by God himself as a revelation of his divine power (Lev. 9:24). God used this fire to consume the sacrifices of the Israelites, which were the center of Israelite worship and represented the coming sacrifice of Christ (e.g., John 1:29; Heb. 10:1, 11–12). So for Christians today, God's gift of the sacrificed Christ is the center of our worship (e.g., 1 Cor. 2:2). Rather than attempting to worship with sparks of our own kindling (Lev. 10:1–2), we need the living Christ and his gift of the divine Holy Spirit (who has been manifested in the form of fire; Acts 2:3–4; cf. Matt. 3:11; Luke 3:16) as the source of transforming power in our worship.

Divine Sovereignty

The tabernacle of the Israelites' king and commander was in the middle of his royal camp (Num. 23:21), just as around 1275 BC the palatial two-room tent of the Egyptian god-king Ramesses II (1279–1213 BC) is portrayed at the center of his rectangular war camp at Qadesh in Syria, in a diagram carved on the stone interior of a temple at Abu Simbel, in southern Egypt.[18] However, whereas the pharaoh was really only human, the monarch of Israel

18. Michael M. Homan, "The Divine Warrior in His Tent: A Military Model for Yahweh's Tabernacle," *BRev* 16 (2000): 22–33, 55; Homan, *To Your Tents, O Israel! The Terminology, Function, Form, and Symbolism of Tents in the Hebrew Bible and the Ancient Near East*, CHANE 12 (Leiden: Brill, 2002), 111–16.

"enthroned on the cherubim" (1 Sam. 4:4; 2 Sam. 6:2) in the holy of holies was the divine YHWH himself.

Several additional factors reinforced the concept of YHWH's sovereignty at his sanctuary. First, the sanctuary functioned as the theocratic administrative headquarters of Israel, from where the Lord gave laws and other communications to Moses for the nation (Exod. 25:22; Lev. 1:1; Num. 7:89), and from where he judged people (Num. 12:4–10; 14:10–12; 16:42–45 [17:7–10 MT]; cf. Lev. 10:2). Thus the words of the prayer that Jesus taught to his disciples—"Your kingdom come, your will be done, on earth as it is in heaven" (Matt. 6:10)—were to be fulfilled in the Israelite community.

Second, the regular rituals performed by the Aaronic priests (Exod. 25:30; 27:20–21; 29:38–42; 30:7–8; etc.) were like the work of a human king's servants for their lord.[19] Everything was to be done just right, according to the directions of their master. YHWH's divine nature and transcendent power made it crucial for them to observe his ritual rules, lest they die (Lev. 8:35; 10:2, 9; 16:2, 13; 22:9).

Third, the high priest was required to give a regular grain offering [*minkhah*] to YHWH, his lord (Lev. 6:19–22 [6:12–15 MT]). The term *minkhah* (cf. grain offerings in Lev. 2) elsewhere refers to a gift or present, including to show respect or homage (e.g., Gen. 43:11, 15, 25–26), or tribute, a required payment acknowledging submission to an overlord (e.g., Judg. 3:15, 17–18; 2 Sam. 8:2, 6). This background suggests that the high priest's required *minkhah* rendered homage or tribute to YHWH. Although the high priest was the highest religious leader in the nation, he was subordinate to the divine sovereign.

Fourth, annual festivals celebrated God's sovereignty over Israel as manifested by his historical deliverance of and provision for his chosen nation. For example, Passover commemorated the transfer of the Israelites from under the control of the pharaoh to the benevolent rule of YHWH, who delivered them (Exod. 12). According to the festival calendar in Lev. 23, on the first day of the seventh month there was to be "a memorial proclaimed with blast [*teru'ah*] of trumpets" (v. 24; cf. Num. 29:1). The text does not specify the function of this trumpet blast, but the Hebrew word is the same as in Num. 23:21: "the shout [*teru'ah*] of a king is among them" in their camp.[20] If this connection is instructive, the trumpets on the first day of the

19. See Menahem Haran, *Temples and Temple-Service in Ancient Israel* (Winona Lake, IN: Eisenbrauns, 1985), 216–19.
20. Both of these verses simply refer to *teru'ah*, without specifying how the sound is produced. Translators have interpreted the word as a "shout" in Num. 23:21 and a "blast of trumpets" (supplying "trumpets," not in the Hebrew) in Lev. 23:24.

seventh month could acclaim and invoke the Lord as the divine monarch and commander of Israel.[21]

Recognition of divine sovereignty is no less vital for Christians, as Jesus indicated in the "Lord's Prayer": "Your kingdom come" (Matt. 6:10). He proclaimed that the "kingdom of heaven" was coming (4:17), taught about this kingdom in parables (e.g., 13:24, 31, 33, 44, 45, 47), and spoke of himself as the divine "King" (25:31–46; cf. 27:11; John 18:37). In the book of Hebrews, Christ serves as a priest after the order of Melchizedek (6:19–7:28), whose name means "king of righteousness" (7:2). Thus Jesus is both king and priest, as Melchizedek was (7:1–2; cf. Gen. 14:18).[22] The book of Revelation prophesies that Christ, the "Word of God" (Rev. 19:13; cf. John 1:14), will return as the conquering "King of kings and Lord of lords" to take over control of planet Earth (Rev. 19:16; cf. Matt. 26:64).[23]

As our world is growing increasingly intense and human values are in conflict, the supreme value that we place in our Lord and his sovereignty will be the anchor point in our lives, including our worship and moral choices. The guidance set by his lordship reaches to everything we do: "Your will be done, on earth as it is in heaven" (Matt. 6:10).

Divine Character and Creatorship

The fact that the Lord wanted to be with his people at his sanctuary indicated his love for them (Exod. 15:13, 17). God's love was especially shown by his provision for sacrifices through which his people could receive ransom for their lives (Lev. 17:11)[24] and forgiveness if they violated his commandments (e.g., Lev. 4:20, 26, 31, 35). Animal sacrifices did cost their offerers something (cf. 2 Sam. 24:24), but they were only tokens by which these individuals accepted divine grace. As Ps. 49:7–9 (49:8–10 MT) recognizes, humans are

21. Gane, *Leviticus, Numbers*, 401–2. After reviewing some options regarding the *teruʿah*, Jacob Milgrom concludes that its purpose on the first day of the seventh month is to arouse YHWH's attention to the need of his people for adequate rain during the upcoming agricultural year. *Leviticus 23–27: A New Translation with Introduction and Commentary*, AB 3B (New York: Doubleday, 2001), 2014–18.

22. God did not permit Israelite kings to function as priests (e.g., 2 Chron. 26:16–21). Rather, he required separation of powers, no doubt to keep kings from being viewed as god-kings like monarchs in some other places in the ANE, such as Egypt. However, the NT views Jesus as legitimately priest + king because he is divine.

23. This is not a pseudotheocratic civil "kingdom" established on earth by humans before Christ's second coming (cf. chap. 8 above).

24. For interpretation of the *piel* of *k-p-r* + preposition *ʿal* + *nefesh* in Lev. 17:11 (cf. Exod. 30:12, 15, 16) as ransom for life, see Jacob Milgrom, *Leviticus 17–22: A New Translation with Introduction and Commentary*, AB 3A (New York: Doubleday, 2000), 1474.

incapable of truly ransoming their lives at any price, so sacrificial expiation was a gift from God.

The ritual laws show the Lord's desire to make it possible for any Israelite to gain the benefit of interacting with him: Options were provided for poor persons to bring inexpensive offerings (Lev. 1:14–17; 5:7–13; 12:8; 14:21–32; cf. 27:8; Deut. 16:17).[25] Most remarkably, a simple offering of grain could serve as a purification offering to expiate for the sin of one who could not even afford two birds (Lev. 5:11–13).[26]

The sanctuary and its services also acknowledged God's love in other ways. The twelve loaves of the "bread of the Presence," one for each tribe and placed every week on the golden table in the holy place (Lev. 24:5–9; cf. Exod. 25:30), served as a token thank offering that acknowledged YHWH's ongoing provision of food. In the wilderness he sent manna, "bread from heaven" (Exod. 16, esp. v. 4; cf. John 6:31–32), of which a sample was kept with the ark of the covenant (Exod. 16:32–34; Heb. 9:4). Firstfruits offerings (Exod. 23:19; 34:26; Lev. 2:14–16; 23:10–14) and the harvest festivals of Weeks/Harvest (later known as Pentecost) and Booths/Ingathering (Exod. 23:16; 34:22; Lev. 23:15–21, 33–36, 39–43) also celebrated and expressed gratitude for blessings of nature by which the Lord supplied the physical needs of his people.

The blessings just mentioned were due to the fact that God is the Creator who continues to sustain his creation (Ps. 145:15–16; Dan. 5:23). Thus the bread of the Presence, acknowledging that YHWH is the Creator-in-Residence, was changed every week on the Sabbath (Lev. 24:8), which serves as a reminder of creation (Exod. 20:11; 31:17).[27] The ritual system also honored the Sabbath with sacrifices in addition to the morning and evening burnt offerings (Num. 28:9–10).[28]

Although many modern Christians are not farmers and we enjoy many advances in technology, we are ultimately just as dependent on God's ongoing creation-maintenance as the ancient Israelites were. Our breath is

25. Thus the ritual system set an example of social justice by including the poor. Cf. J. David Pleins, *The Social Visions of the Hebrew Bible: A Theological Introduction* (Louisville: Westminster John Knox, 2001), 64–65; Richard H. Hiers, *Justice and Compassion in Biblical Law* (New York: Continuum, 2009), 180.

26. Hebrews 9:22 recognizes this case: "Indeed, under the law *almost* everything is purified with blood, and without the shedding of blood there is no forgiveness of sins" (emphasis added).

27. See Gane, "'Bread of the Presence,'" 199–203.

28. The sanctuary was linked to creation and Sabbath by the facts that the sanctuary altar and priesthood were consecrated in seven days (Exod. 29:35–37; Lev. 8:33–35), paralleling the seven days of creation (Gen. 1:3–2:3), and laws regarding the Sabbath are strategically located at the end of the instructions for constructing the sanctuary (Exod. 31:12–17) and at the beginning of the narrative that describes the fulfillment of those instructions (35:2–3).

in his hands (Dan. 5:23), so there is no question that God works for us. Therefore the Sabbath continues to remind us of our dependence on care from our Creator, and we can also give thanks to God whenever we enjoy food and drink that he has provided for us (cf. Matt. 15:36; 26:27; Luke 22:17, 19; etc.).

Now Jesus has given the ultimate demonstration of love through his life, teachings, and death, thereby elevating our understanding of what it means to follow God's law of love. Christ's truly efficacious expiatory sacrifice has gained reconciliation for all members of the human race (2 Cor. 5:18–19), including "the poor in spirit" (Matt. 5:3), so we can directly come to God through prayer to receive his merciful forgiveness (1 John 1:7, 9).

Approaching God in Worship

Protocol

As the divine sovereign of the Israelites, YHWH set the rules for approaching him. The priests were authorized for activities that brought them into the closest proximity to the Deity, including officiation at the outer altar and entering the tabernacle (e.g., Num. 3:38; 18:7).[29] Only the high priest was permitted to approach the glorious presence of the Lord in the holy of holies, and then only once per year on the Day of Atonement and with special procedures (Lev. 16). Nonpriests, both men and women, could enter the courtyard of the sanctuary in order to bring their sacrifices to the priests and to carry out parts of the sacrificial process that did not involve putting anything on the altar (e.g., Lev. 1:4–5a, 6, 9a).[30] However, only the priests were permitted to apply the blood to the altar and place body parts or fat on it to burn (e.g., vv. 5b, 7–8, 9b). Thus ordinary Israelites could interact with God through sacrificial worship only with the assistance of priestly mediation.

A Christian church is not a sanctuary/temple in the sense that the Deity resides there on earth as he dwelled in the Israelite sanctuary. However, Jesus promised that even "where two or three are gathered in my name, there am I among them" (Matt. 18:20). So although our worship need not include the ritual elements performed at the ancient sanctuary, it does involve interaction with the Divine. The Lord is superior to us, so if we want our worship to be

29. In Num. 18:7 "all that concerns the altar and that is within the veil [*paroket*, i.e., inner veil]" appears to be a merism, referring to everything from the altar to the holy of holies, including the holy place (outer sanctum) in between.
30. On women offering sacrifices, see chap. 13 above.

acceptable to him, rather than merely to us,[31] it will be according to his principles. The NT leaves plenty of leeway for various Christian worship styles within different cultural environments, but worship should be God-directed rather than focused on human worshipers (including worship leaders), and it should be sincere and humble rather than a hypocritical show of pride (see, e.g., Matt. 6:1, 5–13; Luke 18:9–14).

At the Israelite sanctuary, any nonpriest who encroached on priestly prerogatives by attempting to do something or go somewhere that was only permitted for a priest was to be immediately put to death by the priestly Levite guards in order to prevent an outbreak of divine wrath on the people (Num. 1:51, 53; 3:10, 32, 38; 18:3–5, 7).[32] At first glance, this makes it sound as though God was mean. But it was crucial that his people understand his nature as the awesomely powerful Creator of the universe, dwelling among them. His strict rules and strong warnings were to protect them by making sure that they stayed within safe boundaries (e.g., Num. 3:38, "guarding the sanctuary itself, to protect the people of Israel"), as modern people must do at a nuclear power plant.[33]

Notice a prominent difference between the two-room tabernacle structure and a Christian church. Because the tabernacle was God's residence on earth, it was necessary to keep people out of it. By contrast, Christians want as many people inside their church as the fire marshal will allow!

It would be well for Christians today to remember with whom we are dealing when we approach God. As his children, we can call him "Abba! Father!" (Rom. 8:15; Gal. 4:6), but he is our Father in heaven, whose name is hallowed, and whose will is done in heaven and similarly should be done on earth (Matt. 6:9–10). We are invited to confidently approach him by faith (Heb. 4:16; 10:19–23), but only through Christ, the "one mediator between God and men" (1 Tim. 2:5), who "always lives to make intercession" for us (Heb. 7:25). No ordinary human should dare to usurp his unique priestly prerogatives by presuming to mediate for others.

Israelite priests or nonpriests who participated in sacrifices or contacted other holy things were required to be in a state of ritual purity (Lev. 7:20–21; 22:1–9). Physical ritual impurities were not to come in contact with the holy sphere of God, the pure, sinless, and immortal Creator and sustainer of life (see chaps. 5, 15 above).

---

31. Cf. the worship of Cain (Gen. 4:3, 5–7) and Jeroboam (1 Kings 12:26–13:5), which YHWH did not accept.

32. Milgrom, *Numbers: The Traditional Hebrew Text with the New JPS Translation*, JPS Torah Commentary (Philadelphia: Jewish Publication Society, 1990), 341–43.

33. Cf. the divinely inflicted death of Uzzah (2 Sam. 6:6–7), whose good intention in grasping the ark to steady it was irrelevant.

Rituals at the sanctuary were like acted-out prayers to accomplish various kinds of transactions with God. But Israelites could also pray toward the sanctuary (1 Kings 8:30; Dan. 6:10 [6:11 MT]) or come to the sanctuary and pray there (1 Sam. 1:10–11). Prayers (often petitions) were like communications of a subject to a ruler.[34] Unlike sacrifices, there was no fixed protocol for prayer,[35] and this form of interaction with the Deity required no human priestly mediation. Now that rituals at an earthly residence of God are no longer possible or necessary for Christians, our physical ritual impurities are irrelevant, and we can accomplish through prayer the transactions that the ancient Israelites carried out through sacrifices. Such transactions can include making a covenant with God (Exod. 24:5–8), paying homage to him as our Lord (Lev. 2; see above regarding the *minkhah*, grain offering), thanking/praising him (7:12–15), or receiving expiation for sin (e.g., 4:1–6:7 [4:1–5:26 MT]).

Praise and Celebration

The sanctuary was not all about atonement for sin. As the place where YHWH dwelled with his people, it was a center of praise and celebration.[36] Even some animal sacrifices were offered for happy motivations, such as to thank and thereby praise the Lord (Lev. 7:12–15), to fulfill a vow (vv. 16–17), or simply as a voluntary expression of loyalty to him (also vv. 16–17). These well-being offerings (so-called peace offerings) did not gain expiation for sins that the offerers had committed, as shown by the fact that the *piel* of k-p-r, "expiate," does not appear in Lev. 3 and 7:11–36 with instructions for well-being offering procedures.

Nevertheless, the statement in Lev. 17:11 that sacrificial blood applied to the altar ransomed the life of the offerer applied to well-being offerings as well as other kinds of sacrifices.[37] This indicates that even praise requires blood ransom, pointing to Christ's sacrifice as the means by which fallen humans can enjoy any access to God. Even our prayers require mediation

---

34. Cf. Moshe Greenberg, *Biblical Prose Prayer*, Taubman Lectures in Jewish Studies: Sixth Series (Berkeley: University of California Press, 1983).

35. The Bible describes individuals praying while kneeling (Dan. 6:10 [6:11 MT]), standing (1 Sam. 1:26), standing with hands spread out toward heaven (1 Kings 8:22–23), or bowed down with face to the ground (2 Chron. 7:3; cf. Num. 16:22, "fell on their faces"). Prayer could be aloud (as in the examples just given) or silent (1 Sam. 1:12–13; Neh. 2:4).

36. Pentateuchal ritual law does not call for music to be performed at the wilderness sanctuary. However, music became a vital part of worship during the reign of David (1 Chron. 16:41–42; 25:6–7; cf. 2 Chron. 7:6). In the book of Revelation, praise for God in the heavenly temple includes singing (Rev. 5:9–10; 14:3).

37. Gane, *Leviticus, Numbers*, 304–5.

in heaven in order to be accepted by God (Rev. 8:3–4). Without Christ's sacrifice, we would be cut off from all communication with God. So as Christians praise God and pray, we can remember that this is not something we do for God to earn his favor. Rather, it is a privilege bought by the blood of Christ.

Annual festivals centered at the sanctuary were occasions for celebrating God's deliverance of Israel from Egypt (Passover and Festival of Unleavened Bread, Exod. 12:1–28, 42–50; 13:3–10), his provision for Israel in the wilderness (Festival of Booths, Lev. 23:42–43), the harvests that he provided in the promised land of Canaan (Festivals of Weeks and Booths, Exod. 23:16; 34:22; Lev. 23:15–21, 33–36, 39–43), and his beneficent sovereignty (Festival of Trumpets and Day of Atonement; Lev. 23:23–32; cf. Lev. 16). All of these festivals required animal sacrifices (Num. 28–29), which are no longer possible without a functioning earthly sanctuary/temple and no longer necessary because the focus of our worship is on the heavenly temple.

However, Jesus has given his followers the Lord's Supper (also known as Communion and Eucharist; Matt. 26:26–29; Mark 14:22–25; 1 Cor. 11:23–26), which is adapted from the Passover service that he and his disciples were observing (see Matt. 26:17–19; Mark 14:12–16) in order to celebrate the greater deliverance that Jesus provides through his new-covenant sacrifice. This Lord's Supper does not require the sacrifice of a lamb (cf. Exod. 12:3–10), because Jesus is the Lamb who has fulfilled the ritual symbol of an animal (1 Cor. 5:7, "For Christ, our Passover lamb, has been sacrificed").

Variety of Sacrifices

The various Israelite sacrifices illustrate different aspects of Christ's sacrifice. By studying these, Christians can better understand and receive the full benefit of what Jesus has done for us.

All flesh of a burnt offering was consumed by the altar fire (Lev. 1:8–9),[38] just as Christ's sacrifice totally consumed his humanity (Heb. 7:27, "he offered up himself"). Sacrificial offerings of grain (Lev. 2), basic food, prefigured Christ's sacrifice of himself as the "bread of life," by which he provides not merely for this present life but also for eternal life (John 6:48–51, 58).[39] The meat of

---

38. The priests received only the hides of the burnt offerings as their "agents' commissions" (Lev. 7:8).

39. A grain offering (*qorban minkhah*, Lev. 2:1, 4) was a sacrifice (*qorban*, cf. 1:2, 14; 4:23) because it was given over to the holy domain of God for his utilization, even though it involved no flesh or blood.

a well-being offering was eaten by the offerer (Lev. 7:15–18),[40] in accordance with the fact that Christ's sacrifice provides life to those who spiritually consume him (John 6:53–57; cf. v. 63).

The blood of the purification offering was uniquely daubed on the horns of the outer altar (Lev. 4:25, 30, 34) or the altar of incense (vv. 7, 18), rather than thrown around on (preposition 'al) the outer altar, as in other sacrifices (1:5, 11; 3:2, 8, 13; 7:2).[41] Thus the purification offering highlighted the role of sacrificial blood in ransoming human life (17:11), foreshadowing the sacrifice of Christ, who ransomed people for God by his blood (Rev. 5:9; cf. Matt. 20:28; Mark 10:45).

An individual who committed sacrilege by inadvertently misappropriating something holy that belonged to YHWH or who deliberately misused God's holy name in an oath to defraud someone was required to pay reparation (restitution + one-fifth penalty) to the wronged party—the Lord or the other person—before the offender's reparation offering was sacrificed (Lev. 5:16; 6:5–7 [5:24–26 MT]; cf. Matt. 5:23–24). Sacrilege carried a price tag that the offender could pay by making monetary/material reparation, but the debt of breaking God's law remained to be remedied by the sacrifice, as Jesus's sacrifice makes it possible for our debts of sin to be forgiven (Matt. 6:12).

The Israelite sacrificial system offered no expiation for defiant sins (Num. 15:30–31).[42] However, Paul affirmed that by Christ "everyone who believes is freed from everything from which you could not be freed by the law of Moses" (Acts 13:39).[43] This explains how even King Manasseh, who committed a plethora of crimes for which there was no expiation through animal

40. Except for portions that belonged to the priests (7:31–36).

41. ESV renders "against the sides of the altar" in 1:5, etc. (cf. NRSV, NJPS, NIV), but NASB's "around on the altar" (cf. NKJV, "all around on the altar") is more correct in light of evidence such as Ezek. 43:18, referring to the outer altar: "to offer burnt offerings on ['al] it and to sprinkle blood on ['al] it" (NASB). Here both the burnt offerings and the blood go 'al the altar. The meaning of 'al with the burnt offerings is clearly "on": they go on the altar. There is no adequate reason to interpret the second 'al in Ezek. 43:18 differently, so the blood also goes "on" (rather than "against the sides of") the altar. For full discussion leading to the conclusion that the blood is to be tossed on the upper surface of the altar, see Naphtali S. Meshel, "The Form and Function of a Biblical Blood Ritual," VT 63 (2013): 1–14. However, the blood of a bird is to be drained out on the qir, "wall/side," of the altar (Lev. 1:15).

42. On defiant sins, see Gane, Cult and Character, 204–13. However, there is evidence that God could forgive such sins without prerequisite expiatory sacrifices of animals if pesha', "rebellious sin" (usually translated "transgression"), in Exod. 34:7 is equivalent to defiant sin. Presumably, divine forgiveness of sins for which there was no ritual remedy (cf. Ps. 51; 2 Chron. 33) would have been based on the coming sacrifice of Christ.

43. However, according to Jesus, blasphemy against the Holy Spirit remains unpardonable (Mark 3:29; Luke 12:10).

sacrifices (2 Chron. 33:1–10), could repent and receive mercy from God (vv. 11–13, 15–16, 18–19).

Removing Sin

The basic purpose of the sanctuary was for the holy YHWH to dwell among his people (Exod. 25:8), but in order for him to do that, it was necessary to remedy their faults. The system of ritual activities that accomplished this served as a dynamic model of God's plan of salvation to restore the divine-human relationship through the sacrifice and mediation of Christ. Christ's one sacrifice is the only basis for salvation (Heb. 10:1–18), but animal sacrifices enabled God's people to witness a limited illustration of the life-and-death consequences of their sins[44] and to experience reconciliation with God by receiving the benefits of Christ's coming sacrifice by faith.

Sin versus Love, and Love = Justice + Mercy

The Israelite system of expiatory sacrifices (burnt, purification, and reparation offerings) illuminated the way in which God deals with acts of sin and the state of sin and mortality resulting from them. Sinful actions violate God's law (1 John 3:4), which is love (Matt. 22:37–40), the only basis on which intelligent beings with free choice can harmoniously coexist in God's universe without destroying each other.[45] The sinner must die (Gen. 2:17; 3:22–24; Rom. 6:23), be permanently eliminated from existence, because sin (= unlove) is destructive. However, the very love of God that condemns sinners also motivates him to save them (e.g., John 3:16).

Saving sinners is problematic because love includes both justice and mercy. To redeem fallen humans in full accordance with love, without which the well-being of the universe would be compromised, God must extend mercy to them with full justice. This is the reason for Christ's sacrifice: to provide the justice for God's merciful forgiveness of sin.

Because Christ is the Creator of the human race (John 1:3–4, 14; Heb. 1:2), he can represent all people, just as an ancestor can represent his descendants (Heb. 7:9–10).[46] Therefore the death of Christ—not simply the first death,

---

44. Sacrificial slaughter was quite humane: The throat of the animal was slit (Milgrom, *Leviticus 1–16*, 154–55) so that it went unconscious from loss of blood. This was a far cry from the agony of Christ's death on the cross (Matt. 27:35–50; etc.).

45. Gane, *Altar Call*, 88.

46. Cf. Isa. 9:6 (9:5 MT), where the messianic child to be born is called "Everlasting Father." At the end of the genealogy in reverse order in Luke 3, Adam is called "the son of God" (v. 38), who created him (Gen. 1–2).

which is like sleep (John 11:11–14), but functioning as the equivalent of the second death, which is eternal (Rev. 20:14–15; 21:8)[47]—could substitute for the death of all humans (2 Cor. 5:14–15).

The Israelite ritual system demonstrated mercy with justice. A person who broke God's law was required to provide an animal that the lawbreaker slaughtered at the sanctuary (Lev. 4:24, 29, 33; etc.), and a priest put the blood and body parts on the altar (vv. 25–26, 30–31, 34–35). The animal served as a substitute/ransom for the life of the sinner (17:11). This was true for sins that were not capital crimes in the sense that the offenders would be executed by the human community. Any sin, even violating a divine command to merely eat a piece of fruit from a certain tree, ultimately results in death (Gen. 2:17; chap. 3; Rom. 6:23) because it constitutes rebellion against God and his way of love.

What Divine Forgiveness Accomplishes

According to Leviticus, when an Israelite commits a sin, "he shall bear [*qal* of *n-s-'*] his iniquity [*'avon*, here referring to culpability]" (5:1). However, if he subsequently "realizes his guilt . . . and confesses the sin he has committed" (v. 5), he shall bring a purification offering, and the priest shall make expiation [*piel* of *k-p-r*] for him (v. 6) so that he can be forgiven ([*niphal* of *s-l-kh*]; cf. vv. 10, 13). Thus expiation by the priest removed the sinner's culpability [*'avon*], which constituted an impediment to the divine-human relationship, prerequisite to forgiveness.

The fact that a purification offering removed the culpability of sin from the offerer is confirmed by the wording of formulas that appear at the ends of prescriptions for this kind of sacrifice: "Thus the priest shall make expiation for him *from* his sin" (Lev. 4:26, my trans., emphasis added; cf. 5:6, 10).[48] Expiation "from his sin" means that the sin is removed from him, as in 1 John 1:9: "If we confess our sins, he is faithful and just to forgive *us* our sins and to cleanse *us* from all unrighteousness" (emphasis added).

---

47. This explains Dan. 9:26, where "an anointed one [*mashiakh*, Messiah; NASB, NKJV] shall be cut off [*niphal* of *k-r-t*]," referring to the terminal divine penalty of being "cut off," by which an offender loses an afterlife (see chap. 5 above). However, Christ came back from the death from which there is otherwise no return because he was righteous, bearing sin on behalf of others (cf. Isa. 53:10–12).

48. The privative preposition *min* in Lev. 4:26 means "from," as correctly represented by NJB ("to free him from his sin") and CEB ("to remove his sin"). Most English versions mistranslate as "for" (NJPS, NRSV, NIV, ESV), "concerning" (NKJV), or "in regard to" (NASB) the sin. For analysis of this important preposition and its implications, see Roy Gane, *Cult and Character*, 106–43; Gane, "Privative Preposition *min* in Purification Offering Pericopes and the Changing Face of 'Dorian Gray,'" *JBL* 127 (2008): 209–22.

Having officiated the purification offering for another person, when the priest ate his portion of the sacrificial meat, he bore [*qal* of *n-s-'*] the culpability ['*avon*] of the offerer as part of the process of making expiation for that person (Lev. 10:17). So the same sacrifice that freed the sinner of culpability that would otherwise lead to punishment transferred the culpability to the priest, who then bore it. Thus the priestly mediators, whose role pointed forward to that of Christ as high priest (Hebrews, esp. chaps. 7–9), participated in the process of removing sin with YHWH, who bears [*qal* of *n-s-'*][49] "iniquity and transgression and sin" when he removes condemnation from sinners (Exod. 34:7).

The Israelite priest did not suffer punishment as a result of bearing the culpability of the sinner whose purification offering he officiated (Lev. 10:17). There were limits to his mediation. Not so with YHWH. When he frees humans from their sins, he bears them to their bitter end on the cross of Christ (e.g., Matt. 27). This is the cost of mercy with justice. Christ died bearing our sins (e.g., Heb. 9:28; 1 Pet. 2:24) in order to free us from condemnation (Rom. 8:1) and give us peace with God (5:1). The fact that Christ bore our sins and died for those sins proves that he died as our substitute.

If we ponder what Christ has done to deliver us from the evil that we have caused and allow this awesome reality to sink into our deepest consciousness, it will remodel our moral landscape. We will cling to our priceless forgiven relationship with him, which has cost his blood, and will not want to throw it away and grieve him by going back to rebellion against him and his loving ways (cf. John 8:11; Heb. 6:4–8; 10:26–31).

When an Israelite priest made expiation for a sinner, the sinner was forgiven, as in Lev. 4:26: "Thus the priest shall make expiation [*piel* of *k-p-r*] for him from his sin, and he will be forgiven [*niphal* of *s-l-kh*]" (my trans.).[50] The priest did not grant the forgiveness. Rather, the passive formulation here ("he will be forgiven"), which does not state the subject, implies that God himself directly granted the forgiveness[51] because it was his law that the sinner had violated. Humans are to forgive one another (Matt. 6:12, 14–15; 18:21–35), but God has never delegated to any ordinary human being, even his authorized Israelite priests, the right to forgive sins as he does. So when Jesus forgave the sins of a paralyzed man, he was either committing blasphemy, as some onlookers alleged, or he was divine, as he claimed to be (Mark 2:5–12).

49. English versions render "forgiving," missing the parallel with the *qal* of *n-s-'* + '*avon* in Lev. 5:1; 10:17.
50. Literally, "and it will be forgiven to him."
51. Explicit references to God forgiving (*qal* of *s-l-kh*) appear in Num. 14:20; 30:5, 8, 12 (30:6, 9, 13 MT).

The Lord knows the heart/mind (e.g., 1 Chron. 28:9; Ps. 139:1–4, 23–24), so even if an expiatory ritual was performed correctly in terms of its physical activities, he could withhold forgiveness if the offerer was hypocritical rather than genuinely repentant (cf. Isa. 1:10–17).[52] The same is true when we pray for forgiveness today. God will surely grant forgiveness and moral cleansing to one who is sincerely repentant (1 John 1:9), but he will not listen to those who cling to sin in their hearts (Ps. 66:18).

We have found that forgiveness following expiatory animal sacrifices freed sinners from divine condemnation. However, this was not the final end of the problem caused by the sin. When the culpability was removed from the sinner, it remained with God (Exod. 34:7; cf. 10:17) because his mercy left a question of justice (see below). Furthermore, divine forgiveness did not necessarily erase natural consequences of the sin. God forgave David so that he did not die for his crimes of taking Bathsheba and then arranging for the death of her husband, but the king suffered serious family tragedies as a result (2 Sam. 11–18).[53] Similarly for Christians now, we can rejoice in freedom from divine condemnation for our moral mistakes, but we may still suffer loss in our human relationships, health, finances, and so forth. Yet these hardships are temporary and are nothing compared to the rich benefits that we will receive in eternity with God.

Holding on to divine forgiveness is our choice. It requires forsaking sin rather than returning to it as a dog returns to its vomit (Prov. 26:11; John 8:11). It also requires passing forgiveness on to others who have wronged us (Matt. 6:12). A person who has been forgiven can lose that forgiveness by refusing to show corresponding mercy (Matt. 18:23–35).

Loyalty, Judgment, and Theodicy

As discussed above, divine forgiveness removed culpability from a sinner, and then YHWH bore it, as represented by the fact that his priests bore it. The Lord's sanctuary also bore effects of sins and serious physical ritual impurities that were expiated by sacrifices there, so that they had to be removed from it on the Day of Atonement (Lev. 16, esp. v. 16). The fact that sins and impurities affected God's holy priests and sanctuary seems to violate a cardinal rule of the Israelite ritual system: holiness and impurity are antithetical and must not be brought in contact with each other (e.g.,

---

52. As Samuel said to King Saul, "To obey is better than sacrifice" (1 Sam. 15:22).
53. Cf. the fact that God's corporate forgiveness of the Israelite nation when they refused to enter Canaan (Num. 14:20) did not keep him from condemning the rebellious adult generation to die in the wilderness (vv. 21–35) and slaying the unfaithful scouts (vv. 36–37).

7:20–21; 15:31). However, only by limited exceptions to this rule could faulty people be freed from these evils.[54]

Correspondingly, God has made himself vulnerable to the effects of human evil by having his most holy Son, Jesus Christ, bear our sins (1 Pet. 2:24; cf. Isa. 53:4–5; 2 Cor. 5:21). If Jesus could expose himself in this way to save us, surely we can become vulnerable in a much more limited sense by reaching out to others in order to carry his teaching to them (cf. Matt. 28:19–20), even to those whom he describes as "the least of these my brothers" (25:40).

At the Israelite sanctuary, defilements resulting from sins and impurities accumulated until the Day of Atonement, when they were removed from the sanctuary, and then the consequences of sins were banished from the Israelite community (Lev. 16, esp. vv. 16, 21). The sanctuary was the place of God's administration, so defilements there stood for problems that temporarily affected his reputation.

The problems involving sins stemmed from two factors. First, God bore judicial responsibility for extending mercy to guilty sinners.[55] It is true that expiation was granted through sacrifice, which provided justice, but would the persons who had been forgiven continue to be loyal to him?

Second, some egregious sins, presumably regarded as defiant, automatically polluted the Lord's sanctuary because they were committed by his covenant people or in his land, thereby sullying his reputation in the world. Those who committed such sins were condemned to the divine penalty of being "cut off" (k-r-t) and were not eligible for sacrificial expiation (Lev. 20:3; Num. 19:13, 20).[56]

Therefore we see that God's sanctuary/reputation was affected both by his forgiveness and his condemnation. Was he saving those who were truly loyal and rejecting those who were disloyal among his nominal people? In other words, was his judgment just? This is a question of theodicy.

The rituals of the Day of Atonement, by which the sanctuary was symbolically purged of defilements, acted out answers to questions of God's justice, thereby vindicating his reputation.[57] The high priest performed two unique purification offerings, one on behalf of himself and his priestly family, and the other on behalf of all other Israelites, in which he applied blood to the sanctuary, beginning in the holy of holies, then moving outward to the holy

54. Cf. Gane, *Cult and Character*, esp. 163–81, 267–84.

55. Cf. 2 Sam. 14:9, where the woman of Tekoa offers to bear David's judicial responsibility if he will grant amnesty to her (fictitious) son, who is guilty of murder (in her juridical parable): "Let the king and his throne be guiltless [lit., "clean"]." Notice the reference to the king's throne, which represents his authority and reputation for administration of justice.

56. This could explain why "rebellious sins" (plural of *pesha‘*) had to be purged from the sanctuary on the Day of Atonement (Lev. 16:16 CEB; ESV, "transgressions"), even though no sacrifice offered expiation leading to forgiveness for this category of sin.

57. Gane, *Cult and Character*, 305–33; Gane, *Leviticus, Numbers*, 284–88.

place, and finally reaching the altar in the courtyard (Lev. 16:14–19). After purging the sanctuary of the physical ritual impurities and sins that had accumulated there, the high priest confessed the sins of Israel with both of his hands on the live goat "for Azazel" (so-called scapegoat, vv. 8, 10), thereby transferring the sins to the goat, which was expelled from the community into the wilderness, thereby disposing of the sins that it carried (vv. 20–22).[58]

The Day of Atonement was Israel's judgment day, when YHWH separated the loyal from the disloyal among his nominal people. To show their ongoing loyalty, Israelites were to humble themselves before God by practicing self-denial and abstaining from work on the Day of Atonement (Lev. 16:29, 31; 23:26–32). Leviticus 16:30 states the motivation: "For on this day shall atonement be made [piel of k-p-r] for you to cleanse you. You shall be clean before the LORD from all your sins." So those who were loyal received personal moral cleansing through the cleansing of the sanctuary by the high priest. This moral cleansing was a second stage of expiation (piel of k-p-r), following the expiation prerequisite to forgiveness that the Israelites had already received earlier in the year (4:20, 26, 31, 35; etc.).

Why was a second stage necessary? Didn't the earlier stage free them from their sins? Yes, but when God's judicial responsibility for having forgiven them was vindicated on the Day of Atonement, the forgiveness that he had already given them was reaffirmed. However, those who (1) had sinned defiantly (Num. 15:30–31), (2) had willfully neglected to offer expiatory sacrifices in order to receive forgiveness for their nondefiant sins, or (3) failed to practice self-denial and keep Sabbath on the Day of Atonement (Lev. 23:29–30, "shall be cut off" and destroyed) did not receive the benefit of the sanctuary being purged on the Day of Atonement, and they were rejected by God.

Divine judgment is not only for the ancient Israelites. Paul said that God "has fixed a day on which he will judge the world in righteousness" by Christ (Acts 17:31; cf. Rom. 2:16). The Lord's people are within the scope of his judgment (Heb. 10:30; cf. 2 Cor. 5:10), which was future from the perspective of the book of Hebrews (cf. Heb. 10:27) and occurs in eschatological time according to the book of Revelation (14:6–7; cf. Dan. 7:9–10).

No doubt the judgment addresses the continuing question of theodicy: Is God saving the right people? As in OT times, the question is not "Who has sinned?" The answer to this is already clear: "All have sinned" (Rom. 3:23). The question is "Who have been forgiven and remain truly loyal to God,

---

58. This goat, which was not slaughtered or offered to God, did not represent Christ (Gane, *Leviticus, Numbers*, 288–91). Hebrews 13:11–12 draws an analogy between carcasses of slain purification offerings that were "burned outside the camp" (cf. Lev. 4:11–12, 21; 16:27) and Jesus as suffering "outside the gate," but Hebrews does not refer to Azazel's goat here.

continuing to receive the gift of grace through living faith in Jesus Christ and his sacrifice (cf. Eph. 2:8; Col. 1:21–23), as demonstrated by the fact that their faith is "working through love" (Gal. 5:6)?

Works provide no merit for salvation, but they show that God's gift is being received by faith. Faith and works are inseparable. Therefore the divine judgment assesses faith on the basis of resulting works (Eccl. 12:14; Rom. 2:13–16; 2 Cor. 5:10). This makes sense because only God can read thoughts of faith, but the judgment is to demonstrate his justice to his created beings (e.g., "myriads" of his attendants in Dan. 7:10 NASB), who cannot read thoughts but can witness works (recorded in books; e.g., v. 10; Mal. 3:16) in order to be assured that God is just in saving the right people.

Assurance of Reconciliation with God

The sanctuary in the community of Israel, with the divine glory cloud hovering above it (Exod. 40:34–38; Num. 9:15–22) and the fire that was lit by YHWH (Lev. 9:24) always burning on the altar (6:12–13 [6:5–6 MT]), assured God's people that he was with them. So long as they were faithful to their covenant relationship with him, they were safe (e.g., 26:3–13), just as Christians enjoy the conditional assurance: "Whoever has the Son has life" (1 John 5:12).

Public sacrifices assured Israelites that expiation was provided for them as a group. Corporate burnt offerings made expiation (cf. Lev. 1:4) for the faults and faultiness of the entire covenant community on every day of the year (including the Day of Atonement), with additional burnt offerings on Sabbaths, new moons, and annual festivals (Num. 28–29). Corporate purification offerings were also performed on certain festival days (including the Day of Atonement) to make expiation for the people (28:15, 22; 29:5, 11, 16; etc.). An individual who sinned was still required to offer an individual expiatory sacrifice, but the person was assured of not being cut off from divine grace before being able to bring the offering to the sanctuary.

Christians have similar assurance: in Christ, God has already reconciled the whole world to himself (2 Cor. 5:19). So the benefits of Jesus's sacrifice are constantly available to anyone who heeds the appeal to accept them (v. 20, "Be reconciled to God"), and they cover us even before we have the opportunity to confess our sins.

The red cow ritual was a unique corporate purification offering for physical ritual impurity that was performed outside the Israelite camp (Num. 19:1–8).[59]

---

59. Labeled as a *khatta't*, "purification offering" (NRSV, CEB), in v. 9. Some English versions mistranslate this as "purification from sin" (NIV, NASB), "for purifying from sin" (NKJV), or "a sacrifice for sin" (NJB).

It produced a supply of ashes (v. 9–10) to be mixed with water in order to purify those who would incur corpse impurity in the *future* (vv. 11–20). Thus Israelites who buried their dead could be assured that provision for cleansing was already stored up for them. Although the red cow ritual was to remedy physical ritual impurity rather than sinful action, it illustrated an aspect of Christ's sacrifice that brings assurance to us: That once-for-all sacrifice made all the provision that was necessary for *future* expiation, including for all of us who live long after the cross event.

Personal interactions of Israelites with the Lord through rituals would enhance their assurance. When a person leaned one hand on the head of a burnt offering victim to signify that he was the offerer—the owner of the animal who was transferring it to YHWH and would receive the benefit of offering this kind of sacrifice (in this case including release from sin)—the individual was assured that "it shall be accepted for *him* to make atonement for *him*" (Lev. 1:4, emphasis added). When someone brought a purification offering and the priest applied its blood and fat to the altar, the sinner could be assured that if he were truly repentant, he would receive fulfillment of the divine promise: "He shall be forgiven" (Lev. 4:26, 31, 35; 5:10, 13). Likewise, when repentant Christians confess the wrongs that we have committed, the Lord "is faithful and just to forgive us our sins" (1 John 1:9).

Leviticus addresses a major human insecurity: How can we receive forgiveness if we sin but do not know what we did wrong? In Lev. 4 sinners are required to bring purification offerings only when they become aware of their commandment violations (vv. 14, 22–23, 27–28). God does not hold people accountable for what they don't know (cf. James 4:17).

Leviticus 5 provides additional assurance:

> If, when a person sins by doing any of the commands of the LORD concerning things that should not be done, without knowing it, he experiences guilt and is punishable, he will bring a flawless ram from the flock at a valuation as a reparation offering to the priest. The priest will purge on his behalf for his inadvertent fault that he has committed, even though he did not know it, so that he may be forgiven. (5:17–18)[60]

Here a person experiences guilt, likely by suffering one or more negative circumstances indicating that God is no longer blessing, and realizes that he must have done something wrong,[61] which could be sacrilege. However, he

60. Trans. Roy E. Gane and William K. Gilders, prepublication draft translation of Leviticus for the CEB.

61. See Bruce Wells, *The Law of Testimony in the Pentateuchal Codes*, BZABR 4 (Wiesbaden: Harrassowitz, 2004), 67–69.

cannot identify the sin, as indicated by the repeated notice that he does not know it, and also by the fact that no reparation is required as it would be if the amount of one or more misused holy things were confirmed (cf. Lev. 5:16).[62]

Rather than worrying, the Israelite can just bring a sacrifice and receive forgiveness. Knowing exactly what one has done is not crucial; what matters is turning the problem over to God. This is also true for Christians, who have assurance that Christ has already died for our sins and we are saved by grace through faith, not through knowledge of our sins.

Becoming Holy

According to OT law, God is (inherently) holy (Lev. 11:44–45; 19:2; 20:26; 21:8), and humans, objects, and places designated by him can have holiness derived from him (e.g., Exod. 26:33–34; 28:4; 30:25–30).[63]

Degrees of Holiness

The Pentateuch defines degrees of derived holiness in proportion to proximity to YHWH. Thus parts of the tabernacle included the holy of holies, the "Most Holy [Place]," the inner sanctum where the Lord's Presence was manifested; and the "Holy Place," the outer sanctum (Exod. 26:33). Outside was the courtyard (27:9–19), which contained the sacred altar of burnt offering and basin (40:29–30, 33).[64] While the Israelites were in the wilderness, the sanctuary was located in their camp, which was treated as holy to a lesser degree (Num. 5:1–4; cf. Deut. 23:9–14).[65]

As people and things got closer to the divine Presence in the sanctuary, several factors correlated with the degrees of holiness just described. First, the value of furniture increased, with gold used for the ark, table, lampstand, and incense altar inside the tabernacle (Exod. 25; 30:1–5) and bronze for the altar and basin outside in the courtyard (27:1–8; 30:18). Second, access of laypersons, priests, and the high priest was in proportion to their degrees of consecration (see above under "Protocol"). Third, in accordance with the high priest's superior access, his garments were more elaborate than those of the ordinary priests (Exod. 28).

---

62. Milgrom, *Leviticus 1–16*, 334–35.
63. Cf. the onetime consecration service prescribed in Exod. 29:1–37 and fulfilled in the narrative description of Lev. 8.
64. However, the courtyard was not consecrated with anointing oil (Lev. 8).
65. Cf. John H. Walton, "Equilibrium and the Sacred Compass: The Structure of Leviticus," *BBR* 11 (2001): 293–304.

There were also degrees of holiness in lifestyle. All Israelites were to be a kingdom of priests and a holy nation (Exod. 19:5–6), and they were to emulate YHWH's holy character (Lev. 11:44–45; 19:2; 20:26). However, consecrated priests were subject to holier standards of living than others in that they were forbidden to incur corpse impurity except to bury close relatives (Lev. 21:1–4), and the high priest was not permitted to contract such impurity at all (v. 11). They were also restricted with regard to the kinds of women whom they could marry (vv. 7, 13–14).

New Testament Christianity recognizes no degrees of cultic holiness now that the sanctuary/temple is gone. In this sense we have no holy places, objects, or people on earth because Christ, our holy high priest, is in God's holy temple in heaven. We dedicate our churches to a special function because there we corporately meet with Christ in a spiritual sense (cf. Matt. 18:20),[66] but the glorious divine Presence does not reside there as in the ancient sanctuary. However, we are to grow in holiness in the sense that our moral character of love increases (1 Thess. 3:12–13), and therefore we make progress in emulating divine love (cf. 1 John 4:8, 16). This is the process of sanctification, which begins at conversion (1 Cor. 6:11, "You were sanctified," i.e., consecrated to the holy God) and continues as long as we live.

Progressive moral wisdom is an important part of the sanctification process: By studying and living the Sacred Scriptures, which are able to make us "wise for salvation through faith in Christ Jesus" (2 Tim. 3:15), we can become "complete, equipped for every good work" (v. 17). But the power for growth in holy, loving living comes from the Holy Spirit, who pours love into our hearts (Rom. 5:5).

Separation from Impurity

Purification offerings contributed to removal of severe physical ritual impurities, which reflected the birth-to-death cycle of mortality that results from sin (Rom. 6:23; see chaps. 5, 15 above).[67] By expiating both for sins and for impurities, which represented physical weakness, purification offerings provided two key benefits from YHWH, "who forgives all your iniquity, who heals all your diseases" (Ps. 103:3).

---

66. The immediate context of this verse is a judicial proceeding within the church (cf. vv. 15–19).

67. Purification of mild one-day impurities required only such remedies as ablutions and waiting until evening (e.g., Lev. 15:5–8), but more serious impurities that lasted a week or more usually also called for purification offerings, often paired with supplementary burnt offerings (e.g., vv. 15, 30).

As was true of other OT sacrifices, purification offerings to remedy physical ritual impurities prefigured Christ's sacrifice. Christ died on the cross to free us not only from our acts of sin but also from our sinful state of mortality (1 Cor. 15:51–54), "that whoever believes in him should not perish but have eternal life" (John 3:16). Our appreciation for the magnitude of what Christ accomplished through his sacrifice expands when we view it not only in terms of legal justification but also from the perspective of healing in light of the purification offerings.

Holiness and impurity were incompatible in ancient Israel. Physical ritual impurities, which were associated with mortality, were not to contact and thereby defile holy things that were linked to YHWH, the pure, holy, immortal Creator and sustainer of all life (e.g., Lev. 7:20–21; 15:31). Another kind of impurity—moral impurity from the serious moral offenses of sexual immorality, idolatry, and murder, for which there were no ritual remedies—was not to defile the Holy Land lest the Israelites ultimately would be exiled from it (Lev. 18, 20; Num. 35:31–34; cf. Lev. 26:30–39).

New Testament Christians do not need to worry about physical ritual impurities, because we have no cultic holy places. We are all physically ritually impure, and it doesn't matter. Some Christians have picked on women, restricting them from church places or functions during their monthly periods or after childbirth, in accordance with the rules of Lev. 12 and the second part of chapter 15 (vv. 19–30) that barred impure women from contact with the sacred. But such restrictions overlook the fact that according to the NT (esp. Hebrews and Revelation), our worship is now focused on the heavenly holy temple.

The invalidity of literally applying the purity rules is shown by what happens if we were to consistently carry that approach to its logical conclusion rather than picking and choosing to discriminate against women. Ancient Israelite men as well as women could become impure from genital flows, as indicated by the entire first part of Lev. 15 (vv. 1–18; cf. Deut. 23:10–11). Moreover, anyone who so much as came under the same roof where a corpse was located became impure (Num. 19:14) and had to be purified with some ashes of the red cow mixed with water (vv. 17–20). If we apply this to Christians, anyone who has attended a funeral but has not been sprinkled with the water containing ashes of the red cow, which has not been available for a couple of millennia, is impure. If ritually impure Christians were to stay away from church, hardly anybody could be permitted to attend!

However, moral purity remains relevant for Christians. Jesus said, "Blessed are the pure in heart, for they shall see God" (Matt. 5:8). Paul exhorted Christians:

But sexual immorality and all impurity or covetousness must not even be named among you, as is proper among saints. Let there be no filthiness nor foolish talk nor crude joking, which are out of place, but instead let there be thanksgiving. For you may be sure of this, that everyone who is sexually immoral or impure, or who is covetous (that is, an idolater), has no inheritance in the kingdom of Christ and God. (Eph. 5:3–5)

Just as physical ritual impurity was necessary to approach YHWH at the OT sanctuary, it is the morally "pure in heart" who will see God face-to-face in the new-creation era. Just as moral purity was vital for Israelites to remain in the land that the Lord had promised to them, so such purity is a condition for inheriting the ultimate promised land, "the kingdom of Christ and God" (Eph. 5:5).

Ministers for God

Functions of the Aaronic priests included worship leadership through performance and officiation of rituals that typified Christ's future mediation (see above), blessing the people (Num. 6:22–27), guarding the sanctuary (3:10, 38; 18:7), administering cultic instructions (e.g., Lev. 13), and teaching God's laws (10:10–11). This priesthood authorized by YHWH was restricted to Aaron and his male descendants. The priests were ordained for life through a ritual service of consecration that included sprinkling them with anointing oil and offering animal sacrifices (Lev. 8).

At one point in the service, Moses took some of the blood of the ram of ordination "and put it on the lobe of Aaron's right ear and on the thumb of his right hand and on the big toe of his right foot" (v. 23). Then he did the same to Aaron's sons (v. 24). It appears that application of blood to these extremities of a priest signified life-and-death accountability to hearing/obeying the Lord, doing his will, and going where he commanded.

The NT recognizes no elite human priests on earth in the Christian religion because Christ's superior Melchizedek priesthood in heaven has superseded the hereditary Aaronic priesthood (Heb. 7). The earthly cult that was "a shadow of the things to come" is gone because the "substance" that "belongs to Christ" (Col. 2:17) has arrived. Therefore, there is no valid earthly cultic service for human priests to perform.

All true new-covenant Christians are ministers in the sense that we constitute "a royal priesthood" (1 Pet. 2:9), just as YHWH gave the conditional promise that if the Israelites were faithful to him and kept his covenant, they would be to him "a kingdom of priests" (Exod. 19:6). It is true that Christian communities and initiatives need designated leaders in various capacities, including worship leaders and teachers, according to their spiritual gifts. It is also true that in the NT church, delegation of responsibilities to individuals who were authorized, in harmony with the Holy Spirit, to carry out certain tasks on behalf of the community of believers could be signified by members of the group praying and laying their hands on them as a symbolic gesture (Acts 6:3, 5–6; 13:2–3). However, this commissioning was nothing close to lifelong ordination of priests, who were thereby elevated in religious status above other members of the community.

Nevertheless, some aspects of the Israelite priesthood can inform our understanding of the Christian priesthood of all believers. First, sacrifices were necessary to authorize and consecrate them. Similarly, it is the sacrifice of Christ that authorizes and consecrates all Christians for our ministry and mission to the world (cf. 2 Cor. 5:14–21).

Second, just as priests were to give wholly devoted service to the Lord, so are Christians (e.g., Rom. 12:11).

Third, although members of the Christian priesthood of believers do not carry out ritual mediation as the Aaronic priests did, we can mediate for others by interceding for them in prayer (e.g., Acts 12:5; James 5:14–16).

Fourth, just as priests were to lead exemplary lives of holiness (see above), so should Christians. We do not represent God to our people to the extent that the Aaronic priests did by typifying Christ in a symbolic system, but we represent the holy, loving character of God to all people of the world (cf. Matt. 5:16; John 17:20–23).

Fifth, as priests were to instruct the Israelites concerning divine laws, Christians are to teach people to observe all that Christ has commanded us (Matt. 28:20).

Conclusion

The Value of Obedience to God

Freedom through Christ as Obedience to God's Law of Love

Modern people tend to view obedience to someone else or to a law, even God's law, as a burden. It is much easier to relate to the concept of freedom, as in Jesus's statement "So if the Son sets you free, you will be free indeed" (John 8:36). But in context, this true freedom from Jesus is liberation from being a "slave to sin" as one who practices sin (v. 34), which "is lawlessness" (1 John 3:4). Lawlessness is breaking God's law, for which one needs his forgiveness (Rom. 4:7–8; Heb. 10:17–18). Therefore the freedom that Christ offers is obedience to God's law. Jesus's freedom and obedience are one!

Rather than being "slaves of sin," converted Christians become "obedient from the heart" as "slaves of righteousness" (Rom. 6:17–18). They have chosen a new master, but this master is God through Christ, whose "yoke is easy" and whose "burden is light" because he is "gentle and lowly in heart," providing "rest for your souls" (Matt. 11:29–30). God's "commandments are not burdensome" to those who have been "born of God," because their faith has gained victory over the sinful world (1 John 5:3–4).

In Jesus's remarkable discourse on the night that he was betrayed, he profoundly illuminated the obedience that he expects of his followers: "If you love me, you will keep my commandments. . . . Whoever has my commandments and keeps them, he it is who loves me. And he who loves me will be loved by my Father, and I will love him and manifest myself to him" (John 14:15, 21). It is love for Christ that motivates true obedience to Christ's commandments, which are to love others (13:34; 15:12, 17; cf. Matt. 22:37–40). Both the environment and the content of commandment keeping is love, which is in harmony with God because his character is love: "God is love, and whoever abides in love abides in God, and God abides in him" (1 John 4:16, cf. v. 8).

Jesus further unpacks the dynamics of obedience: "As the Father has loved me, so have I loved you. Abide in my love. If you keep my commandments, you will abide in my love, just as I have kept my Father's commandments and abide in his love. These things I have spoken to you, that my joy may be in you, and that your joy may be full" (John 15:9–11). Jesus is to his disciples what his Father is to him. By instructing his followers to keep his commandments, he is only asking them to emulate what he has done by obeying his Father. He is their example (cf. 1 Pet. 2:21–22). The purpose of obeying Christ is relational: to abide in his love, which he has already demonstrated for his disciples (cf. John 13:1), just as the Father has loved him. So obedience is acceptance of a loving relationship, and the result is joy.

Jesus continues: "This is my commandment, that you love one another as I have loved you. Greater love has no one than this, that someone lay down his life for his friends" (John 15:12–13). Jesus's commandment is to pass on the love that he received from his Father (cf. v. 9) and gave to his disciples, who in this way emulate him. He defines such love: "as I have loved you" (cf. 13:34). This is the highest and purest kind of love. It is epitomized by prioritizing the lives of friends over one's own life, as Jesus is about to demonstrate through his self-sacrifice.

Jesus counters the idea that obedience to him downgrades his followers: "You are my friends if you do what I command you. No longer do I call you servants, for the servant does not know what his master is doing; but I have called you friends, for all that I have heard from my Father I have made known to you" (15:14–15). "Slaves of righteousness" (Rom. 6:18) who obey Christ enjoy an intimate relationship with him as his friends. Compare Daniel, a "man greatly loved" by God (Dan. 10:11), whose faithfulness in obeying divine law to maintain a holy lifestyle (1:8–16) was rewarded by "understanding in all visions and dreams" (v. 17; chaps. 2, 4–5) and special revelations from God that were made known to him (chaps. 7–12).

Jesus's teaching concerning obedience provides a foundation for addressing five common misconceptions, which the following sections of this conclusion will address:

1. Christians who are saved "by grace, . . . through faith, . . . [and] not a result of works" (Eph. 2:8–9) do not need to keep God's law.
2. Obedience to God's law is too difficult.
3. Christ's commandment to love one another supersedes OT law, except perhaps for the Ten Commandments.

4. Genuine obedience is unthinking.

5. Concern for obedience to God's law is legalism.

Need to Keep God's Law

Misconception 1: *Christians who are saved "by grace, . . . through faith, . . . [and] not a result of works" (Eph. 2:8–9) do not need to keep God's law.* Divine grace through faith, not works, is how we are saved *from* slavery to sin, which is lawlessness, meaning disobedience to God's law of love (cf. above and vv. 1–5). Verse 10 tells what we are saved *to*: "For we are his workmanship, created in Christ Jesus for good works, which God prepared beforehand, that we should walk in them." Obedience is not the cause of salvation from sin but the inevitable result. We are released from the law in the sense that we are freed from its condemnation for breaking it (Col. 2:14, "the record of debt that stood against us"), not so that we are free to disobey its enduring principles (Rom. 6:15), but so that having been forgiven (Col. 2:13), "we serve in the new way of the Spirit" (Rom. 7:6; cf. v. 5; 8:1–4).[1] Jesus's entire life, death, and resurrection proclaim the meaning of his name: "for he will save his people *from* their sins" (Matt. 1:21, emphasis added), not *in* their sins.

Good works of a converted Christian are not in opposition to faith; rather, the works result from faith. Belief and obedience work together, as shown by the functional parallelism in John 3:36: "Whoever *believes* in the Son has eternal life; whoever does not *obey* the Son shall not see life, but the wrath of God remains on him" (emphasis added). The gospel is to be believed (Mark 1:15; Acts 15:7; Rom. 1:16) and also obeyed (Rom. 10:16; 2 Thess. 1:8; 1 Pet. 4:17).

No amount of law-keeping can remedy past failure (Gal. 3:10–12); only Christ's sacrifice, received by faith, can do that (vv. 5–9, 13–14). But persons who refuse or neglect to keep Jesus's commandments show that they do not love him (cf. John 14:15, 21), abide in his love (15:10), or have true, living faith (James 2:26). So such an individual does not accept the free gift of saving grace through faith in Christ that results in eternal life (cf. John 3:16, 36) and is left with the alternative: "The wages of sin is death" (Rom. 6:23; cf. vv. 21–22).[2]

---

1. Removal of our condemnation (cf. Rom. 8:1) does not wipe out divine law any more than a police officer or judge tearing up a traffic ticket would annul the law that was violated. God's law expresses love (Matt. 22:36–40) that is eternal and can never pass away (1 Cor. 13:8). Regarding the ongoing relevance of OT law for Christians and compatibility between the law and grace, see Daniel I. Block's three-part series, "Preaching Old Testament Law to New Testament Christians," in *Ministry: International Journal for Pastors* 78, no. 5 (May 2006): 5–11; no. 7 (July 2006): 12–16; no. 9 (September 2006): 15–18.

2. On the reason for such death, see chap. 16 above.

Like Moses, Jesus sets before us the free choice between "life and good, death and evil" (Deut. 30:15). The Scriptures, including OT law, explicate the options so that the choice can be intelligent: "to make you wise for salvation through faith in Christ Jesus" (2 Tim. 3:15). This "wisdom preserves the life of him who has it" (Eccl. 7:12).

Profoundly affecting our view of salvation and law is the fact that there is both continuity and discontinuity between the OT and the NT. Throughout the Bible, the divine covenants function as phases of cumulative development in God's overall covenant plan. At strategic points in biblical history, God's covenant initiatives have provided fresh waves of grace and divine self-revelation, with timely emphases to advance his purposes in the world, culminating in the new covenant (Luke 22:20; 1 Cor. 11:25; 2 Cor. 3:6, prophesied in Jer. 31:31–34).[3]

The difference between the OT covenant phases and the "new covenant" is not the difference between salvation through law in the former and grace in the latter. Ever since the fall, the only way to salvation has been by grace through faith (Eph. 2:8) in the "seed"/posterity of Eve (Gen. 3:15), understood to mean Jesus Christ (Gal. 3:16).[4] The new covenant builds on and completes the earlier covenant phases, but it does not supersede them in terms of introducing a different way of salvation.[5]

Possibility of Obedience to God's Law

Misconception 2: *Obedience to God's law is too difficult.* Without divine assistance, the most challenging of all commandments is the one that Jesus reiterated: to love one another as he has loved his followers (see above). In

3. O. Palmer Robertson, *The Christ of the Covenants* (Phillipsburg, NJ: Presbyterian and Reformed, 1980); cf. John H. Walton, *Covenant: God's Purpose, God's Plan* (Grand Rapids: Zondervan, 1994).

4. On the significance of Gen. 3:15, see, e.g., Afolarin Ojewole, "The Seed in Genesis 3:15: An Exegetical and Intertextual Study" (PhD diss., Andrews University, 2002).

5. Cf. Skip MacCarty, *In Granite or Ingrained? What the Old and New Covenants Reveal about the Gospel, the Law, and the Sabbath* (Berrien Springs, MI: Andrews University Press, 2007). The "old covenant" in Jer. 31:31–34 was not a divine provision for salvation based on human works. At Sinai, as elsewhere, God offered a relationship based on grace, as shown by the fact that he had already delivered the Israelites (Exod. 19:4; 20:2). The "[old] covenant" was "my covenant that they broke, though I was their husband, declares the LORD" (Jer. 31:32). God wanted to replace this relationship, which was faulty because his people were unfaithful, with the "new covenant," really the "renewed covenant" (cf. Fredrick Holmgren, *The Old Testament and the Significance of Jesus: Embracing Change—Maintaining Christian Identity* [Grand Rapids: Eerdmans, 1999], 73–81, 86–95). The "new covenant" was to restore the kind of internalized heart relationship that YHWH had offered at Sinai, but on a stronger basis of forgiveness (Jer. 31:34b).

fact, it is impossible for us to keep this law by our own strength of will. But the Lord does not require Christians to keep his commandments on their own. "His commandments are not burdensome" for those who have been "born of God" so that they "overcome the world" by faith in him (1 John 5:3–4). The key is the miracle of new birth through the transforming Holy Spirit (John 3:3–8; Titus 3:4–7), who pours love into the heart (Rom. 5:5) as a free gift of grace received through faith in Jesus Christ. This love brings the Christian into harmony with God's character and law of love. To receive God's gift is to accept, cooperate with, and live out the moral transformation that he offers by the strength that he makes available.

In other words, it is for those who "turn to the LORD" their God with all their heart and with all their soul (Deut. 30:10) that obedience to God's commandments is possible, as Moses affirmed:

> For this commandment that I command you today is not too hard for you, neither is it far off. It is not in heaven, that you should say, "Who will ascend to heaven for us and bring it to us, that we may hear it and do it?" Neither is it beyond the sea, that you should say, "Who will go over the sea for us and bring it to us, that we may hear it and do it?" But the word is very near you. It is in your mouth and in your heart, so that you can do it. (Deut. 30:11–14)

According to the NT, the Lord is able to keep his people from "stumbling" (Jude 24) into disobedience and does not allow them to be tempted (to disobedience) beyond their ability, "but with the temptation he will also provide the way of escape, that you may be able to endure it" (1 Cor. 10:13). Thus God enables the obedience that he requires. Without this divine intervention, obedience is impossible.

The fact that obedience is possible does not mean that a true believer instantaneously attains it. Obedience is a learning and growing process, and God's grace is available when we falter (1 John 1:9; 2:1–2). In fact, we are constantly dependent on a fresh supply of divine grace through the saving blood of Christ every day of our lives, no matter how obedient and sanctified we become through the power of the Holy Spirit, because our faulty nature will continue until we receive glorious, sinless, immortal, new bodies (1 Cor. 15:51–54). Even then, when we will no longer be sinners, there will be no end to our moral growth because it is growth in love, and love is as limitless as the infinite heart of God. The closer we come to God in character, both in the present flawed life and the next perfect life, the more we will see how much room for further growth in love invites us to even greater joy. Harmony with God's love is a journey with him rather than a destination.

Love in Relation to Old Testament Law

Misconception 3: *Christ's commandment to love one another supersedes OT law, except perhaps for the Ten Commandments.* When Jesus said, "A new commandment I give to you, that you love one another" (John 13:34; cf. 15:12, 17), he was not giving a commandment that was new in the absolute sense. Rather, he was renewing it as a sign of discipleship (cf. 13:35) and clarifying its definition by adding, "Just as I have loved you, you also are to love one another" (v. 34). Jesus knew that he was reiterating the OT law, "You shall love your neighbor as yourself" (Lev. 19:18), which he had singled out as the second-greatest commandment of OT law after the command in Deut. 6:5 to love God (Matt. 22:35–40; cf. Mark 12:28–31; Luke 10:25–28).

Paul pointed out that the OT law to love your neighbor as yourself summarizes the Ten Commandments concerning responsibilities to other humans and fulfills God's ongoing law (Rom. 13:8–10; cf. Gal. 5:14). So Jesus's command to love one another embraces rather than replaces the OT laws that unpack this overarching principle. Jesus was summarizing, but a summary refers to, rather than supersedes, what it summarizes.

In fact, a summary is defined by what it summarizes. When Jesus commanded "love," he was referring to God's kind of love, which includes both justice and mercy (e.g., Exod. 34:6–7), as it is defined by the whole Bible, including OT law (Matt. 22:37–40). "God is love" (1 John 4:8, 16), so he defines love by all that he does, including things that we don't comprehend. God's love is a huge concept because he is huge.

It is hazardous for Christians to latch on to the word "love" as their only responsibility if they assume that they know what it means, according to their own subjective notions, while disregarding the biblical revelation that defines love and corrects human misunderstandings of it. This approach lacks adequate external controls for calibrating moral compass and can lead to the arrogant view that one's own version of love is superior to that of God, as demonstrated in some parts of the Bible, where he was faced with tough choices when people persisted in rejecting his mercy and therefore were left with the justice part of his love.[6]

Our study of OT law has shown that the Decalogue exemplifies the great principles of love for God and for other human beings, which Jesus affirmed, and which also form the foundation for the rest of OT law.[7] The NT

---

6. See, e.g., 2 Kings 17, 24–25; 2 Chron. 36; and the examples of divine destruction in chap. 14 above.
7. See esp. chaps. 7, 11–12.

prominently reiterates the Ten Commandments (e.g., Matt. 19:17–19; Rom. 2:21–22; 7:7; James 2:11), but there are several reasons why Christians should not ignore the other OT laws as we have for many centuries.[8]

First, the fact that the Lord gave laws outside the Decalogue through Moses does not negate their divine authority. They came from God, who could have given them directly to the Israelites, but he conveyed them through Moses because the people were afraid to continue hearing his voice (Exod. 20:18–21; Deut. 5:23–31). So "Mosaic" laws are divine laws. The fact that these laws were given to Israel does not separate them from the Decalogue, which God also gave to the world through Israel. The Israelite descendants of Abraham "were entrusted with the oracles of God" (Rom. 3:2) as a channel of revelation to bring God's blessing to all peoples of the earth (Gen. 12:3; 22:18).

Second, the NT cites laws outside the Decalogue as applicable to Christians (e.g., 1 Cor. 5:1–5, applying Lev. 18:8; 20:11).

Third, many OT laws exemplify and apply principles of the Ten Commandments in helpful ways (e.g., Exod. 23:4, exemplifying 20:15), and some OT laws summarize Decalogue principles (Lev. 19:18; Deut. 6:5, as recognized by Jesus in Matt. 22:37–40).

---

8. Minnie Warburton, "Letting the Voice of Leviticus Speak," *STRev* 37 (1994): 164:

> The early Church Fathers dealt with Leviticus, Numbers, Deuteronomy, and chunks of Exodus very simply: We keep the Ten Commandments, and the rest of the Law and Commandments do not apply to Christians. One might ask how they squared that with what Jesus himself had to say about Torah, that he did not come to change a single "jot or tittle" of it; further, when asked what were the greatest of the commandments, Jesus gives two, neither of which comes from the ten. Rather, one is from Deuteronomy, and the other from Leviticus. Nevertheless, the Church Fathers deemed those extra 603 laws to be superfluous. There were those who thought they should be removed from the Christian canon entirely, but fortunately they did not prevail.

The main historical reason why Christian tradition turned away from OT law during patristic times was not biblically based; it was anti-Semitic overreaction to Judaism. See, e.g., Justin Martyr, *Dialogue with Trypho*, chaps. 12, 13, 16–24; and later John Chrysostom, *Eight Homilies against the Jews*; cf. Wayne A. Meeks and Robert L. Wilken, *Jews and Christians in Antioch in the First Four Centuries of the Common Era*, Sources for Biblical Study 13 (Missoula, MT: Scholars Press, 1978); Robert L. Wilken, *John Chrysostom and the Jews: Rhetoric and Reality in the Late 4th Century* (Berkeley: University of California Press, 1983). I am grateful to my Andrews University colleague John Reeve for these references.

Consider Roy Gane, *Leviticus, Numbers*, NIV Application Commentary (Grand Rapids: Zondervan, 2004), 311:

> A venerable Christian fallacy is the idea that the more Christian we want to become, the less Jewish our religion must be. This anti-Semitic notion, which has wreaked havoc on Jewish-Christian relations for more than a millennium and a half, is not supported by Scripture. Rather, the more Jews and Christians absorb and live up to the essential ideals of our respective biblical holy books, the more common ground we will discover.

Fourth, some OT laws express moral principles that are subprinciples of love but are not found in the Decalogue as such (e.g., Lev. 19:11, "You shall not lie to one another"; Exod. 22:21 [22:20 MT]).[9]

Fifth, even when Christians cannot keep a law, they can learn from it about God's character and the way he works with people to save them. For example, the divine instructions regulating the ancient Israelite ritual system (e.g., Lev. 1–16) profoundly illuminate the way Christ saves us as our sacrificial victim and priest (esp. Heb. 7–10; see chap. 16 above).

Lest there is any doubt that Jesus retained all of OT law as valuable for his followers, he explicitly said so (Matt. 5:17–19; cf. Luke 16:17; Rom. 3:31). This makes sense because Jesus also said that the Scriptures, which include OT law, "bear witness about" him (John 5:39). In fact, Jesus claimed to be the "I am" (John 8:58), meaning the God of Israel, who is YHWH (Exod. 3:14–15, "I AM WHO I AM"). If so, it appears that the preincarnate Christ, the Word (John 1:1–5; cf. v. 14), whose "goings forth are from long ago" (Mic. 5:2 NASB [5:1 MT]), was the giver of OT law, which reflects and therefore bears witness to his character.

The OT values do not lose the authoritative force of their wisdom when they move into the NT era.[10] If anything, new-covenant Christians, who have received the superior revelation of God in Christ (2 Cor. 3), bear a greater responsibility for wise and holy living than the ancient Israelites did (cf. Matt. 5:17–48).

Learning to live in harmony with God in the present life by emulating his holiness (Lev. 11:44–45; 19:2; 20:26; 1 Pet. 1:15–16) is indispensable preparation for living with him and holy created beings for all eternity (cf. 1 Cor. 6:9–11; Rev. 21:3–8, 22–27; 22:14–15). Those who will live with God for all eternity will be those who have persisted in choosing him and his way of love, those who have accepted his gift of moral transformation. Simply being "nice" isn't enough.

9. Although the Decalogue includes a law against false witness, which involves lying or deception (Exod. 20:16).

10. Affirmed by Walter C. Kaiser Jr., *Toward Old Testament Ethics* (Grand Rapids: Zondervan, 1983), 312 (emphasis original):

> There is no contrast between what the Old Testament law required and what the New Testament enjoined. James, in a similar style to the Old Testament, names the law of brotherly love the "royal law" and urges Christians to fulfill it (James 2:8). Likewise, John refers to the law as if it were a well-known rule of righteousness and defines sin as a transgression of the law (1 John 2:7, 8; 3:7, 8, 23, 24; 5:2, 3; 2 John 5, 6). In fact, Peter's summary of a Christian lifestyle is the same as that of Old Testament law, "be holy in all you do; for it is written: 'Be holy, because I am holy'" (1 Peter 1:16). The moral law, as revealed in the Old Testament, was the recognized standard of holiness that remained authoritative for Christ, the apostles, and the early church *because it was written.*

Obedience and Thinking

Misconception 4: *Genuine obedience is unthinking.* The present book demonstrates in detail the need for Christians to think in order to understand and follow God's revealed will within the settings of their lives. Paul wrote to Timothy: "Do your best to present yourself to God as one approved, a worker who has no need to be ashamed, rightly handling the word of truth" (2 Tim. 2:15). "Rightly handling" includes a process of interpreting a divine message in accord with its intent, as indicated by its context and relationship to other messages. This allows for neither avoidance of obedience through rationalization (e.g., Mark 7:9–13) or unnecessary debate (e.g., 2 Tim. 2:14) on the one hand nor unthinking knee-jerk compliance on the other.

It may appear pious to thump one's Bible and declare, "I just read and do!" But "rightly handling" inserts another step: read, *think*, and then do. This is common sense. When we receive instructions from any source, we need to understand them at least to some extent in order to know when they apply to us, and if so, how to properly carry them out. Those who lack an adequate grasp of what is involved may cause unnecessary problems by their attempted obedience.[11] My response to the "just read and do" approach is simply to say: "Take Deuteronomy 25:5–10, for example." What would happen if we tried to unthinkingly and literally implement the law of levirate marriage in the modern Western Christian church? Does God really expect us to do that?[12]

"Rightly handling" is not limited to unaided human reason. Thus Paul counseled: "Think over what I say, for the Lord will give you understanding in everything" (2 Tim. 2:7). God's will can be understandable to one whose mind is renewed to harmony with him instead of being "conformed to this world" (Rom. 12:2), with its myopic self-absorption, changing fads, and subjectivity. Therefore true obedience and the thinking behind it can be countercultural, not making sense to those who are not attuned to God's will.

Obedience does not require full comprehension of the reason(s) for a divine instruction (cf. Deut. 29:29). For instance, the Lord commanded the Israelites to maintain their personal holiness by abstaining from the meat of certain animals that he defined as unfit to eat, but he did not explain the rationale for regarding these kinds of animals as impure (Lev. 11; cf. Deut.

---

11. See, e.g., some episodes in the fascinating experiment of A. J. Jacobs, *The Year of Living Biblically: One Man's Humble Quest to Follow the Bible as Literally as Possible* (New York: Simon & Schuster Paperbacks, 2007).

12. See chap. 9 above.

14).[13] Obedience calls for humble faith in God's character and superior wisdom.[14]

Faith to obey God is not blind. Rather, it is trust that is based on experience with his goodness. The faith of those who venture to obey him is reinforced when they receive the corresponding benefits of cause and effect with divine blessing (cf. Lev. 26:3–13; Deut. 28:1–14). Thus the results of obedience encourage further obedience.

Obedience and Legalism

Misconception 5: *Concern for obedience to God's law is legalism.* If this were so in an unqualified sense, Jesus and Paul were legalistic because they were concerned for obedience to God's law (see above). But God gave his laws within the covenant framework of grace to those who were already delivered (cf. Exod. 20:2, followed by the Decalogue) and for the benefit of those who keep them. They are for the good of human beings (Deut. 10:13) because their principles of cause and effect are in harmony with the way we are created. Adherence to these principles not only constitutes obedience to God; it is also obedience to the laws of our nature.

Compare the fact that instructions in a car manual are designed for the way a particular model is manufactured. Nobody would think to call someone who studies such a manual and uses the specified kinds of oil, gas, and replacement parts "legalistic." So why should Christians who study the Bible and seek to optimize their well-being by following its guidance be labeled "legalistic"? If obedience to a car manufacturer frees one from excessive worry and breakdown, so does obedience to the Creator. Here is another sense in which freedom and obedience are one (see above).[15]

God's law is not "legalistic," and genuine obedience to it is not "legalism." People are legalistic when their concern for obedience is twisted so that they misuse divine law for purposes other than that for which it was intended, such as the following:

13. There are rules of thumb for identifying certain kinds of creatures as pure or impure, but these do not give the reasons why the animals should belong to those categories.

14. Even for scientific, intellectual, independent modern people, "although we do gain wisdom from the exercise of analysis and discourse on God's commandments, we gain character from our decision to obey in spite of our limited human capability to understand." Laura Schlessinger and Stewart Vogel, *The Ten Commandments: The Significance of God's Laws in Everyday Life* (New York: Cliff Street Books, 1998), xxv.

15. Of course, in a broken world this does not mean that only good things happen to good people and bad things happen to bad people (cf. Ps. 73).

1. To avoid "the weightier matters of the law" while attempting to appear righteous by focusing on minutiae (Matt. 23:23) or inventing loopholes (15:3–9; Mark 7:6–13).

2. As a basis for pride and elitism (Matt. 23:5–7; Luke 18:11–12).

3. For hypocritical harsh condemnation of others (John 8:3–9).

4. To supposedly protect divine law through excessively stringent interpretations of it or humanly devised expansions around it (e.g., Mark 2:23–24).

5. As a political tool through which legalists seek to gain and maintain social control by making standards that they impose on others (Matt. 15:1–2; 23:4; Mark 7:1–5). Insofar as they usurp God's authority by putting their authority in place of his, "teaching as doctrines the commandments of men" (Matt. 15:9; Mark 7:7), they commit a form of blasphemy (cf. John 10:33).

6. To earn merit for salvation or have assurance that one is saved (e.g., Gal. 3:10–12, 21–22; cf. John 5:39), failing to see that God's law is much bigger than an external bottom line (e.g., Matt. 19:16–22) and attempting to substitute limited human obedience for infinite divine grace. Tragically, millions today are basing their hope for salvation on the popular legalistic notion that if they are good enough by achieving a minimum standard of performance, they can be saved. This is false assurance. People will not be excluded from eternal life because they have failed to *earn* salvation (which no fallen human can do), but because they have failed to *receive it as a gift* (Rom. 3:24; 6:23).

7. By fixating on and becoming overwhelmed with all the requirements of divine law and the difficulty of obedience due to the extreme depravity of human nature, without corresponding trust in God's enabling power and the reasonableness of his instructions. This can lead to discouragement that gives up on the possibility of and need for obedience. Ironically, therefore, this kind of legalism can result in a reaction of cheap grace, false assurance (with an exhilarating sense of liberation), and practical antinomianism that masquerades as "righteousness by faith" but undermines a full relationship with God that involves comprehensive surrender to his will.[16]

Legalists misrepresent God and his law. True obedience is not simply to this law or that law but basically to God, who requires obedience to all his

16. Cf. Roy Gane's two-part series, "Legalism and 'Righteousness by Faith,'" in *Ministry: International Journal for Pastors* 80, no. 1 (January 2008): 5–9; no. 3 (March 2008): 14–18.

commands (Lev. 26:14–15). This relational principle explains James 2:10–11: "For whoever keeps the whole law but fails in one point has become accountable for all of it. For he who said, 'Do not commit adultery,' also said, 'Do not murder.' If you do not commit adultery but do murder, you have become a transgressor of the law."

Growth in Love Guided by Law

God's law itself is love (see above), so it is fulfilled, it is truly obeyed, by showing love to others (Rom. 13:8–10) for the right reason: We love God "because he first loved us" (1 John 4:19; cf. John 14:15; 15:9; Rom. 5:6–8). Therefore our obedience depends on divine grace, which supplies unselfish love (Rom. 5:5) that works through faith (Gal. 5:6) to keep God's law. Without this love, even extreme manifestations of external obedience are worthless (cf. 1 Cor. 13:3).

As the guide to true love, the law plays two crucial roles. First, as the standard of love, it exposes unlove, which is sin, thereby serving as a crucial diagnostic tool that reveals the need of faulty people for redemption by grace (Rom. 3:19–20; 7:7, 13). Second, it provides the manual for progressive moral wisdom in holy living that is in harmony with God's character and will (cf. 2 Tim. 3:14–17). This process, requiring diligent cooperation with God (Phil. 2:12–13; cf. v. 5), is growth in love, which is sanctification, growth in holiness (1 Thess. 3:12–13).

The fact that sanctification is growth in love, which reaches out for the benefit of others, indicates that it is not a kind of self-focused piety. As Jesus showed, a holy life is a life of service. Peter affirmed the outgoing nature of holy new-covenant people when he applied the covenant promise of Exod. 19:5–6 to them: "But you are a chosen race, a royal priesthood, a holy nation, a people for his own possession, that you may proclaim the excellencies of him who called you out of darkness into his marvelous light" (1 Pet. 2:9). By God's grace, all Christians are to conduct their lives as his consecrated ministers in order to effectively let others know about his transforming goodness, so that they too may hear and answer God's call and enjoy his wonderful light.

Selected Bibliography

Barmash, Pamela. *Homicide in the Biblical World*. Cambridge: Cambridge University Press, 2005.

Barton, John. *Understanding Old Testament Ethics: Approaches and Explorations*. Louisville: Westminster John Knox, 2003.

Block, Daniel I. *Deuteronomy*. NIV Application Commentary. Grand Rapids: Zondervan, 2012.

Boecker, Hans Jochen. *Law and the Administration of Justice in the Old Testament and Ancient East*. Translated by Jeremy Moiser. Minneapolis: Augsburg, 1980.

Bovati, Pietro. *Re-Establishing Justice: Legal Terms, Concepts and Procedures in the Hebrew Bible*. Translated by Michael J. Smith. JSOTSup 105. Sheffield: JSOT Press, 1994.

Burnside, Jonathan. *God, Justice, and Society: Aspects of Law and Legality in the Bible*. New York: Oxford University Press, 2011.

Cochran, Robert F., Jr., and David VanDrunen, eds. *Law and the Bible: Justice, Mercy and Legal Institutions*. Downers Grove, IL: IVP Academic, 2013.

Daube, David. *Studies in Biblical Law*. Cambridge: Cambridge University Press, 1947. Repr., New York: Ktav, 1969.

Davidson, Richard M. *Flame of Yahweh: Sexuality in the Old Testament*. Peabody, MA: Hendrickson, 2007.

Davis, John Jefferson. *Evangelical Ethics*. 4th ed. Phillipsburg, NJ: P&R, 2015.

Enns, Peter. *Exodus*. NIV Application Commentary. Grand Rapids: Zondervan, 2000.

Falk, Ze'ev W. *Hebrew Law in Biblical Times: An Introduction*. 2nd ed. Provo, UT: Brigham Young University Press; Winona Lake, IN: Eisenbrauns, 2001.

Feinberg, John S., and Paul D. Feinberg. *Ethics for a Brave New World*. 2nd ed. Wheaton, IL: Crossway, 2010.

Gane, Roy. *Leviticus, Numbers*. NIV Application Commentary. Grand Rapids: Zondervan, 2004.

Green, Joel B., ed. *Dictionary of Scripture and Ethics*. Grand Rapids: Baker Academic, 2011.

Green, Joel B. and Jacqueline E. Lapsley, eds. *The Old Testament and Ethics: A Book-by-Book Survey*. Grand Rapids: Baker Academic, 2013.

Greengus, Samuel. *Laws in the Bible and in Early Rabbinic Collections: The Legal Legacy of the Ancient Near East*. Eugene, OR: Cascade, 2011.

Hallo, William W. *The Context of Scripture*. 3 vols. Leiden: Brill, 2003.

Hiers, Richard H. *Justice and Compassion in Biblical Law*. New York: Continuum, 2009.

Jackson, Bernard S. *Wisdom-Laws: A Study of the Mishpatim of Exodus 21:1–22:16*. Oxford: Oxford University Press, 2006.

Janzen, Waldemar. *Old Testament Ethics: A Paradigmatic Approach*. Louisville: Westminster/John Knox, 1994.

Kaiser, Walter C., Jr. *Toward Old Testament Ethics*. Grand Rapids: Zondervan, 1983.

Milgrom, Jacob. *Leviticus 1–16: A New Translation with Introduction and Commentary*. AB 3. New York: Doubleday, 1991.

———. *Leviticus 17–22: A New Translation with Introduction and Commentary*. AB 3A. New York: Doubleday, 2000.

———. *Leviticus 23–27: A New Translation with Introduction and Commentary*. AB 3B. New York: Doubleday, 2001.

Miller, Patrick D. *The Ten Commandments*. Interpretation: Resources for the Use of Scripture in the Church. Louisville: Westminster John Knox, 2009.

Nardoni, Enrique. *Rise Up, O Judge: A Study of Justice in the Biblical World*. Translated by Seán Charles Martin. Grand Rapids: Baker Academic, 2004.

Patrick, Dale. *Old Testament Law*. Atlanta: John Knox, 1985.

Paul, Shalom M. *Studies in the Book of the Covenant in the Light of Cuneiform and Biblical Law*. VTSup 18. Leiden: Brill, 1970. Repr., Eugene, OR: Wipf & Stock, 2006.

Phillips, Anthony. *Essays on Biblical Law*. JSOTSup 344. London: Sheffield Academic, 2002.

Rae, Scott B. *Moral Choices: An Introduction to Ethics*. 3rd ed. Grand Rapids: Zondervan, 2009.

Rodd, Cyril S. *Glimpses of a Strange Land: Studies in Old Testament Ethics*. OTS. Edinburgh: T&T Clark, 2001.

Roth, Martha T. *Law Collections from Mesopotamia and Asia Minor*. SBL Writings from the Ancient World 6. Atlanta: Scholars Press, 1995.

Sarna, Nahum M. *Exodus: The Traditional Hebrew Text with the New JPS Translation*. JPS Torah Commentary. Philadelphia: Jewish Publication Society, 1991.

Sprinkle, Joe M. *Biblical Law and Its Relevance: A Christian Understanding and Ethical Application for Today of the Mosaic Regulations*. Lanham, MD: University Press of America, 2006.

Tigay, Jeffrey H. *Deuteronomy: The Traditional Hebrew Text with the New JPS Translation*. JPS Torah Commentary. Philadelphia: Jewish Publication Society, 1996.

Walton, John H. *Ancient Near Eastern Thought and the Old Testament: Introducing the Conceptual World of the Hebrew Bible*. Grand Rapids: Baker Academic, 2006.

———, ed. *Zondervan Illustrated Bible Backgrounds Commentary*. Vol. 1, *Genesis, Exodus, Leviticus, Numbers, Deuteronomy*. Grand Rapids: Zondervan, 2009.

Watts, James W. *Reading Law: The Rhetorical Shaping of the Pentateuch*. BibSem 59. Sheffield: Sheffield Academic, 1999.

Webb, William J. *Slaves, Women & Homosexuals: Exploring the Hermeneutics of Cultural Analysis*. Downers Grove, IL: IVP Academic, 2001.

Welch, John W. *Biblical Law Cumulative Bibliography*. CD-ROM. Provo, UT: Brigham Young University Press; Winona Lake, IN: Eisenbrauns, 2005.

Wells, Bruce. *The Law of Testimony in the Pentateuchal Codes*. BZABR 4. Wiesbaden: Harrassowitz, 2004.

Westbrook, Raymond, ed. *A History of Ancient Near Eastern Law*. 2 vols. Handbook of Oriental Studies, Section 1, The Near and Middle East 72. Leiden: Brill, 2003.

———. *Law from the Tigris to the Tiber: The Writings of Raymond Westbrook*. Edited Bruce Wells and Rachel Magdalene. 2 vols. Winona Lake, IN: Eisenbrauns, 2009.

———. *Property and the Family in Biblical Law*. JSOTSup 113. Sheffield: JSOT Press, 1991.

———. *Studies in Biblical and Cuneiform Law*. CahRB 26. Paris: Gabalda, 1988.

Westbrook, Raymond, and Bruce Wells. *Everyday Law in Biblical Israel: An Introduction*. Louisville: Westminster John Knox, 2009.

Wright, Christopher J. H. *Old Testament Ethics for the People of God*. Downers Grove, IL: InterVarsity, 2004.

Index of Modern Authors

Entries for frequently cited authors identify topics discussed.

414

Index of Scripture and Other Ancient Sources

Index of Subjects